Introduction to Business

The Economy and You

2d Edition

Anne Scott Daughtrey
Emerita Professor of Management
College of Business and Public Administration
Old Dominion University

Robert A. Ristau
Professor of Business Education
Department of Business and Industrial Education
Eastern Michigan University

Steven A. Eggland
Professor of Vocational Education
Teachers College
University of Nebraska

Les R. Dlabay
Associate Professor of Business
Department of Economics and Business
Lake Forest College

GB16BA
PUBLISHED BY
SOUTH-WESTERN PUBLISHING CO.
CINCINNATI, OH   DALLAS, TX   LIVERMORE, CA

Acquisitions Editor: Robert E. Lewis
Senior Developmental Editor: Willis S. Vincent
Production Editors: Angela Crum, Rebecca Roby
Associate Editor/Production: Melanie A. Blair
Cover and Internal Designer: Craig LaGesse Ramsdell
Pagination Specialist: Mary Mullins
Production Artist: Nicola Jones
Senior Photo Researcher: Devore M. Nixon
Unit Opener Photographers: Diana W. Fleming, Mimi Ostendorf-Smith
Marketing Manager: Donald H. Fox

Copyright © 1992

by

SOUTH-WESTERN PUBLISHING CO.
Cincinnati, Ohio

All Rights Reserved

ISBN: 0-538-61217-7

Library of Congress Catalog Card Number: 90-62303

3 4 5 6 7 8 9 0 D 9 8 7 6 5 4 3 2

Printed in the United States of America

Preface

These are exciting economic times. We are experiencing evolutionary and—in some instances—revolutionary changes in our economy and in the world. The spirit of enterprise, along with technological advancements, constantly invigorates our economy. Computers, once large and costly and used primarily for accounting purposes, not only have invaded the entire workplace but have also become commonplace in homes and schools. We know that change will certainly continue to be a fact of life in the years ahead, yet the fundamental principles of business stay virtually the same from year to year. Social, economic, technological, and regulatory developments have introduced new ideas and methods into business practices and have, therefore, impacted the study of business.

The study of business, a major component of our economy, is increasingly important to all. Everyone in our economy interacts with business—through the products we buy, the advertisements we see and hear, the jobs we hold, and the money we invest. From many perspectives, it is important that young people understand the role of business in our society and begin to comprehend what their relationship is to business and the economy in which they live. The basic objectives of this book focus on introducing students to the world of business and helping prepare them for a more meaningful and beneficial interaction with businesses and our economy.

A BOOK FOR CHANGING TIMES—CONTEMPORARY TOPICS AND FORMAT

Introduction to Business: The Economy and You, 2d edition retains much of the well-established content developed through twelve editions of *General Business for Economic Understanding* and continues to expand and develop the business orientation of topics introduced in the first edition of *Introduction to Business: The Economy and You*. State-of-the-art textbook production techniques have been used to present materials in an attractive and easy-to-read format to support and enhance the sound education methodology employed throughout the textbook.

TEXT ORGANIZATION

Introduction to Business: The Economy and You is divided into eleven units.

- Units 1, 2, and 3 introduce students to our economic system, business in our economy, and the role of labor and government in our economy. These three units in a sense "interlock" to give students a broad perspective of the context of business. Chapter 7 in Unit 2 introduces the important topic of world trade, while Chapter 8 in Unit 3 introduces careers and the labor market.
- Units 4 and 5 focus on two important roles in our economy: the worker /producer role and the consumer role. Students are given a start on career planning in Unit 4 and learn the basics of being a good consumer in Unit 5.
- Unit 6 describes the impact of technology on our society. The use of computers in business is described, and the future of technology is addressed.
- Unit 7 explores the dynamic, ever-changing world of financial institutions. While the section focuses on the operations and services of banks, it also includes a discussion of the most common financial institutions.
- Units 8 and 9 relate to two important concerns of the American consumer: the prudent use of credit and the saving and investing of money. How to establish credit and how to maintain a good credit record are important aspects of Unit 8. Various savings and investment opportunities are described in Unit 9.
- Unit 10 introduces students to the need to recognize financial risks and how to protect against financial losses through insurance.
- Unit 11 concludes the study of business by focusing on an important personal business concern: the management of personal business affairs. Budgeting and planning for a sound financial future are appropriate culminating activities for this text.

SPECIAL FEATURES

This edition continues to present material and features that were well received in the previous edition. The Business Briefs, which open each unit, present new and updated information on special events in business and successful businesspeople. The Glossary incorporates the specialized Computer Glossary, which was introduced in the previous edition.

The Career Focus sections of the textbook and career planning activities in the workbooks have been retained and updated. Students continue to verify their need for career information and assistance with the career planning function.

Each chapter has been rewritten using multiple-level headings to better lead students through concepts and ideas. Activities at the end of each chapter of *Introduction to Business: The Economy and You* have been carefully planned to facilitate teaching and learning.

End-of-chapter activities involve students in writing, applying, computing, investigating, interviewing, problem solving, demonstrating, and reporting. Students are given opportunities to learn and practice basic life skills needed to perform their economic roles in today's complex society. The variety of activities presented allows the teacher to select and use those which best accommodate students based on their interests and abilities. All activities are keyed to performance objectives as shown in the matrices provided in the teacher's guide, and they are divided into the following sections:

- *Increasing Your Business Vocabulary.* This section increases word power by asking students to identify definitions of commonly used business and economic terms.
- *Reviewing Your Reading.* This section measures students' comprehension through oral or written responses to questions directly related to the content of each chapter.
- *Using Your Business Knowledge.* Through the activities in this section, students apply what they have learned in the chapter to problem situations relevant to their everyday lives.
- *Computing Business Problems.* By solving the business/economic problems in this section, students strengthen and refine their basic mathematics abilities. Problems vary in level of difficulty; the first problem in each section is designed for easy and quick solution. Many chapters contain a metric activity to familiarize students with the metric system.
- *Expanding Your Understanding of Business.* The activities in this section are intended mainly as optional experiences for students. The solutions require students to exercise careful thought, to investigate sources of information beyond the textbook, and in some cases, to conduct studies using basic and practical research methods. Students may be expected to report their findings and to make decisions or recommendations. This section is designed particularly, but not exclusively, for the more able or resourceful students.

Finally, the workbooks that accompany *Introduction to Business: The Economy and You* have been revised with many new activities and projects in each chapter.

In addition a short, classroom-tested business simulation has been included in each workbook. Students should find the simulation activities instructive and fun. Teachers should find them very useful in expanding the explanation of material covered in the text chapters.

ACKNOWLEDGMENTS

Specialists from many levels of business and education have provided substantive data, reviewed some manuscripts, offered suggestions, and otherwise contributed to the improvement of this edition of *Introduction to Business: The Economy and You*. Authorities, including national trade and professional organizations, have helped significantly in updating content and illustrations relating to computer technology, financial institutions, investments, credit, and financial management.

We are especially grateful for the following special group of teachers from seven states who, with the cooperation of their students, provided significant input into the revision process for this edition. From Arizona: Ann Allison, Independence (Glendale) High School; Steven M. Glass, McClintock (Tempe) High School; and Tim McBurney, Tempe High School. From Illinois: Sharon E. Arnold, Bismarck-Henning High School; Mary Kay Hencken, Charleston High School; Thomas E. Jeske, Fenton (Bensenville) High School; and Sue Phipps, Shiloh (Hume) High School. From Indiana: Augustine Watts, West Side (Gary) High School. From Michigan: Bettye Harris, Flint Central High School; and Maynard Leigh, Grosse Pointe South High School. From Nebraska: Jeff Alfrey, Millard North (Omaha) High School; D. C. Beckenhauer, Columbus High School; Mark King, Daniel J. Gross (Omaha) High School; and Gary Schleppenbach, Crete High School. From Ohio: Marden Herr, Pandora-Gilboa High School. From Virginia: Pamela Altieri, Glenvar High School; Jeff Highfill, William Byrd High School; Jean Holbrook, Supervisor, Roanoke County Schools; Becky McClellan, Cave Spring High School; Gladys Morris, Northside Junior High School; and Mary T. Sutphin, Northside High School. From Wisconsin: Julee Dredske and Thomas Tempas, Poynette High School.

And to all teachers who used the previous edition, furnished helpful suggestions, and provided feedback on possible changes and innovations, we owe a special debt of gratitude and express a hearty "thank you."

Anne Scott Daughtrey
Robert A. Ristau
Steven A. Eggland
Les Dlabay

Contents

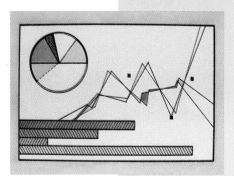

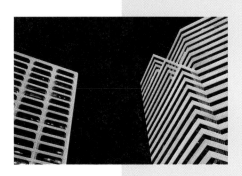

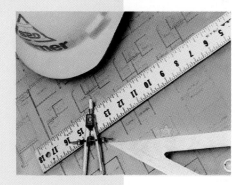

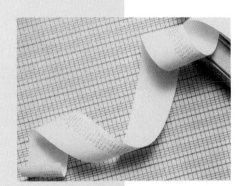

Our Economic System

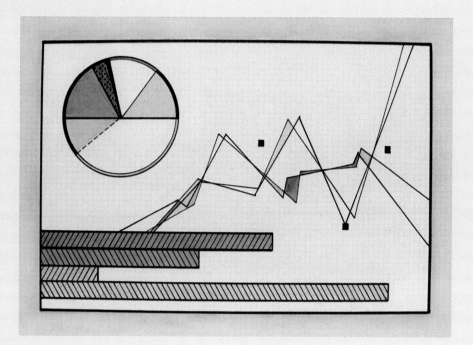

Unit Goals

After studying the chapters in this unit, you will be able to:

1. *Explain the basic economic problem.*
2. *Describe several features of our market economy.*
3. *Give examples to show how each of your three economic roles plays a part in our economic system.*
4. *Discuss three ways to measure economic progress.*

Entrepreneurship Is Alive and Growing

Business Brief

The American dream! It excites people. The free enterprise system has always encouraged entrepreneurs—people willing to invest time and money to turn ideas into profits. People seeking to "make a million" or to be their own boss have

been venturing out on their own in growing numbers. These entrepreneurs are bringing new products and services to the marketplace and are helping to create new jobs. Consider a few of the things modern-day entrepreneurs have given us— the laser, optical scanner, personal computer, turbojet engine, insulin, penicillin, FM radios, zippers, ball-point pens, Velcro strips, stenciled T-shirts, jogging shoes, and fast-food restaurants.

The success of Steven Jobs and Steven Wozniak's Apple Computer, Inc., is now a classic story in commercial innovation. When their company, after only a few years in operation, went public in 1989, the two young men became millionaires. Many changes have taken place in the company since then, but the personal computer is a commonplace communications tool today due in large measure to their entrepreneurial venture.

Entrepreneurs often move from one venture to another, putting their ideas to the test in the marketplace. Separated from the company in the mid-1980s, Jobs started a new company, Next, Inc., and in 1988 introduced a new computer. Again, innovative in design and targeted to academic research, the new product has been cited as a future benchmark in personal computer development.

Sophia Collier was just turning 21 years old when she created her all-natural-ingredients soft drink by cooking up batches of fruit punch in her kitchen. She sold her first order of Soho Natural Soda to a local health-food store. During the time it took for her product to catch on, she paid her bills by operating a typing service from her home. Eight years later, with Soho Soda well established, Collier is a millionaire and, as she noted, "working on her first hundred million."

Entrepreneurs often start when they are quite young. Geary Christ, at age 13, spends his summers tending his 50 crab pots in the bay near his home. He pulls in a tidy haul of crabs that nets him about $50 a day. Taking his motorboat out into the bay at 5 a.m. each day to gather the crabs is not so bad, Geary said. "There's nothing else that pays like this with these hours. On a good day, it's two hours for $80." After a sizable investment for his equipment and supplies, Geary is now following a financial plan drawn up by his parents and other backers and is making his loan payments ahead of time.

Not all entrepreneurial ventures succeed, of course. History shows that 40 percent of new businesses fail within five years. However, those that do succeed supply us with many new products and services. One economist has predicted that improving economic conditions will sweep us into the next century as a "new country" with new jobs and new opportunities. A great many entrepreneurs will help us get there.

Sources: "What's Next: Gala Debut Could Outdazzle Computer," *The Virginian-Pilot and Ledger Star*, 11 October 1988; "You Can Still Make a Million Dollars," *Parade* (January 26, 1986); and "Early Bird Catches the Seafood," *The Virginian-Pilot and Ledger Star*, 11 July 1988.

Satisfying Needs and Wants

Chapter 1

Chapter Objectives

After studying this chapter and completing the end-of-chapter activities, you will be able to:

1. *Give an example to show that human wants are unlimited.*

2. *Give an example of each of the three kinds of resources that are needed to produce goods and services.*

3. *Explain the importance of human resources in the production of goods and services.*

4. *Give an example to show that economic resources are limited.*

5. *Explain why the basic economic problem forces you to make choices.*

6. *State the six steps in the decision-making process.*

"Hi, Dad," Greg Santos called as he entered the kitchen and headed for the refrigerator. "What's to eat? I'm starving."

"Hi, Son. First, sit down and tell me about your first day in high school. Do you like it as well as middle school? How were your teachers? Here, have a sandwich while you tell me about it. What did you learn?"

"Hey, what's with all the questions? I learned I need some hi-tops! Could we go to the mall tonight to look for some?"

"Hi-tops? We just bought you jogging shoes and sneakers. Now, hi-tops? When do you think you'll have enough shoes?"

"Gotta have 'em, Dad. Every guy at school has them. Oh, and I also need a couple of school T-shirts. The plain ones won't cut it this year."

"Will your wants never end, Greg? I have a few wants, too, but I can't buy everything I want. So, I make no promises. We'll see what we can do."

"OK, Dad, but hurry and see," Greg said as he finished his sandwich. "Say, how soon is dinner?"

EVERY PERSON HAS NEEDS AND WANTS

Does Greg's conversation with his father sound familiar? No doubt this scene is being repeated in the homes of many of Greg's classmates. They have wants, too, as do their parents. Every person has needs and wants.

Needs Are Basic to Survival

Things that are necessary for survival are called **needs**. Food, clothing, and housing are the basic needs that most people have, but we also desire things beyond our basic needs. It is doubtful that the hi-tops Greg wants are necessary to his survival, but he wants them anyway.

Wants Make Life More Pleasant

Things which are not necessary for survival but which add comfort and pleasure to our lives are called **wants**. You may want a new tennis racquet, a stereo headset, and a school ring. You could live without them, but having them would make life easier and more fun for you. When we talk about needs and wants, we often lump them together and just call them wants.

WANTS ARE UNLIMITED

Needs and wants never end. Greg's sandwich satisfied him for a while, but he is already thinking about dinner. Look at your own wants. You may have bought that tennis racquet that you had wanted for a long time. That want was fulfilled, but then you wanted tennis balls, a tennis outfit or two, tennis lessons, and a tennis bracelet.

Illus. 1-1
Some items, such
as food, clothing,
and housing,
meet our basic
needs.

Your family may want to trade in a large car for one that uses less gas in order to save money and conserve energy. You may learn about a new product that has just arrived in the stores. You decide that you want the new product because it is useful or just because it is new. So, for many reasons, our wants keep changing. We can never satisfy all of them. This is true for everyone—our wants are unlimited.

GOODS AND SERVICES SATISFY WANTS

Some of our wants are classified as goods and some as services. We satisfy most of our wants with goods and services; these are key words in the study of business, and you will use them often. **Goods** are things you can see and touch. Greg's hi-tops and T-shirts, and your tennis racquet, stereo headset, and school ring are goods. All of the things that satisfy our material wants are goods—food, a television set, gasoline, cement, books, a bicycle, and clothes are examples. Goods are also called products.

Not all of our wants can be met with things that you can see and touch. Some wants are satisfied through the efforts of other people or by equipment. These efforts are called **services.** When you go to a movie, play a video game, make a deposit at the bank, get a haircut, take a swimming lesson, use your telephone, or ride a bus, you are using services. When you pay the hairstylist to cut your hair, you are buying a service performed by a person. When you put a coin in the video machine to play a game, or deposit coins

Illus. 1-2
Some wants are
satisfied through
the efforts of
other people.

at the car wash before you drive into the washing stall, you are buying a
service performed by a piece of equipment. We need both goods and services
to satisfy our wants. Supplying goods and services is what business is all
about.

GOODS AND SERVICES REQUIRE ECONOMIC RESOURCES

Goods and services do not just appear as if by magic. You cannot create
goods from nothing or supply a service without some effort. The means
through which goods and services are produced are called **economic
resources** or **factors of production**. There are three kinds of economic
resources: natural, human, and capital resources. All three are needed to
produce the goods and services that satisfy our wants.

Natural Resources

The raw materials supplied by nature are called **natural resources**. All of the
materials that come from the earth, the water, or the air are natural resources.
We take iron ore, gold, and oil from the earth to use in making goods. We
also grow vegetables in the soil and take fish from the water for food. We use
oxygen from the air in hospitals to help sick people breathe and to make such
products as carbonated water for colas. All of the goods we use today began
with one or more natural resources.

Human Resources

Natural resources do not satisfy our wants by themselves. It takes people to turn them into goods and make the products and services available to us. **Human resources** are the people who work to produce goods and services. **Labor** is another name for this factor of production. Human resources include people who run farms and factories, manage banks, design machines to mine coal, process food, announce the news on television, check out our purchases at the supermarket, police the streets, or teach Introduction to Business. Human resources are very important in producing goods and services.

Illus. 1-3
Can you identify the types of resources shown in these photos?

Capital Resources

The tools, equipment, and buildings that are used to produce goods and services are called **capital resources**. Office buildings, factories, tractors, carpenters' tools, computers, delivery trucks, and display cases are examples of capital resources. If you use a bicycle to deliver newspapers, your bicycle is a capital resource because it is the equipment you use to provide the newspaper delivery service. Likewise, a computer used by a bank to prepare a report of a customer's account is a capital resource. The grill used to cook the hamburger you buy for lunch as well as the restaurant building are capital resources.

The word **capital** is often used in place of capital resources, especially when referring to the factors of production. Capital is also thought of as money that is needed to run a business. A person may say she or he is trying to raise $40,000 capital to expand a business or that she or he has a $10,000 capital investment in a store operated by friends.

All three economic resources—natural, human, and capital—are necessary to produce goods and services to satisfy our wants. Unfortunately, we do not have an endless supply of these resources.

RESOURCES ARE LIMITED

If Greg's family had enough money, they could buy all of the things that both he and his father want. However, as his father suggested, their money is limited, and they cannot buy everything. No doubt, you have already had the experience of wanting many things you could not buy because you did not have the money to pay for them. This is true for people everywhere. Economic resources that can be turned into goods and services are limited.

Newscasts often report about shortages of certain items. In recent years, oil, lumber, and sugar have been reported as scarce. There were not enough of these items for all of the people who wanted them. We do not have an endless supply of economic resources. Because of pollution, we do not have endless supplies of clean air, water, and land. We also have shortages in certain kinds of human resources, such as accountants, nurses, secretaries, and others with the skills and education to satisfy our unlimited wants. Since our natural and human resources are limited, our manufactured capital resources—such as buildings and tools—cannot be made and are therefore also limited.

Scarcity Affects Everyone

Just as meeting your unlimited wants with limited resources is a problem for you, so it is for everyone—your family, your neighbors, and your school club. People all over the world are affected by scarcity. For this reason, we

Illus. 1-4
Shortages of
certain kinds of
human resources,
such as skilled
teachers for the
disabled, occur in
our society.

refer to the conflict between unlimited wants and limited resources as the
basic economic problem, or **scarcity**.

The members of your family may not be able to afford many of the things
they want because the wages of your father or mother are needed for food,
clothing, the house payment, the electric bill, or your school expenses. Your
neighbors and the families of your friends face the same economic problem.
Your school club might want to hire a live band to play for its annual dance,
but because its money is scarce, the club may have to use cassette tapes
instead.

Businesses and Governments Must Also Deal with Scarcity

Just as individuals face the basic economic problem, so do businesses,
governments, and all agencies that supply goods and services. A business
might want to enlarge its plant and parking lot to take care of its growth, but
because the land it owns is limited and locating elsewhere would cost more
than it can afford, it cannot do both.

All levels of government face the problem of supplying the almost
unlimited wants of the citizens with limited resources. For example, your
town may wish to give a large wage increase to police officers and fire
fighters. However, because taxes may not provide enough money, the
increase might have to be smaller in order to provide other services, such as
a new school building or additional employees to collect the garbage. Cities,

states, the United States, and all other nations must cope with the problem of providing the many services the citizens want from limited resources—the taxes collected to pay for the services. Someone must decide which services will be provided. How do you, other individuals, businesses, and governments decide which of the unlimited wants to supply?

INDIVIDUALS MAKE ECONOMIC CHOICES

Since you cannot have everything you want, you must choose which of the things you want most and can afford. Suppose you earn $10. If you spend it on movies and pizza with your friends on Friday night, you will not have enough left to go to the amusement park on Saturday. So you must make a choice. You must decide which of your wants—the movie and pizza with friends or the trip to the amusement park—is more important to you and will satisfy you more. One of the purposes of this book is to help you learn how to make wise economic decisions. Learning and following a logical process will help you make better decisions (see Figure 1-1).

Figure 1-1
Individuals, businesses, and nations must decide how to use limited resources.

The Decision-Making Process

There is a process that you can use to make almost any kind of decision. Let us look at the way economic decisions are made. **Economic decision making** is the process of choosing which wants, among several wants being considered at a certain time, will be satisfied. Once you learn the process, your decision making will be easier and your decisions may be better.

Steps in Making a Decision

You will study more about decision making later in this book when you read about choosing a career and buying wisely. For now, however, let's look briefly at the following steps.

1. *Define the problem.* If you have only $10 and want to buy several items, the problem is how to spend the money in a way that will give you the most satisfaction. In each situation, the problem must be defined in order to make a decision that will lead to its solution.
2. *Identify the choices.* There may be many choices or only two or three. In the movies/amusement park decision, you identified two wants or choices. Other choices, or alternatives, also might be considered. For example, you might decide to save your money instead of going to either place. It is important to consider all of the alternatives in making a decision.
3. *Examine the advantages and disadvantages of each choice.* If you go to the movie, you will enjoy seeing the show and being with your friends;

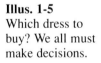
Illus. 1-5
Which dress to buy? We all must make decisions.

but you will have the disadvantage of missing the trip to the amusement park. You also might miss the opportunity of being with your family on a Saturday outing. If you save the money and do neither, you will have the money for other things later. However, you will miss out on being with your friends and enjoying the recreation of either the movie or the amusement park. Sometimes actually writing down your choices and listing the advantages and disadvantages of each will help with the next step.

4. *Choose*. This is really getting down to the "nitty gritty" of the problem. Even if you have done the first three steps as best you can, this is often a difficult step. You must learn to select from your alternatives the one that you believe will be the best for you and your interests at this particular time.

5. *Act on your choice*. This is the "take-action" step. If you have chosen to go to the movie, go and enjoy it. Try not to worry about the other choices that you decided against. Some people agonize so much over the choice they made that they cannot enjoy the activity they decided upon. Life is full of choices, and no doubt everyone regrets a decision from time to time. Using the decision-making process each time, however, will help you improve your ability to make choices.

6. *Review your decision*. Was your decision a good one? On a scale of one to ten, what score would you give your decision for the satisfaction it provided? What was right about it? What was wrong with it? If you had it to do over, would you make the same choice? Did you miss one of the alternatives that might have been a better choice, or did you fail to examine all of the advantages and disadvantages of each choice? This step gives you the opportunity to evaluate your decision and learn from any mistakes you believe you made so that you can make a better decision in the future.

Of course there are occasions when decisions must be made quickly and you will not have time to use all of these steps. For example, if your home

I REALLY HATE MAKING DECISIONS!

catches on fire, you will not have time to consider many choices before you decide to get out! For most decisions, however, following this process will help you make better choices.

As you progress through this course, you will have an opportunity to practice decision making. Furthermore, you will learn how the six-step process can be used by everyone--individuals, businesses, and governments--to cope with the problem of choosing which of the unlimited wants to satisfy with the limited resources available.

Increasing Your Business Vocabulary

The following terms should become part of your business vocabulary. For each numbered item, find the term that has the same meaning.

basic economic problem or scarcity   *human resources or labor*
capital resources or capital   *natural resources*
economic decision making   *needs*
economic resources or factors of   *services*
  production   *wants*
goods

1. The process of choosing which want, among several wants being considered at a certain time, will be satisfied.
2. The means through which we produce goods and services.
3. The problem—which faces individuals, businesses, and governments—of satisfying unlimited wants with limited resources.
4. Raw materials supplied by nature.
5. The things you can see and touch.
6. Tools, equipment, and buildings used in producing goods and services.
7. Things that are necessary for survival, such as food, clothing, and shelter.
8. The people who work to produce goods and services.
9. Things which are not necessary for survival but which add pleasure and comfort to our lives.
10. Things that satisfy our wants through the efforts of other people or equipment.

Reviewing Your Reading

1. Give two examples each of needs and wants.
2. Give three examples to explain why wants are unlimited.
3. Does business play a part in satisfying our needs and wants? Explain.
4. Give one example each of a service provided by a person and a machine.
5. How are economic resources involved in satisfying our needs and wants?
6. Name the three kinds of economic resources and give an example of each.

7. Can goods be produced with only capital and human resources? How important are human resources in producing goods and services?
8. Give two examples to show that economic resources are limited.
9. Explain what is meant by the basic economic problem.
10. Give one example each to show that businesses and governments must also deal with scarcity.
11. What are the six steps in the decision-making process?

Using Your Business Knowledge

1. Review the examples of limited resources given in the chapter. For each of the three economic resources, give two examples not listed in the text.
2. Mr. Santos, Greg's father, told him that with the family's limited resources, he will have to choose between a pair of hi-tops and season tickets to the ball games during the school year. This means Mr. Santos has put Greg on Step 3 of the decision-making process. List the advantages and disadvantages of Greg's two choices.
3. Everyone must cope with the basic economic problem. Give one example to show how this was done and what choice was made for each of the following: your family, one of your school's sports teams, your town or city, and the federal government.
4. Think about the clothes you own. Name one piece of clothing that you own but no longer wear. Give two reasons why you do not wear the item and tell how this situation contributes to unlimited wants.
5. List two businesses in your community that sell goods, two that sell services, and two that sell both.
6. Name some of the natural resources that were used in making each of the following: denim jeans, a pizza, jogging shoes, and this textbook.

Computing Business Problems

1. The Jenkins family has a monthly take-home pay of $1,080. Each month they pay for the following needs:

House payment	$310
Electric bill	95
Water bill	15
Food	250
Clothing	50

   a. What is the total monthly payment for the needs?
   b. How much is left for other needs and wants?
   c. What percentage of the Jenkins' take-home pay is being spent for needs?
2. Greg Santos entered an open 10-K (kilometer) Run sponsored by his class to raise money for the local children's hospital. The 10-K Run drew 110 runners from the school and the community.

Each paid a $4 entrance fee, $1.50 of which was used to cover publicity, awards, and other expenses, with the remainder going to the hospital. (For help with problems involving metrics, see Appendix D.)

a. How long is the 10-K run, expressed in miles?
b. If all of the participants completed the run, how many kilometers did they cover in total?
c. How many miles did they cover?
d. How much could the class donate to the children's hospital?

3. Forest fires take a heavy toll on land and timber resources, as shown recently in the Wildfire Report below for protected areas (those which are under the control of state and federal agencies, such as the Department of Agriculture or the Department of the Interior). Study the table and answer the questions that follow it.

	Acres of Protected Land	
	Federal	**State and Private**
Total land area	685,552,000	840,163,000
Area burned by wildfires	946,000	3,235,000
Number of fires reported	15,400	173,800

a. What is the total acreage of protected land?
b. What was the total number of fires reported in protected areas for the year?
c. How many acres were burned in the protected areas?
d. What was the average number of acres (show in rounded numbers) of federally protected land burned per fire?
e. How do these wildfires affect the problem of limited resources?

4. To protect natural resources, businesses and various levels of government recently spent the following amounts in one year for water and air quality control activities.

Agency	**Quality Control Expenditures (In Millions of Dollars)**	
	Water	**Air**
Business	$18,857	$18,396
Federal government	110	639
State and local governments	10	403

a. How much did business spend on pollution control for air and water?
b. How much did each level of government spend during the year to protect the quality of air and water?
c. What was the total spent by all levels of government for air and water control?
d. What percent of the total amount was spent by all levels of government?
e. For which resource was the most money spent? What was the amount spent on the resource?
f. In what way might the action by business and government help to alleviate the problem of scarcity?

Expanding Your Understanding of Business

1. What changes might occur for you and your family if any of the three factors of production—natural, human, or capital—were no longer available?

2. Most of the goods and services we want can be bought from various kinds of businesses, but many of our wants are satisfied by some level of government. On a sheet of paper, write three column headings: local, state, and federal. List under each heading five wants that are supplied by each level of government. How do we pay for these wants?

3. One of the economic decisions you will be making soon is whether or not you will go to college. It is an economic issue because your decision will affect your ability to earn money (a resource) in order to satisfy your needs and wants. While you cannot act on your decision at this time, you can begin thinking about the decision now. Follow this decision through the first three steps of the decision-making process. Write down your responses for each step. If you had to complete Step 4 now, what would be your choice?

4. Make a list of all your purchases for one week. To simplify recording, list food items bought for home preparation together as "home food" and food eaten at restaurants as "restaurant meals." Since it is easy to forget small purchases, you should record the items daily. At the end of the week, classify each of the items as a good or service. For which did you spend the most money?

5. The Department of Labor issues information on human resource needs for the present and for the next few years. The department recently stated that we will have a shortage of certain skilled workers for several years into the future. Two of these were accountants and secretaries. List as many ways as you can think of to ease the scarcity of these two groups of workers.

Our Market Economy and Other Economic Systems

Chapter 2

Chapter Objectives

After studying this chapter and completing the end-of-chapter activities, you will be able to:

1. *State the three economic questions that must be answered by every society.*

2. *Describe three types of economic systems.*

3. *Identify five features of our market economy.*

4. *Explain the statement that people are entitled to make profits from their business ventures.*

5. *Explain why competition generally results in better service and more goods at lower cost.*

6. *Explain who owns or controls the economic resources under capitalism, socialism, and communism.*

17

At this time of your life, you are beginning to think about choosing a career. Your freedom to make that choice yourself is a cherished feature of our economic system. Think about the following conversations in which two teenagers from different countries discuss their futures.

"I want to be a doctor," Andrea said to her school counselor as they planned her program of courses. "I need to take courses to prepare me for college and then medical school."

"That is your choice to make, Andrea," the counselor replied. "But your grades are not as high as they should be. You'll have to improve that. In the meantime, you might want to look at some alternative careers to choose from—just in case."

"No, my mind is made up. I'll improve my grades," Andrea said confidently.

While in another part of the world . . .

Mikelov looked with disappointment at the work assignment list from the Labor Ministry.

"But I wanted to be an engineer," he told his teacher.

"Sorry, Mikelov. You don't meet the criteria of the Labor Ministry. The engineering quota is closed. We are told that more workers are needed for our factories. You have been assigned as a production worker in the tractor factory."

Andrea and Mikelov represent decisions about resource use in two very different economic systems. As you have learned, resources to satisfy our many wants are limited. Every country, including the United States, must use whatever resources it has to provide as many of its members' wants as it can. This is a fact of life that all societies have had to cope with since time began, and a fact that will apply to all societies in the future. The limited economic resources available to each nation force the nation to make choices on how the resources will be used. These economic resources or factors of production, you will recall, are natural, human, and capital resources. How does a nation decide how to use these resources to its best advantage?

THREE BASIC ECONOMIC QUESTIONS

In order to decide how to use its scarce resources, each nation must answer three economic questions: (1) What goods and services are to be produced? (2) How should the goods and services be produced? (3) For whom should the goods and services be produced? A nation's plan for answering these questions is called its **economic system** or its economy. Since these questions help us to understand different economic systems, let us think about each one.

What Goods and Services Are to Be Produced?

Nations differ in their wants just as individuals do. One country might decide to use its resources to produce spaceships and to explore other planets. Another might want to use its resources to build the biggest and best military force. Some might want to use most of their resources to provide such consumer goods as cars, television sets, dishwashers, and recreational parks. Still other countries might have such limited resources that they must concentrate on providing the basic needs of food, clothing, and shelter. If a country wants to meet some or all of its people's wants, it must learn how to best use its resources. A nation that concentrates too much of its resources on military goods will not have enough left for consumer goods and services. On the other hand, a nation that uses all of its resources to supply consumer goods and services may not be able to protect its people from outside forces. Each nation must decide which kinds of goods and services it values most.

How Should the Goods and Services Be Produced?

A country that has a great many people but not much money or equipment might build roads by having many workers use picks and shovels to do the job. In another country, road building may be accomplished by using only a few people to operate heavy equipment, such as bulldozers and power earth movers. In the first case, the country is making use of its human resources to offset its lack of capital resource. In the second case, the country is doing the job with more capital resources and less labor. In either case, the road will get

Illus. 2-1
Nations, like individuals, differ in their wants. For example, a nation might want to use its resources to build a large military force.

built. The second method, however, is more efficient and will enable the country to complete the road much sooner. As you can see, economic resources can be combined in different ways to produce the same goods and services. Each nation decides which combination of resources will best suit its circumstances.

For Whom Should the Goods and Services Be Produced?

For whom should the goods and services be produced? How will the goods and services be distributed? Should the goods and services be shared equally among the people? Should people who contribute more to producing the goods and services be able to get a larger share of them? If you have the money, shouldn't you be able to buy anything you want? These are some of the questions that have to be considered.

In some economic systems, you can buy whatever you want and can afford. But in others, your ability to buy may be limited by the country's answer to the question, ''What shall be produced?'' For example, a country might be using a large share of its resources to produce capital goods, such as tractors or industrial robots. The country might, therefore, limit its production of consumer goods, such as high-fashion clothes and television sets. In the United States, the share of goods and services that you are able to have is largely determined by the amount of money you have to spend. In addition, the amount of money that you receive in wages will be affected by many things, including your abilities and how you use them. Figure 2-1 illustrates a variety of responses to the three basic economic questions.

Figure 2-1
Every economic system must answer the three basic economic questions.

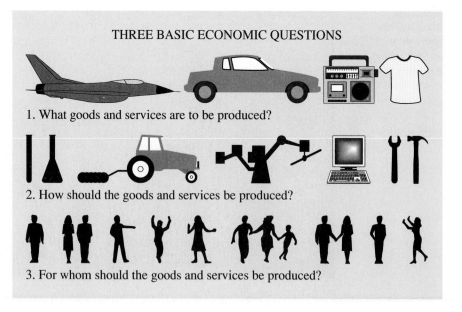

THREE BASIC ECONOMIC QUESTIONS

1. What goods and services are to be produced?

2. How should the goods and services be produced?

3. For whom should the goods and services be produced?

TYPES OF ECONOMIC SYSTEMS

Another way to understand a nation's economic system is to look not only at how the three economic questions are answered, but also at who answers them. In some countries, the answers are established by custom. In a **custom-based economy**, goods are produced the way they have always been produced. Children of each generation are taught to use the same method to make the same goods their parents and grandparents produced, and a tradition develops over the years. The custom may be weaving cloth on a hand loom, making straw baskets, or planting rice by hand. Goods are typically produced by hand, by using primitive tools, and by using people or animals for energy. Change and growth occur slowly in countries whose economies follow customs and in which the people are poor in material goods.

In some countries, economic questions are answered by the owners of the resources. In a **directed** or **planned economy**, resources are owned and controlled by the government. The officials of the government decide what and how goods will be produced and how they will be shared. They decide how much of the nation's resources will be spent on military uses and how much will be used to produce consumer and capital goods. They decide how much grain will be grown, how many pairs of shoes will be produced, and how many people will be used to produce tractors. As in Mikelov's case, government leaders assign people to careers based largely on their view of the needs for producing the goods and services. They plan all phases of the

Illus. 2-2
Methods of production are slow to change in a custom-based economy.

economy and command that the plans be carried out, using military or police force to do so if necessary. In directed economies, the average citizen has very little to say about how the three economic questions are answered. While directed economies work for some countries, the freedom of the people is always limited.

In a third type of economy, the three questions are answered by the buying and selling activities in the marketplace. The **marketplace** is any place where buyers and sellers exchange goods, services, and some form of money. People who order goods from a mail-order catalog, go to a movie, buy food in a supermarket, lease a telephone, buy a share of stock, or have a sweater cleaned are operating in the marketplace. When an airline orders a new jet, a business launches a satellite, or the government hires computer operators, each is operating in the marketplace. No one tells the consumers what to buy and no one tells businesses what to sell. Consumers and businesses make economic decisions based on their own interests. For example, you may use your money to buy a leather jacket, while one friend spends his or her money to take tennis lessons and another buys a compact disc player. A system in which economic decisions are freely made by buyers and sellers in the marketplace is called a **market economy**. When people in a market economy buy a product, they are helping to answer the question, ''What will be produced?'' Resources are combined in such a way that goods which people want and buy will be produced. This answers the question, ''How will goods and services be produced?'' Since people buy what they want and can afford in a market economy, they largely answer the question, ''For whom will goods and services be produced?''

LABELS FOR OUR ECONOMIC SYSTEM

Were you able to identify our economy as you read the three types? If you selected ''market economy,'' you were correct. As you know, the main differences among economic systems involve who owns the economic resources and who makes the decisions about production and distribution. Our system fits the definition of a market economy—a system in which economic decisions are freely made by buyers and sellers in the marketplace. But our economic system also has other labels.

Capitalism is another name used to identify the economic system in the United States. This term refers to the fact that economic resources are mostly owned by individuals rather than by government. Since most of the resources are privately owned, the individual owners are free to decide what they will produce with them. This freedom of the individual to choose what to produce provides the rationale for two other names given to our economy—a **free enterprise system** and a **private enterprise system**. All four of these terms—market economy, capitalism, free enterprise system, and private enterprise system—mean about the same thing: a system in which most economic resources are privately owned and decisions about production and distribution are largely made by free exchange in the marketplace. The terms ''market economy'' and ''private enterprise system'' will be emphasized in our discussion.

FEATURES OF OUR MARKET ECONOMY

There are many aspects of our economic system that make it different from other systems of the world. You are aware that the words ''freedom'' and ''individual choice'' are frequently used in discussing our economy. Let us examine five major features of our market economy.

Private Enterprise

A **business** is an establishment or enterprise that supplies us with goods and services in exchange for payment in some form. The right of the individual to choose whether to own a business, what business to enter, and what to produce with only limited government direction is referred to as **private enterprise**. Private enterprise ensures your freedom to decide how you will earn a living. In a private enterprise system, you may start or invest in any business you wish as long as you obey the law in doing so. You are free to choose to be a bricklayer, minister, karate instructor, business owner, astronaut, teacher, dancer, or anything you wish. Andrea can freely choose to

Illus. 2-3
The U.S. economic system is best described as a market economy.

be a doctor, but it is up to her to qualify for medical school through scholastic achievement and other criteria.

As a businessperson, you are generally free to offer goods and services at times, prices, and places of your choice. You are free to succeed or even to fail in the business of your choice. Of course, there are some regulations that prevent you from performing activities that would harm others. For example, you may not dispose of chemical wastes in a way that would pollute the environment. Nor can you practice surgery unless you have been granted a medical license by the appropriate agency in the state in which you plan to practice surgery. These regulations are not designed to limit freedom but to protect people from harmful practices.

Private Property

If your family owns the home in which you live or the television set you watch, the family is enjoying the right of private property. The **private property** feature is the right to own, use, or dispose of things of value. You may dispose of things you own by selling them, giving them away, willing them to anyone you wish, or even by throwing them away. In our country, you can own any item and do what you want with it, as long as you do not violate a law in doing so. You also have the right to own, use, and sell whatever you invent or create.

Businesses also have the right to own property. This property may be things such as land, buildings, tools, and the goods they produce. Businesses also have the right to use and dispose of their property in any lawful way, just as individuals do.

The Profit Motive

Businesses supply goods and services to the marketplace for one main reason—to earn money. Unless business owners can expect to make a profit, they would not want to put time, energy, and money into an enterprise. **Profit** is the money left from sales after subtracting the cost of operating the business. Business owners are entitled to make profits because they run the risk of losing the money they invested to start the business and because of the extra work and stress that are part of owning and running a business.

The desire to work for profit is often called the **profit motive**. This profit motive helps make our economy strong. Because of it, people are willing to invest money in business and to develop new products to satisfy consumers' wants. But the profit motive is not the only reason for putting time, money, and effort into businesses. Some people enjoy bringing out new products or improving existing ones. Others get pleasure from knowing that the goods or services they produce make other people happier, and others like the

Illus. 2-4
Businesses
supply goods and
services to the
marketplace for
one main
reason—to earn
money.

excitement of starting and running new businesses. But the profit motive is
the heart of the private enterprise system.

Competition

An ad on television urges you to buy ''Superior'' brand instead of
''DeLuxe'' brand. A supermarket ad in the newspaper claims in bold letters,
''Ours are the lowest prices in town.'' An ad in a magazine urges you to buy
the designer jeans being modeled by a famous video star. The rivalry among
businesses to sell their goods and services to buyers is called **competition**.
This feature of our economy gives you the opportunity to make choices
among countless goods and services that are available. You make these
choices by comparing prices, quality, appearance, usefulness, and appeal of
the goods and services you buy. And, if you are not satisfied with a purchase,
you are free to buy from a competing business next time. Competition
encourages business owners to improve products, offer better services, keep
prices reasonable, and produce new things.

Freedom of Choice

You have learned that the private enterprise system gives you the right to
enter a business or career of your choice, to own property, to make a profit,
and to compete. You also have other rights that contribute to your economic
freedom of choice.

You have the right to buy where and what you please, even though sales
of some products and services that the government declares harmful to you
or others may be prohibited or required to carry a warning of danger. You
have the right as a worker to organize with other workers. Through

organization, you can strive to improve working conditions. You have the right to travel when and where you please in this country and to many other countries. Finally, you have the right to express your opinions in newspapers, over radio and television, and in talking with others as long as you do not slander another person. The private enterprise system provides greater freedom of choice to the individual than any other economic system.

OTHER ECONOMIC SYSTEMS

There are many different economic systems operating in the world today. The major ones are known as the three ''isms'': capitalism, socialism, and communism. We have already examined capitalism, or private enterprise, as it operates in the United States.

If you examined all three systems in detail, you would find that it is difficult to define them and explain how they work. This is true partly because none of the systems exists anywhere in a pure form. Two countries operating under the same system may differ in a variety of ways. Therefore, economic systems are usually identified by the major features of their organization and operation. Under pure capitalism, for example, all enterprises would be privately owned and managed. This is not true in the United States, but we call our system capitalism because most of its enterprises are privately owned and managed. Likewise, neither of the other two major economic systems exists in pure form. Each country modifies the system it chooses to suit its own needs and makes changes in the system as its needs change.

Under **socialism**, the government owns and operates certain basic enterprises, such as steel mills, railroads and airlines, power plants, radio and television stations, hospital and health-care services, and banks. However, the extent of the government ownership and control is decided by the people. If they want more government control, they can vote for it. If they want less, they can vote against it. Some enterprises are also privately owned, but there is less frequency of private business ownership than in a private enterprise economy.

Under **communism**, the government owns or controls most of the economic resources and has tight control over them. All economic activities are planned and directed by the state. Farms, mines, factories, stores, newspapers, railroads, telephone services—all are owned and run by the government. Officials of the government decide what goods and services are to be produced and in what quantities. They also decide how the goods are to be produced. It is true that people are free to buy whatever goods and services are offered for sale. However, the prices and supplies of such products as clothing, television sets, watches, and cars are set by the government. The wages of the workers are also set by the government. These actions by government basically answer the question of how goods and services will be distributed.

Most people living under communism today do not have the freedom to decide how far they will go in school or what job they will have. Job opportunities, like wages, are primarily determined by government. Even the size of an apartment or house in which people are to live may be assigned by the government in directed economies.

MIXED ECONOMIC SYSTEMS

An economic system usually gets its name from the way its economic resources are owned and controlled. However, most modern economic systems cannot be easily and neatly placed under such labels as capitalism, socialism, or communism. As you have read, there is no pure form of any of these systems in any country today. In general, we think of most countries as having mixed economic systems. While countries are usually predominantly one system, they often combine some features of others. Socialism combines government ownership and control of basic industries with some private ownership of consumer-goods businesses. In some communist countries, a limited amount of private enterprise and profit motive is tolerated. For example, after farmers in some communist countries meet the government's quota for their crops, they may be allowed to sell the rest and keep the profit.

In our country, there is some government regulation of business. There are also some government-operated enterprises, such as post offices, schools, and city water agencies. Our economic system is not pure capitalism, so it is often called modified or mixed capitalism. In Unit 3, you will learn about how government and business work together in our economic system.

Increasing Your Business Vocabulary

The following terms should become part of your business vocabulary. For each numbered item, find the term that has the same meaning.

business
capitalism, free enterprise system,
    market economy, or private enter-
    prise system
communism
competition
custom-based economy
directed or planned economy

economic system
marketplace
private enterprise
private property
profit
profit motive
socialism

1. A nation's plan for making decisions on what to produce, how to produce, and how to distribute goods and services.
2. An economic system in which goods are produced the way they have always been produced.
3. An economic system in which government owns and controls the economic resources and makes all of the decisions regarding the production of goods and services.
4. Any place where buyers and sellers exchange goods and services for some form of money.
5. An economic system in which most economic resources are privately owned and decisions about production are largely made by free exchange in the marketplace.
6. The right of the individual to choose what business to enter and what to produce with only limited direction from the government.
7. The right to own, use, or dispose of things of value.
8. Money left from sales after subtracting the cost of operating the business.
9. The right to work for profit.
10. The rivalry among businesses to sell their goods and services to buyers.
11. An economic system in which government owns and operates a number of industries while providing for some degree of private property and private enterprise.
12. An economic system in which government owns most of the economic resources and has tight control over the production and distribution of goods and services.
13. An establishment or enterprise that supplies goods and services in exchange for some form of payment.

Reviewing Your Reading

1. What are the three economic questions that every society must answer to set up an economic system?
2. State the major feature of the three types of economic systems.
3. Who owns and controls most economic resources in a system of capitalism?
4. In addition to capitalism, give three other names by which the U.S. economic system is known.
5. What are the five features of our market economy?
6. Why are business owners entitled to make a profit from their business ventures?
7. What does the right of private property entitle the owner to do?
8. Give three ways in which consumers benefit from competition among businesses.
9. In addition to the profit motive, give two other reasons that might encourage people to invest their time, money, and energy in operating their own businesses.
10. In addition to private property and private enterprise, what are four other rights that are included in our economic freedom of choice?
11. How does ownership of resources differ under socialism and communism?
12. Do citizens have any influence on the extent of government control under socialism? Explain.
13. Is freedom to buy goods and services in a communist system restricted in any way?
14. What is meant by the term "mixed economy"?
15. Why is it more accurate to refer to our economic system as modified or mixed capitalism rather than as pure capitalism?

Using Your Business Knowledge

1. How is the question of what goods and services will be produced chiefly determined under a custom-based system?
2. Who chiefly decides what will be produced in a directed economic system?
3. Explain and give examples showing how enterprises stay in business which sell, at higher prices, goods and services also sold by other businesses.
4. For each of the three types of economic systems, give one example of a country operating under that system in the world today. Explain your choices.
5. If we can choose any kind of work we wish under the right of free enterprise, why can't individuals open a law office, practice dentistry, or pilot a plane when they feel they are ready to do so?
6. If the United States operated as pure capitalism, what are several changes that might occur?
7. It has been said that the term "market" in our market economy refers to an idea and not to a place. What do you think this means?
8. Explain how the decisions of buyers and sellers in the marketplace largely answer the question of what to produce in our private enterprise system.
9. Even though we have many freedoms under our economic system, there are many activities that we are not free to do. For example, we are not permitted to hunt and kill animals that are designated as endangered species. List several activities that we are not allowed to do in our society.

Computing Business Problems

1. Countries that make efficient use of capital goods can produce more with fewer people in a shorter time than countries in which many workers perform the work by manual labor. Study the figures below for farm workers and their output and then answer the questions that follow.

	United States	Soviet Union
Agricultural labor force	4,380,000	34,350,000
Number of people supplied from output of each farm worker	49	7

   a. How many more people were working in agricultural jobs in the Soviet Union than in the United States in the year quoted?
   b. In which country was each farm worker more productive?
   c. In terms of people supplied from the output of each farm worker, how much more productive was the worker cited in item (b)?

2. Lani Oolan compares food prices in newspaper ads each week before doing her grocery shopping. One week she found these prices for Grade A eggs at three competing supermarkets: Food Mart, $1.09 per dozen; Farm-to-You, $1.17 per dozen and 20 cents off with a newspaper coupon; and Kitchen Pride, special, 2 dozen for $2.09.
   a. At which store would Lani pay the lowest price per dozen?
   b. Will the coupon be an advantage? Explain.

c. Do you think the fact that there were three stores from which Lani could buy eggs benefited her in any way?

3. The table below shows the average number of hours a worker in the capitals of the United States, United Kingdom, and the Soviet Union would have to work to earn enough money to buy the items listed at the left. The data are from the National Federation of Independent Business.

	Washington, D.C.	London	Moscow
Hamburger meat, 1 pound	17.0 min.	29.0 min.	56.0 min.
Color television, large screen	65.0 hrs.	132.0 hrs.	701.0 hrs.
Toothpaste	16.0 min.	13.0 min.	27.0 min.
Bus fare (2 miles)	7.0 min.	11.0 min.	3.0 min.
Men's shoes, 1 pair	8.0 hrs.	7.0 hrs.	25.0 hrs.
Week's food for family of four	18.6 hrs.	24.7 hrs.	53.5 hrs.

a. How much longer than a U.S. employee must a Soviet employee work to earn enough to buy food for four for a week?

b. How much longer than a U.S. employee must a British employee work to earn enough to buy the weekly food basket?

c. How many 8-hour days would a worker in each country have to work to earn enough to buy the color television?

d. If the color television costs $650, what would U.S. workers' wages per hour be?

Expanding Your Understanding of Business

1. Using library resources, such as *The Statistical Abstract of the United States*, prepare a report on the two largest directed economies, the Soviet Union and the People's Republic of China. Find as much as you can of the following information about each of the two countries:

- Population.
- Percent of the world's population living in each country.
- Output per person (check under the listing "GNP—per capita").
- Amount of goods exported.
- Amount of goods imported.
- An example of an exported and an imported good. Do the exported/imported goods give you an idea about the advantage and the disadvantage of each country's resources? Explain.

2. Visit a mall or a shopping center in your community and list the businesses that sell the same or similar products. List ways in which these businesses compete with one another to get customers to buy.

3. Several countries operating under communism have, in recent years, allowed their citizens to engage in some capitalistic activities. For example, under a program called *perestroika*, the Soviet Union allows enterprises to make business decisions in response to market demand and profit potential rather than in response to a state quota. From the local media or from library sources, compile a list of capitalistic activities that have been allowed in the Soviet Union recently.

4. In our market economy, you and other consumers make most of the decisions regarding what to produce by what you

buy. Some products that are put on the market succeed because many people buy them. Others stay on the market only a short time because no one buys them. Consumers are saying with their purchases, ''Produce this'' or ''Don't produce this.''

From discussions with your parents and other adults, identify three products that have remained on the market over a long period of time and three that were put on the market but failed in a short time.

You and the Market Economy

Chapter 3

Chapter Objectives

After studying this chapter and completing the end-of-chapter activities, you will be able to:

1. *Identify three economic roles each person plays.*

2. *Identify an example to show how dollar votes help create demand.*

3. *Identify one example each to show how demand and supply affect prices.*

4. *Explain the effect that competition has on prices.*

5. *Explain how your worker role supports your consumer role.*

6. *Cite one example to show the importance of productivity in your worker role.*

7. *Identify two examples of economic citizenship.*

At 6:30 in the morning, after a ride across town to his job, Nuyen Shao got off the bus and dashed into a restaurant for a quick breakfast. To earn money for college in the fall, Nuyen has been working at the city zoo, helping to build new living quarters for the animals. After work, he rode the bus back across town to the voting precinct near his home. At age 18, Nuyen is voting in elections for the first time. He takes pride in having studied the issue to be decided this election day. Nuyen is preparing to be a veterinarian and has a special interest in the vote regarding a tax issue for city projects, which would include expansion of the zoo. As he leaves the voting booth and heads home, he feels good about his day. He may not be aware of it, but Nuyen has played three economic roles during the day.

YOUR THREE ECONOMIC ROLES

You play three economic roles, too, just as Nuyen did. A look at his activities will help you to identify those roles. First, Nuyen was a consumer; he purchased goods (breakfast) and services (the bus ride). As a worker, Nuyen helped produce a service (zoo maintenance). As a citizen, he voted on an economic issue.

You and everyone you know will play many different roles in life. You may become a famous recording star, a business executive, or even the president of the United States. A friend of yours may become a swimming coach, an electrician, a minister, or a computer programmer. While you and

Illus. 3-1
As citizens, we make economic decisions collectively by voting.

your friend may follow different career paths, some of the roles you play will be the same.

The three roles that all people share are those of consumer, worker, and citizen. It is true that some people do not work outside the home for wages, and some people may not exercise their right to vote, but we all will be affected in some way by these three economic roles. As you play these roles, you will make decisions that affect not only you, but the entire economy as well. Understanding how the private enterprise system works will help you understand the importance of your decisions—and may even help you make better ones—in each of your economic roles. In the remainder of this chapter, you will look at how the American economy works and how your roles fit into the picture.

YOUR ROLE AS A CONSUMER

As you learned in Chapter 2, the American economic system is a market economy in which buyers and sellers freely make economic decisions in the marketplace. You also learned that these decisions basically answer the question of what will be produced. The buying decisions of all consumers—individuals, businesses, and governments—provide the answer to how we will use our scarce resources. The important role you and all other consumers play in making these decisions is one of the most interesting characteristics of our system. Individual buying decisions have a great influence on our market economy; individual consumers buy more than two-thirds of all goods and services produced in it. As you can see, consumers play a central role in a private enterprise system.

It may seem to you that the American economy is a big, unorganized system in which everyone does just about as he or she pleases. You may wonder how the system can work when each business makes its own decision about what to produce and each buyer makes a decision about what and where to buy. But the system does work and it works well. Let's explore how your consumer decisions affect the system.

Your Dollar Votes Help Create Demand

As a consumer, you help businesses make their decisions. You do this by buying—or not buying—certain goods and services. When you buy something, you are casting a *dollar vote* for it. You are saying to a business, "I like this product or service, and I'm willing to pay for it." When a business sees your dollar votes and those of all other consumers, it knows the demand for the product. **Demand** means the quantity of a product or service that consumers are willing and able to buy at a particular price.

Demand Helps Determine Supply

Knowing the demand tells a business what type and what quantity of products and services to supply. **Supply** means the quantity of a product or service that businesses are willing and able to provide at a particular price. Suppliers usually will produce a product or service as long as it can be sold at a price that covers the costs of operating the business to make and sell it, plus a reasonable profit. This is why you can buy a hamburger for about $1.50, but you will not find any for 10 cents. Suppliers of hamburgers could not cover their costs and make a profit at the 10-cent price.

Together, supply and demand play an important part in our market economy. The buyers and sellers in the marketplace that you read about in Chapter 2 help to determine not only what will be produced, but also what the price will be. Let's see how that works.

Demand and Supply Affect Prices

Have you ever wondered how a business decides what price to charge for a product or service? Why does a sweater cost $40 and a new car $12,000? Why does the price of a swimsuit drop in the fall of the year or the cost of food go up after a long summer's drought?

In addition to deciding what to produce, a business must set a price on a product or service. Generally speaking, prices are very carefully determined after a good deal of study. Supply and demand are among the most important factors to be considered.

The demand for a product affects the price. If many people want (demand) a particular product or service, its price will tend to go up, as illustrated in Figure 3-1. The price of Christmas cards is usually at its peak in November and early December, when many people want to buy them. Have you noticed, however, that the prices of the cards are often cut in half the day after Christmas? When demand is low, prices are usually low.

Supply also affects the price of a product. Remember that a supplier needs to cover the costs of operating the business and make a reasonable profit. Prices are set to do these two things. If a supplier of jogging shoes, for example, sets a price too high, people will not buy the shoes. Therefore, the supplier will have to lower the price in order to sell the shoes. Of course, if the price is set too low, operating costs will not be covered; the supplier will lose money and soon go out of business. All this means that the supplier must produce a good product and operate in an efficient way. Prices can then be set at reasonable levels so that consumers will be willing and able to buy the products.

Of course, other factors may be involved in the pricing process. The prices of some products tend to stay high, for example, because the materials from which they are made are limited by nature. Diamonds have been found

Figure 3-1
Prices are
affected by the
demand for and
the supply of
goods and
services.

in only a few countries of the world and in relatively small quantities. Therefore, the price of diamonds is very high.

In recent years, the people of the United States have also come to understand that the supply of oil is not unlimited as was once thought. When suppliers of oil produce less and the supply of products made from oil—such as gasoline—is reduced, the prices rise. On the other hand, when suppliers produce more oil and make it available, the prices tend to fall.

Competition Keeps Prices Reasonable

Earlier you read that suppliers set prices to cover operating costs and earn some profit. What is to prevent a seller from charging an unreasonably high price in order to earn larger profits? The answer is competition. You will remember from Chapter 2 that competition is one of the main features of the private enterprise system. If one store offers cassette tapes for $12.95 but another offers the same tapes for less, you probably would say to the merchant with the higher price, "Forget it. I can buy that same tape at a store down the street for $10.95." If the owners of the store keep the price at $12.95, and do not compete in other ways—such as delivery or other services—they will soon go out of business because not many people will buy tapes at the higher price.

Competition affects prices in another way, too. When a product has a very high demand and is making money for one supplier, other businesspeople will begin to offer the product also. With several businesses offering the product, one of the suppliers could not afford to sell at extremely high prices. Consumers would go to the competitors to buy. This also tends to cause suppliers to produce goods and services efficiently. If a supplier cannot produce the product at a low cost so that it can be sold at competing prices, other suppliers who do so will get all of the business and the inefficient producer will be forced out of the market. In this way, competition tends to allow only efficient producers—those who can supply good products at competitive prices—to survive in the marketplace. Competition, then, aids the consumer by helping to keep prices and profits at reasonable levels.

YOUR ROLE AS A WORKER

No matter what price is set on products and services in the marketplace, you cannot enjoy the products and services unless you have the money to buy them. This is where your worker role comes into the picture.

Your Earnings Help Set Your Standard of Living

Most people earn their money by working. Of course, people work for many reasons. One of the main reasons you will work, however, is to earn money to buy the things you need and want. While your parents may be supplying most of your needs now, before long you will be meeting your own needs with the money you earn. How well you succeed in your chosen career will be the most important factor in setting your standard of living. We use the term **standard of living** as a measure of how well people in a country live; that usually means the quality and quantity of wants and needs which are satisfied. We use our incomes to buy the things we need to maintain and improve our standard of living. Your worker role, then, supports your consumer role.

Your Worker Productivity Affects You and the Economy

The main way we improve our standard of living is to produce more in our worker roles. When you begin your worker role, you will join more than 116 million other workers in the United States. These workers produce the goods and services that consumers demand. One of the reasons this country has progressed so far in such a short time is that it has had a varied and skilled work force. We have combined with this work force better capital goods and a high level of technology to increase our productivity. That is, we have

Illus. 3-2
Your role as a
worker supports
your role as a
consumer.

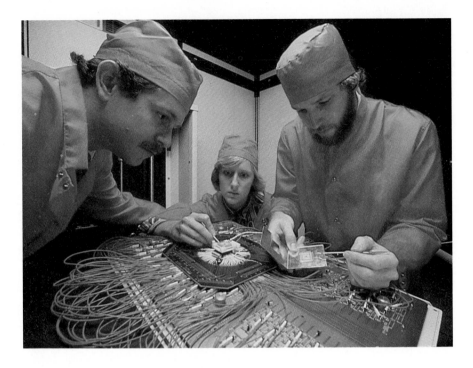

learned to work more efficiently. **Productivity** refers to the quantity of a
good that an average worker can produce in an hour. High productivity has
enabled us to achieve a standard of living that is among the highest in the
world. As a worker, you will want to improve your productivity so that you
can increase your earnings and your standard of living. If you produce less
than is expected of a worker in the job you choose, you help to lower the
productivity and thus the standard of living for the nation. You will learn
more about productivity and about your worker role in other chapters in this
text. Now, let us consider the third role you play in the private enterprise
system.

YOUR ROLE AS A CITIZEN

So far, we have considered how you will satisfy your own wants and needs
through your worker and consumer roles. But there are some needs and wants
that you will not be able to satisfy for yourself. In your citizenship role, you
will join other citizens in making some economic decisions for the common
good.

Some Decisions Are Made Collectively

You probably will not earn enough to have your own fire department to
protect your home. Furthermore, you will not earn enough to build your own

highways on which to drive your car. Even if you did earn enough money, it would not be very practical for each person to provide his or her own fire department or road system. Think of the confusion, to say nothing of the waste! There are many other services such as schools, courts, and police protection, that neither individuals nor businesses can usually provide for themselves. In your role as citizen, you will join others, through different levels of government, in providing for these goods and services. Thus, we collectively decide how some of our scarce resources will be used and what will be provided for our common use.

Taxes Help Pay for Common Services

To pay for the goods and services that the government provides for our common use, you and other citizens will pay taxes. There are many kinds of taxes collected by local, state, and national governments. You will learn more in Unit 3 about meeting the costs of government services. In your citizenship role, you should remember that the government cannot supply all that you and other people want. It, too, must make choices as to which services it can afford to provide. When Nuyen Shao voted for the expansion of the city zoo through increased taxes, as discussed in the opening of this

Illus. 3-3
Taxes help to pay for goods and services provided by the government.

chapter, he helped his city decide which of the many goods and services would be provided. When you vote, as a part of your citizenship role, you will be helping to make some of these decisions.

Increasing Your Business Vocabulary

The following terms should become part of your business vocabulary. For each numbered item, find the term that has the same meaning.

demand   *standard of living*
productivity   *supply*

1. The quantity of a good that an average worker can produce in one hour.
2. The quantity of a product or service that businesses are willing and able to provide at a particular price.
3. As a measure of how well people in a country live, this term indicates the quantity and quality of wants and needs that are satisfied.
4. The quantity of a product or service that consumers are willing and able to buy at a particular price.

Reviewing Your Reading

1. State the three economic roles that most people in the United States play.
2. Explain the way your dollar votes help to create demand.
3. Give one example each to show how demand and supply affect prices.
4. Suppliers usually set their prices to cover what two factors?
5. If a business has overstocked a product, would it be likely to raise or lower the price of the product?
6. Would the price of a product made with scarce natural resources tend to be high or low?
7. What effect does competition have on prices?
8. Give an example to show how competition tends to make businesses more efficient.
9. In what way does your worker role support your consumer role?
10. In what way might your selection of a career affect your future standard of living?
11. Give one example to show the importance of productivity in your worker role.
12. Give two examples of activities you perform in your citizenship role.

Using Your Business Knowledge

1. When the demand for small cars increases, what might the suppliers of large models do to sell their cars?
2. Name two products other than those cited in the text that are usually high-priced because they are scarce.
3. Discuss the importance of the consumer in a market economy.
4. If workers produce fewer goods and services than they are expected to produce, what effect will their lowered productivity have on the nation's standard of living?

5. Since Americans have the freedom to make individual choices in the marketplace, why would they make some decisions collectively?
6. Choosing your career is one of the most important economic decisions you will make. Can you explain why?

7. In your citizenship role, you will be performing a variety of activities in addition to voting on economic issues. After discussing this with friends and members of your family, list several activities that a good citizen does for either his or her personal satisfaction or for the common good.

1. The Video Rental Center purchased 24 dozen videotapes of a blockbuster new movie, at a cost of $20 per tape, to sell during the Christmas season.
   a. How many individual tapes did Video Rental Center buy?
   b. What was the total cost of the tapes?
   c. In January, the shop had one-fourth of the tapes left. How many tapes were unsold?
   d. If demand had dropped after the holidays, would the shop be more likely to increase or decrease the price to sell the tapes?
2. Below is a table showing information about the voting activity of young people in three national election years. One year, 1984, was a presidential election year; 1982 and 1986 were congressional election years. Study the data and answer the questions that follow.

Year	Number of People Age 18 to 20 Years Old (In Millions)	Percent Reporting They Are Registered to Vote	Percent Reporting They Voted
1982	12.1	35.0%	19.8%
1984	11.2	47.0	36.7
1986	10.7	35.4	18.6

   a. How many 18- to 20-year-olds voted in each year?
   b. How many 18- to 20-year-olds reported they registered but did not vote in 1986?
   c. How many more 18- to 20-year-olds reported they voted in the presidential election year than in 1982?
   d. Why do you think so many more voted in a presidential election year than in a congressional election year?
3. Diamonds are called precious gemstones because they are so scarce. Diamonds are used not only in jewelry but also in industrial production for cutting and grinding other materials. They are found in only a few places in the world. The leading producers are Zaire, Botswana, and the Soviet Union. Below is a table showing the gemstone diamonds imported by the United States in two recent years.

Year	Volume (In Millions)	Value (In Millions)
1983	6.3 carats	$2,275
1985	8.2 carats	$3,007

a. What was the increase in value of the imported diamonds in 1985 over 1983?
b. What was the percent of increase in the carat weight of the imported diamonds in 1985 over 1983?
c. If the percent of increase remained the same for each two-year period, how many million carats of diamonds would the United States have imported in 1989?

Expanding Your Understanding of Business

1. Local newspapers at midweek often feature many ads from food stores. Examine the ads from your local paper for several stores and list all forms of competition other than price.
2. Interview the manager of a local retail store, such as K mart. Ask the manager whether there have been any items recently for which there was a surge of demand. If so, did the store have enough of the item to supply the demand? Did the price change? Ask the manager to explain also how such things as bad checks and theft affect prices in the store.
3. As a class project, survey a senior homeroom or social science class about the voting habits of the members. Prepare a survey form in your class so that all students will be asked the same questions. Some suggested items for the survey form are: What is your age? If you are 18, have you registered to vote? Why or why not? Do you plan to register before the next election? Do you think 18-year-olds should vote? Why or why not? Have you ever voted? Tally all of the survey forms and discuss the results in class.
4. Visit three gasoline service stations in your area and list the price each charges for unleaded regular gas. Find out how much of the cost represents taxes and from what levels of government the taxes are imposed. Ask the owners how they compete with other stations other than by the price of the gasoline.
5. Make a list of ten "dollar votes" that you have cast within the past week. When demand is high, one sometimes has to go to two or more stores to cast dollar votes for the item. Was that the case for any item on your list? If so, explain.

Measuring Economic Progress

Chapter 4

Chapter Objectives

After studying this chapter and completing the end-of-chapter activities, you will be able to:

1. *Explain how GNP is used as a measure of economic growth.*

2. *Explain how per capita output is determined.*

3. *Cite an example to explain how productivity is related to the standard of living.*

4. *Describe economic conditions in the four phases of the business cycle.*

5. *List three economic problems that our country faces.*

How many ways do you measure your growth? Probably in more ways than you think. Two obvious ways are your age and your size. They keep changing. You add another year to your age every birthday. As you grow, your shoe size gets bigger every year. Your clothes seem to be shrinking; your body is just reminding you of your growth.

You grow in many other ways, too. As you mature, your abilities increase. You depend less on your parents and begin to plan for your future—looking at careers, working part time and saving some of your wages for the future, and improving your grades to enable you to enter college.

Your mirror, the scales, and your shoe size measure your body growth. Your interests, actions, and achievements measure your mental and psychological growth. Improvement in grades and the size of your savings account measure the extent to which you are meeting your goals. These are just a few of the ways by which you can measure various growth factors in your life.

MEASURING THE GROWTH OF THE ECONOMY

Just as you can use different ways to measure your own growth, we can use different methods to check on the growth of our economy. A high rate of employment and a low rate of business failures are two indications that our economy is doing well. However, the most important ways by which we can measure how well we are doing relate to how much we produce to help satisfy the needs and wants of our people. Today more than 116 million Americans work in thousands of different jobs and produce thousands of different products and services—hamburgers, snowmobiles, amusement parks, nail polish, electronic games, fire engines, carry-out chicken dinners, garbage collection, medical services, concerts. The list is almost endless. The total of all the goods and services that Americans produce is the output or production of our nation. We have only about 7 percent of the world's land and about 5.4 percent of the world's population, but our output accounts for more than 25 percent of all goods and services produced in the world.

MEASURING THE NATION'S OUTPUT

One way to find out how well our economy is doing is to compare output from year to year. The federal government collects information from producers and estimates our national output. The most widely used estimate is the gross national product. The **gross national product** or **GNP** is the total dollar value of all final goods and services produced in our country during one year.

GNP includes what consumers spend for food, clothing, and housing. It includes what businesses spend for buildings, equipment, and supplies. It also includes what government agencies spend to pay employees and to buy

Illus. 4-1
Millions of
Americans are
employed in
thousands of
different
occupations.

supplies. There are a few things not included, of course. For example, GNP does not include the value of the work we do for ourselves, such as cutting our own lawn or building a picnic table for our yard. However, if we buy the

Illus. 4-2
Some activities,
such as
babysitting, are
not included in
the GNP. Can
you name some
others?

lawn service or the picnic table from businesses, they would be included. Only final goods, such as a house, are counted when we measure GNP. If intermediate goods, such as the lumber used to build the house, were counted as well, the value of the intermediate goods would be counted twice.

If the GNP increases from year to year, this is a good sign that our economy is growing. Even though we have had some bad years, our economy has enjoyed a steady climb over its history. GNP was more than $4 trillion in a recent year. Writing that figure down—a 4 followed by 12 zeros—will give you an idea of how big our economy really is when we measure it in dollars.

There is one big difficulty in comparing a country's GNP from year to year, however. Prices of what we produce do not stay the same from year to year. Prices go up and down—mostly up. In order to make comparisons that are fair and accurate, we need to take the current prices and adjust them each year so that they are equal in value over a period of years. Let's look at a very easy example.

Suppose the tiny make-believe country of Bananaland produces only banana chips. The output of Bananaland is shown in Figure 4-1.

Figure 4-1
Output of
Bananaland.

Year	Cartons of Banana Chips Produced	Current Price per Carton	GNP at Current Prices	Prices Adjusted to 1980	GNP at Constant Price
1980	1,000	$ .50	$ 500	$ .50	$500
1985	1,000	$1.00	$1,000	$ .50	$500
1990	1,000	$1.50	$1,500	$ .50	$500

Note that under current prices the GNP for 1990 is reported at $1,500. On this basis, you could say that the GNP (or total output) increased three times since 1980. However, this would be wrong. Actually, Bananaland made no progress in producing banana chips. In each of the years, 1,000 cartons of banana chips were produced. If prices had remained the same, the dollar value would have been $500 each year.

Now let's look at a different example for Bananaland. Figure 4-2 shows that in 1990 Bananaland produced three times as many banana chips as in 1980. If the GNPs at current prices are compared, the GNP increase in 1990 was nine times that of 1980 ($4,500 ÷ $500 = 9). However, in constant prices, the GNP in 1990 was three times that of 1980—exactly the same as the actual increase in the total number of banana chips produced. In this example, we have used 1980 as the year the price is held constant so that we can use it as a measuring device. We call 1980 the base year. **Base year** means the year chosen to compare an item, such as price, to any other year. We can choose

Figure 4-2
A Second Look at
Bananaland's
GNP.

Year	Cartons of Banana Chips Produced	Current Price per Carton	GNP at Current Prices	Prices Adjusted to 1980	GNP at Constant Price
1980	1,000	$ .50	$ 500	$ .50	$ 500
1985	1,500	$1.00	$1,500	$ .50	$ 750
1990	3,000	$1.50	$4,500	$ .50	$1,500

any year as the base year, just as we chose 1980 to compare the GNP of
Bananaland.

MEASURING OUTPUT PER PERSON

An even better way than GNP to measure economic growth is the per capita
output or the output per person. The **per capita output** is found by dividing
GNP by the total population (see Figure 4-3). For example, suppose that
there is no change in GNP this year over last year. Suppose, also, that the
population increases. You can see that the same output would have to be
divided among more people. An increase in per capita output means that our
economy is growing. A decrease may mean that our economy is having
trouble.

Figure 4-3 Per capita output is determined by dividing GNP by the total population.

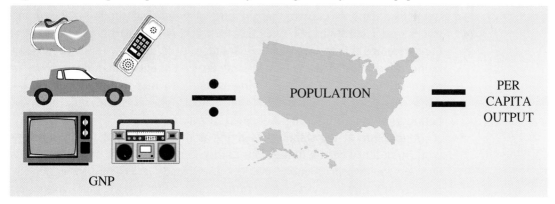

GNP ÷ POPULATION = PER CAPITA OUTPUT

MEASURING PRODUCTIVITY

As you learned in Chapter 3, productivity is the quantity of output for the
average worker in an hour. Our economic history shows a steady upward
climb in productivity until recently. During the past 20 years, productivity
has had some ups and downs (see Figure 4-4). While there has been an

Figure 4-4
Can you explain
the importance of
the relationship
between wages
and productivity?

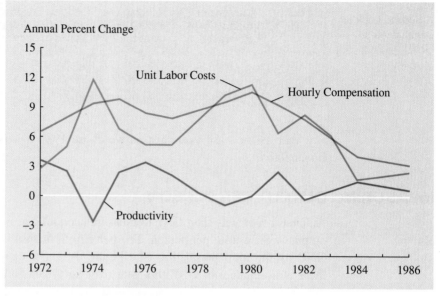

Source: U.S. Bureau of the Census.

increase in productivity in many of those years, the amount of the increase
has become smaller than in the past. And in a few cases, productivity has
actually decreased. At the same time, wages were steadily climbing. In one
recent ten-year period, wages increased five times more than did productivity. This means, of course, that the cost of producing goods increased and
prices rose accordingly. So even though workers were earning more money,
they were not able to improve their standard of living very much because of
rising prices. For that reason, a great deal of attention has been given in
recent years to ways of motivating workers to increase productivity. By
doing so, the workers will be contributing to a higher standard of living in the
nation as well as improving their own life-styles.

A measure of the standard of living is the number of hours one has to
work in order to earn a living. Our ability to produce more and more goods
and services as our country developed has made it possible to reduce the
number of hours in a workweek. In the early 1890s, the average worker put
in about 60 hours a week. Today the average workweek is a little less than 40
hours. Even though we work fewer hours and have more leisure time, we
produce more and earn more than our labor force ever has before. We can
produce more in less time because we use modern equipment and efficient
work methods, and we have many highly skilled workers. Although
productivity in our recent past has increased nearly every year, it has been
pointed out that the amount of the increase has been getting smaller. Some
improvement in productivity was noted in the late 1980s.

COPING WITH ECONOMIC PROBLEMS

You probably have heard people talking about the many changes in the economy. They speak about bad times and good times, rising prices, a new business coming to town and providing new jobs, or a factory closing and causing hundreds of workers to lose their jobs. What do these changes mean? We have learned over the decades that our economy has its ups and downs and that good times and bad times seem to run in cycles.

The Business Cycle—Changing Economic Conditions

It has been said that bad times go away and good times return—if you wait long enough. If we look at the economic changes that have occurred during our country's history, we can see that they do form a pattern—good times to bad times and back to good times. This movement of our economy from one condition to another and back again is called a **business cycle**. There are four phases of the business cycle. Let's look at the good times first.

PROSPERITY

At the high point of the business cycle, we enjoy **prosperity**. During prosperous times, most people who want to work are working, wages are good, and the GNP is high. Consumers are buying and business is booming. Then for some reason, the economy begins to slow down. For example, after the successful moon landing in 1969, the U.S. government severely decreased its spending for space exploration. Jobs of engineers, technicians, and other workers in the program ended. Businesses that had contracts to supply the technology and labor for the space program had to cut production and lay off workers. The nation had some serious economic adjustments to make. In the late 1980s, an increase in oil supply caused a significant decrease in oil prices. Many businesses in states with oil-based economies, such as Texas and Oklahoma, were forced to curtail spending. They began to lay off large numbers of workers to cut expenses. When people lose their jobs or hear of many others losing jobs, they begin to worry and cut down on spending. Business begin to feel this reduced spending through decreased sales.

RECESSION

When demand falls and businesses lower production, unemployment begins to rise; this phase of the business cycle is called a **recession**. It may not be too serious nor last very long. It may signal trouble only to certain groups of workers in certain areas, such as Texas and Oklahoma during the recent oil glut, or it may spread through the entire economy. For example, businesses in other states that sold equipment and supplies to Texas and Oklahoma companies begin to feel the pinch of reduced sales. These firms may then

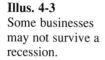

Illus. 4-3
Some businesses
may not survive a
recession.

start laying off workers and the process spreads. GNP then slows and may
even decrease, causing some recessions to be longer and worse than others.

DEPRESSION

If a recession deepens and spreads through the entire economy, the nation
may move into the third phase, **depression**. This phase of the business cycle
is marked by high unemployment and business failure. GNP is at its lowest
point during a depression. Fortunately, our economy has not had a deep
depression for more than half a century. The last one was the Great
Depression of 1930-1940. Approximately 25 percent of the American labor
force was unemployed. Many people could not afford even the basic needs.
Food and clothing were given out in the "bread line" of churches and other
charitable agencies. Depression was not only an appropriate name for the
state of the economy, it fit the people well also. They were emotionally as
well as economically depressed.

RECOVERY

By the end of the 1930s, the economy began to recover. **Recovery** is the
phase of the business cycle in which unemployment begins to decrease and
GNP rises. People begin to find jobs, and consumers regain confidence about
their futures and begin buying again. This new demand causes businesses to

produce more and to employ more people to do this. Recovery may be slow or fast. As it continues, the nation moves into prosperity again.

Inflation and Deflation

Another problem with which our nation has had to cope is inflation. **Inflation** is an increase in the general price level. Inflation occurs when the demand for goods and services is greater than the supply. When a large supply of money, earned or borrowed, is spent for goods that are in short supply, prices increase. Inflation was a serious problem in the 1970s and early 1980s. Government, business, and individuals continued to increase their spending and prices continued to rise. Even though wages (the price paid for labor) tend to increase during inflation, prices of goods and services usually rise so fast that the wage earner never seems to catch up.

Controlling inflation requires reduced spending. Cuts in spending require a great deal of discipline. In addition, reduced spending by government, business, and individuals often leads to other economic problems, such as unemployment. As you have read, this can also lead to a change in the business cycle.

There is an opposite to inflation. It is called deflation. **Deflation** means a decrease in the general level of prices. It usually occurs in periods of recession and depression. Prices of products are lower, but people have less money to buy them. You will learn more about inflation and deflation in Chapter 15 when you study about the changing value of money.

Other Economic Problems

We have come a long way under our private enterprise system. We know it works well. We also know that it can be made to work even better as we find solutions to the economic problems that confront us, in addition to coping with business cycles and controlling inflation.

All of us may be harmed by pollution. Air, land, and water are being polluted by gases, smoke, and waste coming from industry, from individuals, and from the products we buy and use. Government now is responding to the people's demand for action. Businesses are cooperating so that we can keep our environment healthy for future Americans. Individuals are also taking more responsibility in protecting the environment. More work needs to be done and you can help. The next time you are tempted to toss a paper cup on the school grounds or onto the highway, stop and think about what you are doing by polluting the environment.

There are still some people who do not have sufficient food or proper health care. Another challenge is that of providing proper housing for all of our people, especially in large cities. Already much of the dilapidated housing is being remodeled or torn down and rebuilt. Efforts are also being made to solve traffic and crime problems in many cities.

We must also find creative solutions to our unemployment problem. As our nation changes from smokestack industries, or factories, to industries that require technology and communications, we must find ways to retrain people whose jobs are lost in the change.

As Americans, we realize that we have some shortcomings. Therefore, as a nation we should work to eliminate economic hardship for our people. Much work needs to be done to control disease and reduce human suffering. We need to find new sources of energy and to conserve our natural resources. Much remains to be done in education, mass transportation, and human relations, and to make our government more responsive to the needs of the people.

BUILDING OUR ECONOMIC FUTURE

What lies ahead for our economy? Robots performing most of the routine tasks in factories? Housekeeping done entirely by machines? Farming under the ocean? Space colonies on the moon or other planets? Replacement of

Illus. 4-4
What does the economic future hold in store for the United States? No one knows for sure.

injured body parts with artificial ones? Working at home and communicating with employers by computer instead of going to offices? Two-way pocket telephones and three-dimensional television? Germproof, tornadoproof, earthquakeproof, soundproof, fireproof, burglarproof houses? These are some of the things scientists have predicted for the year 2000, which is not far away. Many of these are already being developed. No one knows for sure how these changes will affect our economy in the future.

To provide a better quality of life for everyone, each of us has the responsibility of understanding how our economic system works, of being aware of our problems, of helping solve our problems, and of realizing the impact of our own productivity on the nation's economy and standard of living.

Increasing Your Business Vocabulary

The following terms should become a part of your business vocabulary. For each numbered item, find the term that has the same meaning.

base year
business cycle
deflation
depression
gross national product or GNP

inflation
per capita output
prosperity
recession
recovery

1. The total value of all goods and services produced in a country in one year.
2. The year chosen to compare an item, such as price, to the same item in another year.
3. The figure that results from dividing the GNP of a country by the population of that country.
4. The movement of our economy from one condition to another and back again.
5. A phase of the business cycle in which employment is high, wages are good, and GNP is high.
6. A phase of the business cycle in which demand decreases, businesses reduce production, and unemployment rises.
7. A phase of the business cycle in which unemployment and business failures are high and GNP is at its lowest point.
8. A phase of the business cycle in which unemployment begins to decrease and GNP rises.
9. An increase in the general price level.
10. A decrease in the general price level.

Reviewing Your Reading

1. Compare the United States with the rest of the world in land size, population, and output of goods and services.
2. "One way to find out how our economy is

doing is to compare output from year to year.'' What does this statement mean?

3. The spending of what three groups is included in GNP?

4. If prices of goods and services remain exactly the same over a long period of time, would it be fair and accurate to compare a country's GNP from year to year at current prices?

5. Explain the use of a base year in measuring output.

6. What is the difference between current prices and adjusted prices of goods and services?

7. How is per capita output determined?

8. How is per capita output used in measuring economic growth?

9. Name three factors that have contributed to the high output over the history of our economy. What changes have taken place in productivity in recent years?

10. Give an example to explain how productivity is related to the standard of living.

11. Describe the general economic conditions in each of the four phases of the business cycle.

12. Is there room for improvement in our economic system? What are some of the economic problems that need solving?

Using Your Business Knowledge

1. The GNP of Kenya, a developing country in Africa, increased 3.6 percent in one year—from $5.6 billion to $5.8 billion. Does this mean Kenya had a 3.6 percent increase in the amount of goods and services produced?

2. If you and your classmates have jobs for which you are paid wages, you are contributing to the GNP. Survey your classmates who work and determine how much your class has contributed to the GNP in one week. (To protect confidentiality, ask the students to report their earnings on a slip of paper without their names.)

3. The GNP of Country A is $400,000. The GNP of Country B is $800,000. Does this mean that the per capita output of Country B is about twice that of Country A? Explain.

4. As you have learned, the GNP of the United States in a recent year was more than $4 trillion in current dollars. Ten years before, it was less than half that amount. In the next few years, the GNP is expected to pass the $5 trillion mark. What difference does it make to you and to other people in your community whether the GNP is increasing or decreasing?

5. Explain how high wages and low productivity can increase the price you pay for goods and services.

6. Explain how productivity has helped to increase the U.S. worker's leisure time.

7. Suppose that many auto and steel plants close throughout a country and that thousands of workers lose their jobs in a relatively short period. If the country has been enjoying prosperous times, it may now be headed into what phase of the business cycle? Describe other conditions that might begin to occur.

8. List several things that you and your classmates could do to prevent or reduce pollution at school. Prepare a summary list for the class, make a poster of the list, and post it in the classroom and on the school bulletin board.

Computing Business Problems

1. The 1990 production schedule of Banana-land listed on page 47 shows its GNP at current prices of $4,500 and at constant 1980 prices of $1,500. If Bananaland's population of 1990 was 500, what was its per capita output?
   a. At current prices?
   b. At constant prices?
2. Some very simple machines such as the wheelbarrow and the hand truck have increased productivity or output per worker hour. Seth Kisco, who works in a warehouse that imports much of its goods, can move from the loading pier to storage one 30-kilo box at a time by hand. Using a hand truck, he can move three 30-kilo boxes at once in the same time.
   a. Seth can move six boxes in one hour without using a hand truck. What is his productivity?
   b. If he uses a hand truck, what is his productivity?
   c. How many workers without hand trucks would it take to do the same work Seth does with a hand truck?
   d. How many pounds can Seth move in an hour with a hand truck? (See Appendix D for information regarding metric conversions.)
3. A small Asian country produces teakwood carvings of water buffalo to sell to tourists. The country's production record is shown in the following table:

Year	Number of Carvings Produced	Current Price per Carving
1980	1,000	$ .50
1985	2,000	$1.00
1990	4,000	$2.00

   a. What is the country's GNP at current prices for each year?
   b. What is the amount of increase in the number of items produced in 1985 over 1980?
   c. What is the rate of increase in the number of items produced in 1990 over 1985?
   d. If the country expects to maintain the same rate of increase for 1995, how many water buffalo carvings will it need to produce?
4. Study the graph on page 48 and answer the questions that follow:
   a. In what year was productivity lowest?
   b. What happened to the cost of producing each unit of goods in the year cited above?
   c. What was the approximate percentage of decrease in productivity from the previous year to the year cited in *a*?
   d. In most years, an increase in productivity is shown, even though the amount of the increase was down from the previous year. In what years was there an actual decrease in productivity?

Expanding Your Understanding of Business

1. GNP does not include many of the services you and your family provide for yourselves and others. List several goods and services that your family provides for itself that it would otherwise have to pay for. Why do you think they are not included in GNP?
2. Look through some recent newspapers and magazines for items that mention any of the nine business terms in the "Increasing Your Business Vocabulary" section.

Mount your clippings on sheets of paper. Below the article, write one statement that the article tells you about the term mentioned.

3. In determining our GNP, only final goods and services are included. This avoids having some items counted more than once. For example, a mining company sells iron ore to a company that makes steel. The steel company sells the steel to an automobile manufacturer who produces finished cars. The iron ore is not counted at each step. Its value is included only once—in the price paid for the final product, the car. Below is a list of goods and services produced in our economy. Tell whether you think each item should be counted as part of GNP. If you do not think it should be counted, tell why.

a. An electric oven bought as a gift
b. A telephone that you buy and plug in
c. Telephone service installed in a government office
d. Fiberglass sold to a company for use in making the boats it produces
e. Grooming services for a cat
f. Paper sold to a publisher of a newspaper
g. Gemstones sold to a jeweler
h. Gemstones sold by a jeweler
i. A computer paid for by the city government
j. A computer for your family's use
k. An automobile for the city police department
l. Videodiscs bought by a music store for resale
m. Broccoli for a food-processing firm

4. Because of economic pressures, many businesses in recent years have been *downsizing*. From library sources, write a definition of the term. List several reasons for downsizing by firms.

5. There have been many reports in the media in recent years focusing on cleaning up the environment. Make a list of the efforts in your city and state to clean up or protect the environment.

Career Focus

A career in the American free enterprise system could be anything you want it to be. If you have enough interest to acquire the training for it, you could be a corporate executive, an opera singer, or a professional clown. The choice is yours.

Each unit in this text will help you prepare to make your choice by outlining career opportunities in the area discussed in the unit. Since this unit introduces you to the economics of our market system, this career section will focus on the people who work in the economics profession; they are called economists.

Job Titles: Job titles commonly found in this career area include:

Economists
Financial Analysts
Financial Managers
Investment Analysts
Consultants
Statisticians
Actuaries
Credit Analysts
Budget Officers
Economics Professors

Employment Outlook: The economics profession is small. In 1986, about 37,000 economists were employed, with about one-third of them in government agencies. An additional 22,000 people taught economics in colleges and universities. Faster-than-average growth is expected in the number of jobs in economics by the year 2000. Competition will be keen for most jobs in economics, especially in teaching, where the number of jobs is expected to decline with decreasing college enrollment. Most of the new jobs will be in manufacturing, financial services, research, consulting, urban and regional planning, health services, and environmental science.

Future Changes: Computers have had and will continue to have a great impact on the economics profession. They have provided economists with more information at rapid speeds; information is the resource with which economists work. Economists who have strong backgrounds in math and computers and the ability to analyze numerical data will have the best job opportunities in the future.

What Is Done on the Job: Economists study the way a society uses its scarce resources—natural, human, and capital—to provide

goods and services. They analyze and interpret their research to find the best ways of using resources to produce and distribute these goods and services. They also measure economic growth, which you learned about in Chapter 4. Some economists are concerned with economic theory; they study how and why economic events, such as recessions, happen as they do. Most economists, however, apply economics in specialized areas such as agriculture, housing, or banking. Some economists collect and analyze data about population changes, such as the number of people in various age groups or the movement of large numbers of people from one section of the country to another. Through their understanding of economic relationships, economists can advise businesses and government about the possible results of various actions or decisions.

Education and Training: A bachelor's degree is usually required to enter the field of economics. Top economists typically have doctoral degrees. Since beginning jobs often involve the collection and compilation of information, the entrant must understand statistics and research methods. The ability to handle details accurately and to analyze objectively are important personal skills. Courses in advanced mathematics and computers, along with advanced degrees in economics and related fields, such as statistics and marketing, provide the best opportunities for advancement.

Salary Levels: Salaries vary widely, depending upon the educational background and experience of the worker and the place of employment. In 1986, the average beginning salary for economists with bachelors or masters degrees was about $22,400. Starting salaries for those with doctoral degrees ranged from $27,200 to $36,600. In 1986, the median salary (half made more, half made less) for economists was $54,000.

For Additional Information: An interview with a banker in your community or an economics professor at a college or university would be helpful if your are interested in exploring a career as an economist. Publications such as *U.S. News and World Report* and *Business Week* regularly feature economic data as well as economists' views on the state of the economy and the outlook for the future. Your school counselor can provide information about colleges and universities offering degrees in economics. The National Association of Business Economists may provide information on careers in business economics. The association's address is:

28349 Chagrin Boulevard
Suite 201
Cleveland, Ohio 44122

Business in Our Economy

Unit Goals

After studying the chapters in this unit, you will be able to:

1. *Describe the four basic types of businesses.*
2. *Cite the main features of the various forms of business ownership.*
3. *Give examples to illustrate how the interdependence of nations makes world trade necessary.*

The Legacy of the Golden Arches

Business Brief

While he did not invent either the hamburger or the "golden arches," Ray Kroc is credited with building a hamburger empire. Ray Kroc's entrepreneurial idea ushered in a new industry and changed the way Americans—and other people in many parts of the world—eat.

Kroc was a man of ideas, energy, and innovative management abilities. He held a variety of jobs before becoming a sales manager for a paper product company where he worked for 17 years. Later, as an agent for a company selling a machine that could make six milk shakes at a time, Kroc was amazed when a California hamburger stand owner ordered eight. Curious about a business that needed to make 48 milk shakes at once, he visited the busy hamburger operation and convinced the owners, Maurice and Richard McDonald, to let him take their golden arches hamburger stand idea back to Illinois as a franchise. They agreed, and in 1955 at age 52, Kroc opened his first McDonald's in a Chicago suburb. Five years and 250 McDonald's outlets later, he bought out the McDonald brothers for $2.7 million.

Kroc insisted that managers of his franchises and of his company-owned stores be skilled in working with people. He stressed cleanliness and strict quality control for his all-beef-patty operation. He applied a streamlined team approach to food preparation. His firm became one of the country's largest employers of part-time teenage workers.

The firm has not been without problems, however. The nutritional value of hamburgers was once debated in Congress. The struggle to keep prices down has been ongoing, and competition from a growing field of fast-food outlets has often been fierce. Kroc always met the problems head-on and survived them. His enormous success has been credited to his genius in innovative management techniques, including fine-tuning the fast-food retailing operation and convincing people worldwide to eat and enjoy his products.

Kroc had other interests along the way. He became influential in the sports world as the outspoken owner (1974-1979) of a professional baseball team, the San Diego Padres. In addition, his humanitarian efforts have benefited many people. Most notable among them are the Ronald McDonald Houses that have been established near several children's hospitals to house parents who are visiting their hospitalized children.

After Kroc's death in 1984, his widow, Joan Kroc, has continued contributing to humanitarian causes. Since his death, she has given more than $35 million to such causes as a research center at Notre Dame University devoted to world peace, a hospice, AIDS research, and a shelter for the homeless.

Sources: Milton Moskowitz, Michael Katz, and Robert Levering, eds., *Everybody's Business: An Almanac—The Irreverent Guide to Corporate America* (San Francisco: Harper & Row, Publishers, 1980), 128-132; "Ray Kroc Dies: Built McDonald's," *The Virginian-Pilot and Ledger Star*, 15 January 1984, 1, 3; "Look Where Joan Kroc is Throwing Her McNuggets," *Business Week* (September 5, 1988): 74-75.

What Business Is All About

Chapter 5

Chapter Objectives

After studying this chapter and completing the end-of-chapter activities, you will be able to:

1. *Give an example of the four basic kinds of businesses.*

2. *Explain how marketing adds value to products.*

3. *Explain the difference between direct and indirect marketing channels.*

4. *Cite seven kinds of activities that are performed by most businesses.*

5. *Explain the difference between gross profit and net profit.*

6. *Give the average percent of profit made by manufacturers.*

7. *Describe two benefits that come to a community as a result of new or expanded business activity.*

8. *Give two examples of ways through which businesses carry out social responsibility.*

Take a moment from your reading to look around and see what your classmates are wearing. Chances are that a good many of them are wearing jeans. You are probably wearing them, too.

When buying the jeans, neither you nor your classmates probably thought much about the chain of businesses involved in making the jeans and getting them to the stores where you bought them. Most people don't. Let's look at the sequence of events that occurred between the creation of your pair of jeans and your purchase of them.

First, the cotton is planted and harvested; then it is made into cloth and dyed different colors. The jeans are designed, made up in various sizes, labeled, boxed, and then stored until they are sold to the store from which you and your friends buy them.

Several businesses are involved in this process. These businesses are different in many ways, but all are alike in one way—they are helping to put a product or service that you want on the market. That is what business is all about. There are more than 16 million business firms in the United States. While there are some differences among them, they all supply or help to supply goods and services to satisfy your wants and needs. Learning about them will help you understand what business does.

BASIC KINDS OF BUSINESSES

You and your family buy from many kinds of businesses. You buy food from a supermarket, shoes from a shoe store, furnace repairs from a plumbing and heating company, financial services from a bank, a car from an auto dealer, and electricity from a utilities company. In all of these cases, you are dealing with businesses that sell products and services to you and to other consumers. Have you ever wondered where they get the products and the materials for the services they sell to you? Often these products and materials have moved through several businesses before they get to the store from which you buy them. There are four basic types of these businesses: extractors, manufacturers, marketers, and service businesses.

Extractors Get Products from Nature

Businesses that grow products or take raw materials from nature are called **extractors**. The farmer who grew and sold cotton for your jeans is an extractor. Silver and coal miners are also extractors, as are those who dig copper in Montana, fish for salmon in Alaska, pump oil in Texas, grow fruit in Florida, and run lumber mills in Washington. Sometimes the extractor's products are ready to be sold just as they come from the earth or the sea, like the clams in New England, oranges from California, or pecans from Georgia. However, most food products and raw materials need some processing or change in form before the consumer can use them.

Illus. 5-1
There are more than 16 million businesses in the United States.

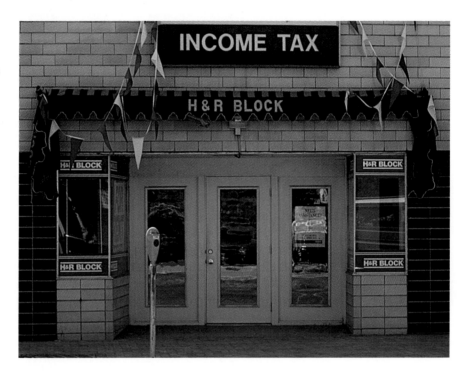

Manufacturers Make Products

The **manufacturer** takes the extractor's products or raw materials and changes them into a form that consumers can use. The manufacturer might make a product such as a moped or process a product such as freezing and packaging vegetables. Other manufacturers may construct sections of a building that, when put together, become a house for people to live in. Some manufacturers are only a part of the total activity of producing goods from the extractor's products. Think about those jeans again. The entire process might require several steps, which may be performed in several different locations, before the jeans are ready for you to purchase. For example, a textile mill in North Carolina takes cotton grown on an Alabama farm, spins it into yarn, and makes the yarn into cloth. A plant in New England then dyes or prints the cloth, and a clothing factory in New York buys the cloth and makes it into jeans. Together, extractors and manufacturers are industries that change the form of resources from their natural states into products for consumers.

Marketers Bring the Products to Consumers

Our skilled labor force and our advanced technology enable producers to make thousands of different products at a reasonable cost. However, if these products are not available where and when you and other consumers want to buy them, they are of no use.

If all of the goods you use had to be bought directly from their producers, it would be extremely difficult and expensive for you to buy things. You might have to go to Central or South America to get a banana. What an expensive banana that would be!

The services of many businesses are often needed before goods actually reach consumers. All of the activities involved in moving goods from producers to consumers are performed by marketers. These activities are called **marketing** or **distribution**.

Marketing includes more than transporting and selling products. Marketers test new product ideas to see whether consumers will like them and buy them. They package goods to protect products and to present them in attractive and convenient sizes, and they also store the goods until they are needed by other marketers or consumers. They even design store windows and arrange displays in supermarkets to attract your attention. All of these marketing activities add value to products by bringing them where the consumer is, at a time they are wanted, in the assortment wanted, and at prices the consumer is willing to pay.

Bridging the gap between producers and consumers can be very complicated. Of course, you can buy certain products directly from the

Illus. 5-2
Marketing includes more than transporting and selling products. Marketers also package goods and arrange displays to attract your attention.

producer. For example, you may buy tomatoes directly from the farmer who grew them or a handmade basket from a basket weaver. However, most products will be handled by several marketers before they reach the store where you buy them. The path that a product travels from producer to consumer is called the **marketing channel** or **channel of distribution**. Figure 5-1 illustrates three possible marketing channels.

When goods are bought by the consumer directly from the producer, the process is called **direct marketing**. The tomatoes and the basket purchases are examples of direct marketing. Most goods, however, will travel through at least one and sometimes several middle firms before they reach the consumer. This process is called **indirect marketing**.

Figure 5-1 Channels of distribution link producers and consumers.

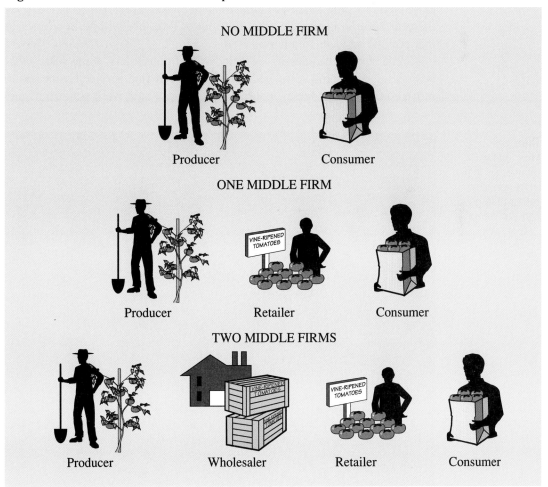

The farmer may sell tomatoes to your local grocery store, a retailer, from which you buy them. A **retailer** is a middle firm that sells directly to the consumer. On the other hand, the farmer may sell the entire crop of tomatoes to a wholesaler, such as a large distribution firm. A **wholesaler** is a middle firm that sells to other wholesalers or to retailers. The wholesaler will then sell the tomatoes to the grocery store, the retailer, which in turn sells them to you. A product may travel through several middle firms in the marketing channel.

Service Businesses Do Things for Us

Firms that do things for you instead of making or marketing products are called **service businesses**. These businesses are perhaps the fastest growing part of our business world. Between 1982 and 1986, the number of people employed full time in service industries increased more than 30 percent. By the year 2000, it is expected that four out of five jobs will be in businesses that provide services to others.

Some service businesses serve individual consumers, some serve other businesses, and some serve both. Today you can find service businesses to move you from New Jersey to Arizona, style your hair, wash your car, figure

Illus. 5-3
How many businesses that offer services rather than goods can you name?

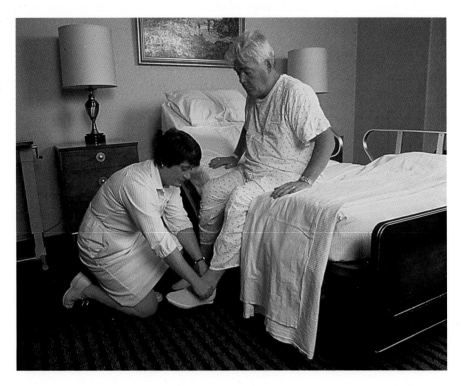

your income tax, board your dog, give you computer lessons, clean your clothes, rent a pair of skis, pull a tooth, take you on a tour, cook the food for your party, or almost any service you need or do not want to do for yourself.

As people have more leisure time and more money to spend, they want more and more businesses to do things for them. Also, as more women enter the labor force, they tend to pay someone to perform many services that they once did for themselves and their families. All this tends to increase the size of the service industry.

ACTIVITIES PERFORMED BY MOST BUSINESSES

Businesses come in many types and sizes. A business may be as small as a newspaper stand on a street corner, or as large and complex as an oil company, which has wells, refineries, and service stations in many different countries. Although individual businesses differ in the way they operate, most of them perform basically the same kinds of day-to-day activities. Let's examine some of these important activities.

Developing Ideas

Every business begins with an idea. Someone must first think about a product, a service, or an improved process or piece of equipment that will meet customer needs before a product or service can be put on the market. Examples are jogging shoes, lawn-care businesses, and automatic can lifters for garbage pickup trucks. All of these examples—stemming from an idea—created not only one, but many businesses.

Established businesses must continue to develop ideas in order to survive. In our market economy, businesses compete with other firms that sell the same or similar products. To compete successfully, they must look for new or improved products and services. Many firms have research and development personnel who work full time creating, researching, and developing ideas that might result in new products and services.

Financing the Business

As you learned in Chapter 1, businesses need capital—money—to operate. Start-up money must be found to create the business. This may come from the owner's personal funds, from loans from banks or other financial institutions, or from others who wish to invest in the business. You will learn more about obtaining start-up money for one firm in Chapter 6.

Established businesses continue financing activities throughout the life of the firm. Companies may need to borrow money to buy equipment or inventory, to redesign a plant or build a new one, or to buy another business.

They may obtain loans from financial institutions, such as banks, or from people who wish to invest in the business.

Financing also includes managing the cash that comes into the business from sales and other sources. Just as you will learn to put your money to work for you, so must a business invest money in banks or other institutions in which it can earn interest and grow.

Buying Goods and Services

Businesses buy goods and services both for resale and for their own use. The owner of a men's clothing store, for instance, must buy slacks, jackets, suits, coats, and other items to sell. The store owner also needs sales tickets, a cash register, display cases, and other supplies. Services offered by other businesses, such as advertising space in a newspaper or a window cleaner to wash the display windows, will be needed.

In addition, businesses that sell products need to buy raw materials to make them. Buying raw materials, such as wheat, oil, plastic, steel, or chemicals, is an important activity in operating goods and services businesses.

Managing Human Resources

Businesses cannot operate without people. Except for the one-person business, all firms need to have a system for carrying out staffing activities. These include recruiting, or finding, the workers; interviewing and testing the applicants; selecting the workers; training and developing both new and experienced employees; and appraising job performance of the workers. Also included are the tasks of analyzing jobs and writing job descriptions to assist in finding employees whose abilities match the requirements of the job. The list also includes developing a system for paying employees fairly and equitably. Human resources management requires a knowledge of equal opportunity laws, health and safety regulations, and employee rights relating to issues such as promotions, transfers, layoffs, and firings. These and other staffing activities are often carried out by a human resources (or personnel) department.

Producing Goods and Services

The heart of a business is the production of a product or service to sell to its customers. The good or service must be produced at the scheduled time, in the appropriate quantity and quality, and at competitive cost in order for the firm to stay in business. Assembling the people, raw materials, processes, and equipment to accomplish this task is essential to all businesses.

A key business decision relates to the control of *inventory*—the amount of raw materials, supplies, and partially completed goods used in production.

Raw materials, supplies, and partially completed goods are needed for production activities. In maintaining control over its inventory, a business must:

- Determine the amount of raw materials and supplies to order and from whom to order.
- Decide when to have the raw materials and supplies delivered and what amount to keep on hand in a storage area.
- Decide what amount of partially completed goods and finished goods to keep in inventory.

If the appropriate amount of raw materials and partially completed goods is not in inventory when needed, production will stop. If production stops, the business will not have an adequate supply of finished goods to sell and the business will probably begin losing money.

Marketing Goods and Services

As you have learned earlier in this chapter, marketing includes a variety of activities, all directed toward getting the product or service to the consumer and persuading him or her to buy it. Businesses must sell their product or service if they expect to stay in operation. You might think of production as one side of a coin and marketing as the other side. Goods must first be produced in order to be sold and the products must be sold, or there is no point in producing them. Together, production and marketing account for most of a business's profit.

Maintaining Accounting Records

All businesses must have some kind of a recording, or accounting, system. You may have heard the expression, ''What's the bottom line?'' This refers to the last line on a report that tells whether a business is making a profit or a loss. Many records must be completed and compiled in the report to enable the owner to know what the bottom line is. Business owners need to know

Reprinted by permission: Tribune Media Services.

how much they have sold, how much of what they sold was returned by customers, and how much they owe to others. They need to know the amount they are spending for building repairs, rent, salaries, and other expenses. Their records show whether their business is making or losing money and give them information they need for government reports.

PROFITS EARNED BY BUSINESSES

As you learned in Unit 1, business owners are entitled to profits because of the risks they take in investing their money and because of the extra work and responsibilities that go with ownership and management. Most, however, do not make the huge profits that some people think. The average percent of profit on sales for manufacturing businesses is usually 4 to 5 percent a year. As you know, competition with other businesses helps keep prices and profits down to reasonable figures. One reason for inaccurate beliefs about profits, however, is that some people do not understand the difference between gross and net profit. **Gross profit**, or **margin**, is the difference between the selling price and the cost of merchandise sold. **Net profit** is what is left after all business expenses have been paid. Suppose Ruby Doss, the owner of a camera shop, sells a camera for $40. She bought the camera for $24, so she has a gross profit of $16. Out of this $16, she must pay rent, supplies, advertising, taxes, and many other expenses. Her records show that all expenses related to the sale of the camera amount to $14. She has therefore made a net profit of $2 on the camera—or a net profit of 5 percent ($2 ÷ $40) on the selling price.

Businesses and the Local Economy

Communities often spend much effort and large sums of money persuading new businesses to locate within their boundaries. Almost everyone is pleased when new businesses open in the community. A new business benefits the local economy in many ways.

The Multiplier Effect

Perhaps the most important benefit of a new business investment in the community is that new jobs are created. This means that the people who work directly for the business have incomes to support themselves and their families. When they spend this income for goods and services, the money multiplies as it is spent again by each person who receives it. The increase in total income caused by the chain of spending by consumers from a new investment by business is called the multiplier effect. Let's see how that works.

When a new factory opens, it begins paying wages to its employees. This is money that has not been in the community before. Workers spend this money for goods and services. The money is then spent again by the businesses from which those goods and services were bought. For example, part of each worker's income is spent for food. The food store manager pays out part of this money for stock. The manager also pays part of it to employees, who in turn spend their money somewhere else for other goods and services. If new people come to the community to work, more houses will probably be needed. This means that local builders will hire more workers and buy more materials. As each dollar is spent, each business is likely to buy more goods and hire more people to meet its customers' demands. This endless spending chain started with the original investment in wages by the new business in the community. Of course, most people and most businesses do not spend all of their income as in this simplified example. People might spend, say, 90 percent of their income and save 10 percent. The multiplier effect works the same way on whatever amount is spent in each round, and it always adds up to more than the original amount (see Figure 5-2). You can see, then, that when new jobs are created in a community, each dollar paid to workers is said to multiply itself. This is why most cities and towns seek new businesses.

Figure 5-2
A new business can benefit the whole community. Here is how the multiplier effect works.

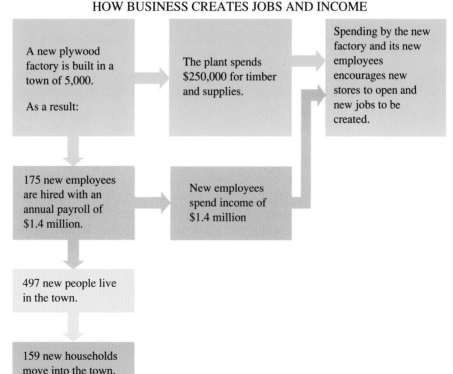

HOW BUSINESS CREATES JOBS AND INCOME

A new plywood factory is built in a town of 5,000.

As a result:

The plant spends $250,000 for timber and supplies.

Spending by the new factory and its new employees encourages new stores to open and new jobs to be created.

175 new employees are hired with an annual payroll of $1.4 million.

New employees spend income of $1.4 million

497 new people live in the town.

159 new households move into the town.

Other Effects on the Local Economy

Another benefit from a new or expanded business is that it pays taxes to the community. This means that the community has more money to build new schools, repair its streets, provide better police and fire protection, and improve other services, such as parks.

When a new business comes to a community, it buys such things as electricity, office furniture and supplies, equipment, and tools. Some of these things will be bought from businesses in other towns, but many will be bought locally. This gives income to local businesses, and, in turn, paychecks to their employees.

Businesses also tend to attract other businesses. When one business settles in a community, other businesses often come to supply it. For example, small businesses may spring up to supply a large factory with such things as small parts, office supplies, cleaning services, and advertising services. Each of these smaller businesses hires people and buys goods and services. Thus, more jobs and more income are created in the community.

Businesses and Social Responsibility

Business owners and managers today must do more than just provide a worthwhile product or service at a reasonable price in order to make a profit and stay in business. They must hire workers without discrimination; they must pay competitive wages and provide other benefits, such as health insurance and paid vacations. They must also provide a safe working environment, and they must show concern for the general welfare of their workers. These are economic benefits that workers in any community expect.

In addition, businesses today assume social responsibilities in the community. Many participate in training programs for unskilled workers. Some businesses provide advice and managerial assistance to members of minority groups in setting up and operating their own businesses. They cooperate with schools in many ways—by providing speakers, by employing students in part-time jobs, and by sponsoring programs such as Junior Achievement. Many businesses contribute generously to education, to charities, and to civic and cultural projects. In fact, business leaders are often the leaders of these projects.

The acceptance of social responsibility by businesses is also seen in the efforts of many firms to avoid polluting the air, the water, or the natural beauty of the countryside. Helping to keep a clean environment is an important part of business planning today. Before they allow a new business to locate in their area, most communities require the firm to show that its operation will not cause pollution. There are still many problems to be worked out to improve the environment and keep it clean, but progress is being made through cooperation between businesses and the communities in

Illus. 5-4
Many businesses provide scholarships for deserving students.

which they are located. Adding the economic and social benefits together, you can see why most communities welcome new businesses.

Increasing Your Business Vocabulary

The following terms should become part of your business vocabulary. For each numbered item, find the term that has the same meaning.

direct marketing
extractor
gross profit or margin
indirect marketing
manufacturer
marketing channel or channel of
    distribution

marketing or distribution
net profit
retailer
service business
wholesaler

1. The activities that are involved in moving goods from producers to consumers.
2. The path that a product travels from producer to consumer.
3. The difference between the selling price and the cost of merchandise sold.
4. The process through which goods are bought by the consumer directly from the producer.
5. A business that takes an extractor's products or raw materials and changes them into a form that consumers can use.

6. The amount left over after expenses are deducted from the gross profit.
7. The process through which goods move through one or more middle firms between the producer and the consumer.
8. A middle firm that sells directly to the consumer.

9. A business that grows products or takes raw materials from nature.
10. A business that does things for you instead of making or marketing products.
11. A middle firm that sells goods to other firms like itself or to other retailers.

Reviewing Your Reading

1. Give an example of the four basic types of businesses.
2. What is meant by the statement that some extractors' products are ready to be sold to the consumer in their natural states?
3. Name several marketing activities other than transporting and selling goods.
4. How does marketing add value to a product?
5. What is the difference between a direct and an indirect marketing channel?
6. To whom do wholesalers and retailers sell their products?

7. Cite seven activities that are performed by most businesses.
8. What is the average percent of profit on sales made by manufacturers?
9. What is the difference between gross profit and net profit?
10. How does the multiplier effect of new businesses result in more jobs and income in the community?
11. Give two examples of ways through which businesses carry out social responsibilities in the community.

Using Your Business Knowledge

1. List three marketing activities that might be involved in getting a home computer from the manufacturer to the retail store that sells it.
2. If two firms make the same percentage of profit on sales, will they also make the same amount of dollar profit from their business operations? Explain.
3. Name two products that you might buy through a direct marketing channel.
4. Kim Sun operates the Sea Isle Treasures shop in the waterfront marketplace of her city. She sells fresh flower arrangements and leis as well as shell jewelry and ornaments. Give two examples of the following:

a. Goods which she would buy for resale.
b. Goods she would buy for use in her store.
c. Services she might offer to her customers.
d. Services she might buy from other businesses.

5. The Chamber of Commerce and the Economic Development Council of Central City have persuaded a fiberglass processing plant to open in the city's industrial park. The company expects to employ 200 people there. Name at least five ways in which the city would probably benefit from the new business.

Computing Business Problems

1. The Juan Iglasias Company is considering building a cannery in Santa Rosa. The company accountants' estimate of the monthly income and expenses for the new plant is as follows:

Income from sales	$200,000
Expenses:	
Salaries	100,000
Raw materials purchased	60,000
Rent on equipment	6,500
Miscellaneous expenses	5,000
Taxes	8,400

   a. What is the total amount of the cannery's monthly expenses, including taxes?
   b. What will be the cannery's net profit if the estimates are accurate? (Calculate net profit by subtracting the total estimated expenses and taxes from estimated income.)
   c. What is the percent of profit based on sales?
2. The fish catch and the value of the catch along the Atlantic coast for 1980 and 1986 are shown below:

Area	Catch (In Millions of Pounds)		Value (In Millions of Dollars)	
	1980	1986	1980	1986
New England states	788	563	$327	$449
Mid-Atlantic states	244	156	97	114
Chesapeake Bay states	718	617	130	131
South Atlantic states	473	249	148	155

   a. What was the total weight of the catch for the Atlantic regions, expressed in full (including the zeros) for 1980 and 1986?
   b. Did the fish catch for any of the areas increase in 1986?
   c. What was the dollar value of the catch in 1980 and 1986?
   d. Did the dollar value of the catch increase in any region in 1986?
3. Joshua Mizell has just received his first semimonthly paycheck of $1,000 from a new firm in his town, Metal Fence Manufacturing, Inc., where he works as production supervisor. He saves 25 percent of his salary. He spends the rest at businesses in town on food, clothing, and a payment on a car. His spending sets the multiplier effect in motion. Each time the money is spent, you can assume that the person who receives the money also saves 25 percent and spends 75 percent.
   a. Carry the multiplier effect through five rounds of the spending/saving chain, beginning with Joshua's $750 spent and $250 saved. List the amount spent and the amount saved for each of the next four rounds.
   b. How much has been added to the local economy at the end of five rounds?
   c. What is the total amount saved by the five people or businesses involved?

Expanding Your Understanding of Business

1. Communities often advertise in newspapers and business magazines to encourage new businesses to locate in their towns. Find out what your community or your state is doing to attract new businesses. Consult such sources as your local newspaper, your Chamber of Commerce publications, *Business Week*, *Fortune*, *The Wall Street Journal*, and *U.S. News and World Report* in your library.

   a. From the ads and other sources of information, list the advantages cited by your city or state to encourage businesses to locate in the area.

   b. Which factors among those listed do you think are the most important? Why?

   c. Would some factors be more important to some kinds of businesses than others? Explain.

2. Read Question 5 from the "Using Your Business Knowledge" section on page 74. Some citizens prefer that businesses not locate in their communities. What are some of the arguments you think they might list when opposing the locating of new businesses, such as the fiberglass processing plant, in their towns? Do you think that the advantages are more important than the disadvantages?

3. When businesses leave a community, the multiplier effect can work in reverse. If several businesses in your community fail during the year, how might the welfare of individual consumers, workers, other businesses, and the local government be affected?

4. Interview the owner or manager of a retail store in your area. Ask him or her if most of the products in the store come through direct or indirect marketing channels. Do any products come through more than one wholesaler? If so, give an example, identifying the types of wholesalers involved. Write a brief report entitled, "The Marketing Channels for (name of store), a Local Retail Store." Share your findings with the class.

Forms of Business Enterprise

Chapter 6

Chapter Objectives

After studying this chapter and completing the end-of-chapter activities, you will be able to:

1. *Explain how ownership differs among sole proprietorships, partnerships, corporations, cooperatives, and franchises.*

2. *State the advantages and disadvantages of the three major types of business ownership.*

3. *Name the five functions of managers.*

4. *Explain how municipal corporations and business corporations differ.*

5. *Explain the difference between a consumers' cooperative and a producers' cooperative.*

When you go to a basketball game, have you noticed how the team runs out onto the court and each member goes to a certain spot on the floor? The center goes to stand opposite the center on the opposing team and the guards take special places around the floor to defend their team's action against moves by their opponents. Their positions determine what role they will play when the ball is put into motion. That didn't just happen. It was carefully organized and important decisions were made by the coach. The players were selected and placed according to their special talents to make it easier to reach the team's goal of winning games.

In a similar way, a business also must organize to produce goods and services for the consumer. Many questions must be answered in the organizing process. Who will make the decisions? Who will buy the goods to sell? Who will keep the records on what is bought and sold? Who will get the profits? If there is a loss, who must bear it? Most of the answers to these questions are found in the way a business is owned and organized.

THREE MAJOR TYPES OF BUSINESS OWNERSHIP

The three major types of business ownership are the sole proprietorship, the partnership, and the corporation. Later in this chapter you will learn about two other types of business ownership, the cooperative and the franchise.

A **sole proprietorship** is a business owned by one person. Most are small firms such as grocery stores, restaurants, gas stations, barber shops, and

Illus. 6-1
More than 70 percent of U.S. businesses are sole proprietorships.

drugstores. As shown in Figure 6-1, more than 70 percent of U.S. businesses are operated as sole proprietorships.

A **partnership** is a business owned and managed by a small group, often not more than two or three people, who become *partners*. By written agreement, these partners share the profits or losses and the responsibilities of their business.

A **corporation** is a business owned by a number of people and operated under written permission from the state in which it is located. The written permission is called a **certificate of incorporation**. The corporation acts as a single individual on behalf of its owners. By buying shares of stock, people become owners of corporations. They are then known as **stockholders** or **shareholders**. A corporation may have very few owners, but most corporations have many owners. Large corporations, such as IBM, Texaco, and General Motors, may have a million or more owners. Even if you own just one share of a company, you are still one of its owners. Most mining, manufacturing, and transporting of goods is performed by corporations. In addition, many of our consumer goods are supplied by supermarkets, department stores, and other businesses organized as corporations.

The size and the nature of a business are key factors in choosing the best type of ownership and organization for it. To help you understand each type of ownership, the next few pages tell a story of how a young man started a business and worked to make it grow.

Figure 6-1
Sole proprietorships, partnerships, and corporations are the major types of business ownership.

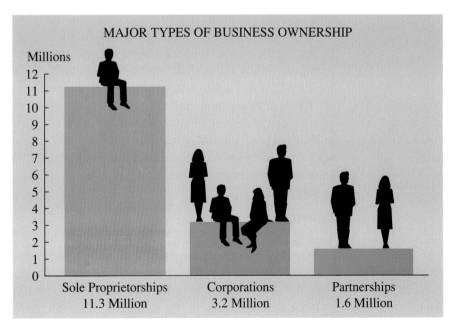

MAJOR TYPES OF BUSINESS OWNERSHIP

Millions

Sole Proprietorships	Corporations	Partnerships
11.3 Million	3.2 Million	1.6 Million

Andy Gable's Proprietorship

While in high school, Andy Gable held a number of different part-time jobs after school and on Saturdays. He thought about retailing as a career and took business courses in school. He was also interested in individual sports and jogged each day before school. During his senior year, he became acquainted with a jogger who was manager of the sporting goods department of a large department store. As a result of this acquaintance, Andy was offered a job as a part-time sales trainee in the sporting goods department. After graduation, he accepted a full-time job with the store.

In the next few years, Andy worked hard and was successful as a salesperson. He prepared for advancement by taking several evening courses at a nearby college. Soon he was promoted to assistant manager of the sporting goods department. Andy was now married, earning a good salary, and saving money. However, he wanted to own his own business. He liked the idea of earning profits for himself and of being his own boss. Therefore, in his spare time, he began planning his own business. Soon he resigned his job in the department store and was on his own.

Due to his experience and interest in selling sporting goods, Andy decided to open a sporting goods store. He chose the name Sports Emporium. He rented a small store in a shopping center and bought showcases and other equipment. With the help of a bank loan, he bought his stock of merchandise.

Andy had learned a great deal about selling sporting goods in the department store, but found that owning his own business required long hours and much decision making. He ordered merchandise, built window displays, and did most of the selling and the stock work. His wife, Connie, helped him keep his business and tax records, and a student was employed part time. Andy owned the business by himself. Therefore, as shown in Figure 6-2, it was a sole proprietorship. All the profits—or losses—were his.

By now, Andy realized how useful his management courses in community college had been. His management experience had given real meaning to the functions of managers, which he had had to learn. These functions were categories for all of the activities he performed in managing his Sports Emporium. As he considered the future of his business, he recalled these functions.

PLANNING

This function includes thinking, gathering and analyzing information, and making decisions about all phases of the business. It means setting goals for the business and strategies for achieving them. Andy did a great deal of planning at the beginning of his business. Now, he felt that he was spending so much time operating the business that he did not have enough time for this important function. He recalled that his instructor had warned the class about this pitfall in managing a business.

Figure 6-2
Andy Gable is the
sole proprietor of
Sports
Emporium.

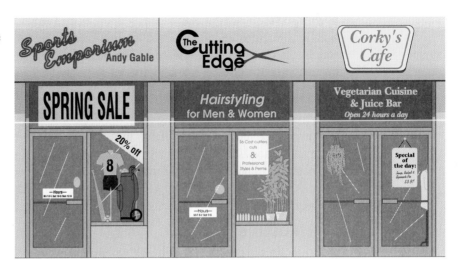

ORGANIZING

This function is the process of determining what has to be done and who is
to do each job. It involves assigning the jobs to workers and showing who
will have the authority over whom to see that the jobs are done. For example,
Andy directed the work of Connie and the part-time worker; they reported
directly to him. The organizing process usually results in a drawing that
shows these work relationships—an organization chart. Andy's business so
far is too small to need one, but if he had wished to make an organization
chart, it would look like Figure 6-3.

    This figure shows that Andy has the authority to direct the work of
Connie and the part-time worker. In turn, they are responsible to Andy to
complete the work he assigns.

Figure 6-3
Organization
chart for Andy
Gable's sole
proprietorship.

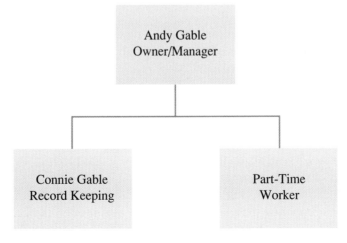

STAFFING

Staffing includes all of the activities involved in finding, selecting, hiring, training, appraising, and rewarding the business's employees. So far, Andy has performed these personnel activities for only two workers.

LEADING AND MOTIVATING

This function involves directing the work of people so that their tasks will be performed correctly and on time. Influencing people to act according to company plans is a difficult task. It must be done in a such a way that the workers will willingly perform their jobs and accept their share of responsibility for accomplishing the business's goals. Leading and motivating require good human relations and communications skills.

CONTROLLING

This function is the process through which management determines to what extent it is accomplishing the goals it set out to reach in the planning stage. Controlling means comparing what actually happens with what was planned to happen. If Andy had planned a 5 percent increase in sales for a three-month period, he would check the actual increase regularly to see whether he was moving toward his goal as planned. If, at the end of the second month, he had a 4 percent increase, he could feel his strategies were working well; however, if the increase was only 1 percent, he would consider changing his strategy.

Controlling also means using the standards you set up in the planning stage for all parts of the firm's operations. If you set a standard of production for workers on an assembly line to be 15 completed units per hour, your controlling activity would be to count the actual units produced per hour for each employee. If your quality standard for each product was that each was to be made without defects, your controlling function would be to check each completed product to see that it had no flaws. As you can see, controlling is directly related to planning.

As Andy thought about these functions of managers, he wondered how long he could handle his business all by himself. Bringing in a partner might be a solution, he thought.

The Partnership of Gable and Lowe

Sports Emporium was a success. Andy paid his bills on time and paid himself, his wife, and his part-time employee fair salaries. Each month he made payments on his bank loan until it was paid off. Profits were put aside in a savings account.

Soon Andy felt that it was time to expand the business, but he needed more money than he had saved. He also needed the help of someone who knew more about advertising and accounting than he did. He knew that his friend and former employer in the sporting goods department had studied advertising, accounting, management, and other business courses in college. His friend, Tom Lowe, also had been a salesperson for a national exercise equipment firm. He knew that this background would add a great deal to his business, so he invited Tom to become a partner in Sports Emporium.

With their combined skills, experience, money, and other property, they could afford to offer a larger variety of sporting goods. They could also afford to add new lines of merchandise—camping supplies, sportswear, and exercise equipment. Offering a greater variety of items would attract more people to the store and increase sales.

They consulted an attorney, Karen Sutton, about setting up the partnership. With her help, Andy and Tom drew up a list of items they wanted to have in their agreement. From this list, Sutton drew up a written agreement called the **articles of partnership**. Among other things, the agreement provided that:

1. The name of the firm will be Sports Emporium.
2. Gable will invest $80,000 in cash and property. Lowe will invest $40,000 in cash.
3. Each partner will draw a salary of $1,800 a month.
4. Profits and losses after salaries are paid will be shared in proportion to each partner's investment: two-thirds to Gable and one-third to Lowe.
5. Gable will have main responsibility for sales, selection, and purchase of merchandise, and customer and community relations. Lowe will handle financial records, payroll, store maintenance, advertising and sales promotion, and other details of operating the business.
6. In the event of the death or the necessary withdrawal of one partner, the remaining partner will have the right to purchase the departing partner's share of the business.

Before Gable and Lowe signed the articles of partnership, their attorney pointed out some of the legal responsibilities of partners. For example, each partner could be held personally responsible for all of the debts of the business. This would even include debts incurred by the other partner without the first partner's consent. Each partner was also bound by the business agreements that the other partner made. To avoid problems, the partners agreed to discuss all important business matters, such as hiring people or buying new equipment.

Under Gable's and Lowe's joint management, the partnership, as shown in Figure 6-4, was very successful. At the end of the first year, there was a profit of $15,000 after the business expenses and the partners' salaries had been paid. Since they had agreed to share the profits in proportion to their investments in the business, Andy received two-thirds, or $10,000, and Tom received one-third, or $5,000.

Figure 6-4
Sports Emporium
is now owned by
partners Andy
Gable and Tom
Lowe.

Sports Emporium and Fitness Center, Incorporated

Sports Emporium continued to grow under the Gable and Lowe partnership, and the partners considered expanding the business even more. They spent much time in developing ideas for improving their business, an activity you read about in Chapter 5. They thought about the new shopping center that was being built on the other side of town. Should they also enlarge the present store? Should they add new sales and storage space and also a line of small boats and boating supplies? Should they open an exercise salon as part of their business? To do these things, they needed more money. They thought about adding more partners; however, they decided against this. They reasoned that they did not need partners to help them manage the business since they could hire qualified assistant managers. Also, there would be personal risks in being responsible for the actions of other partners.

Karen Sutton advised Andy and Tom that if they formed a corporation, they would not be personally responsible for the debts of the business. In case of a business failure, each member of the corporation could lose only the amount he or she had invested. Again with Karen's help, Andy and Tom dissolved the partnership and drew up a plan for a corporation, Sports Emporium and Fitness Center, Incorporated. The corporation was to represent a total investment of $240,000. Their financial records showed that the partnership was worth $180,000; therefore, they needed to raise another $60,000.

Andy and Tom decided to divide the $240,000 into 24,000 shares, each with a value of $10. Based on the partnership agreement and the corporation plans, they divided the 24,000 shares this way: (1) Andy received 12,000 shares worth $120,000, (2) Tom received 6,000 shares worth $60,000, and (3) they offered for sale 6,000 shares valued at $60,000.

The information about the division of shares of stock and other information about the corporation was included in an application that was submitted to the state government. The application requested permission to operate as a corporation. After approving the application, the state issued a certificate of incorporation authorizing the formation of Sports Emporium and Fitness Center, Inc.

Andy and Tom were no longer owners of the partnership. They had sold their partnership to the new corporation. In return, they had received 18,000 shares of stock, or a part ownership in the corporation amounting to $180,000. These 18,000 shares were divided in proportion to the investment in the former partnership. The 6,000 shares offered for sale were bought by 30 people who had confidence in the new corporation, including their attorney, Karen Sutton, who bought 1,000 shares. The corporation now had a total of 32 individual stockholders, or owners. The owners received stock certificates like the one shown in Figure 6-5 as evidence of their ownership of the corporation.

Andy and Tom called a meeting of the stockholders to elect officers, to make plans for operating a branch store, and to conduct other business. Each stockholder had one vote for each share of stock that she or he owned. Since Andy and Tom together owned 18,000 shares, they had enough votes to control the operation of the business.

Figure 6-5
A stock certificate shows ownership in a corporation. Karen Sutton owns 1,000 shares of Sports Emporium and Fitness Center, Inc.

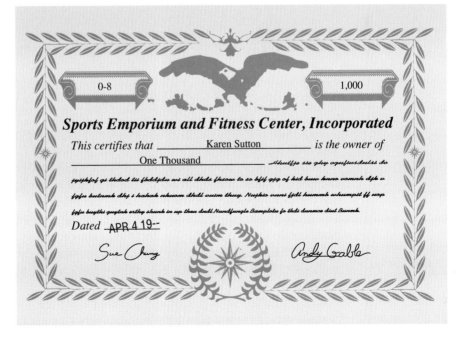

At the stockholders' meeting, seven people, including Andy and Tom, were elected as directors of the corporation. These seven people made up the **board of directors**. The board's responsibility was to guide the corporation. The board's first act was to elect the executive officers of the corporation. The directors elected Andy Gable as president, Jo Rabinski as vice president, Sue Chung as secretary, and Tom Lowe as treasurer. As full-time employees, the officers receive regular salaries for managing the business. An organization chart for Sports Emporium and Fitness Center, Inc. might look like Figure 6-6.

Figure 6-6
The organization chart for Sports Emporium and Fitness Center, Inc.

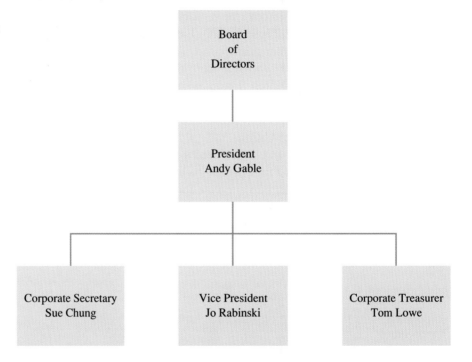

The chart shows that the board of directors has the responsibility to guide the corporation. It is placed on top in the position of highest authority and will make large policy decisions. When the board elected three of its members to hold corporate offices, it assigned authority and responsibility for the daily operation of the business to the officers.

Andy Gable, as president, will have the highest authority and will be responsible to the board for his decisions. The other officers will be assigned specific functions. Sue Chung, the corporate secretary, may be assigned the responsibility for managing the office function and any office personnel employed to carry out the communication and clerical activities of the firm. As corporate secretary, she will also sign legal documents and reports of actions taken by the board of directors. The elected office of corporate secretary is an executive position and is not the same as a secretary employed to take and transcribe dictation from a manager.

Jo Rabinski, vice president, may be assigned the responsibility for all of the sales and marketing of the company's products. Tom Lowe, the treasurer, will be the financial officer of the business. His function will include preparing the budget, preparing financial reports, and managing the firm's investments.

The vice president, treasurer, and secretary will have separate but equal authority over their assigned functions, and each will be responsible to Andy Gable, the president. Gable, in turn, will report to the board of directors.

At the end of the year, after all taxes were paid, the corporation had a net profit of $31,600. The board of directors voted to keep $10,000 of this in the business for expansion and to divide the other $21,600 among the stockholders. Since the corporation had issued 24,000 shares, each of the 32 stockholders received 90 cents for each share of stock that he or she owned ($21,600 ÷ 24,000 = $.90). The part of the profits that each stockholder receives is called a **dividend**. In addition to their salaries, Gable received $10,800 ($.90 x 12,000 shares) and Lowe received $5,400 ($.90 x 6,000 shares). Figure 6-7 shows the prospering corporation.

Figure 6-7
Ownership of a corporation can change without affecting the organization and life of the business.

TYPES OF OWNERSHIP COMPARED

You have read about Andy Gable as a sole proprietor, as a partner with Tom Lowe, and as a major stockholder in a corporation. As you have seen, Gable found some good features and some not-so-good features about each experience. Figure 6-8 shows a summary of the main advantages and disadvantages of the three types of ownership.

Figure 6-8
There are
advantages and
disadvantages to
each type of
ownership.

Type of Ownership	Advantages	Disadvantages
Sole Proprietorship	It is easy to start the business.	Capital is limited to what the owner can supply or borrow.
	The owner makes all of the decisions and is his or her own boss.	The owner is liable (responsible) for all debts, even to losing personal property if the business fails.
	The owner receives all of the profits.	Long hours and hard work are often necessary.
		The life of the business depends upon the owner; it ends if the owner quits or dies
Partnership	It is fairly easy to start the business.	Each partner is liable for business debts made by all partners, even to losing personal property if the business fails.
	More sources of capital are available.	Each partner can make decisions; there is more than one boss.
	More business skills are available.	The partnership ends if a partner quits or dies.
		Each partner shares the profit.
Corporation	More sources of capital are available.	It is difficult and expensive to start the corporation.
	Specialized managerial skills are available.	The owners do not have control of the decisions made each day, unless they are officers of the company.
	The owners are liable only up to the amount of their investments.	The business activities of the corporation are limited to those stated in the certificate of incorporation.
	The ownership can be easily transferred through sale of stock; the business is not affected by this change of ownership.	

Service-Oriented Corporations

When driving into towns, you probably have seen signs like ''Centreville—Incorporated.'' An incorporated town is called a **municipal corporation**. Unlike a business corporation, it is organized to provide services for its citizens with money from their taxes rather than to make a profit. It does not issue stock representing ownership. It has its own officials, its own schools, and its own police and fire departments. It repairs its own streets, and it provides its own water supply, street lighting system, and other services for its citizens. It levies taxes and passes rules and regulations to operate effectively. It buys supplies, equipment, and services just as any business does and pays for them under the corporate name of the city. However, it is not a business that has incorporated in order to make a profit.

Other groups are also organized as nonprofit corporations. Like the municipal corporation, nonprofit organizations are those that operate to provide a service but not for profit. Among these are churches, private colleges and universities, American Red Cross, Boy Scouts of America, Future Business Leaders of America, and Distributive Education Clubs of America. Both community governments and nonprofit agencies find that the corporate form of organization provides the most effective way for them to deliver their services to the public.

Cooperatives—Businesses Owned by Members

In addition to proprietorships, partnerships, and corporations, there are other forms of organization for doing business. Sometimes people join together to operate a business known as a cooperative. A **cooperative** is owned by the members it serves and it is managed in their interest. One type is a **consumers' cooperative**—an organization of consumers who buy goods and services more cheaply together than each person could individually. For example, farmers and members of labor unions may form cooperatives to buy products such as groceries and gasoline and services such as insurance and electricity. Farmers also form cooperatives from which they buy products needed to run their farms.

Another type of cooperative is a **producers' cooperative**. It is usually a farmers' organization that markets products such as fruits, vegetables, milk, and grains. Sometimes the cooperative operates processing plants such as canneries. A producers' cooperative lets farmers band together for greater bargaining power in selling their products.

A cooperative is much like a regular corporation. Its formation must be approved by the state. It may sell one or more shares of stock to each of its members. A board of directors may be chosen by the members to guide the cooperative. However, a cooperative differs from corporations in the way that it is controlled. In a regular corporation, a person usually has one vote for each share she or he owns. A cooperative may be controlled in two ways: each owner-member may have one vote, or each member's vote may be based on the amount of service he or she has received from the cooperative.

Most consumers' cooperatives sell to nonmembers as well as members. Prices in cooperative stores are set at about the same level found in other local stores. Most of the profits a cooperative earns may be refunded directly to members at the end of the business year; part may be kept for expansion of the business.

Franchises—Selling Another's Product

If you have stayed in a Holiday Inn or a Howard Johnson's motel, or have eaten Kentucky Fried Chicken or a Burger King hamburger, you have bought services and goods from a company that operates as a franchised business. A **franchise** is a written contract granting permission to sell someone else's product or service in a prescribed manner, over a certain period of time, and in a specified territory. Franchises can be operated as a proprietorship, partnership, or corporation.

In a recent year, there were 499,000 franchised businesses. More than 81 percent of these were owned by one person or a group of people who had received the franchise from a parent company to sell its products or services. This person or group is called the **franchisee**. Ownership of the remaining 19 percent was retained by the parent company granting the franchise, the **franchisor**.

Illus. 6-2
Many restaurants are part of a franchise system.

The franchise agreement states the duties and rights of both parties. The franchisee agrees to run the business in a certain way. This often includes the name of the business, the products or services offered, the design and color of the building, the price of the product or service, and the uniforms of employees. This standardizing of the franchised businesses means that customers can recognize a business and know what to expect when they buy a product or service from any one of them. You know approximately what kind of hamburger you will get when you buy at the "golden arches," whether you are in Miami, Kansas City, or Tokyo.

A franchise is a relatively easy business to start and the franchisor agrees to help the franchisee get started. Also, the national advertising of the product or service by the parent company serves all of the franchises all over the country. For its service, the franchisor collects a percentage of sales or an agreed-upon fee from the franchisee each year. Franchises usually require a large investment of capital to start and they are often very competitive. You may have seen in your town a fast-food restaurant or other franchise fail because it was not competitive or because it was not in a good location. Nevertheless, franchises are a popular way of doing business.

Increasing Your Business Vocabulary

The following terms should become part of your business vocabulary. For each numbered item, find the term that has the same meaning.

articles of partnership
board of directors
certificate of incorporation
consumers' cooperative
cooperative
corporation
dividend
franchise

franchisee
franchisor
municipal corporation
partnership
producers' cooperative
sole proprietorship
stockholder or shareholder

1. A group of people elected by stockholders to guide a corporation.
2. An organization that farmers form to market their products.
3. A business owned by one person.
4. A written agreement made by partners in forming their business.
5. An association of two or more people operating a business as co-owners and sharing profits or losses according to a written agreement.
6. An incorporated town or city.
7. An organization of consumers who buy goods and services together.
8. A business made up of a number of owners but authorized by law to act as a single person.
9. A document, generally issued by a state

government, giving permission to start a corporation.

10. The part of the profits of a corporation that each stockholder receives.
11. A person who owns stock in a corporation.
12. A business that is owned by the members it serves and is managed in their interest.
13. A written contract granting permission to sell someone else's product or service in a

prescribed manner, over a certain period of time, and in a specified area.

14. The person or group of people who have received permission from a parent company to sell its products or services.
15. The parent company that grants permission to a person or group to sell its products or services.

Reviewing Your Reading

1. What advantages did Andy Gable find in starting his own business?
2. What disadvantages did Andy find as the operator of a sole proprietorship?
3. Name the five functions that Andy Gable performed as a manager.
4. What advantages over his original organization resulted when Andy Gable entered into a partnership with Tom Lowe?
5. Name six items that should be agreed upon and recorded in the articles of partnership.
6. State two advantages that a corporation has over a partnership.
7. Name two disadvantages of a corporation.
8. What evidence of ownership did Andy Gable and Tom Lowe receive when they changed from a partnership to a corporation?

9. Who actually manages a corporation?
10. Why does a corporation's board of directors keep part of the profit before dividing the remainder among the stockholders?
11. What is the difference between a municipal corporation and a business corporation?
12. What is the purpose of a consumers' cooperative?
13. In what ways does a producers' cooperative serve its members?
14. How does a cooperative differ from a regular corporation?
15. What are the three conditions of a franchise agreement?
16. Name one advantage and one disadvantage of operating a business as a franchise.

Using Your Business Knowledge

1. Features of the five types of business organizations, which you studied in this chapter, are given in the following statements. Name the type of organization to which each statement applies. Some statements may apply to two types of organizations.
   a. The owner is his or her own boss.
   b. If one of the owners makes a large, unwise purchase and the business cannot pay the bill, another owner might have to do so.
   c. The business can sell stock to raise more money.
   d. If a profit is made, the owner receives all of it.
   e. Owners agree on how they will divide profits and share losses.
   f. Owners allow a board of directors to make decisions about the business.
   g. Owners/operators agree to operate the business in a prescribed manner set forth by the parent company.

h. Farmers join together to transport, store, and sell their crops.

i. Owners must get written permission from the state in which the business is located before it can operate.

j. An owner may be added to help make business decisions.

k. The amount of control a person has in the business may depend upon the value of the products and services bought from the business during the year.

l. A percentage of sales or a set fee must be paid annually to a parent company.

2. Explain how the planning function is related to the controlling function.

3. Explain how the policies and management of a corporation with more than 10,000 stockholders could be controlled by just one stockholder.

4. The community of Grandview has petitioned its state government for a certificate of incorporation so that it can become a town. When Grandview becomes a corporation, can it sell stock and issue dividends to stockholders? Explain.

5. Sarah Gray and her partner, John Tolkin, fail in their business venture. The debts are about $8,000 greater than the value of the business. Gray has personal property worth more than $10,000, but Tolkin owns nothing. Could Gray's personal property be taken to settle the debts of the business? Explain.

Computing Business Problems

1. Jake Simmons and Maury Gertz operate a small convenience store under a franchise agreement with a national company. The franchisor requires an annual payment of 5 percent of gross sales. At the close of the current year, the accountant who keeps the records for the Simmons-Gertz store reported gross sales of $523,250. How much will Simmons and Gertz pay to the franchisor for the year?

2. As an art major at a university, Lu-yin Chang specializes in creating inexpensive gemstone jewelry. To earn extra money, Lu-yin rents a stall in the new festival marketplace in the revitalized downtown area. Her income and expenses for the month of December were as follows:

Income from sales	$850
Expenses:	
Rent for stall and utilities	125
Polishing/mounting tools	45
Gemstones and supplies	110
Ad in the university paper	20

a. What was the total of Lu-yin's expenses for December?

b. How much profit did Lu-yin make in December?

c. If Lu-yin puts 20 percent of her profit into a savings account before spending on personal needs, how much will she save in December?

3. Scott and Kristie de la Garza own stock in four corporations. On the next page is a record of their stockholdings and the dividend they received for each share at the end of the first quarter.

Company	Number of Shares Owned	Quarterly Dividend per Share
IBM	50	$1.10
Avon Products	20	.25
William Wrigley, Jr.	50	.18
PepsiCo	100	.21

a. How much dividend income did the de la Garzas receive from each of their four stocks for the quarter?
b. What was their total dividend income for the quarter?
c. If each corporation paid the same amount per share for the remaining three quarters, how much dividend income would the de la Garzas receive from each corporation for the year?
d. What total dividend income would the de la Garzas receive for the year?

4. After all expenses were paid, Grant Valley Consumer Cooperative had $13,000 of profit left over. Of this amount, $3,000 was set aside for expansion of the business. According to its policy, Grant Valley would refund to each member an amount in proportion to the amount he or she bought during the year. Since total sales for the year were $500,000, the refund would be 2 percent, or 2 cents for every dollar each member had spent at the cooperative during the year. The following were among the members; their total purchases are shown in even dollars:

Randy Likins	$1,000
Jill Peery	650
Sam Peery	750
B. E. Fonza	100
H. E. Reynolds	1,250

a. How much refund did each of these members receive?
b. What was the total amount refunded to these five members?

Expanding Your Understanding of Business

1. Be prepared to give an oral report about an interview with the owner of a local business. Plan carefully in advance for your interview. Ask the business owner questions such as these:
   a. Why did you choose to go into this particular kind of business?
   b. What risks do you take in operating your own business?
   c. What methods do you use to compete with similar businesses for customers?
   d. What training and experience should a person have before attempting to start his or her own business?

2. Visit a local shopping center. Take a pad and pencil with you and write down the names of at least ten businesses located in the center. Beside each name, write down whether you believe the business to be a proprietorship, a partnership, a corporation, or a franchise. Be able to explain to the class what part of the business's name led you to identify it as you did. If you could not identify the type of organization by name, be able to explain why.

3. Corporations are required to issue an annual report to their stockholders. Several ways in which you might get such a report

to review are listed below:

a. Borrow one from a member of your family or a friend who owns stock.
b. Ask your school or community librarian if the library has corporation annual reports.
c. Visit a corporation in your community and ask for a copy of its report.
d. Write to a corporation and ask for a copy of its report.

   Using these suggestions, try to obtain annual reports from two corporations. Write a brief report showing the types of information contained in both reports.

4. In most partnerships, the partners are general partners, but sometimes there are limited partners and silent partners. Explain the differences among these types. (Refer to business law and business principles textbooks in your library.)
5. Franchise businesses are particularly common in the motel, restaurant, and prepared-food fields. List the names of four or five other franchise businesses in your area and describe the product or services provided by each.

World Trade and Our Economy

Chapter 7

Chapter Objectives

After studying this chapter and completing the end-of-chapter activities, you will be able to:

1. *Explain how people, communities, and nations throughout the world depend upon each other.*

2. *Give an example to show the difference between foreign trade and domestic trade.*

3. *Explain how we depend upon world trade for many goods and services.*

4. *Describe how tariffs, quotas, and embargoes affect world trade.*

5. *State an advantage and a disadvantage associated with world trade.*

Do you own a radio or cassette player? A watch? Jogging shoes? A pocket calculator? A wool sweater? A television set? Chances are that you and members of your family own several of these items. You probably purchased them in a local store, but few of them may have actually been made in your city or town—or even in the United States. The cassette player, the pocket calculator, and the television set may have been made in Japan; the jogging shoes may be from Korea, Taiwan, or Brazil; and the wool sweater may have come from Scotland or New Zealand.

As you learned in Unit 1, our hometowns cannot supply all of the things we want, so we trade with other communities, states, and countries to help fulfill our needs. Likewise, other communities, states, and countries buy from suppliers in our town and from others who have the things they want. This trading is an important part of our economy.

SPECIALIZING IN GOODS AND SERVICES

Each region of our country has certain special advantages. These advantages may include climate, deposits of minerals, rich soil, a favorable location, or many workers with special skills and abilities. These kinds of advantages make it possible for a state or region to produce a certain good or service of higher quality or at a lower cost than another state or region. Thus, Florida has an advantage over Wisconsin for growing oranges, and Minnesota has an advantage over Florida for producing iron ore. Georgia has an advantage over Wyoming in growing peanuts, and Michigan has an advantage over Maine in making cars.

Trade allows each state or region to specialize—to devote most of its resources to producing the kinds of goods it produces best. In addition, each state exchanges its special products for the special products of other states. Trade among people and businesses in the same country is called **domestic trade**. What is the result for you as a consumer? You benefit by having many different kinds of products that are generally better in quality and lower in price than if each state or region tried to supply most of the things its people need.

For example, a person in Omaha, Nebraska, might buy from a local dealer a car that was made in Detroit. The heater, battery, tires, and other parts may have been produced in communities in other states and shipped to Detroit to be assembled in the car. Furthermore, at least 30 raw materials used to make the car parts came from other nations.

You can see the problem of the automobile customer in Omaha. He would not have been able to obtain a car if it were not for trade among communities in the United States and trade between the United States and other countries.

TRADING AMONG NATIONS

Just as we specialize and trade among our states and communities, other countries also take advantage of special factors of production that they have. They produce goods according to these advantages and trade with other countries to help provide for the wants of their citizens. This trading affects your daily life more than you realize.

What did your family have for breakfast this morning? Coffee, cereal, and sliced bananas, perhaps? If it were not for trading with Brazil for the coffee and with Honduras for the bananas, you might have had only cereal. The sugar on your table may have come from the Philippines. Even your morning newspaper was printed on paper that may have come from Canada.

While our country has many natural resources, a skilled labor force, and modern machines and methods of production, we cannot provide ourselves with all of the things we want. We go beyond our borders to get many things. We conduct trade with as many as 150 foreign countries in one year. Trade among different countries is called **world trade**. It is also referred to as **foreign** or **international trade**.

Most nations of the world have special advantages. Brazil, for example, has an advantage over the United States in producing coffee. Saudi Arabia has an advantage over most other countries in crude oil. Australia has an advantage in wool. Korea and Taiwan have an advantage in the number of skilled laborers who can assemble radios and make textiles and shoes. Compared with these and many other countries, the United States has advantages in the production of airplanes, tractors, computers, office equipment, and many varieties of food and other agricultural products. Because of trade and modern means of transportation, nations everywhere can specialize in the kinds of production they can do best.

Illus. 7-1 As do most nations, the United States has advantages in the production of certain products.

IMPORTING GOODS—BUYING FROM OTHER COUNTRIES

The things we buy from other countries are called **imports**. Imports account for our total supply of bananas, coffee, cocoa, spices, tea, silk, and crude rubber. About half the crude oil and fish we buy comes from other countries. Imports also account for 20 to 50 percent of our supply of carpets, sugar, leather gloves, dishes, and sewing machines. In order to produce industrial and consumer goods, we must import tin, chrome, manganese, nickel, copper, zinc, and several other metals. Figure 7-1 shows the percentage of various materials imported by the United States in a recent year.

Figure 7-1
The United States imports some of the raw materials used in the production of many products.

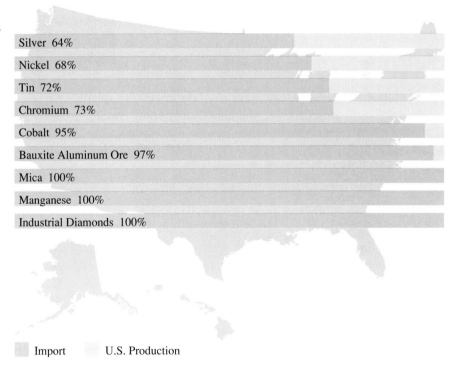

Silver 64%
Nickel 68%
Tin 72%
Chromium 73%
Cobalt 95%
Bauxite Aluminum Ore 97%
Mica 100%
Manganese 100%
Industrial Diamonds 100%

Import   U.S. Production

We depend upon imported raw materials for many of the products we use today. Also, without world trade, many of the things we buy would cost more. This is due to the fact that other countries' advantages allow them to produce goods and services at lower costs. These lower production costs are largely the result of labor costs being lower in many foreign countries than they are in the United States.

Many people prefer to buy certain imported goods, even at higher prices, if the quality is better. You might be willing to pay a higher price for a pair of German binoculars, a Swiss watch, or an imported cashmere sweater

Illus. 7-2 The United States also imports finished products from other nations.

because you have confidence in the quality and workmanship of these products. Or, you may simply enjoy owning products made in other lands.

EXPORTING PRODUCTS—SELLING TO OTHER COUNTRIES

The goods and services we sell to other countries are called **exports**. Just as imports benefit you, exports benefit the people of other countries. People in nations throughout the world operate their factories with machinery made in the United States. They work their land and harvest their crops with American-made tools. They eat food made from many of our agricultural products. They use our chemicals, fertilizers, medicines, and plastics. They watch our movies and read many of our publications. Producing these exported goods employs many of our workers. One out of every six jobs in the United States depends upon world trade. Figure 7-2 shows some of the countries with which the United States trades.

Two segments of the American economy—machinery and agriculture—are especially dependent on selling in foreign markets. Our exports in the machinery and transport-equipment fields include diesel engines, buses, tractors, oil-drilling rigs, earth-moving equipment, jet planes, computers, and air-conditioning and refrigeration equipment. Large amounts of farm products are also sold abroad each year. American farmers who grow crops such as cotton, wheat, soybeans, and rice depend on selling in foreign markets.

The jobs and incomes of millions of American workers depend directly upon success in exporting. In addition, the profits of many businesses depend in part upon the demands of other countries for American products and services.

Figure 7-2
The United States has many trading partners.

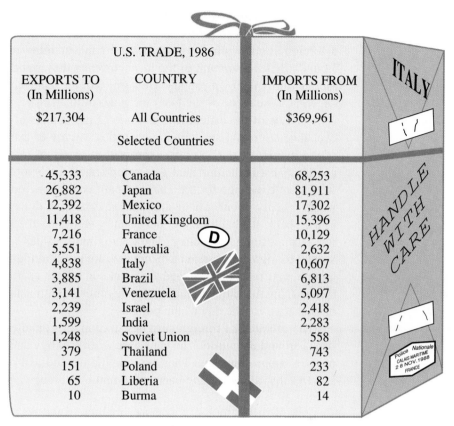

U.S. TRADE, 1986		
EXPORTS TO (In Millions)	COUNTRY	IMPORTS FROM (In Millions)
$217,304	All Countries	$369,961
	Selected Countries	
45,333	Canada	68,253
26,882	Japan	81,911
12,392	Mexico	17,302
11,418	United Kingdom	15,396
7,216	France	10,129
5,551	Australia	2,632
4,838	Italy	10,607
3,885	Brazil	6,813
3,141	Venezuela	5,097
2,239	Israel	2,418
1,599	India	2,283
1,248	Soviet Union	558
379	Thailand	743
151	Poland	233
65	Liberia	82
10	Burma	14

PAYING FOR FOREIGN GOODS

Suppose that each of the 50 states had a different kind of money, each with a different value. Imagine the trouble you would have in traveling through New England if you had to change your "Massachusetts money" into "Rhode Island money" and then into "Connecticut money." If you lived in Chicago, and were ordering products from Oregon, you would need to convert your "Illinois money" into "Oregon money" to make the payment. This is what we must do when we travel in or trade with other countries. It is one reason for the fact that world trade is so much more complicated than domestic trade.

Each nation has its own type of money and its own banking system. In the United States, we use dollars; Mexico uses pesos; France uses francs; Japan uses yen; and so on. When American businesses buy olive oil from Italy, for example, arrangements are made to change American dollars into lire, the Italian currency. If you were to visit Spain, you would need to have pesetas to pay for meals and other expenses. When Spanish people come to this country, they need to change their pesetas into dollars.

For experienced travelers or businesspeople, the exchange of money from one currency to another is not as difficult as it might seem. Travelers in a foreign country simply go to a local bank or other money changer and "buy" whatever amount of the local currency they want and pay for it with money from their own country. How much of the local currency they get will depend on the value of the two currencies at that time.

Because of the differences in value of the monies of the world, rates of exchange are established among countries. A **rate of exchange** is the value of the money of one country expressed in terms of the money of another country. This is the part that gets complicated. Let's look at an example. If the rate of exchange for the Thailand baht is .04, this means that the baht is worth 4 cents in our money and that an American dollar could be changed into 25 baht. A Thai tourist in our country would need 250 baht to exchange for $10 in American money. The approximate values of the currencies of several foreign countries on a recent date are given in Figure 7-3. Remember, though, that rates of exchange vary and sometimes change from one day to the next. In international trading, the buyer or seller must be aware of the rate of exchange for the day of the purchase.

The problem of foreign currency exchange is handled mainly by major banks around the world. The banks are willing to buy and sell the currencies of the various countries. They provide the needed and often very complex services that allow trading partners to make and receive payments.

Figure 7-3 Exchange rates of currencies change frequently.

COUNTRY	MONETARY UNIT	EXCHANGE RATE	VALUE IN U.S. MONEY
Canada	Dollar	0.8309	83¢
England	Pound	1.8220	$1.82
Japan	Yen	0.008054	4/5 of a cent
Portugal	Escudo	0.006944	69/100 of a cent
Sweden	Krona	0.1641	16¢
Thailand	Baht	0.039888	4¢
Venezuela	Bolivar	0.1333	13¢
West Germany	Deutsche mark	0.5683	57¢

REGULATING TRADE

World trade affects and is affected by the economy, but there are other factors that may be involved as well. Chief among these is our political relationship to other countries. Our government establishes a foreign policy that guides our activities, including trade, with other countries. Several devices may be used to control the importing and exporting of a product or service. Among these controls are quotas, tariffs, and embargoes.

Quotas

One of the devices used by governments to regulate foreign trade sets a limit on the quantity of a product that may be imported or exported within a given period of time. This limit is called a **quota**. Quotas may be set for many reasons. Countries that export oil may put quotas on crude oil so that the supply will remain low and maintain prices at a certain level. Quotas may also be imposed by one country on imports from another to express disapproval of the policies or behavior of that country. Quotas can also be set by one country to protect an industry from too much foreign competition. This is often done by a nation to shield its ''infant industries,'' which need protection to get started. Our government in the past has imposed quotas on sugar, cattle, dairy products, and textiles.

Tariffs

Another device that governments use to regulate foreign trade is the tariff. A **tariff** is a tax that a government places on certain imported products. Suppose you want to buy an English bicycle. The English producer of the bicycle sets a price of $140, but our government places a 20 percent tariff on the bicycle when it is imported. This means that you will have to pay $168 plus shipping charges for the bicycle. The $28 tariff goes to the government. Tariffs make up only a small part of the government's revenue. Tariffs are used not so much to produce income as they are to regulate imports. By increasing the price of an imported product, a high tariff tends to lower the demand for that product and, therefore, to lower the number imported. If a country wants to increase imports of a product, it can remove the tariff or put a very low one on it. The product can then be sold at a lower price, which encourages people to buy it and results in more being imported.

Embargoes

If a government wishes, it can stop the export or import of a product completely. This action is called an **embargo**. Governments may impose an embargo for many reasons. They may wish to protect their own industries from foreign competition to a greater degree than either the quota or tariff will accomplish. The government may wish to prevent sensitive products, particularly those important to the nation's defense, from falling into the hands of unfriendly groups or nations. As with the quota, a government may sometimes impose an embargo as a strong measure to express its disapproval of the actions or policies of another country. When it needs to do so, a government may use any of the three devices to improve its trade position. Let's take a look at the way a government measures its trade position.

KEEPING TRACK OF TRADE FLOWS

As you learned in Unit 1, a major reason people work is to get money to buy the things they need and want. That is, they sell their labor for wages that they then spend for products and services. People usually try to keep their income and spending in balance, knowing that if they spend more than they earn, they can have some economic problems. So it is with nations regarding their trade positions.

Balance of Trade

Countries pay for their imports with the money they receive for their exports. Keeping the two in balance is often a problem, however. The difference between a country's total exports and total imports is called the **balance of trade**. If a country exports (sells) more than it imports (buys), it has a *trade surplus* or its trade position is said to be favorable. But, if it imports (buys) more than it exports (sells), it has a *trade deficit* or an unfavorable balance of trade.

A country can have a trade surplus with one country and a deficit with another. Overall, however, a country tries to keep its trade in balance. If it does not, and it has no other way of making up the deficit, its money will flow out of the country to other countries. Figure 7-4 shows the three possible trade positions. After a long history of a favorable balance of trade, the United States had a trade deficit every year of a recent ten-year period. In

Figure 7-4   In recent years, the United States has experienced a deficit in its balance of trade.

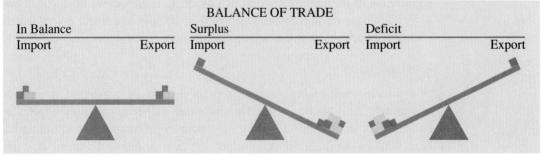

BALANCE OF TRADE

In Balance		Surplus		Deficit	
Import	Export	Import	Export	Import	Export

a recent year, the trade deficit was almost $152.7 billion. This has been a serious problem for our economy.

Balance of Payments

In addition to export and import flows, other forms of exchange occur between nations that affect the economy. Money flows from one country to another through investments. For example, a citizen of one country might buy stock in a firm in another country, or a business may set up a plant in a foreign country. Also, one government might give financial or military aid to another nation. Furthermore, banks may deposit funds in foreign banks. When tourists travel, they also contribute to the flow of money from their country to the country they are visiting. Some countries limit the amount of money their citizens can take out of the country when they travel.

The difference between the amount of money that flows into and the amount of money that flows out of a country for investments, tourism, and nontrade items is called the **balance of payments**. A country can have a surplus in the balance of trade and a deficit in the balance of payments. A balance of trade deficit, for example, can be made up by a high level of tourism to effect a balance of payments surplus. However, if a balance of payments deficit continues over a long period of time, the country could bankrupt its treasury. Nations try to review regularly their balance of trade and balance of payments positions in the interest of the health of their economies.

UNDERSTANDING BENEFITS AND PROBLEMS OF WORLD TRADE

You have already learned that there are many benefits to world trade. Since countries cannot supply all of their citizens' wants and needs, trade offers a way to provide them from other countries. By increasing the abundance of products available to us, often at prices lower than we could set, world trade enables us to increase our standard of living.

Trade also creates jobs. Firms that make and market products for export may depend upon foreign trade to exist. Other firms may sell in both the domestic and foreign markets. Ships and planes which carry cargo and tourists overseas are manufactured and operated by firms that provide jobs based heavily on world trade.

Many people view world trade as a way to promote international understanding. Nations that are trading partners usually try to maintain friendly relations for economic reasons; this sometimes promotes better relationships and understanding between the countries.

Even though there are many benefits, world trade also creates some problems. The competition that brings in better products at lower prices can also lower demand for domestic products and cause people working in our industries to lose their jobs. In some cases, it can cause domestic businesses to close when demand for their products falls in favor of imported products. The United States in recent years has experienced such problems in several of its industries, including shoes, textiles, television sets, and cars. Some people argue that when Americans buy Italian shoes, Korean sweat suits, or Japanese cars, they are exporting American jobs to those countries. This means that their purchase of imported products creates demand for those products in the countries where they are made, and therefore, creates jobs in those countries. At the same time, as demand for the same domestic products decreases in favor of the import, American businesses must lay off workers and sometimes close down their plants. On the other hand, competition is bringing about more efficient production in our country and enabling American businesses to recapture the market through better products at reasonable prices.

In addition to the jobs/trade dilemma, countries also may become too dependent upon a trading partner. If one country depends heavily upon another for certain products and the exporting country decides to cut production, the importing country may have serious problems. This could be especially critical for strategic products such as energy and food.

Even though there are problems, the benefits of world trade are believed to outweigh the disadvantages. With today's high-speed transportation and instantaneous communication creating demand for products from all over the world, international trade will increase.

Illus. 7-3
What changes would you expect if all world trade stopped tomorrow?

Increasing Your Business Vocabulary

The following terms should become part of your business vocabulary. For each numbered item, find the term that has the same meaning.

balance of payments
balance of trade
domestic trade
embargo
exports
imports

quota
rate of exchange
tariff
world, foreign, or international trade

1. Goods and services sold to another country.
2. A limit on the quantity of a product that may be imported or exported within a given period of time.
3. The buying and selling of goods and services among people and businesses within the same country.
4. The value of the money of one country expressed in terms of the money of another country.
5. Trade among different countries.

6. Goods and services bought from another country.
7. Stopping the importing or exporting of a certain product or service.
8. The difference between a country's total exports and total imports of merchandise.
9. A tax that a government places on certain imported products.
10. The difference between the total amount of money that flows into a country and the money that flows out of a country for investments, tourism, and nontrade items.

Reviewing Your Reading

1. Give an example to show the difference between domestic and foreign trade.
2. Give three examples of regional advantages in production in the United States and in the world.
3. Name a food, a raw material, and a manufactured good that we would not have without world trade.
4. What percent of our supply of aluminum ore is imported?
5. State one reason why you might prefer to buy an imported product, even at a higher cost.

6. What two segments of the American economy particularly depend upon international trade?
7. Why are rates of exchange established?
8. State three reasons that are given by countries for placing tariffs on imports.
9. How does a quota limit trade?
10. What is the difference between balance of trade and balance of payments?
11. What is meant by the term "unfavorable balance of trade"?
12. State one advantage and one disadvantage associated with world trade.

Using Your Business Knowledge

1. It is said that no community or nation today can be completely independent. Do you agree or disagree? Explain.

2. How does world trade contribute to a better standard of living for many people in various countries?

3. An American manufacturer of electric toasters wants to sell its products to the people of China. Can you think of some difficulties that this business might have in entering the Chinese market?

4. What is meant by "infant industries"? Give two examples of infant industries either in the United States or in other countries. Do you think that such industries should be protected by high tariffs? If so, how long should they be protected?

5. Some people believe that the United States should place stiff controls on imports of goods that compete with our businesses to prevent the "exporting of American jobs" to other countries. Give arguments for and against such a position.

Computing Business Problems

1. The table below shows the approximate value of some imported foods for 1985 and 1986. The values are stated in millions of dollars.

Food	1985	1986
Meat and meat products	$2,339	$2,367
Fruits and nuts	2,717	2,781
Coffee	3,130	4,293
Sugar	936	670
Fish	3,985	4,691
Cocoa	564	418

   a. What is the total value in millions of dollars of the foods imported by the United States in 1985?
   b. What is the total value in millions of dollars of the foods imported in 1986?
   c. Was there an increase or a decrease from 1985 to 1986?
   d. What was the amount of the increase or decrease?

2. Using the information in Figure 7-3 on page 102, tell what the equal amount in U.S. dollars would be for these amounts in foreign currency:
   a. In Portugal, 100 escudos
   b. In Japan, 136 yen
   c. In Canada, one Canadian dollar
   d. In Thailand, 20 baht

3. To make their exports suitable for use in other countries, U.S. manufacturers must produce goods that are measured in the metric system. Many of our measures do not convert exactly into a standard measure of the metric system. For example, if a manufacturer wanted to export paint, which is sold in gallon cans in this country, it would probably export the paint in 4-liter (about $1^1/4$ gallons) cans. To what sizes would the items listed below be converted for export to countries using the metric system? (Refer to Appendix D.)
   a. A quart bottle of liquid detergent
   b. A 50-yard bolt of polyester fabric
   c. An automobile engine measured in cubic inches

d. A 12-inch ruler

e. A bathroom scale that measures in pounds

4. The table below shows the approximate values of the exports and imports going through the nine customs ports in a recent year.

City	Exports (In Millions)	Imports (In Millions)
Boston	$18,300	$40,300
New York	33,400	67,000
Baltimore	12,100	31,300
Miami	18,600	31,500
New Orleans	14,400	17,100
Houston	21,700	27,700
Los Angeles	22,200	53,100
San Francisco	32,100	44,100
Chicago	33,700	54,800

a. What is the total value in millions of dollars of the exports for the year? the imports?

b. Which port city reported the largest business in terms of value? What is the value?

c. Which port imported and exported the least amount? What was the value for each?

Expanding Your Understanding of Business

1. When travelers enter a country, including their own, they are required to go through a customs check. Talk to someone who has traveled to a foreign country and ask him or her to relate this experience to you. Ask what procedure was followed at the customs check, what forms had to be filled in, how much exemption they were given on items purchased abroad before having to pay a customs levy, and what amount, if any, the traveler had to pay. Report your findings to the class.

2. Using a reference that gives governmental statistics, such as the *Statistical Abstract of the United States* or *The World Almanac*, prepare a brief table showing the U.S. balance of trade position for a recent four-year period.

3. Look in the classified section of your local paper or in the Yellow Pages of your telephone directory in the "car dealer" or "cars for sale" section. List all of the foreign cars sold in your area. Indicate the country of origin for each make of car on your list.

4. Agencies are often referred to by an acronym, which is a word made up of the initials of the agency's name. OPEC, relating to world trade, is an example of such an agency. EEC and OAS, relating to regional trade, are other examples. For each of these three terms, find the complete name, the purpose of the organization, and the nations that are involved.

In this unit, you have learned about the type of businesses, what they do, and how they carry on trade with each other in the United States and throughout the world. The people who operate these businesses are called managers. It takes many managers to operate our businesses, government agencies, and other organizations. Therefore, career opportunities in management are numerous.

Job Titles: Job titles commonly found in this career area include:

    Bank Managers and Officers
    Public Administrators
    Sales Managers
    Hospital/Health Service Managers
    Administrative Managers
    General Managers and Top Executives
    Store Managers
    Supervisors
    Restaurant Managers
    Personnel and Human Resources Managers
    Department Managers
    Management Consultants

Employment Outlook: Managers, officials, and proprietors make up one of the largest career categories. In 1987, there were more than 10.6 million managers, officials, and proprietors. This number is expected to increase by 29 percent to 13.6 million by the year 2000. This means that more than 333,000 new managers will be needed each year. Bank managers and health service administrators are expected to be in high demand.

Future Changes: As the United States moves toward becoming a service-oriented economy and high technology changes the way we produce goods, management is increasing in scope and importance. As more use is made of computers to supply data used by managers to make decisions, preparation for management careers will require superior decision-making skills and an understanding of computers. In order to direct today's more sophisticated and demanding work force, managers must also have a high level of human relations ability.

What Is Done on the Job: Managers get things done by people. They plan what has to be done, how it is to be done, by whom it is to be done, and when it is to be done. They assign tasks and see that the work is completed. Managers also evaluate the performance of workers and see that

they are paid. Activities of managers fall into five functions: planning, organizing, staffing, leading and motivating, and controlling. All managers perform all of these functions in varying degrees. However, there are many types of managers who perform specialized duties. Sales managers plan and organize sales departments. They assign sales quotas and territories to salespeople; plan ways to motivate them, such as giving bonuses for exceeding quotas; require reports from the salespeople; and evaluate them on their performances. Personnel managers handle employee-related matters including recruiting, selecting, training, and appraising the performance of employees. A manager's specialization, therefore, will dictate in which function the manager spends most of his or her time.

Education and Training: While it is still possible for high school graduates to become managers, it is becoming increasingly less likely. High school graduates who are experienced workers with a record of excellent performance are sometimes promoted to a supervisory or lower level management jobs. However, they are usually required to get additional training through college courses or company-sponsored development programs. A bachelor's degree in business administration is a typical requirement for entering a management career. Management courses in such a program usually include management principles, human resources management and labor relations, business policy and strategy, organizational behavior, and information management technology of computer science. People with college degrees in management usually begin their careers as management trainees. Vacancies in management are usually filled from the pool of trainees. Graduate study will become increasingly necessary.

Salary Levels: Factors affecting salary vary widely in management; among them are the level of management in which one works, and whether one works in business, for the government or another nonprofit agency, or for oneself. In 1986, beginning salaries for management trainees with bachelor's degrees ranged between $17,000 and $25,000. During that year, the top managers in several U.S. businesses earned more than $1 million. As you can see, the range of salaries for managers is broad.

For Additional Information: To learn more about managers, visit a local business and ask the manager to describe his or her job to you. Your school counselor can advise you about colleges and universities that offer degree programs in management and business administration. Visit your library and ask for information on management careers. See also sources of information on management in *The Occupational Outlook Handbook*, published each year by the U.S. Department of Labor.

Labor and Government in Our Economy

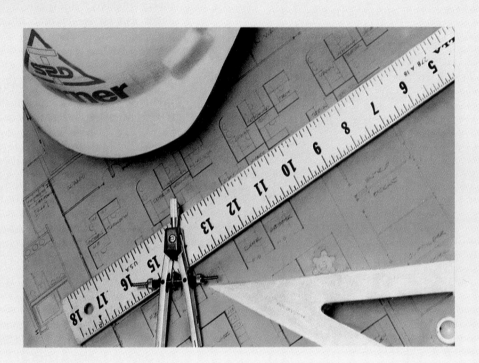

Unit Goals

After studying the chapters in this unit, you will be able to:

1. *Discuss the role of labor in our economy.*
2. *Describe the activities of labor organizations.*
3. *Explain how government serves you as a citizen, consumer, and worker.*
4. *Describe how we pay for government services.*

Public Services Are Going Private

Business Brief

The public sector is that part of our economy owned by and operated for the benefit of the whole society. We have come to expect the public sector to provide certain services, such as fire protection, street repairs, and the upkeep of public

parks. However, in recent years, some public services have been performed by private businesses. The privatization of public services has been the result of two factors. First, the cost of paying a public work force to provide services is very expensive. Second, some public services can be provided more efficiently by private enterprise. Private enterprise can often achieve maximum productivity from the resources that it uses.

One of the first services that was turned over to private companies was trash collection. Now several cities and states have local businesses operating their jails, fire departments, and computer facilities. The President's Commission on Privatization in the late 1980s recommended that more services be transferred from government-owned operations to private businesses. The committee's report suggested that airport control towers, mail delivery, and management of public hospitals be considered for privatization.

Transferring services from public control to private companies does not always mean better and less expensive service. For example, while the U.S. Postal Service has competition in certain areas, such as packages and overnight mail delivery, some people believe its monopoly on first- and third-class mail delivery should end. Private companies, however, would most likely compete for the most profitable mail routes, leaving other routes—namely, rural and inner-city areas—either without service or with service but at a higher cost.

Another concern of privatization is whether the public interest will continue to be served. Privately owned businesses operating a hospital cafeteria or maintaining city parks may adequately serve the needs of citizens. However, few people want to let police protection be handled by private organizations operating for a profit.

Many people do not believe private businesses can do a better job than government in providing public services. However, competition between private companies and government agencies can provide a cost-effective, high-quality service. To maintain a competitive situation, some governmental agencies have some services, such as trash collection or street maintenance, handled partially by a government agency and partially by a private business. This situation prevents a private company from getting into the business by offering to provide a low-cost service, and then raising its fees after the city has sold its garbage collection trucks or maintenance equipment.

In the future, who will provide your public services will depend on who can provide the most efficient services. Some basic questions need to be answered before this economic decision is made. What tasks does government do best? Why do we assign these tasks to government? Can private enterprise perform certain services better than government? If so, which ones? What is it that government cannot do as well as private enterprise and should not be involved in? Can government and private enterprise share responsibility in providing public services?

Human Resources and the Economy

Chapter Objectives

After studying this chapter and completing the end-of-chapter activities, you will be able to:

1. Explain why labor is a vital economic force.

2. Identify who is included in our work force.

3. List examples of businesses in the two major industry groups.

4. Identify occupational categories that will be in demand in the future.

5. Discuss several factors that affect job opportunities.

6. Describe efforts that are important for future success in the job market.

Jim Nishimura recently completed a training program to qualify for a position in the insurance industry. Although his current job as an agricultural equipment sales representative was still secure, Jim believed that there would be greater employment opportunities in the insurance industry. He had read several news articles which indicated that there would be fewer job opportunities in agricultural occupations. One important factor influencing Jim's decision to change jobs was the demand for agricultural equipment. Jim realized that as the demand for farm equipment declined, fewer sales representatives would be needed.

Think about the kind of job you want to do. You may want to be a computer operator, a police officer, a salesperson, or an office worker. Whatever your choice, try to determine the future demand for people in that line of work. Do you plan to work in an occupation in which demand for a product or service is high? Do you have, or can you develop, the skills necessary to be productive in the work you desire? Thinking about these questions can help you make a wise career decision

ECONOMIC INFLUENCES OF LABOR

The contributions of workers in our society are vital to economic growth. As presented in Chapter 1, labor includes all of the men and women involved in obtaining products from nature, converting raw materials into useful products, selling products, providing services, or supervising or managing others. As also discussed in Chapter 1, three types of economic resources are needed for production. These are natural resources, capital resources, and human resources. Although labor is only one of the needed resources, many people believe it is the most important resource. Without labor, tools, machinery, and buildings could not be created. Furthermore, without labor, equipment could not be operated to produce goods and services for consumers.

In some industries, products or services are provided mainly through the efforts of labor. Many personal services, such as automobile repair, child care, and food preparation, are *labor intensive*. Workers are the main economic resource in the productive process in these industries. In contrast, some industries are *capital intensive*. Equipment is heavily used for creating goods or in providing services. Manufacturing companies and utilities are examples of capital-intensive industries.

OUR WORK FORCE

There are more than 120 million people like Jim Nishimura who have full-time and part-time jobs in our nation. Some jobs require extensive education and special training, while others require only basic skills and a willingness to work hard and learn on the job. Some jobs are high paying and some are low paying; some involve working mainly with machines, while others involve working mainly with people and information.

All of the people age 16 and over who hold jobs or who are seeking jobs make up our **work force**. That work force is an important part of our economy. In spite of advancing technology and electronic innovations in business and industry, people continue to be the most important economic resource.

Industry Categories

The business world consists of thousands of companies and jobs. These jobs may be organized in a variety of ways. The Bureau of Labor Statistics (BLS), which is part of the U.S. Department of Labor, researches thousands of different jobs held by people in our work force. The BLS publishes many materials about current and projected employment opportunities. Two BLS publications, *The Occupational Outlook Handbook* and *Occupational Outlook Quarterly*, offer up-to-date information about many types of jobs.

The Occupational Outlook Handbook divides jobs into two major categories as shown in Figure 8-1. The **service-producing industry** includes businesses that satisfy the needs of other businesses and consumers. For example, service companies include health care facilities, insurance companies, retail stores, and transportation organizations. The **goods-producing industry** includes businesses that manufacture various products. These companies are involved in construction, manufacturing, mining, and agriculture.

Figure 8-1
Our work force is employed in two major industry categories.

Industry Categories

Service-Producing Industries	Goods-Producing Industries
• Personal and business services • Retail and wholesale trade • Finance, insurance, and real estate • Government • Transportation, communications, and public utilities	• Construction • Manufacturing • Mining • Agriculture

Our economy has experienced a long-term shift from goods-producing to service-producing employment. The BLS estimates that by the year 2000 nearly four out of five jobs will be in service industries.

Employment Categories

Another way of studying our work force is to look at employment categories. While industry trends indicate the job opportunities in certain types of businesses, occupational groups are helpful for specifying which jobs will be in demand. The job categories used by the BLS, along with future employment prospects, are shown in Figure 8-2.

Figure 8-2
Do you know people who have jobs in some of these employment categories?

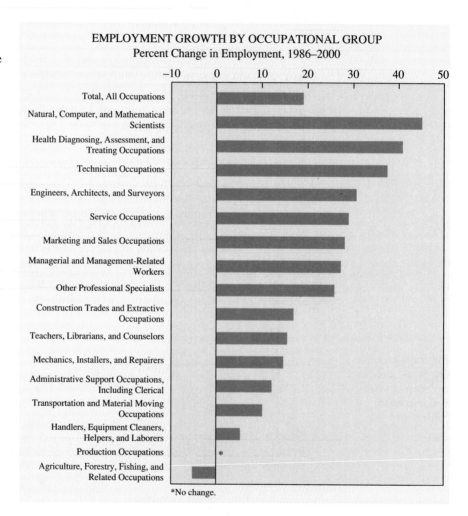

EMPLOYMENT GROWTH BY OCCUPATIONAL GROUP
Percent Change in Employment, 1986–2000

*No change.

White-Collar and Blue-Collar Workers

Two categories that have been used traditionally to group workers are white-collar and blue-collar. Both white-collar and blue-collar workers are important in our work force. Both types of workers are needed to help meet our economic needs and wants.

Illus. 8-1 Our work force consists of people in many different occupations.

White-collar workers are people whose work involves a great deal of contact with other people and who work with or process information. Most white-collar workers are employed in offices and stores and include professional, managerial, and clerical workers. **Blue-collar workers** are people whose work involves the operation of machinery and equipment. They are employed in factories, in machine shops, and on construction sites. Increased use of computers and information technology in factories and offices is changing the role of blue- and white-collar workers. These terms are being replaced in usage by goods-producing industry worker (for blue collar) and service-producing industry worker (for white collar).

FACTORS AFFECTING JOB OPPORTUNITIES

The jobs held by people in our work force are subject to a variety of factors that can cause these jobs to change. Some of these influences may cause jobs to be eliminated, while others will cause jobs to be modified, often requiring employees to have more skills or different training. Consumer preferences, economic conditions, the changing job market, new technology, business costs, and social factors are strong influences on the work force.

Consumer Preferences

Consumer preferences affect the availability of jobs in our work force. Jobs are affected by **derived demand**; that is, the demand for factors of production, such as labor, are dependent on the demand for a product or service. For instance, if most consumers decided to wear clothing made of blue denim, workers who make blue denim clothing would be needed. If consumer choice shifts away from blue denim, fewer workers would be needed by those companies.

Sometimes new products entering the market make those already available obsolete—at least in the mind of the consumer. Workers producing the old product may find that their jobs will be eliminated, while new jobs will be created by the demand for the new product.

Economic Conditions

When businesses are expanding and consumers are buying more and more goods and services, new jobs are created to meet the growing demand. As workers earn more money, they spend more on goods and services that they need, and the growing demand continues.

High prices cause consumers to decrease their buying. When interest rates increase and both businesses and consumers find it difficult to borrow money, demand for goods and services decreases. As a result, jobs may be eliminated or the number of workers reduced. The workers in turn have less money to spend for their needs and wants and are hesitant to spend what money they do have because they are not sure of their future earnings. This tendency to spend less further decreases demand for goods and services.

The Job Market

In the same way that supply and demand affect the prices of goods and services, wages and salaries are influenced by supply and demand. When only a few trained workers are available to fill certain jobs, these individuals will be offered higher salaries to attract their services. In contrast, if more workers are available than needed for certain types of work, lower wages will result and some individuals will not be employed. A knowledge of which jobs will be in demand is vital for successful career planning.

Technological Change

Technology refers to the use of automated machinery and electronic equipment to help increase the efficiency of labor. Computers and robots are examples of technology. Robots are changing the types of jobs available in manufacturing companies, while computers are strongly influencing the office environment.

Today, microcomputers—small-sized or desktop computers with a keyboard and screen—are commonly used in most offices. Through the use of microcomputers at workers' desks, information is available almost instantly when it is needed. Another important change has been in the preparation of written materials. **Word processing** is an office function that involves the use of electronic equipment, such as microcomputers, to

Illus. 8-2
Technology will continue to create new and exciting employment opportunities.

produce reports, letters, memorandums, and other forms of written communication. Word processing equipment makes it easier to revise written communication, and final copies can be reproduced quickly on high-speed printing devices.

Telecommunications involves the transmission of information through the use of television, telephones, communication satellites, computers, and other electronic devices to allow both visual and audio communication. Telecommunications can be used for meetings and conferences so that people will not need to travel to one location. Money is saved on travel expenses, and more time is available for other organizational tasks. Telecommunications also allows the transmission of a document from one place to another almost instantly. The influences of technology on our lives and work will be discussed further in Unit 6.

Business Costs

The cost of running a business also affects jobs and workers. When profits begin to decrease, the business must look for ways to improve its profits. Installing new equipment that allows workers to produce more goods and services in less time may be one solution. In the end, there may be a decrease in the number of workers employed in these companies.

Social Trends

Social factors such as the makeup of our population and the location of jobs also influence work opportunities. The 16- to 24-year-old category in our population will be a smaller portion of the work force by the year 2000. This will mean greater employment opportunities for young people, especially women, minorities, and immigrants who will be needed to fill the demand for entry-level positions requiring very little training or experience.

In recent years, many businesses have relocated to warmer climates. While this has created additional jobs in these areas, other locations have attempted to attract companies with special tax programs and other incentives. The potential for employment opportunities in a geographic area should be considered when planning a career.

THE FUTURE JOB MARKET

Given the factors that affect jobs, is it possible to look ahead and determine which jobs will be needed in the future? This is not a simple task. Some of the factors that affect jobs are difficult to predict. However, there are certain actions every person can take to be successfully employed in our economy.

Planning a Career

Because your employment will have an impact on nearly every aspect of your life, the choice of a career is a very important decision. Your ability to obtain and maintain employment will depend on various career planning skills. As you will learn in Chapter 12, career success will be the result of:

- Knowing your personal interests and talents.
- Exploring different types of careers.
- Assessing the changing job market.
- Obtaining skills and knowledge to fulfill the requirements of the career you desire.

People who do not give career planning careful thought often spend years in unsuitable employment. When they discover their mistake, they may find it difficult, if not impossible, to change careers.

Assessing Job Opportunities

An important part of your career planning activities is knowing in which specific job areas there will be future needs. Estimates of the need for workers in any particular job category are based upon two major factors: (1) the number of new jobs to be created, and (2) the number of people who will be replaced because of transfers and separations. Certain career areas such as

Illus. 8-3
The employment
opportunities for
women and
minorities will
continue to
expand.

health care, financial services, data processing, and retailing are expected to grow faster than the average for our economy. Other employment fields such as communications, manufacturing, and agriculture will have slower growth.

The best way to keep informed on careers with strong future opportunities is to conduct personal research. By reading newspaper and magazine articles you will learn about our changing job market and the demand for certain types of employment. Television and radio news reports on business and economic conditions can provide additional knowledge about current and future job opportunities. This information can help you select a career field that not only will be interesting but also will provide strong economic security for your future.

Continuing Education

Many research studies reveal that employers look for people who have a good general education and who have been trained in some technical area. Technological developments, competition in our economy, and the desire to make a reasonable profit require that businesses employ people who can perform their job tasks well. Increased education and advanced training will serve the needs of business as well as help you secure employment.

Increasing Your Business Vocabulary

The following terms should become part of your business vocabulary. For each numbered item, find the term that has the same meaning.

blue-collar workers
derived demand
goods-producing industry
service-producing industry
technology

telecommunications
white-collar workers
word processing
work force

1. The use of automated machinery and electronic equipment to help increase the efficiency of labor.
2. All of the people age 16 and over who hold jobs or who are seeking jobs.
3. Businesses that satisfy the needs of other businesses and consumers.
4. The use of television, telephones, communication satellites, computers, and other electronic devices to transmit both visual and audio communication.
5. Businesses concerned with manufacturing various products.
6. A demand for factors of production affected by the demand for a product or service.
7. People whose work involves the operation of machinery and equipment.
8. An office function that involves using electronic equipment to produce written material rapidly.
9. People whose work involves a great deal of contact with other people and who work with or process information.

Reviewing Your Reading

1. How does labor influence our economy?
2. How many workers are in the work force?
3. Name two publications of the Bureau of Labor Statistics that offer information about the job market.
4. What types of businesses are expected to provide the most jobs in the year 2000?
5. What occupational groups are expected to have the largest growth by the year 2000?
6. What are some factors that influence job opportunities?
7. Describe some of the technologies that are causing changes in the world of work.
8. What are two social trends that affect job opportunities?
9. What career planning activities will help you in your future job success?
10. Why is education and training important to both businesses and workers.

Using Your Business Knowledge

1. What type of businesses would require the majority of their operating expenses be spent for labor expenses? Name some organizations that have extensive costs for buildings, equipment, and machinery.
2. Prepare a list of service-producing and goods-producing industries that are represented in your community. List some of the job titles for each business on your list.
3. How could each of the following changes

in our economy affect the job market?

a. Increased government spending for highway repairs

b. Lower interest rates

c. Decreased consumer spending on travel

d. Higher prices for food products

4. Give examples of technology you have observed in banks, retail stores, and offices.

Computing Business Problems

1. Mining employment is expected to decline from 783,000 workers to 725,000.
   a. How many jobs will be lost in the mining industry?
   b. What is the percent of decrease for jobs in this industry?

2. One of the large stores in a shopping center employs 48 salespeople, 6 department managers, 2 credit clerks, 2 secretaries, 1 accountant, and 1 store manager.
   a. How many employees, including the store manager, are there in this store?
   b. If the credit clerks, secretaries, and accountant make up the office staff, the office staff is what percent of all employees?
   c. If two-thirds of the salespeople work part time, how many part-time salespeople are there? How many salespeople are full-time workers?

3. In the year 2000, 11 percent of the work force is expected to be 55 years old and over, 73 percent will be between 25 and 54 years old, and 16 percent will be between 16 and 24 years old. If there are 139 million people in the work force in the year 2000, how many will be in each age category?

4. For the following occupational categories, the current number of workers and the expected growth rate through the year 2000 are given.

Category	Current Employment (In Millions)	Expected Growth Rate (Percent)
Government employees	8.6	9%
Construction	4.9	18
Finance, insurance, and real estate	6.3	26
Wholesale trade	5.7	27

a. For each job group, how many new employment positions are expected?

b. For each group, what will be the total number of jobs by the year 2000?

c. What will be the total employment for these four job categories by the year 2000?

d. What is the average expected growth rate for these four occupational categories?

Expanding Your Understanding of Business

1. Use *The Occupational Outlook Handbook* or *Occupational Outlook Quarterly* to obtain information about an occupational area in which you may be interested in the future. Prepare a short essay or oral report on the training requirements and type of work done in this occupational area.

2. The demand for many workers depends in

part on the preferences of consumers for certain goods and services. Make a list of some of the goods and services you and your friends demand that help create jobs. Then identify the kinds of jobs that are affected by these consumer preferences.

3. The percentage of women, minorities, and immigrants entering the work force is increasing. What are some of the reasons for this change? How will this affect employment opportunities for all workers?

4. Obtain information about the impact of technology on businesses in your community. Discuss with business owners, managers, and employees their experiences with technology and the effect it has had on their jobs, if any. Topics to be discussed might include expanded job opportunities, changes in job titles and descriptions, higher productivity, increased need for education and training, and the use of new products and services.

Labor-Management Relations

Chapter 9

Chapter Objectives

After studying this chapter and completing the end-of-chapter activities, you will be able to:

1. *Discuss the growth of unions in our society.*

2. *Explain the difference between a closed shop and a union shop.*

3. *Name six concerns of workers.*

4. *Describe the collective bargaining process of organized labor.*

5. *List the actions used by workers and management to solve labor disputes.*

Carla Lopez recently started a new job operating a computer on the assembly line for a manufacturing company. Her salary is comparable to her previous position, but the opportunity for advancement with this new job is much better. After a few weeks on the job, one of Carla's coworkers told her about the benefits of joining the union that represents a portion of the company's employees. Carla, however, wants to learn more about labor unions before she makes a decision about union membership.

ORGANIZATIONS FOR PROTECTING WORKERS' RIGHTS

An old saying states that ''there is strength in numbers.'' This is the idea behind a **labor union**, an organization of workers formed to give workers greater bargaining power in their dealings with management. One worker would have limited influence in dealing with the management of a company. However, when several employees speak as a group, management is more likely to seriously consider workers' demands. Today organized labor ranks with business and agriculture as one of our country's major economic ''power'' groups.

Not all people believe it is necessary for workers to organize. Some individuals believe government will protect the rights of employees. Chapter 10 will discuss the actions of government on behalf of workers.

The Growth of Unions

Before the 1800s, our economy was mainly agricultural. Most businesses were small and owners hired only a few workers. Problems of salary and working conditions were usually settled between the owner and each worker. As the use of machines increased and mass production grew, businesses became too large for owners and managers to know each employee personally.

Increased business size found many workers laboring in conditions that we would consider unbearable today. Workdays of 12 to 14 hours were common, and working conditions were often unsanitary and unsafe. Pay was frequently so low that workers could buy only basic necessities. If employees banded together to express their discontent, they risked prosecution in court. In some cases, conflicts between employers and employees ended in violence.

Despite opposition, groups of employees continued to organize unions in order to improve their working conditions. In 1935, the legal status of unions in the United States was firmly established. In that year, the National Labor Relations Act, sometimes called the Wagner Act, was passed. This law assures the right of employees to join unions and to hold fair elections to decide which union they want. It also states that workers have the right to choose representatives from the unions to make agreements with employers about working conditions.

In the beginning, involvement in labor organizations was usually limited to blue-collar workers. Factories, shops, and construction sites were the main sources of union members. This is changing as more white-collar and professional workers have united to express their concerns.

Organized Labor

Many people in the work force—nearly 20 million workers—express themselves through labor unions. Almost 14 million of these workers belong to unions that are affiliated with one very large labor organization. This is the American Federation of Labor—Congress of Industrial Organizations, commonly known as AFL-CIO. There are also strong independent unions such as the United Mine Workers.

As unions increased in size, they also became a powerful influence in the operation of businesses. Laws were created to maintain the balance of power between labor and business. For example, federal law makes the closed shop illegal. A **closed shop** exists when an employer agrees to hire only union members. At the same time, however, a union shop is permitted. A **union shop** exists when an employer may hire nonunion workers who must then join the union within a specified time period after employment.

Illus. 9-1
Unions allow groups of workers to express their views and concerns to management.

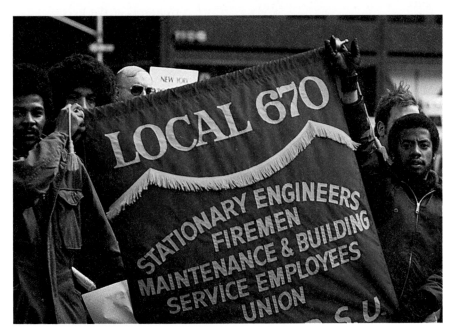

Some states have enacted **right-to-work laws** which state that no one can be required to join a union in order to get or to keep a job. In the states that have right-to-work laws, unions are sometimes more difficult to organize. Even in those states, however, workers are still allowed the choice of whether or not to join a union. Unions oppose right-to-work laws because in unionized companies nonunion members receive the same benefits as members even though they do not pay union dues.

Workers often organize, though not as a labor union, to promote interests of those working in their field. Examples include the American Farm Bureau, the American Medical Association, and the National Education Association. There are also special societies for sales managers, computer programmers, and office administrators, to name a few.

THE CONCERNS OF LABOR

All workers are concerned about matters such as job safety and a fair pay rate. Many are also interested in other matters such as paid vacations, health insurance, and company training programs. Figure 9-1 illustrates some of the main concerns of workers. The agreements reached between union leaders and management regarding these concerns are usually written as a legally binding contract. A labor contract is designed to protect both employees and management.

Figure 9-1
Workers have a variety of concerns.

Concerns of Workers		
Financial Concerns	**Human Concerns**	**Other Concerns**
• Compensation	• Working conditions	• Grievance procedures
• Fringe benefits	• Training programs	• Union representation
• Job security	• Flexible work hours	• Collective bargaining
	• Performance appraisal	
	• Promotions	

Financial Concerns

The main concern of most workers is their wage rate or salary. As they obtain additional skills and experience, employees desire pay increases. Workers frequently receive a raise when living costs increase. This can cause further inflation. However, when a salary increase is a reward for higher productivity, improved economic stability rather than inflation results. As a company increases output and sales, higher wages and other benefits are possible.

Compensation is the payment given to an employee by a business in return for the employee's labor. The compensation of workers is affected by the following factors:

- Their level of training and education.
- Their experience and length of time with the company.
- The quality of performance such as the number of items produced or the amount of sales.
- The demand for people in this type of work.

Compensation levels are also affected by the federal government. The Fair Labor Standards Act regulates the types of employment for which a minimum wage must be paid. This law also requires that workers be paid overtime rates for more than 40 hours of work in a week. The Equal Pay Act requires that women and men be paid at the same rate for comparable work when they have equal training and experience.

The benefits provided by employers in addition to pay have a monetary cost. The value of benefits must be considered by both workers and management. For example, consider the benefits offered by two similar jobs.

	Job A	Job B
Salary	$28,000	$24,600
Paid holidays (per year)	10	13
Paid vacation days (per year)	10	12
Life insurance	none	$25,000
Health insurance	none	full coverage
Pension plan	none	employer financed

While Job A pays more than Job B, the value of the additional benefits may make Job B a more attractive situation.

In recent years, some companies have allowed individual workers to decide which benefits they will receive. Within a set limit, an employee may choose the benefits desired. A worker with several dependents may want additional health or life insurance coverage. A single employee may want extra vacation days. These flexible benefit programs allow workers the freedom to choose a plan that meets their needs.

Many factors affect whether one worker—or many workers in one industry—will keep his or her job. Unions try to get *job security* for their members in several ways. They try to persuade employers not to discharge large numbers of employees suddenly. Unions may try to get employers to agree to retain workers and place them in other jobs. Unions may ask employers to guarantee their workers enough employment to earn a minimum annual income. Unions also try to get employers to recognize *seniority rights*, that is, to consider the length of time a worker has been with the company.

Human Concerns

A basic right of employees is safe working conditions. Unfortunately, certain methods of production can create dangers. Manufacturing equipment, factory chemicals, and building materials can be hazardous. Many labor contracts require that workers be protected from dangerous substances and conditions. Poor working conditions lower employee morale, contribute to job dissatisfaction, and unfavorably affect the quality of and amount of work accomplished.

An emphasis on technology demands workers who have the education and training to handle sophisticated equipment. The effects of technological improvements have reduced the number of jobs available for workers without special skills and training. In recent years, unions have been concerned about retraining programs. As the skills of workers become outdated by technology, labor and management can both benefit from retraining current employees.

In recent years, training programs within companies have become more important. Even though many people learn work skills in school, equipment and work tasks are constantly changing. *On-the-job training* refers to learning that occurs in the actual work setting, such as in an office, store, or factory. Classes, reading materials, videos, decision-making exercises, and group discussion are other training methods used within business organizations. Each teaching technique is used to help employees update current skills or to obtain new knowledge. In addition, an experienced employee may demonstrate various tasks to newer employees.

Advancements in technology make it possible for people to work at home using a computer-to-telephone hookup. This allows an individual to be employed and still have the flexibility of caring for a family. With more working parents, other arrangements have been created to help people balance work with family needs. Many organizations offer financial assistance for child care costs, while others have day-care facilities at the place of work. Flexible schedules in some companies allow employees to select desired working hours. In addition, some parents take advantage of job sharing, with two individuals dividing a full-time job so that each can handle personal and family needs.

Your academic achievement is measured through homework assignments, tests, and grades. Success on the job also needs to be evaluated. *Performance appraisal* assists business organizations in their efforts to:

- Measure the quality and quantity of work activities.
- Encourage workers to improve their level of performance.
- Reward employees through increased compensation and promotions.

The factors that are usually the basis of a performance appraisal include personal characteristics and work performance. Personal traits such as completing work on time and works well with others are commonly evaluated by a worker's supervisor. Also measured is your quality of completed tasks, such as typed reports that follow the format required in your company.

One of the most important goals of performance appraisals is rewarding employees with promotions. A *promotion* refers to a person's advancement in an organization to a position of more responsibility and higher pay. Employees who are promoted are those individuals who have demonstrated excellent work performance.

Other Concerns

Differences of opinion about a labor contract can and do occur. For example, an employee may believe extra pay is due for certain duties; the supervisor may disagree. Most union contracts outline a process for solving these disputes. This process is called a **grievance procedure**. Grievance procedures usually contain steps that allow each side to present its views of the situation.

In many industries, the right to union representation is still very important. In some major industries, particularly manufacturing, the percentage of union membership is high. Major industries such as automobiles, mining, transportation, and clothing are highly unionized. Furthermore, in some industries, even nonunion workers are covered by union contracts. In actual numbers, however, union membership has declined over the last few decades and is no longer growing vigorously. Membership has decreased from about 27 percent of the work force in 1970 to about 16 percent today. The composition of union membership has changed because of the trend toward a service-producing economy. More white-collar employees are now joining unions.

THE COLLECTIVE BARGAINING PROCESS

A union contract is the result of many hours of meeting between representatives of workers and the employer. The negotiations that take place between an organized body of workers and an employer which deal with wages and working conditions are called **collective bargaining**. This process usually involves several steps before an agreement between the two sides is reached.

Starting the Process

Collective bargaining starts with a meeting in which representatives of labor and management present what they believe should be in the contract.

Attempts then follow to settle differences about wages, working hours, employee benefits, and other issues affecting workers. Ideally, an agreement will be reached and a contract will be signed. If, however, neither side will compromise on an item, other actions may be necessary. In many cases, others are asked to help resolve points of disagreement.

Using Third-Party Assistance

Sometimes negotiations between labor and management can go no further than the discussion stage. When this happens, a mediator may be used to settle the differences. A **mediator** is a neutral person, neither a member of management nor of labor, who attempts to resolve the dispute. A mediator can only recommend solutions, not enforce them.

If a disagreement cannot be settled by mediation, an arbitrator may be called in to decide the issue. An **arbitrator** is a person who makes a legally binding decision to resolve labor-management differences. Both sides present their views after which the arbitrator makes a ruling to which all are bound. Before an arbitrator can be called in, however, both sides must agree to the use of an arbitrator.

Mediation and arbitration are frequently used to settle differences as part of the grievance procedure. The people who serve as mediators and

Illus. 9-2
Differences between labor and management can be resolved through negotiations.

arbitrators are selected from approved lists of individuals who are acceptable to both labor and management.

Problems arising from contract disputes are also decided by the National Labor Relations Board (NLRB). This federal government agency investigates unfair practices of unions or management. The NLRB can, for example, stop union members from pressuring nonunion members to join. Or, employers can be forced to stop giving special treatment to nonunion employees.

LABOR AND MANAGEMENT ACTIONS

The collective bargaining process may not always be successful. When neither party is willing to compromise, other actions can result. Procedures are available to both workers and management that can be used to encourage the settlement of differences.

Organized Labor's Actions

Workers who are dissatisfied with management's contract offer may vote to strike. A **strike** is a refusal to work until demands are met. A strike affects many people. Workers are not paid; the business may not have items to sell; and consumers may have to do without needed goods and services. For example, during a transit strike, buses, trains, and subways do not operate. People must find other ways of getting where they need to go. Since many suffer during a strike, it is usually used only as a last resort.

During most strikes, union members carry signs at the work site to publicize their complaints. This is called **picketing**. Picketing can encourage support from others. Customers and members of other unions often refuse to do business with a company that is being picketed.

Another action of labor is a boycott. A **boycott** is the refusal by workers to handle or buy products of a company involved in a labor disagreement. A boycott may also be a type of consumer action. If consumers believe a business is unfair to its workers, they might refuse to buy the company's products.

Management's Actions

When workers go on strike, the company may take certain actions. First, the business may try to operate as usual by hiring new employees. These people are referred to as strikebreakers. Using strikebreakers, however, may not be possible since some jobs require special training and experience.

Second, management may close all of its facilities in an attempt to put pressure on the striking union. Such action is called a **lockout**. If one union strikes, management may decide to close all offices and factories, thus involving employees not in the striking union. With many others out of work, pressure may be put on the strikers to compromise.

A third effort to stop a strike is legal action. An **injunction** is a court order directing striking employees to go back to work. Some strikes affect many people, such as a truck drivers' strike. In some cases, the president of the United States may obtain an injunction to get goods and services flowing again.

THE FUTURE ROLE OF WORKERS AND UNIONS

As new types of jobs develop, the role of workers and labor organizations will change. In recent years, the number of employees in manufacturing industries, such as automobile and steel, has decreased. This is the result of two main factors. First, competition from other countries has increased. Other countries can manufacture more efficiently many of the goods we once sold. People are now buying more products made elsewhere in the world, meaning fewer jobs for Americans. Second, technology has changed the work skills that are required. Robots and computers have replaced people in various jobs.

Many new job opportunities are related to information and technology. Many employees in these industries will be white-collar workers. If unions are to grow, they will have to meet the needs of these workers. The needs and expectations of white-collar workers may differ from those of blue-collar workers. Unions will have to be aware of those differences. Organizing efforts will focus on clerical, professional, service, and government workers.

While various factors in our economy will be different, one thing will not change. A cooperative effort among workers, business, and government will be necessary for economic success.

Illus. 9-3
A cooperative effort between labor and management is essential for economic success.

Increasing Your Business Vocabulary

The following terms should become part of your business vocabulary. For each numbered item, find the term that has the same meaning.

arbitrator
boycott
closed shop
collective bargaining
grievance procedure
injunction
labor union

lockout
mediator
picketing
right-to-work laws
strike
union shop

1. Exists when workers are required to join a union within a specified time after employment.
2. A neutral person who recommends solutions to disputes between labor and management.
3. A situation in which employees refuse to work until their demands are met.
4. A business in which an employer agrees to hire only union workers.
5. A refusal by workers to handle or buy the products of a company involved in a labor disagreement.
6. Negotiations that take place between an organized body of workers and an employer which deal with wages and working conditions.
7. A court order directing striking employees to go back to work.
8. A process in a labor contract for solving differences between workers and management.
9. A person who makes a legally binding decision to resolve labor-management differences.
10. A situation in which management closes all of its facilities in an attempt to put pressure on striking employees.
11. Laws which state that no one can be required to join a union to get or to keep a job.
12. A situation in which union members carry signs to publicize their complaints.
13. An organization of workers formed to give workers greater bargaining power in their dealings with management.

Reviewing Your Reading

1. How do labor organizations help workers be heard?
2. Why do some individuals believe that it is not necessary for them to become a member of a labor organization?
3. What conditions in the past contributed to the rise and growth of unions?
4. Why is the National Labor Relations Act of special importance to workers?
5. What is the name of the largest labor organization in the United States?
6. Explain the main difference between closed shops and union shops.
7. Why do unions oppose right-to-work laws?
8. Name three examples of employee benefits.
9. How has technology affected the demands of workers?
10. How do performance appraisal systems assist business organizations?

11. What is the purpose of a grievance procedure?
12. How does the collective bargaining process work?
13. Describe the difference between a mediator and an arbitrator.
14. What is the National Labor Relations Board?

15. What techniques does organized labor use to persuade management to accept their demands?
16. In what ways can management reduce the effectiveness of a strike?

Using Your Business Knowledge

1. Only a portion of our total work force is in a union. What are some of the reasons why more workers are not union members?
2. Certain products, such as clothing, have a label on them which indicates the manufacturer is a unionized company. Members of unions are encouraged not to buy products that do not have union labels on them. Do you think this is fair? Give reasons for your answer.
3. The demands of workers and business owners are frequently negotiated through collective bargaining. Decide if each item listed would most likely be a demand of labor, of management, or of both.
   a. A day off for an employee's birthday.
   b. Every employee works one Saturday a month.
   c. No overtime pay for cleaning machines after working hours.
   d. Promotions from within the company.
   e. Life insurance coverage for employees.
4. The workers at the Superior Food Processing Company are on strike. What groups, other than the workers and the owners of the company, are affected by the strike? In what ways?
5. Many people believe that government workers who perform vital services, such as police officers and fire fighters should not be allowed to strike. What do you think? Why?

Computing Business Problems

1. In one city, there are 10,000 people in the work force. Of those, 21 percent are members of labor unions.
   a. How many people in the work force are members of labor unions?
   b. How many people in the work force are not members of labor unions?
2. To join a certain union, you must pay an initiation fee of $75 and monthly dues of $25.
   a. How much will it cost to be a union member in the first year?
   b. How much will it cost the second year?
3. Members of the work force are not always paid by the hour. Sometimes they are paid by the amount of work they do. Consider the following two choices that were offered to a truck driver going from Washington, D.C., to Buffalo, New York, a distance of about 560 kilometers: (1) receive 24 cents per kilometer for the entire trip; or (2) receive $16 per hour for the trip, driving at an average speed of 80 kilometers per hour.
   a. How much would the truck driver earn working by the kilometer?
   b. How much would the truck driver earn working by the hour?
4. Listed on the next page are the hourly wages for six workers:

J. Adams	$8.65
L. Blake	8.27
K. Lomton	7.43
R. Morton	7.61
D. Roundtree	7.23
T. Washington	8.51

a. What is the average hourly rate for these six workers?
b. If Blake works 40 hours a week for one year, what will be his yearly earnings?

Expanding Your Understanding of Business

1. Through library research, obtain information about the growth and development of organized labor in the United States. What is the difference between a craft (or trade) union and an industrial union? What laws protect and restrict the rights of unions?

2. Discuss the questions below with relatives and friends who are members of labor unions. Summarize in writing the information you receive from your discussion and be prepared to give an oral report to the class.
   a. What social and welfare advantages do unions provide for their members?
   b. What does it cost to maintain membership in a union?
   c. What voice does the membership have in the operation of the local union? in the national union?

3. Talk to friends, relatives, and others who work and obtain information about the types of employee benefits they receive. Prepare a list of the most common benefits.

4. Collect news articles about various labor and management actions. Examples could include strikes, contract agreements, or other labor issues. Prepare a display of this news for your class.

5. Contact local employers to obtain information on programs and benefits offered to workers related to child care, flexible work schedules, and training programs. Write a two-page report on your findings.

Government Services

Chapter 10

Chapter Objectives

After studying this chapter and completing the end-of-chapter activities, you will be able to:

1. *List five services provided by government.*

2. *Describe how government protects you as a citizen, consumer, and worker.*

3. *List at least three ways government influences our economy.*

4. *Describe government's role as a purchaser of goods and services.*

5. *Explain how government activities are changing.*

Each day you are free to make many decisions as a consumer, worker, and citizen. You are usually allowed to buy the goods and services you desire. Sometimes, however, restrictions are placed on consumers buying products such as alcoholic beverages, cigarettes, and medications. Government tries to protect consumers from purchasing potentially dangerous items.

In a similar manner, you have the freedom to select a career. However, for some jobs, such as a doctor, lawyer, or teacher, you must meet certain requirements. These requirements are designed to protect consumers. You certainly do not want an untrained doctor treating you when you are ill.

Government also requires business owners to follow certain safety and labor laws. Government attempts to balance and serve the interests of everyone in our economy.

GOVERNMENT IN OUR ECONOMY

As explained in Chapter 2, government plays a role in every economic system. In our private enterprise system, the amount of government involvement is much less extensive than in socialist or communist systems.

The main actions of government that influence economic and business activities are:

- Providing services for members of our society.
- Protecting citizens, consumers, businesses, and workers.
- Regulating utilities and promoting competition.
- Providing information and assistance to businesses.
- Purchasing goods and services.

Each of these efforts has either a direct or indirect impact on business expansion and economic growth in our economy.

GOVERNMENT AS A PROVIDER OF SERVICES

Government is organized into three levels—federal, state, and local—as shown in Figure 10-1. The main goal of the federal government is to oversee the activities that involve two or more states or other countries. Business transactions involving companies in more than one state are called **interstate commerce**. Therefore, a trucking company that ships products to several states would be regulated by the federal government.

State governments regulate business activities within their own boundaries. **Intrastate commerce** refers to business transactions involving companies that do business only in one state.

Local governments include county boards and city or town councils. These local government units provide many of the day-to-day necessities for an orderly society, such as police and fire protection.

Figure 10-1
Different levels
of government
have different
duties, concerns,
and responsi-
bilities.

Levels of Government		
Local	**State**	**Federal**
Government units include: • county • city • park district • library district • school district	Concerned with the regulation of intrastate commerce	Concerned with interstate commerce and trade between the United States and other countries

Government officials are elected or appointed to serve you. Their job is to serve all citizens based on the choices made by voters. As a citizen, one of your responsibilities includes participation through the ballot box in our society's decision-making process.

Participating in Decision Making

Choices about who will govern result from voting. In an election citizens decide who will represent them. Our elected officials then have the task of making choices that will affect everyone. For example, state legislators may decide to spend more money for schools and provide less funds for building new highways.

Although many believe political power to be in the hands of a few, decisions are really made by many in our form of government. By voting, citizens influence the choices that will be made by our public officials. As discussed in Chapter 3, a vote to increase or decrease taxes will affect the government services available.

Meeting the Needs of the People

We enjoy freedom and safety because of the services furnished by government. The efforts of government that benefit citizens are called **public services**. Examples include fighting fires, maintaining roads, and teaching young people. Protecting our basic rights and providing economic stability are also fundamental government activities.

GOVERNMENT AS A PROTECTOR

Our personal health and safety are important factors that influence government actions. Many governmental activities are concerned with protection of our environment, property, and national security. Government also protects our rights as consumers, business owners, and workers.

Protecting Society

Providing local police and fire-fighting services is a basic duty of government. The protection of property is necessary for our survival. On a larger scale, the armed forces provide for our national defense. The security of our country is a major concern of the federal government.

Government regulations also attempt to protect us from an unsafe environment. Several laws exist to prevent air, water, noise, and chemical pollution. If people could do as they pleased, we might not have clean air or water for future use. Federal, state, and local government agencies enforce laws that prevent the dumping of chemicals and waste in rivers and lakes. Other regulations forbid the burning of substances that make our air unsafe to breathe. Protection of our communities from pollution is an important government service for everyone.

Protecting Consumers and Businesses

Every business transaction involves an agreement to exchange goods or services for something of value, usually money. This agreement is called a **contract**. A contract may be written or unwritten. Figure 10-2 highlights the main elements of every contract. Examples of contracts include a lease to rent an apartment, a credit card agreement, and documents that state the terms of a purchase.

The enforcement of contracts is necessary for an orderly economic system. If you agree to have repairs made on your car for $45, the work must be paid for when completed. If you fail to make the payment, legal action can be taken to force you to pay. Both consumers and businesses benefit from contract enforcement. Without it, dishonest consumers or business owners

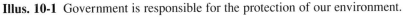

Illus. 10-1 Government is responsible for the protection of our environment.

Figure 10-2
Every contract
must have these
parts.

For a contract to be valid, you must have:

AGREEMENT An offer must be made, and an acceptance must occur.

COMPETENT Those entering into the contract must be of legal
PARTIES age and must be mentally competent.

CONSIDERATION Something of measurable value must be
exchanged by the parties involved.

LEGALITY The contract must be for a product or service
that may be legally sold; also no fraud or
deception exists in the agreement.

could refuse to honor their agreements, and our daily business activities would be very confusing.

Consumers frequently receive special attention when it comes to government protection efforts. Since we are all consumers, each of us benefits from various consumer protection laws. Government regulations exist to make sure that the food, drugs, and other products we consume are safe. In addition, labeling and advertising laws are designed in order to provide consumers with fair and correct information about the purchases they make. Consumer protection laws are discussed further in Chapter 17.

We are also protected by special property rights. When individuals or companies create new products or ideas, they may obtain a patent. A **patent** gives the inventor the exclusive right to make, use, or sell the item for 17 years. For example, a company that creates a new method to record programs from television could obtain a patent for this process to prevent other companies from making or selling recorders using this process.

In a similar manner, a **copyright** protects the work of authors, composers, and artists. This protection continues for 50 years after the person's death. Examples of copyright statements can be found on the front pages of most books. Patent and copyright laws were passed to reward and to protect creative efforts.

Another form of protection given to a business by government is a trademark. **Trademarks** are words, letters, or symbols that are associated with a specific company or product. Company names, team emblems, and label designs may be registered with the government. A trademark can be very valuable since many are famous throughout the world. What are some trademarks you see frequently?

Protecting Workers

Employees are also protected by government. As a worker, you have a basic right to safe working conditions. For example, safety standards for buildings, machines, and chemicals are set by government agencies. Government inspection and regulation of work areas helps to reduce the number of job-related accidents. For example, when machine operators wear safety glasses, the number of eye injuries can be reduced.

Additional government regulations stem from the need to protect the basic human rights of workers. For example, government does not allow people to be denied work because of their race, religion, sex, or age. Selection for a job must be based on training and experience. As discussed in Chapter 9, government does not permit wages below a set amount for certain jobs.

Other government efforts to protect basic human rights of workers include the following:

- Government training programs assist workers in obtaining necessary employment skills.
- Job placement services help workers find employment.
- Unemployment benefits provide financial assistance to workers who have lost their jobs due to poor economic conditions.

GOVERNMENT AS AN ECONOMIC MANAGER

Our economic system is based on freedom of choice for individuals. Buying items, selecting a career, or starting a business are usually necessary to preserve economic stability. The regulation of utilities and prevention of unfair business activities help to provide a stable business environment.

Regulating Utilities

Most goods and services you use are obtained from private businesses that are relatively free of government regulation. However, a **public utility** is an organization that supplies a service or product vital to all people. These include companies that provide local telephone service, water, and electricity. Most public utilities do not compete with other companies. One is selected to serve the whole community. If your city had six different electric companies, each with its own utility poles, lines, and expensive equipment,

Illus. 10-2
Government regulates utilities to ensure that these vital services are available to all citizens.

the service you would get would be more expensive and less efficient. Also, the extra poles and wires would create an unsightly environment.

While many utility companies are privately owned, they are closely regulated by government. Therefore, public utilities cannot set prices as they wish. This would be unfair since there is no competition to keep prices reasonable. The rates charged for items such as electricity, water, or natural gas must be approved by a government agency.

Promoting Competition

Most businesspeople are fair and honest, but a few may try to take advantage of their customers or competitors. Government attempts to prevent this. If a company charges different prices to different people for the same product, it is treating its customers unfairly. Likewise, if one business gets lower rates for the same quality and quantity of supplies than others, it has an advantage. Such action results in unfair competition.

A **monopoly** exists when a business has control of the market for a product or service. While a public utility monopoly may be beneficial by making sure people receive a needed service at a fair price, other monopolies may not be good for the economy. For example, if all food stores in your city were owned by the same company, consumers might not be treated fairly. This business could charge high prices and provide poor-quality products. Competition exists to give customers the best items at a fair price.

One government action designed to promote competition and fairness and to prevent monopolies was the passage of **antitrust laws**. Antitrust laws also prevent other unfair business practices such as false advertising, deceptive pricing, and misleading labeling. Each of these unfair practices hurts competition and reduces consumer choice.

Providing Business Assistance

Government also helps business by collecting and reporting valuable information. Data collected by the government can assist in planning for the future. Information about incomes, prices, worker availability, and business failures can help a businessperson make wiser decisions. For example, census information can help a business decide where the most potential customers live. The Bureau of Labor Statistics, the Department of Agriculture, and the Department of Commerce are a few of the government agencies that provide information.

Financial assistance is another government effort to help business. Loans can be obtained to help new businesses get started. Also, farmers and others may receive financial help in times of extreme hardship such as drought, flooding, or other natural disasters. Destruction of home and property by a tornado may qualify a person for a low-interest government loan. These programs are designed to promote the economic well-being of our society.

GOVERNMENT AS A PURCHASER OF GOODS AND SERVICES

All levels of government buy and use a wide range of items. They are also consumers of human services. More than 12 million people in our country work full time for federal, state, and local governments.

Buying Goods and Services

The federal government spends a great deal of money each day to buy a variety of goods and services. Buying everything from file cabinets to jet planes, government is major customer and an important economic force. Many businesses depend on government contracts and spending for their survival. Companies in your state most likely do business with the federal government, supplying such things as computers, processed foods, and automobiles.

Hiring Public Employees

Government is the single largest employer in our economy. About one of every nine workers is a public employee. Most people think only of police officers, fire fighters, and sanitation workers as government workers, but government employs the same types of workers employed by private industries. Secretaries, lawyers, meat inspectors, and computer programmers, for example, are employed by government. In recent years, although the number of federal employees has grown slowly, job opportunities in many state and local governments have increased at a faster rate as citizens have demanded additional public services.

The Changing Role of Government

The services provided by government units are constantly changing. Government today is involved in many more activities than ever before. In addition, areas of government activity have changed. For example, because government has removed certain regulations, the airline and banking industries have been allowed to compete more freely than in the past. Many people believe government should have less involvement in business and economic activities. Others believe that government involvement in such matters as the health and safety aspects of products must increase.

Government will continue to play a major role in our economic system. The specific areas of involvement will depend on your future decisions as a citizen and as a voter.

Illus. 10-3
Many people are hired by federal, state, and local governments to provide public services.

Increasing Your Business Vocabulary

The following terms should become part of your business vocabulary. For each numbered item, find the term that has the same meaning.

antitrust laws
contract
copyright
interstate commerce
intrastate commerce

monopoly
patent
public utility
public services
trademark

1. A business that supplies a service or product vital to all people and whose prices are determined by government regulation rather than competition.
2. Business transactions involving companies that do business only in one state.
3. Efforts of government, such as fire and police protection, which benefit citizens.
4. Laws designed to promote competition and fairness and to prevent monopolies.
5. Protection of the work of authors, composers, and artists.
6. An agreement to exchange goods or services for something of value.
7. The exclusive right given to a person to make, use, or sell an invention for a period of 17 years.
8. Business transactions involving companies in more than one state.
9. A word, letter, or symbol associated with a specific product or company.
10. A business that has complete control of the market for a product or service.

Reviewing Your Reading

1. What are the three levels of government?
2. How do interstate and intrastate commerce differ?
3. In what ways do individuals influence the decisions of public officials?
4. How does government protect society?
5. Explain how the enforcement of contracts helps consumers and businesses.
6. Why does the government grant special property rights such as copyrights and patents?
7. List four ways in which government protects and assists workers.
8. Why can one public utility serve a city better than several similar public utilities?
9. When is a monopoly not in the best public interest?
10. Name two ways in which government assists private businesses.
11. What types of products and services do governments buy?

Using Your Business Knowledge

1. Below is a list of some of the public services provided by government. For each service, tell whether the federal, state, or local government would most likely have the responsibility for the service. (Some services may be provided by more than one level of government.)
   a. Fire protection

b. Education
c. Parks and recreation
d. Water supply
e. Highways between cities
f. Assistance to low income families
g. Sewage and trash disposal
h. Public buses
i. Police protection
j. Public libraries
k. City street maintenance
l. National defense

2. Make a list of public utilities that serve your community
   a. What services do they provide?
   b. Do you think it would be better for these services to be offered by several competing businesses? Explain your answer.

3. Each day people enter into many contracts both written and unwritten.
   a. Give examples of contracts between a consumer and a business, between two businesses, and between a worker and a business.
   b. What services are provided by government to enforce contracts?

4. Two students are discussing the topic "Government is Our Biggest Business." Cindy believes that some government activities are in direct competition with private businesses and that this is unfair. She believes that government should limit its activities to those activities that private businesses cannot or will not undertake. Chuck thinks that government should undertake any business activities that it can perform better or less expensively than private business. What do you think? Give some examples of business activities undertaken by both private businesses and by government-owned businesses.

Computing Business Problems

1. A city government spends $186,000 a month on public services. Of that amount, 46 percent is used for fire and police protection.
   a. How much is spent each month for fire and police protection?
   b. How much is spent each month for other services?
   c. How much is spent by the city in a year for fire and police protection?

2. In a city in which there are 90,000 employed workers, 18,000 are public employees. Of this number, 6,000 are employed by the federal government, 8,000 by the state, and 4,000 by the city.
   a. What percent of all workers are public employees?
   b. What percent of the public employees are employed by the federal government?
   c. What percent of all employees are employees of the state government?

3. The town of Clarksville wants to expand the main street from two to four lanes. To do so, 150 feet of land is needed. How many meters of land will be used for the road-widening project?

4. Listed below is the cash income and expenditures record of the Midland Public Library for one year.

Income:

Cash on hand, beginning of year	$ 1,250
Town and state appropriations	52,000
Income from investments	1,795
Gifts	1,645
Fines on overdue books	550
Miscellaneous income	325

Expenditures:

Salaries	$23,500
Books and periodicals	6,775
Utilities	1,525
Insurance	780
Equipment and supplies	1,455
Cleaning and repairs	420
Community service programs	1,800
Library binding	675
General administrative expenses	715

a. What was the total of the cash on hand and cash received during the year?

b. How much was paid out during the year?

c. What percent of the total cash received was accounted for by town and state appropriations? (Round your answer to the nearest whole percent.)

d. What percent of total expenditures was accounted for by salaries? (Round your answer to the nearest whole percent)

Expanding Your Understanding of Business

1. Make a list of businesses in your community involved in interstate and intrastate commerce. Information can be obtained from newspaper advertisements, customers, and employees of local companies.

2. You have seen many trademarks on products as well as in advertisements, on television, on billboards, and in newspapers and magazines. Make a display of ten trademarks you recognize to show to your class. See if your classmates can tell the name of the company represented by each trademark. Why is government protection of trademarks important?

3. The salaries paid to government employees are matters of public record; that is, the public can know what these people are paid. Do you think it is fair to these employees for you to know how much money they earn? Why or why not?

4. Using a business law book or information gained through library research, find out the extent to which minors are liable for the contracts they sign?

5. Government control of monopolies in the United States has had an interesting history. Many important laws have been passed to control monopolies. Through library research find out the major provisions and some of the results of these laws.
   a. Sherman Antitrust Act
   b. Clayton Act
   c. Federal Trade Commission Act

Government and Taxation

Chapter 11

Chapter Objectives

After studying this chapter and completing the end-of-chapter activities, you will be able to:

1. State at least two reasons for the increasing costs of government services.

2. Identify three sources of government revenue.

3. List four items that are taxed.

4. Name three factors that are considered when a tax is created.

5. Explain how government can meet its expenses if taxes do not provide enough revenue.

On most mornings, the Ramos family's breakfast includes food products that the government has inspected for safety. Mrs. Ramos later drives her daughter and son to school on roads built and repaired by government workers. The car Mrs. Ramos drives was built to meet federal pollution standards. The school the children attend is a service provided with local, state, and federal government funds. After school, Maria and Carlos Ramos often go swimming in the community-supported pool of the park district.

These are just a few of the services provided by various levels of government. But how are these services financed? Government must raise money to cover the costs of public services. Since we all benefit from government services, we should also share in paying government expenses.

THE COST OF GOVERNMENT

Most goods and services you buy come from private businesses, but other items are provided through government efforts. Over the years, government has become more involved in serving the public. People now demand more from government than in the past. We have come to expect good highways, up-to-date libraries, and other public services. This demand for more public services results in higher government costs.

Another reason for increased government spending is the complexity of our economy. A growing population and an expanding business structure require a high degree of government effort. Providing services for more than 250 million people is no small task.

We have all had to cope with higher costs because of inflation, and government is no different. As prices increase, it costs more to provide public services and the rising cost of government is likely to continue. As costs continue to rise, finding new ways to pay government expenses may be necessary.

SOURCES OF GOVERNMENT REVENUE

As with businesses and individuals, income is necessary for government to operate. Government income is called **revenue**. Taxes are the main source of government revenue. To pay for services it provides, government levies taxes based on earnings, property, estates, and goods and services.

There are other sources of revenue in addition to taxes. Fines for traffic violations and other violations of the law provide income for government. Fees and licenses are also a source of revenue. Certain types of enterprises require a business license. For example, insurance and real estate agents pay a fee for the privilege of conducting business. Other examples of government fees are charges for drivers' licenses and fishing licenses.

Illus. 11-1
To pay for the
services it
provides, such as
building and
maintaining
highways,
government
levies taxes.

Taxes Based on Earnings

Your earnings as an individual are subject to an income tax. **Income taxes** are levied on the income of individuals and corporations. This is the largest source of revenue of the federal government as shown in Figure 11-1. Federal income tax deductions are also the largest wage deductions for most workers. Employers are required to withhold a portion of their employees' earnings from each paycheck for taxes. Employers then send this money to the government. Self-employed people are usually required to make quarterly tax payments to the federal government.

By April 15 of each year, taxpayers must file their federal income tax returns. An *income tax return* is a form used to determine the amount of tax owed for the year. Taxpayers may have to make an additional payment to the government, or they may receive a refund for any overpayment. Figure 11-2 on page 156 illustrates the steps involved in calculating your taxable income for federal income tax purposes.

Most states and many cities also tax the incomes of individuals. This revenue helps to cover the costs of services provided by state and local governments.

Corporate income taxes also provide government revenue. These are based on business profits. As you learned in Chapter 6, the corporate form of business ownership has several advantages, but there is the disadvantage of *double taxation*. First, the corporation pays a tax on its profits. The dividends that are paid to the shareholders by the corporation must then be reported as income on the shareholders' individual tax returns.

Figure 11-1
Government
revenue comes
from several
sources. The
largest source is
the individual
income tax.

SOURCES OF FEDERAL GOVERNMENT REVENUE

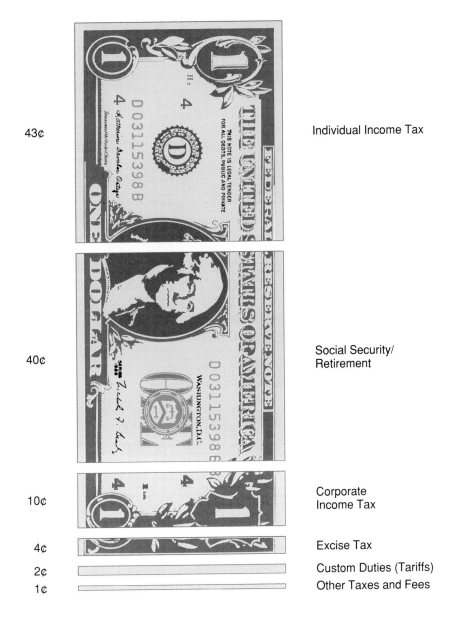

43¢ — Individual Income Tax

40¢ — Social Security/ Retirement

10¢ — Corporate Income Tax

4¢ — Excise Tax

2¢ — Custom Duties (Tariffs)

1¢ — Other Taxes and Fees

The Ramos family owns stock in a corporation. The company pays corporate income tax on its profits and pays dividends to Mr. and Mrs. Ramos. They must then report the dividends as income on their personal income tax form.

Figure 11-2
Your federal
income tax is
based on several
factors.

	GROSS INCOME	Earnings from wages, salary, commissions, profits, and investments.
—	**DEDUCTIONS**	Expenses that reduce the amount of taxable income for a person such as interest on a home mortgage, contributions to charity, or certain types of business expenses.
—	**EXEMPTIONS**	A reduction in the amount of taxable income for yourself and each family member who qualifies as a dependent.
	TAXABLE INCOME	The amount on which income tax is calculated using either a tax rate or tax table.

The Social Security program, discussed in Chapter 42, is supported by a tax on earnings. A percentage is deducted from your pay, up to a set limit. Your employer then contributes a similar amount based on your earnings to Social Security. These funds provide retirement and disability benefits for workers.

Taxes Based on Property

A major source of revenue for local governments is the real estate **property tax**. This tax is based on the value of the land and the buildings attached to the land. Most property tax revenue is used to pay for schools and other local government services, such as police protection and community parks. Businesses also pay a property tax. This amount, like salaries and advertising costs, is an operating expense of the company and is included in the prices charged for goods and services.

Some state and local governments also tax personal property. This tax is based on the value of items such as automobiles, boats, furniture, and farm equipment.

Taxes on Estates

In addition to taxes on property, the government also collects revenue based on the total worth of a person. Such a tax may take one of two forms. An **estate tax** is an assessment or tax based on the value of a person's property when he or she dies. The person's property may include cash, investments, a house, and land. When the property is transferred to someone else, it may be subject to an inheritance tax. An **inheritance tax** is a tax based on the value of property or the amount of money received from a person who has died. Both estate and inheritance taxes are sources of revenue for federal and state governments.

To avoid estate and inheritance taxes, some people give away their property before they die. At present, the federal government allows you to give a person tax-free $10,000 each year to as many people as you wish. When amounts greater than $10,000 are given to an individual, the value of the property is subject to a **gift tax**.

Taxes on Goods and Services

The cost of buying things can be increased by a sales tax. A **sales tax** is a state or local tax on goods and services that is collected by the seller. If you buy a can of paint for $15.00 and the state sales tax is 6 percent, the seller collects $15.90 from you. The seller then will pay 90 cents to the state, but you were the one who provided the money for the tax.

Some states do not tax the cost of food and medicine. This is to assist low-income individuals and families who spend a large portion of their income on these necessities. In recent years, only five states have not imposed a general sales tax.

Another type of tax that consumers pay on the purchase of certain goods and services is known as an **excise tax**. This tax is imposed on such goods

Illus. 11-2
Sales tax adds to the cost of consumer purchases.

and services as gasoline, cigarettes, air travel, and telephone service, and is usually included in the price of the item. The excise tax is a revenue source for federal and state governments.

As you learned in Chapter 7, taxes on imports are called tariffs. Only the federal government can impose an import tax. States cannot put a tariff on goods that are imported from foreign countries or shipped from other states.

TAXATION POLICIES

The establishment of completely fair tax policies is quite difficult. People usually believe that they should pay less and benefit more. To some people, the only fair tax is the one someone else pays.

Like the Ramos family, we all benefit from government services. As a result, most people are willing to share in the cost of government operations. Throughout history, attempts have been made to create taxes that are fair for everyone. Several factors are usually considered when selecting a method of taxation. These are burden of payment, ability to pay, and benefits received.

Burden of Payment

Taxes are paid by two groups, individuals and businesses. A tax that cannot be passed on to someone else is called a **direct tax**. Sales taxes and personal income taxes are examples of direct taxes. These are paid directly by individuals.

An **indirect tax** is one that can be passed on to someone else. For example, corporate income taxes are paid by the business, but these taxes are paid from money received from customers. The price of products you purchase includes an amount that will be used to pay the corporate income tax.

People who rent an apartment or house also pay real estate property tax indirectly. While the tax is paid to government by the property owner, the funds come from the amount paid in rent. Every tax, both direct and indirect, is eventually paid for by individuals.

Ability to Pay

At one time, property taxes were based on the number of farm animals owned or the number of windows in a person's house. Today, most taxes are related to some monetary value. This amount may be earnings, purchase price, or property value. A **progressive tax** is a tax whose rate increases as the amount taxed increases. For example, our federal income tax system requires a person earning $60,000 to pay a larger portion for taxes than a person earning $25,000. This is based on the belief that the person with the higher income is better able to pay.

Another common tax formula is the proportional method. A **proportional tax** is a tax in which everyone pays the same rate; it is commonly called a **flat tax**. Most sales, Social Security, and some state income taxes are examples of proportional taxes.

Proportional taxes may seem fair. Unfortunately, low-income individuals and families frequently pay a larger share of their income as a result of a proportional tax. This is true because of their lower ability to pay. For example, in a state that has a 5 percent sales tax on all products, including food, the following can occur:

	Family A	Family B
Family income	$50,000	$20,000
Food budget	$ 7,000	$ 4,000
Sales tax on food (5%)	$ 350	$ 200
Portion of income spent on food sales tax	0.7%	1.0%

Although Family A pays more than Family B in sales tax, Family B is paying a larger percentage of its income. Even though the tax is said to be proportional, the family with the lower income pays a larger portion of its income in taxes. This example suggests why many states do not tax the sale of food.

Benefits Received

Some people believe that taxes should be paid by those who benefit directly from the revenue. For example, these people would argue that only people with school-age children should be taxed for the cost of public schools because these parents receive the value. Others would say this is not completely true, since all citizens benefit from an educated population. There is less unemployment, better production output, and more technological discoveries with a well-educated population. The benefits-received idea may be appropriate for a toll road, but for services like police protection, for example, it would be a difficult rule to follow.

GOVERNMENT BORROWING

Government income from taxes and other sources may not always be enough to cover the costs of providing services. In a recent year, $980 billion in tax revenue was collected by the federal government. During that year, however, expenses were more than $1 trillion. When government spends more than it collects, a **deficit** results. This requires borrowing; borrowing increases the

national debt, which is the amount of money owed by the federal government.

The federal government borrows by selling Treasury bills, notes, and bonds to individuals, banks, insurance companies, and other financial institutions. In part, some of the national debt is financed by people or governments outside of the United States.

The federal government uses tax revenues to pay the interest on the debt. At the federal level, about 14 cents of each dollar spent goes for interest on the national debt.

A CITIZEN'S RESPONSIBILITIES

One responsibility of every citizen is to help decide how to use tax money. The people who are elected to government positions should represent your desires. You can be involved in public decision making by:

- Being informed about government activities.
- Electing capable, honest people to government positions.
- Studying and then voting intelligently on the issues presented.
- Expressing your views to elected officials.

The wise use of your tax dollars will only come from citizen participation. Your actions will result in well-managed government at all levels.

Illus. 11-3
The federal government borrows money by selling bonds to individuals and financial institutions.

Increasing Your Business Vocabulary

The following terms should become part of your business vocabulary. For each numbered item, find the term that has the same meaning.

deficit
direct tax
estate tax
excise tax
gift tax
income tax
indirect tax

inheritance tax
national debt
progressive tax
property tax
proportional tax or flat tax
revenue
sales tax

1. The amount of money owed by the federal government.
2. A tax that cannot be passed on to someone else.
3. Income that government receives from taxes and other sources.
4. A tax imposed when an individual receives an amount of money or property greater than $10,000.
5. A tax levied on the earnings of individuals and corporations.
6. A tax on certain goods and services, generally included in the price of the item.
7. A tax on goods and services that is collected by the seller.

8. A tax whose rate increases as the amount taxed increases.
9. A tax based on the value of a person's property when he or she dies.
10. A tax that is passed on to someone else for payment.
11. A situation that exists when government spends more than it collects.
12. A tax based on the value of property or the amount of money received from a person who has died.
13. A tax method in which everyone pays the same rate.
14. A tax based on the value of the land and the buildings attached to the land.

Reviewing Your Reading

1. How has inflation affected government spending?
2. List three sources of income for the federal government? for state governments? for local governments?
3. List four items on which taxes are levied.
4. How is corporate income tax a form of double taxation?
5. How are Social Security taxes paid?
6. For which level of government are property taxes a major source of revenue? How is this money usually spent?

7. What is the difference between a sales tax and an excise tax?
8. Who may impose tariffs on imports?
9. Give an example of an indirect tax.
10. Why is it that some states do not have a sales tax on food?
11. How can the federal government pay its expenses if taxes do not provide enough revenue?
12. How can you help make sure that good business management is practiced in government?

Using Your Business Knowledge

1. As the size of a country's economy grows, the cost of government usually increases. Name some services that may not be necessary in a small country.
2. Income taxes are withheld from your paycheck throughout the year. Why do you think the government collects the taxes in this way rather than just once a year, such as when you file your income tax return?
3. What do you think would happen if states were permitted to place import taxes on goods brought in for sale from other states?
4. Taxes can be classified as either direct or indirect. Tell whether consumers pay the following taxes directly or indirectly:
   a. Sales tax
   b. Tariff
   c. Corporate income tax
   d. Excise tax
   e. Property tax for renters
   f. Property tax for homeowners
   g. Personal income tax
5. How is money that the federal government received through borrowing different from money received through taxes?

Computing Business Problems

1. When Amelia Degado received her first paycheck, she was quite upset. She had been hired at a rate of $350 a week. However, her check was for an amount much less than that. The stub of her check showed that the following deductions were made from her pay:

Federal income tax	$52.50
Social Security tax	$27.75
State income tax	$10.50

   a. What was the total amount of deductions from Amelia's check?
   b. What was the amount of her paycheck?
2. A state government received $3.7 million in tax revenue during a year. The costs of services for that same year were $4.1 million.
   a. What was the amount of deficit for the state for the year?
   b. If the interest rate is 8 percent, how much will the state have to pay in interest?
3. The state in which Thomas Sheehan lives has a 4 percent sales tax on all consumer purchases except food. At the supermarket one day, Mr. Sheehan bought the following items:

   1 box of sandwich bags, 72¢
   2 liters of milk, 60¢ per liter
   1 can of tomato juice, 76¢
   2 rolls of paper towels, 65¢ per roll
   1 box of detergent, $2.43
   1 package of frozen fish, $1.78

   What was the total of Mr. Sheehan's bill, including sales tax?
4. The Mount Sherman School District is located in a city of 20,000. The student enrollment is 4,000. The property tax rate is $42.00 per $1,000 of assessed valuation. Of this tax rate, $20.16 is for educational needs. The total assessed valuation of all property in the city is $126 million.
   a. How much revenue should the city receive this year from the property tax?
   b. What percent of the property tax is budgeted for education?
   c. How much of the total annual revenue is budgeted for educational needs?
   d. What is the average amount of revenue received by the school district per student enrolled?

Expanding Your Understanding of Business

1. Make a list of local government services that have increased in cost over the past few years. Obtain information from articles in local newspapers or by contacting government officials.

2. The federal income tax is levied against taxable income. When you file an income tax return, taxable income is determined by subtracting certain exemptions and deductions from your total income. Through library research, find out what some allowable exemptions and deductions are. Why do you think the government allows these exemptions and deductions?

3. Besides using them as a source of revenue, government can also use taxes as a means of control. If a product is scarce and the government wants to discourage consumers from buying that product, the government can place an additional tax on that item. Is this a good way of controlling shortages? Explain your answer.

4. The federal government borrows money by selling U.S. Treasury bills, notes, and bonds. Using the financial pages of the newspaper, find the current rates people can earn by lending money to the government. Why are the interest rates for U.S. Treasury bills, notes, and bonds different from each other?

Career Category: Government

As you read Unit 3, did you find yourself wondering what it would be like to be involved in government directly — as an employee? Perhaps no other career category offers more variety in employment opportunities than does working for a government agency.

Job Titles: Job titles commonly found in this career area include:

Police Officer
City Manager
Postal Worker
Highway Maintenance Worker
Legislator
Armed Services
Health and Safety Inspector
Fire Fighter
Government Accountant
Public Librarian
Customs Agent
Social Worker

Employment Outlook: There are approximately 17 million people employed by local, state, and federal governments. Job opportunities include teachers, postal workers, accountants, computer programmers, custodians, and clerical employees. The variety of government careers is almost as diverse as that in private business. Nearly 1 million new government jobs will be created during this decade.

Future Changes: The number of federal government employees will remain fairly constant. At the same time, more local and state governmental agency workers will be needed as our population grows and people want more public services. Government careers that will be in demand in the future include office workers, maintenance employees, and those with technical skills in areas such as engineering, computers, and law.

What Is Done on the Job: Because there are so many types of government jobs, we cannot describe them all here. Let's look at two that you might find interesting, the city manager and the health inspector. Local government officials responsible for the coordination of the day-to-day operations of a city are called city managers or public administrators. A city manager usually works closely with the mayor or the city council.

A major duty of the city manager is handling finances. Tax money has to be collected and bills

have to be paid. In addition, city managers work with various departments that provide police and fire protection, education, traffic control, and other government services.

City managers are also responsible for the preparation of budgets and the creation of future plans. Writing and reading reports are another major part of the job. A career as a local government administrator usually requires long hours and many meetings with department heads and community groups.

Health and safety inspectors are the people responsible for the safety of food products, places of employment, and our environment. Thousands of people are employed by federal, state, and local governments to protect citizens from potential dangers.

A health inspector can be involved in checking processed foods, medicines, or restaurants. Inspections are designed to insure the safety of consumer products and services. When necessary, legal action may be taken to force a business to comply with government regulations. Government inspectors are also employed in the areas of air safety, construction, customs, labor laws, mines, and occupational safety. The work in this career can be interesting and exciting as inspectors frequently encounter unusual situations.

Education and Training: Requirements for government positions vary greatly. Certain jobs are available to high school graduates; other careers require specialized training. The college subjects most frequently recommended for government work are courses in business, office skills, communication, law, economics, and polit-

ical science. Many federal government jobs require that the applicant take a civil service test. This exam is designed to measure a person's ability and potential for advancement.

Salary Levels: Just as there are many different jobs in government work, salaries also vary widely. Incomes can range from $14,300 for starting office clerks to more than $100,000 for public administrators of large cities.

For Additional Information: Additional information about this career area is available from numerous sources, including the following:

Office of Personnel Management
1900 E Street, N.W.
Washington, DC 20415

American Federation of State, County, and
   Municipal Employees
1625 L Street, N.W.
Washington, DC 20036

National Association of Government
   Employees
2139 Wisconsin Avenue, N.W.
Washington, DC 20007

American Federation of Government
   Employees
1325 Massachusetts Avenue, N.W.
Washington, DC 20005

Careers in Our Economy

Unit 4

Unit Goals

After studying the chapters in this unit, you will be able to:

1. *Explain how to plan for a career.*
2. *Tell how to obtain a job that can begin your career.*
3. *Describe career opportunities in small businesses.*

Chapter 12
Planning Your Career

Chapter 13
Entering the World of Work

Chapter 14
Career Opportunities in Small Business

Quiet!
Entrepreneur at Work

Business Brief

Many entrepreneurs in American business started in a small way in jobs not considered to be especially glamorous. Take John Barfield, for instance. In 1949, he worked as a janitor on the custodial staff at the University of Michigan. In

1988, John Barfield headed two businesses with combined sales of more than $40 million. Was it luck or hard work that brought success? Let's take a look at his business record.

While working as a janitor, he supplemented his income by washing and waxing cars of university professors. This work paid him well, and he looked for other ventures. He noticed many new homes being built and observed that building contractors did not clean houses very thoroughly for their new owners. He suggested cleaning the new houses on a contract basis. The builders liked the idea, and he had another business venture under way.

Success followed and he had to hire others to help him. His reputation for dependability and quality work was an important factor in attracting new business.

In 1955, he signed his first contract for cleaning a commercial building. The commercial business proved to be profitable and kept grow-

ing. Within 15 years, he established both a national and international reputation. He had started the first school for training janitorial workers, and a training manual he wrote became a national model.

A large corporation offered to buy John Barfield's company, so in 1970 he sold his business and "retired." Although he had achieved his financial goals, he continued to work as a manager in the business for three years at the new owner's request.

In 1975, John Barfield started over again in the same business he had operated for 20 years. Within one year, his new company was a success and became one of Michigan's largest service firms.

In 1977, John Barfield was encouraged by several local business managers to start a manufacturing business that would employ black workers to supply parts for an automobile plant. Michigan's economy was weak at that time, and he considered this to be his most risky venture. Among the many challenges he faced were upgrading an old plant with old equipment, keeping the machinery running, motivating his three employees to stay with him when things did not look very good, and meeting schedules with quality products. The first year of operation resulted in a net loss of $160,000. In his own words, "It took courage to keep going." Today that firm employs 120 people and has sales of more than $20 million.

Another opportunity came along the following year when the need for technical employees in the auto industry was brought to his attention. He hired six students from a community college and started Barfield and Associates. Today that firm has offices throughout the United States, employs more than 700 people, and has sales exceeding $23 million.

Can you note any luck in this story? In a conversation, John Barfield said that too often the fear of failure keeps people from taking the risks necessary to be successful. He was able to meet every challenge that faced him and his business. Hard work and courage were the elements of success that paid off for him, not luck.

168

Planning Your Career

Chapter 12

Chapter Objectives

After reading this chapter and completing the end-of-chapter activities, you will be able to:

1. *Explain what a career is and why career planning is important for students.*

2. *List at least four important sources of career information.*

3. *Identify a desirable approach to planning and conducting a career information interview.*

4. *State at least three questions that help students think about their values.*

5. *Explain why it is important to develop one's talents, abilities, and basic skills as part of career planning.*

6. *Describe five steps to follow when making career decisions.*

7. *List at least three sources for financing additional education.*

Carrie Nees was reading the local newspaper. The Winthrop cartoon caught Carrie's fancy; it went as follows: Winthrop's friend is talking to him and says, "I'd like to be a teacher, but I don't like kids. Or maybe I could be a tightrope walker, but I'm afraid of heights." As Winthrop walks away he muses, "And I thought I had problems!" Carrie considered what the cartoon was saying and agreed that Winthrop's friend did indeed have a problem. Carrie also reflected on the fact that many of us have problems when it comes to making decisions about careers.

Career planning is a real-life process; it involves making some decisions about the jobs for which we want to prepare. When planning is done correctly, it can relieve frustrations and help point us in the right direction. Making decisions about the future, though, is never an easy matter. You learned some facts and figures about the world of work and our work force in Chapter 8. Understanding the world of work is a good first step in career planning. Finding the job that is right for you, among the thousands of different jobs in the world of work, is a challenge. A study of careers is necessary before good career decisions can be made.

Planning your career is important, and the planning needs to begin while you are in school. Career planning involves looking into possible careers. It also means looking at yourself and deciding what you want to do and do not want to do in your future. Selecting the career that is right for you means finding out things about jobs and yourself.

STUDYING CAREERS

Before we go on, let's consider what is a job and a career. A **job** is a task or series of tasks that are performed to provide or help to provide a good or service. People are hired to fill jobs, and they are paid for the work they perform. A **career** is a goal in life that is fulfilled through a job or series of jobs. Some people would say that you have a kind of career now; the goal is to complete your schooling. Your job is to pass the courses you take and to earn good grades. When your career is in the world of work, your goal may be to become a department store manager. Your first job then could be as a salesperson in a department store; later you might be promoted to assistant department manager as you move toward the fulfillment of your career goal.

There are specific facts to be learned about jobs. You must find out about the duties performed, the education and training required, the wages paid in different jobs, and financial requirements. You should learn about what it takes to succeed and about the advantages and disadvantages of certain career areas. Done correctly, your job study will answer some important questions for you.

Career planning is the process of studying careers, assessing yourself in terms of careers, and making decisions about a future career. You do not just decide to study careers for one day or one week. The study of careers is a continuous process because new career opportunities occur all the time. You should view learning about careers as a lifelong activity, something that continues even after you begin your career.

We all need help in career planning. There are several sources of help for you right in your own school and community. Some information covers careers in general; other information is more specific about careers in your local area. You should look into as many sources of information as possible.

WHERE TO FIND INFORMATION

Your own school is a good place to start looking for information about careers. Many school libraries have career resource materials. You may find *Occupational Outlook Quarterly* or other publications of the Department of Labor and the Bureau of Labor Statistics to be quite helpful. For example, *The Occupational Outlook Handbook* gives detailed information on 225 occupations. Included are job duties, working conditions, education and training requirements, advancement possibilities, employment outlook, earnings, and a list of other occupations that require similar aptitudes, interests, or training.

Career World magazine publishes information about a variety of careers, often looking at careers of the future. *The Encyclopedia of Careers* can give you basic information about many jobs and career areas. Organizations, such as The Administrative Management Society (AMS) and the Insurance Information Institute, publish materials dealing with their particular career areas. The AMS publication, *The Office and You*, is helpful for those interested in business careers.

Some books are written specifically to help students with career planning. *Business Careers*, *Secretarial and Office Careers*, *Accounting and Data Processing Careers*, and *Marketing Careers* are four books that give some helpful information on planning a career in business. Books that deal with other career areas are also available. Materials such as these often include activities that help with career planning.

Your school may have a career resource center. Some schools locate them in the library, some in the counseling office, and others in departments such as business education and vocational education. These resource centers normally have a wide variety of materials available. You may find magazines, brochures, pamphlets, films, and videotapes on careers. You may also have computer terminals in your school that are connected to centralized computer files of career and education information.

Newspaper help-wanted ads are also useful in career planning. Reading the help-wanted ads in your local newspaper or a large metropolitan paper can give you a good idea of what jobs are in demand. Reading those ads can

Illus. 12-1 *The Occupational Outlook Handbook* and current help-wanted ads can provide information useful for career planning.

 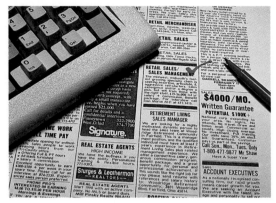

help you discover what employers are looking for in the people they hire. Sometimes ranges of beginning salaries are shown.

Another good source of information in many communities is the **government employment office**. These offices, which are tax supported, help people find jobs and provide information about careers. Employers who need workers often contact government employment offices for help. They may also contact private employment agencies for the assistance they need. Employment offices can provide up-to-date information about the job market in your local area. They also can help you look for part-time, summer, or full-time work.

GETTING INSIGHT INTO WORK

Part-time or summer jobs can also be part of your career planning. You can learn useful information by being alert to what is going on around you as you work. You may have already had experiences with part-time or summer jobs. Think about what they taught you about certain jobs and the work that had to be performed.

Would you like to talk to people about their jobs and careers? Career information interviews are an excellent way to get valuable information about careers. A **career information interview** is a planned discussion with a worker to find out about the work that person does, the preparation necessary for that career, and the person's feelings about his or her career. Interviews will help you gain insight into what actually happens in a particular career area and can often reveal how important it is to select and prepare for the right career.

You will find that most workers like to talk about their career experiences. However, before you begin a career information interview, you

Illus. 12-2
Part-time and summer jobs can provide a wealth of career information.

should think about the questions you want to ask. Here are some questions that often are asked:

- How did you get your present job? Did other jobs lead you to this one? What were those jobs?
- In what ways do you find your job to be satisfying? In what ways is it dissatisfying?
- What are some tasks you perform in your job?
- In what ways do you think your job is better than other jobs? In what ways is it not as good?
- What do you believe are some of the most important qualifications for the work you do? What training and education are needed?
- What advice would you give a young person who is considering this line of work?

You should keep notes on what you learned through the career information interviews. The job experiences of others will provide important career planning information that you will continue to find valuable.

LIFE-STYLE NEEDS AND WANTS

Your way of life is influenced by your needs and wants. As you consider your future career, you may have to decide whether you want to work in the area in which you now live or whether you are willing to move to where the

Illus. 12-3
Interview several people about the career area in which you are interested.

job you really want is located. There may be reasons why you would prefer to live and work near your home. However, people who successfully pursue the careers of their choice often need to move to another area.

Mobility is the willingness and ability of a person to move to where jobs are located. The lack of mobility of our work force leads to locational unemployment. **Locational unemployment** occurs when jobs are available in one place but go unfilled because those who are qualified to fill those jobs live elsewhere and are not willing to relocate.

Your career goals and your feelings about where you want to live influence your mobility. You may prefer to work and live where your family and friends live, or you may be willing to venture into a new community where new friends and relationships have to be established. Your desires and personal qualities are important in several ways when it comes to career planning. You need to know about careers and about yourself.

A SELF ASSESSMENT

As you look into careers and learn about jobs and the work involved, you get a feel for certain jobs and career areas. You may like or dislike certain jobs and career areas without knowing why. There are personal aspects of career planning and decision making that are important. Becoming aware of these personal aspects and learning about yourself in the process are important in career planning.

Your Goals and Values

Your own **values**, the things that are important to you in life, must be considered along with facts about jobs and careers. There are a number of ways you can learn about your values. Your counselors or business teachers may have exercises or activities that can help you learn about your values. These exercises show how you rank items such as prestige, money, power, achievement, independence, leadership, security, or belonging. Each of these may influence you, directly or indirectly, when you select your job or career.

You can begin to examine some of your values by answering certain questions. Your answers will help you to understand some values you consider important. Each answer should be thought through and analyzed. Here are some examples of those kinds of questions:

- Is it important to me to earn a lot of money?
- Am I mainly interested in work that provides a service for others?
- Is it important for me to have a job that others think is important even if I do not really care for it?
- Do I want a job that is especially challenging and may require additional schooling?
- Would I be willing to start in a job that pays a lower salary than another if that job were more challenging and offered better opportunities for future advancement?
- Do I consider investing in education or job training to be as important as spending for other things?

There may be other questions you can think of, but these will give you a good start.

Another activity is to consider what you would do if someone gave you a large sum of money to be used in any way you desire. Would you start your own business? Would you hire a jet and travel throughout the world? Would you develop a foundation to support athletics for underprivileged children? Would you help build up a run-down neighborhood? Would you buy the biggest wardrobe someone your age ever had? Would you use the money to finance an expensive education? Your answers will tell you something about your personal values.

Some jobs and careers will let you achieve your goals, use your talents and abilities, and fit your values. Those jobs bring the highest levels of satisfaction to the worker. Your talents and abilities, and your willingness to use and develop them, determine to a large extent the career that you should follow.

Talents, Abilities, and Basic Skills

Each of us has certain talents and abilities. You may have some that your friends and classmates do not have. Your talents and abilities, along with your career goals and interests, are important in career planning.

There are a number of ways you can learn about your own abilities. Think about the courses you have taken and the grades you have received in school. What kinds of courses have you taken? In which ones have you done your best work? Which courses have been easiest for you? Which have been the most difficult? Answers to questions such as these will identify your talents and abilities.

Your courses and your grades also tell you something about your likes and dislikes. You may have talent and ability but are not applying yourself. To get a good look at your talents and abilities, you should discuss this matter with your parents, counselors, teachers, and friends.

Just as there are exercises to help you examine your values, there are also tests and exercises that analyze your abilities. Your school counselors may have these tests available. Sometimes employment agencies have applicants take these special tests so that they can better match people with jobs requiring certain talents and abilities.

Illus. 12-4
Making a career decision involves looking at yourself, your values, and your goals.

Abilities can be developed, and that is an important point to keep in mind. If you are weak in a certain area, you may want to take courses that will improve that area. For instance, employers continue to tell us that basic skills in writing, reading, and computing are very important to them. If you are not strong in composing letters and reports, you should take additional courses in English, preferably business English. If reading is a problem for you, get help in that area, too. If computations, including working with fractions and decimals are difficult for you, additional courses in math, including business math, would be desirable. The idea is to strengthen your weak areas *before* you go into full-time work. You can plan your courses and future activities to help you grow toward your chosen career.

THE CAREER DECISION

Each person must eventually make his or her own career decision. Too often the decision is made when full-time work begins. But that is too late, especially if certain training and education are required.

Making initial career decisions while you are in school has many advantages. One advantage is that in school you have a lot of good information readily available. But more important, early career planning will help you select the right courses. An early career decision can also encourage you to become involved with organizations such as Future Business Leaders of America, Distributive Education Clubs of America, and Junior Achievement that teach you about business and help you prepare for a career.

Your decision may be a **tentative career decision**; that is, a decision that is subject to change or modification as new information is received. A tentative decision is much better than no decision at all. Your career decision will give you a direction that is needed, and you will find a new kind of interest in what you do.

How can you be sure that you are making the best career decision possible? There is no way to guarantee a perfect decision. But good decisions generally are made by those who follow the right steps. Here are some steps to follow in making your career decision:

1. Gather as much information as you can.
2. Analyze what you have learned about careers and about yourself.
3. Think about different plans of action and what might happen if you follow each one.
4. Select what seems to be the best plan of action and follow it.
5. Evaluate your career decision from time to time.

Your search for the right career could continue for a long time. In the years ahead, some of your values and goals will change. You will develop new interests and abilities. New jobs and careers will come along for you to learn about. You should be ready to make career-decision changes when they are called for in your situation.

PURSUING AND FINANCING ADDITIONAL EDUCATION

Some jobs require education and training beyond high school. Two-year schools—usually called community colleges or junior colleges—offer a wide variety of training in many career areas. Four-year colleges and universities, both public and private, provide education and training for many career areas and professions. Private business schools that specialize in certain job training, such as radio and television or computer technology, are other sources for additional career preparation.

You should consider the cost for additional schooling as an investment in your future; an investment that will earn for you higher wages in the future. There are a number of ways in which you can get help financing additional schooling. Most schools have financial aid programs that you should investigate. These programs include scholarships, student loans, and work-study opportunities. Some financial aid programs are based on your record as a student while others are based on financial need. Part-time work also is a common way in which young people finance the additional education needed to pursue the career of their choice. You should consider these as you continue your career planning and decision making.

CARRIE NEES—A GOOD APPROACH

Carrie Nees learned about career planning in a number of ways. Carrie prepared a career report on becoming a corporate lawyer as a requirement for her Introduction to Business class. She also interviewed the legal counsel for a local corporation. Her report gave her doubts about whether she really wanted to pursue a career in law and whether she could afford the additional schooling.

A course in accounting that Carrie completed in her junior year led her to believe that the accounting field was one that she would like to enter. She did some reading about accounting careers. With her computer skills, she was able to get a part-time job in an accounting office the following summer. While on the job, she learned about how an accounting office operates. Her job gave her an opportunity to talk to several accountants and auditors about their careers. When school began again in the fall, she took the second-year accounting course. She also enrolled in additional courses in math and English. The accountants had recommended that she get more course work in both of those areas. She also took the office laboratory course to become more familiar with office procedures. Carrie worked hard to get good grades;

Illus. 12-5
Carrie's accounting background helped her get started on her career.

she knew that those grades would be important later if she were to achieve her future goal. With her good grades and attendance, she was confident that she could receive some financial aid when she entered college.

The accountants had suggested that she should "reach for the top"—and that meant more schooling along with accounting work experience. Carrie wants to eventually take the state accounting examination. If she passes it, she will become a certified public accountant (CPA).

Carrie continues to work part time for the accounting firm. She also is enrolled in her local college, where she is majoring in accounting. She has a career plan and is following it. Very likely some day it will be "Carrie Nees, CPA."

Increasing Your Business Vocabulary

The following terms should become part of your business vocabulary. For each numbered item, find the term that has the same meaning.

career
career information interview
career planning
government employment office
job

locational unemployment
mobility
tentative career decisions
values

1. The process of studying careers, assessing yourself in terms of careers, and making decisions about a future career.
2. A tax-supported office that helps people find jobs and provides information about careers.
3. A planned discussion with a worker to find out about the work that person does, the preparation necessary for that career, and the person's feelings about that career.
4. The willingness and ability of a person to move to where jobs are located.
5. Jobs are available in one place but go unfilled because workers who are qualified to fill those jobs live elsewhere and are not willing to relocate.
6. The things that are important to you in life.
7. A career decision that is subject to change or modification as new information is received.
8. A task or series of tasks that are performed to provide or help to provide a good or service.
9. A goal in life that is fulfilled through a job or a series of jobs.

Reviewing Your Reading

1. Why should you study careers?
2. What are several sources of information about careers?
3. Name three books that are written specifically about business careers.
4. Explain how a career resource center can be helpful.
5. What information can be gained from reading newspaper want ads?
6. For what purposes have government employment offices been established?
7. How can career information interviews help you in career planning?
8. Why is mobility important in looking ahead to future careers?
9. Why are basic skills important to consider in career planning?
10. What are some of the things you should learn about your values?
11. How can courses and grades tell you something about your talents, abilities, and interests?
12. What steps are involved in career decision making?
13. What help is available to assist you in financing additional schooling?

Using Your Business Knowledge

1. There is a great deal of information that can be learned about business operations, interpersonal and customer relationships, and other experiences from working a part-time or summer job. Give some examples of what might be learned through these kinds of experiences.
2. Describe how you would conduct a career information interview. What would you do to prepare for it in advance?
3. What are some good sources of information about jobs in your local community?
   Comment on how you might use each one.
4. Make a list of your talents and abilities, and then note the ones in which you feel you are strong or weak. Indicate how you might use your strengths in career planning. Also indicate what action you might take to strengthen your weaker abilities.
5. When you discover what your values are in relation to such things as prestige, power, and recognition, how will your values affect your thinking about future careers?
6. Why should your career decisions be con-

sidered tentative rather than once-and-for-all decisions?

7. Why is investing in additional education

Computing Business Problems

1. Emilio Ramirez works as a nurse in a local hospital. He works 40 hours per week and is paid $11.25 per hour. He saves one-third of what he earns to create a fund so that he can go to medical school.

   a. How much does Emilio earn in one week? How much is he able to save each week?

   b. Without considering interest he would earn on savings, how much would he save in 10 weeks? in 15 weeks? in 25 weeks?

   c. If Emilio needs to save at least $8,000 before he can consider going to medical school, for how many weeks will he have to save in order to reach or exceed the $8,000 goal?

2. Bobby Holihan works as a manager for a trucking firm. Bobby has to keep records of the number of trucks going out and coming in each day, and he must keep a record of the number of miles driven by each driver. Last Monday there were 17 trucks on the road, 3 on the lot being loaded, and 2 in the shop being repaired.

   a. On Monday, the trucks on the road averaged 175 miles each. How many total miles were driven that day? If all of the trucks were on the road the following day and averaged the same number of miles, how many total miles would be driven?

   b. If all of the trucks were driven for 5 days, and the average miles per truck increased to 190 miles, what would be the total number of miles driven?

   c. If the cost of operating a truck is $3.75 per mile, how much did it cost the

something that should be considered in career planning?

company to operate their trucks in each of the three previous situations?

3. Lindsay Nees works in an office that is 12 feet wide and 14 feet long. The ceiling is 10 feet high. (See Appendix D for information regarding metric conversions.)

   a. What are the dimensions of her office in meters?

   b. Her desk is 30 inches high, 54 inches long, and 36 inches wide; what are the dimensions of her desk in centimeters?

   c. A cleaning fluid that is used to keep her furniture looking nice comes in 1-liter, 2-liter, and 5-liter containers. How many quarts of cleaning fluid are there in each container? If the firm uses 50 gallons of cleaning fluid per year, how many 2-liter containers do they use in one year?

4. Michael Inannocone sold $10,000 worth of merchandise the first week of this month. His second-week sales totaled $12,500, his third week $17,500, and his fourth week $24,500.

   a. What were his total sales for the four-week period?

   b. What were the percentage gains in sales each week?

   c. What was the percentage gain from the first week to the last week?

   d. If he improves his sales by 10 percent in the first week of the next four-week period (over the total for the fourth week of the first four-week period), what will be his total sales?

   e. What would be the approximate percentage gain in sales from his first week to the end of the first week of the second four-week period?

Expanding Your Understanding of Business

1. Make a list of all of the career resources in your school that could be of help to someone looking into careers. Be sure to check the reference shelves, card catalog file, and periodicals in the library or resource center. Your counselor's office and the business education department are also places to look for materials to be included on your list.

2. Develop a career information interview questionnaire. When you have it in usable form, practice using it with someone in class or with a teacher or administrator in your school. After using it, make any changes you think would be desirable and use it in a career information interview as part of a career project.

3. Talk with a friend who has worked on part-time or summer jobs and find out what that person has learned about the world of work and how the information may affect his or her career planning. In particular, determine if his or her work values have changed in any way and whether work itself is viewed differently.

4. Invite a job counselor, an employment interviewer, or someone who hires young people for jobs in your community to come to your class to talk with you about career planning and job opportunities. Develop a list of at least six specific questions that you would like to have answered.

5. From the list of library resources you compiled in Question 1, select two or three pamphlets or books that describe a job about which you know nothing or very little. Read those materials and write a report on why you believe that career could be a good one for you or someone else (even if you decide it is not the one for you). List at least three advantages and three disadvantages of that job. Give a report to the class on your findings.

6. Collect from newspapers and magazines cartoons that deal with career planning and career decision making. For each one, write a commentary on how each applies to real-life situations. Consider making a bulletin board display of your cartoons.

7. Write a short report on how you believe your values will influence your selection of a career. Be specific when relating to how such things as power, independence, security, money, and prestige could cause you to choose or reject certain occupations. Use a wide range of occupations, such as a lawyer, teacher, minister or priest, welder, auto mechanic, nurse, factory worker, sales clerk, politician, secretary, accountant, marketing manager, and small business owner.

8. Contact a financial aid office at a community college or university and learn what financial aid programs are available and what are the requirements.

Entering the World of Work

Chapter 13

Chapter Objectives

After studying this chapter and completing the end-of-chapter activities, you will be able to:

1. *Write an ideal letter of application.*

2. *Prepare a personal data sheet.*

3. *Identify sources of information about job openings.*

4. *Fill out a job application form that would be acceptable to an employer.*

5. *Explain how preemployment tests might be used by employers.*

6. *List several questions that are often asked in a job interview.*

7. *State five actions that a job applicant can take that will result in a favorable job interview.*

8. *Describe employer requirements and what is required to succeed on the job.*

Shana Holihan scanned the help-wanted ads once more. Each week for the past several weeks she has been searching for a particular job that she wants. "After all," she remarked, "I have completed an excellent high school business education program, and I am ready to start on my career. In the fall, I will enroll in our local college, but I want to get started on a good job this summer. If I can find the right one, I will take courses at night and work toward my degree while working full time."

Shana has applied for a job through the local government employment agency, and she has let her school counselors know about her intention to find employment. She has also talked over her plans with several friends and relatives. Shana's career goal is to become a certified professional secretary and to one day work as an administrative assistant to a corporate executive. She knows that she will start out as a secretary or word processing operator, but she is hoping to get a job where she can be promoted if she does good work. She is being somewhat selective in her search for a job that will let her enter the world of work and begin her career.

Then it finally happened; a job opened that Shana believed was "just the one for her." It was for an assistant secretary position in the office of the vice president of a local university. It required some of the skills Shana had developed in high school, and it was an organization large enough to have promotional opportunities. Shana was excited and applied for the job.

PREPARING A LETTER OF APPLICATION AND A PERSONAL DATA SHEET

The job notice Shana read asked applicants to write a letter of application. Although it is not always required when applying for a job, it is important to know what a letter of application is and how to write one.

A **letter of application** is a sales letter about yourself written for the purpose of getting a personal interview. It should be a courteous letter focusing on your interest in and qualifications for the job.

Like any good sales letter, your letter of application should attract the employer's attention and interest. It should create a desire to meet you. You should urge the reader to invite you to come for an interview. Figure 13-1 shows Shana Holihan's well-prepared letter of application. The letter is neat, courteous, and to the point. A carelessly written letter may cause the employer to think that you will be a careless worker. Your letter represents you, and it must compete with other letters of application for the reader's attention.

Shana's letter mentions that a personal data sheet is enclosed with the letter. A **personal data sheet** is a summary of important job-related

Figure 13-1
Your letter of
application will
introduce you to
your prospective
employer. It
should represent
you well and
make the reader
want to meet you
in person.

520 Nancy Blvd.
Phoenix, AZ 85027-2392
June 25, 19--

Dr. Ruth Collins
Vice President
Uptown University
Tempe, AZ 85076-4261

Dear Dr. Collins:

The advertisement in the *Daily Chronicle* for an assistant secretary describes just the job I want. Please consider me as an applicant for that position.

The ad said that you are looking for a bright and alert person who is conscientious and interested in long-term employment. I believe that my record at Upper Mountain High School and part-time employment record will show that I have the qualities you desire. My career goal is to some day be an administrative assistant. An assistant secretary position in your office will allow me to get an important start on my career.

My business education program at Upper Mountain High School included courses in introduction to business, computers, word processing, office procedures, and accounting. I also took four years of English and three years of math. For each of my last semesters, I was on the honor roll. In our cooperative education program, I worked ten hours a week during my senior year for the Tempest Tea Pot Company, where I learned a great deal about secretarial work and human relations.

Enclosed is a personal data sheet giving my qualifications in more detail. It would be a privilege to have an interview with you. I may be reached by telephone at 555-0308 any time during the day.

Sincerely yours,

Shana Holihan

Shana Holihan

Enclosure

information about yourself. It describes your education and work experience and lists the names of people who have agreed to be your personal references. **Personal references** are people who can give a report about your character, your education, and your work habits. The people you might select as references could include teachers, religious leaders, adult friends, former employers, and others. Look at Shana Holihan's data sheet in Figure 13-2.

Figure 13-2
Shana's personal
data sheet
summarizes
important job-
related
information that
is of interest to an
employer.

PERSONAL DATA SHEET

NAME: Shana Holihan

TELEPHONE: 555-0308

ADDRESS: 520 Nancy Blvd.
                       Phoenix, AZ 85027-2392

EDUCATION: Upper Mountain High School
                       Graduated June 10, 1990
                       Major: Business Education

                       Business Subjects Studied:
                         Introduction to Business
                         Word Processing Operations
                         Accounting I and II

                       Activities:
                         Member of Pep Club
                         Treasurer, Future Business Leaders of America

**WORK
EXPERIENCE:**   Word Processing Operator, Tempest Tea Pot
                       Company; one year, part-time

**OTHER
ACTIVITIES:**   Member of Alpha Chi youth group at First Christian Church
                       Member of West Side YMCA swim team

REFERENCES: Mr. Tim Schilling, Business Teacher
                       Upper Mountain High School
                       1234 Lovers Lane Road
                       Phoenix, AZ 85098-2392

                       Mrs. Phyllis Lipton
                       Office Manager
                       Tempest Tea Pot Company
                       707 Coffee Lane
                       Phoenix, AZ 85029-2367

                       Rev. David R. Crane
                       First Christian Church
                       937 Culpepper Court
                       Phoenix, AZ 85027-2392

FINDING OUT ABOUT JOB OPENINGS

Shana correctly carried out her job search. She had thought about the type of job she wanted. She used several sources to obtain job leads. Furthermore, she looked for the job she wanted and was willing to wait for the appropriate job opportunity.

Finding job openings is an important part of getting that first job. No one source is necessarily better than others. You need to let as many people as possible know that you are looking for a job. Your relatives, friends, neighbors, and others will be good potential sources of job leads.

The sources you use for information about career planning are also good sources of job leads. Your school counselors and business teachers can be very helpful. If your school has a placement office, be sure to register with that office. You should also contact employment agencies. Newspaper want ads are also helpful. You should also visit businesses and inquire about their openings. Some businesses post help-wanted signs in their windows. Getting a job means going out and looking around. Finding a job can be hard work, but it is worth the effort.

COMPLETING AN APPLICATION FORM

Shana's phone rang one day, and it was the university vice president's administrative assistant calling. Shana was invited to come to the university for an interview. Needless to say, she was excited.

The receptionist in the vice president's office made Shana feel welcome when she arrived. Shana was asked to fill out an application form and was taken to a desk where she could complete it.

An employer frequently has each job applicant complete an application form even after a letter of application and a personal data sheet have been provided. An **application form** is a document used by an employer that asks for information related to employment. The form contains information about each job applicant. Most application forms ask for your name, address, Social Security number, education, work experience, the job for which you are applying, references, and other qualifications.

The information on your personal data sheet will help you complete the application form. Completing the job application form should be seen as the first job task your employer asks you to perform. Supply each item requested; do not leave questions unanswered. Take the assignment seriously. A poorly prepared application form may give the wrong impression about you. Observe the application form prepared by Shana Holihan in Figure 13-3.

SCREENING EMPLOYEES THROUGH TESTING

In addition to the information provided on application forms, some employers also use preemployment tests to screen applicants for skills and abilities that are needed to perform certain jobs. Examples of preemployment tests include typing tests, word processing tests, computation tests, and number and word arranging (filing) tests. These are frequently called ability tests. An **ability test** is one that measures how well a job applicant can perform certain job tasks.

Figure 13-3
Be sure that you are neat, accurate, and thorough when completing a job application form.

UPTOWN UNIVERSITY
APPLICATION FOR EMPLOYMENT

Name _Shana Susan Holihan_
      (First)   (Middle)   (Last)
Social Security No. _399-48-6951_
Date _July. 15.19--_

U.S. Citizen _X_ yes

_____ no, if not, Type of Visa _____

Do you have any physical condition that may prevent you from performing certain kinds of work? _No_

Have you ever been convicted of a felony or misdemeanor or are there any felony charges against you pending disposition? _No_

If yes, give date(s) and nature of the act(s) and disposition. _____

Have you ever been compensated for an on-the-job accident? _No_ If yes, explain _____

Have you served in the U.S. Armed Forces? _No_ What branch _____ Type of discharge _____ Rank _____

Dates of service _____ If you were deferred—why? _____

In case of emergency, notify _Barbara Holihan_   _520 Nancy Blvd., Phoenix. AZ_   _555-0308_
                              (NAME)   (ADDRESS)   (PHONE)

EMPLOYMENT HISTORY

List all employment within the past ten years

NAME OF EMPLOYER and Immediate Supervisor	ADDRESS and Telephone Number	POSITION HELD Occupation and Duties	Monthly Rate	Dates Employed From	To	Reason for leaving
Tempest Tea Pot Company Mrs. Phyllis Lipton	707 Coffee Lane Phoenix, AZ 555-1010	Word Processor; produced letters and reports	$5/hr.	9/89	6/90	Temporary-Coop.

EDUCATION

Level	Name	Address	Years Attended From	To	Date Graduated	What did you specialize in? Degree(s) Received
Elementary	Hillside Elementary	16 N. 45th St.	1978	1986		
High School	Upper Mountain	1234 Lovers Lane	1986	1990	June 10	
Trade School						
Business College						
College						
Graduate						
Other						

PERSONAL REFERENCES

Other Than Immediate Relatives

Name	Address	Telephone Number	Occupation	Years Known
Mr. Tim Schilling	1234 Lovers Lane, Phoenix	555-1099	Teacher	3
Rev. David Crane	937 Culpepper Ct., Phoenix	555-4661	Pastor	12
Mrs. Susan Haugen	1602 Woodrale, Tempe	555-0065	Secretary	5

Type of work you would consider _Secretarial_   Full, or part time? _Full time_

Minimum salary you would consider _12.000_ Would you consider temporary work? _Yes_ Date available for employment _Immediately_

The information contained here is true to the best of my knowledge and belief. I realize that any falsification in this application constitutes grounds for rejection or dismissal. In this connection, I authorize all previous employers to provide Uptown University with any information concerning my employment. I further authorize Uptown University to verify any other information I have provided on this application. *I FURTHER UNDERSTAND THAT THIS APPLICATION BECOMES INACTIVE AFTER THREE MONTHS.*

Signature _Shana Holihan_   Date _July. 15. 19--_

Testing makes it possible to compare each job applicant on the same basis. Each applicant, for example, may have completed a high school course in word processing and each received a B average. High school teachers, however, do not all grade using the same standards. By testing each applicant, the employer can use the test results to compare the skills of each person being considered for the job.

A test should be viewed as just another instrument used by employers to evaluate the abilities of a job candidate. If you do the best you can on a test under whatever circumstances the test may be given, you should not worry about the results. Employers realize that taking a test in an office, perhaps using unfamiliar equipment, can affect test results.

HAVING A SUCCESSFUL JOB INTERVIEW

The job interview is one of the important steps in the hiring process. A **job interview** is a two-way conversation in which the interviewer learns about you and you learn about the job and the company.

Job interviews are often conducted by personnel interviewers. A **personnel interviewer** is someone who has special training in talking with job applicants and hiring new employees. The interviewer will be able to find out about your appearance, manners, use of language, and general suitability for the job. Plan for your interview as carefully as you planned your letter of application and personal data sheet. The following are some good points to keep in mind:

- Be on time for the appointment.
- Go alone to the interview. Do not take friends or relatives with you.
- Dress properly. Do not be too formal or too informal. Wear the type of clothing that is appropriate for the company and the job in which you are interested.
- Try to be calm during the interview. Avoid talking too much, but answer each question completely. Ask questions intelligently. Let the interviewer guide the discussion.
- Leave when the interviewer indicates that the interview is over.
- Thank the interviewer for the opportunity to discuss the job and your qualifications.
- After the interview, send a brief thank-you letter to the person with whom you interviewed.
- Be patient after the interview. It may take several weeks for the company to complete all of its interviews and make its selection.

There are many different approaches that an interviewer may take. Most interviewers will try to put you at ease when your interview begins. As the interview progresses, there are a number of questions that could be asked by the interviewer. Here are some examples:

- Why are you interested in this particular job?
- What are some of the activities you like to do in your spare time?
- What courses have you taken that will help you on this job?
- What are your career goals?

Illus. 13-1
A good first
impression in an
interview is
important.

- Do you plan to continue your education now or in the future?
- Do you have any friends or relatives who work here?

The interviewer may also review your test results and discuss specific job requirements with you.

Shana had two interviews. Her first was with the administrative assistant, Edward Bailley, and then she was interviewed by the vice president herself. The interviews were a pleasant experience for Shana, and she felt good about her interviews when she left the university. She had come prepared, and what she learned made her eager to work there if a job were offered.

SUCCEEDING ON YOUR FIRST JOB

Shana was offered the job of assistant secretary. She began her first day with enthusiasm and high expectations. She was started on her career, and the job she had was just what she had planned for.

Shana remembered what she had been taught by her business teachers about proper behavior for success on the job:

- *Ask questions.* If you do not understand directions, have them repeated and listen carefully. It is important that you understand what is expected of you.
- *Avoid complaining about a heavy workload.* If you seem to have more work to do than you can handle, talk with your supervisor about it. It is

not good to try to do more work than you can reasonably handle in an attempt to impress your employer.

- *Honor the time provided for breaks.* Abuse of rest periods and lunch breaks by extending the time limits is a bad business practice. Even if others seem to do it and get by with it, you will do better by following the company's policy.
- *Be attentive to your appearance.* Dressing neatly and being well-groomed is important in several ways: It lets others know that you believe your job to be important, and employers often find that sloppy dress and appearance reflect sloppy work habits and attitudes.
- *Be on time.* Arriving late or leaving early is a poor practice for any employee, especially a new one. On occasion, tardiness or having to leave early might be necessary—but tardiness should be explained, and early departures should be approved in advance.
- *Be friendly.* Success on the job involves human relations. Respect your coworkers and learn to get along with them. One caution here: Do not become so friendly with others that it interferes with either your work or theirs.
- *Do work that is well done and on time.* Work that is sloppily done or turned in late can affect others in the office. You are part of a team; take pride in what you do as part of that team. Paying attention to detail displays a positive attitude and lets your coworkers know that you can do the job assigned to you.
- *Follow the rules.* Rules are developed for the good of the coworkers in your work unit. Not paying attention to company policy can bring trouble to you and others. If a rule seems unfair or unreasonable, discuss it with others and find out why it has been established. You may eventually be able to influence changes in rules that are not desirable.

When you begin a new job, remember that your employer is just as eager as you are for you to succeed. Generally you will find the other employees willing to help you through the first few days. You probably will make a few mistakes in the process of learning your job. The important thing is to learn from each mistake and to avoid repeating it. You will need to be a good listener, too. Your job will test your ability to follow directions and to produce good work. It should be a challenging experience for you.

In the one small word *attitude* lies the difference between having just another job and being happy and successful in your work. Your attitude toward your new job is important. For example, a negative attitude may result in frequent absences from work. A positive attitude, on the other hand, may mean you are willing to learn and grow in your job, and to cooperate with other workers. As a result, you will probably find your job more satisfying.

Shana has demonstrated readiness for her new job. She has progressed from her work as a student into a career as a full-time worker. The record she built as a student—her good attendance record, the courses she took, the activities in which she participated, and the grades she earned—was important when she was considered for her job. Her school record showed that she was conscientious and capable of good work. Career planning plus a good school record adds up to a successful start in the world of work.

BUILDING GOOD RELATIONSHIPS WITH COWORKERS

Getting along with the other workers in your work unit will make your workplace more pleasant, improve your own efficiency, and influence your future. The following are a few fundamental rules that can help you get along with others.

1. Learn from the others with whom you work, even if they do things differently from the way you were taught in school. Avoid assuming you are right and they are wrong. If you have an idea for improving work procedures, find the right time to suggest improvements.
2. Be on friendly terms with as many people as you can. The person who delivers the mail, the person who cleans the office, the secretary to the president, and others are important people in many ways. Any of your

Illus. 13-2
A positive relationship with your coworkers can influence your future success.

coworkers may be able to help you some day in ways unknown to you now.

3. Learn to accept and give praise when it is due. When you have done something well and you are given credit for it, accept it graciously and appreciatively. When others do something nice, say a good word to them. Learn not to overdo praise, however. False praise will get you nowhere and will raise suspicions about your motives.

4. Show others that you are dependable. Little things, such as returning phone calls promptly and responding to messages without unnecessary delay, tells others that you care about what you do and can be trusted to do your work. When others have a positive impression of you, they will want to work with you and will want to help you succeed.

5. Look ahead to future opportunities. People with whom you develop good relationships may be promoted to higher positions in a business. Having ''friends in high places,'' as the saying goes, may help you get ahead. The people you help today, and those who respect you for what you can do on the job, may have a major influence on your future career.

Increasing Your Business Vocabulary

The following terms should become part of your business vocabulary. For each numbered item, find the term that has the same meaning.

ability test
application form
job interview
letter of application

personal data sheet
personal references
personnel interviewer

1. A sales letter about yourself written for the purpose of getting a personal interview.
2. A summary of job-related information about yourself.
3. A document used by an employer that asks for information related to employment.
4. A two-way conversation in which the interviewer learns about you and you learn about the job and the company.
5. Someone who has special training in talking with job applicants and hiring new employees.
6. People who can give a report about your character, education, and work habits.
7. A test that measures how well a job applicant can perform certain job tasks.

Reviewing Your Reading

1. In what ways does your attendance record, grades, and school activities influence an employer when considering applicants for a job?
2. Identify at least eight sources of information on job openings.
3. What is the purpose of a letter of application?

4. List six categories of information that should be included on a personal data sheet.
5. Why are preemployment tests used by employers?
6. What is the first job task that you will perform for an employer? Why is it important to perform this task correctly?
7. What are some questions commonly asked during a job interview?

8. What four characteristics do personnel interviewers evaluate about the person being interviewed?
9. What four points should you remember after the interview ends?
10. What are some of the reasons why a positive attitude is important in your first job?
11. What are some job behaviors that will help you succeed?

Using Your Business Knowledge

1. Name at least six people you know whom you could ask for help in finding a full-time job. Also identify several local organizations or agencies you could contact for help in finding a job.
2. If you were in charge of hiring people for jobs, what information would you want to get about applicants? How would you go about getting this information? What are some specific questions you would ask if you were to interview the applicants?
3. Your personal data sheet should list several references. Application forms also ask for references to be listed. Make a list of three or more references you could use right now. Then note the type of information each reference could give that would be of help to a potential employer.
4. Write a personal data sheet that you could use right now if you were to apply for a part-time or full-time job. After it is completed, think about whether or not you need to consider being more involved in school, church, or community activities. Think about whether or not your personal data sheet would impress an employer and what you could do that could be included in future personal data sheets to better present yourself.

5. Information has been received about three job openings in your community. Each is quite different and requires different kinds of backgrounds and preparation. Assume that you are qualified for only one position. Make up whatever qualifications you think you would like to present to a prospective employer. Then write a letter of application for the position.
   a. Reliable person is needed to handle a variety of responsibilities in a small business office. Must be able to work without supervision and communicate effectively with people who call in for information. Word processing and filing skills are desirable. Salary is better than average in this community.
   b. Salespeople are needed for an auto parts department and for a cosmetics department of a major retail establishment. Applicants should have some familiarity and/or experience with selling. Hours are flexible, although some evening and weekend work will be required. Benefits are especially attractive; incentive bonus policy can provide a good income for the right person.
   c. Ours is a leading bank in this region. We are in need of capable people who

want to begin a career in banking. Our training program starts at the bottom, but provides a great opportunity to learn the in's and out's of the banking industry. Business majors are preferred, but liberal arts majors may apply. We are an equal opportunity employer; salary is competitive.

6. Design an application form similar to the one in Figure 13-3 on page 188 and supply whatever information you think necessary to apply for one of the jobs mentioned in Question 5.

7. Give several examples of what you might do and not do as a new employee in order to develop positive relationships with your coworkers.

Computing Business Problems

1. Mercedes Castillo is a personnel interviewer. On Monday, she interviewed 7 job applicants; on Tuesday, 6 applicants; on Wednesday, 9 applicants; on Thursday, 5 applicants; and on Friday, 8 applicants.

   a. How many job applicants did Mercedes interview that week? What was the average number per day?

   b. On Wednesday, the first interview took 50 minutes; the next 2 each took 40 minutes; the next 4 took 35 minutes each; and the last 2 took 45 minutes each. How many total hours did Mercedes spend in these interviews? What was the average length of the interviews?

2. The Personnel Department of the Tempest Tea Pot Company has 1 personnel manager, 1 administrative assistant, 2 word processing operators, 2 personnel interviewers, 1 affirmative action-union affairs specialist, and 1 clerk-receptionist. The manager and administrative assistant each have worked for Tempest for 17 years; each of the word processing operators have worked there for 5 years; and the others have worked there just 1 year.

   a. How many total years of employment do the 8 Personnel Department employees have? What is the average number of years of employment per worker?

   b. The administrative support staff consists of the 2 word processing operators and the clerk-receptionist. The word processing operators are paid $8 per hour, and the clerk-receptionist is paid $7.50 per hour. They each work 35 hours per week. What total wages do these three workers earn in a week? in a month? in a year?

   c. According to the union contract, the administrative staff workers receive a 6 percent increase in wages each year. What will be the hourly wages next year of the word processing operators? of the clerk-receptionist? How much will each earn in a 40-hour week that year?

3. Two data sheets were received by the Personnel Department. The data sheets listed the height and weight of the applicants and contained the following data:

   Mr. Buring:
   height: 175 cm   weight: 79 kg

   Mr. Dowses:
   height: 185 cm   weight: 72 kg

   a. Which of the applicants is the tallest? by how many inches?

   b. Which of the applicants weighs the most? by how many pounds?

Expanding Your Understanding of Business

1. Assume that you are a personnel interviewer. Make a list of ten specific questions you would like to ask an applicant for a job as a salesperson in a men's or women's fashion clothing store. Then have someone from your class play the role of an applicant and conduct a mock interview. After the interview is over, discuss whether the questions were relevant and what was learned from the questions.

2. Ask for copies of some of the letters that were written for Question 5 in the "Using Your Business Knowledge" section. After reading and evaluating the letters, decide which of the applicants you would like to interview and why. Then talk with the people who wrote those letters and see if your impression of the letter writers was the same impression that the letter writers wanted to convey. Discuss the effectively written letters of application and how they conveyed the message the writer desired.

3. Check to see what governmental and private employment agencies are located in your community. Contact one or more of them and make an appointment to interview the director or manager. Find out (1) how they learn of job openings, (2) how they screen or test those who register with them for work, (3) what they charge for their services, and (4) what their success rate is in filling jobs that are listed with them. Write a report on your findings and be prepared to share it with the class.

4. Visit with some personnel managers about their policies with respect to testing prospective employees. Find out what kind of tests are given and how the results are used.

5. Role play office work situations in which good and bad behaviors can be demonstrated. Students who are not role playing should critique the situation and identify the good and bad behaviors.

Career Opportunities in Small Business

Chapter 14

Chapter Objectives

After studying this chapter and completing the end-of-chapter activities, you will be able to:

1. *Explain why there are career opportunities in small businesses.*

2. *Give a definition of a small business.*

3. *Describe how the Small Business Administration helps small-business owners.*

4. *Explain why small businesses are important in the economy of the United States.*

5. *State at least five reasons why small businesses fail.*

6. *List at least seven characteristics of successful small-business owners.*

7. *Discuss ideas for new small businesses.*

Courtney Greer has been working with a local photographer for the past five years. In high school, she majored in business education and was an active member of the school's photography club. After graduation, she worked in a photo supply store for several years while taking college courses at night. After earning an associate of arts degree in photography, Courtney got her present job as an assistant to photographer Paul A. Roid. Paul Roid owns and operates a portrait studio, takes pictures at weddings, and does some special public relations work on a contract basis. He has been in business for many years.

Courtney enjoys her work and has learned a great deal about the photography business. Paul Roid has told her several times that she is good at what she does. Courtney has done a few small jobs on her own in which she contracted with some friends and acquaintances for special-event pictures.

Courtney has a dream of owning her own business. In fact, she is eager to do so. She lives a simple life, drives an old car, has no debts, and saves as much of her wages as possible—she has more than $5,000 in her bank account. She shares an apartment with a friend, and she has no expensive habits.

Courtney believes she is ready to venture out on her own—to be her "own boss." Yet, she knows that there are risks in starting a new business.

Illus. 14-1
Entrepreneurs are willing to contribute time, energy, and economic resources to a business.

She wonders what new things she will have to learn about the business. Should she ask Paul Roid for advice?

What kind of help is available if she needs help while she is on her own? What are some of the questions she must answer for herself if she is to be successful? These are all good questions.

If Courtney follows through on her plans, she will become one of several million small-business owners in the United States. She will be an **entrepreneur**; that is, someone who takes a risk in starting a business to earn a profit. Entrepreneurs are people willing to contribute time, energy, and economic resources to a business with the hope of earning a profit. Courtney wonders if she will be a good risk taker.

There are many things to be learned about small-business ownership. Let's look at some facts about small-business operations.

NEW JOB OPENINGS IN SMALL BUSINESSES

When you begin your career, you very likely may be working in one of our nation's small businesses. During the past decade, the majority of *new* job openings were in small businesses. As shown in Figure 14-1, more than half of the new jobs created in 1988 came from businesses with fewer than 100 employees. In a recent six-year period, more than 4 million jobs were created by businesses with fewer than 20 employees. Small businesses provide excellent employment opportunities.

Figure 14-1
Small businesses account for most of the new jobs in our economy.

Number of Employees in the Firm	New Jobs Created	
	Number	**Percent**
1-19	840,284	35%
20-99	377,149	16
100-999	709,934	30
1,000-9,999	251,812	10
10,000-24,999	64,617	3
25,000 +	159,855	6
Total	2,403,651	100%

Source: Dun & Bradstreet Corporation and ''USA Snapshots—A Look at Statistics That Shape Your Future,'' *USA Today*, 19 April 1988.

You may also consider going into business for yourself. There are many small-business opportunities for people who, like Courtney, are ready to take that step. More than 230,000 businesses were started in recent years, and it is expected that new business growth will continue to be high. Starting your own business can be an exciting, although risky, beginning to a career.

WHAT IS A SMALL BUSINESS?

When we use the term **small business**, we are referring to a business that:

- Usually has the owner as the manager.
- Is not dominant in its field of operation.
- Employs fewer than 500 people.
- Usually is local, serving the nearby community.

You may be surprised that a small business may employ up to 500 people. However, businesses with only one to four employees are a major factor in our work force. Figure 14-2 shows that more than half of the employees of private business firms are employed in businesses that have four or fewer employees.

Figure 14-2
Small businesses employ the greatest percentage of employees in private businesses.

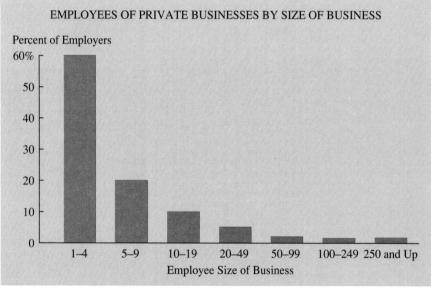

EMPLOYEES OF PRIVATE BUSINESSES BY SIZE OF BUSINESS

Source: National Federation of Independent Business, Research and Education Foundation, *Small Business Primer* (1988), 5.

Most small businesses begin as sole proprietorships. It is not unusual, however, for a person to begin his or her own business through a franchise agreement (see Chapter 6). Many small businesses eventually become incorporated. The advantages of a corporation, as pointed out in Chapter 6, are reasons why some small-business owners decide to incorporate their businesses. The most common form of ownership for small businesses, however, continues to be the sole proprietorship.

Our government has an agency set up to help small businesses; it is called the **Small Business Administration (SBA)**. The SBA is a government-funded organization that helps small-business owners borrow money as well as manage their businesses more efficiently. Information about the SBA and its services can be obtained by contacting an office in your city or state or by writing to the SBA, 1441 L Street, Washington, DC 20416.

Small businesses are found in all of the industries you learned about in Chapter 8. A recent analysis showed that the largest percentage of small businesses are found in retailing—28 percent—and in services—24 percent (see Figure 14-3). Courtney's new business venture would place her in the services industry.

Figure 14-3
The largest percentage of small businesses are found in retailing and services.

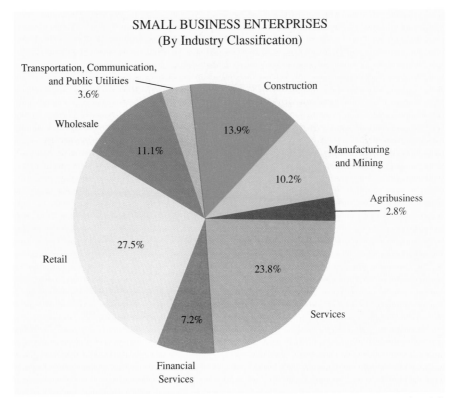

SMALL BUSINESS ENTERPRISES
(By Industry Classification)

Transportation, Communication, and Public Utilities
3.6%

Construction
13.9%

Wholesale
11.1%

Manufacturing and Mining
10.2%

Agribusiness
2.8%

Retail
27.5%

Services
23.8%

Financial Services
7.2%

Source: *The State of Small Business: A Report of the President* (Washington, D.C.: U.S. Government Printing Office, 1989).

Some businesses are classified as venture businesses. A **venture business** is one that has been in operation for less than three years and has no employees other than the owner. In one year, more than 1,600 new venture businesses were started every day in the United States. Courtney would operate of those 1,600 venture businesses.

HOW SUCCESSFUL ARE SMALL BUSINESSES?

Small businesses make many contributions to our economy as innovators of new products and developers of new production processes. Small businesses adjust more quickly to changing market demands than do large businesses. They can experiment with new products and new methods of production without waiting for approval from management committees.

Not all small businesses succeed; in fact, their failure rate is quite high. Figure 14-4 shows the number of business closings due to bankruptcies and failures for the period from 1981 through 1987. A **bankruptcy** is a situation in which a business does not have enough money to pay its creditors even after selling its equipment and other capital resources. A **creditor** is a person or business that is owed money. A **failure** is the closing of a business with a loss occurring to at least one creditor. Although these figures represent a small percentage of small businesses, the number of failures is of some concern. In addition to these official figures, some small enterprises just quietly go out of business when the owner believes that he or she is not doing well enough to continue.

Figure 14-4
Small businesses close because of bankruptcies and failures.

Business Closings, 1981-1987			
Year	**Bankruptcies**	**Failures**	**Total**
1981	48,086	17,044	65,130
1982	69,242	25,346	94,588
1983	62,412	31,334	93,746
1984	64,211	52,078	116,289
1985	81,277	57,067	128,344
1986	80,400	61,601	142,001
1987	60,828*	61,236	122,064*

* Only the first nine months of 1987 are included.

Source: *The State of Small Business: A Report of the President* (Washington, D.C.: U.S. Government Printing Office, 1988), 25.

WHY SMALL BUSINESSES FAIL

In a typical year, more than half of the businesses that fail have been in operation less than five years and are classified as small businesses. The reasons for failure are quite varied. The following are the most common reasons for failure:

- Not keeping adequate records.
- Not having enough start-up money.
- Lack of sales and management experience.
- Lack of experience with the type of business.
- Not controlling operating expenses.
- Poor location for the business.
- Failure to manage payments due from customers for purchases made.

Each of the above causes of failure can be overcome with the right kind of assistance. As a prospective small-business owner, you may need special help in the areas of management, accounting, personnel, and finance.

ASSISTANCE AVAILABLE FOR SMALL BUSINESSES

Small-business owners can get assistance from a number of sources. Universities and colleges have individuals on their faculties who can give advice and assistance to people who are starting or have started their own businesses. Local organizations of businesspeople, such as Junior Chambers of Commerce and the Administrative Management Society, have members who can help other members with business problems.

The Small Business Administration, as noted earlier, was set up for the specific purpose of aiding small-business owners. The SBA fulfills its mission through a variety of means. The SBA has a large number of publications designed to assist small-business owners, such as *Management Aids for Small Manufacturers*, *Starting and Managing a Small Business of Your Own*, and *Managing for Profits*. The SBA provides assistance with financing and offers special programs on how to operate small businesses. **Small Business Institutes (SBIs)** are programs offered in cooperation with colleges and universities to provide management counseling.

The SBA is also responsible for the formation and operation of two organizations known as SCORE and ACE. **SCORE** stands for the **Service Corps of Retired Executives** whose members can provide assistance in special areas of operation, such as finance, accounting, and marketing.

Illus. 14-2
SCORE members can provide assistance in special areas of business operation, such as finance and marketing.

Members of SCORE are local businesspeople who volunteer their services and are paid only a basic amount to cover their travel expenses. ACE is the Active Corps of Executives that provides services similar to those of SCORE.

Other special services provided by the SBA include the Small Business Investment Companies (SBICs) and a specialized Section 301(d) SBIC, commonly called a Minority Enterprise SBIC (MESBIC). SBICs are set up to provide venture capital and management services. The providing of **venture capital**—money used to start up a new small business or help a business expand during a growth period—is an important service. Section 301(d) SBICs deal specifically with minority-owned businesses. Minority business owners can also be helped through the Minority Small Business-Capital Ownership Development (MSB-COD) program and the Minority Business Development Agency (MBDA).

A large number of small-business owners are women. The SBA operates an Office of Women Business Owners. It also has special publications dealing with women who are small-business owners, such as *Women Business Owners: Selling to the Federal Government.*

WHAT IT TAKES TO SUCCEED

You probably have already concluded that small-business owners must know certain facts and perform certain functions in order to be successful. In addition to knowledge of business operations and management skills, small-business owners must have certain personal characteristics. Some characteristics of successful small-business owners are as follows:

- Can do things on their own; they are self-starters.
- Have leadership abilities; they can get others to do what has to be done.
- Can take charge of things; they assume responsibility.
- Like to plan what must be done; they are good organizers.
- Are hard workers; they work long hours on the job.
- Are decision makers; they can make decisions quickly when necessary.
- Can be trusted; they mean what they say.
- Are achievers; they will work on a task until it is finished.
- Have good health; they exhibit energy.

The above characteristics are based on an SBA publication called a *Checklist for Going into Business*. In addition, some researchers also have discovered the following characteristics to be important:

- Would rather work for themselves, even if they made considerably less money than working for someone else.
- Are at least 24 years old (see Figure 14-5).

Figure 14-5
Twenty-five percent of business owners start their own businesses before the age of thirty.

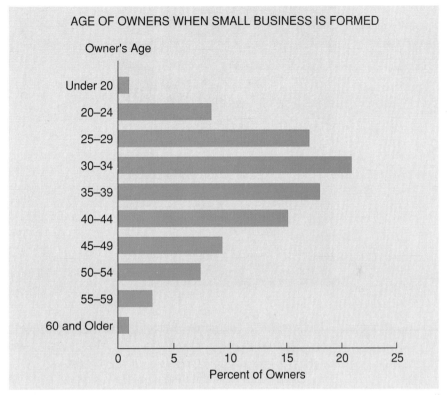

AGE OF OWNERS WHEN SMALL BUSINESS IS FORMED

Owner's Age

Percent of Owners

Source: National Federation of Independent Business, Research and Education Foundation, *Small Business Primer* (1988), 11.

- Have had a variety of business experiences, often with someone who is a successful small-business owner.

IDEAS THAT LED TO NEW BUSINESS VENTURES

Having a real desire to be your own boss, developing a good initial plan for a business, and coming up with some innovative ideas are important factors in starting your own business. You might begin in a small way, and then establish a long-range plan for the growth of your business.

Can you think of some service or product that is not being offered that could be in demand? Is there some service or product that you personally could offer more efficiently or with better results than others are doing now? Is there some special talent that you have that could become the foundation for a business of your own?

There are still good opportunities for entrepreneurship in small businesses. **Entrepreneurship** is the process of starting, organizing, managing, and assuming the responsibility for a business. Here are some real-life examples taken from reports of the SBA:

Illus. 14-3
Small-business
owners are self-
starters and
achievers.

1. *Compos-It.* Margaret Carpenter started her venture business with "three little rooms on Perry Street" in Montgomery, Alabama. Equipment consisted of one typewriter, one varityper, and one headline machine. Three years passed before a profit was made. A decision to pursue a U.S. Air Force contract took courage, but it paid off. A few years later, there were 99 employees who worked three shifts to keep up with the demand for the firm's typesetting and composing services.

2. *Carl's Cycle Sales.* With $800 in savings, a $2,000 loan from a friend, and a $3,000 bank loan, Carl and Liz Struthers opened their Boise, Idaho, motorcycle and snowmobile dealership. Carl's enthusiasm for his product helped them succeed. To finance a business expansion, they sold their home and lived in a trailer for a few years. Within a few years, 12 full-time and 4 part-time employees made up their work force, and annual net sales were more than $2 million.

3. *Action Packets.* The idea for this business venture came to Judith Kaplan while visiting a planetarium. She and her husband wanted to go into the stamp collecting business, and she got this idea: Why not package stamps along theme lines? They eventually had to move out of their basement quarters in Ocala, Florida, to a larger facility in order to handle the demand for their product. Their business has surpassed the $2.1 million annual sales level.

4. *Take-A-Break Vending Machines.* Jerry Blum left a traveling job in the mid-1960s to set up a family business. By use of innovative coffee brewing equipment and one of the first computerized vending machines,

the business became successful. He and his sons now manage a growing Delaware business that employs 25 people and has sales of more than $2 million per year.

5. *O'Neale's Trucking and Trailer Transport.* During his first year of employment after leaving Trinidad, Kenneth O'Neale worked as a shipping clerk for a trucking company. He noticed that shipments of goods for small companies often sat on the docks in favor of shipments going to larger businesses. Kenneth invested in a pickup truck and began hauling small shipments after his normal work hours. Word got around that he was reliable and delivered on time. The firm he now heads has expanded to 35 employees with annual net sales exceeding $1 million in St. Croix, Virgin Islands.

YOUNG ENTREPRENEURS SUCCEED

Sam Salter II was president of his own company in 1984 at age 19. Sam started his company when he was 16 years old, but his business experience started earlier than that.

At the age of 8, he helped keep business records for his father's auto repair shop. He listened to tapes on money market information and how to be a manager. When he was 14, he talked a real estate firm into letting him work with some of the agents. From his real estate experience, he observed that one of the most important needs of buyers was getting financing for their homes. And he had an idea about how he could help people finance a home.

His business firm, Continental Financial Corporation, located in New Jersey, helps people apply for loans. In a two-year period, his business processed 275 loans; 207 were approved.

Sam Salter's goal is for his company to become a "financial supermarket," one of the largest of minority-owned businesses. His plans also include earning his college degree through part-time study. Sam Salter II was named a "Young Entrepreneur of the Year" by the Small Business Administration.

Todd Dorn discovered the value of innovation on his tenth birthday while selling flowers on a street corner. By arranging special displays of his flowers, he outsold all of his competitors. In the next few years, he went into other business ventures, including buying and selling stamps and coins, making and selling puka shell jewelry, and selling car stereo equipment. He later sold real estate and became a top salesperson using innovative sales techniques that he willingly shared with others.

His biggest business was organized from a need he observed while selling real estate: firms that wanted to relocate in California needed special kinds of help in deciding just where to locate and how to set up their offices. As a result, he established Dorn and Company. Success again came with the use of innovative marketing and communication techniques. He also received an SBA Young Entrepreneur of the Year Award.

Increasing Your Business Vocabulary

The following terms should become part of your business vocabulary. For each numbered item, find the term that has the same meaning.

bankruptcy
creditor
entrepreneur
entrepreneurship
failure
Service Corps of Retired Executives (SCORE)

Small Business Administration (SBA)
Small Business Institutes (SBIs)
small business
venture business
venture capital

1. A business that has been in operation for less than three years and has no employees other than the owner.
2. A group of retired executives who can provide assistance to small-business owners.
3. Someone who takes a risk in starting a business to earn a profit.
4. A situation in which a business does not have enough money to pay its creditors even after selling its equipment and other capital resources.
5. A person or business that is owed money.
6. The closing of a business with a loss occurring to at least one creditor.
7. Money used to start up a new small business or help a business expand during a growth period.
8. Programs offered in cooperation with colleges and universities to provide management counseling.
9. A business that usually has the owner as manager, is not dominant in its field of operation, employs fewer than 500 people, and usually serves its nearby community.
10. A government-funded organization that helps small-business owners borrow money as well as manage their businesses more efficiently.
11. The process of starting, organizing, managing, and assuming the responsibility for a business.

Reviewing Your Reading

1. What size firms, based on the number of employees, have created the greatest number of jobs during the past several years?
2. What are three specific things that the SBA does to help small businesses?
3. In which industries are the greatest percentages of small businesses found?
4. State seven common reasons for business failures.
5. Name several publications of the SBA.
6. What is SCORE, who are members, and what assistance does it provide for small businesses?

7. What are some characteristics of successful small-business owners?
8. Name three important factors to be considered before starting your own small business.

9. Give several examples of opportunities for starting a small business.

Using Your Business Knowledge

1. What are some reasons why people start their own businesses?
2. Why is your career likely to begin in a small business?
3. In what ways are small businesses major contributors to our economy?
4. Why are most of the small businesses found in the retailing and service industries?

5. How could each of the reasons why small businesses fail be overcome?
6. Why do you think the government established the SBA?
7. Which of the 12 characteristics of successful small-business owners do you presently have? Which ones do you believe you could develop while in school?

Computing Business Problems

1. Jack Sheard wants to open a sporting goods store. He has been told that he should have at least $35,000 to invest in his new business. He has $3,000 in his bank account, a friend will lend him $4,000, and he can get a bank loan for $10,000.
   a. How much money does Jack have available for investing now?
   b. How much will he have to borrow to come up with the $35,000?
   c. If he can get an additional $5,000 loan on his credit card account, how much will he still need?
   d. If a local bank is willing to lend him $10,000, will he have enough then to start his business? If not, how much short will he be?
2. Sandy McIntosh owns and operates a beauty salon. On Monday, she worked 12 hours; on Tuesday, 8 hours; on Wednesday, 9 hours; on Thursday, 8 hours; on Friday, 11 hours; on Saturday, 6 hours. She earned $1,595 that week, and her expenses were $785.

   a. How many total hours did Sandy work that week? What was the average number of hours per day?
   b. How much did she have as profit after subtracting expenses from the money she took in? How much profit did she make per hour worked?
   c. If Sandy worked for the Shear Delight Beauty Parlor, she would be paid $12.50 per hour. How much more does Sandy earn a week in her own business compared to working for another beautician if she worked the same number of hours?
3. Larry Maynor operates a fleet of five trucks. Three trucks cost him $18,000 each, and two trucks cost him $31,000 each. Last week the five trucks averaged 250 kilometers of driving. Larry's business makes $17.25 for each mile driven by the trucks.
   a. How much does Larry have invested in his five trucks? If Larry's goal is to earn 10 percent on his investment, how much should he earn on those trucks?

b. How much does Larry earn on the total miles driven by his trucks in the situation described above?

c. If four of the trucks each carried an average load of 1,125 kilograms of materials, how many pounds did each truck carry? How many pounds did the four trucks carry? If one truck hauled liquids and averaged 1,900 liters per haul, how many gallons were there per haul?

d. Does Larry's business earn enough to meet his goal? How much short or over the goal are the actual earnings? What is the percentage that was actually earned?

4. Look at Figure 14-2 on page 200. Assume that it represents a state with a total of 550,000 workers, and that the state has the same percentage (round off percentages to the nearest tenth) of workers for each size of business.

a. How many employees does each of the following groups of firms have?

(1) 1-4 employees

(2) 5-9 employees

(3) 10-19 employees

What would be the total number of employees in those three firms?

b. Based on the total number of employees calculated in *a*, what percentage (round percentages to the nearest whole number) of that figure are employed in each of the following groups of firms?

(1) 1-4 employees

(2) 5-9 employees

(3) 10-19 employees

c. If the 550,000 firms were distributed in the same proportion as shown in Figure 14-3 on page 201, how many firms would there be in each of the following industries? (Round percentages to the nearest whole number.)

(1) Services

(2) Retail

(3) Financial Services

(4) Wholesale

(5) Transportation and Communication

Expanding Your Understanding of Business

1. Look through the Yellow Pages of a telephone book or scan back issues of a newspaper to identify small businesses in your community. Or just be alert to small businesses you observe as you move around in your community. Make an appointment with one of the owners to discuss his or her business, including how he or she got started, problems he or she had to face, and other significant experiences he or she had as an entrepreneur. Be prepared to report your findings to the class.

2. Read through the list of brief stories of successful small-business owners on pages 206 and 207, and then review the list of characteristics of successful small-business owners. Analyze each of the brief stories of successful owners and identify ways in which they illustrate the success characteristics. Make a list of the three characteristics you believe are most important; be ready to defend your list.

3. Today there continues to be many opportunities to start small businesses. Review this chapter and make a list of ideas that are included for small-business operations. Then brainstorm with a group of students on additional ideas for small-business operations. Don't hold back on any idea. Your idea could be an innovative one that just might work!

4. Form a small business as a class or as a group of students. Find out about some product or service that would be of interest to your student body—in other words, do a market survey. Then find some way of providing that product or service, come up with a means of financing your operation, sell your product or service, and determine whether or not you made a profit. Many of the characteristics of small-business owners will have to be present in your group for a venture of this type to succeed.

Career Focus

Many people start business careers in administrative support occupations. Rewarding and challenging careers can be found in these occupations. The increased use of computers and new office systems are factors influencing opportunities in these occupations.

Job Titles: Job titles commonly found in this career area include:

Bank Tellers
Bookkeepers
Clerical Supervisors
File Clerks
General Office Clerks
Postal Clerks
Receptionists
Travel Agents
Secretaries
Statistical Clerks
Stenographers
Stock Clerks
Telephone Operators
Typists
Word Processing Operators

Employment Outlook: In 1986, there were 14.3 million workers employed in the occupations listed above. It is expected that there will be more than 17 million employed in those occupations by the year 2000. The occupations that will have the greatest increases are secretaries, general office clerks, stock clerks, receptionists, and clerical supervisors. Opportunities for employment will be based on new jobs and the need for replacements. A decrease is expected in the number of people employed as statistical clerks and as stenographers because of a contin-

ued increase in the use of office technology. Overall, the growth in this area will be moderate compared with some other career areas.

Future Changes: New developments in computers, office machines, and office systems will help secretarial and clerical workers do more in less time. Many routine jobs will be handled through computerized systems or electronic processing. Skilled workers with appropriate training and good work habits will still be needed.

What Is Done on the Job: Workers in this career area prepare and keep records; operate office machines; arrange schedules and make reservations; collect, distribute, or account for money; deliver messages, mail, or materials; type and file reports; take minutes at meetings and

prepare transcripts; greet people and answer telephones; and provide a variety of important supportive work for administrators and managers.

Education and Training: High school graduates frequently find good employment opportunities in this career area. However, job applicants with specific job training beyond high school—in either two-year or four-year pro-grams—generally find opportunities in higher level positions and are promoted more frequently. The nature of the training, however, is important, as is the job performance of the employee, when it comes to salary increases and promotions.

Salary Levels: Salaries vary widely in this career area, depending in part on the section of the country in which the employee is located, the level of the job, and the work record of the employee. Salaries for secretaries averaged $16,326 in 1986, with the top 10 percent receiving an average of $28,051.

For Additional Information: Additional information about this career area is available from several sources including the following:

Hopke, William E., ed., *Encyclopedia of Careers and Vocational Guidance.* New York: Doubleday and Co., Inc., 1984.

Can I Be an Office Worker? Public Relations Department General Motors Detroit, MI 48202

Careers, Inc. Largo, FL 33540

Administration, Business and Office, No. 1. 3d ed. Career Information Center, 1987.

Consumers in Our Economy

Unit Goals

After studying the chapters in this unit, you will be able to:

1. *Explain why it is so important to become an informed consumer.*
2. *List and describe the steps in the buying decision process.*
3. *Describe six rights and five responsibilities that consumers have.*
4. *Describe why understanding inflation and deflation is important to consumers.*

Chapter 15
Consumer Information

Chapter 16
Consumer Buying Decisions

Chapter 17
Consumer Rights and Responsibilities

Chapter 18
The Changing Value of Money

The Customer Is Always Right

Business Brief

The attitude that the customer is always right is alive and well in business today, and it suggests that consumers' wants and needs guide business practices. From engineering through manufacturing to final delivery of a product or service, the customer's wishes are important.

Concern for the customer was not always the case. The folklore of American business attributes the following statement to Henry Ford: "The public can have any color (automobile) it wants, so long as it's black." Even if this statement was not actually made by Ford, it was expressed in his attitude toward customers during the years the Model T Ford dominated the auto market. During that time, the Ford Motor Company and many other businesses were guided by what manufacturing wanted to make, not by what customers wanted to buy. Eventually, however, the Ford Motor Company reacted to customer demand and began to manufacture cars in a variety of colors.

Today the Ford Motor Company marketing executives are very interested in their customers. They are constantly at work trying to learn more about auto customer's wants and needs. The Ford Motor Company, for example, uses a method to gauge the thought processes that precede the decision to buy a new car. They carefully study various target groups of car buyers through the use of focus group interviews. These interviews are conducted with small groups of people to learn about their needs and wants. Information gained from these interviews is used by Ford executives to make decisions about colors, styles, prices, options, engines, and other factors that would influence consumer decisions.

If a business is committed to customer satisfaction, it will prosper in the long run. The Richman Gordman Company of Omaha, Nebraska, has for years offered its "Happiness Guarantee." This upscale retail chain promises that every customer will be happy with every purchase "no matter what." If, for any reason, customers are dissatisfied with something purchased from one of the Richman Gordman stores, they need only to bring it back to the store for a free exchange or a full refund. The exchange or refund is given with a smile and with no questions asked. Sometimes customers are reluctant to buy because they are unsure whether the product will fully suit their needs once they get it home. The "Happiness Guarantee" removes that barrier to buying.

All of this attention to the buyer has resulted in putting the needs and wants of the customer first. Companies that employ wise marketing techniques are satisfying their own objectives and wants, too. In general, companies that truly satisfy customers' needs and wants will earn a profit. Never in history has so much effort been given to satisfying customers. Hence the phrase, "The customer is always right."

Sources: David L. Lewis, *The Public Image of Henry Ford* (Detroit: Wayne State University Press, 1986), 57; and "Ford Gauges Thought Processes," *Advertising Age* 56 (December 9, 1985): 68.

Consumer Information

Chapter 15

Chapter Objectives

After studying this chapter and completing the end-of-chapter activities you will be able to:

1. *Describe the role of the consumer in our economic system.*

2. *Describe how consumer information can contribute to an improved standard of living.*

3. *Name two product-testing agencies.*

4. *List at least two periodicals containing consumer information.*

5. *Explain how advertising can help you become a well-informed consumer.*

6. *Describe the kinds of information contained on a product label.*

7. *Describe the services provided by a Better Business Bureau.*

8. *List the important decisions you should make before buying a product or service.*

Everyone is a consumer. We all consume or use products or services every day. We buy snacks, tape recorders, clothing, and bicycles. We also purchase movie tickets, telephone services, and legal advice. All of these activities make us consumers. It is the job of American businesses to provide goods and services for us to consume, and it is our job to be wise consumers.

In order to be a wise consumer, it is important to have knowledge about goods and services. You cannot be a wise consumer without information about what you are buying. The best consumers constantly work at acquiring reliable information about the products and services they purchase.

THE CONSUMER

A **consumer** is a person who buys and uses goods or services. More than two-thirds of the U.S. gross national product represents products and services sold to consumers. As a consumer, you are very important to businesses and to the economy. The buying decisions that you and other consumers make can lead to either the success or the failure of many businesses. Consumers are, therefore, obviously important to businesses. As a result, businesses expend great efforts to attract and please consumers. Without consumers, businesses would not make sales, earn profits, or remain in business.

Illus. 15-1
An informed consumer is a wise consumer.

THE IMPORTANCE OF BEING A GOOD CONSUMER

Most people seek the highest standard of living that their incomes will allow. You can raise your standard of living by becoming an informed consumer. In fact, your standard of living is probably determined more by how wisely you spend than by how much money you earn.

How you consume, to some degree, defines who you are. Your consumer habits reflect and determine your life-style. On one hand, you may choose to be thrifty and buy only the products and services you need to live. On the other hand, you may buy products and services that you could easily do without. To some extent, you are known by your spending habits. Have you ever heard of a person being called a "real tightwad," a "cheapskate," or a "big spender"?

In a larger sense, we have an obligation to society to be wise and efficient consumers. Our world has only a limited supply of natural resources, such as petroleum, metals, clean air, and clean water. Sometimes consumer behavior unnecessarily wastes these irreplaceable resources and/or contributes to damaging our environment.

INFORMATION FROM PRIVATE CONSUMER ORGANIZATIONS

In an effort to help inform consumers, several organizations or branches of organizations have been developed. The testing they do and the advice they give is usually objective. They may publish magazines, award seals, and in some cases, endorse products for quality and safety.

Product-Testing Agencies

Some organizations have as their main purpose the testing of products and services. U.S. manufacturers pay these private firms to perform safety tests on products produced. The organizations highlighted here comprise only a small sample of product-testing agencies.

Perhaps the most well-known of these organizations is the Underwriters Laboratories, Inc. Underwriters Laboratories tests electrical components of products from all over the world for fire and electrical safety. The symbol of the Underwriters Laboratories is an indication that the product has been tested and judged safe for normal use.

Another organization is the Association of Home Appliance Manufacturers (AHAM). This group develops and updates the performance standards of such appliances as refrigerators, air conditioners, and freezers. The AHAM seal signifies that a product has met the association's performance standards. Other seals include the Factory Mutual Approved Mark and the seal of the American Gas Association.

Illus. 15-2
The UL seal
indicates the
product is
approved by the
Underwriters
Laboratories.

Print and Broadcast Sources

Certain other organizations have as one of their goals the reporting of scientific, technical, and educational information. Some are nonprofit organizations. One well-known nonprofit organization is Consumers' Union, Incorporated, which performs independent tests on consumer goods and publishes articles on the quality of the goods. Consumers Union publishes its findings in a monthly magazine called *Consumer Reports*. Consumers' Research, Incorporated, is an independent, nonprofit organization that presents articles on a wide range of topics of consumer interest. The magazine *Consumer's Research* analyzes products, services, and consumer issues.

Some magazines that are published for a profit endorse products. *Good Housekeeping* and *Parent's Magazine* are examples. Any product advertised in these magazines can display the magazine's seal. The Good Housekeeping Seal promises the product will be replaced or your money will be refunded if the product is found to be defective within one year of purchase.

In the financial world, there are many periodicals that cover topics of interest to consumers. *Money, Changing Times, Fortune,* and *The Wall Street*

Journal, for example, evaluate and report on the performance of investments such as stocks, bonds, mutual funds, real estate, precious metals, art, and coins.

There are also specialty magazines or newspapers that provide information about specific kinds of products or services. These publications cover topics such as cars, computers, boats, sound equipment, travel, and education. They help consumers understand technical or complex products and services. Sometimes even comparative ratings are given for products or services.

Like magazines and newspapers, radio and television are sources of consumer information. Many stations carry regular programs that inform the public about product safety, care and use of products, and shopping tips, such as the best food buys of the week. In addition, many stations now broadcast talk shows designed to help listeners with their consumer problems.

CONSUMER INFORMATION FROM GOVERNMENT

Federal, state, and local governments also provide assistance to people wishing to become informed consumers. The federal government, for example, formed the Consumer Information Center to serve as headquarters for consumer information. This agency issues catalogs four times a year. Each catalog lists approximately 250 publications of special interest to consumers. In addition to making government publications available, the Center publishes the results of government research and product tests. The agency has distribution centers in several major cities.

The U.S. Department of Agriculture (USDA) is another source of consumer information. USDA publications specialize in information about food—judging quality, buying wisely, improving buying practices, planning meals, improving nutrition, and other farm- and home-related topics.

The USDA also inspects and grades foods and makes that information available to consumers in the form of a grade. A **grade** indicates the quality or size of a product. For example, beef may be stamped ''prime,'' ''choice,'' or ''select.'' The USDA shield means that the product has been inspected and approved by that government agency.

Other government agencies that provide information to consumers include the Office of Consumer Affairs, the Federal Trade Commission, the Food and Drug Administration, the Consumer Product Safety Commission, the National Highway Traffic Safety Administration, the Department of Health and Human Services, and the Environmental Protection Agency. In each case, the name of the agency suggests its area of concern and responsibility. Cities and counties also have some type of consumer agency from which you can get information.

CONSUMER INFORMATION FROM BUSINESSES

As a public service and in an effort to sell goods and services, businesses provide consumer information. Businesses make information available through advertising, labels, customer service departments, business specialists, and Better Business Bureaus.

Advertising

Advertising is a very popular source of consumer information. Since the main purpose of an advertisement is to convince you to buy a product or service, you should use it with care as a source of consumer information. Advertising can be useful to you if you know what product or service you want and if you can overlook strong appeals to buy a particular product or service.

Useful advertisements tell you what the product is, how it is made, and what it will do. These advertisements give facts that you can use to compare the product with other competing products. Beware of claims made that really tell you nothing about the product. If an advertisement states, "Buy Gizmos, they're better!" you should ask, "Better than what? How are they better?" and "Show me."

Product Labels

A **label** provides written information about the nature or content of a product. The label may tell you what the product is made of, its size, how to care for it, and when and where it was made. For example, if you want to buy a pair of running shorts, you need to know whether or not they will shrink when washed or dried. The label on the shorts should tell you what they are made of and provide laundering instructions.

A label may be printed on a carton, can, wrapper, or tag attached to the product. It may also be stamped or sewn onto the product. Whatever the form, a label gives useful information about a product. Study it carefully and you will be a better-informed consumer.

Customer Service Departments

Many businesses have special departments devoted to customer service. Some firms provide customers with booklets on a variety of consumer topics. Banks and insurance companies publish booklets to help consumers manage their money. Some large retail firms provide printed materials to help consumers with their buying problems. J.C. Penney and Sears, for example, publish pamphlets to help customers improve their buying skills.

Illus. 15-3
Clothing
manufacturers
provide care
labels on their
garments. It is up
to the consumer
to read and follow
the instructions.

Business Specialists

Sometimes it is wise to get advice from an expert before purchasing a product. This is especially true if you have never bought such an item, if the item is very complicated, or if it is very expensive. Houses, business machines, and used cars are examples of products that should not be purchased without an expert's advice. For example, most of us could not judge whether a used car's transmission is worn or its brakes need to be replaced. An automobile mechanic, however, could give reliable advice about the condition of the car.

Better Business Bureaus

In an effort to improve credibility, businesses all across the country have joined together in a self-regulation effort and created Better Business Bureaus. Many communities have a Better Business Bureau. Better Business Bureaus are supported by dues paid by member businesses. The bureaus work to maintain ethical practices in the advertising and selling of products and services and to combat consumer fraud. They are chiefly concerned with problems arising from false advertising or misrepresentation of products and services.

Illus. 15-4
Better Business
Bureaus can
provide
consumers with
helpful
information on
products and
businesses.

Better Business Bureaus can provide helpful information. For example, suppose you were planning to buy a used car from a particular dealer. You could call the Better Business Bureau to find out what experiences others have had with that dealer. If consumers have reported problems with the firm, you could find out about these complaints. Better Business Bureaus give facts only; they do not recommend products or firms. They give you the information they have, but you are free to interpret it and to make your own decision.

GOOD CONSUMER PRACTICES

You may not always use good consumer skills in the purchase of every product or service. Sometimes there will not be time to do so, and at other times, it may not be worth the effort when making a minor purchase. You can, however, develop the habit of using good judgment in making most of your purchases.

Whenever you plan to buy anything, you must make a number of important decisions. Your answers to the following questions will help you choose the best product or service for you:

1. Would you rather buy this item instead of another desired item that costs the same amount of money?
2. Which business or businesses should you visit?
3. What quality of goods or services do you want to buy?
4. What price are you willing to pay?
5. Should you pay cash or buy now and pay later?
6. Do you really need this item now, or can you wait awhile?
7. If you make this purchase, what other important item may you have to do without?

Use reliable consumer information to judge each purchase according to whether it will meet your needs better than something else you could buy. Not buying one article so that you can buy another article can be viewed as an opportunity cost. An **opportunity cost** is the value of any alternative that you give up when you buy something else or make another choice. For example, suppose you want both a new sweater and a seat for your bicycle, but have only enough money for one or the other. If you choose the seat, you must give up the sweater. Part of the ''cost'' of the seat, then, is the opportunity to have a new sweater.

Increasing Your Business Vocabulary

The following terms should become part of your business vocabulary. For each numbered item, find the term that has the same meaning.

consumer
grade

label
opportunity cost

1. A person who buys and uses goods or services.
2. An indication of the quality or size of a product.
3. The value of any alternative that you give up when you buy something else or make another choice.
4. A written statement attached to a product giving information about its nature or contents.

Reviewing Your Reading

1. Why are consumers vitally important to businesses?
2. What are common activities of consumers?
3. In what way do we have an obligation to society to be wise and efficient consumers?
4. What are two examples of product-testing agencies?
5. Name one form of consumer information provided by businesses.

6. What are two nonprofit organizations that publish consumer magazines?
7. How can advertising help you become a better consumer?
8. What kinds of information can you find on labels?

9. Explain the services a Better Business Bureau can provide for you.
10. What are the seven important decisions you should make before purchasing a product or service?

Using Your Business Knowledge

1. List four sources of consumer information about a bicycle.
2. Why do you think a good businessperson with good products or services to sell would like to have customers who are well informed?
3. Why do you think specialty newspapers and magazines are published and sold?
4. What kinds of advertisements are most valuable to consumers? Give an example.
5. If you were to purchase the following items, for which of them would you seek the advice of a specialist? Give reasons for each answer.
   a. A study desk
   b. A microcomputer
   c. A pair of jeans
   d. A used car
6. One autumn day a woman and a man came to Dorothy Franklin's door. They said they were chimney sweeps and would like to clean her chimney before she began using her fireplace. They said it would be inexpensive and make her home safer because it would reduce the chances of a chimney fire. Mrs. Franklin looked out her window and saw the name "Chim Chim Chimney Sweeps" on the truck they were driving. How can she find out if the firm is reliable?
7. Why do you believe businesses are willing to support Better Business Bureaus?

Computing Business Problems

1. While studying an automobile buyer's guide, Jan learned that the value of three new cars she was considering would decrease over the next four years. The figures were as follows:

Car Brand	Original Price	Total 4-Year Reduction in Value
Sunglow Convertible	$16,400	47%
Grocery-Getter	$ 9,850	23%
Flash Car	$12,200	33%

   a. At the end of four years, what will be the value of the Sunglow Convertible?
   b. At the end of four years, what will be the value of the Grocery-Getter?
   c. At the end of four years, what will be the value of the Flash Car?
2. The advertisement on the next page appeared in a newspaper during the month of March:

```
SAVE

CLEARANCE SALE

Buy NOW! Buy for NEXT YEAR!
A small deposit will hold your selection!
Don't miss these fine values!
```

	Regular Price	Sale Price
Fur-Trimmed Coats	$259.95	$174.95
Finer Winter Coats	$199.95	$149.95
Raincoats	$ 74.95	$ 59.95

```
SAVE
```

a. By how much money were the fur-trimmed coats reduced?
b. By how much money were the finer winter coats reduced?
c. By how much money were the raincoats reduced?

3. Near the end of the summer, Wheeler's Garden Store marked down a number of items for quick sale. The regular selling price, reduced price, and cost of each item to the store are shown below. Each item was sold at the reduced price.

Item	Regular Price	Reduced Price	Cost
21-inch power mower	$194.99	$179.25	$151.50
Riding lawn mower	675.00	599.95	562.50
Electric hedge trimmer	54.00	49.32	40.50
Deluxe barbecue grill	97.45	74.52	81.75
Lawn furniture set	224.99	169.32	135.00
Total			$971.25

a. By what amount was each item reduced?
b. How much was realized on the sale of each item?
c. What was the total amount received from the sale of the five items?
d. By what percentage of the regular price was each item reduced?

Expanding Your Understanding of Business

1. You have found that there are many sources of consumer information available. Why would information from an independent agency (such as Consumers Union) be

more objective and reliable than information provided by a business?

2. Use a telephone book to find the address and telephone number of the nearest Better Business Bureau. List the kinds of information it has available.

3. Make a list of all the information contained on any food package label. Write a short statement explaining how a consumer might use this information to make a good consumer decision.

4. Newspapers carry stories about consumer events and columns that provide consumer information. Examine one issue of your local newspaper and make a list of all articles about consumers. Indicate which articles are published as a consumer information service.

5. Look through your weekly local radio or television listing to see if you can find a program designed to provide information to consumers. Watch it or listen to it, and write a paragraph about the kind of information it broadcasts. The public station(s) may be your best source.

6. Use the telephone to call two or three local retail stores, such as K mart or Wal-Mart, and ask them to describe their policy regarding the return of goods. Write one paragraph describing each store's return policy.

Consumer Buying Decisions

Chapter 16

Chapter Objectives

After studying this chapter and completing the end-of-chapter activities, you will be able to:

1. *Describe the steps in the buying process.*

2. *Define comparison shopping.*

3. *Calculate unit prices.*

4. *Identify different types of sales.*

5. *Identify national, house or store, and generic brands.*

6. *Name seven types of stores.*

7. *State the role of timing in wise buying.*

In order to be a good consumer, you must understand the buying process. When buying, the consumer is faced with a wide variety of choices. These choices center on price, quality, quantity, variety, location, timing, and other factors. When faced with many choices, a consumer might behave in two different ways. A poor consumer might make random, thoughtless purchases, while the wise consumer will make thoughtful, orderly purchases that will lead to personal satisfaction.

MAKING BUYING DECISIONS

Economic decision making was first discussed in Chapter 1. The buying process follows a similar series of steps. They are:

1. Identify your needs or wants. Be able to state clearly why you intend to buy something.
2. Know the choices that are available to you. These choices include price, quality, location, variety, reputation, and the like.
3. Determine the criteria for satisfaction of your needs and wants. You will develop answers to questions such as "How much am I willing to pay," "What quality level will be adequate?" and "How long am I willing to wait for the product?"
4. Evaluate the alternatives. At this stage, you will shop for the products and services that might satisfy your needs. You will compare them in terms of the criteria you have identified.
5. Finally, you will make the decision to buy.

The important thing to recognize is that we all have a set of values on which we base our buying decisions. The next time you make a purchase, ask yourself "Which of my values is causing me to buy this?"

DEVELOPING BUYING SKILLS

You can become a wiser consumer; all it takes is a little buying skill. Once you gain that skill, you should get greater value for your money each time you make a purchase. You can learn how to compare prices, services, and value. You can also learn about sales and how to examine what you buy. You can become more efficient in your buying activities.

Compare Price, Quality, and Service

A skillful consumer is a comparison shopper. **Comparison shopping** means comparing the price, quality, and services of one product to those of another product. Except for utilities, such as water and electricity, or for very specialized goods, there are few things that are produced or sold by only one

Illus. 16-1
Many of our
purchases are
motivated by our
values.

business. Therefore, you can choose where to buy and you can compare prices, quality, and services.

Smart consumers, of course, compare the prices of products. They question advertisements that use such phrases as ''normally sells for'' or ''sold elsewhere for.'' Usually these ads are honest, but sometimes the prices mentioned in them are not really the prices normally charged. The wise consumer compares prices to find out if what is being offered is a real value.

All consumers want to get their money's worth. Good quality merchandise and services generally cost more, but buying lower quality items can sometimes turn out to be even more costly. For example, if you buy a blank tape on which you plan to record music for a very low price, it may break or fail to give you the quality of sound you want. A good-quality tape may cost more, but it may last twice as long as the poor-quality tape and will probably give you more pleasure.

The wise buyer also compares services offered by businesses. Most dealers try to give good service, but types of services may differ. Some businesses sell for cash only; others extend credit. Some businesses deliver goods; others do not. Some keep a very large stock from which selections may be made; others may have fewer items in stock.

Service is important, but you should not pay for more service than you actually need. You should know what you want, seek out what you want, and buy what you want at the best prices. In short, develop your skills as a comparison shopper.

Look for Unit Prices

Unit price is a price per unit of measure. To compute unit price, you must divide the price of the item by the number of units per measure. For instance, suppose you need to buy a bag of frozen peas. In the supermarket, you see that a 16-ounce bag of Big Green Peas costs $1.26. Nearby in the freezer case, are 8-ounce boxes of Perfection Peas for $.69 per box. Which is the better buy? Comparing the total prices only, it is not easy to decide. However, if each container also showed the cost per ounce—the unit price—you could quickly compare prices. In this case, the 16-ounce bag would show a unit price of 7.9 cents an ounce ($1.26 ÷ 16). The 8-ounce box would be 8.6 cents per ounce ($.69 ÷ 8). Unit pricing would quickly tell you that the 16-ounce bag is a better buy per ounce. Larger sizes do not always mean better value, though. You often are not aware of this if the label does not show the unit price. Also, you should not buy a larger size if it is more than you need. Buying more of a product than you can use is not wise.

To help consumers compare value among various brands and sizes of the same product, many stores show the total price and the price of one standard measure, or unit, of the product. In the case of peas, a standard unit would be

Illus. 16-2
Unit prices enable shoppers to compare the costs of various sizes and brands of products.

one ounce. If the store showed how much one ounce of each brand of peas costs, you could easily tell whether Big Green or Perfection was a better buy regardless of the size of the containers.

The wise consumer, then, will look for the store that features unit pricing. Or, as an alternative, it might be a good idea to take a pocket calculator with you when you go shopping. Armed with this inexpensive tool, unit prices are easy to determine.

Understanding a Genuine Sale

The word "sale" may be the most over-used and least-trusted word in marketing. You have probably seen "sale" signs a thousand times. They are used so much as gimmicks to try to sell goods that many buyers no longer know when a real sale is occurring. When an item is really on sale, it is offered at a price lower than its normal selling price. Many so-called sales are not really sales at all, and you should check them carefully. Sometimes they consist of regular goods at regular prices being heavily advertised with the word "sale."

Retailers run three main types of sales. With **promotional sales**, businesses promote the sale of their regular merchandise by making temporary price reductions. They may do this to open a new store or to publicize the new location of an established store. They may have promotional sales to build acceptance for new products by offering them at low introductory prices. The retailers hope that customers will buy the products at the reduced prices, like them, and then buy them at the regular prices in the future. Retailers also use promotional sales to draw customers into their stores. They hope that customers who buy the sale merchandise will buy other products at the regular prices.

Clearance sales are used to clear merchandise that stores no longer wish to carry in stock. This may be shopworn stock; leftovers, such as odd sizes and models; or a line of merchandise that the store no longer carries. Clearance sales usually offer some bargains, but it is important to be sure that you can use a sale item before you buy it.

There are sales, however, which feature special-purchase merchandise. This is merchandise bought for a special sale rather than regular merchandise that has been reduced in price. Special-purchase merchandise may include goods purchased from a manufacturer who is overstocked, goods that are no longer made, or stock from a company that is going out of business.

To be able to take advantage of sales, you have to look for sales that are genuine and that are truthfully advertised. Even then, you must know the regular price of the product so that you can buy only those items that represent a real savings.

Illus. 16-3
Sales are a way of
life in American
business. What
kind of sale is this
one?

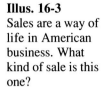

Examine a Product Before Buying

To be certain the quality of a product will satisfy your needs, you should always try to examine a product before you buy it. Even if you are not an expert, you can often tell whether it is exactly what you want. With experience, you will learn to recognize differences in quality.

As you examine the quality of a product, remember an important rule of buying: "Don't buy quality you don't need." This means that the intended use of the product determines the level of quality you need. For example, you would not need to buy expensive designer jeans for working in the yard. Less expensive, strong jeans would serve just as well.

DECIDING WHERE TO BUY

In today's competitive business environment, you have a wide variety of choices when buying a product or service. You can buy from a local business or a nationwide retail chain. You can buy from a store in your neighborhood or from one across town. You may buy goods from a mail-order catalog or you may buy from a door-to-door salesperson. As a consumer, you should be familiar with the goods and services you wish to buy.

Consider the Business's Reputation

You should make every effort to judge the quality of goods and services for yourself. Sometimes, however, you may have no way of knowing exactly what you are getting. One of the best assurances you can have that the products you buy are of good quality is to buy from businesses that have good reputations. The wise business owner knows that a satisfied customer is likely to return. Businesses with good reputations have salespeople who know the uses and the quality of the goods being offered for sale. They are also concerned about matching the proper goods with customers' needs. If you buy from a business with a good reputation, you can usually rely on its salespeople to help you make wise selections.

Know Brand Names

A **brand name** is a name given to a product or service that is intended to distinguish it from other similar and/or competitive products or services. The brand name is created by the business that is selling the product or service. A brand name is designed to build customer loyalty to a product or service.

Many brand-name goods and services are advertised nationally and are sold in almost every community. Among these goods are clothing, shoes, tools, canned foods, toothpaste, cosmetics, furniture, and appliances. Manufacturers of such goods often place brand names on the items they make. General Electric, for example, is the brand name of a world-famous line of electrical appliances. These are called *national brands*.

Learning to recognize national brand names can help you in two ways. First, you can usually expect uniform quality, even when brand-name goods are bought from different businesses. Buying brand-name goods is especially helpful when it is difficult to inspect for quality, such as canned goods. Second, brand names make comparison shopping possible.

Some stores have their own brand names. These are called *house brands* or *store brands*. For example, Kenmore has been one of the house-brand names for appliances sold by Sears. House brands are usually sold at a lower cost than national brands. Buying house brands, therefore, may often save you money and offer good quality at the same time.

Some supermarkets carry unbranded items at reduced prices. They are called *generic products*. Generic products are less expensive because they do not require advertising and fancy packaging, thus saving the manufacturer money. These savings are passed on to consumers. The labels on generic products are usually written with large bold print identifying the contents. There are sometimes only minor differences in quality and uniformity between generic and branded products.

Choose from a Variety of Stores

When deciding where to buy, the consumer has a wide variety of choices available. The stores that sell goods are organized with unique characteristics. The choice of which type of store will depend upon the consumer's wants and needs.

Full-service stores offer a wide variety of goods and emphasize customer service. For example, they are likely to have a repair department, to make deliveries, and to wrap gifts. Their prices, however, will be higher. **Discount stores**, on the other hand, emphasize reduced prices on products sold. Most discount stores base their success on a high volume of sales and low prices. If service is not important to you, this may be where you should shop. Stores that have a special line of products for sale are known as **specialty stores**. They carry a wide variety of products in a narrow line such as sporting goods, jewelry, and women's shoes. Some specialty stores may also be discount stores. **Factory outlet stores** are becoming more and more popular and often have a reputation for selling high-quality merchandise at low prices. Products are direct from the factory and sometimes have minor flaws. These stores offer goods at bargain prices.

In food retailing, there are three types of stores. The first is the **supermarket**, a large, full-service store that carries a wide variety of national, store, and generic brands at moderate prices. The **warehouse market** is a no-frills food outlet emphasizing the sale of large quantities of items at reasonable prices. The **convenience store** is a small store that emphasizes the sale of food items, an accessible location, and long operating hours. These stores usually stock popular items at higher prices.

DECIDING WHEN TO BUY

Timing is a key part of good buying. It takes time to buy wisely. A smart consumer spends time planning a shopping trip. Once in the marketplace it is important to go slowly and thoughtfully to find the best buys. Smart shoppers also know that there is often a right time of the day, month, or year to buy.

Take Your Time

"I just don't have the time" is the complaint of many people. It is often tempting to spend only a little time shopping. This is usually not a good practice. Spending more time planning purchases and shopping usually results in savings that reward you for the time spent. Taking your time usually means slowing down, visiting more stores, and giving yourself a chance to look for the best values. If you learn to pace yourself, you will probably find that your money goes farther toward buying the goods and services you need and want. As a good shopper, you should refuse to be hurried into buying anything. In this way, you avoid buying merchandise that you really do not want or need.

Sometimes consumers become impatient. They want to buy right now which often costs them money. Being patient might mean postponing a purchase until you have saved enough money to pay cash, until you can afford to make a larger down payment, or until you can take advantage of special sales.

Buy at the Right Time

In some businesses, prices are lowest at predictable times. A good shopper will learn about those times and take advantage of them. Certain seasons and conditions favor goods and services being sold at reduced prices. Here are just a few examples:

- When fresh fruit and vegetables are at their peak, they are usually lower in price.
- Automobiles are usually less expensive at the end of the model year (September) before the new models are displayed.
- Winter clothing is often on sale in January.
- February ''White Sales'' are a good time to buy bedding and towels.
- Airline tickets cost less when travel is at off-peak times of the week and year, such as flights to Florida in the summer.
- Chimney sweeps often charge less in the summer.

You can probably add to the list of products and services that are less expensive on a seasonal basis. Consumer magazines and newspaper articles, as well as radio and television programs for consumers, can help you add to this list.

Don't Be Impulsive

The opposite of spending time and thought in shopping is buying too rapidly without much thought. This type of buying is called **impulse buying** and should be avoided to keep from making costly mistakes. Impulse buying often happens when you see an item attractively displayed and suddenly decide to buy it. Sometimes impulse buying is harmless. Purchasing some small item like a bag of popcorn, a small gift for a friend, or a magazine is a pleasant part of life. The cost is small and the item is usually worth the price. However, buying more expensive items such as clothing, radios, or especially automobiles on impulse can be costly. You may not really need the item, or it might not be the best value for the price, as you might discover if you collect information about the item and then carefully shop for it.

Illus. 16-4
Wise consumers
stick to their
shopping lists and
avoid impulse
buying.

One of the best ways to avoid impulse buying is to make a shopping list and stick to it. Many people use lists when shopping in grocery stores and supermarkets. Market research firms that study consumers' buying habits have found that, in supermarkets, people without shopping lists tend to buy more items (many of them luxury items) than do people with shopping lists. Since most consumers are open to suggestion, an attractive display of products can tempt them to buy something that they had not planned to buy. You can save money if you make and stick to a shopping list whether it is for groceries, hardware, or clothing.

BECOMING AN EFFICIENT SHOPPER

Skillful consumers are efficient in their shopping activities. They save time, energy, and money by planning. You can become a skillful shopper, too. There are at least three specific steps you can take. First, plan your purchases carefully and make a shopping list. As you already know, a consumer with a list makes better decisions in the store and avoids impulse buying. Next, use the telephone to help you. Using the classified ad section of the telephone book and calling businesses to find out if they have what you need is a very efficient practice. Often you can order goods and services by telephone. Finally, you can save fuel by carefully planning the route of your trip. Unnecessary travel can add to the cost of a shopping trip.

Increasing Your Business Vocabulary

The following terms should become part of your business vocabulary. For each numbered item, find the term that has the same meaning.

brand name	*impulse buying*
clearance sale	*promotional sale*
comparison shopping	*specialty stores*
convenience store	*supermarket*
discount stores	*unit price*
factory outlet stores	*warehouse market*
full-service stores	

1. Stores that offer a wide variety of goods and emphasize customer service.
2. Buying too rapidly without much thought.
3. Large stores that sell large quantities of goods at low prices.
4. Comparing the price, quality, and services of one product to those of another product.
5. Stores that carry a wide variety of products in a narrow line.
6. A name given to a product or service by a manufacturer that is intended to distinguish it from other similar and/or competitive products or services.
7. Stores selling products at low prices that sometimes have minor flaws.
8. A large, full-service food store that carries a wide variety of national, store, and generic brands at moderate prices.
9. The price per unit of measure of a product.
10. A no-frills food outlet emphasizing the sale of large quantities of items at reasonable prices.
11. A sale in which a price reduction is used to sell items that a store no longer wishes to carry in stock.
12. A small store that emphasizes the sale of food items, an accessible location, and long operating hours.
13. A sale in which items are sold below their regular price to publicize the opening of a new store or location and to build acceptance for new products.

Reviewing Your Reading

1. What is the first step in the buying process?
2. How does unit pricing help consumers?
3. What does the phrase, ''Don't buy quality you don't need'' mean?
4. What is the difference between a house brand and a national brand?
5. Name advantages of buying a product that has a national brand name.
6. What are generic products?
7. Why are automobiles usually a good buy in September?
8. How should you avoid impulse buying?
9. Name two steps you can take to become an efficient shopper.

Using Your Business Knowledge

1. Explain how values influence purchases.
2. How would you describe the buying habits of consumers possessing brand loyalty?
3. In what ways is timing important to a shopper?
4. When would you consider an impulse purchase a harmless activity?
5. What are some factors you might consider when deciding which store to buy from?

Computing Business Problems

1. Popper's peanut butter comes in an 18-ounce jar and is priced at $2.38. Georgia Pride peanut butter comes in a 24-ounce jar and is priced at $2.92.
   a. What is the unit price of each brand?
   b. Assuming the quality of each is equal, which is the better buy?
2. A consumer has two choices regarding where to buy a microwave oven. One option is an appliance specialty store. This store is located 10 kilometers round-trip from the consumer's home. A microwave oven can be purchased there for $154. A second option is a discount store located 100 kilometers round-trip from the consumer's home. The identical microwave oven can be purchased there for $135. Assume that the consumer's car costs 40 cents per mile to drive and that either purchase would require one round-trip to the store. Based on the price of the microwave oven and transportation costs alone (not service, reputation, etc.), which is the better buy?
3. Western Furniture and Appliance is moving to a new store. To avoid having to move a lot of merchandise, it is having a pre-moving clearance sale. Western has advertised that it will reduce the price of all merchandise in the store by 20 percent for one day.
   a. What would be the sale price of a $979 sofa?
   b. A customer paid $304 for a video cassette recorder. What was the original price of the VCR?

Expanding Your Understanding of Business

1. One businessperson has said "Our highest goal is to achieve the best match between our products and services and our customers' needs and wants." Tell why you think this is a good goal.
2. For each item listed below, tell whether you would choose to buy a higher quality item, or whether you would choose a lower, but acceptable, quality item.
   a. Outdoor paint for your two-story frame home
   b. Tires for the car your brother drives a few miles into town to work each day
   c. Shoes for school
   d. A wallet to give to your father, who is a salesperson
   e. A ball-point pen for school use
3. Many supermarkets carry three types of brands—national, house, and generic. Name two food products you would feel comfortable buying under each type of brand. Tell why you made the selections you did.

Consumer Rights and Responsibilities

Chapter 17

Chapter Objectives

After studying this chapter and completing the end-of-chapter activities, you will be able to:

1. List six rights you have as a consumer.

2. Name three governmental agencies concerned with consumer interests.

3. Describe a monopoly.

4. List four organizations a consumer might contact to help solve a problem.

5. Explain express and implied warranties.

6. Name five consumer responsibilities.

Lynne and Dwight Osmund recently purchased a home in the suburbs of a Colorado city. The home was built on a tract of land that was somewhat barren. It needed trees to enhance its beauty and to protect it from the wind and sun.

They decided to order six bare-root aspen trees from a mail-order nursery. Aspens are native to the area and normally thrive in a mountain climate. The trees were described in the Pike's Peak Nursery Catalog as "six feet tall and guaranteed to live."

The six trees arrived promptly and were eagerly planted by the Osmunds. They began to sprout leaves. Soon, however, three of them died. The Osmunds were disappointed, but they followed the instructions in the catalog regarding what to do if a tree died. They called the customer service representative of Pikes Peak Nursery and told her of their problem. She asked how they planted and cared for the trees. Satisfied that they had treated the trees properly, the customer service representative agreed to send them three more trees.

This consumer problem had a pleasant ending; most of them do. It is usually not necessary to get upset or angry in order to get satisfactory results from businesses. In fact, most businesses are eager to solve problems that consumers may have. They want happy, satisfied customers that will return to their businesses again and again.

Solving consumer problems is usually a matter of practicing good two-way communication. It is up to you to let the business know what you want. The job of the business is to tell you what you can expect to get. It is within this context that the study of consumer rights and responsibilities fits.

KNOWING YOUR RIGHTS AS A CONSUMER

The rather pleasant relationship that is enjoyed by businesses and consumers now was not always so. In fact, at one point in our history, some businesses were viewed as frequently trying to take advantage of consumers. False claims were made about products, prices charged were too high, and some products that were sold were unsafe. If a consumer was cheated, there was nowhere to turn—except away from the offending business. To fight against unfair business practices, consumers joined together to demand fair treatment from businesses. This banding together gave rise to what is known as the *consumer movement*. As a result of this movement, public and private agencies, policies, laws, and regulations were developed to protect consumer interests.

A highlight of the consumer movement came in 1962 when President John F. Kennedy presented his Consumer Bill of Rights in a message to Congress. He declared that every consumer has the following rights:

1. The right to be informed—to be given the correct information needed to make an informed choice.
2. The right to safety—to be protected from goods and services that are hazardous to health or life.
3. The right to choose—to be assured of the availability of a variety of goods and services at competitive prices.
4. The right to be heard—to be assured that consumer interests will be fully considered by government when laws are being developed and enforced.

In 1969, President Richard M. Nixon added a fifth right to the list, and in 1975, President Gerald R. Ford added the sixth:

5. The right to a remedy—the assurance of the right to legal correction of wrongs committed against consumers.
6. The right to consumer education—to learn about consumer rights and responsibilities as economic citizens.

EXERCISING YOUR CONSUMER RIGHTS

As was suggested by Kennedy, consumers have the right to expect honesty and fair treatment from businesses. Few businesses are ever dishonest on purpose. However, being a skillful consumer means that you know what your rights are and how to exercise them.

The Right to Be Informed

Most products and services that you buy are described in advertisements, on labels, or by a salesperson. You are entitled to know what the product or service is and what it will do for you. Sometimes we buy carelessly. We may not weigh the facts provided in advertising or by a salesperson, and we blame the seller for our poor purchases.

There are other times, though, when inaccurate information is given to a customer in an effort to make a sale. This type of dishonesty is known as **fraud**. Fraud occurs when false information is given to a customer in order to make a sale. If a salesperson knowingly sells you a pair of hiking boots that are made of vinyl while telling you they are made of leather, a fraud has occurred.

Suppose, on the other hand, you were looking for a small desk for your personal computer. If a salesperson told you she thought the desk would be sturdy enough to hold the computer—but it was not—you were not deceived, even though the salesperson may not have been accurate in judging the strength of the desk.

When a salesperson exaggerates the good qualities of a product—says "It's the best," or "It's a great buy"—there is no fraud. If, however, the salesperson tells you the desk is made of oak when, in fact, it is made of pine, this is fraud.

The Right to Safety

People could be endangered by taking harmful medication. Children have been hurt playing with unsafe toys. Consumers have a right to be safe from harm associated with using products or services.

Several agencies work to assure the safety of consumers. The Consumer Product Safety Commission (CPSC) is one of them. The CPSC has the authority to set safety standards, to ban hazardous products, and to recall dangerous products from the market.

The Food and Drug Administration (FDA) makes certain that food, drug, and cosmetic products are not harmful to consumers. This federal government agency enforces laws and regulations that prevent the distribution of unsafe or misbranded foods, drugs, and cosmetics. The FDA also works to assure that product labels do not mislead consumers.

The U.S. Department of Agriculture (USDA) also helps insure consumer safety by setting standards for the grading of farm products that are sold from one state to another. It also controls the processing of meat, the inspection of meat, and the stamping of meat products with grades according to their quality.

Illus. 17-1
The USDA insures consumer safety by setting standards for the grading of farm products.

The Right to Choose

The right of consumers to choose from a variety of goods and services has become well established. In fact, one of the main activities of the Federal Trade Commission (FTC) is to prevent one firm from using unfair practices to run competing firms out of business. When a business has no competitors and controls the market for a product or service, it is said to have a *monopoly*. Competing firms try to get your business by offering a variety of products and services at various prices. By driving away this competition, monopolies limit your right to choose.

The Right to Be Heard

Most large businesses have a department to hear the concerns or complaints of customers. In smaller businesses, one person is usually assigned that responsibility. Most businesses are glad to take care of problems you have with their products or services.

Several federal government agencies have the responsibility to assure the consumer's right to be heard. The Office of Consumer Affairs (OCA) coordinates and advises other federal agencies on issues of interest to consumers. Its primary concerns are to represent the interests of consumers, to develop consumer information materials, and to assist other agencies in responding to complaints. The OCA normally refers consumer problems to

Illus. 17-2
Competition is the cornerstone of our economic system. As consumers, we have the right to choose from among competing products.

other appropriate agencies and uses complaints from consumers to promote legislation.

The FTC also protects your right to be heard. As a consumer, you can complain directly to the FTC if you believe that any of your rights which come under its protection have been violated. The FTC regulates advertising and encourages informative and truthful advertising. It also requires textile companies to label wool and other fabrics with information telling what the material is made of and how to care for it.

State governments also support public agencies that are interested in hearing consumers' concerns. Usually the Office of the Attorney General and the Department of Consumer Affairs have some responsibility for protecting the rights of consumers. They can prosecute businesses for violation of state consumer-protection laws and inspect advertising practices. They can also handle other types of consumer matters such as automobile-repair problems, credit problems, and door-to-door sales practices.

In addition to publicly supported consumer protection agencies, there are some privately funded groups that help to make sure that you are heard. Perhaps the best known of these is the Better Business Bureau.

As discussed in Chapter 15, the Better Business Bureau is chiefly concerned with problems that arise from false advertising or misrepresented products and services. If you believe that your consumer rights have been violated by such practices, you can get help from the Better Business Bureau in your community. The bureau will usually ask you to report your problem in writing so that it can get all of the details correct. It will then try to persuade the business to remedy the problem or fulfill its promises for the product or service in question. Most businesses willingly carry out the bureau's requests.

There are a number of other private organizations that help protect your right to be heard. Groups of like businesses frequently form **trade associations**. These are organizations of businesses engaged in the same line of business. Many trade associations establish standards of quality for the products that their members manufacture. These standards of quality help assure that customers receive the quality they expect when purchasing a product. Some trade associations also publish codes of ethics that members are urged to follow. Several trade associations now serve as central complaint departments to resolve consumer problems that may have been mishandled on the retail or manufacturer levels.

Many newspapers and radio and television stations have added features designed to publicize consumer complaints and to help consumers solve problems. They respond to complaints by trying to resolve grievances between consumers and businesses.

The Right to a Remedy

As a result of the consumer movement, many laws were passed. These included the Fair Packaging and Labeling Act, the National Traffic and Motor Vehicle Safety Act, the Truth in Food Labeling Act, and the Fair Debt Collection Practices Act, to name a few. All of these acts were designed in part to provide assurances that consumers could seek a legal remedy if they were wronged.

Another form of remedy that consumers have is the protection provided through a guarantee. With some purchases, a consumer can expect a guarantee, or a warranty. A **guarantee** is a promise by the manufacturer or dealer, usually in writing, that a product is of a certain quality. A guarantee may apply to the entire item or only to some parts of it. It may promise that defective parts will be replaced only if a problem occurs during a specified period of time. No guarantee, however, covers damages caused by misuse.

When making a purchase, a skillful consumer asks about a guarantee. A guarantee is frequently in the form of statements like these: "The working parts of this watch are guaranteed for one year." "This sweater will not shrink more than 3 percent." "This light bulb is guaranteed to burn for at least 5,000 hours." These kinds of guarantees are sometimes called **express**

Illus. 17-3
The consumer has a right to a remedy when something is wrong with a product or service.

warranties. They are made orally or in writing and promise a specific quality of performance.

You should insist on seeing a copy of the guarantee when you buy an item. You can also require the business to put in writing any other guarantees that have been offered. Written guarantees are useful if you need to seek replacement of a faulty product. Guarantees are sometimes included in ads for the product. Keep a copy of the ad as evidence of the guarantee. Read the guarantee carefully to find out just what is covered and for what period of time.

Some guarantees are not written. They are called **implied warranties**. They are imposed by law and are understood to apply even though they have not been stated either orally or in writing. In general, the law requires certain standards to be met. For example, it is implied that health care products purchased over the counter at a pharmacy will not harm you when used properly.

The Right to Consumer Education

In proclaiming this right, President Ford made a commitment on the part of the federal government to support consumer education. Traditionally the focus of consumer education programs has been on individual decision making related to the purchase of goods and services. Although consumer buying decisions are important, educated consumers need to understand how their decisions affect our economy as well. Today consumer education focuses on consumer decisions that relate to the interaction between consumers and producers in our economic system. Educated consumers are aware that their decisions not only affect their life-styles, but also have economic implications.

PERFORMING YOUR CONSUMER RESPONSIBILITIES

Consumers in our country are protected through hundreds of laws, yet every day examples of consumer difficulties are reported. Why? The answer probably lies with consumers themselves. They sometimes do not carefully meet their responsibilities as consumers. What are those responsibilities?

Be Honest

Most people are honest, but those who are not cause others to pay higher prices. Shoplifting losses have been estimated to be in the billions of dollars each year. Businesses usually make up losses that result from shoplifting by charging everyone higher prices.

Some people who would not think of shoplifting may be dishonest in other ways. Businesses report many dishonest acts by customers. For

Illus. 17-4
Shoplifting is
costly to
everyone.

example, a customer might wear an outfit once for a formal occasion and then return it. Another customer might buy a stereo from a discount store, but have it repaired at a retail store that has a generous repair plan on the same brand of stereos. Also, customers have been seen taking lower priced tags from articles and putting them on the more expensive items they buy. There have also been many complaints about customers who try to use discount coupons for merchandise they have not purchased.

As a responsible consumer, you must be as honest with a business as you want it to be with you. You should be as quick to tell the cashier that you received too much change at the checkout counter as you are to say that you received too little. Remember that dishonesty, in addition to being illegal and unethical, usually results in higher prices for all consumers.

Complain Reasonably

As a buyer, you are usually responsible for what you buy if the business has been honest with you. If you are dissatisfied, however, and wish to complain, you should complain in a reasonable way.

You should first be sure that you have a cause for complaint. Be sure that you have followed the directions for using the product. One consumer angrily returned a record player because it would not work. The store found that the customer had failed to remove a piece of plastic placed under the turntable for safe shipping.

After you have confirmed the details of your complaint, calmly explain the problem to an employee of the business from which you bought the item. In most cases, the business will be glad to correct the problem because it does not want to lose you as a customer. If you become angry or threatening, you risk getting an angry response that will only delay the solution to your problem.

If you believe that your complaint is not handled fairly by the salesperson or the customer service department, take the matter up with the owner or an official of the firm. If that fails and the firm is a part of a national company, a letter to the customer relations department at the headquarters often gets results. If you do not get a response within a reasonable time, a second letter with copies sent to several consumer agencies will often bring a quick reply. If you fail to receive what you think is a fair adjustment, you may contact one of the following organizations:

- The Better Business Bureau.
- The local or state consumer affairs agency or the attorney general's office in your state.
- Your social welfare agency if you or your family are receiving aid from the government.
- A lawyer or the Legal Aid Society if the problem is quite serious.
- In larger cities, the small claims court, which is operated for filing small claims only.
- A consumer help department of a local or national newspaper or radio or television station.

Report Unethical Practices

As a responsible consumer, you should report unethical business practices to prevent other consumers from becoming victims. For example, the hand brake on your two-week-old bicycle fails to work. The shop from which you bought the bike refuses to honor its guarantee to replace all parts that break under normal use within 90 days. After several unsuccessful attempts to get the bicycle fixed, you might be tempted to give up, pay someone else to fix your bicycle, and mark it off as a bad experience. However, that action will not prevent other people from losing money as you did. By reporting the matter to an agency discussed in this chapter, you might be able to get the shop to keep its word both to you and to future customers.

Be Informed

The most important responsibility you have as a consumer is to be informed. Just having the right to be informed will not make you an informed consumer. You must find and use the information available to you. A producer might put a complete label on a product, but it is up to you to read and use the information on the label. To be an informed consumer, you should continually learn about the many goods and services available. You should also keep informed about your rights as a consumer. Learn about the laws and agencies that protect your rights and how to report a violation of your rights. Being an informed consumer is hard work, but the extra effort spent in making your dollars go as far as possible will be worth it.

Be Involved

In our democratic government, involvement is an important consumer activity. As a citizen, you have a responsibility to participate in government—even if only to be an informed voter. As a consumer, you also have responsibilities. When the opportunity arises, make your concerns known to government officials or consumer agencies. Only when you become involved as a consumer can agencies do their jobs and legislative bodies pass appropriate laws. You may also have an opportunity to serve on a consumer panel or advisory group. As an active participant on the panel or in

Illus. 17-5
Reading consumer information contributes to a good consumer education.

the group, you can help to assure that appropriate consumer legislation is passed and that government agencies fairly represent the interests of consumers.

Increasing Your Business Vocabulary

The following terms should become part of your business vocabulary. For each numbered item, find the term that has the same meaning.

express warranty
fraud
guarantee

trade association
implied warranty

1. When inaccurate information is given to a customer in an effort to make a sale.
2. A guarantee made orally or in writing that promises a specific quality of performance.
3. A promise by the manufacturer or dealer, usually in writing, that a product is of a certain quality.

4. A guarantee imposed by law that is not stated orally or in writing which requires certain standards to be met.
5. An organization of businesses engaged in the same type of business.

Reviewing Your Reading

1. What is usually the best way to solve a consumer problem?
2. What are the six consumer rights?
3. What are three governmental agencies that are concerned with consumer safety?
4. What is the difference between exaggerating the good qualities of a product and fraud?
5. How do monopolies harm consumers?
6. How does the Federal Trade Commission help consumers?

7. What are the responsibilities of the Office of Consumer Affairs?
8. What are five responsibilities that every consumer has?
9. Give an example of an express warranty.
10. Give at least three examples of consumer dishonesty.
11. Why should you report businesses that are following unethical practices?

Using Your Business Knowledge

1. Why, with all of the laws and organizations to protect consumers, do we continue to hear of examples of consumer fraud?
2. Give a real or imaginary example of a business monopoly. Tell why it is a monopoly.

3. Which of the consumer rights are you exercising right now?
4. Which of the following would be considered fraud? Explain your answers.
   a. A salesperson says the sound system you are looking at is the best brand

made. After you buy it, you find it rated in a consumer magazine as second best.

b. The label in a shirt says the colors will not fade. After washing it, you find that instead of a bright red shirt you now have a pale pink one.

c. The person who sells an electric corn popper says it is completely washable. Before using it, you put it into a sink filled with water to wash it. The first time you try to make popcorn, there is a flash and the popper's electrical unit catches fire. When you return the popper to the store, the salesperson tells you that she did not mean the popper could be put under water. She says you should have known that electrical appliances should not be put in water. She refuses to give you either a refund or an exchange.

5. Suppose that the first time you wash a new wool sweater it shrinks so much that it no longer fits you. You washed the sweater in hot water, but you notice that the label in the sweater says to use cold water. Would you have a fair complaint against the business that sold you the sweater? Why?

Computing Business Problems

1. The Art Mart Gallery, a shop dealing mainly in prints and drawings, guarantees satisfaction with every purchase for a month. That means a customer can return a print or a drawing anytime within 30 days of purchase for a full refund. Last year's sales are given below:

Total sales	$320,000
Products returned for refund	$ 6,400

a. What percent of total sales was returned for refund?

b. What was the total amount of net sales, deducting the cost of refunds?

2. The Jones family ordered a new car from Germany. The express warranty said the average driver would get 48.3 kilometers for every 3.8 liters of gasoline used.

a. How many miles per gallon is this?

b. If they traveled 90 miles and used 10.5 liters of gasoline, had the car performed better or worse than the warranty claimed?

3. Jane Franklin is thinking about subscribing to a weekly consumer magazine so that she can be better informed. The magazine is offering a special trial subscription of 26 weeks for $19.50. The normal subscription rate for 26 weeks is $32.50.

a. What is the normal cost per issue?

b. What is the cost per issue under the special subscription rate?

c. How much would Jane save per issue by taking advantage of the special subscription rate?

Expanding Your Understanding of Business

1. Gather four written guarantees and read them carefully. Make two lists from the guarantees. First, list all statements that give you specific information or instructions. Second, list all statements that are vague or general.

2. If you were a businessperson selling tools, what two express warranties would you put on your tools? Tell why you chose these two kinds.

3. The Fair Packaging and Labeling Act was passed to encourage businesses to package

and label their products in such a way that the consumer would be better informed. Using your school library, find out what the provisions of this law are. Then find some packages or labels that illustrate how businesses are complying with the law.

4. Because business losses to shoplifters have been growing so rapidly, more and more businesses are prosecuting offenders who are caught. Through your school library and interviews with local businesspeople, the police department, and the Chamber of Commerce, prepare a report on this problem. Consider these questions:

a. What is the extent of the problem in your area?

b. What is the estimated amount of loss by all local businesses in a year?

c. What are businesses doing to prevent shoplifting?

The Changing Value of Money

Chapter 18

Chapter Objectives

After studying this chapter and completing the end-of-chapter activities, you will be able to:

1. *Explain how the value of money changes over time.*

2. *List several causes of inflation.*

3. *Explain how changes in demand for goods and services without an increase in supply cause changes in the value of money.*

4. *Describe what happens to prices during periods of inflation and deflation.*

5. *Explain three actions the government can take to control inflation or deflation.*

6. *Explain the Consumer Price Index.*

255

As the saying goes, there are only two things in life that are certain—death and taxes. A third thing could be added—change. Sometimes change occurs gradually; sometimes change is radical or violent. Almost everything changes. The weather, technology, and even the value of money are examples of things subject to change. As you will learn, the value of a dollar, as measured by what it can buy, changes from year to year.

THE VALUE OF A DOLLAR CHANGES

Prices of goods and services are changing all the time. These changes in the value of a dollar have been a source of confusion and frustration to consumers for many years. Buyers are engaged in a constant guessing game—wondering if prices will go up or down, or if certain businesses will give the best, or lowest, prices.

One way to measure the value of a dollar is by the amount of goods and services it will buy. In general, the prices of goods and services tend to rise over the years, making a dollar worth less from one year to the next. Suppose that a quart of motor oil cost $1.10 a few years ago, and that it now costs $1.54. This is an increase of 40 percent. If the average price of all goods and services has risen 10 percent, the consumer will need $1.40 to buy what $1.00 used to buy. Sometimes prices for items double or even triple in just a few months.

Illus. 18-1
The changing value of the dollar usually means that the prices of goods and services have increased.

INFLATION

As you will recall from Chapter 4, the tendency for prices to rise is called *inflation*. Inflation is a general increase in prices that usually occurs whenever the demand for goods and services tends to be greater than the supply.

Types of Inflation

Economists do not completely agree about what causes inflation. In general, inflation is the result of a disturbance in the balance between supply and demand.

Cost-push inflation results from a rise in the general level of prices that is caused by increased costs of making and selling goods. For example, an increase in the cost of producing goods as a result of an employee pay raise will normally cause cost-push inflation. Large increases in the cost of raw materials, such as cotton, is another cause of cost-push inflation.

In a period of prosperity, the demand for goods and services of all kinds tends to increase rapidly, causing prices to rise. **Demand-pull inflation** is a general rise in prices in response to increased demand for products or services. The classic definition of demand-pull inflation is "too much money chasing too few goods." Too much money may be available for spending when most people have jobs and are optimistic about the future. Demand-pull inflation may also occur as a result of tax cuts or other government policy changes that increase the amount of money people have to spend.

Illus. 18-2
As the cost of cotton increases, the cost of cotton products will increase.

During a period of high employment, most people have jobs and regular paychecks. In this case, some people tend to buy a new house or move to a better apartment. What usually results is an increase in the price of houses or the cost of rent if an adequate supply of houses or apartments is not available.

A Reduction in Buying Power

During inflationary periods, there is reduced buying power. If increases in wages and salaries are greater than increases in productivity, more dollars are spent on a limited supply of goods and services. That gives prices an upward push. To meet the demand or the expected demand for more goods and services, businesses must expand. They build new stores and factories and spend large amounts of money for equipment. In turn, all of this spending increases demand and adds to the upward movement of prices.

Local and federal governments may also contribute to inflation. Governments spend money for defense, education, welfare, roads, and many other goods and services. If governments collect enough in taxes to match their spending, their expenditures do not increase demand. However, if governments borrow large amounts of money and then spend that money, they increase demand. As the governments spend borrowed money, the amount that people have to spend is not decreased if taxes have not been raised.

Illus. 18-3
People tend to buy houses during periods of full employment and, thereby, drive up housing prices.

Ways to Combat Inflation

Sometimes wages and salaries do not increase at the same rate as prices. When this happens, an individual's standard of living is reduced. People who receive fixed payments, such as retirement benefits, are harmed by rising prices.

Government can help to reduce the effects of inflation. Among other things, it can:

1. *Increase taxes.* An increase in taxes takes money away from consumers and thus reduces their demand for goods and services.
2. *Reduce government spending.* A reduction in spending, especially when accompanied by higher taxes, decreases demand and thus decreases prices.
3. *Encourage higher interest rates.* Higher interest rates increase the cost to borrow money to buy things such as a car or a house. Higher interest rates also increase what a business must pay if it wants to borrow to expand its facilities. Some buying may, therefore, be postponed or avoided entirely. Decreases in purchases may result in a decrease in the demand for goods. A smaller demand for goods may help bring down prices.

On the positive side, moderate inflation can be beneficial in some cases. For example, it is helpful when you owe a long-term debt that you have agreed to pay at a fixed amount per year. With inflation, the amount paid becomes relatively smaller each year.

DEFLATION

The opposite of inflation is deflation. As you read in Chapter 4, *deflation* exists when the general level of prices falls. With deflation, there is an increase in the purchasing power of a dollar. Deflation tends to occur when the supply of goods and services is greater than the demand.

When prices increase during inflation, consumers may cut down on their purchases. Consumers may stop buying either because they think that prices are too high or because they have already bought to the limit of their incomes. Because of the decreased buying of consumers, there is less demand for goods and services. Businesses may lay off employees or have employees work fewer hours. The employees then have less money to spend and decrease their buying. The decreased buying by employees further decreases demand and makes deflation even more serious. As business becomes less active, stores and factories may delay expansion. This again decreases demand and helps push prices down. While there is generally decreased buying during a period of deflation, a dollar might buy more goods or services because prices may be lower.

Occasionally government collects more in taxes than it spends. When this occurs, government takes money from consumers that otherwise might be spent. Government spending decreases the total demand for goods and services and tends to cause prices to decrease. Although prices are lower, unemployment is higher. While the dollar's buying power is increased, consumers have less money to spend.

Ways to Combat Deflation

To combat deflation, government can follow policies just the opposite of those used to combat inflation. Among other things, it can:

1. *Decrease taxes.* A decrease in taxes leaves more money in the hands of consumers. Consumers then can increase their purchases of goods and services.
2. *Increase government spending.* An increase in spending that is not offset by an increase in taxes increases demand and, thus, prices.
3. *Encourage lower interest rates.* Lower interest rates tend to encourage individuals and businesses to borrow in order to buy. With increased borrowing, consumers have more money to spend. This helps to increase the demand for goods and eventually may encourage higher prices.

The Seriousness of Deflation vs. Inflation

When deflation threatens, quick action is usually taken. Everyone notices the slowing down of business and the loss of jobs that deflation brings. Government officials do whatever they can to avoid the hardships that deflation causes. Furthermore, the actions taken to combat deflation are usually welcomed. Almost everyone likes to have taxes reduced. Few people object to increased spending by government for public works or services that benefit them. Also, few object to lower interest rates, especially if they want to borrow to buy a home or some other major item.

When inflation threatens, however, such prompt action is not as likely to be taken. The strong demand for goods and services that usually occurs during inflation makes businesses prosperous and jobs plentiful. Wages and salaries increase. Prices also increase, but the increases are not as noticeable at first. Therefore, before inflation becomes serious, most people do not want anything done that will affect what seems to be a good condition.

Usually the methods of fighting inflation are unpopular. Few people like to pay higher taxes or higher interest rates. The idea of reduced government spending is approved by many people, but few favor reductions in the public works or services that affect them and their jobs.

Illus. 18-4
Serious deflation
can bring about
the loss of jobs
with serious
social
consequences.

THE CONSUMER PRICE INDEX

The federal government's Bureau of Labor Statistics (BLS) publishes several price indexes. These indexes are published in an effort to establish an objective measure of what is happening to prices in our economy and to help guide the consumer. A **price index** is a series of figures showing how prices have changed over a period of years.

The **Consumer Price Index (CPI)** shows the changes in the average prices of goods and services bought by consumers over a period of time. Actually, the BLS compiles and publishes two CPIs. The CPI-W (wage earners and clerical workers) represents the buying experience of urban wage-earners and clerical workers. It includes approximately 32 percent of the population. The CPI-U is a broader index. It covers about 80 percent of the population. The CPI-U (all urban consumers) includes such diverse groups as salaried workers, the unemployed, the retired, and the self-employed. The CPI-U is the most frequently quoted of the two.

The BLS checks prices throughout the country on a collection of goods and services often referred to as a "market basket." Categories of items included in the "market basket" are purchases you or your family might make for such things as clothing, food, fuel, and housing. As the average level of prices for a number of typical items changes, the CPI either goes up or down. The trend of the CPI has been upward.

Figure 18-1 shows the percentage increase in the Consumer Price Index during the years 1982-1989. Changes in prices may not seem important from day to day, but over a number of years the changes may be very important.

Figure 18-1
The prices of goods and services have risen each year since 1982.

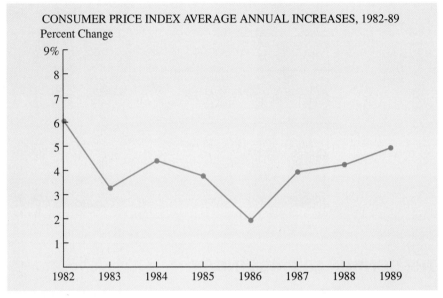

CONSUMER PRICE INDEX AVERAGE ANNUAL INCREASES, 1982-89

Source: U.S. Department of Labor, Bureau of Labor Statistics, *CPI Hotline* (Washington, D.C.: U.S. Government Printing Office, January 21, 1990).

THE CONSUMERS' RESPONSE

Even economists have difficulty predicting the specifics of inflationary and deflationary trends. So how should you respond as a consumer to the changing value of money? There is little you can do to affect the trends, but that does not suggest inactivity. A consumer can:

1. Avoid the temptation to carelessly spend money during a period of inflation just because it is available.
2. Elect responsible government officials who will try to stem inflation and/or deflation through sound economic policies.
3. Try to have money invested during inflationary times in assets that will increase in value, such as a home.
4. Have a savings account that can tide you over if deflationary times result in unemployment.

Increasing Your Business Vocabulary

The following terms should become part of your business vocabulary. For each numbered item, find the term that has the same meaning.

Consumer Price Index (CPI)   *demand-pull inflation*
cost-push inflation   *price index*

1. A general rise in prices in response to increased demand for products or services.
2. A rise in the general level of prices that is caused by increased costs of making and selling goods.

3. An index that shows the changes in the average prices of goods and services bought by consumers over a period of time.
4. A series of figures showing how prices have changed over a period of years.

Reviewing Your Reading

1. What causes inflation?
2. During a prosperous time in our society, what usually happens to prices?
3. Is the demand for goods and services generally strong or weak during an inflationary period?
4. What has happened to the general price level of goods and services over the past years?
5. When does deflation occur?
6. What kind of inflation might result from an increase in the cost of producing automobiles caused by a jump in the price of steel?

7. What happens to the average price level during deflation?
8. What agency publishes the Consumer Price Index?
9. Does a dollar buy relatively more or less during a deflationary period?
10. Why is quick action usually taken against deflation?
11. Name three things that the government can do to act against inflation, and three things it can do to act against deflation.
12. How much did the Consumer Price Index increase from 1988 to 1989?

Using Your Business Knowledge

1. If you were going to use the past performance of the Consumer Price Index to help you predict the future value of the dollar, what would you predict? Explain your answer.
2. What is meant by the phrase, "Too much money chasing too few goods"?
3. If Congress reduced income taxes dramatically and people spent the resulting extra income on houses, what would happen to the price of houses? What kind of inflation is this?
4. The average family spends from 18 to 25 percent of its take-home pay on food. If prices for food increase rapidly, what effects would such increases have on a family's life-style?
5. Describe the process the Bureau of Labor Statistics uses to compile the Consumer Price Index.
6. If Erik Larson puts $5,000 away in a safe place in his home, can he expect that at the end of five years the money will buy more, the same, or less than it would have when he put it away? Explain your answer.

Computing Business Problems

1. Suppose a cord of firewood delivered and stacked cost $20 in one year. Assuming the Consumer Price Index increased a total of 17.2 percent over four years, how much do you think that same cord of wood would cost in four years?

2. Chris Howard is required by a court to pay $400 each month in child support payments. This payment is to increase in accordance with the CPI-U increase. After the first year, the CPI-U increased by 5.1 percent. How much were his payments each month during the second year?

3. The Yokimura family buys and consumes 16 liters of milk per month. Determine how many gallons of milk the Yokimura family consumes each month.

4. Karen Swisher bought a pair of shoes that cost $45. Just one year ago, a similar pair of shoes sold for $42. Two years ago, they cost $38.

   a. How much did the cost of the shoes increase in the last year? in the last two years?

   b. Was the increase in cost greater last year or the year before? What was the difference in the amount of the increase from the year before last year?

Expanding Your Understanding of Business

1. Explain why people on fixed incomes are especially vulnerable to the effects of inflation.

2. Possible trends toward inflation and deflation in our economy are important to consumers. Look through last month's newspapers and magazines, and clip any stories that you find which deal with economic problems. Do they indicate that the country is in good or bad economic shape? Are we in a period of inflation, deflation, or neither? Report your findings to the class.

3. Using a long-term debt (such as a home mortgage) as an example, explain how modest inflation can be an advantage to a person owing money.

4. Why might you want to have money invested in items that will increase in value during times of inflation? Give some examples of items that might increase in value.

5. Two problems that our economy has had to face in the past are recession and depression. (You may want to review the information about recessions and depressions in Chapter 4.) Perhaps you have read about the depression that the United States experienced during the 1930s. Do some library research about depressions. What usually causes them? What brought the United States out of the 1930s depression?

Career Category: Retailing

This unit has concentrated on the activity of consumers in our economy. Consumers, by definition, are involved in buying goods and services from various businesses. Many of these businesses are retail businesses—businesses in which you might someday like to become employed.

Retailing is the final connection between manufacturers and consumers. The retailing field typically consists of chain stores, specialty stores, variety stores, franchise stores, mail-order houses, supermarkets, and department stores. They buy goods from wholesalers or manufacturers, transport them, stock them, merchandise them, and resell them to individual consumers in smaller quantities. Retailers must know their customers' needs and wants and promote the goods they sell.

Job Titles: Job titles commonly found in this career area include:

Advertising Assistant
Advertising Manager
Aisle Manager
Assistant Store Manager
Buyer
Cashier/Checker
Counter Clerk
Department Manager
Department Store Salesperson
Divisional Merchandiser
Fashion Buyer
Fashion Coordinator
Home Furnishings Salesperson
Marketing Manager
Merchandise Checker
Rack Jobber
Retail Buyer

Retail Sales Worker
Salesperson
Sales Manager
Stock Clerk

Employment Outlook: Retailing is all around us. Most of us buy something from a retail business almost every day. Retailing as a potential career, however, is frequently overlooked. It should not be. On the contrary, it merits serious consideration as a career field for women and men.

The future of employment in retailing looks very bright. In a recent year, retail sales workers alone held about 4.3 million jobs. They worked in

stores ranging from the small drug or grocery store employing one part-time salesperson to the giant department store with hundreds of employees.

Employment of retail personnel is expected to grow faster than the average for all workers through the year 2000 due to the anticipated growth in retailing. Retailing will continue to provide more job openings than almost any other occupation for the next ten years. This growth prediction is due largely to the increased volume of retail sales over the same time period.

Future Changes: While the volume of goods sold is expected to grow rapidly, the adoption of self-service and computerized checkout systems by more retailers will limit the need for additional retail workers. During recessions, retail business usually declines. Purchases of expensive items such as cars, appliances, and furniture tend to be postponed by consumers during difficult economic times. Significant layoffs, however, are unlikely. Since retail worker turnover is usually very high, employers often can cut unemployment simply by not replacing all those who leave.

What Is Done on the Job: Most employees in retailing work in clean, comfortable surroundings. While helping customers make purchases, many retail workers must stand for long periods. Although many retailers have a 5-day, 40-hour week, in some stores the standard workweek is longer and includes weekend employment. Longer-than-normal hours may be scheduled before holidays and during other peak buying periods. Many employees in retailing regularly work one evening or more per week. Part-time workers in retailing generally work during peak business hours, which are daytime rush hours, evenings, and weekends.

In addition to selling, most retail workers also make out sales checks, receive cash payments, make change, and give receipts. They also handle returns and exchanges of merchandise and keep their work areas neat. In smaller stores, they may help order merchandise, stock shelves or racks, mark price tags, take inventory, and prepare displays.

Education and Training: In the early history of retailing, much of the training was com-
pleted while working in small businesses. More recently formal education has provided the best entry into the field. Marketing education programs in high schools, community colleges, private career colleges, and four-year colleges now prepare people to enter retailing.

Education beyond high school is not required for some of the beginning jobs in retailing. However, those people who progress through the ranks into managerial or executive positions find that an educational background in marketing and retailing is important.

Salary Levels: The starting wage for most entry-level retail employment is the federal minimum wage. Weekly earnings of full-time retail workers in large stores are about $410. Sometimes employees in retail stores receive salaries plus commissions based on a percentage of sales. Other employees are paid only commissions. An additional fringe benefit that many retail sales workers receive is a discount on merchandise that they purchase from the store.

For Additional Information: You may wish to speak with your marketing education teacher at the high school you attend. You may also receive information on careers in retailing by writing the following organizations:

National Mass Retailing Institute
570 Seventh Avenue
New York, NY 10018

National Association of Trade & Technical
  Schools
2021 K Street N.W.
Washington, DC 20006

Marketing Education Resource Center
1375 King Avenue
Columbus, OH 43212

The Marketing Education Association
1908 Association Drive
Reston, VA 22091

Living and Working with Technology

Unit Goals

After studying the chapters in this unit, you will be able to:

1. *Describe the components of a computer system.*
2. *Identify methods in which computer systems are used in businesses and other organizations.*
3. *Explain how technology is changing our business and personal lives.*

Chapter 19
Computer Systems

Chapter 20
Computer Applications

Chapter 21
Technology in Your Future

Voice-Activated Computers

Bob inserted his access card into the automated teller machine. Then he heard, "Hello Robert Conway. How may I help you today?" He looked around, but no one was there! Bob finally realized that the computer was doing the talking and that

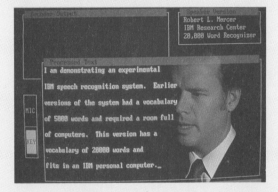

this computer system was voice activated. All he had to do was say, "I want to deposit $245 in my checking account." The computer terminal accepted his paycheck, gave Bob a receipt, and said "Thank you."

The computers of the future will allow you to enter, process, store, and retrieve data through a series of voice commands. Instead of entering a complex series of computer instructions, you will be able to say, "Subtract the amount of this payment and determine how much money I have left in my account." The computer will be able to translate your words into instructions it can understand and will be able to perform the necessary processing.

A voice-activated computer (VAC) system operates by breaking a person's spoken words into codes that represent the sounds of your speech pattern. Then the system must compare these codes to those stored in its memory and

attempt to determine the proper word, the pronunciation, and the correct usage. Next the system must translate the codes into words or other instructions for the computer to take action. Finally, a computer voice creates the sounds to respond to your request.

The system must recognize many words in our language with similar but different meanings. For example, the same sound can be used for different words, such as "to," "too," and "two." In addition, every person has a distinctive voice pattern along with different rates of speaking. The first VAC system required that a person had to pause between each word to give the computer time to record, code, and translate the sentence. Eventually systems were developed to handle all speech patterns as well as understand and respond in different languages.

Because of the complexity of the process, the first VACs were only able to understand a few words. As with all technology, however, research improvements have resulted in systems that can recognize more than 20,000 words and understand almost any speaker. In the future, you can expect to see expanded use of voice-activated computers in toys, games, household appliances, automobiles, and stores. Perhaps someday while shopping you will hear, "May I help you?" You will state your purchases out loud, and the system will request these items. The VAC system will tell you the prices, which items are not available, and announce the total of your purchases. VAC systems are just one type of computer application that will change the way we work and live. VACs can help to make the use of computers in our lives much easier, since the only command we will need may sound something like this: "Please prepare my monthly financial report," and the VAC system will respond.

Computer Systems

Chapter 19

Chapter Objectives

After studying this chapter and completing the end-of-chapter activities you will be able to:

1. *Describe the uses of computers in our society.*

2. *Identify the four components of every computer system.*

3. *Explain methods for entering data into a computer system.*

4. *Discuss the importance of a computer program.*

5. *Describe different types of storage devices.*

6. *Explain how processing results are reported.*

7. *Describe how a computer system processes data.*

Technology is changing our business world and society. Recently you may have:

- Purchased an airline ticket with the reservation, flight information, cost, and seat number recorded and stored by computer.
- Ordered clothing by mail from a company that maintains its inventory and customer records by computer.
- Paid a utility bill with the use of your Touch-Tone telephone system.

Each of these business activities was made easier as a result of computers, which have become a vital part of our society. Many businesses have turned to the computer as a way to stay competitive, to control the costs of business operations, and to manage resources. To be an effective employee in most of today's businesses, you must have an understanding of the uses and functions of computers.

COMPUTERS IN OUR SOCIETY

Computers are electronic devices designed to store, process, and report information. If you consider the amount of information that is used each day in our society, you can see that computers make life easier. School records, business reports, letters, sales records, family budgets, and team sport statistics are some of the information stored in computers and used by people each day.

Computers enable businesses and others to handle data quickly and efficiently. **Data** consist of facts in the form of numbers, alphabetic characters, words, or special symbols. Because computers handle data quickly, they save time and money. Because they store information so efficiently, they save space. Today's computers are much less expensive and smaller than the first computers. The first computers were large and expensive, but technology has resulted in computers that can be held in your hand.

An early computer inventor was American engineer Herman Hollerith who designed a punched-card system for the 1890 census. Each punched hole represented a unit of data. Computers read the holes in the cards and stored the data. As a result, the 1890 census was completed in two and a half years, five years faster than the 1880 census! In recent years, the electronic computer has been developed for a faster, more efficient method of storing the increasing volume of data. Preliminary results from the 1990 census were available immediately after data were entered into computers.

At first, computers were owned only by large companies. Now most small- and medium-sized organizations use computers to collect data and to solve business problems. Frequently, the data collected must be rearranged before it is useful. This rearrangement or processing of data to make it more useful is called **data processing**.

ELEMENTS OF A COMPUTER SYSTEM

While many different types and sizes of computers are used by organizations, all systems have four basic components:

- An input unit.
- The processing unit.
- Memory and storage.
- An output unit.

The combination of these components working together through the use of software make up a *computer system*. All of the basic components of a computer are called **hardware**. Examples of hardware are the keyboard, monitor (or screen), chips, and the printer. **Software** refers to the instructions that run the computer system.

A large computer system is called a **mainframe**, which can handle more instructions and process data faster than smaller computers. In recent years, very large mainframe computers, called *supercomputers*, have been created for use in large organizations. A **minicomputer** is smaller and less powerful than a mainframe. The smallest computers, such as desk-top or portable models, are referred to as **microcomputers**. A microcomputer is frequently referred to as a *personal computer*.

Illus. 19-1
Microcomputers include all of the elements of a computer system.

Input

While most people are concerned with the results of a computer operation, there has to be a starting point. The data you enter into the computer is called **input**. The most common input device is the keyboard, similar to that of a typewriter, with which you can enter letters, words, numbers, and other symbols or commands that the computer can understand. The keyboard and visual display screen may be referred to as a **terminal** and may be part of a communications network, which connects other computers.

Another common input device is the **mouse**, which is a hand-held device used to point to a certain command on the computer screen. For example, if you want to store a report, point the mouse toward a drawing of a filing cabinet on the screen. When the symbol lights up, press the command button marked ''yes'' on the mouse. The report will then move to storage in the computer.

Technology has further automated data entry activities for computers. Recent developments in this area include:

- A touch-sensitive screen that allows you to touch or point at the correct command to enter data.
- Scanning devices that can read numbers, letters of the alphabet, and symbols directly from a typed, printed, or handwritten page and translate them into a format which can be recognized by the computer.
- Voice-activated systems such as those discussed in the Business Brief at the beginning of this unit.

Illus. 19-2
Scanning devices are a fast method of data input.

Processing

How does a group of related data become meaningful information, which can be used by organizations and individuals? This activity occurs in the **central processing unit (CPU)**, which is the control center of the computer. The CPU is capable of sorting, comparing, and calculating data based on the instructions it is given.

The processing of data is done on tiny wafers or chips, no bigger than your thumbnail. **Chips** are tiny pieces of silicon that are located in the CPU and contain imprinted circuits. Electronic pulses, which carry instructions and data, flow along tiny paths on the circuits that cover the chip.

Despite the automated process by which a computer operates, your efforts are still needed. You must always tell the system what task you want it to perform. The most common way to give instructions to a computer is with a program. A **program** is a series of detailed, step-by-step instructions that tell the computer what functions to complete and when to complete them.

Most computer programs are not written with a format that is easily understood by people. Instead, instructions are most frequently written in a manner that is understood by the computer. A **computer language** is a system of letters, words, numbers, and symbols used to communicate with a computer. Figure 19-1 lists some of the most common computer languages. These languages are used by **programmers** who write the instructions to tell the computer what functions to perform. The wide availability of

Illus. 19-3
Tiny computer chips are powerful sources for computer processing.

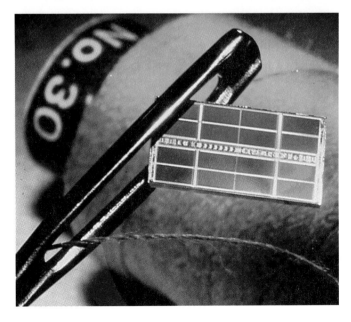

Figure 19-1
If you plan to do any programming, you will need to know a computer language.

Common Computer Languages
Ada
ALGOL (ALGOrithmic Language)
APL (A Programming Language)
ASCII (American Standard Code for Information Interchange)
BASIC (Beginner's All-purpose Symbolic Instruction Code)
C
COBOL (COmmon Business-Oriented Language)
FORTRAN (FORmula TRANslation)
LOGO
Pascal
PL/1 (Programming Language)

ready-to-use programs makes it unnecessary for most people to do their own programming.

Memory and Storage

The third major component of a computer system is known as memory. The instructions that the computer follows are stored in locations called **memory**. Memory may also be referred to as internal storage or *primary storage*. From memory, the program is carried out by the CPU. Likewise, the data placed into a computer by an input device for processing is stored in memory.

The internal storage capacity of a computer depends upon the size of its memory. These amounts are measured using computer terms such as bit, nibble, byte, and kilobyte (K). Figure 19-2 shows these measures. To give you an idea of a computer's internal storage capacity, it would take at least a 1K computer to store the information on an average page in this book. Large computers can store thousands of pages of information.

Figure 19-2
The amount of information that can be stored depends upon the size of the computer's memory.

Measurements Used to Store Information
Bit (smallest unit of code a computer reads)
Nibble (four bits; a half-byte)
Byte (eight bits)
Kilobit (1024 bits)
Kilobyte (1024 bytes)
Megabit (a million bits)
Megabyte (a million bytes)
Gigabit (a billion bits)
Terabit (a trillion bits)

Primary storage, however, cannot store all of the programs and all of the data needed by computer users. Therefore, *auxiliary* (or *external*) *storage* that is not part of memory is available for storing both programs and data. Auxiliary storage devices, such as disks, are often used to store programs and volumes of data that cannot fit into the computer's primary storage or memory all at one time.

A **disk drive** is used to store information onto a magnetic medium so that information can be recalled and used again. Disks on which programs or data are stored come in two basic forms. **Floppy disks** are small, pliable oxide-coated plastic disks in protective covers that may be used to store programs and data. A **hard disk** is built into the computer and is made from rigid material that does not bend. It allows storage of tens of millions of characters. Both types of disk systems use coded magnetic spots to represent information.

As with other aspects of the computer system, new technology has expanded storage capabilities. Compact discs (CDs) were originally used for music, but these laser-beam systems are now commonly used for data processing applications.

Output

The phase of computer operations that is of greatest interest to most people is the output. When the processing of data is completed, output is the result. **Output** is data that has been processed into a form that can be used by a person for later retrieval or for immediate communication. Examples of

Illus. 19-4
Disks store programs and data for future use.

output include a sales report, an inventory record, a school report card, or a church financial statement.

Frequently output will be displayed on a computer screen. When viewing this information on a screen, you can quickly see various aspects of your data processing efforts. For example, you can view sales by a salesperson, by geographic area, or by product. However, the screen will only allow you to see a limited number of lines at one time.

Quite often you may instruct the computer to print a copy of the processed data on a **printer**, an output device that produces written results on paper. A printed report is commonly referred to as a *hard copy* or *printout*, which is in contrast to the *soft copy* that appears on the screen or is stored on a disk. Printers are available in a variety of speeds and with different features. They range from dot-matrix devices, which print 40 to 80 characters per second, to laser printers that produce several thousand lines per minute and may print in several colors. Laser printers produce high-quality documents compared to other types of printers.

COMPUTER PROCESSING IN ACTION

So far, we have looked separately at each element of a computer system. But how do these elements work together to handle company data or to do problem solving? For example, you may ask the computer to compare your

Illus. 19-5
The quality of printed processing results varies by type of printer.

company's financial statements for the last three business years in order to determine the increase or decrease for certain expenses. Or, if you sell three different products, you might ask the computer to indicate what percentage of all expenses should be assigned to each product. For the CPU to provide meaningful information for a logical decision, certain steps must be followed:

1. Data concerning expenses for three years are recorded and entered into the computer's memory by using a keyboard or other input device.
2. A program instructing the computer how to use the information is also entered or loaded into memory.
3. The computer operator enters any new data into memory and instructs the computer to follow the program to provide the information needed.
4. When the computer begins to follow the instructions, electronic pulses flow along the circuits of the computer. The pulses cause the computer to follow the program step by step, using the data stored in memory. The data is rearranged almost instantly as the computer completes the required operations.
5. The computer operator can request a printed copy of the rearranged data, which also appears on the screen.

Remember that computers do not make decisions. By following the instructions given in the program, however, computers process and provide data needed by the people who will make business decisions.

Increasing Your Business Vocabulary

The following terms should become part of your business vocabulary. For each numbered item, find the term that has the same meaning.

central processing unit (CPU)	*mainframe*
chips	*memory*
computers	*microcomputer*
computer language	*minicomputer*
data	*mouse*
data processing	*output*
disk drive	*printer*
floppy disks	*program*
hardware	*programmers*
hard disk	*software*
input	*terminal*

1. Tiny pieces of silicon that contain imprinted circuits.
2. Data that has been processed into a useful form.
3. A computer that is smaller and less powerful than a mainframe.
4. Small, pliable oxide-coated plastic disks in protective covers that may be used to store programs or data.
5. A hand-held device used to point to a certain command on the computer screen.
6. The rearrangement or processing of data to make it more useful.
7. The control center of the computer.
8. Electronic devices designed to store, process, and report information.
9. A series of detailed step-by-step instructions that tell the computer what functions to complete and when to complete them.
10. A large computer system, which can handle more instructions and process data faster than smaller computers.
11. Data entered into a computer.
12. Facts in the form of numbers, alphabetic characters, words, or special symbols.
13. A disk that is built into the computer and is made from rigid material, which does not bend; allows storage of tens of millions of characters.
14. People who write the instructions to tell the computer what functions to perform.
15. A device that is used to store information onto a magnetic disk so that the information can be recalled and used again.
16. The smallest type of computer.
17. The keyboard and visual display screen used to enter and view data.
18. An output device that produces written results on paper.
19. Storage locations for the instructions and data that the computer will use.
20. A system of letters, words, numbers, and symbols used to communicate with a computer.
21. The components or equipment of a computer system.
22. Instructions that run a computer system.

Reviewing Your Reading

1. What are the uses of computers in businesses and other organizations?
2. What are the four basic components of a computer system?
3. What methods can be used to input data into a computer system?
4. What role does a programmer play in the operation of computer system?
5. What is the difference between primary storage and auxiliary storage?
6. What are the common types of output of a computer system?
7. How does a hard copy differ from a soft copy?

Using Your Business Knowledge

1. Which of the following items are hardware and which are software?
   a. Monitor (screen)
   b. Data
   c. Chips
   d. Keyboard
   e. Program
   f. Disk drive
2. What are the advantages of a mouse as an input device over a keyboard?
3. Is a visual display screen an input device or an output device? Explain.
4. What types of business activities can be performed more efficiently by using a computer system than if these tasks were done manually?

Computing Business Problems

1. Using the measurements in Figure 19-2 on page 274, how many bytes of information could be stored in a 256K computer?
2. Ivana Dvorsky requested sales information from the computer about the Lightning pickup trucks from each of five sales districts in the United States. The computer-generated report is shown below. Calculate the data that is missing in the report.

U.S. Region	Trucks Allocated	Percentage Sold	Number of Trucks Sold	Current Inventory*
East	4,200	18%	--	--
Southern	6,425	27%	--	--
North Central	8,625	--	--	5,175
Southwest	--	20%	550	--
Northwest	100	--	--	83

*Trucks Allocated - Trucks Sold = Current Inventory

3. A minicomputer sells for $7,800. The printer costs $2,500 and the yearly maintenance fee is $700.
   a. How much will the buyer pay for all three items if it is a cash purchase?
   b. How much will the monthly payments be if there is a 12 percent interest charge and there will be 12 payments if all items are purchased?
   c. How much will the buyer save if there is a 2 percent discount on the computer and printer for paying cash within ten days of purchase?
4. The Second Bank of Atlanta installed an automated teller machine. It costs $15,000 plus $2,000 maintenance per year. If the machine replaced $2\frac{1}{2}$ tellers whose salaries were $16,000 a year, how much was saved per year by installing the computer?

Expanding Your Understanding of Business

1. Report on the different functions of computers used in your school, at local businesses, and by other organizations in your community.
2. Collect advertisements, photos, and articles from newspapers and magazines that show different types of computer equipment, including input, storage, and output devices.
3. Prepare a five-person panel presentation about the evolution of the computer. The first person should be responsible for the 1890-1950 period. The last four people should research and report on the 1950s, the 1960s, the 1970s, and the 1980s to the present. Obtain information for your report from library books and articles.
4. A *flowchart* is a visual presentation of the steps in a process or procedure. Computer programmers use this device to break down a process so that it can be understood by the computer. Design a flowchart bulletin board to show the processing of data on page 277 or show some other business use of computers.

Computer Applications

Chapter 20

Chapter Objectives

After studying this chapter and completing the end-of-chapter activities, you will be able to:

1. *Describe the benefits of an automated word processing system.*

2. *Identify uses of database, spreadsheet, and graphics software packages.*

3. *Explain the benefits of electronic mail.*

4. *Discuss uses of integrated software and desktop publishing.*

5. *Identify uses of computers and technology in retailing, education, and public service.*

6. *Describe how computers are allowing people to work at home.*

In Chapter 19, you learned that software is used to control the operation of the different components of a computer system. In this chapter, you will learn about the software designed to perform particular operations related to problem solving and record keeping. For example, a manager needs a complete record of each employee in the department. To obtain this information, the manager can consult the database file of all employees. An office worker needs to write letters to all current customers. This task can be easily accomplished with word processing software that will prepare a personalized letter for each customer. A student wants to plan a budget for a year. The budget will show expected income and expenses, making it possible for the student to develop a plan for spending available income. A spreadsheet can be used to prepare the budget.

OFFICE COMPUTER APPLICATIONS

Extensive use of computer systems can be found in most offices. Computers are used to create letters and reports, to maintain records, and to handle financial data. The software used to meet a particular processing need of the user is known as *applications software*.

Word Processing Software

A common use of the computer in the office is for word processing. **Word processing software** is used to create and revise written documents. Word processing allows the user to enter, store, revise, and print text in the form of

Illus. 20-1
Computers are used for a variety of business tasks.

letters, memos, reports, or standard business forms. Office workers can quickly recall text from a disk, display it on the screen, make changes, and print a final copy without having to rekey the entire document. The normal computer system operations you have learned—input, processing, storage, and output—apply to word processing software just as they do to other software.

The benefits of computerized word processing are many and include:

- An ability to create, store, and retrieve frequently used letters, memos, and reports.
- Ease of editing (or revising) text; you can quickly move an entire paragraph or add and delete words, sentences, and paragraphs.
- An ability to check spelling and grammar by pushing one or two special keys.
- The creation of personalized letters or memos to different people without rekeying the entire document.

Each of these activities is quite easy to do with word processing software. Most software allows you to select a task from a **menu**, which is a list of computer functions that appear on the screen (see Figure 20-1). For example, you may be asked if you want to save, edit, or create a new document. After you make your selection from the menu, you will be able to perform that task.

Figure 20-1
A menu makes it easy to select commands for operating the software.

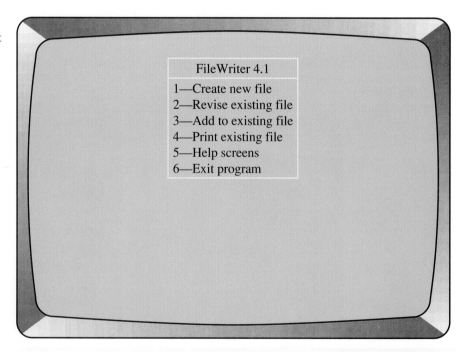

FileWriter 4.1

1—Create new file
2—Revise existing file
3—Add to existing file
4—Print existing file
5—Help screens
6—Exit program

Database Software

Quite often an organization requires data to be sorted in a certain manner. A **database** is a collection of organized data whose elements are in some way related to one another. For example, an inventory clerk may require a list of products sold, while the sales manager may need similar information sorted by customer or salesperson. Each of these reports would come from the same database, but would require different sorting and rearranging.

Database software processes a database. As shown in Figure 20-2, a database program can arrange and sort information in different ways. A

Figure 20-2
Database software is used to arrange information into needed reports.

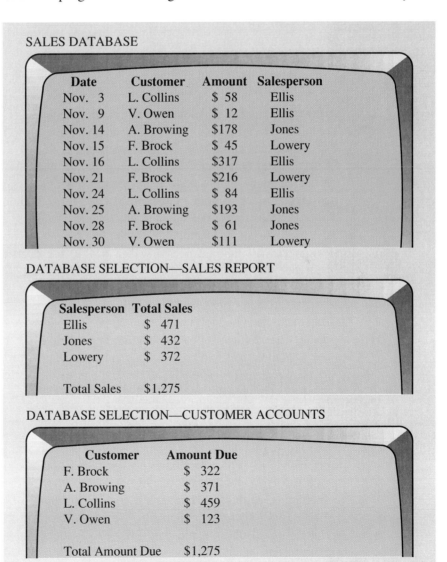

SALES DATABASE

Date	Customer	Amount	Salesperson
Nov. 3	L. Collins	$ 58	Ellis
Nov. 9	V. Owen	$ 12	Ellis
Nov. 14	A. Browing	$178	Jones
Nov. 15	F. Brock	$ 45	Lowery
Nov. 16	L. Collins	$317	Ellis
Nov. 21	F. Brock	$216	Lowery
Nov. 24	L. Collins	$ 84	Ellis
Nov. 25	A. Browing	$193	Jones
Nov. 28	F. Brock	$ 61	Jones
Nov. 30	V. Owen	$111	Lowery

DATABASE SELECTION—SALES REPORT

Salesperson	Total Sales
Ellis	$ 471
Jones	$ 432
Lowery	$ 372
Total Sales	$1,275

DATABASE SELECTION—CUSTOMER ACCOUNTS

Customer	Amount Due
F. Brock	$ 322
A. Browing	$ 371
L. Collins	$ 459
V. Owen	$ 123
Total Amount Due	$1,275

typical organization will use database software to handle records for employee information, sales and inventory, and accounting. Business owners and managers depend upon different databases for making decisions about day-to-day operations and for meeting long-term organizational goals.

The data stored in a database is used and shared in several ways. Data may be stored in one microcomputer, and only the user can access the data in the computer. The data may be stored in a minicomputer or mainframe and can be accessed by several people who use terminals or microcomputers. A **modem** is a device that allows you to communicate with other computers through the use of telephone lines. With a modem, your computer can receive data from other computers or it can access data provided by various publishers and commercial data banks, such as *CompuServe*. A modem also allows you to send data.

Spreadsheet Software

Have you ever seen an accountant's worksheet with numerous rows and columns of information? This is an example of a manually prepared spreadsheet. A *spreadsheet* is simply a row and column arrangement of data. **Spreadsheet software** is a computer program that uses a row and column arrangement of data to perform calculations. This software makes data entry easier and more accurate. Also, spreadsheets make certain kinds of computations, such as totals, percentages, and averages, quickly and accurately with the use of built-in formulas. Computations are more accurate because the computer will not make errors as a person might. However, if the user instructs the computer to use the wrong formula, the results will be inaccurate.

Spreadsheets are used frequently to prepare payroll records, financial statements, and budgets (see Figure 20-3). This software may also be used to do a ''what if '' analysis of a situation. For example, a company may want to see what the effect will be on operating costs and profit for different levels of sales revenue. The spreadsheet will automatically calculate the situation when certain data are entered in the computer.

Graphics Software

The processing results from a spreadsheet or database program are frequently presented in a report format. However, rather than just listing numbers, the data can be communicated clearly and quickly with the use of a graph or diagram. **Graphics software** is a computer program that prepares charts, graphs, and other visual elements. This software can be used to create bar charts, line graphs, and pie charts as well as specialized graphics in the form of maps and other drawings.

Figure 20-3
A spreadsheet may be used to prepare the financial reports and documents of a business organization.

	A	B	C	D	E	F	G	H
1				1991 PROJECTED INCOME STATEMENT				
2								
3	ESTIMATED SALES			1000000				
4								
5	COST OF GOODS SOLD			722000				
6								
7	GROSS PROFIT			278000				
8								
9	LESS EXPENSES:							
10	SALARIES			150000				
11	ADVERTISING			50000				
12	UTILITIES			30000				
13	INSURANCE			30000				
14								
15	TOTAL EXPENSES			260000				
16								
17	PROFIT BEFORE TAX			18000				
18								
19								
20	ESTIMATED SALES			950000				
21								
22	COST OF GOODS SOLD			685900				
23								
24	GROSS PROFIT			264100				
25								
26	LESS EXPENSES:							
27	SALARIES			142500				
28	ADVERTISING			47500				
29	UTILITIES			30000				
30	INSURANCE			29000				
31								
32	TOTAL EXPENSES			249000				
33								
34	PROFIT BEFORE TAX			15100				
35								
36								
37			1991 PROJECTED INCOME STATEMENT WITH VARIABLE RESULTS					
38								
39				PERCENT OVER /UNDER FORECAST				
40				0%	-5%	-10%	+5%	+10%
41								
42	ESTIMATED SALES			1000000	950000	900000	1050000	1100000
43								
44	COST OF GOODS SOLD			722000	685900	649800	758100	794200
45								
46	GROSS PROFIT			278000	264100	250200	291900	305800
47								
48	LESS EXPENSES:							
49	SALARIES			150000	142500	135000	157500	165000
50	ADVERTISING			50000	47500	45000	52500	55000
51	UTILITIES			30000	30000	30000	30000	30000
52	INSURANCE			30000	29000	28000	31000	32000
53								
54	TOTAL EXPENSES			260000	249000	238000	271000	282000
55								
56	PROFIT BEFORE TAXES			18000	15100	12200	20900	23800
57								

Computer graphics are included in television and magazine advertisements, training materials for employees, and business documents. In general, the use of graphics makes communication much clearer than the use of words alone.

Communications Software

Sending and receiving letters, memos, and reports is vital to businesses. In the past, these messages have usually been sent using the U.S. Postal Service.

Illus. 20-2
Graphics are used to clearly and quickly communicate data.

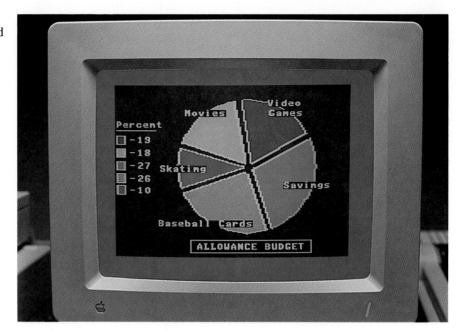

Computers are now being used to save time and money in the delivery of correspondence. **Electronic mail**, also referred to as EM or E-mail, is software that gives users the ability to send textual messages through a computer system. After an office worker prepares a letter or memo on a computer, the document may be sent electronically to another computer terminal. Electronic mail allows messages to be exchanged without preparing a hard copy of the document or requiring the receiver to be at his or her computer.

A form of electronic messaging has been around since the early 1800s when Samuel F.B. Morse invented the telegraph. That system, however, required a knowledge of codes for each letter of the alphabet, and the receiver of the message had to be present to record it. Today, all that is required of electronic mail users is a basic knowledge of computer systems and writing skills.

ADDITIONAL COMPUTER APPLICATIONS

In the previous section, several types of applications software for the office were discussed. These programs included word processing software, database software, spreadsheet software, graphics software, and communications software. These programs represent the most common software applications used with microcomputers today. However, there are combinations of software that are available for almost any type of use you can imagine. This section will introduce integrated software packages as well as cover desktop publishing and computer usage in retailing, public service, and education.

Integrated Packages

Word processing, database, and spreadsheets software are referred to as *single-function software packages*. These programs each have one purpose. The data from a spreadsheet, for example, may not be transferred to a word processing document. To make it possible to work with several types of software at one time, combination packages are available. **Integrated software** is a computer program capable of performing more than one basic function. Common integrated software packages combine word processing, database, and spreadsheet applications; others include graphics as well.

The major advantage of integrated software is the convenience of moving or transferring data from one portion of a package to another. For example, a spreadsheet or graph might be combined with text in a word processing document. In addition, integrated software packages allow the user to use the same command for all of the functions. Printing a document from a word processing program, a database, or a spreadsheet requires knowledge of only one command.

Desktop Publishing

Word processing activities have been expanded to include production of newsletters, brochures, and other publications with the use of a personal computer. **Desktop publishing** is the process of writing and designing high-quality publications with the use of microcomputers. A desktop publishing system includes the computer hardware and a software package that allows the user to create professional formats with creative designs and graphics. The software that performs desktop publishing can produce a wide variety of type styles on a laser printer and can combine graphics with the text. Many businesses and other organizations are using this method to publish high-quality materials at a low cost, compared to traditional printing techniques.

Sales and Retailing

Other than in the office, the impact of computers is probably greatest in the stores at which you shop. Salespeople enter information about a customer's purchase electronically as the sale takes place. The computer automatically updates the inventory record when an item is bought, sold, or returned. In addition, at the time a sale is made, a form known as an *invoice* is printed and given to the customer. The amount of the sale and other important information is recorded in the computer. When a customer pays an amount owed, the amount of the payment is also recorded in the computer.

Illus. 20-3
Technology helps store workers to do their jobs better and faster.

Banks, grocery stores, and gas stations rely heavily on computers for handling business transactions. As you will learn in Unit 7, a bank card allows you to deposit or withdraw money from your account at an automated teller machine. At many supermarkets, the price of an item is recorded by a computer, which reads the price and even states the price so that customers know what they are being charged. Shopping by computer will continue to expand as home usage of computers makes it possible to view and order everything from clothing to concert tickets.

Public Service

Government agencies use computers to keep the many records they need. For example, the federal government must keep the Social Security records of all past and present workers in the United States and the military records of all people who have served in any branch of the military. Other service agencies are also increasing their use of computers. Medical information can be found within seconds to save lives. Police records can be sent from state to state minutes after a crime has occurred, thus assisting in solving the crime. Social agencies and schools can transfer records easily when someone moves to another area of the country.

Education

The computer is probably the most important new teaching device of the past 100 years. Computers have made it possible to train and test new and current workers in a variety of professions. Office workers learn to use word processing software, while also receiving instruction on the proper use of grammar, spelling, punctuation, capitalization, and document forms. Airline pilots used computerized simulators to learn and improve skills needed for flying new types of aircraft.

Computer-assisted instruction (CAI) is the use of computers to help people learn or improve skills at their own pace. With CAI, every student can work at a speed that best serves her or his needs. The student also does not have to go to a school building for instruction. The student can learn at home on a computer or with a system connected to a television.

TELECOMMUTING

Telecommuting is a term used to describe the activities of a worker using a computer at home to perform a job. Each year more and more people are becoming telecommuters. Telecommuters can get up from the breakfast table, go into another room, turn on their computer, and report to work. This working arrangement is especially attractive to people who have difficulty

Illus. 20-4
Students can learn at their own pace with computer-assisted instruction.

leaving their home to go to work, such as handicapped individuals or parents who desire to be near their children.

A growing number of people are working at home through the use of computers. Sales representatives, authors, and software programmers can easily send their reports, documents, and ideas to the office by computer. Work-at-home arrangements save travel time and costs and result in less traffic and less noise and air pollution. Opportunities for working at home have also resulted in many people starting their own businesses, such as consulting, newsletter publishing, software development, and mail-order companies.

A modem allows your at-home computer to communicate with a larger computer. You, or the company you work for, pays the cost of transmitting data over the telephone lines. Working at home has become even more practical as a result of the development of a system in which a copy of a document is transmitted from one location to another. **Facsimile**, or **FAX**, allows the rapid sending or receiving of copies through an electronic device that is connected to the telephone lines. Telecommuters can easily submit completed work and obtain new assignments with the use of a FAX machine.

Increasing Your Business Vocabulary

The following terms should become part of your business vocabulary. For each numbered item, find the term that has the same meaning.

computer-assisted instruction (CAI)
database
database software
desktop publishing
electronic mail
facsimile or FAX
graphics software

integrated software
menu
modem
spreadsheet software
telecommuting
word processing software

1. A computer program that uses a row and column arrangement of data to perform calculations.
2. The use of computers to help people learn or improve skills at their own pace.
3. A list of computer functions that appear on the screen.
4. A computer program that processes an organized collection of information.

5. A term used to describe the activities of a worker using a computer at home to perform a job.
6. A computer program used to create and revise written documents.
7. A process of writing and designing high-quality publications with the use of microcomputers.

8. The delivery of correspondence through a computer system.
9. A computer program that prepares charts, graphs, and other visual elements.
10. A device that allows you to communicate with other computers through the use of telephone lines.
11. A system in which a copy of a document is

transmitted from one location to another through an electronic device that is connected to the telephone lines.
12. A collection of organized data whose elements are in some way related to one another.
13. A computer program capable of performing more than one basic function.

Reviewing Your Reading

1. How does word processing save time and money for businesses?
2. What are the benefits of computerized word processing?
3. What purpose does a menu serve in a computer program?
4. What function does database software serve?
5. What types of office work can be prepared using spreadsheet software?
6. What is the value of graphics software for businesses?
7. What are the main advantages of integrated software?
8. In what ways have computers helped businesses involved in sales and retailing?
9. What aspects of public service have been made more efficient by computers?
10. What are the benefits of computer-assisted instruction (CAI)?
11. What types of careers are best suited to telecommuting? What are some advantages of telecommuting for individuals and businesses?

Using Your Business Knowledge

1. List three manual on-the-job tasks that a person might perform more efficiently with the help of a computer.
2. Identify which of the following computer applications would be performed using word processing software, database software, spreadsheet software, and graphics software.
   a. Preparing a report of new equipment for each office of a company.
   b. Preparing a list of employees that is sorted by ZIP code.
   c. Creating a form letter to go to new customers of a mail-order business.
   d. Creating a pie chart showing the portion of sales of each product.
   e. Preparing a document listing the total sales for each geographic area of the country.
   f. Listing the employees who have not missed a day of work in five years.
   g. Sending a letter to each employee who has not missed a day of work in five years.
   h. Creating a budget for the new office that will be opened in another city.
3. Explain how a modem would make it possible for people to work at home rather than going to work at an office.
4. Who would benefit from schools that would allow students to take classes at home by computer?

Computing Business Problems

1. Roger Friedman bought a personal computer for $1,850. He also bought a disk-drive unit for $1,125 and a printer for $2,740. If he bought five floppy disks at $1 each, how much did he pay for everything?
2. After Roger Friedman (Question 1) had his computer, disk-drive unit, and printer for a year, he decided to sell them. If he sold them for 65 percent of what he paid for them, how much did he receive for the three items?
3. Loretta Fremont paid the following monthly rates for her modem service during the year.

January	$32.00	July	$32.80
February	16.50	August	19.64
March	28.38	September	27.72
April	55.13	October	29.75
May	46.05	November	76.22
June	29.60	December	45.11

a. How much was Loretta's yearly expense for the modem service?
b. How much was Loretta's average monthly cost for this special feature?

Expanding Your Understanding of Business

1. Using a copy of a typed one-page report, explain how you could use word processing software to delete text, insert text, move text, and check spelling.
2. Research the types of documents that could be prepared with the use of spreadsheet software. Talk to people who use this type of software. What special commands are built into most spreadsheet programs?
3. Obtain examples of newsletters, brochures, and other publications that have been prepared with the use of desktop publishing. Use these materials to prepare a class display of desktop publishing documents.
4. Visit a store to observe the uses of computers in retailing. What activities are performed by computers or other technology that were previously performed manually?
5. Prepare a class bulletin board showing pictures of and articles about people using computers and other technology in their homes to work and do household tasks.

Technology in Your Future

Chapter 21

Chapter Objectives

After studying this chapter and completing the end-of-chapter activities, you will be able to:

1. Explain how computers and technology are affecting employment.

2. Describe computer literacy.

3. Discuss how computers are helping to expand international business.

4. List the benefits of using robots and other technology in business operations.

5. Identify the services that technology can bring to your home.

6. Explain the uses of SMART cards.

7. Discuss the social concerns associated with computers and technology.

Joan Williams starts each day with the following greeting from her clock radio: "It's 6 a.m." A few minutes pass, and she hears "It's 6:05 a.m." Joan finally says, "I'm up!" Her voice-activated radio stops the message. Breakfast is ready when she gets to the kitchen since her microwave was programmed the night before. On the way to work, Joan handles some routine business calls, along with making plans for a weekend trip, using her car phone. A few years ago, most people could not imagine these devices.

We live in an exciting age! New uses for computers and other technology are discovered almost daily. Medical researchers have built computerized body parts that respond when the brain gives the command for action. Researchers expect to be able to store billions of bits of data in an area that is so small it cannot be seen with the human eye. Computers are even used to create special effects for motion pictures and at amusement parks. Currently, there are thousands of people developing new uses for computers.

TECHNOLOGICAL CHANGES IN OUR ECONOMY

Many people think computers are replacing them in their jobs. What is actually occurring, though, is a shift in the job duties and skills needed to work in business and industry. Companies will need to retrain those workers

Illus. 21-1
Computer technology is influencing almost every aspect of our lives.

who are replaced by computers with skills in programming, operating, or repairing computer systems. **Displaced workers**, or workers who are unemployed due to changing job conditions, must adapt to the changing job market in order to have continued employment.

As computers become more important in our lives, the ability to use this technology is vital to each person's economic survival. **Computer literacy**, which is the ability to use computers to process information or solve problems, has become a major goal of schools, businesses, and other organizations. While you do not have to understand how to program a computer to use it, you do need to know how to enter, store, process, and retrieve information.

Most software currently used in schools and businesses is **user-friendly software**, meaning the program will tell you what to do next and will also help you when you make a mistake. For example, with the use of a menu and other on-screen information, a user-friendly program will tell you how to enter data or how to proceed. Quite often the software will also have *help screens* to provide additional assistance and instructions.

While typing was once reserved for secretaries, the ability to keyboard is now needed by most workers in offices as well as in factories. Keyboarding as a means of entering and processing data is a skill you are likely to find of value.

CHANGES IN THE WORKPLACE

The computer is being used in business to help improve efficiency and productivity in every area of an organization. You can find computers in oil fields, warehouses, retail stores, hospitals, offices, and factories. Computers are used to perform business operations requiring the handling of large volumes of data.

The Global Office

International computer systems, along with programs that translate information from one language to another, are making it possible to conduct business in a foreign country without leaving your keyboard. Instant transmission of data with the use of satellites makes even the farthest point on earth as close as a button on your computer. Increased global business will have an important impact on world trade and international relations.

Imagine import and export trades taking place within a computer system with the goods being moved from the closest location, perhaps another country, to save time and money. For example, you may be able to order an item from South Korea by using a computer terminal. When South Korean marketers receive your order on their terminal, they check their database and discover there are five such items in Canada. They instruct the Canadian

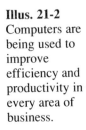

Illus. 21-2
Computers are being used to improve efficiency and productivity in every area of business.

importers by electronic mail to ship the items, which you receive the next day. You pay the South Korean company, and the South Korean and Canadian companies settle their accounts later—by computer.

Robots

Most of us have seen robots and special computers in science fiction movies set in outer space and in the future. But **robots**, mechanical devices programmed to do routine tasks, are commonly used in many factories. Assembly line work that requires the same repeated tasks is a situation in which robots are used. Early robots performed only simple tasks such as connecting a bolt to hold together an automobile part. Today, robots have been created that can see, hear, smell, and feel. Robots have the advantages of being able to work 24 hours a day without a coffee break; they can work in outer space without space suits, under water without air, and in coal mines without fear.

Expert Systems

Artificial intelligence (AI) involves programs that enable computers to reason, learn, and make decisions using logical methods similar to the way in which humans do. One step toward artificial intelligence is a computer program that makes decisions about a complex topic. For example, software exists in which people can answer questions about their health in order to determine solutions to potential problems. Programs that assist people in problem solving on technical topics are called **expert systems** and are currently available for medical services, financial planning, and legal matters. Expert systems are expected to provide intelligent answers in many specialized areas as effectively as human experts in those subject matters.

Computer-Assisted Design

Computers are also changing the workplace in the area of product design. **Computer-assisted design (CAD)** refers to technological assistance used to create product styles and designs. CAD allows you to try different sizes, shapes, and materials for a new machine, automobile, or food package. This process can be used to experiment with many variations before spending time and money building a model or actually going into production. CAD is also used to design homes to meet specialized needs such as for handicapped or elderly individuals.

TECHNOLOGY AT HOME AND ON THE ROAD

At home, your computer system can help with shopping, financial matters, and entertainment. Almost every kind of transportation has been influenced

Illus. 21-3
With CAD, a designer may experiment with many variations before spending time and money on an actual production model.

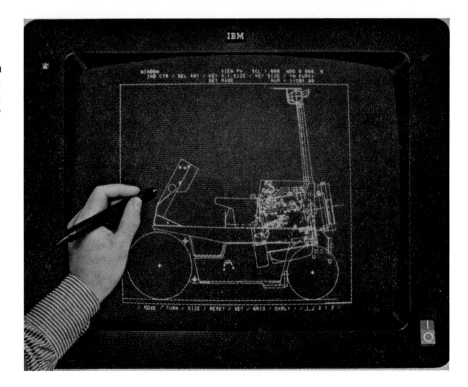

by computers. Each new car introduced seems to have more computerization. Many aircraft can fly to their destinations under the control of computers. Rapid transit trains are scheduled and operated by computer systems.

Your Window to the World

Imagine having access to every book, magazine, and newspaper ever published at the touch of a button. Or, imagine the convenience of shopping at home by video for food, clothing, and other products. Integrated communication systems involving your personal computer, telephone lines, and cable television will eventually make these activities possible. Each day more and more people are banking at home, making travel arrangements, checking the community event calendar, and comparing prices at several stores before leaving home. Each of these is possible as homes are connected to major databases.

Software packages are also available to perform specific household activities on a personal computer. Database programs, as discussed in Chapter 20, can be used to create and update lists. You can keep a list of names and addresses of people to whom you send greeting cards, or you may wish to store your favorite recipes by categories. The family's medical history can be kept on file, or you can have an inventory of household items for insurance records in case of theft or damage.

Other home software packages will help with your personal financial record keeping (discussed in Chapters 40 and 41). These programs can help you set up a budget, balance your checkbook, or prepare your income tax return on your computer. For example, a software package designed to help you complete your federal income tax forms would guide you step-by-step through the process. The program would contain screen presentations for all of the necessary forms. As you answer each question with a yes or no response or enter the amount of money, the software would move on to the next item that needs a response. Other personal finance software allows you to prepare net worth statements or maintain a record of investments. You may also wish to keep detailed automobile records that show gas and oil usage, repair costs, and mileage. Such records are easy to keep and can help you decide whether to keep, sell, or trade your car.

While most people are familiar with credit cards and electronic banking cards, few may be aware of the existence of a **SMART card**, a plastic card with a silicon chip for storing information. The chip within the card stores data such as your current account balance, credit history, and even medical information in case of an emergency. A SMART card has the potential of taking the place of money and checks because each transaction is recorded on the chip as it occurs. Every time a purchase is made, the amount of the transaction would be deducted from the balance in your SMART card account. When you receive a paycheck or other income, the deposit would be added to your balance. In addition to financial matters, the SMART card could be used to access databases, to gain access to your place of work, or to open and start your car without keys.

Automotive Technology Systems

Our daily transportation is also being greatly influenced by the computer. Computers were first used in automobiles to regulate speed, climate, and audio systems. The use of technology in your car has been expanded to include computer-voice safety systems that warn drivers and passengers about unfastened seat belts, open doors, and engine problems. Future expectations for the automobile are in the form of radar systems to alert drivers about potential collisions, video screens with maps to plot your route, and sensing devices that will allow you to travel with the use of ''automatic pilot.''

SOCIAL CONCERNS OF COMPUTER USERS

As with every new development, the advantages are accompanied by potential problems. Expanded usage of computers has resulted in concerns about health and safety, criminal activities, and privacy. While computers have been beneficial in many areas, the wise person will not place complete faith in the reliability or safety of computer systems.

Illus. 21-4
Computers have improved the safety and convenience of driving.

Potential Health Dangers

During our lifetimes, we have learned that certain products and substances can be dangerous. While little danger exists from using computers and other technology, some people have encountered discomfort from on-the-job activities. For example, eye strain and vision problems have been associated with prolonged work with computer screens. Muscle tension can also be caused by too many hours at a keyboard. These and other concerns have resulted in guidelines from labor organizations and government agencies for safe computer operation.

Computer Crime

Wide use of the computer has led to an increase in **white-collar crime**, an illegal act performed by office or professional workers while at work. Some workers steal money, information, or computer time by improper use of databases or illegal access to computer systems. While the average bank robbery results in a $10,000 loss, computer crimes involving bank records average hundreds of thousands of dollars. Theft of a physical item is obvious, but theft of computer time or information from a database is more difficult to detect.

Crimes such as **piracy**, stealing or illegally copying software packages or information, are also a growing problem. Some companies that develop software may lose more than half of their profits to information pirates who violate the law. Copyright laws, which were discussed in Chapter 10, apply to software as well as books and music.

Destructive efforts are also a concern to computer users. A **computer virus** is a program code hidden in a system that can later do damage to software or stored data. The virus may be programmed to become active on a certain date or when certain data is accessed. While some computer viruses are harmless, only showing up as a funny message, others have been known to destroy critical government records.

The Ethics of Confidentiality

One of the greatest challenges facing computer users is the need to guarantee privacy. Some people have learned how to illegally access computer databases. While laws exist to protect your privacy, many believe these regulations are not strong enough. Some businesses are becoming stricter in regard to who can access and use company information. Also, tighter security systems are being developed. Some organizations change the password needed to access information several times a day to protect their databases.

Illus. 21-5
Some computer
viruses may be
harmless, while
others may
destroy critical
records.

Increasing Your Business Vocabulary

The following terms should become part of your business vocabulary. For each numbered item, find the term that has the same meaning.

> *artificial intelligence (AI)*　　　　*piracy*
> *computer-assisted design (CAD)*　*robots*
> *computer literacy*　　　　　　　　*SMART card*
> *computer virus*　　　　　　　　　*user-friendly software*
> *displaced workers*　　　　　　　*white-collar crime*
> *expert systems*

1. Mechanical devices programmed to do routine tasks.
2. Technological assistance used to create product styles and designs.
3. A plastic card with a silicon chip for storing information.
4. A program that will tell you what to do next and will also help you when you make a mistake.
5. Workers who are unemployed due to changing job conditions.
6. Stealing or illegally copying software packages or information.
7. Programs that assist people in problem solving on technical topics.
8. An illegal act performed by office or professional workers while at work.
9. A program code hidden in a system that

can later do damage to software or stored data.

10. The ability to use computers to process information or solve problems.

11. Programs that enable computers to reason, learn, and make decisions using logical methods similar to the way in which humans do.

Reviewing Your Reading

1. How have computers affected employment?
2. How can a computer system and software be user friendly?
3. What effect might computers have on international business activities?
4. What are the advantages of using robots for various job tasks?
5. How can computer-assisted design save time and money for business?
6. What types of home activities can be made easier and faster with computers?
7. What types of information might be stored on a SMART card?
8. How is technology making automobile driving safer?
9. What types of health concerns are associated with computer use?
10. What types of crimes are committed by computer users?

Using Your Business Knowledge

1. How is it possible for the increased use of computers to create more jobs than are lost?
2. How can expert systems be used to help people solve medical, legal, financial, and other technical problems?
3. What would be the potential benefits from the use of SMART cards in handling everyday transactions?
4. How might a person's right to privacy be affected by widespread use of computers?

Computing Business Problems

1. Essex Corporation usually sends about 3,500 pieces of mail per month at 25¢ each. If the firm switches to electronic mail service at a cost of $1,125 per month, how much money would it save or lose?
2. Lydia Mosier can buy 500 radios from a U.S. business for $35 each. She can buy the same radios from a Chinese company for $27 each, but she must pay a 10 percent import tax. Which is the better buy? How much will she save by buying the cheaper radios?
3. A scientist working 8 hours a day can analyze 14 medical reports per hour using a computer. Before using the computer, the scientist could analyze 3 reports per day. How many more medical reports per five-day workweek can the scientist analyze by using the computer?
4. A robot can do as much work in eight hours as three workers earning an average of $23,000 a year. If a company buys a robot for $135,000 and uses it 24 hours a day:
   a. How many eight-hour-a-day workers will the robot replace?
   b. How much money will the company save or lose each year?
   c. How many workers can the company keep in addition to the robot without increasing operating costs?

Expanding Your Understanding of Business

1. Present an original idea to the class for which computers are not yet used. Tell the class how the product or service functions, who would use it, how you would advertise it, and how much it might cost.

2. Talk to people who use computers in their work. Ask them what basic computer literacy skills are needed in today's offices, stores, and factories.

3. Conduct library research on how technology is changing our work and leisure activities. Suggest changes that are likely to take place over the next ten years.

4. Locate articles on health problems caused by computers or articles on the effects of computer crime. Report to the class on one of these topics.

Career Focus

As you know, computers and technology are influencing the lives of almost everyone, both at work and at home. No other career area offers more challenging or exciting employment opportunities.

Job Titles: Job titles commonly found in this career area include:

Computer Operator
Computer Programmer
Computer Systems Analyst
Computer Teacher (schools and industry)
Computer-Assisted Design (CAD) Technician
CAD Terminal Parts Catalogers
Computer-Assisted Graphics (CAG) Technician
CAG Terminal Input Artist
Computer-Assisted Manufacturing (CAM) Specialist
Computer Modeling and Simulation Technician
Computer Research and Design
Computer-Terminal Information Processor
Computer Vocational Training Technician
Data Processing Machine Mechanic
Editor/Proofreader
Electronic Data Processing (EDP) Equipment Operator
Industrial Robot Production Technician
Sales Representative for Computer Systems and Software
Word Processing Operator
Word Processing Supervisor

Employment Outlook: The Bureau of Labor Statistics expects an increase of 40 to 50 percent in computer and technology-related jobs by the year 2000. It is predicted that by that time four out of every five workers will be in service industries. At least half of these workers will collect, manage, and distribute information. Computer knowledge will be required for these positions.

Data processing jobs are found in a wide range of industries from finance and electronics to manufacturing and transportation. Any organization with data and records to be stored, such as banks, insurance companies, or government agencies, must have computer departments. These organizations need employees to enter data, code information, develop programs, and

manage databases. As emphasis on information storage grows, so will employment in these areas.

Future Changes: Computer use will become commonplace in most occupations. Technology-related careers will make up one of the fastest growing employment categories. While the demand for programmers will continue to be strong, new types of computers with voice-activated commands and an ability to respond to written documents will change the types of employment opportunities in this field.

What Is Done on the Job: Workers in this area collect information, enter data, code information, and manage records. Others develop programs, design software, and apply techniques such as graphics, desktop publishing, and computer-assisted design. Still others are involved with the marketing and sales of hardware and software. There is a great demand for teachers at all levels in the computer field as well as systems analysts and researchers to create new uses for computers and computer technology.

Education and Training: While the type and technical level of a job will influence the required preparation, most computer-related jobs require education beyond high school. This training may be achieved through a specialized vocational program or a college degree program. Many positions also require a master's degree. One basic need for every position is that an applicant be computer literate with a basic understanding of computer systems and an ability to solve problems using a computer.

Salary Levels: Salaries vary widely in this career area, depending on the level of the job and training required. Computer operators, for example, receive salaries ranging from $15,000 to $35,000. Computer programmers earn from $20,000 to $60,000, while systems analysts have salaries that range from $28,000 to more than $70,000. Many individuals have earned millions of dollars by developing computer systems and successful software.

For Additional Information: Additional information about this career area is available from several sources, including the following:

Data Processing Management Association
505 Busse Highway
Park Ridge, IL 60068

Association for Systems Management
24587 Bagley Road
Cleveland, OH 44138

Financial Institutions and Banking Services

Unit 7

Unit Goals

After studying the chapters in this unit, you will be able to:

1. *List six services provided by banks.*
2. *Explain how to open and maintain a checking account.*
3. *Write an error-free check.*
4. *Reconcile a bank statement.*
5. *Name five means of payment other than cash or personal checks and tell when each should be used.*

Banking Has Come a Long Way

Business Brief

Many developments have occurred in our banking system through the years. Let's look at a brief sketch of how banks have changed.

The 1930s and 1940s. Banking meant a trip downtown. Bars separated tellers from customers,

but the tellers knew most customers by name. Transactions were recorded by hand. The 1930s and 1940s ushered in banking for the masses. Consumer banking was growing. A run on banks during the Great Depression brought about the birth of the Federal Deposit Insurance Corporation to protect customers' deposits.

The 1950s. America was becoming a mobile society. We fell in love with cars and the freedom they gave. They took us to drive-in hamburger stands and drive-in movies. Banks took the cue. Drive-up windows added convenience and come-as-you-are informality to banking.

The 1960s. Americans were still on the move—from the cities to suburbia. Shopping malls followed. Banks took their services to the suburbs, and branch banking was born. By the mid-1960s, branch banks outnumbered main banks by three to one.

The 1970s. Big things happened in the 1970s. The automatic teller machines (ATMs) meant 24-hour banking and they moved into malls, airports, supermarkets—everywhere. Through electronic funds transfer (EFT), ATMs allow us to deposit money, withdraw cash, pay bills, or transfer money instantly.

A savings bank in Massachusetts found a legal way to allow customers to write special checks—negotiable orders of withdrawal—on savings accounts, introducing the concept of interest on checking. The NOW account idea would soon spread throughout the industry.

The 1980s. Federal deregulation of banking in the early 1980s erased many differences among financial institutions. Rules allowing savings and loan associations (S&Ls) to pay higher interest rates than banks were erased, putting both in competition for the same savings dollars. S&Ls and credit unions began allowing checks on savings. Financial institutions were allowed to transact business formerly assigned to specific types of firms. Department stores, brokerages, and other firms began offering certain financial services, giving birth to "nonbank" banking. Increased uses of EFT began reducing the need for checks. Home computers began to be viewed as tools for "home banking."

The 1990s. In spite of decades of predictions that we would become a "checkless society," Americans have stubbornly adhered to the use of checks. Only through technology, such as EFT, has the financial system been able to keep pace. Deregulation will probably allow more changes in the way depository institutions expand in size, location, and variety of services. At the same time, federal regulations to provide security for deposits will probably be strengthened. Technology will continue to expand and to affect the way we do our banking.

Sources: Laura Zinn, "Electronic Banking May Have to Log Off," *Business Week* (April 10, 1989): 75; and "CheckFree Automates Personal Bill-Paying Nationwide with Low-Cost PC Software," *Personal Technology Times,* (March 15, 1989): 1.

The Banking System

Chapter 22

Chapter Objectives

After studying this chapter and completing the end-of-chapter activities, you will be able to:

1. *Give three reasons for depositing your money in a bank or other financial institution rather than keeping it at home.*

2. *Explain how banks earn most of their income.*

3. *Give three examples of ways in which the Federal Reserve System serves its member banks.*

4. *Name two federal government agencies that insure depositors' money.*

5. *Explain the difference between demand deposits and time deposits.*

6. *List six services provided by banks.*

7. *Give two examples of electronic funds transfer.*

"I had a crazy dream last night," Maria Melendez told her husband, Carlos, as she rushed to the breakfast table.

"Yeah? First your coffee; the eggs will be ready in a second. So—what did you dream this time?" Carlos asked.

"I dreamed that all of the banks and financial institutions in the whole country had closed—for good. We had to keep our money in a gift box in the closet. I loaded my backpack full of money and drove all over town paying bills—to the phone company, to the power company, to city hall to pay the water and waste disposal bills, to the department store to pay for the sweater you bought last month—everywhere! I kept thinking I'd never get around to pay them all, especially those that go to other cities and states. It was a nightmare! Wouldn't that be awful?"

"Sure would," Carlos replied. "You dreamed up some problems all right. Where would we borrow money to build our new house? And remember that our money in the closet wouldn't be earning any interest for us, either."

"Yeah, and someone might break in and steal it, too," Maria said.

"We'd sure be in a mess. Go back tonight and dream those banks open again! Meantime, let's get on the road, or we'll be late for work. Remember, we planned to stop by the bank on the way to work this morning and get some cash for grocery shopping tonight. That is, unless you have dreamed our automatic teller machine closed!" Carlos said laughing.

Fortunately, we do not have to handle money as Maria did in her dream because banks and other financial institutions are in business and open to provide us with convenient services, and the safety and growth of our money. They provide services that help you and the community to carry out daily business activities. These services are available to individuals, to businesses, and to government agencies in the community. One of the major ways banking serves you is by providing a safe place to keep your money until you need it. Banks can also help your money grow by putting it to work in the community through loans. Banks also offer advice on how to manage money so that it will be used in the best way. There are more than 150 ways in which banks and other financial institutions serve their customers.

BANKING AS A BUSINESS

Have you ever thought of a bank as a business and yourself as its customer? Many people do not think of banks in this way, yet a bank is a business just as stores and factories are businesses. As a business, a bank sells services. For their services, banks expect to earn a profit. Banks earn most of their income by charging for loans they make to individuals, businesses, and government and by investing part of the money customers deposit in the bank. Later in this chapter, you will learn about other sources of income for banks.

Since banks are businesses, can anybody start one? Well, not exactly. People who wish to start a bank must meet certain qualifications set up by federal and state governments. Since the bank owners are going to handle other people's money, they are expected to be responsible citizens of high moral character. They must also have enough capital to start the business operations.

People who want to start a bank must apply for a charter from their state or from the federal government. If they apply to their state and a charter is granted, the bank will operate as a state bank. If the charter is from the federal government, the bank will operate as a national bank. In bank titles, N.A. stands for National Association and is used today in place of the word "national." Many bank names today, however, do not convey the type of bank. A bank once named "Virginia National Bank" is now Sovran Bank, N.A.

REGULATION OF BANKS

A bank's operations are regulated more strictly than the operations of most businesses. If a business other than a bank fails, only a few people lose money. If a bank fails, thousands of people are affected. Government regulation is necessary to assure the safety of customers' money. Regulation of banks is assigned to the Treasury Department and its agencies. Even though Congress removed many regulations in 1983 and 1984, the government still exercises a great deal of control over the financial industry. State banks operate under the banking laws of the state in which the banks are located. National banks operate under federal laws as well as those of the state in which they are located.

The Federal Reserve System

The federal government set up the **Federal Reserve System (Fed)** to help banks serve the public efficiently by supervising and regulating member banks. All national banks are required to join the Federal Reserve System, and state banks may join. Banks that join the system are known as *member banks*. The United States is divided into 12 Federal Reserve districts, with a central Federal Reserve Bank in each district, as shown in Figure 22-1.

As an individual, you cannot open a savings account in a Federal Reserve Bank or borrow money from it. A Federal Reserve Bank is a bank for banks. Its relationship to member banks is similar to that of your bank to you.

Figure 22-1 Locate the Federal Reserve district in which you live. Is there a Federal Reserve Bank in your town or city?

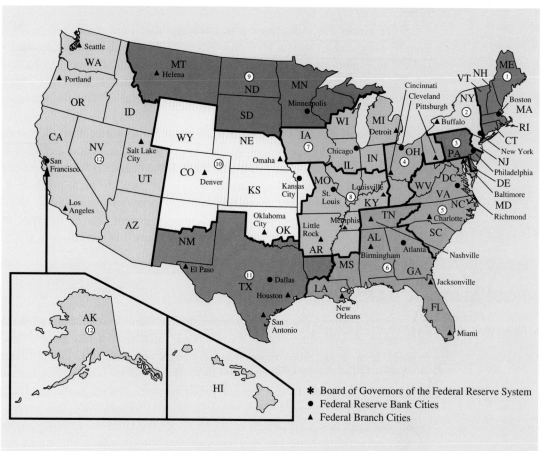

You may go to your bank to deposit money or to get a loan. The Federal Reserve Bank serves its member banks in the same way. It accepts their deposits, lends them money, and provides them with other banking services.

The Federal Deposit Insurance Corporation

Another federal agency that helps to regulate banks and certain savings institutions is the **Federal Deposit Insurance Corporation (FDIC)**. It protects depositors' money in case a bank or financial institution that it regulates fails. At present, the FDIC insures each account grouping—that is, all accounts at each bank in the same name—up to $100,000. Although the FDIC is a government agency, money for its operation is provided by banks rather than by government. Also, member banks of the Federal Reserve

Illus. 22-1
Federal Reserve
Banks serve other
banks.

MCMXXII

FEDERAL RESERVE
BANK
BUILDING ENTRANCE

System are required to join the FDIC. Nonmember banks may join by meeting certain requirements. Almost 99 percent of all banks are FDIC members. Other federal agencies regulate other types of financial institutions, as you will learn in the next section.

TYPES OF FINANCIAL INSTITUTIONS

Financial institutions are usually classified by the number and kinds of services they offer. They are also called *depository institutions*. There are several types. Let's look at some of the most common ones.

Commercial Banks

Most banks are organized as **commercial banks**. These are often called **full-service banks** because they offer a full range of financial services. Commercial banks handle checking accounts, make loans to individuals and to businesses, and provide a variety of other services. These services may be handled in different departments, such as a savings department, a trust department, a real estate department, or an investment department. Because commercial banks have so many different departments, they have been called "financial department stores." There are more than 14,000 commercial banks in the United States.

Special Purpose Banks

Some banks are organized for special purposes. **Savings banks**, for example, often provide a variety of services, but they are organized mainly to handle savings accounts and to make loans to home buyers. The major purpose of **trust companies** is managing people's money and property for them. As noted above, commercial banks also usually have a trust department that serves this purpose.

Banking Services from Other Financial Institutions

Other financial institutions, often called *thrifts*, also offer banking services. Among these are savings and loan associations, credit unions, and consumer finance companies.

Savings and loan associations (S&Ls) specialize in savings accounts and making loans for mortgages. Savings in S&Ls are usually protected by a government agency, which insures accounts in much the same way that the FDIC insures bank accounts. Until 1989, only the Federal Savings and Loan Insurance Corporation (FSLIC) insured accounts in S&Ls. At that time, because many S&Ls were having serious financial difficulty, the FDIC was given the added responsibility of closing or merging about 350 insolvent or financially unstable S&Ls. Although these S&Ls represented only a small percentage of the S&Ls in operation, their financial problems caused much concern in the economy. Transition of the insolvent S&L's from FSLIC to FDIC started in February 1989. While the FDIC was assigned the responsibility for handling the insurance for both banks and S&Ls, the insurance funds of the two industries remained separate.

In August 1989, to bring stability to the troubled thrift industry, Congress passed legislation to reorganize the industry. The Resolution Trust Corporation Oversight Board (RTC) was created to take over the task of closing, merging, or selling the S&Ls that could not meet the government's standards of solvency. In addition, a new insurance agency, the Savings Association Insurance Funds (SAIF, pronounced ''safe'') was created to keep S&L funds separate from bank funds in FDIC. SAIF has the responsibility of insuring depositors' funds in S&Ls. To further restore public confidence in thrifts, the legislation also required that, beginning immediately after the passing of the law, S&L firms display a new sign stating that savers' funds are ''backed by the full faith and credit of the United States government.''

Recently, many S&Ls have changed to savings banks and now include the words ''savings bank'' in their titles. For example, Lifetime Savings and Loan Association has become Lifetime Savings Bank.

A **credit union** is a type of bank that is formed by workers in the same firm, government agency, labor union, or other agency. Credit unions serve members only. They accept members' savings deposits and make loans to them for a variety of purposes. In recent years, credit unions have begun to offer other services such as special checking accounts, credit card services, electronic funds transfer services, auto loans, and loans to small firms in the credit union's business communities. Almost 15,000 credit unions were in operation in a recent year. They are regulated by the **National Credit Union Administration (NCUA)**, a federal agency similar to the FDIC. NCUA also insures a depositor's funds, up to $100,000, through its National Credit Union Share Insurance Fund.

Consumer finance companies specialize in making loans for durable goods, such as cars and refrigerators, and for financial emergencies. Because they make loans, they are a part of the financial services industry; however, they do not accept savings as do banks and other financial institutions.

As a result of decreased government regulation of the banking industry, the differences among banks, S&Ls, and credit unions are not as evident as they once were. Some banks now compete with S&Ls and credit unions for savings and other services. At the same time, some S&Ls and credit unions offer special checking services on their savings accounts.

Other changes are also occurring. Firms not usually associated with banking now sometimes offer selected financial services. These "nonbank" financial institutions include brokerage firms and credit agencies. For example, brokerage firms that buy and sell stocks for their customers now also provide special savings accounts on which customers can write checks. Some credit agencies, such as MasterCard and VISA, sometimes send a limited number of checks with a customer's statement, allowing them to write a check to obtain cash or to pay a bill. If the customer uses the checks, the amount of each check is charged to the customer's credit card account.

SERVICES OF BANKS

Whatever financial needs consumers or businesses may have, there is a financial institution to serve it. As depository institutions, most banks offer a common range of services, as well as specialized ones. Let's take a look at the most common services.

Accepting Deposits

One of the main services that financial institutions offer is accepting money from their customers for safekeeping. Sachi Kinoshita, a student who works part time and summers, is an example of a customer who uses this service. Sachi earns a take-home salary of $180 a week from her summer job on a road construction crew. She wants to save part of her earnings for a down payment on a car. Sachi knows that if she carries the money with her or keeps it at home, she may be tempted to spend it or it may be lost or stolen.

To protect her money, Sachi puts most of her weekly pay in the bank. The money she puts in the bank account is called a **deposit**. When she makes a deposit to her account, she becomes a *depositor*.

DEMAND AND TIME DEPOSITS

Sachi could deposit her money into a checking account where she can use it at any time by writing a check. A **check** is a depositor's written demand to a bank to pay out money from his or her account. Money put into a checking account is called a **demand deposit**. Since Sachi does not plan to use her money until she saves a large amount, she has chosen a savings account and will make time deposits instead. A **time deposit** is one that usually will be left in the bank for a period of time. Since Sachi's money is in a savings account, she is saying to the bank, "I'm going to leave this money in my account for a fairly long period of time—maybe six months to a year or longer—and you can use it until I need it." The bank can then make loans to other customers with Sachi's money, along with the funds of other depositors, and Sachi will be paid by the bank for the use of her money. The amount paid for the use of money is called **interest**. Let's say that Sachi deposits $500 of her summer wages in a savings account and leaves it there for a year. If the bank pays 6 percent interest on savings, Sachi's savings will have earned $30 in interest at the end of the year, and her car fund will have grown to $530.

CHECKING AND SAVINGS ACCOUNTS

At one time, there were two clear differences between checking and savings accounts: (1) Checking accounts did not earn interest as did savings accounts, and (2) you could not write checks on savings accounts. The differences between checking and savings accounts no longer exist to the extent that they once did. Certain types of checking accounts earn interest. Some types of savings accounts permit check writing. The bank may require the depositor to keep a minimum balance, such as $1,000, to earn interest on the account. These accounts are called **NOW (negotiable order of withdrawal) accounts.** A NOW account can be viewed as either a savings account on which checks can be written or a checking account that earns interest. There are many types of NOW accounts. Technically, a NOW account is not considered a demand deposit. Financial institutions may limit the number and frequency of checks that can be written on Now accounts.

Transferring Funds

Suppose that Edo Chan has a checking account that he uses to pay bills. He can pay his bills by instructing the bank to pay out, or transfer, a certain amount from his account to someone to whom he owes money. The bank provides different ways through which Edo can do this. One of the most common transfer methods is by check. When Edo writes a check to his rental agent to pay his rent, for example, the bank subtracts the amount of the check from Edo's account and, if the rental agent has an account at the same bank, the bank adds the amount to the rental agent's account. If the agent's account is at another bank, Edo's bank will transfer the funds to the agent's bank where they will be added to the agent's account. The transfer of funds is simply an accounting entry in the records; no actual cash has been handled in the transaction.

More and more banking is done through electronic funds transfer. **Electronic funds transfer (EFT)** is a system through which funds are moved electronically from one account to another and from one bank to another. You can instruct your bank to transfer funds automatically, for example, from your savings to your checking account without writing a check. Or you can pay monthly bills, such as your phone bill or your rent, by instructing your bank to transfer the amount automatically each month from your account to the phone company or the rental agent.

You can go to your bank in person or write a letter instructing the bank to make electronic transfers for you. You can also give the instructions to the bank at an automatic teller machine. An **automatic teller machine (ATM)** is a computer terminal provided by a bank to receive, dispense, and transfer

Illus. 22-2
Thanks to ATMs, customers can complete many banking transactions even when the bank is closed.

funds electronically for its customers. ATMs provide automatic teller service quickly and easily and are available 24 hours a day. Their popularity has brought about considerable growth in the EFT system, which is changing the way people do their banking. A fee may be charged by some banks for certain types of EFT transactions.

Lending Money

Many people, businesses, and government units need to borrow money at some time. For example, a business may want to borrow money to expand, to build a new warehouse, or to buy merchandise for resale. Individuals may borrow to buy a car or to pay college tuition. Banks will lend money to those who need to borrow if it seems likely that the loans will be repaid when due. In fact, a bank needs to make loans. You will recall that a bank receives most of its income from the interest it charges borrowers. Even when you buy items such as clothing or sports equipment and pay for them with a bank credit card, such as MasterCard or Visa, you are borrowing money from the bank.

Banks cannot lend all of the money they receive from their customers. The government requires banks to keep a certain amount of their customers' money on deposit with the Federal Reserve System so that the banks can meet the daily needs of their customers. Therefore, a bank will lend only a certain percentage of its customers' deposits and keep the rest in reserve. For example, if a customer deposits $1,000 and the bank is required by the Federal Reserve System at that time to hold 15 percent of all deposits in reserve, it can lend $850 ($1,000-15% or $150 = $850). This regulation is designed to help the banking system and the economy operate efficiently and to protect depositors' money.

Storing Valuables in Safe-Deposit Boxes

Besides offering a place to deposit money, banks offer **safe-deposit boxes** where you can store valuables. Since these boxes are in well-guarded vaults, they are the safest places to keep such things as jewelry, bond and stock certificates, birth records, a list of insurance policies, and a copy of a will. Not even a bank has the right to open your safe-deposit box unless it is ordered to do so by a court of law. The box can be opened only by you or by someone who has been given the right to open it for you. Safe-deposit boxes are rented by the year and you can choose from a variety of sizes to suit your needs.

Providing Financial Advice and Investment Services

Many banks help their customers by offering financial advice and investment services. Officers of a bank can advise customers about such things as

Illus. 22-3
Safe-deposit boxes provide a secure place to store your valuables.

whether it is wise to buy a certain house, how to manage money better, or how to exchange U.S. currency for foreign currency.

Most banks offer advice on investments that customers can make. **Investments** are savings that are put to work to earn more money. For example, money in a savings account is an investment because the savings account earns interest. Federal government bonds are another kind of investment that can be bought through a bank. If a depositor wants to buy bonds regularly, once a month, for example, the bank can automatically deduct the cost of each bond from the depositor's account. A bank can also cash government bonds for its customers and pay them whatever interest the bond has earned. Usually depositors are not charged for these services. You will learn more about investing in government bonds in Unit 9.

Banks also buy for their customers bonds issued by businesses, by state and local governments, and by school districts. Since the deregulation of the banking industry, banks can buy and sell stock for their customers. At present, however, banks cannot advise customers as to which stocks to buy or sell, as stockbrokers can, but this may change in the future.

Managing Trusts

Many banks manage investments for their customers. When they do this, the money or other property that is turned over to the banks for investment is said to be held in trust. This service can be offered through a trust company or through trust departments in banks.

Trust departments are used by people of all ages, but they are especially useful for very young people and for elderly people. A young person who inherits money may not have the skill and experience to manage it wisely. Elderly people may have the trust department of a bank manage their money because they no longer want to do it. The bank makes investments and keeps the customers informed about what is happening to their money.

BANKS AND COMMUNITY GROWTH

There is a great deal more to banking than that which you have read in this chapter. But from what you have learned so far, you can see that banks are important to all of us. More than 1.6 million people work in America's 62,000 banking offices. Banking services help build homes, start new businesses, plant crops, finance educations, buy goods, pave streets, build hospitals, and buy new equipment. These services are made possible because of the savings of many people.

Bank deposits do not remain idle in bank vaults. They are put to work. When you deposit money in your bank, you are making your money work for you and your community.

Increasing Your Business Vocabulary

The following terms should become part of your business vocabulary. For each numbered item, find the term that has the same meaning.

automatic teller machine (ATM)
check
commercial or full-service bank
consumer finance companies
credit union
demand deposit
deposit
electronic funds transfer (EFT)
Federal Deposit Insurance Corporation (FDIC)
Federal Reserve System (Fed)

interest
investments
National Credit Union Administration (NCUA)
NOW (negotiable order of withdrawal) accounts
safe-deposit boxes
savings and loan associations (S&Ls)
savings banks
time deposit
trust companies

1. Banks that mainly handle savings accounts and make loans to home buyers.
2. A bank that offers a full range of financial

services; sometimes called a "financial department store."

3. Money that is placed in a bank account by a customer.

4. A nationwide banking plan set up by our federal government to assist banks in serving the public more efficiently by supervising and regulating member banks.

5. An amount paid for the use of money.

6. A depositor's written demand to a bank to pay out money from his or her account.

7. Banks that specialize in managing the money and property of others.

8. Financial institutions that specialize in savings accounts and loans for mortgages.

9. A financial institution formed by workers in the same organization that serves only its members.

10. Financial institutions that specialize in making loans for durable goods and financial emergencies.

11. A federal agency that protects depositors'

12. money in case a bank or financial institution that it regulates fails.

12. A savings account on which checks can be drawn or a checking account that earns interest; each may require a minimum balance and may limit withdrawals.

13. A deposit that usually will be left in the bank for a period of time.

14. Boxes in a bank vault for storing valuables.

15. A system through which funds are moved electronically from one account to another and from one bank to another.

16. Savings that are put to work to earn more money.

17. A computer terminal provided by a bank to receive, dispense, and transfer funds electronically for its customers.

18. Money put into a checking account.

19. A federal agency that insures depositors' funds in credit unions up to $100,000.

Reviewing Your Reading

1. State three reasons for depositing your money in the bank rather than keeping it at home.

2. How do banks earn most of their income? Name two other ways in which banks earn income.

3. Why is government regulation of banks thought to be necessary?

4. Name three services the Federal Reserve System provides for its member banks.

5. Name federal agencies that insure depositors' money.

6. How is a full-service bank different from a special-purpose bank?

7. How does a credit union differ from a savings and loan association?

8. How are banks and S&Ls becoming more alike?

9. Explain the difference between demand deposits and time deposits.

10. What do the letters "NOW" mean in a NOW account? Explain the account.

11. Give an example of an electronic funds transfer.

12. List six services provided by banks.

13. What two age groups find trust departments of banks especially helpful? Why?

14. Give three examples to show the importance of banks to the economy of the community.

Using Your Business Knowledge

1. Alicia Perez and Miguel Morales operate a small film rental store. Each day they deposit all of the cash they received except a small amount of change and a few bills

that they keep in their safe. Explain why they are wise to follow this method of handling their money.

2. List the type of banking service that you think each group or individual below would be most likely to use. Explain your answer.
   a. A person planning to open a fitness center
   b. A pop vocal group
   c. A wealthy senior citizen
   d. A buyer of a van
   e. A high school recycling club

Computing Business Problems

1. Sachi Kinoshita, as you remember, is saving money for a car. She worked 12 weeks during the summer on a road construction crew. Her take-home pay was $180 a week.
   a. If she deposited each paycheck in the bank, what was the total amount she deposited during the summer?
   b. If she put $75 each week in her savings account, how much had she saved during the summer?
   c. If she leaves her accumulated summer savings in the bank for a year at 6.5 percent interest, how much will she have available for a down payment on a car at the end of the year?
2. On October 1, Susan Pohlnik had a checking account balance of $120. She has her paychecks automatically deposited into her account. Her earnings for October were $920. During the month, she wrote checks for $75, $125, $25, and $250. She also had $100 automatically transferred from her checking account to her savings account. In addition she used her EFT card at an automatic teller machine to withdraw $50 in cash. The bank charges 50 cents for each EFT transaction. Find Susan's bank balance after these transactions.

3. Jake Olsen's "Great Jake's Great Brownies" won for him $1,000 in an original recipe bake-off contest sponsored by the local television station. He has decided to put all of his winnings in the bank. List several questions Jake might want to ask before choosing whether to put the money in a checking or a savings account.

4 "In a private enterprise system, anybody who wants to open a bank should be allowed to do so." Do you agree with this statement? Give reasons for your answer.

3. To raise money for a Christmas party for patients at a local children's hospital, a business club at Martin Luther King High School sold cans of trail mix. The 0.5 kilogram cans sold for $2.50 each. The students deposited the total amount of their sales each week in the school's accounting office. During one month, the records of the three students with the highest sales showed the following:

Date	Jose Santos	Darlana Jones	Carl Perlman
Nov. 5	12 cans	3 cans	5 cans
12	7	5	4
19	5	9	4
26	13	10	6

a. How many cans did each student sell?
b. How much did each student deposit during November?
c. How many kilograms of trial mix did each student sell?
d. Find the number of pounds sold by each of the three students. (See Appendix D for information regarding metric conversion.)

e. If the trail mix cost the students $1.25 per can, what was the amount of their profit on sales for November?

4. Deposits in banks and S&Ls are insured up to $100,000 by FDIC or SAIF. The insurance is paid for by the banks and S&Ls just as individuals buy insurance for their homes or cars. The regulating agency sets the amount charged to the financial institutions based on the amount of deposits in the firm. The data in the right-hand column show the rate charged to S&Ls in a recent year and a proposed rate change.

Fidelity S&L Association

Deposits: $5,650,000

Current insurance rate per $100
  of deposits: 20.3 cents

Proposed rate per $100
  of deposits: 23 cents

a. What is the percent of increase in the rate?

b. What is the cost of Fidelity's insurance at the current rate?

c. What will Fidelity's cost of insurance be at the proposed rate?

d. What is the amount of the increase?

Expanding Your Understanding of Business

1. Many changes have taken place in banking during the last 25 years. You have read about some in this chapter. Talk with your parents and neighbors and see how many changes in banking you can list that have taken place during that period. As a start, you might list evening banking hours. Compile a single list from all of the changes noted by all of the members of your class.

2. Find the following information about at least one bank in your community:
   a. What is the name and address of the bank?
   b. Is it a state bank or a national bank?
   c. Has the bank changed its name in recent years? Why?
   d. Does it belong to the Federal Reserve System?
   e. Is it a commercial bank, or has it been organized for a special purpose?
   f. Does it provide safe-deposit facilities for its customers?
   g. Does the bank offer services other than those presented in this chapter? If so, give a brief explanation of each.

3. Five examples of items that might be kept in a safe-deposit box were given in this chapter. Talk with several adults and try to find out at least five other items that are stored in safe-deposit boxes. For example, one bank gives its customers a list of 27 items to be stored in safe-deposit boxes. Also ask if there are items that should not be kept in safe-deposit boxes and tell why they should be kept elsewhere.

4. Interview someone who works for a credit union, such as a teller or a manager in a credit union office. Find out what services the credit union offers its members. Why are people who use the credit union called members instead of depositors? Write a brief report of your findings to share with the class.

5. Interview a manager of a credit union or savings and loan association and find out how NOW accounts work. You might include such questions as these in your interview:
   a. How is a NOW account opened?
   b. Must a certain balance be maintained?
   c. Is there a limit to the number of checks (negotiable order of withdrawals) that may be written on the account?

d. What are the advantages and disadvantages of NOW accounts?

6. Some people prefer to continue to use checks rather than use electronic funds transfer. Talk with several people who have bank accounts and find out their opinions about EFT. Report your findings by listing several advantages and disadvantages of the EFT system.

7. Some banks have ATMs that accept not only their own ATM cards, but also other banks' cards and credit cards such as VISA and MasterCard. Find out if a bank in your city has multiple-card ATMs. Write a brief report on the bank's ATM process and share it with the class.

Using a Checking Account

Chapter Objectives

After studying this chapter and completing the end-of-chapter activities, you will be able to:

1. List four advantages of having a checking account.

2. Explain the difference between the two major types of checking accounts.

3. Explain why a bank requires you to sign a signature card when you open a checking account.

4. Describe the procedure for making a deposit.

5. Show how to record your first deposit on a check stub or register.

Every once in a while, a comedian will repeat the old joke about the unsophisticated checking account owner. It goes something like this: The bank informs the customer that several checks have been returned because the account is overdrawn. "But that's impossible!" the surprised customer responds. "I can't be overdrawn—I have some checks left in my checkbook."

That little anecdote continues to get laughs because we all remember all of the questions we had about using our first checking account. This chapter and the two that follow are designed to help you open your first checking account and understand and manage it with confidence. Many people before you have learned to do this. From 1980 to 1990, the volume of checks written each year in the United States increased from 34 billion to 52 billion. A look at some of the advantages will show why checking accounts are so popular.

ADVANTAGES OF PAYING THROUGH A CHECKING ACCOUNT

When you open a checking account, you will find that it will be a convenient way to handle your business affairs. With a checking account, you can write checks at home and pay your bills by mail. Or, as you have learned, you can make payments automatically through the EFT system. Both methods will save time, energy, and money.

In addition to convenience, using a checking account to make payments also has many safety advantages. People who keep a great deal of money on hand risk losing it by fire, theft, or carelessness. When money is at home, there is also a greater temptation to spend it needlessly. With a checking account, you will need to keep only a little cash on hand for small purchases.

Another safety feature is that you can safely send a check through the mail because it can be cashed only by the person or business to whom it is made payable. It is not safe to send cash through the mail because if it is lost, there is no way to recover it. However, if a check is lost in the mail, it can be replaced.

As you learned in Chapter 22, the money you deposit in the bank is protected in another way. If the bank is a member of the Federal Deposit Insurance Corporation, your deposit will be insured up to $100,000. You should always check to see that the bank in which you deposit your money is an FDIC bank. If you deposit your money in a savings and loan association, you should verify that it is a member of a federal insuring agency. The same caution applies wherever you deposit your money: first find out what kind of insurance protection your money will have.

A third advantage of paying by check is that, once cashed, a check is legal proof of payment. For example, suppose you write a check each month for $20 to pay for tennis lessons at the Indoor Tennis and Fitness Center. The

Illus. 23-1
Checking accounts provide a safe and convenient way to make payments.

Center will deposit your check at its bank. The Center's bank will then send the check to your bank where it will be subtracted from your account. Most banks return checks to depositors with "paid" stamped on the back. If the Center makes an error in its records and later tells you that a past month's fee has not been paid, your returned check will prove that you made the payment. Even if your bank does not return checks, it keeps a record of all checks paid and you can request that a copy of the check be sent to you. You can use the copy as proof of payment.

Another advantage of checking accounts is that they provide a record of your finances. With a checking account, you must record every deposit you make and every check you write. You can tell from these records how much you are spending, where your money is going, and how much you have remaining in your account. The organized records you keep help you manage your money. It is obvious that the bank customer in the opening anecdote was not keeping a record of the checks that were written. You will learn how to keep these records in Chapter 24.

There are many advantages to paying through a checking account. Now that you know some of the main ones, your next step is to learn what kinds of checking accounts are available.

KINDS OF CHECKING ACCOUNTS

Many things in banking have changed in recent years; the kinds of checking accounts offered by banks are among those changes. Checking accounts differ from one bank to another and from one part of the country to another. They differ in the features they offer customers. They also differ in costs, such as service charges. A **service charge** is a fee a bank charges for handling a checking account. When you are ready to open a checking account, you should visit several banks to find out what each offers. A bank employee will explain the advantages and disadvantages of each kind of account the bank offers. Shopping for your checking account will enable you to choose one that best suits your needs.

While there are still many types of accounts in use, recent changes have tended to put them into two basic groups: regular checking accounts and interest checking accounts.

Regular Checking Accounts

If you write a large number of checks each month, you probably should use a regular checking account. With some banks, there is no service charge for a regular checking account as long as the account balance does not fall below a certain amount during a month. This balance varies, but it may be as high as $300 or more. Sometimes the charges are figured on the average balance of the account during the month. This means that the account may fall below a certain minimum on some days, but must average at or above the minimum at the end of the month to avoid a service charge. Figure 23-1 illustrates the minimum and average balance requirements for regular checking accounts at Gulfstream Bank. Some banks also do not charge service fees on checking accounts to people who keep a certain balance, often $1,000, in a savings account in the bank. Service charges are also waived by some banks for people 65 years old or older.

Interest Checking Accounts

If you are able to keep a rather large balance in your account, you may choose an interest checking account. Banks differ in their requirements. Some banks may require a minimum balance of $500 or an average daily balance of $1,000. A *minimum monthly balance* is a stated amount that an account must not fall below. An *average monthly balance* is the sum of the daily balances divided by the number of days in the month. As long as the account meets the balance requirement, the bank will pay interest on the checking account. If the account falls below the required amount, the bank usually pays no interest and may also add a service charge to the account. The charges may include a monthly charge, a fee for each check written, or both of these service charges.

The rates of interest that banks pay their customers also vary. Typical rates are 5 or $5^1/_4$ percent a year when required balances are maintained. In some cases, a bank may offer a higher rate of interest for a higher maintained

Figure 23-1 Fees charged and interest rates paid by banks may vary from bank to bank.

Interest rates and service charges.

	Minimum Balance		Average Monthly Balance	Interest	Monthly Service Charge
Regular Checking	$300 $0—299	or and	$600 $0—599		$0 $6
Interest Checking	$500 $0—499	or and	$1,500 $0—1,499	5 1/4%	$0 $7
Preferred Interest Checking			$10,000 + $5,000—9,999 $2,500—4,999 $0—2,499	premium rate money market rate money market rate 5 1/4%	$0 $0 $5 $8

Interest Checking and Preferred Interest Checking Accounts closed between interest payment periods will not receive interest for that monthly period.

GULFSTREAM BANK

Member FDIC

balance. The interest rate may be based on the current cost of money in the marketplace. This rate is known as the **money market rate**. It is the interest rate that big users of money, such as governments and large corporations, pay when they borrow money. For example, the federal government announces each week what interest rate it has to pay to borrow money from citizens, banks, and businesses. The rate, along with other rates that make up the money market rate, may vary from day to day.

Banks offer interest checking accounts with varying rates tied to the money market rate. As this rate changes, so does the rate the banks pay depositors in certain types of accounts. To avoid changing rates daily or weekly, the bank, at the end of a month or a three-month period, determines the average of the daily money market rates for the month and pays the depositor that average rate for the period. Even higher rates than money market rates are sometimes available for very large accounts. Gulfstream Bank's interest checking account requirements are shown in Figure 23-1 as an example.

Variations of Basic Checking Accounts

In addition to the two basic kinds of checking accounts, there are several other types that you may want to examine as you shop for an account.

You may need to write only a few checks each month and may wish to keep only a small balance in your checking account. For depositors with such needs, many banks offer special checking accounts. Charges on the accounts vary, but the basic charge is about 10 cents to 20 cents for each check written and paid by the bank. There may also be a small monthly service charge for the account.

Some banks also offer a variety of banking services along with the usual checking account services in a package-plan account. With such an account, you may use a variety of bank services for a monthly fee. The fees vary from bank to bank according to the number of services included in the package. The package plan eliminates separate fees usually charged for services such as checking account maintenance, traveler's checks, and credit card privileges.

In Chapter 22, you learned that financial institutions other than banks offer checking services. Savings and loan associations, for example, also offer NOW accounts. You will recall that these accounts earn interest and allow you to write checks called negotiable orders of withdrawal. These accounts usually require that a minimum balance be maintained in order to earn interest. The required balances vary among types of accounts and among institutions.

Some credit unions also provide NOW accounts to their members. Members in credit unions are called *shareholders* when they have money on deposit, and their checks are called **sharedrafts**. This means a draft (withdrawal) is made on the member's shares of ownership (deposits) in the credit union. Interest rates may vary and the number of shared drafts may be limited.

As you also learned in Chapter 22, brokerage firms also offer for their investment customers accounts on which checks can be written. These accounts usually earn interest at money market rates.

Now you know the most common kinds of checking accounts that are available. Which kind would you choose if you were opening a checking account?

YOUR CHECKING ACCOUNT

The procedure for opening a checking account is the same regardless of the kind of account you choose. Opening a checking account is easy. You can simply take your paycheck or cash to the new-accounts desk in any bank and say that you want to open an account. The representative will help you sign a signature card, make your deposit, and select your checks. Some banks may require you to be 18 years old or older to open a checking account.

Signing the Signature Card

A bank will take money from a checking account only when authorized to do so by the depositor. Therefore, the bank must keep the depositor's signature on record to compare with the signature that appears on his or her checks. For this reason, you will be asked to sign your name on a card when you open your account. This card is called a **signature card** and is the banks's official record of your signature. You must use the same signature on each check you write. Figure 23-2 shows a signature card for Alan Edwards.

Figure 23-2
The signature on your checks must match the one on your signature card that is on file at your bank.

Second National Bank
PERSONAL CHECKING ACCOUNT

○ JOINT AND SEVERAL (Payable to the order of either or the survivor)
● INDIVIDUAL (If payable on death to named survivors, fill in section below)
— Indicate number of signatures required

Alan Edwards
SIGNATURE

_____
SIGNATURE

Alan Edwards   or _____
PRINT OR TYPE NAME(S)

19684 La Paloma Dr., Houston, TX 77083-5549   2 years
ADDRESS   CITY AND STATE   ZIP CODE   HOW LONG? MO. YRS.

555-6403   720J64 – TX
HOME PHONE   DRIVERS LICENSE NO./STATE

PAYABLE ON DEATH OF DEPOSITOR TO SUCH OF THE FOLLOWING NAMED AS SURVIVE DEPOSITOR:

(PRINT OR TYPE NAME - DESIGNATION BY OTHER MEANS IS NOT SUFFICIENT.)

Office: _____   Date: ____ April 10, 19--

OFFICER APPROVAL	201-24-1590	1648-7214
	SOCIAL SECURITY NUMBER	ACCOUNT NUMBER

Sometimes two or more people have an account together. This is known as a **joint account**. Each person who will write checks on the account must sign the signature card. Any signer of the card in a joint account can write checks on the account as if he or she were the only owner. A signature card for a business would show the name of the business and the signatures of everyone authorized to sign checks for the business.

Making Your First Deposit

When you deposit money in your checking account, you will fill out a **deposit slip** or a **deposit ticket** that must accompany your deposit. This is a form on which you list all items you are depositing—currency, coins, or checks.

The deposit slip shows your name as depositor, your account number, the date, the items deposited, and the total amount of the deposit. Most banks print the depositor's name, address, and account number on deposit slips and checks. Since these will not be ready when you open your new account, you will use a blank deposit slip. Figure 23-3 shows a deposit slip made out by Alan Edwards. His deposit consisted of $60 in currency, $1.75 in coin, and his paycheck for $270.10, for a total of $331.85.

Figure 23-3
Alan Edwards has completed a deposit slip for a total deposit of $331.85.

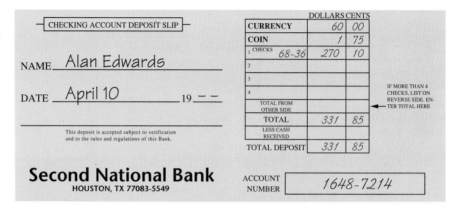

ENDORSING THE CHECK FOR DEPOSIT

Before Alan can deposit his paycheck, he must endorse it by writing his name on the back of the check near the trailing edge, or left end. The right edge is the leading edge. An **endorsement** is written evidence that you received payment or that you transferred your right of receiving payment to someone else. Because space must be reserved for the bank's stamp showing the date of payment, the endorsement must be in the top 1¹/₂ inches of the trailing edge of the check. You will learn about different kinds of endorsements in a later chapter. Here you will see how Alan endorsed his check to deposit it to his new account.

To endorse a check, sign your name in ink exactly as it is written on the face of the check. The endorsement should match your signature on the signature card. If the name on the check is different from your official signature, you will need to endorse the check twice. In Figure 23-4, Alan first endorsed his paycheck "A. C. Edwards" as it appeared on the check. Then he signed it "Alan Edwards" as he had written it on the signature card. Alan is now ready to list his endorsed check on the deposit slip.

RECORDING CHECKS ON THE DEPOSIT SLIP

Each check is identified by the number of the bank on which it was drawn. This number is assigned to each commercial bank by the American Bankers

Figure 23-4
Why did Alan
have to endorse
this check twice?

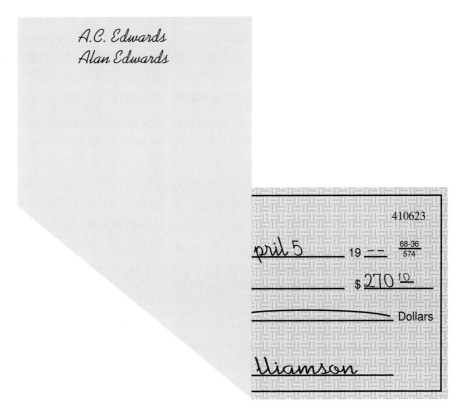

A.C. Edwards
Alan Edwards

410623

pril 5 _____ 19 _ _ $\frac{68-36}{574}$

$270 $\frac{10}{}$

_____ Dollars

Uiamson

Association. You can see the three parts of this number in Figure 23-5. The
first part of the number above the line indicates the city or state in which the
bank is located. The second part is the number assigned to the individual
bank. The number below the line is a Federal Reserve number that banks use
in sorting checks.

Figure 23-5
Each commercial
bank in the
United States is
assigned a
number by the
American
Bankers
Association.

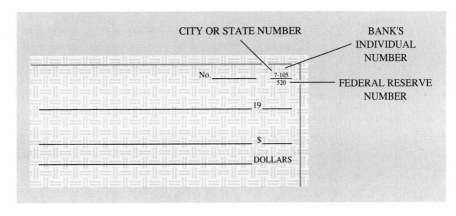

CITY OR STATE NUMBER   BANK'S
                                        INDIVIDUAL
                                        NUMBER

No._____ $\frac{7-105}{520}$

                                        FEDERAL RESERVE
                                        NUMBER

_____19____

$_____

DOLLARS

The two top numbers may be listed on the deposit slip, as shown in Figure 23-3 on page 332. Checks may also be listed on the deposit slip by the name of the person from whom the check was received or by the name of the bank on which it was drawn. You should use the method your bank prefers.

GETTING A RECEIPT FOR YOUR DEPOSIT

When you make a deposit to your checking account, the bank teller will give you a receipt. The receipt may be printed by a machine at the same time that it registers the deposit in the bank's records. This type of receipt is shown in Figure 23-6.

Figure 23-6
No matter how you make deposits to your account, be sure to get a receipt each time.

FIRST NATIONAL BANK OF DAWSON

MEMBER
FEDERAL DEPOSIT INSURANCE CORPORATION   DAWSON, ALASKA

ALL ITEMS ARE CREDITED SUBJECT TO PAYMENT
THIS IS YOUR RECEIPT
THE BANK SYMBOL, TRANSACTION NUMBER, DATE AND AMOUNT OF YOUR DEPOSIT ARE SHOWN BELOW

FNB 425 ⅏JUN **1**   **50.00** D44

ALWAYS OBTAIN OFFICIAL RECEIPT WHEN MAKING A DEPOSIT

Another type of receipt has a stamped or written acknowledgment of the deposit on a duplicate copy of the deposit slip. Deposits may also be made at automatic teller machines located away from the bank building. Figure 23-7 shows a receipt for a deposit made at an automatic teller station.

Deposits may also be sent through the mail. The bank records your deposit and mails a receipt back to you. Remember, mail deposits should not include cash because it may be lost.

Selecting Your Checkbook

When you become a depositor, your bank will supply you with blank checks bound in a **checkbook**. Checkbooks may be supplied without charge on some kinds of accounts, but usually banks charge a fee when the depositor's name and address are printed on each check and deposit slip. Today checks may be personalized in ways other than just printing the depositor's name.

Figure 23-7
This receipt for a deposit to a checking account was issued at an automatic teller station.

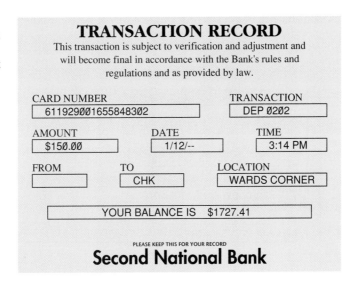

TRANSACTION RECORD

This transaction is subject to verification and adjustment and will become final in accordance with the Bank's rules and regulations and as provided by law.

CARD NUMBER
6119290016558483Ø2

TRANSACTION
DEP Ø2Ø2

AMOUNT
$15Ø.ØØ

DATE
1/12/--

TIME
3:14 PM

FROM

TO
CHK

LOCATION
WARDS CORNER

YOUR BALANCE IS $1727.41

PLEASE KEEP THIS FOR YOUR RECORD

Second National Bank

You may also choose from a variety of colors and designs; an example is shown in Figure 23-8.

Besides the checks, a checkbook also contains forms on which a depositor writes a record of deposits made and checks written. In some checkbooks, this record is kept on the **check stub**, which is attached to each check, as shown in Figure 23-9. Another type of checkbook provides a **check register**, which is a separate form for recording deposits and checks. Checkbooks also often contain deposit slips.

When checks are printed, the bank number and the account number are usually printed in magnetic ink. These magnetic ink numbers enable banks

Figure 23-8
Depositors may now choose from a wide variety of check designs.

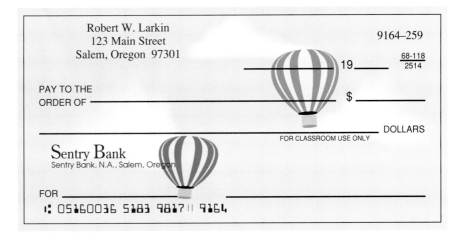

Robert W. Larkin
123 Main Street
Salem, Oregon 97301

9164–259

19_____

68-118
2514

PAY TO THE
ORDER OF _____

$ _____

_____ DOLLARS

FOR CLASSROOM USE ONLY

Sentry Bank
Sentry Bank, N.A., Salem, Oregon

FOR _____

⑈: Ø5⅃6ØØ⅃6 5⅃83 98⅃7⑈ 9⅃64

Figure 23-9 The check stub attached to a check provides one way to keep checking account records. The stub is completed when the check is written.

347	$ _____
	_____ 19 _____
TO _____	
FOR _____	

	DOLLARS	CENTS
BAL. FOR'D		
DEPOSITS		
TOTAL		
THIS CHECK		
OTHER DEDUCTIONS		
BAL. FOR'D		

Delena Kolberg
984 Birchwood Drive
Mystic, CT 06355–7582

347

92-403
1241

_____ 19 _____

PAY TO THE
ORDER OF _____ $ _____

_____ DOLLARS

FOR CLASSROOM USE ONLY

Riverview National Bank
Mystic, CT 06355-7582

FOR _____

⑆124404035⑆   326�011016622⑈

to sort checks quickly using machines that electronically read the numbers. Figure 23-8 shows magnetic ink numbers in the lower left corner of the check.

Recording Your Deposit

When you make a deposit to your checking account, you should immediately enter the amount on the check stub or in the check register. Figure 23-10

Figure 23-10 A check register is one way to maintain checking account records. Like the stub, the register is completed at the time each check is written or a deposit is made.

PLEASE BE SURE TO **DEDUCT** CHARGES THAT AFFECT YOUR ACCOUNT

ITEM NO. OR TRANSACTION CODE	DATE	DESCRIPTION OF TRANSACTION	AMOUNT OF PAYMENT OR WITHDRAWAL (–)	✓	TAX OR OTHER	AMOUNT OF DEPOSIT OR INTEREST (+)	BALANCE FORWARD
		SUBTRACTIONS				ADDITIONS	
D	19-- 4/10	TO *Opening deposit* FOR *Paycheck 271.10; cash 61.75*				331 85	331 85 B A L 331 85
		TO FOR					B A L
		TO FOR					B A L
		TO FOR					B A L
		TO FOR					B A L
		TO FOR					B A L
		TO FOR					B A L
		TO FOR					B A L

shows how Alan Edwards recorded the information for his deposit in his check register. Since Alan is opening a new account, there is no balance to be entered on the "Balance Forward" line.

Alan Edwards is now ready to write checks up to the amount he has deposited in his account. In the next chapter, you will learn how this is done.

Increasing Your Business Vocabulary

The following terms should become part of your business vocabulary. For each numbered item, find the term that has the same meaning.

checkbook   *joint account*
check register   *money market rate*
check stub   *service charge*
deposit slip or deposit ticket   *sharedrafts*
endorsement   *signature card*

1. A form that accompanies a deposit and lists the items deposited—currency, coins, or checks.
2. A form attached to a check on which a depositor keeps a record of the checks written and any current deposit.
3. Written evidence that you received payment or that you transferred your right of receiving payment to someone else.
4. A separate form on which the depositor keeps a record of deposits and checks.
5. A card, kept by a bank, that shows the signatures of all individuals authorized to draw checks against the account.
6. A bank account that is used by two or more people.
7. A bound book containing blank checks and forms on which a depositor writes a record of deposits made and checks written.
8. A fee a bank charges for handling a checking account.
9. The current cost of money in the marketplace.
10. Withdrawals made on a member's shares of ownership (deposits) in a credit union.

Reviewing Your Reading

1. What are the advantages of paying bills through a checking account?
2. Why should a person who wishes to open a checking account be interested in knowing whether or not the institution is a member of the FDIC or SAIF?
3. Explain the difference between the two major kinds of checking accounts.
4. Describe several variations of the two basic kinds of checking accounts.
5. Name two kinds of fees that can be included in the service charges.
6. What is the difference between a minimum balance and an average monthly balance?

7. Why does a bank require you to sign a signature card when you open a checking account?
8. Describe the process for making a deposit.
9. If the name on the face of a check and the depositor's official signature are not alike, how should the depositor endorse the check?
10. Explain the meaning of each of the three parts of an American Bankers Association number.
11. By what three methods may checks be listed on a deposit ticket?

12. If you have both cash and checks to deposit, should you send the deposit by mail? Why?
13. Explain the difference between check stubs and a check register.
14. Why are account numbers printed in magnetic ink on checks and deposit tickets?
15. Explain the procedure for recording the first deposit to a new account on a check register.

Using Your Business Knowledge

1. "You should shop for the best place to open a checking account as carefully as you shop for the best buy in any product or service." Give two reasons to support this statement.
2. If you sign your full name on the signature card and when you open your checking account and then sign your nickname on a check, do you think the bank should pay the check? Give a reason for your answer.
3. Ann and Walter Neal have a joint checking account and both have signed the signature card. Must they both sign each check? Why?
4. Akeo Mori attends a technical school in the morning and works afternoons and weekends as a receptionist at a skating rink. He believes that if he deposits his earnings in a checking account and writes checks to pay the few monthly bills he has, he could better manage his money. What kind of checking account would you recommend for Akeo? Why?

Computing Business Problems

1. Shana Brown wrote a check to make a deposit to her savings account and three checks to pay her monthly bills. The checks were written for the following amounts: savings, $100; rent, $325; electric bill, $92.50; gasoline bill, $72.25. This left a new checkbook balance of $290.25.
   a. What is the total amount of Shana's monthly bills?
   b. What is the total amount of Shana's four checks?
   c. What was Shana's checkbook balance before she wrote the four checks?
2. Service charges for Tom Harding's regular checking account at Second National Bank are based on the bank's rate schedule, which follows:

Minimum Balance	Charge
0 - $199	$6
$200 - $399	4
$400 and over	no charge

During a recent six-month period, his balances were April, $142; May, $194.20; June, $97.70; July, $402.43; August, $238.74; and September, $254.36.

a. How much was Tom's service charge for each month?

b. What was the total service charge for the six-month period?

3. The rate schedule at Gulfstream Bank is shown in Figure 23-1 on page 329. Wanda Settle's interest checking account at Gulfstream had an average monthly balance for June of $1,621.80.

a. Is Wanda eligible to earn interest on her account for June?

b. If the bank paid $5\frac{1}{4}$ percent annual interest on the average monthly balance, how much interest will she earn for June?

Expanding Your Understanding of Business

1. The numbers printed in magnetic ink in the lower left corner of a check are written in a kind of computer language called Magnetic Ink Character Recognition or MICR. In Figure 23-8 on page 335, you will notice two groups of MICR numbers. The first group is the bank's number for identification and routing and the second group is the customer's account number. When the bank pays a check you have written, the check is returned to you with another MICR number printed in the lower right corner. Ask your parents or another person who has a checking account to let you examine the returned check and find out what the added MICR number is. Report your findings to the class.

2. Many banks today do not have a minimum age requirement for a person who wants to open a checking account. Visit a local bank or talk with a bank employee to find out if there is an age requirement at the bank. Find out if the bank's policy is based on a state banking regulation or if the decision is left to the individual bank. Write a brief report on the reasons given for having or not having an age requirement.

3. Find out what a split deposit is and prepare a deposit slip to show how such a deposit is made.

4. Below is a list of terms that relate to joint bank accounts. Write a short definition of each term. You might refer to a high school business law textbook or ask a bank employee to help you with your definitions.

a. Joint and several

b. Tenants in common

c. Joint tenants with right of survivorship

d. Tenants by entirety

Writing and Receiving Checks

Chapter 24

Chapter Objectives

After studying this chapter and completing the end-of-chapter activities, you will be able to:

1. *Correctly maintain checking account records on check stubs or in a check register.*

2. *Write error-free checks.*

3. *State three purposes of endorsements.*

4. *Identify three types of endorsements and explain when each is used.*

5. *Correctly endorse a check.*

Now that Alan Edwards, whom you met in Chapter 23, has opened his checking account and has made his first deposit, he is ready to write and receive checks through the account. As you learn, along with Alan, how easy and convenient it is to manage a checking account, you will probably wonder how you ever got along without one. You will join more than 100 million other owners of checking accounts who write more than 52 billion checks each year.

Checks are important pieces of paper. They travel across town and across the country to make both personal and business payments. Each check is finally either returned to the person who wrote it or stored at his or her bank. Most people consider their checking accounts an important part of their money management. If you learn to write checks and record your banking activities correctly, you will find that using your checking account is easy and enjoyable.

GETTING ACQUAINTED WITH YOUR CHECKS

A good way to get acquainted with checks is to examine several different checks belonging to relatives or friends. You will find that the checks look alike even though they are from different banks. Compare them to the check shown in Figure 24-1. Note that all checks have basically the same kind of information printed in the same places.

As you study the parts of the check in Figure 24-1, you will find some terms that are used to identify the parts which appear on its face or front. At the upper left and the lower right, you will see the word "drawer." The **drawer** is the owner of the account and the person who signs the check. The **payee** is the person to whom the check is written. The payee's name always appears after the words "Pay to the order of." The **drawee** is the bank or other financial institution in which the account is held. Three parties, as you see, are shown on each check: the drawer, the payee, and the drawee. You may want to refer to the parts of a check in Figure 24-1 as you learn to write checks in the next section.

WRITING A CHECK

In addition to checks, your checkbook will have a form for recording the activities of your account. Two types of forms are available. A check stub is a form attached to the check by a perforated line. After the check is written, it is torn off at the line and the stub remains in the checkbook. A check register is a separate book of forms, usually the same size as the checkbook. Compare the two forms shown in Figure 24-2 on page 343. Note that both provide blanks to fill in the same type of information about the check.

Figure 24-1 The parts of a check.

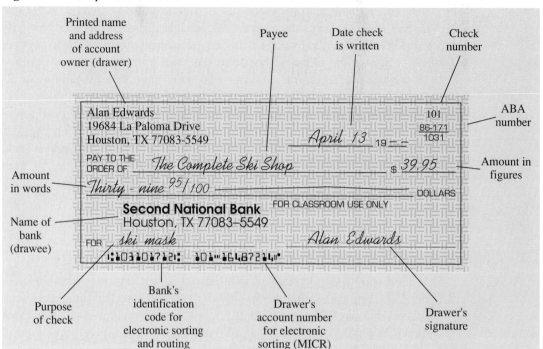

Filling Out Your Check Stub or Register

The check stub or register is your record. Fill out the stub or register first. If you write the check first, you may forget to record the information. Later, when you need to refer to the information, you may not remember the amount of the check or to whom it was written.

Figure 24-2 shows how Alan Edwards would record his check for $39.95 to The Complete Ski Shop, using both a check stub and a register. Of course, he would use only one type, but you can see from Figure 24-2 that he would record the same information on either form.

Let's consider the check register here. Recall that in Chapter 23 Alan opened his account with a deposit of $331.85. That is his first entry in the register. It is entered in the Additions column and Balance column. Since this is his first deposit, there is no balance forward to record.

The second entry is for the check that Alan wrote to The Complete Ski Shop (Figure 24-1). Alan has entered the check number in the first column and the date of the check in the second. In the next column, he has recorded the payee and noted that the payment was for a ski mask. The amount of the check has been written in the amount of Payment or Withdrawal column and subtracted from the beginning balance of $331.85. He recorded his new

Figure 24-2
Which form
would you
prefer?

ITEM NO. OR TRANSACTION CODE	DATE	DESCRIPTION OF TRANSACTION	AMOUNT OF PAYMENT OR WITHDRAWAL (–)	✔	TAX OR OTHER	AMOUNT OF DEPOSIT OR INTEREST (+)	BALANCE FORWARD —	
D	4/10	TO *Opening deposit* FOR *Paycheck 271.10; cash 61.75*				331 85	331 85 / 331 85	
101	4/13	TO *Complete Ski Shop* FOR *ski mask*	39 95				39 95 / 291 90	
102	4/15	TO *Second National Bank* FOR *cash-current expenses*	50 —				50 00 / 241 90	
D	4/16	TO *Deposit* FOR *Birthday-Dad*				50 —	50 00 / 291 90	
103	4/21	TO *Skiing Update* FOR *one yr. subscription*	32 97				32 97 / 258 93	
104	4/22	TO *J. T. Gore Sports* FOR *postage due on 4/20 order*	— 87				87 / 258 06	
VOID 105	4/22	TO ~~*Johnson Motors*~~ FOR *VOID*					—	
AT	4/23	TO *Cash from ATM* FOR *game tickets and dinner*	50 —				50 00 / 208 06	

PLEASE BE SURE TO **DEDUCT** CHARGES THAT AFFECT YOUR ACCOUNT   SUBTRACTIONS   ADDITIONS   BALANCE FORWARD

101	$ 39.95	
April 13	19	
TO Complete Ski Shop		
FOR Ski mask		
	DOLLARS	CENTS
BAL FOR'D		
DEPOSITS 4/10	331	85
TOTAL	331	85
THIS CHECK	39	95
OTHER DEDUCTIONS		
BAL FOR'D	291	90

balance, $291.90, in the Balance column on the same line as the amount of the check.

Filling Out the Check

After you have completed the entry in the check register, you are ready to fill out the check. Remember that a check is an order to the bank to pay out your money, so fill out the check completely and carefully.

There are usually seven items that you will write on the check: the check number, the date, the payee, the amount in figures, the amount in words, the purpose of the check, and your signature. Complete the following steps in writing your checks:

Step 1. Number your checks in order. These numbers help you to compare your records with the checks that have been paid and returned to you. If the numbers are not already printed on the checks, write them in the space provided. Check numbers are usually printed on both the checks and the check stubs. Check registers have a space for you to write the check numbers.

Step 2. Write the date, which was entered in the register, in the proper space on the check.

Step 3. Write the payee's name on the line following ''Pay to the Order of.'' The payee for Alan's first check is The Complete Ski Shop, as shown in Figure 24-1 on page 342.

Step 4. Write the amount of the check in figures after the printed dollar sign. Write the amount close to the dollar sign so that a dishonest person cannot insert another number between it and the amount. A check on which the amount has been dishonestly increased is called a **raised check**. Cents are usually written somewhat smaller so that the amount in dollars and the amount in cents can be easily distinguished. Write cents figures close to the dollar figures so that additional numbers cannot be inserted.

Step 5. Write the amount in words on the line below the payee's name. Spell out the amount in dollars. Write the cents in figures as a fraction of a dollar. Begin writing at the far left end of the line so that the amount cannot be changed by adding a word at the beginning of the line. Draw a line from the fraction to the printed word ''Dollars'' to fill all unused space. If a check must be written for less than a dollar, write the amount as shown in Figure 24-3.

Figure 24-3
Most people would rather not write a check for less than $1. However, sometimes it is necessary, and this is how it should be done.

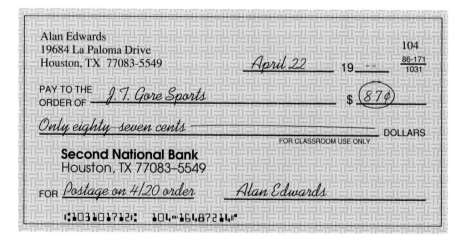

If the amount written in figures does not agree with the amount written in words, the bank may pay the amount written in words. However, the bank is not obligated to pay a check containing errors. If there is a considerable difference between the two amounts, the bank may call you and ask for instructions concerning payment. The bank may also return the check to you and ask you to replace it. There is usually a charge, often as much as $20, when a check is returned for any reason. If a business receives a check from you on which the amounts disagree, the business will probably return it to you and ask for another check.

Step 6. Write the purpose of each check on the line labeled "For" at the bottom of the check. Writing the purpose will later help you remember why you wrote the check. Note that Alan Edwards wrote "ski mask" as the purpose of Check No. 101.

Step 7. Sign your checks with the same signature that you wrote on your signature card. A married woman should use her given name in signing checks. For example, she should sign Racquel Waterman, not Mrs. Jack Waterman. Alan Edwards is the drawer of the check in Figure 24-1 and has signed his name on the proper line.

On checks issued by a business or other organization, the firm's name may appear as a printed signature and is often followed by the word "By." The person who signs the check writes his or her name after "By." This shows that the firm is the drawer and that the check should not be charged to the person who has signed the check. An example of a business signature is shown in Figure 24-4.

Figure 24-4
Who is the drawer of a business check? Should Sarah Adams' account be charged for this check?

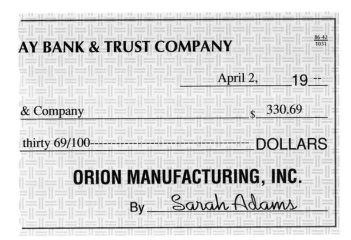

The bank may subtract from the depositor's account only the amounts of checks and electronic funds transfer (EFT) transactions that the depositor has authorized. Your signature as drawer on a check tells the bank to pay the amount from your account. EFT payments require special arrangements with the bank. By using your private code number at an automatic teller machine to give instructions for EFT payments, you authorize the bank to subtract money from your account.

If a bank cashes a check signed by someone who had no right to use the depositor's signature, the bank may be held responsible. Writing another person's signature on a check without his or her authority is a crime called **forgery**. A check with such a signature is a *forged check*.

FOLLOWING TIPS FOR GOOD CHECK WRITING

Anyone who writes checks has a great deal of responsibility. However, if you remember the tips listed below, there is little chance of losing your money because of poorly written checks.

1. *Write checks only on the forms provided by your bank.* It is possible to write checks on just about anything—even a paper bag. Sorting and exchanging the millions of checks that are written every day is a tremendous job for banks. This job is done at a reasonable cost due to the use of machines that sort the checks according to the MICR numbers printed on the check (see Figure 24-1). If the check does not have these numbers, the sorting will be interrupted, the check may be delayed, and a charge for handling the check may be made.

2. *Tear up all checks on which you make errors.* Do not try to erase or retrace your writing. No one who handles your check can be sure whether the changes were made by you or by someone who had no right to make them. Before destroying the check, record its number and write the word "void" on the register to show that the check was not used. Note that Alan voided Check No. 105.

3. *Avoid making checks payable to cash or to bearer.* If such a check is lost, it can be cashed by anyone. For this reason, you should never make a check payable to cash unless you are going to cash it at the time it is written—at the teller's window in the bank. Even then, it is usually preferable to make the check out with the bank as payee. That is what Alan did with Check No. 102.

4. *Always fill in the amount.* If you leave it blank, you may be held responsible for amounts filled in by others.

5. *Write a check only if you have enough money in your account to cover it.* A bank is not expected to cash checks for more than the amount that is in your account. Writing a check for more than you have in your account is called **overdrawing**. When an account is overdrawn, the bank may not pay the check. In addition, most banks charge the depositor for checks they have to return marked "insufficient funds." Special arrangements can be made with the bank to give you an automatic loan

if you overdraw your account unintentionally. Intentionally overdrawing without an arrangement with the bank, however, is against the law.

6. *Use the current date.* A **postdated check** is one that is dated later than the date on which it is written. For example, a check written on October 1 but dated October 5 is postdated. You might postdate a check because you do not have enough money in your account on October 1 to cover the check but plan to deposit money on October 3. This is a bad business practice because you may not be able to make the deposit or may forget to make it as planned. Also, you must be sure that your deposit is actually entered into your account by the bank before you write checks using the money. This usually takes one or two days after the deposit reaches the bank, but it may take longer. Writing checks before your deposit is put into your account will result in an overdraft. To avoid an overdraft, you must have funds to cover the check amount in your account before your deposit is made. Before you open an account, get information on when the bank enters deposits into customers accounts.

7. *Record every payment from your checking account, whether the payment is by check or EFT.* Some people carry a few blank checks in their wallets instead of carrying their checkbooks. When one of these checks is used, the drawer should make a note of it and record it in the register as soon as possible. It is also important to record promptly all transactions made at an ATM. Since no check is written, it is easy to forget to record withdrawals. However, a receipt is given for each transaction. Note the last entry in the register in Figure 24-2 on page 343.

8. *Write all checks in ink.* This prevents someone from raising the amount of the check. Some businesses use small machines called check protectors or check writers to guard against possible changes in the amount of a check. These machines stamp the amount on the proper line of the check so that the amount cannot be changed. Many businesses, especially large ones, use computers to print their checks, this also helps to prevent raising of checks.

Following these eight guidelines will help prevent losses on checks that you write.

STOPPING PAYMENT ON A CHECK

In certain situations, you may want to instruct your bank not to pay a check that you have written. Suppose Alan Edwards' Check No. 118 for $52.67 to Joseph Fields was lost. Before he writes a new check, Alan should ask the bank not to pay the first one. This is called **stopping payment**. The bank will ask Alan to fill out a stop-payment form, such as the one shown in Figure 24-5. This form is a written notice from the drawer telling the bank not to pay a certain check. Note the items included on the stop-payment form: date,

Figure 24-5
A stop-payment
form tells your
bank not to pay a
check that you
have written.

Second National Bank   June 5, 19 --

Received: Office_____ Date_____ 19_____ Time_____

☒ Please **STOP PAYMENT** on the following described check, issued by the undersigned.

Amt. $52.67	Date 6/1/--	Ck. No. 118	Payee Joseph Fields

It is understood that you agree to indemnify
us for said amount and losses, expenses
and costs incurred by us arising from our
compliance with the above order

Account Number _1648-7214_

Account
Name
and
Address

Alan Edwards
19684 La Paloma Drive
Houston, TX 77083-5549

☐ Please cancel the above stop payment.
Date_____ 19_____
Signature_____

Signature____ *Alan Edwards*

AUTHORIZATION

check number, amount, payee, and the drawer's signature. Most banks charge a substantial fee for stopping payment on a check.

Payment of a check should be stopped only for good reasons. You may learn, for example, that a check you have written to pay a bill was lost in the mail. Or, a check you have written may be stolen. Before you write a new check, you should stop payment on the one that was lost or stolen. To prevent the wrong person from cashing the check, you should notify the bank immediately. The bank is responsible for verifying the validity of the signature on a check. Alerting the bank may save you the fee that you would have been charged to stop payment. Remember that once you have issued a check, it may be legally passed from one person to another. You can be held responsible for damages that stopping payment on a check may cause to rightful holders of the check.

Now you have learned how to write your own checks correctly and to stop payment on a check if a problem arises that demands this action. But what about checks written by others which you receive? How do you handle those?

HANDLING CHECKS YOU RECEIVE

You will no doubt receive many checks in your lifetime. You should learn to handle them as carefully as you do cash. As the payee, you can do one of three things with a check: you can cash it, deposit it to your bank account, or transfer it to another person or business as a payment. To do any of these things, you must first endorse the checks you receive.

As you remember from Chapter 23, Alan Edwards had to endorse his paycheck before he deposited it to his account. In doing so, he was following one of the basic purposes of endorsements.

The Purpose of Endorsements

When you endorse a check, your responsibilities are almost as great as if you had written the check yourself. As an endorser, you are actually making this promise: "If this check is not paid by the bank, I will pay it." To enable you to handle properly the checks you receive, you should understand the following three purposes of endorsements:

1. Endorsements allow the payee of the check to carry out his or her plans for the check, either to cash it, deposit it, or transfer it to someone else.
2. Endorsements serve as legal evidence that the payee had the check and that he or she cashed it or transferred it to someone else.
3. Endorsements mean that the endorser will pay the check in case the next owner of the check cannot collect the money. Studying the kinds of endorsements will help you understand these purposes.

Placement of Endorsements

In 1988, the federal government set up guidelines for all financial institutions which require that money deposited to customers' accounts be available to them in a certain period of time. The time between the receipt of the deposit by the bank and its availability to the depositor is called the **float**. Evidence that the bank followed the time regulations is its stamped endorsement on the check. Because these stamps are usually large, the guidelines also set a specific space on the check for the payee's endorsement. As you learned in Chapter 23, your endorsement must be made in the $1^1/2$-inch space on the trailing edge of the check. Figure 24-6 shows a diagram for the payee's endorsement; this diagram was sent by a bank to its customers when the regulations went into effect.

These space regulations are very specific. If you put anything outside the $1^1/2$-inch limit, it may cause the check to be returned. Further, you may be liable for losses stemming from late returns as a result of endorsements that are unreadable, misplaced, or incomplete. Banks have the right to refuse your check for any of these faults.

Kinds of Endorsements

Different endorsements serve different purposes. As you handle the checks you receive, you will probably use each of the four types of endorsements discussed below. Let's start with the endorsement that Alan Edwards used for his paycheck in Figure 23-4 on page 333.

BLANK ENDORSEMENT

An endorsement that consists of only the endorser's name is called a **blank endorsement**. Alan Edwards signed his name exactly as it was written on the

Figure 24-6
The payee's endorsement is limited to 1¹/₂ inches on the back of the check at the trailing edge.

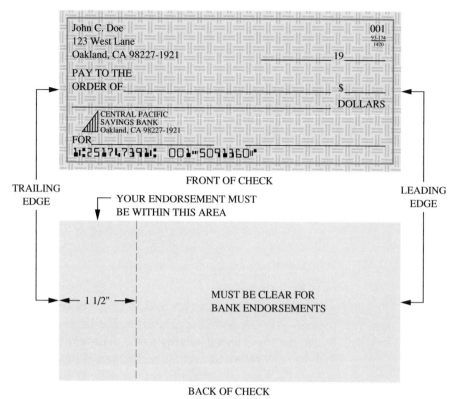

John C. Doe   001
123 West Lane   93-174
Oakland, CA 98227-1921 _____ 19 _____   1420

PAY TO THE
ORDER OF_____ $_____
_____ DOLLARS

CENTRAL PACIFIC
SAVINGS BANK
Oakland, CA 98227-1921
FOR_____

⑈:251747391⑈ 001⑈5091360⑈⑈

FRONT OF CHECK

TRAILING
EDGE

YOUR ENDORSEMENT MUST
BE WITHIN THIS AREA

LEADING
EDGE

1 1/2"

MUST BE CLEAR FOR
BANK ENDORSEMENTS

BACK OF CHECK

face of the check. He then signed his name as he had written it on the signature card.

✓ A blank endorsement makes a check payable to anyone who has the check. This endorsement may be used whenever a check is to be transferred, but sometimes another type is better.

SPECIAL ENDORSEMENT

Suppose Nancy R. Brooks receives a check made payable to her. She then wants to make that check payable to Kunio Shinoda, who operates a service station where she buys gas. The check is a payment on the bill she owes Mr. Shinoda. If she uses a blank endorsement and sends the check to Mr. Shinoda, he can cash it when he receives it. However, if the check is lost before it reaches him, anyone who finds it can cash it.

✓ To make sure that no one except Kunio Shinoda will be able to cash the check, Miss Brooks may use a **special** or **full endorsement**, which includes the name of the person to whom the check has been transferred. With this endorsement, she places the words "Pay to the order of Kunio Shinoda" before her signature as shown in Figure 24-7. Mr. Shinoda must sign the check before it can be cashed.

Figure 24-7
A special or full endorsement.

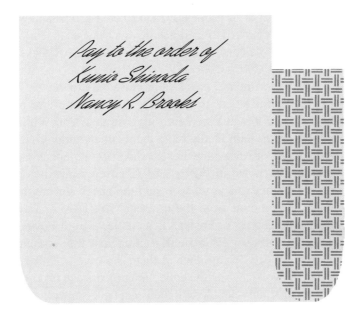

RESTRICTIVE ENDORSEMENT

A **restrictive endorsement** limits the use of the check to the purpose given in the endorsement. For example, you may have several checks that you want to mail to the bank. If you write "For deposit only" above your signature, as in Figure 24-8, you have restricted the use of the check so that it can only be deposited to your account. If a check with such an endorsement is lost, it cannot be cashed by the finder.

Businesses often use rubber stamps to imprint restrictive endorsements that require checks to be deposited to their accounts. A business thus has no risk of loss if an unauthorized person uses the stamp to endorse a check.

Figure 24-8
A restrictive endorsement. If this check is lost, it cannot be cashed by the finder.

MULTIPLE ENDORSEMENTS

After endorsing a check, the payee usually cashes it or deposits it in a bank. The payee may, however, transfer the check to another person who in turn may transfer it to someone else, and so on. Each person who transfers a check should be required to endorse it, because each endorsement is another promise that the check will be paid. In actual use, checks with more than one endorsement are rare.

An endorsement serves as a promise only to those who receive the check after the endorsement is written. It does not apply to people who held the check before the endorsement. Suppose that Jean Whitfield writes a check and gives it to Sam Corbett and that Corbett endorses it and gives it to Earl Foster. Suppose also that Foster endorses the check and gives it to Harry Paulsen. As shown in Figure 24-9, Paulsen sends the check to his bank for deposit. If the bank refuses to pay the check for any reason, Paulsen may collect the amount from the drawer (Whitfield) or from either of the two endorsers (Corbett or Foster). If he collects from Foster, Foster has a claim against the drawer (Whitfield) and against the first endorser (Corbett). If Paulsen collects from either of them, however, neither has a claim against Foster. As you can see, the collection process can become quite involved; for this reason, many people will not accept checks with multiple endorsements.

Figure 24-9
A check with multiple endorsements. Remember to observe the 1¹/₂-inch regulation.

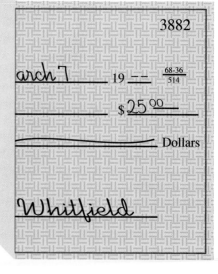

FOLLOWING TIPS FOR ACCEPTING AND CASHING CHECKS

It is important that you understand your responsibility as a signer and as an endorser of checks. According to law, a check is payable on demand, that is, at the time the holder of the check presents it for payment at the bank on which it is drawn. However, a bank may refuse to accept a check if it is presented for payment long after the date on which it was written. Some checks carry a printed notation, ''Please cash within 60 days.'' Therefore, you should present a check for payment within a reasonable time after you receive it.

A check is valuable only when it is drawn on a bank in which the drawer has money on deposit. For this reason, you should accept checks only when they are written or endorsed by people whom you know and trust or those who can provide clear identification. A check received from a stranger who cannot provide acceptable identification may turn out to be worthless, and it may be impossible for you to find the person to collect the money.

Just as you should be cautious in accepting checks, you should not expect strangers to cash checks for you. If you must ask a business or a person who does not know you to cash your check, you will probably have to prove your

Illus. 24-1
A check acceptance policy may vary from store to store. Remember that no one is legally bound to accept checks.

form of identification. Some businesses require a second identification before accepting a personal check. Some banks furnish identification cards that can be used on a credit-check terminal in a business to verify electronically that a customer presenting a check has funds on deposit to cover the amount of the check.

Checks are so commonly used in place of cash that you will usually have no trouble cashing them where you are known. However, legally, no one has to accept your checks.

Increasing Your Business Vocabulary

The following terms should become part of your business vocabulary. For each numbered item, find the term that has the same meaning.

blank endorsement
drawee
drawer
float
forgery
overdrawing

payee
postdated check
raised check
restrictive endorsement
special or full endorsement
stopping payment

1. The owner of the account and the person who signs the check.
2. The crime of writing another person's signature on the check without his or her authority.
3. A check dated later than the date on which it is written.
4. The person to whom the check is written.
5. The bank or other financial institution in which the account is held.
6. Instructing a bank not to pay a certain check.
7. Writing a check for more money than is in one's account.

8. A check on which the amount has been dishonestly increased.
9. An endorsement including the name of the person to whom the check has been transferred.
10. An endorsement that limits the use of a check to the purpose given in the endorsement.
11. An endorsement consisting of the endorser's name only.
12. The time between the receipt of a deposit by the bank and its availability to the depositor.

Reviewing Your Reading

1. Name the three parties involved with a check and tell where their names are shown on the face of a check.

2. What two numbers are included in the MICR figures printed on the lower left edge of the check? For what are they used?

3. Why should the check stub or register be filled in before the check is written?

4. Explain the difference between the way check numbers are recorded on a check stub and on a register.

5. Name the seven steps in writing a check and tell how each part of the check should be written.

6. How does the signature section of a business check usually differ from that of a personal check?

7. What is a forged check?

8. What risk is involved in making a check payable to cash or to bearer? What can you do to avoid the risk?

9. Is it always illegal to overdraw intentionally? Explain.

10. Under what conditions might you stop payment on a check? How would you stop payment?

11. What are the three purposes of endorsements?

12. Describe the placement of the payee's endorsement. For what is the remaining space used?

13. If you wish to transfer ownership of a check from yourself to another person, would you use a blank, a special, or a restrictive endorsement? Explain.

14. Which endorsement would you use to limit the use of your payroll check to being deposited in your bank account?

15. What is meant by multiple endorsement?

Using Your Business Knowledge

1. Cher Alonso likes the convenience of the automatic teller machine for her banking. She often makes deposits at the ATM that she passes on her way to work. However, she frequently forgets to record these banking activities in her check register and never seems to know how much money she has in the bank. Also she has overdrawn her account twice and has had to pay a fee each time. Can you suggest a plan for Cher to follow that would allow her to use the automatic teller services and still be sure of having an accurate record?

2. Matt Huffman believes that it is a waste of time to record information on check stubs. "The bank sends me a statement each month; that's all I need," he says. How could you convince Matt that he should keep records?

3. On October 28, Arvind Bluestone selected a $59.95 sunshield helmet to wear when he commutes to work on his motorbike. The merchant agreed to take his personal check, using Arvind's driver's license and his company ID card for identification. However, when the merchant saw that Arvind had dated his check November 1, he refused to accept it. Arvind explained that he would deposit his paycheck on October 30, and that by the time the merchant sent the check through the bank, it would be covered. The merchant still refused to take the check. Do you agree with the merchant? Why?

4. The NaturFresh Supermarket requires its checkers to follow four rules in the following order when accepting checks: (1) Get two forms of identification (ID) from the customer. (2) Hand the check and the ID's to the manager for approval. (3) Stamp the check with the store's rubber endorsement stamp. (4) Place the check under the cash tray in the register drawer.

   a. Why do you think the store requires two ID's?

   b. Why do you think the check must be approved by the manager?

c. What kind of endorsement would most likely be on the rubber stamp?

d. What are the advantages of stamping the check immediately after accepting it?

e. Why do you think checks are placed under the cash tray instead of with the cash?

5. For each of the following situations, (a) tell which endorsement should be used, (b) write the endorsement, and (c) explain why you selected that endorsement and why you signed the endorsement in the manner in which you did.

a. John C. Houchens is in the bank and wants to cash his payroll check.

b. Michi Okano wants to deposit her pay-check by mail.

c. Lloyd B. Kilgore uses a check received from Howard W. Sloan to pay for groceries at TruValu Supermarket.

d. Martha S. Markowski gives two checks to a friend, Caron Ann Talbot, who is to deposit them to Martha's account.

e. Thomas Browne deposits a check on which his name has been misspelled as Tomas Brown.

6. Harvey Graham owed Leonard Saunders $58. He wrote a check to Mr. Saunders and mailed it to him. Later, Mr. Graham decided that he did not want to pay all of the debt at once. Therefore, he asked his bank to stop payment on the check. Do you think it was wise for Mr. Graham to make this request? Why?

Computing Business Problems

1. Kathy Whiteside opened a checking account on June 1 and deposited $122.47, the amount of her first paycheck from her summer job as a day-camp counselor. During the month, she deposited three more paychecks of the same amount.

a. What was the total of Kathy's deposits?

b. During June, Kathy wrote four checks for the following amounts: $37.50, $25, $7.35, and $4.20. What was the total amount paid out in checks?

c. What was Kathy's balance at the end of June?

2. As treasurer of the Seneca Valley High School Student Council, in Troy, New York, you are to fill out check stubs and write checks for the following transactions of the council. If check stubs and checks are not available, draw forms similar to the ones shown in Figures 24-1 and 24-2. The beginning balance is $277.60. Use the current date. Number the stubs and checks beginning with Check No. 26.

a. Pay $9.25 to the New York Bookstore for the book, *Parliamentary Procedure*.

b. Pay 82 cents to Sandy Graham for a record book (79 cents plus tax).

c. Pay $27.50 to Latimer's Trophy Shop for a scholastic trophy.

d. Pay $43.04 to Don Smedke for his traveling expenses to the state convention of student councils.

3. On September 1, Yuan Shen had a balance of $678.25 in his checking account. By arrangement with his bank, his electric bill is automatically paid each month through EFT. The amount of his electric bill is deducted from his account and added to the account of the utility company. He also has his payroll check automatically deposited to his account by his employer. His checks and deposits for the month are shown below. Record the beginning balance, the checks, the deposits, and his EFT transactions in a check register similar to the one in Figure 24-2 on page 343.

September	Check No.	To	For	Amount
1	AD	Automatic deposit	8/15-31 check	$575.24
3	AT	City Public Util.	August electric	98.65
4	134	Century Realty Co.	September rent	395.00
9	135	Mary Scartarige, M.D.	Sprained ankle	52.50
13	136	Jerome's Fashions	Balance on suit	64.22
16	137	Luma's Hardware	Paint, wallpaper	72.20
16	AD	Automatic deposit	9/1-15 paycheck	575.24
20	138	Bryan Fuel Co.	Oil contract	88.20
24	139	Charters SuperFood	Groceries	97.91
25	AT	Automatic withdrawal	Cash for expenses	50.00
28	140	United Fund Drive	Contribution	35.00
30	141	L&M's Pharmacy	Medicine	18.11

4. Paul D. Redford stopped at an automatic teller machine to deposit three checks he had received. The amounts were $142.75, $64.50, and $13.80.
   a. What was Paul's total deposit?
   b. Write the correct endorsement that Paul would use. His name was spelled out on two of the checks; on the other, it was P.D. Redford.
   c. In order to prepare a deposit slip, what other information would Paul need?

Expanding Your Understanding of Business

1. Listed below are some errors that were made in filling out checks. Explain which errors would probably not affect the use of the checks and which would probably cause the checks to be void. You may need to do some research or check with a local financial institution to find the answers.
   a. The check number is omitted.
   b. The check stub was not filled out.
   c. The drawer forgot to sign the check.
   d. The check was dated 1989 instead of the current year.
   e. The drawer forgot to fill in the name of the payee.
   f. The payee's name was misspelled.
   g. The amount of the check was $54.50. It should have been $45.50.
   h. The drawer omitted the amount of the check since that information was not available, and in a letter instructed the payee to fill in the correct amount.
   i. The back of a check at the trailing edge had been used as note paper to jot down a name and phone number.

2. Visit two or three banks in your area and find out what the banks' policies are on the float. Ask if there has been much difficulty with endorsements since the regulations went into effect in 1988. Write a brief report of your findings.

3. Some large supermarkets have rules posted about cashing checks. Some of these rules include the following: only checks in the amount of the purchase will be accepted; no checks will be accepted unless ID cards are on file in the store; anyone paying by check will be photographed; each person paying by check must record her or his thumbprint on the back of the check. Find out whether these or other rules are posted in a supermarket near you. Ask the manager whether the amount of bad-check loss

has gone down since the store began using these methods. Report your findings to the class.

4. Some banks offer special ID cards to their customers. These cards allow the customer to have checks approved electronically in businesses that have credit-check terminals connected to the computers in the customer's bank. Visit a large supermarket, drugstore, or department store and find out if the store has a credit-check terminal. Ask for a demonstration. Write a brief description of the procedure and report to the class.

Reconciling a Checking Account

Chapter Objectives

After studying this chapter and completing the end-of-chapter activities, you will be able to:

1. Explain how a check is cleared.

2. Explain why a canceled check is valuable to the drawer.

3. Explain how a depositor whose bank does not return paid checks can prove that a certain payment was made.

4. Reconcile a bank statement.

In the last chapter, you learned, along with Alan Edwards, how to write checks and how to handle the checks you receive. You also learned that the checks you write will be processed with the billions of other checks written each year by people in the United States. In this chapter, you will learn how your checks are returned to you and how to calculate the accuracy of the bank statement that accompanies them.

Checks travel around the country in wallets, handbags, envelopes, mail pouches, planes, trucks and on trains. They crisscross the nation's cities and towns and travel to farms, to ships at sea, and to foreign countries. They go in and out of houses, businesses, government offices, and banks of all shapes and sizes. They are written on, typed on, stamped on, and imprinted with oddly shaped characters in magnetic ink. They are shuffled by hand, stored temporarily under money trays in cash registers, and stacked and bound with rubber bands. They are sped through machines that read and sort them by the thousands a minute. Finally, they find their way, still in good shape, back to the bank of the drawer. The bank will microfilm the checks before returning them to the drawer, as most banks do. Some financial institutions, especially credit unions and brokerage firms, may show the deduction on the customer's monthly statement instead of returning the checks. In either case, the checks will be available to the depositor as proof of payment. For many checks, the journey from drawer and back is a long one. You may wonder how all of the checks ever find their way back to the right person. Let's see how that happens.

PROCESSING OF YOUR CHECKS

Though returning checks to their original drawers may seem an impossible task, it happens through a carefully planned system. You have learned how

Illus. 25-1
Checks are sorted by high-speed document-handling equipment.

checks are passed from one person to another by an endorsement. Therefore, the check you write or receive may be owned by several people before it is returned to you as the drawer. However, it is eventually returned to the drawer's bank to be paid and charged to his or her checking account. This process is called **clearing a check**. Clearing may be done locally on the books of one bank, through a specially designated place for clearing, or through the Federal Reserve System.

Clearing Checks Locally

Check clearing may involve one, two, or several banks and drawers within the same city. Let's see how these differ.

THE SAME BANK

If both the drawer and the payee have accounts in the same bank, clearing is simple. The bank subtracts the amount from the drawer's account and adds it to the payee's account. It is simply an accounting transaction.

TWO BANKS

When two different banks are involved, clearing is somewhat different, although it is still fairly simple if the two banks are in the same small town.

Suppose Jon Gable's neighborhood rock group believes its new song will be a big hit if the group can get more practice time and get the song recorded. Jon persuades his father to rent a garage on the outskirts of town for rehearsals. The rent for one month is $50. Mr. Gable sends the rental check, written on his account with the North River National Bank, to Arlene-Bayne Realty. Look at Figure 25-1 and follow the check as it travels to the two banks in the town where the Gables live and back to Mr. Gable.

Arlene-Bayne Realty endorses the check and deposits it in its account in the First Federal Trust Company. When First Federal receives the check, it adds $50 to the account of Arlene-Bayne Realty, endorses the check, and sends it to North River National for payment. After North River National receives the check, it pays First Federal $50 and subtracts that amount from Mr. Gable's account. The check is then marked paid by North River National and returned to Mr. Gable as his record of payment.

SEVERAL BANKS

When there are several banks in the same town, the banks usually agree on a certain time each day to clear checks. Each bank makes up one package of its paid checks that were drawn on the other banks—one package for each bank. A messenger may be sent to each bank to exchange packages of checks and pay or collect any difference that might be due. Or, each bank may send a representative to a central place that the banks have selected as an exchange

Figure 25-1 Follow Mr. Gable's check through the clearing process.

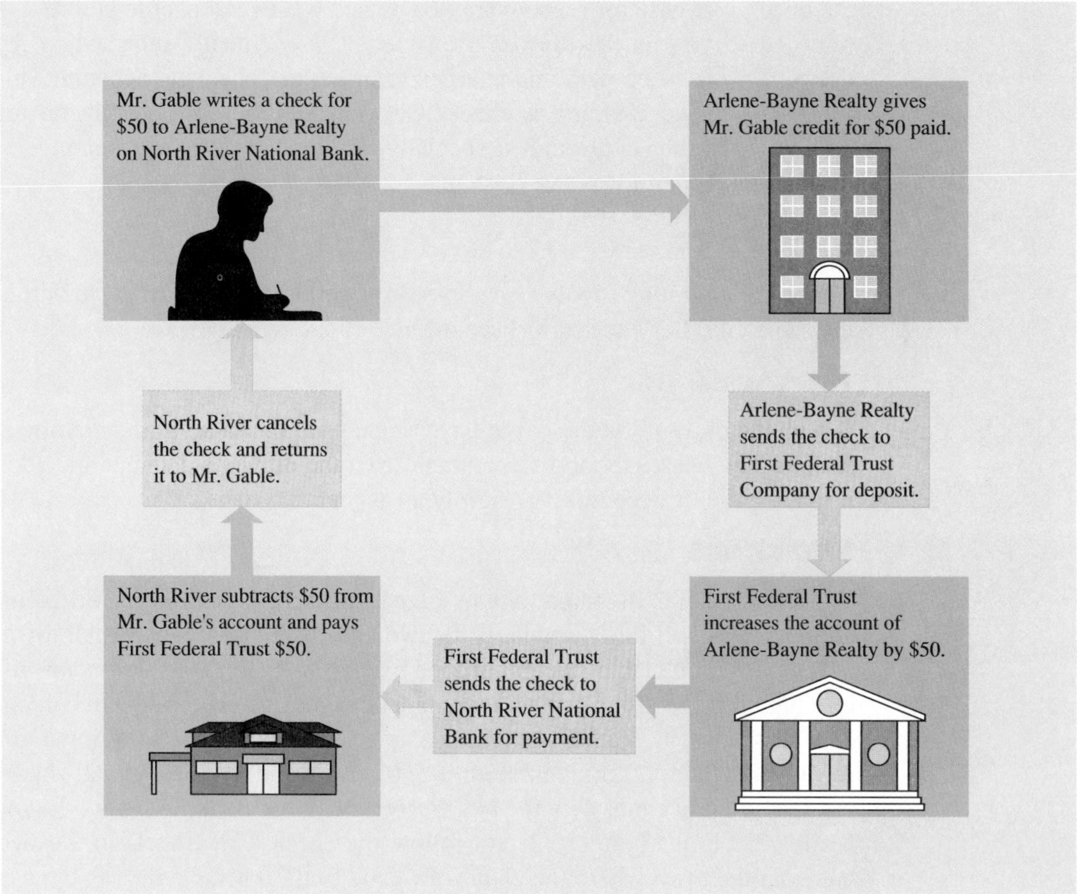

Mr. Gable writes a check for $50 to Arlene-Bayne Realty on North River National Bank.

Arlene-Bayne Realty gives Mr. Gable credit for $50 paid.

North River cancels the check and returns it to Mr. Gable.

Arlene-Bayne Realty sends the check to First Federal Trust Company for deposit.

North River subtracts $50 from Mr. Gable's account and pays First Federal Trust $50.

First Federal Trust sends the check to North River National Bank for payment.

First Federal Trust increases the account of Arlene-Bayne Realty by $50.

office where they will exchange checks and settle the accounts with each other.

Suppose that when the bank representatives meet, it is discovered that the First Federal Trust Company has checks totaling $4,000 drawn on the North River National Bank. Also, the North River National Bank has checks totaling $4,250 drawn on the First Federal Trust Company. First Federal thus owes North River National $250. It may pay this amount in cash, but usually a method is worked out that makes the handling of cash unnecessary. For example, both banks may maintain accounts with the same bank in a neighboring city. In this case, the bank in the other city may be notified to transfer $250 from the account of First Federal to the account of North River National.

Clearing Checks Through a Clearing House

In large cities where there are many banks, it would not be practical for each bank to send checks for payment to all banks on which the checks were written. Usually city banks are members of an association that operates a place for members to clear their checks every day. This place is called a **clearing house**.

The method of clearing checks through a clearing house is similar to the method followed between banks in a small town, except that thousands of checks are handled for many banks. Each bank sends a delivery clerk and a settling clerk to the clearing house with the bundles of checks. The clerks turn over the checks drawn on other banks, pick up checks drawn on their banks, and settle the net differences among themselves. In Figure 25-2, you see a simplified accounting entry showing the net balance settlement for

Figure 25-2
An accounting record of a net settlement may look like this.

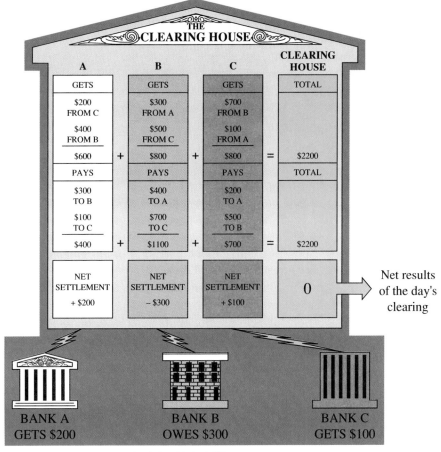

Source: Federal Reserve Bank of New York, 1987.

three banks through the clearing house fund. Note that the function of the clearing house is simply to redistribute the amounts. The $2,200 received was balanced by the $2,200 paid out, with no net change in the clearing house fund.

Instead of paying net balances in cash as in former years, electronic entries are usually made in accounts that the banks maintain with the clearing house or with a Federal Reserve Bank.

Clearing Checks through the Federal Reserve System

One of the services of the Federal Reserve System, which you learned about in Chapter 22, is clearing checks between banks in different cities. This process is more complex than clearing through a clearing house because of the volume of checks that must be cleared. Just as banks use a clearing house and their district Federal Reserve Bank for settlement of net balances, the Federal Reserve uses the Interdistrict Settlement Fund in Washington, D.C., to settle net amounts due among banks in the 12 districts. The Interdistrict Settlement Fund can be viewed as the Federal Reserve clearing house. Settlements are made through EFT.

The Federal Reserve System handles millions of checks every business day. In a recent year, for example, the Federal Reserve System handled more than 16 billion checks, more than a third of the 45 billion checks handled that year by all financial institutions. Because of the services of the Federal Reserve System, checks can be used to make payments in any part of the country as easily as they can be used locally. Even so, you can see that the actual handling of the checks to return them to the drawer is expensive. Banks use EFT whenever they can to speed up the process.

Other financial institutions, such as credit unions, savings and loan associations, and brokerage firms, usually handle a small volume of checks. These firms usually have an account with a large bank, which they use in the same way as any other customer uses an account. For example, let's say that Ivy University Credit Union (IUCU) has an account at Pilgrim Bank. After Pilgrim Bank has cleared all of its checks, it sorts them and returns them to its customers. IUCU will receive its bundle of checks with its statement. The difference between the IUCU bundle of checks and an individual customer's bundle received from Pilgrim Bank is that the IUCU bundle contains all of the checks written by all of its account holders, while the individual's bundle contains only those written by him or her. When IUCU receives its bundle, it then does the same thing that a bank does. It microfilms the checks, sorts them by customer, subtracts the checks from the customers' accounts, and either returns them to the customer or stores them.

After your bank subtracts all of your cleared checks from your balance, the checks will either be filed at the bank or sent back to you with a report of your account. Reviewing this report will be the last step in the process of maintaining your checking account.

REVIEWING YOUR BANK STATEMENT

As a depositor, you will need to review the record of your account that the bank keeps. At regular intervals, usually monthly, the bank will send you a report on the status of your account known as a **bank statement**. Statement forms vary, but most of them show the following items of information:

- The balance at the beginning of the month.
- The deposits made during the month.
- The checks paid by the bank during the month.
- Any electronic or automatic teller transactions made during the month.
- Any special payment the bank has made at your request, such as a transfer of funds from your checking to your savings account, or the automatic payment of a monthly bill, such as a car payment.
- Service charges for the account for the month, including charges for special services, such as stopping payment on a check.
- The balance at the end of the month.

See if you can locate an example of each of these items on the bank statement shown in Figure 25-3.

EXAMINING YOUR RETURNED CHECKS

If your bank returns checks, it will return all of the checks that it has paid during the month with your statement. Before the bank sends you your checks, it cancels each one, usually using a machine that stamps a cancellation number on the front or back of the check. The paid checks are called **canceled checks**. Be sure to save them; they are valuable records. Your check stub or register is your own record, but the canceled check is evidence that payment was actually received. Since the payee must endorse a check before it can be cashed, the endorsement proves that the payee received the check.

Suppose your bank does not return checks to depositors, and you need a certain check to prove that a payment was made. Banks that do not return checks often send a more detailed statement than banks that return checks. In most cases, information on the statement will be sufficient to prove payment. However, if the check showing the endorsement is needed, a copy of it can be obtained by giving the bank enough of the details of the check to allow a clerk to identify it. Banks keep a photographic record of all checks paid. Your check will be located in this record and a copy will be sent to you. There will probably be a small service charge for this service.

Figure 25-3
Alan Edwards'
bank statement
showing
transactions
completed during
April.

Second National Bank

Checking Account Statement

ACCT. 1648-7214
DATE 5/1/--
PAGE 1

Alan Edwards
19684 La Paloma Drive
Houston, TX 77083-5549

Please examine at once. If no errors are reported within 10 days, account will be considered correct.

BALANCE FORWARD	NO. OF WITH-DRAWALS	TOTAL AMOUNT	NO. OF DEP.	TOTAL DEPOSIT AMOUNT	SERVICE CHARGE	BALANCE THIS STATEMENT
0 : 00	14	433 : 89	4	826 : 95	3 : 00	390 : 06

CHECKS AND OTHER DEBITS		DEPOSITS AND OTHER CREDITS	DATE	BALANCE
		331.85	4/10	331.85
101	39.95		4/13	291.90
102	50.00		4/15	241.90
		50.00	4/16	291.90
103	32.97		4/22	258.93
104	.87		4/22	258.06
	50.00 ATW		4/23	208.06
106*	16.30		4/24	191.76
107	25.78		4/24	165.98
		175.00	4/24	340.98
109*	65.33		4/26	275.65
110	33.46		4/27	242.19
111	24.33		4/27	217.86
112	5.80		4/27	212.06
113	12.85		4/27	199.21
		270.10 AD	4/29	469.31
114	4.25		4/30	465.06
	72.00 AP TexPower		4/30	393.06
	3.00 SC		4/30	390.06

KEY TO SYMBOLS

AD-	AUTOMATIC DEPOSIT	PC-	PAID OVERDRAFT CHARGE
AP-	AUTOMATIC PAYMENT	PR-	PAYROLL DEPOSIT
ATD-	AUTOMATIC TELLER DEPOSIT	RC-	RETURN CHECK CHARGE
ATW-	AUTOMATIC TELLER WITHDRAWAL	RT-	RETURN ITEM
CC-	CERTIFIED CHECK	SC-	SERVICE CHARGE
EC-	ERROR CORRECTED	ST-	SAVINGS TRANSFER
OD-	OVERDRAFT	TC-	TRANSFER CHARGE

*Where this asterisk is shown, a preceding check is still outstanding or has been included on a previous statement.

You receive computer-printed receipts for all transactions made at an automatic teller station. Some banks send another receipt of the transaction with your statement; other banks do not. In either case, your statement will show a record of each transaction. You should have kept your own record of each EFT transaction in your register.

Now you have your returned checks and your bank statement. Your next step is to compare your record of your account with the bank's record.

RECONCILING YOUR BANK STATEMENT

You have learned about keeping a record of your account on check stubs or in a register. The bank statement gives you a copy of the bank's record of your account. The balances on the two may differ. Bringing the balances into agreement is known as reconciling the bank balance. The statement showing how the two balances were brought into agreement is called the **bank reconciliation**. Forms for reconciling are often printed on the back of the bank statement.

The balances shown on your records and the bank statement may be different for several reasons. Here are the most common reasons:

- Some of the checks that you wrote and subtracted from your balance may not have been presented to the bank for payment before the bank statement was made. These checks, therefore, have not been deducted from the bank-statement balance. Such checks are known as **outstanding checks**.
- You may have forgotten to record a transaction in your register. This is especially true if you use an automatic teller machine or have other EFT transactions. Failure to record these is a frequent cause of errors.
- A service charge that you have not recorded may be shown on the bank statement.

Illus. 25-2
Record all transactions, including those at ATMs, as they are completed.

- You may have mailed a deposit to the bank that had not been received and recorded when the statement was made.
- If yours is an interest-bearing account, you may not have added to your balance the interest shown on your statement.
- You may have recorded the amount of the check incorrectly in your check register or on the check stub.

Let's see how a bank reconciliation is made. On May 4, Alan Edwards received the bank statement shown in Figure 25-3. The statement balance is $390.06. Alan's checkbook balance is $416.56. He examined his canceled checks, which were returned with the statement, and found that his checks numbered 108, 115, and 116 were missing. Check No. 105, you will recall, had been voided. The others are outstanding. He listed these on the reconciliation form with the amounts for each and recorded the total. His bank reconciliation is shown in Figure 25-4.

Figure 25-4
A bank reconciliation helps you bring your records and the bank's records of your account into agreement.

YOU CAN EASILY
BALANCE YOUR CHECKBOOK
BY FOLLOWING THIS PROCEDURE

FILL IN BELOW AMOUNTS FROM YOUR CHECKBOOK AND BANK STATEMENT

BALANCE SHOWN ON BANK STATEMENT	$ 390.06	BALANCE SHOWN IN YOUR CHECKBOOK	$ 416.56
ADD DEPOSITS NOT ON STATEMENT	$		
TOTAL	$ 390.06	ADD ANY DEPOSITS NOT ALREADY ENTERED IN CHECKBOOK	$

SUBTRACT CHECKS ISSUED BUT NOT ON STATEMENT
108 $ 10.00
115   21.00
116   17.50

TOTAL $ 416.56

SUBTRACT SERVICE CHARGES AND OTHER BANK CHARGES NOT IN CHECKBOOK

$ 3.00
Tex Power   72.00

TOTAL	$ 48.50	TOTAL	$ 75.00
BALANCE	$ 341.56	BALANCE	$ 341.56

THESE TOTALS REPRESENT THE CORRECT AMOUNT OF MONEY YOU HAVE IN THE BANK AND SHOULD AGREE. DIFFERENCES, IF ANY, SHOULD BE REPORTED TO THE BANK WITHIN TEN DAYS AFTER THE RECEIPT OF YOUR STATEMENT.

By using the reconciliation form, Alan proved the accuracy of the bank statement and his record by (1) subtracting the total of the outstanding checks he had listed on the form from the bank statement balance, and (2) subtracting the service charge and the automatic payment of his electric bill from his checkbook balance.

In some cases, other additions or subtractions might have to be made in the reconciliation. For example, a charge made for stopping payment on a check should be subtracted from the checkbook balance. Also, a deposit made so late in the month that it did not appear on the bank statement should be added to the balance on the bank statement.

If the balances do not agree, either you or your bank has made an error. In that case, you should compare your canceled checks with those listed on the bank statement and with those recorded in your check register. Be sure that you have recorded all EFT transactions. Then carefully go over the calculations on your register. If you do not find an error in your calculations, take the matter up with the bank right away.

After you have reconciled your bank statement, correct any errors that you made on your register. Note how Alan has entered his reconciliation in his check register in Figure 25-5. Some people like to note the reconciliation entry in a different color so that next month they will know where to start with the new bank statement. On Alan's reconciliation entry, he has subtracted the service charge and the electric bill payment. The new balance now agrees with the bank statement. With his account now in order, he can feel free to write checks on his new balance.

Figure 25-5 Alan finds it helpful to make reconciliation entries in his check register in a different color.

ITEM NO. OR TRANSACTION CODE	DATE	DESCRIPTION OF TRANSACTION	AMOUNT OF PAYMENT OR WITHDRAWAL (−)		✓	TAX OR OTHER	AMOUNT OF DEPOSIT OR INTEREST (+)		BALANCE FORWARD	
PLEASE BE SURE TO **DEDUCT** CHARGES THAT AFFECT YOUR ACCOUNT			SUBTRACTIONS				ADDITIONS		455	06
115	19-- 4/30	TO Beechcraft & Ball, Ltd. FOR Shirt	21	00					21 434	00 06
116	4/30	TO Nelson's Garage FOR auto repairs	17	50					17 416	50 56
Recon	4/30	TO Service charge FOR April	3	00					3 413	00 56
AP	4/30	TO Tex Power FOR automatic payment-electric	72	00					72 341	00 56
		TO FOR								
		TO FOR								

Increasing Your Business Vocabulary

The following terms should become part of your business vocabulary. For each numbered item, find the term that has the same meaning.

bank reconciliation

bank statement

canceled check

clearing a check

clearing house

outstanding checks

1. A place where member banks exchange checks to clear them.
2. Returning a check to the drawer's bank to be paid and charged to his or her checking account.
3. A report sent by the bank to a depositor showing the status of his or her account.
4. A check that has been paid by the bank.
5. Checks that have not been deducted from the bank-statement balance.
6. A statement showing how the checkbook balance and the bank statement were brought into agreement.

Reviewing Your Reading

1. How are checks cleared in the same bank? How are they cleared between different banks in a small town?
2. In large cities where there are many banks, how are checks cleared?
3. Explain the role of the Federal Reserve System in clearing checks.
4. What seven items of information are included on a bank statement?
5. How does a depositor know that his or her checks have been paid?
6. Explain how you can prove that a certain payment was made if your bank files your checks instead of returning them to you.
7. Why should you save canceled checks?
8. For what six reasons might your bank statement and your checkbook balance differ?
9. When EFT transactions are involved in a bank statement error, what is the usual cause?
10. How do you reconcile a bank statement? State the steps briefly.
11. How would you record a service charge on your check stub or in your register?

Using Your Business Knowledge

1. Helen and Jim Hogan were talking about whether or not to save their canceled checks from their joint account. Jim says, "Throw them out; I hate a cluttered house." Helen reminds him, "Remember what happened last year when you tried to use your check register to prove you paid the furniture bill? I think we should save the canceled checks." Do your agree with Helen or Jim? Why?

2. Isaac Ahlred has received his bank statement for the month of May. The bank statement shows a balance of $401.19, but his check register shows a balance of only $364.52.
   a. What is the most likely reason that the bank balance is larger than Isaac's?
   b. What steps should Isaac take to bring his balances into agreement?
3. Look at Alan Edwards' bank statement in

Figure 25-3 on page 366 and answer these questions:
a. What is his account number?
b. How many deposits did he make? What was the total amount?
c. How many withdrawals were made? What was the total amount?
d. Does the statement show any outstanding checks? How is this indicated on the statement. If there are none indicated, how would Alan find out if there are any?
e. Is there a service charge? If so, how much is it?
f. How many EFT transactions were made during the month?

4. Burt Engles maintains a checking account at the Fulton Trust Company. He drew a check on his account for $97.31 and sent it to the Edison Electric Company. The Edison Electric Company deposited the check in the Fifth National Bank, which in turn sent the check to the Fulton Trust Company for payment. Assuming that all parties concerned were located in the same city, draw a chart similar to the one in Figure 25-1 on page 362 showing the movement of the check from the time it was issued by Burt Engles until it was returned to him.

Computing Business Problems

1. When Gizella Ott began to reconcile her bank statement, she discovered that four checks she had written had not been paid by the bank. The amounts of the checks were $24.50, $7.28, $20, and $46.72.
   a. What is the total amount of unpaid checks?
   b. In order to reconcile the statement, should Gizella subtract this total from the bank statement balance or from her checking account balance?
2. When the four banks in the town of Butler prepared to clear checks one day, they found that they had paid checks drawn on the other banks as shown in the following table:

	Drawn On			
Checks Held By	First National	Farmers' Trust	Merchants' Mutual	Butler Bank
First National	—	$938.57	$644.63	$1,158.64
Farmers' Trust	$443.74	—	$711.44	$ 208.45
Merchants' Mutual	$304.36	$522.82	—	$ 639.28
Butler Bank	$988.95	$326.31	$783.30	—

Assuming that each bank makes an individual settlement with every other bank, calculate the amount that each bank will either pay or receive from every other bank.

3. In October, Tom Jones received his bank statement that showed a balance of $378.65. The service charge was $3. In examining his statement, he found that the following checks were outstanding: No. 31, $7.16; No. 34, $15.10; and No. 35, $9.95. His checkbook balance at the end of the month was $349.44. Reconcile his bank statement.

4. Olivia Cardona operates Spectacular Candles, a shell-candle gift shop in a stall at the TriCity

Mall. Her bank balance on June 1 was $471.04. During the Area Festival Week of June 1, she made the following deposits: $57.10, $101.96, $231, $198.04, $172, $298.30. During that week, Olivia wrote the following checks: to herself for salary, $225; to TriCity Mall, for stall rental, $390; to Wrapping Classics, Inc., for wrapping supplies and bags, $154.80; and to TriCity Herald, for an ad, $75. If her account falls below $50 on any day of the month, she pays a $10 service charge to her bank.

a. What balance should her check register show at the end of the week?

b. Should Olivia's June bank statement show a service charge based on her checking account activities for the first week? If so, how much?

5. Stephanie Moore's April bank statement has arrived. Her interest-bearing account incurs a service charge of $8 if it falls below $1,500 on any day during the month. She has stopped payment on one check during the month. An examination of her statement shows the following: statement balance, $1,486.20; service charge, $8; stop payment fee, $13; automatic loan payment, $200; outstanding checks: No. 27, $82.50: No. 30, $17.13, No. 31, $6.24: No. 32, $50; and interest earned, $59.58. Stephanie's checkbook balance was $1,491.75. Reconcile Stephanie's bank statement.

Expanding Your Understanding of Business

1. Among the EFT programs offered by some banks are debit cards and smart cards. By interviewing a banker or using library sources, answer the following questions:

   a. What is the basic use of debit cards?

   b. What are several uses of the smart card?

   c. Is there a difference between debit cards and smart cards? If so, what?

   d. Are these cards offered by banks in your community?

2. Statements of interest-bearing checking accounts show interest earned each month. The statement will be the first record of the interest earned that the customer sees. The statement will therefore be out of balance with the customer's records. Using the form in Figure 25-4 on page 368, show how this interest on checking will be handled in reconciling the account.

3. The following is a list of items for which many banks charge a fee. State briefly the meaning of each item. Find out if a local bank charges for these services, and, if so, what amount?

   a. Overdraft

   b. Insufficient funds

   c. Stop-payment order

   d. Photocopy of a paid check

   e. Extra statement

   f. Dormant account

   g. Postdated check

   h. Returned deposit item

   i. Counter check used on restricted account

   Collect from three banks their schedule of fees and charges. List and define any additional charges that you find on their schedules.

4. Visit a bank in your community that has automatic teller service. Write a brief report describing how a customer would use the automatic teller for the following transactions:

   a. To obtain $50 in cash.

   b. To pay a utility bill of $87.92.

   c. To transfer $200 from a savings to a checking account.

Other Ways of Making Payments

Chapter 26

Chapter Objectives

After studying this chapter and completing the end-of-chapter activities, you will be able to:

1. *State three points to consider in choosing the best method of making a payment or transferring money.*

2. *Name four basic methods of payment other than cash or personal checks.*

3. *Explain how four kinds of money orders are purchased and used.*

4. *Explain why traveler's checks are considered to be a good way for travelers to make payments.*

5. *Explain how payments are made through electronic funds transfer.*

6. *State where you could go for advice on the best method of making a payment.*

A television ad tells the story in two brief scenes. In Scene I, the young bride and groom, on a limited budget and driving an old car that has broken down, call the bride's parents for help. "Please send the money soon, Mom," the bride pleads tearfully, "or there won't be a honeymoon." In Scene II, the happy couple is pictured a short time later reaching across the counter at the telegraph office where the cash from home is counted out to them.

In this situation, a check would not have arrived in time to help the young couple. A faster means, with arrangements for transferring money electronically, was necessary. In this chapter, you will learn about the telegraphic money order used by the bride's parents as well as other means of making payments.

As safe and convenient as checks are, there are times when personal checks are not the best way to transfer money. There are even situations in which personal checks may not be accepted. People traveling far from home may have difficulty in cashing a check because they are not known. People making large purchases may find that the seller questions whether or not there is enough money in the purchaser's account to cover the check offered in payment. For a variety of reasons, other means of making payments are needed. Fortunately, other means are available. These include money orders, traveler's checks, certified checks, bank-guaranteed checks, and electronic funds transfers. In choosing the best method, you will need to consider where and to whom the money is going, how fast it must get there, and how much you are sending.

MONEY ORDERS

A person who does not have a checking account and who wants to send a small payment through the mail may purchase a money order. A **money order** is a form of payment that orders the issuing agency to pay the amount printed on the form to another party. When you buy a money order, you pay the issuing agency the amount of the payment you want to make and a service fee.

Money orders are convenient because they can be purchased in many places. They are sold by banks, post offices, express companies, and telegraph offices. Many retail stores, such as supermarkets and drugstores, also sell them.

Let's look at an example of how money orders work. Jill Carter wants to order a metric tool kit from the Precision Tool Company. The company does not take personal checks on first orders and it would take several weeks for Jill to establish credit with the company. She needs the tools right away to work on her car. How should she pay for the tool kit? There are several kinds of money orders that she could buy.

Illus. 26-1
Money orders are
sold in many
locations. Service
fees may vary.

Bank Money Orders

One way Jill Carter could pay for her metric tool kit is to buy a money order
from her bank. A *bank money order* is a form sold by a bank stating that
money is to be paid to the person or business named on the form.

In the bank money order shown in Figure 26-1, Jill Carter is sending
$72.50 to the Precision Tool Company. She pays the bank $72.50 plus a
service charge, which may be about $2.

Figure 26-1
After payment is
made, a bank
money order is
returned to the
issuing bank.

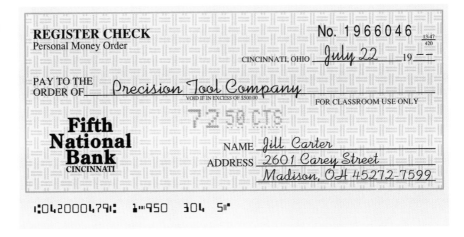

When this money order has been paid, it will not be returned to Jill as a canceled check would be. It will be returned to the bank that issued it. However, the money order can be obtained if Jill wants to prove that payment was made. Since bank practices in issuing money orders vary, check with your bank to find out what its practice is before you buy a money order.

Postal Money Orders

Jill Carter may also purchase a money order from the post office. When you buy a *postal money order*, the postal clerk registers by machine the amount in figures and words. You then complete the form by filling in the payee's name, your name and address, and the purpose of the money order. Figure 26-2 shows a sample postal money order.

Figure 26-2 A postal money order can be cashed only after it is signed by the payee.

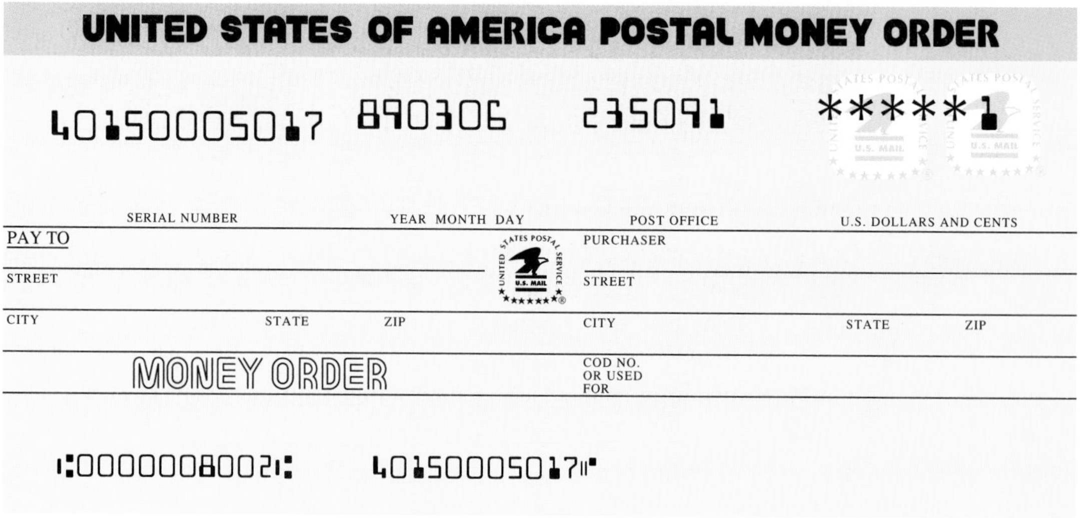
UNITED STATES OF AMERICA POSTAL MONEY ORDER

40150005017 890306 235091 *****1

SERIAL NUMBER | YEAR MONTH DAY | POST OFFICE | U.S. DOLLARS AND CENTS

PAY TO | PURCHASER

STREET | STREET

CITY STATE ZIP | CITY STATE ZIP

MONEY ORDER | COD NO. OR USED FOR

⑆000000800 2⑆ 40150005017⑈

You can send a postal money order safely through the mail because it can be cashed only after it is signed by the payee. If a money order is lost or stolen, the receipt copy that you receive may be used in making a claim with the post office. The payee may cash the postal money order at a post office or a bank or may transfer it to another person by filling in the information requested on the back of the money order.

Postal money orders are issued only in amounts up to $700. If you want to send a larger amount, you may buy more money orders. Fees for postal money orders vary with the amounts that are purchased, but the charge is small.

Express Money Orders

Jill Carter could also use an *express money order* to pay for her tool kit. Express money orders are sold by offices of the American Express Company, Traveler's Express Company, Federal Express Services Corporation, some travel agencies, and many retail stores, such as supermarkets, pharmacies, and convenience stores. A Traveler's Express money order is shown in Figure 26-3.

An express money order can be written only for amounts up to $299.99, but you may buy as many as you want. Charges are usually $1 per money order. If you buy an express money order, you should keep the receipt as proof that you bought the money order.

Figure 26-3 An express money order.

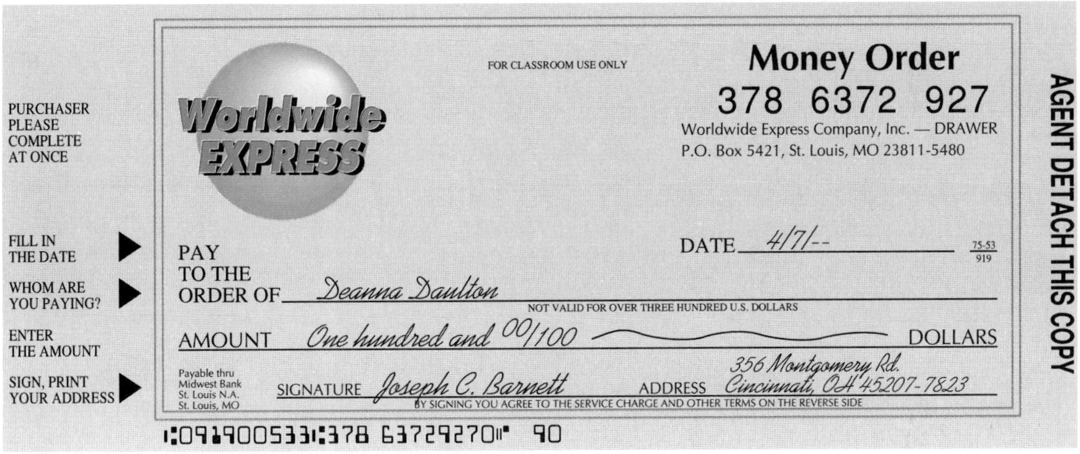
PURCHASER PLEASE COMPLETE AT ONCE

Worldwide EXPRESS

FOR CLASSROOM USE ONLY

Money Order
378 6372 927
Worldwide Express Company, Inc. — DRAWER
P.O. Box 5421, St. Louis, MO 23811-5480

FILL IN THE DATE ▶ DATE 4/7/-- 75-53/919

WHOM ARE YOU PAYING? ▶ PAY TO THE ORDER OF Deanna Daulton

NOT VALID FOR OVER THREE HUNDRED U.S. DOLLARS

ENTER THE AMOUNT AMOUNT One hundred and 00/100 DOLLARS

SIGN, PRINT YOUR ADDRESS ▶ Payable thru Midwest Bank St. Louis N.A. St. Louis, MO SIGNATURE Joseph C. Barnett ADDRESS 356 Montgomery Rd. Cincinnati, OH 45207-7823

BY SIGNING YOU AGREE TO THE SERVICE CHARGE AND OTHER TERMS ON THE REVERSE SIDE

⑆0919005331⑆378 63729270⑈ 90

AGENT DETACH THIS COPY

Telegraphic Money Orders

When buying a *telegraphic money order*, you buy a message directing a telegraph office to pay a sum of money to a certain person or business. Although her situation is not urgent, Jill Carter could use a telegraphic money order. Telegraphic money orders are used mainly in an emergency—when money must be delivered quickly. That's why the bride's parents chose the telegraphic money order to send money to the bride and groom in the introduction to this chapter—so they could get their car repaired and continue driving to their destination. Let's look at another example.

Suppose that while Sami Peery is on a senior class trip to Washington, D.C.—2,000 miles from home—she loses her wallet with all her money. Sami may phone her parents requesting $100 spending money for the rest of the trip. A telegraphic money order will probably be the best way to get the money to her fast. Her father will pay the $100 plus a handling fee to his telegraphic office in Denver, Colorado. A telegram like the one shown in Figure 26-4 will be sent ordering the Washington, D.C., telegraph office to pay Sami $100. If the message is sent promptly, Sami should have the money soon after her call is made or the telegram is sent. To receive the money, Sami will be required to fill out Western Union's "To Receive Money" form and present it with valid identification. If she lost her identification with her wallet, she may be asked a personal test question by the Western Union agent.

To be sure that the right person receives the money, a test question may be sent free. The sender may choose to ask a personal question, such as "When is your mother's birthday?" Sami's father would tell the clerk the answer to the question. In order to get the money, Sami would have to give the Washington, D.C., clerk the correct answer. Mr. Peery could request a report that the money was paid to Sami. For this service, he would pay an additional fee.

Figure 26-4 Telegraphic money orders are usually used in emergencies—when money is needed quickly.

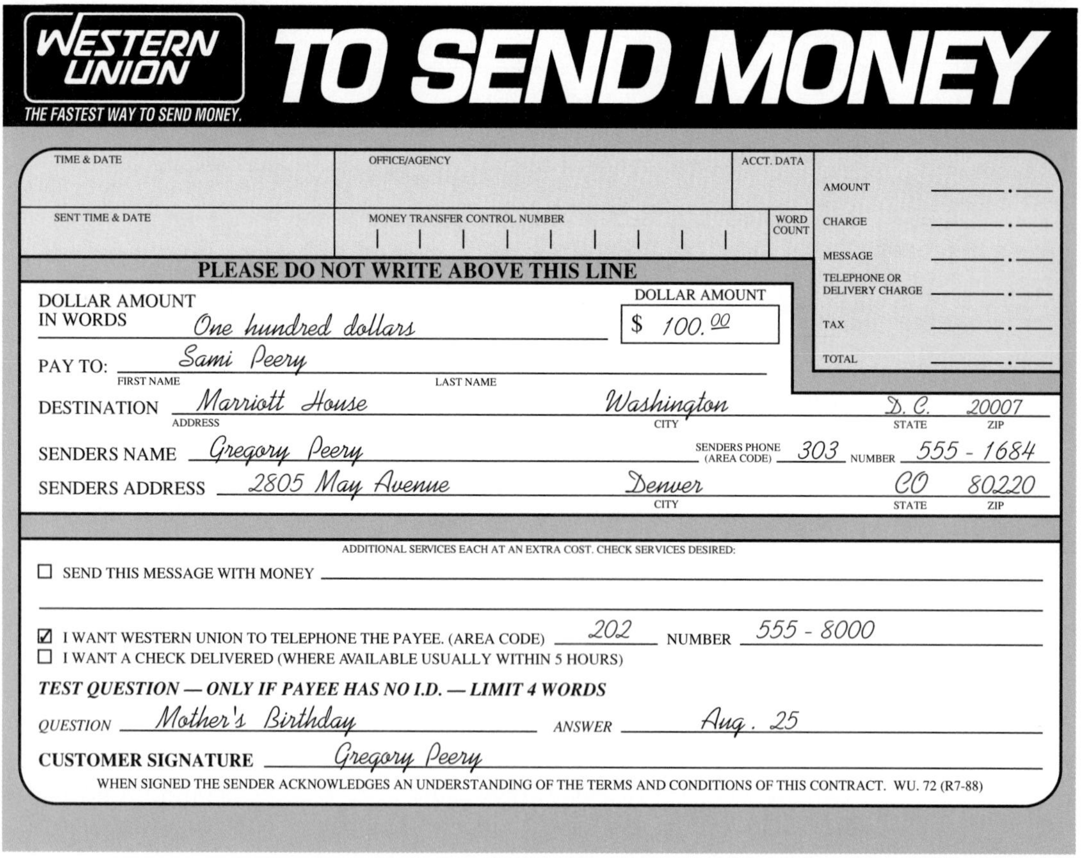

WESTERN UNION **TO SEND MONEY**

THE FASTEST WAY TO SEND MONEY.

TIME & DATE | OFFICE/AGENCY | ACCT. DATA

SENT TIME & DATE | MONEY TRANSFER CONTROL NUMBER | WORD COUNT

AMOUNT ____ . ____
CHARGE ____ . ____
MESSAGE ____ . ____
TELEPHONE OR DELIVERY CHARGE ____ . ____
TAX ____ . ____
TOTAL ____ . ____

PLEASE DO NOT WRITE ABOVE THIS LINE

DOLLAR AMOUNT IN WORDS *One hundred dollars* DOLLAR AMOUNT $ *100.00*

PAY TO: *Sami Peery* (FIRST NAME, LAST NAME)

DESTINATION *Marriott House* (ADDRESS) *Washington* (CITY) *D.C.* (STATE) *20007* (ZIP)

SENDERS NAME *Gregory Peery* SENDERS PHONE (AREA CODE) *303* NUMBER *555 - 1684*

SENDERS ADDRESS *2805 May Avenue* *Denver* (CITY) *CO* (STATE) *80220* (ZIP)

ADDITIONAL SERVICES EACH AT AN EXTRA COST. CHECK SERVICES DESIRED:

☐ SEND THIS MESSAGE WITH MONEY

☑ I WANT WESTERN UNION TO TELEPHONE THE PAYEE. (AREA CODE) *202* NUMBER *555 - 8000*
☐ I WANT A CHECK DELIVERED (WHERE AVAILABLE USUALLY WITHIN 5 HOURS)

TEST QUESTION — ONLY IF PAYEE HAS NO I.D. — LIMIT 4 WORDS

QUESTION *Mother's Birthday* *ANSWER* *Aug. 25*

CUSTOMER SIGNATURE *Gregory Peery*

WHEN SIGNED THE SENDER ACKNOWLEDGES AN UNDERSTANDING OF THE TERMS AND CONDITIONS OF THIS CONTRACT. WU. 72 (R7-88)

A charge is made for any other message sent with the telegraphic money order. Sending money in this way is somewhat expensive when one considers the cost of telegrams both ways and the cost of the money order. However, this form of payment is very useful in an emergency.

TRAVELER'S CHECKS

It is risky to carry a large sum of money when you travel, since it can be lost or stolen easily. It is also difficult to pay traveling expenses with personal checks. You will be dealing mostly with strangers, and, as you have learned, strangers may not accept personal checks. Even money orders may not be useful when traveling, as you may not have the identification that is necessary for cashing them.

Special forms designed for the traveler to use in making payments are called **traveler's checks**. You can buy them at banks, express companies, credit unions, and travel bureaus. They are sold in several denominations, such as $10, $20, $50, and $100. In addition to the value of the checks, there is usually a charge of 1 percent of the value with a minimum charge of 50 cents. This means that $100 worth of traveler's checks will cost $101. However, some banks and credit unions do not charge for traveler's checks if customers have certain types of accounts. Some travel agencies, such as the American Automobile Association, also provide free traveler's checks to their members.

Traveler's checks have two places for your signature. When you buy the checks, you sign each one in the presence of the selling agent. When you cash a check or pay for a purchase with it, you sign it again in the presence of the person accepting it. That person checks to see that the two signatures are alike. At that time, you also fill in the date and the name of the payee.

Illus. 26-2
You must sign traveler's checks twice, once when you purchase them, a second time when you make a purchase with them.

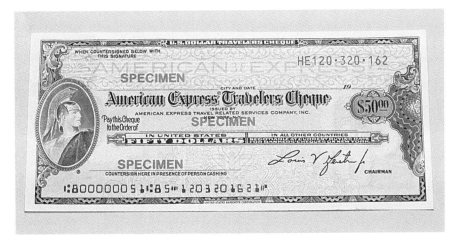

Traveler's checks, especially those widely advertised, are commonly accepted throughout the world. Almost any business is willing to accept a traveler's check since there is little chance of its not being signed by the right person.

When you buy traveler's checks, you should immediately record the serial number of each check on a form that is generally given to you by the issuing agency. Then, on the same form, record the place and date you cash each check. Keep this record separate from your checks so that you can refer to it if your checks are lost or stolen. If they are lost or stolen, report it at once to the nearest bank or office where such checks are sold. The company that issued them will replace them.

BANK-GUARANTEED CHECKS

There are many times when a personal check will not be the best means of paying for a product or service. But there is a way to have a bank guarantee that the check will be good, and this makes the check acceptable when it otherwise would not be. Banks provide several kinds of checks that they guarantee. Learning about these will give you several options to choose from when deciding the best way to make a payment. Let's look at three bank-guaranteed checks.

Certified Checks

A **certified check** is a personal check on which the bank has written its guarantee that the check will be paid. The certification is stamped on the face of the check and is signed or initialed by a bank officer. Suppose Hazel Canton wants to make a payment to someone who does not know her and who does not want to accept her personal check. She could use several forms of payment, as you have learned, but she may want to have the transaction recorded in her checking account. Ms. Canton could have her bank certify her check, as shown in Figure 26-5. If she has an account at the bank, she may pay a fee of about $4. If she does not have an account there, the fee may be $8 or more.

When the bank certifies Ms. Canton's check, the amount of the check is immediately subtracted from her account. This makes it impossible for her to withdraw the money or to use it for other checks. If the check is not used, it may be returned to the bank and credited to her account.

Bank Drafts

For certain large payments, a bank's own check may be purchased. Banks usually deposit part of their funds in other banks. An officer of a bank may draw checks on these deposits in the same way that you may draw on funds that you have deposited in your bank. A check that a bank official draws on

Figure 26-5
The Merchants Bank guarantees that this certified check will be paid.

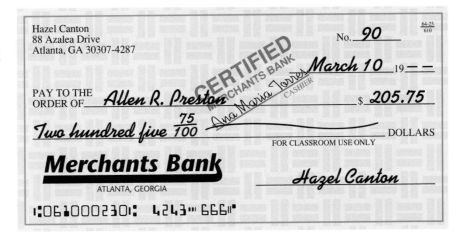

the bank's deposits in another bank is known as a **bank draft**. Anyone can buy a bank draft simply by going to a bank and requesting one for a certain amount. Let's see how that works.

Suppose Juan Quintero, a newly established contractor in Salem, Oregon, wanted to make a large payment to the TriState Prefab Company (TSPCo) in Eugene, Oregon. TSPCo does not accept personal checks from new customers. Juan could pay the $14,720.62 with a bank draft. In this case, the draft would be a check that Juan's Salem Bank wrote on funds it has on deposit in another bank. The other bank may be a commercial bank in Eugene or a western district Federal Reserve Bank. Juan would pay his bank $14,720.62 plus a fee for issuing the draft. The service charge is usually based on a small percentage of the amount of the draft, with a set minimum fee. Juan's bank draft is shown in Figure 26-6.

Figure 26-6
A bank draft may be used when a personal check is not acceptable.

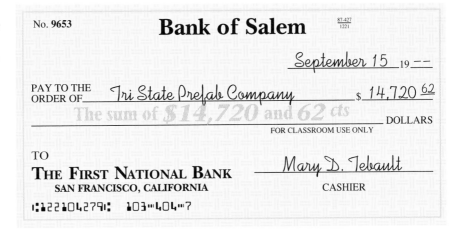

Cashier's Checks

Banks also keep funds within their own banks on which they can write checks. A **cashier's check** is a check that a bank draws on its own in-house funds. It was so named because such checks were originally written by a bank employee known as a cashier. Some banks refer to checks drawn on their own funds as officer's checks, treasurer's checks, or manager's checks, depending upon who is authorized to sign them. A cashier's check is shown in Figure 26-7. As with bank drafts, a cashier's check costs the amount of the check plus a service fee. Both are often used to make rather large payments. These banker's checks are more acceptable than the personal checks of an individual whom the payee may not know.

Figure 26-7
A cashier's check is drawn on a bank's own in-house funds.

November 13 19 --

No. **1081**

GRAND CANYON NATIONAL BANK

Kingman, Arizona

91-153
1221

PAY TO THE
ORDER OF___Kenneth C. Adler_____ $ 239.50

The sum of *239 DOLS 50 CTS*

FOR CLASSROOM USE ONLY

_____ DOLLARS

CASHIER'S CHECK

Yoko Matsumi
CASHIER

⑆221015361⑈ 423 996 6⑈

Bank checks, as well as money orders, can also be used for sending payments to other countries. Information about the methods of making payments to businesses or individuals in foreign countries may be obtained from the bank or from the place where the money order is purchased. Any time you do not know the best means of making a payment, ask your bank for advice.

ELECTRONIC FUNDS TRANSFER

As you learned in Chapter 22, electronic funds transfer (EFT) is the moving of funds from one account to another and from one bank to another by computer. This means that payments can be made without a written form, such as a check. Electronic funds transfer gives faster and less costly service than has been possible the past. Let's discuss some of the EFT services that are now becoming commonplace.

Individuals can instruct their banks to pay automatically such monthly bills as utility and telephone charges. Each month the utility company, for example, sends to the bank the bills for everyone who has instructed them to do so. The bank subtracts the amounts due from the accounts of the customers who have instructed the bank to make monthly utility payments automatically for them. The amounts from the customers' accounts are added to the utility company's account.

Many businesses hesitate to accept a personal check as payment without proof that the customer's account contains at least the amount of the check. With EFT, however, customers can often have their checks approved at a terminal located in the store where they are shopping. The information from the terminal tells the merchant that the amount of the check is covered by the current balance in the customer's account. This verifies the check at the point of sale and the merchant then is willing to accept the personal check for payment.

As you have learned, automatic teller machines are increasing in popularity. ATMs—actually computer terminals—allow customers to make payments or transfer money for a variety of reasons at any hour of the day or night. Bank customers can also make deposits and withdrawals, transfer money from savings to checking accounts, make a loan payment, or even get a loan at these electronic terminals. Automatic tellers are placed in convenient locations, such as in shopping malls, in airports, and on street corners.

Your employer can also pay your salary through EFT. Some businesses have practically eliminated payroll checks by directing their bank to pay their employees through EFT. The bank subtracts the total amount of the payroll from the business's account and adds the amount earned to each employee's account, even if the employees' accounts are in several different banks. The computer is programmed to transfer electronically the amount of the salary to the appropriate bank for each employee.

Reprinted by permission: Tribune Media Services.

Other EFT services are available and more are being developed all the time. As more people buy their own personal computers, more payments will be made electronically. The customer's computer will be able to communicate with the bank's computer, permitting the customer to do a great deal of banking electronically. EFT has helped banks reduce paperwork and it has sped up the transfer of funds. EFT is not, however, expected to eliminate checks or traditional banking methods completely.

Increasing Your Business Vocabulary

The following terms should become part of your business vocabulary. For each numbered item, find the term that has the same meaning.

> *bank draft*   *money order*
> *cashier's check*   *traveler's check*
> *certified check*

1. A personal check on which the bank has written its guarantee that the check will be paid.
2. A check that a bank official draws on the banks's deposits in another bank.
3. A form designed for the traveler to use in making payments.

4. A form of payment that orders the issuing agency to pay the amount printed on the form to another party.
5. A check that a bank draws on its own in-house funds.

Reviewing Your Reading

1. Why are personal checks not always the best way to make payments?
2. In choosing the best method of making a payment, what three things should you consider?
3. Name five methods of payment other than cash or personal checks.
4. What happens to a bank money order after it has been paid?
5. Why is it considered safe to send a postal money order through the mail?
6. In what ways is an express money order different from a bank money order and a postal money order?

7. What is the procedure for sending money by telegraphic money order?
8. Why are traveler's checks better for the traveler to carry than personal checks or cash?
9. What does a bank do to show that it has certified a check?
10. What is the major difference between a bank draft and a cashier's check?
11. Explain how payments are made through EFT. Give an example of an EFT payment.
12. If you do not know which type of special money payment to use in a certain situation, where can you find out?

Using Your Business Knowledge

1. While on a vacation trip, the Mendoza family found an old jukebox made in the 1930s and in good working order in an antique shop. The family decided that it would be a good addition to the family recreation room. The jukebox cost $500 and the dealer would not accept a personal check or credit cards. What method could be used to pay for the jukebox?
2. Suppose you want to send $76 to Classic Car Parts, Inc., in another city for parts needed to repair an old car. You have no checking account. Would you make the payment with a certified check, money order, or a bank draft? Explain.
3. Frieda and Ned Scopi are moving to a distant city where Frieda has been transferred by her employer. The moving company has instructed them to have a cashier's check ready to pay the driver when their furniture is delivered to their new home. Give several reasons for the mover's request for this type of payment.
4. The Edfield family made the following money payments during a six-month period. In each case, tell what method of making payment you would recommend.
   a. Mrs. Edfield paid the phone bill at the local office.
   b. Mr. Edfield made the monthly payment on the house at the local bank.
   c. The Edfields paid their federal income taxes.
   d. Mr. Edfield bought his automobile license plates.
   e. The Edfields paid $150 for goods they ordered from an Atlanta mail-order house. They wanted the goods shipped at once, but they had never bought from that firm before and they do not use credit cards.
   f. Mr. Edfield had an automobile accident 300 miles from home. Mrs. Edfield sent him $300 by the fastest method.
   g. Mr. Edfield paid $27.82 for repairs at a local garage.
   h. Mrs. Edfield paid $177 each month for a loan from her bank.

Computing Business Problems

1. Michaela Jarrett bought traveler's checks from her credit union to pay for her family's vacation. She must pay a fee of 1 percent of the value of the checks. The denominations she chose were $400 in $50 checks and $200 in $20 checks.
   a. How many $50 checks did she receive? How many $20 checks did she receive?
   b. How much was the bank's charge for the checks?
   c. What was the total cost of Mrs. Jarrett's checks?
2. Tiffany Taylor is a Dixieland jazz fan. She ordered a tape to add to her collection. The tape was advertised on television as available only through the station address. Customers could pay the $9.95 cost by credit card, check, or money order or, for an additional fee, could order COD (collect on delivery). Since Tiffany did not have a credit card or a checking account, she used a postal money order for the tape. The cost of the order was 75 cents.
   a. What was the total cost of the tape?
   b. If the postage and handling fee for delivery to Tiffany's home were $2.64, how much would the tape cost if it came COD?
   c. How much did Tiffany save by sending the payment with her order?
3. Julio Costa's ability to repair bicycles has developed into an after-school business.

He can get parts cheaper by ordering them from wholesale houses in several cities. He pays by postal money order. During the last three months, he made the following payments:

Honda Cycle House:
$12.72, $17.96, $29.80
Harley Wheels, Inc.:
$81.04, $9.16, $47.08, $20

The post office fee schedule is as follows:

Amount of Order	Fee
$ 0.01 to $ 35	$ .75
$35.01 to $700	$1.00

a. What was the cost of each postal money order? List the payments in a column and write the fee beside each.
b. What was the total cost of Julio's postal money orders for the three months?
c. What was the total cost of the bicycle parts Julio ordered, including the cost of the money orders?

4. On August 10, Grace Whiteside of Seattle suddenly remembered that it was the twenty-first birthday of her twin grandsons, Tom and Terry of Athens, Georgia. She had forgotten to send her usual gift of $1 per year of age to each grandson. To get her gift to them on time, she decided to send a telegraphic money order for the total amount, addressed to both young men, and have it delivered to their home. She included this message: "Happy Birthday, Tom and Terry. Our love and a dollar per year." The fee schedule was as follows:

Base Fee for Office Delivery

Amount	Fee
$0 - $50	$12
$50 - $100	$14

Additional Fee for Home Delivery	Message
$10	$2 minimum, 10 words 20 cents per word over minimum

a. How much money was sent by money order as a combined gift?
b. What was the fee for the delivered money order, not including the message?
c. What was the charge for the message?
d. What was the total cost of Mrs. Whiteside's gift to Tom and Terry?

Expanding Your Understanding of Business

1. A memo from an employer gave employees the option of receiving their paychecks as usual or having their wages deposited automatically to their accounts at their individual banks. List some advantages and disadvantages of the automatic deposit plan that you would consider if you were one of the employees. Which method would you choose? Why?
2. List the name of at least one place in your community where each type of money order can be bought. What is the cost of each kind of money order for $10? for $50?
3. Certified checks are often required in real estate closings. Why might a personal check not be acceptable? Find the cost of a certified check at a local bank or savings and loan association. A real estate agent, lawyer, or banker might help you with your answer.
4. Some banks include in their certifying stamp on certified checks the words, "Do

not destroy.'' To whom is this addressed? Why are the words included? If the words were not included, is it all right to destroy the check?

5. There are several types of traveler's checks. Illus. 26-2 on page 379 shows the American Express traveler's check. Find out what other types are sold in your community. Is there a difference in the cost?

6. Certified checks sometimes are imprinted with the words, ''collectible at par.'' Find out what this means and whether a bank in your community issues certified checks including these words.

Career Focus

The financial industry offers a variety of career opportunities. More than 2.25 million people are employed in over 61,000 banks and their branches and over 20,000 other financial institutions. Most of these workers are employed in commercial banks. Others work in specialized banks and in savings and loan associations, credit unions, and finance companies.

Approximately two-thirds of all bank employees are clerical workers. Bank officers and managers make up about 30 percent of the total. A small percentage are professional workers, such as economists, attorneys, and investment analysts, and specialists in computer technology, marketing personnel, and public relations. The remaining employees include guards, maintenance workers, and other service personnel.

Job Titles: Job titles commonly found in this career area include:

Trust Officer
Branch Manager
New Accounts Clerk
Word Processing Specialist
Loan Officer
Commercial Teller
Systems Analyst
Financial Manager

Employment Outlook: The Department of Labor estimates that growth in the service occupations of finance, insurance, and real estate will increase by approximately 27 percent by the year 2000. Employment in management-related occupations tends to be related to industry growth. The outlook for bank managers and officers may be somewhat slower than the aver-

age, since growth in the number of banks and financial institutions has been slowing somewhat during the past few years. According to the Labor Department, the number of bank tellers, which make up a large portion of bank employees, is expected to increase more slowly than the average for all occupations by the year 2000. Employment growth among bank tellers is not expected to keep pace with the overall employment growth in banks and other financial institutions because of the increased use of automatic teller machines and other electronic equipment. Nevertheless, qualified applicants should have good prospects for both full- and part-time employment, since bank tellers provide a relatively large number of job

openings. Replacement needs will probably provide most of the job opportunities.

Future Changes: As the financial industry continues to expand the use of electronic technology, a large number of these specialized workers will be needed. Also, as deregulation allows banks to expand their services into other fields such as investment counseling, real estate, and insurance there will be a need for employees for these special fields.

What Is Done on the Job: The type of jobs in financial firms are about the same across the industry. However, all of the jobs are not found in all institutions.

Tellers spend most of the time working directly with customers, receiving and paying out money. At the end of the day, tellers must count the money, balance their cash drawers, and reconcile their daily computer-terminal printouts with their cash transactions. They may then help sort and file checks, notes, and other papers. In a large bank, tellers duties are often specialized. A loan teller, for example, receives only loan payments, while a payroll teller handles payroll accounts for businesses that are the bank's customers.

Most clerical workers perform their jobs behind the scenes, handling routine paperwork and record keeping. They may operate computer terminals, word processors, and sorting machines. They may write computer programs, record transactions in customers' accounts, or sort and file checks and other papers. Some clerks handle specialized duties. An interest clerk, for example, is responsible for keeping the records of notes on which the bank must collect or pay interest.

The bank may have many officers and managers. A loan officer is responsible for making loans to businesses and individuals. The operations officer is responsible for seeing that the daily operations of the bank flow smoothly and efficiently. This officer usually directs the work of tellers, clerks, data processors, and word processing specialists.

Education and Training: Most beginning jobs in banking require at least a high school education. Many entry-level employees also have had additional business preparation in community or technical colleges. Officers, professional personnel, and executives usually have college degrees.

Bank workers who meet the public must be able to communicate well. They must be accurate and have businesslike appearances. Most bank workers must be able to handle details and to work well under stress. They must also be able to work at routine tasks for long periods. Knowledge of computers is increasingly important.

Salary Levels: Salaries for banking officers vary widely among banks and financial institutions. A chief executive officer in a large bank in a metropolitan area may earn $250,000 or more annually, while a management trainee in a smaller bank may earn from $14,000 to $20,000. Salaries of specialized managers also vary. The average salary of a banking chief financial officer in a recent year was $54,834, within a range of $45,897 to $72,473. Average earnings of head bank tellers that year were $15,008, within a range of $12,431 or $18,041; beginning bank tellers that year earned a salary of $9,700. In general, a greater range of responsibilities results in a higher salary. Type, size, and location of the bank, as well as the experience and length of service of the worker, also influence salaries in the financial services industry.

Additional Information: One of the best ways to learn about banking careers is to talk to a banker. Many banks have brochures that describe opportunities in banking. *The Occupational Outlook Handbook* usually lists with its banking sections several organizations relating to banking and careers within the financial industry. Consult a current edition of this publication for addresses of these organizations.

The Business of Credit

Unit Goals

After studying the chapters in this unit, you will be able to:

1. *Explain what credit is and why it is important in our economy.*
2. *Discuss and compare the use of charge accounts, credit cards, and installment loans as forms of credit.*
3. *Explain why credit costs and give several examples of costs of credit.*
4. *Discuss why credit records are important and give examples of ways in which good credit records are built.*

Chapter 27
Credit in the Economy

Chapter 28
The Use of Consumer Credit

Chapter 29
The Cost of Credit

Chapter 30
Credit Records and Regulations

A Man with a Lot of Credit

Business Brief

This is the true story of a businessperson who today is successful and rich. He was not always that way, however. As a young boy, Tom was an orphan who earned money selling newspapers on a street corner in Ann Arbor, Michigan. When he

was 23 years old, he and his brother opened a small pizza shop at the edge of Eastern Michigan University's campus in Ypsilanti. As Tom put it, my brother and I "went into hock up to our eyebrows to buy the place." The partnership did not last long. The business got off to a very slow start, and six months later his brother quit the business.

A few years later, Tom had established a record of success in opening new pizza shops in other cities. An Ann Arbor bank gave him a $400,000 line of credit to open 40 black-operated franchise stores in Detroit. The franchising operation continued to grow, and Tom's reputation as a successful businessperson grew, too.

Even though he took very little money out of his business for himself—his annual salary was about $10,000—his business developed financial problems. He had to sell some of his stores in order to raise enough money to continue operat-

ing, but even that was not enough. Nine years after opening his first store and after several years of business success and prosperity, his business faced financial difficulty. To avoid bankruptcy, he agree to have a local businessperson take over the operations of his business. During a period of rapid expansion of his business, a number of problems occurred. Among the problems that had to be solved were a lack of proper training for store managers, poor use of credit, too much debt, expansion without a long-range plan, and inadequate financial reports needed for sound business management.

Some creditors began demanding that they be paid; they were promised payment of every cent owed—a promise that was kept. A long-range plan for reorganizing the business was developed, a better accounting system was installed, and the expansion of new franchises was established on an orderly basis. Tom again became the leader of his business, and today he is one of our successful business entrepreneurs.

The story of Tom Monaghan and Domino's Pizza, Inc., is a "rags to riches" story for its owner. Success was achieved through hard work, a good business plan, an unwillingness to give up when things looked bad, the wise use of credit, and the help of others when it was needed. A boyhood dream of Tom Monaghan came true in 1983 when he bought the Detroit Tigers baseball team for $53 million—that was quite an accomplishment for a man who got his business experience selling newspapers on a street corner and later selling pizza in a small store.

Source: Based on excerpts from Tom Monaghan with Robert Anderson, *Pizza Tiger* (New York: Random House, Inc., 1986).

Credit in the Economy

Chapter Objectives

After studying this chapter and completing the end-of-chapter activities, you will be able to:

1. *Explain what credit is.*

2. *Give examples of how credit is used by consumers, businesses, and governments.*

3. *State the difference between loan credit, sales credit, and trade credit.*

4. *Discuss at least two sources of loans.*

5. *Explain how businesses use the three Cs of credit.*

6. *Give several advantages and disadvantages of using credit.*

7. *State at least four questions to be answered before using credit.*

At times, businesses, governments, and consumers borrow money. Whether the amount borrowed is large or small, being able to borrow money at a time of need is an important aspect of our economic system. The following are examples of the use of credit:

- Alex buys gas for his car and uses his oil company credit card.
- Biando's Boutique sells a blouse to a customer who charges the purchase to her charge account.
- Chi-luan applies for and receives a government loan to help with his college expenses.
- Diana borrows $1,000 from her credit union to pay for her summer cruise.
- Eduardo takes his family out to dinner and pays the bill using his bank charge card.
- Faye's family pays its telephone and electricity bills the month after those services have been used.
- Ginger and her husband apply for and receive a mortgage so that they can build a new house.
- Hiawatha County borrows $250,000 to make needed road repairs.
- Nesgiv, Inc. receives a $2 million loan to build a new tire store in the downtown area.
- Karie asks a friend for a $10 loan until payday.
- Louisiana borrows $25 million through a bond issue to construct new community college buildings.

THE USE OF SOMEONE ELSE'S MONEY

Credit is the privilege of using someone else's money for a period of time. That privilege is based on the belief that the person receiving credit will honor a promise to repay the amount owed at a future date. The credit transaction creates a debtor and a creditor. Anyone who buys on credit or receives a loan is known as a **debtor**. The one who sells on credit or makes a loan is called the **creditor**.

Although the credit system uses forms and legal documents, it also depends on trust between the debtor and creditor. **Trust** means that the creditor believes that the debtor will honor the promise to pay later for goods and services that have been received and used. Without that trust, our credit system could not operate.

When you borrow a large amount of money or buy on credit from a business, you usually will be asked to sign a written agreement. The agreement states that you will pay your debt within a certain period of time. For example, when Diana borrowed $1,000, she signed a paper which stated that she would make a payment on the first day of each month for 24 months. Chi-luan had to agree to pay his tuition loan in full within two years after graduation. When Alex used his credit card to buy gas and signed the receipt form, he agreed to pay for his purchase when the bill came at the end of the month or pay interest charges. A credit agreement means that the debtor promises to pay and the creditor trusts that the debtor will pay the amount that is owed.

THREE TYPES OF CREDIT

If you borrow money to be used later for some special purpose, you are using **loan credit**. Loans are available from several kinds of financial institutions. Banks, credit unions, savings and loan associations, and consumer finance companies are the primary businesses that make consumer loans. As you learned in Chapter 22, these institutions lend money to earn a profit through interest and other loan charges.

Loan credit usually involves a written contract. The debtor often agrees to repay the loan in specified amounts, called installments, over a period of time. You will learn more about installment and other types of loans in Chapter 28.

If you charge a purchase at the time you buy the good or service, you are using **sales credit**. Sales credit is offered by most retail and wholesale businesses. Sales credit involves the use of charge accounts and credit cards by consumers. **Trade credit** is used by a business when it receives goods from a wholesaler and pays for them at a later specified date. Trade credit terms often are stated "2/10, n/30." This means that the business can take a 2 percent discount if the bill is paid within 10 days from the billing date; the full or net amount must be paid within 30 days.

Different types of charge accounts and credit cards will be discussed in Chapter 28. All forms of credit—loan credit, sales credit, and trade credit—are important and used often in our economy.

THE USERS OF CREDIT

The dollar volume of credit in our country is very high. Here are a few figures from a recent year that show how extensively credit is used in the United States:

- Total consumer debt totaled $723 billion.
- One major retailer had a long-term debt of more than $6.5 billion.
- A large midwestern state owed $9.8 billion.
- Our federal government borrowed $236.3 billion from the public.

If you are a typical American consumer, you will use credit for many purposes. You may use credit to buy fairly expensive products that will last for a long period of time, such as a car, house, or major appliance. Or you may use credit for convenience in making smaller purchases, such as meals and CDs. Paying for medical care, vacations, taxes, and even paying off other debts are other common uses of credit.

Businesses may secure long-term loans to buy land and equipment and to construct buildings. They may also borrow money for shorter time periods, sometimes for only 1 or 2 days but usually for 30 to 90 days, to meet temporary needs for cash. For example, merchants buy goods on credit, and manufacturers buy raw materials and supplies on credit. Businesses borrow on a short-term basis to get the cash they need while waiting for goods to be sold or for customers to pay for their purchases.

Local, state, and federal governments often use credit in providing for the benefit of the public. Governments may use credit to buy items such as cars, aircraft, and police uniforms. They may also borrow the money that is needed to build hospitals, highways, parks, and airports.

BASIS FOR GRANTING CREDIT

You have already read that trust between the debtor and the creditor is essential if credit is to be granted. To become a debtor, you must be able to prove that you are dependable. Not everyone who desires credit will receive it.

The business that is considering you as a credit risk will generally ask you about your financial situation and request credit references. **Credit references** are businesses or individuals from whom you have received credit

Illus. 27-1
Businesses may secure long-term loans to buy land and to construct buildings.

in the past and/or who can help verify your credit record. The answers to the financial questions and the information received from your credit references will help the business decide whether loan or sales credit should be extended to you.

You should be willing to give all required information readily and honestly. You may be asked some of the following questions: How much do you earn? How long have you worked for your present employer? What property do you own? Do you have any other debts? Consumer protection laws, such as the Consumer Credit Protection Act, regulate the kinds of information that can be used in evaluating credit applicants. The questions listed above can be legally asked. Credit decisions cannot be made without reliable information.

THE THREE Cs OF CREDIT

In deciding whether or not to grant you credit, businesses consider three factors, known as the three Cs—character, capacity, and capital.

Character refers to your honesty and willingness to pay a debt when it is due. If you have a reputation for paying bills on time, you probably will receive credit. How you will pay your bills in the future usually can be predicted by how you have paid them in the past.

Capacity refers to your ability to pay a debt when it is due. The lender or seller must consider whether your income is large enough to permit you to pay your bills. If your income is too small or unsteady, granting you additional credit may not be wise even though you have had a good credit record in the past. On the other hand, your income may be very high, but if you already have many debts, you may not be able to handle another one.

Capital is the value of the borrower's possessions. Capital includes the capital resources you learned about in Chapter 1. It can also include the money you possess and the property you own. You may also have a car that is paid for and a house on which a large amount has been paid. You also may have a checking account and some savings that add to your capital, or you may have nothing except your present income. The value of your capital helps give the lender some assurance that you will be able to meet your credit obligations.

CREDIT CAN BE BENEFICIAL

Both businesses and consumers benefit from the use of credit. Businesses benefit in several ways. By allowing their customers to buy on credit, customers will tend to purchase more and the business will increase its profits. If the business buys its merchandise using trade credit, the merchandise can be paid for after it has been sold to customers.

As a consumer, you also can benefit from the wise use of credit. Here are some ways in which consumers benefit from their use of credit.

- *Convenience.* Credit can make it convenient for you to buy. You can shop without carrying much cash with you. There may be times when you do not have enough cash and have an urgent need for something. If your car needs emergency repairs, you may have to wait until payday unless you can have the work done on credit.
- *Immediate possession.* Credit allows you to have immediate possession of the item that you want. A family can buy a dishwasher on credit and begin using it immediately rather than waiting until enough money has been saved to pay cash for it.
- *Savings.* Credit allows you to buy an item when it goes on sale, possibly at a large saving. Some stores, especially department and furniture stores, often send notices of special sales to their credit customers several days before sales are advertised to the general public. Therefore, credit customers have first choice of the merchandise and may obtain good bargains.
- *Credit rating.* If you buy on credit and pay your bills when they are due, you gain a reputation for being dependable. In that way, you establish a favorable **credit rating**, your reputation for paying debts on time. This credit rating is valuable during an emergency when you must borrow money or when you desire to make a major purchase. It is also valuable in obtaining credit if you move to another community.

Illus. 27-2
Using credit may allow you to take advantage of special sales.

CREDIT CAN CAUSE PROBLEMS

Buying on credit is convenient and is usually beneficial. However, there are some disadvantages if you are not careful in your use of credit. Some problems you as a consumer can encounter with unwise use of credit include the following:

- *Overbuying is one of the most common hazards of using credit.* There are several ways in which this can happen. One way is to purchase something that is more expensive than you can afford. It is easy to say, "All right, charge it," for a suit that costs $190 when you would purchase a less expensive one if you had to pay cash. Attractive store displays and advertisements attract us and invite us to make purchases. As a credit customer, you may be tempted to buy items that you do not really need.
- *Careless buying may result if you become lazy in your shopping.* You may stop checking advertisements carefully. You may fail to make comparisons, causing you to buy at the wrong time or the wrong place. Smart buyers know that at certain times of the year, the prices of some goods decrease. Credit can tempt you not to wait for a better price on an item you want.
- *Higher prices may be paid.* Stores that sell only for cash are able to sell at lower prices than stores that offer credit. Extending credit is expensive. It requires good accounting to keep accurate records of each charge sale and each payment. When customers do not pay as agreed, there are collection expenses. Increased costs are passed on to customers in the

Illus. 27-3
Be careful!
Buying on credit
may lead to
overbuying.

form of higher prices. The cost of credit will be discussed in greater detail in Chapter 29.

- *Consumer's overuse of credit can result in too much being owed.* "Buying now and paying later" may sound like a good idea, but if too many payments are to be made "later" the total amount that must be paid can become a problem. Consumers must keep records of the total amount owed to creditors so that they do not have a total of monthly payments that exceeds their ability to pay.

Businesses and governments, too, can get into trouble with the overuse of credit. Too much borrowing can lead to bankruptcy if the organization is not managed properly. Too many debts place a damaging strain on the finances of businesses and governments. Using credit wisely is important for consumers, businesses, and governments.

SOME QUESTIONS TO BE ASKED

Before making a final decision on whether to buy on credit, there are some questions you as a consumer should answer: How am I benefiting from this use of credit? Is this the best buy I can make or should I shop around some more? What will be the total cost of my purchase including the cost of charging the item? What would I save if I paid cash? Will the payments be too high considering my income? Answers to these questions will help you make wise credit decisions.

Increasing Your Business Vocabulary

The following terms should become part of your business vocabulary. For each numbered item, find the term that has the same meaning.

capacity	*credit reference*
capital	*debtor*
character	*loan credit*
credit	*sales credit*
creditor	*trade credit*
credit rating	*trust*

1. The factor in credit that refers to a customer's honesty and willingness to pay a debt when it is due.
2. Credit that is offered at the time of sale.
3. The factor in credit that refers to a customer's ability to pay a debt when it is due.
4. A person's reputation for paying debts on time.

5. One who buys on credit or receives a loan.
6. Borrowing money to be used later for some special purpose.
7. The privilege of using someone else's money for a period of time.
8. A business receives goods from a wholesaler and pays for them at a later specified date.
9. Businesses or individuals from whom you have received credit in the past and/or who can help verify your credit record.
10. The factor in credit that refers to the value of the borrower's possessions.
11. The creditor's belief that the debtor will honor the promise to pay later for goods and services that have already been received and used.
12. One who sells on credit or makes a loan.

Reviewing Your Reading

1. Our credit system is based in part on trust. Who does the trusting, the debtor or the creditor? What does this person trust?
2. As a debtor, what are you promising to do?
3. Name several sources of loans.
4. What are some typical uses of credit by consumers? by businesses? by governments?
5. What does the term "2/10, n/30" mean? With what kind of credit is it used?
6. What kinds of information do creditors need before extending credit?
7. What are the three Cs of credit? Why is each one important?
8. What are some ways in which the use of credit is important to a business?
9. What are four advantages of buying on credit for consumers?
10. Name four problems that can be caused by the unwise use of credit.
11. What are some questions you should ask yourself when considering whether to use credit?

Using Your Business Knowledge

1. Why is trust so important in a credit transaction? Why is it necessary to have written agreements to repay a loan?
2. Some people think it is a good idea to buy a few things on credit, even when you could pay cash. Why might this be a good idea?
3. Edward Adiska buys everything he possibly can on credit. If he does not have enough money to cover his monthly payments when they are due, he borrows money to pay them. His sister, Debbie, likes to buy things only after she has saved enough money to pay cash for them.
   a. Whose plan do you think is better? Why?
   b. What suggestions about the use of credit might you make to Edward and Debbie?
4. Gerry Shadle owns and operates a flower shop. She is considering expanding her shop to include home decorating items. At present, Gerry sells for cash only. How might extending credit help or hurt this business?
5. Here are some statements that people have made about credit. Read each statement and tell whether you agree or disagree and why.
   a. "I should buy as many things as I can on credit because credit increases sales and helps business."
   b. "If things were sold for cash only, in the long run, prices would be lower and everyone would be better off."
   c. "Buy on credit at least occasionally; make your payments on time; and keep

a good credit rating, which will be valuable in an emergency.''

d. ''Credit should be used only in making expensive purchases, such as houses and cars, and never for everyday purchases, such as food and clothing.''

Computing Business Problems

1. The following amounts of consumer credit in the United States were reported for the three years shown below:

Year	Consumer Credit (In Billions of Dollars)
1980	$369
1982	410
1984	562
1986	724

   a. What was the increase in consumer credit, in billions of dollars, from 1980 to 1982? from 1980 to 1984? from 1980 to 1986?
   b. What was the average increase per year, in billions of dollars, for the six-year period from 1980 to 1986?
   c. If consumer credit continues to increase by the 1980-1986 annual rate of increase, what will be the total of consumer credit (in billions of dollars) in 1990? in 2000?

2. Last year O'Leary's Cycle Shop sold 2,200 ten-speed bicycles. The average sale price was $145, including tax. Seven out of every ten customers bought their bikes using O'Leary's credit plan.
   a. What was the amount of the total sales of ten-speed bicycles?
   b. What was the amount of total credit sales of ten-speed bicycles?

3. The Capital Area Transit System borrowed $1,800,000 to buy six new buses to expand its service to the suburbs. It is estimated that each bus will earn about $6,500 per month. It will cost approximately $1,500 per month for fuel, operating costs, and repairs on each bus. How many months will it take to pay for the six buses?

4. Amy Markson would like to be an airline pilot someday. Right now, she wants to learn to fly and get a private license. Her parents have agreed to pay half the cost of the lessons if Amy pays the other half. Amy checked with the Superior Air Service and was told that the cost would include the following:

Fees and materials for ground instruction:	$480
24 hours of in-flight instruction:	$50 per hour
20 hours of solo flight time:	$32 per hour
Third-class student's license:	$80

   a. How much will Amy's cost be to learn to fly and to get her license?
   b. If Amy borrows her share of the cost, how much will she borrow?
   c. If Amy repays her loan in 50 equal weekly payments, how much will each weekly payment be? If she repays $75 each month, how many months will it take to repay the amount she borrowed?

Expanding Your Understanding of Business

1. In addition to the three Cs of credit, some add a fourth called *collateral*. Find the meaning of collateral as it is used in connection with credit and explain how it is used.

2. A family with relatively low income and

little property might have a better credit rating than a family with a large income and considerable property. Likewise, a small business might have a better credit rating than a much larger business owning millions of dollars worth of property. Explain the circumstances under which each of these conditions might exist.

3. Suppose that you and your parents decide to open a snack shop near your school to sell light lunches and snacks. Most of the customers will be junior and senior high school students. Since many students will forget to bring money or will want to treat friends when they do not have enough money, they will sometimes ask you to charge their purchases. Make up a set of rules that you would use to make it sound business to extend credit to teenage customers.

4. Suppose everybody decided to stop extending credit to customers. What do you think would be the effects on each of the following:
   a. A recently married couple who have to buy furniture for their apartment
   b. A small retail store that is trying to build its sales
   c. A large manufacturer that wants to expand its line of machines
   d. A local school district similar to the one your school is in

5. Do some reading in current periodicals, such as *The Wall Street Journal*, the business section of a metropolitan newspaper, and consumer magazines, to learn how credit is being used today. Report to your class on problems you discover.

The Use of Consumer Credit

Chapter 28

Chapter Objectives

After studying this chapter and completing the end-of-chapter activities, you will be able to:

1. Describe open charge accounts, budget charge accounts, and revolving accounts.

2. Explain how a teenager may obtain his or her own charge account.

3. Describe the process by which bank credit card transactions are handled.

4. Compare bank charge cards, travel and entertainment credit cards, oil company credit cards, and retail store credit cards.

5. Explain how installment credit sales differ from credit card sales.

6. Describe three kinds of loans available to consumers.

7. List seven questions that should be answered before signing an installment sales contract.

Consumers in the United States use a great deal of credit. Charge accounts, installment sales credit, and bank or finance company loans are common forms of consumer credit. The following are examples of common, everyday transactions involving credit.

Tanya was shopping in her favorite department store. After selecting her purchase, she was asked by the sales clerk, "Will this be cash or charge?" "Charge," replied Tanya, "I will use my bank charge card." Tanya also has a revolving charge account at that store, which she could have used.

Max purchased a color television with remote control and advanced electronic tuning. He agreed to make equal monthly payments, which included a charge for the use of credit, and signed an installment sales contract.

Jessica talked with the loan officer at the Savings and Loan Company. She needed a loan to pay off her many charge accounts and to make some home improvements. Jessica signed a promissory note to get a loan.

Kuang-fu needed to build an addition to his print shop. He applied for a loan. His banker said that Kuang-fu could get either a personal loan or a secured loan. The secured loan seemed like a better deal. Several pieces of Kuang-fu's printing equipment were used to secure his loan.

Denise drove into the local gasoline station. She filled her gas tank, added some oil to her engine, and paid for these transactions using her oil company's credit card.

From the above situations, you can see that there are a number of ways to obtain and use credit. In deciding what kind of credit to use, you should understand the different kinds of credit that may be available. Let's consider charge accounts first.

TYPES OF CHARGE ACCOUNTS

If you are able to get credit, you may open an account at a retail store, a public utility, or a supplier, if you are in business. When you make a purchase from the business that extended you credit, the amount you owe is added to your account with that business. Three types of charge accounts generally are available for your use. You may have an open, budget, or revolving account.

Open Charge Accounts

An **open charge account** is one in which the seller expects payment in full at the end of a specified period. A common open period is one month. The seller may set a credit limit on the total amount that may be charged during a period. Open accounts generally are used for everyday needs and small purchases.

Illus. 28-1
Open charge
accounts are
convenient for
making small
purchases.

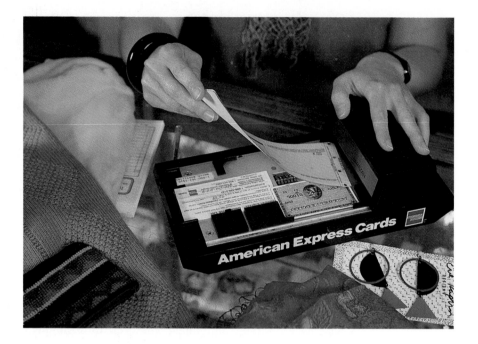

At times, a cashier may call the credit office when you present your card for a charge sale. This call is to verify that your account is in good standing. It also may be to check the credit limit if a limit has been set for your account.

Budget Charge Accounts

Some merchants and public utilities offer budget charge accounts. **Budget charge accounts** require that payments of a certain fixed amount be made over several months. One budget plan offered by businesses is the 90-day, 3-payment plan. Under this plan, you pay for your purchase in 90 days, usually in 3 equal monthly payments. There is generally no finance charge if payments are made on time. The **finance charge** is the additional amount you must pay for using credit, including interest and other costs such as credit insurance. The cost of finance charges will be discussed in more detail in Chapter 29.

In a budget plan offered by many utility companies, an estimate is made of how much you will be charged for gas or electricity during a certain period of time, such as a year. You then agree to pay a certain amount each month to cover those purchases. For example, you may be permitted to pay a certain amount of money each month to cover the cost of energy used for heating. This plan avoids large payments during winter months. However, you pay the same amount during warm months when heating is not required.

Revolving Charge Accounts

The revolving charge account is a popular form of credit. With a **revolving charge account** purchases can be charged at any time but at least part of the debt must be paid each month. It is similar to an open account but has some added features. There is usually a limit on the total amount that can be owed at one time. A payment is required once a month, but the total amount owed need not be paid at one time. A finance charge is added, however, if the total amount owed is not paid.

Revolving charge accounts are convenient, but they can tempt you to overspend. The finance charges on unpaid balances are usually quite high, often $1^1/2$ percent per month or higher. Since they are commonly used for low-priced, frequently purchased items, revolving accounts can be expensive unless you watch charges and payments carefully. Many customers do not pay the full amount when it is due and thus remain in debt for long periods of time.

CHARGE ACCOUNTS FOR TEENAGERS

Under contract law, minors cannot be held liable for their personal debts. Therefore, businesses are not willing to open charge accounts in a teenager's name if he or she is a minor. There are special circumstances, however, under which a special charge account may be opened in a teenager's own name.

Charge accounts for teenagers have a limit on the amount that can be charged, and the limit is usually lower than the amount set on charge accounts for adults. Generally a parent or guardian must agree to pay any balance due if the teenager does not. Sometimes the parent or guardian also must have a charge account with the business granting the credit.

Charge accounts for teenagers may be open or revolving. The accounts give teenagers a privilege and a freedom in buying that they otherwise would not have. If a teenager has an income of his or her own, the charge account can be the first step toward proving an ability to manage money wisely. It also is an opportunity to show that he or she is a good credit risk and can use credit wisely. Responsibility comes along with the privilege.

THE USE OF CREDIT CARDS

Credit cards are the most popular form of credit today. In a recent year, it was reported that 62 percent of the families in the United States used one or more credit cards. Fifty-four percent used retail store credit cards and 40 percent used bank credit cards. In that year, 38 percent of credit card users were under the age of 25. A total of almost 300 million credit cards were in use. Needless to say, the credit card business is a big one!

Accounts for these cards are set up by banks, oil companies, retail stores, or by businesses that specialize in extending credit for special purposes such as travel and entertainment. A special card, showing the person's name and account number and a place for the person's signature, is issued to identify the customer as one having a charge account.

Bank Charge Cards

You read about bank charge cards in Chapter 22. These charge cards have become very popular. MasterCard and VISA are two of the best known. Most of the banks in the United States are part of a worldwide bank charge-card system. There usually is an annual fee that must be paid for the privilege of using the card.

Bank charge cards are issued to people whose credit ratings meet the bank's standards. A bank charge card, in effect, indicates that the credit rating of the cardholder is good. Agreements are made between banks and various merchants to accept the charge cards.

When you use your bank charge card, a credit sales slip that requires your signature is made out. The merchant collects all credit sales slips prepared during the day and sends them to the bank.

The bank charges your account for your charge purchases and bills you once a month for all the purchases you made. You usually do not pay a finance charge if you pay your bill in full. However, if you pay only part of your bill, there is a substantial finance charge on the unpaid balance.

The bank totals all of the sales slips received from each business. The businesses are paid for the amount of the sales minus a service fee. This fee is usually about 4 to 6 percent. At the 4 percent rate, a retail store would receive $960 from sales totaling $1,000 ($1,000 - 4 percent or $40.) This fee covers the bank's expenses of processing the sales slips and collecting amounts owed from customers. The bank is doing the work that the business's own credit department would have to do otherwise.

Business owners like bank charge cards for several reasons. For one thing, the bank decides if a customer is a good credit risk. The bank also assumes most of the trouble and expense of granting credit. Businesses receive their money, minus the service fee, immediately.

Customers like bank charge cards because they are accepted by so many businesses throughout the United States and in many foreign countries. Bank charge-card users also like the fact that they receive only one monthly bill rather than many from the various businesses where they charge purchases.

There are some disadvantages to bank charge cards, too. There is the additional record keeping for a business. At the time of the sale, a credit slip must be written out. Some businesses can handle their credit sales for less than the fee charged by the banks. Consumers often find it too easy to use

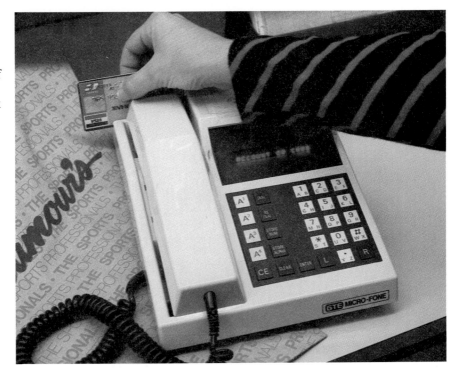

their "plastic" money and may find themselves buying more than they can afford.

Travel and Entertainment Credit Cards

Travel and entertainment (T&E) cards are similar to bank charge cards. However, an independent business performs the functions for T&E accounts that a bank performs for bank charge-card accounts. The T&E cards are used mainly to buy services such as lodging in hotels and motels, meals, and tickets for entertainment. Purchases are billed in the same way that bank charge-card purchases are, and T&E card users also pay annual fees for the privilege of having the card. Examples of nationally known T&E are Diners' Club, Carte Blanche, and American Express.

Travelers especially like T&E credit cards because they do not have to carry much cash with them. The cards are accepted at many different businesses in all parts of the world. Businesses that accept T&E credit cards often find that their sales increase because more customers are attracted if T&E cards can be used. Customers also often buy more than they might buy if they had to pay cash.

Illus. 28-3
Many travelers
enjoy the
convenience of
using T&E credit
cards.

Oil Company Credit Cards

Oil companies, such as Texaco, Standard Oil, and Shell, issue their own credit cards. As with banks, accounts are opened for customers who apply for credit and have their applications approved. Oil company credit cards can generally be used only for purchases from gasoline stations selling that company's brand of gasoline. It may also be possible to charge car maintenance service and merchandise sold by that station.

Some consumers find it advantageous to have credit cards with oil companies from whom they frequently purchase gasoline. The oil companies like to extend credit to encourage consumers to buy their products.

Retail Store Credit Cards

Many retail stores offer their own credit cards to their customers. These cards carry the name of the store that issues the card and are similar to bank credit cards. However, these cards can be used only at the store that issued it. The credit that is extended is on a revolving charge account basis.

Having a retail store credit card is a convenience for the consumer. The store also knows that the consumer is more likely to shop there if he or she has one of its credit cards. Some stores have special sales that are advertised just to their credit card holders.

INSTALLMENT SALES CREDIT

For some types of purchases, especially those that are quite expensive and will last for long periods of time, installment sales credit is often used. **Installment sales credit** is a credit contract issued by the seller that requires periodic payments to be made at times specified in the agreement. Finance charges are added to the cost of the item or items purchased, and the total amount to be paid is shown in the agreement. Furniture and household appliances frequently are purchased using installment sales credit.

Using installment sales credit differs from using credit cards. Instead of just handing your credit card to a salesperson, you must fill out a credit application at the time of the purchase and receive credit approval. There are some special features of installment sales credit with which you should be familiar. Under an installment credit plan you will:

- Sign a written agreement (a sales contract) that shows the terms of the purchase, such as payment periods and finance charges.
- Receive and own the goods at the time of purchase. However, the seller has the right to repossess them (take them back) if payments are not made according to the agreement.
- Make a **down payment**, which is a payment of part of the purchase price; it is usually made at the time of the purchase.
- Pay a finance charge on the amount owed, because this amount is actually loaned to you by the seller.
- Make regular payments at stated times, usually weekly or monthly. For example, if a total of $120 is to be repaid in 12 monthly installments, $10 is paid each month. In some cases, a penalty is charged if a payment is received after the due date. In others, all remaining payments may become due at once if only one payment is missed.

TYPES OF LOANS

A loan is an alternative to charge-account buying or installment sales credit. There are several kinds of loans available. The terms of the loans and the requirements for securing the loans differ.

One type of loan is called an installment loan. An **installment loan** is one in which you agree to make monthly payments in specific amounts over a period of time. The payments are called installments. The total amount you repay includes the amount you borrowed plus the finance charge on your loan.

Another kind of loan is called a single-payment loan. With a **single-payment loan**, you do not pay anything until the end of the loan period, possibly 60 or 90 days. At that time, you repay the full amount you borrowed plus the finance charge.

A lender needs some assurance that each loan will be repaid. If you are a good credit risk, you may be able to get a promissory note. A **promissory note** is a written promise to repay based on a debtor's excellent credit rating. The amount borrowed, usually with some interest, is due on a certain date. The names given to the different parts of a promissory note are shown in Figure 28-1.

Figure 28-1 A promissory note.

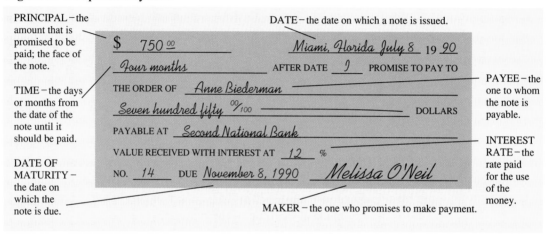

In some cases, you may be asked to offer some kind of property you own, such as a car, a house, or jewelry, as security. Property that is used as security is called **collateral**. You give the lender the right to sell this property to get back the amount of the loan in the event you do not repay it. This is called a **secured loan**.

If you do not have a credit rating established or property to offer as security, you may be able to get a relative or friend who has property or a good credit rating to also sign your note and become the legal cosigner. The **cosigner** of a note is responsible for payment of the note if you do not pay as promised.

THE LEGAL CONTRACT

Credit is important in many ways. It is a privilege that millions of consumers and businesses enjoy. No matter what kind of credit is involved, legal responsibilities are created for both parties.

"KWYS" are four letters to keep in mind when signing any legal form; the letters stand for "know what you're signing." This applies to all credit contracts.

The installment sales contract is one of the most important forms you may sign. Before signing one, answer the following questions:

- How much are the finance charges? The total financing cost must be clearly shown in your contract.
- Does the contract include the cost of services you may need, such as repairs to a television or a washing machine? If there is a separate repair contract, is its cost included in your contract? Will you be billed for anything separately?
- Does the contract have an add-on feature so that you can later buy other items and have them added to the balance that you owe?
- If you pay the contract in full before its ending date, how much of the finance charge will you get back?
- If you pay the contract within 60 or 90 days, will there be any finance charge or will it be as if you had paid cash?
- Is the contract you are asked to sign completely filled in? (Do not sign if there are any blanks. It is proper and businesslike to draw a line through any blank space before you sign the contract.)
- Under what conditions can the seller repossess the merchandise if you do not pay on time? *Repossess* refers to the right of the seller to take back merchandise in partial or full settlement of the debt.

Illus. 28-4
Understanding the agreement you sign is important!

Increasing Your Business Vocabulary

The following terms should become part of your business vocabulary. For each numbered item, find the term that has the same meaning.

budget charge account
collateral
cosigner
down payment
finance charge
installment loan

installment sales credit
open charge account
promissory note
revolving charge account
secured loan
single-payment loan

1. A credit contract issued by the seller that requires periodic payments to be made at times specified in the agreement with finance charges added to the cost of the purchase.
2. A type of loan in which you do not pay anything until the end of the loan period, possibly 60 or 90 days.
3. A type of loan in which the lender has the right to sell property used as collateral to get back the amount of the loan in the event the loan is not repaid.
4. A credit plan in which the seller expects payment in full at the end of a specified period, usually a month.
5. A credit plan that allows purchases to be charged at any time but requires that at least part of the debt be paid each month.

6. A type of loan in which you agree to make monthly payments in specific amounts over a period of time.
7. A credit plan which requires that payments of a certain fixed amount be made over several months.
8. Someone who becomes responsible for payment of the note if you do not pay as promised.
9. A payment of part of the purchase price that is made as part of a credit agreement.
10. A written promise to repay based on the debtor's excellent credit rating.
11. Property that is offered as security for some loan agreements.
12. The additional amount you must pay for using credit.

Reviewing Your Reading

1. What are three common forms of consumer credit?
2. What does it mean to have an open charge account?
3. How does a budget charge account help a consumer with his or her budgeting? Give an example.
4. What is the advantage of having a teenage charge account?
5. List two dangers of using revolving charge accounts.
6. How many credit cards were used in the

United States in a recent year? What percentage of families in the United States used one or more credit cards?
7. Describe briefly how bank charge-card plans work.
8. What special features do installment sales credit contracts normally contain?
9. How do installment loans and single-payment loans differ?
10. What kind of person can get a loan through a promissory note?

11. What is the difference between a promissory note and a secured loan?

12. What does a cosigner agree to when signing a loan agreement?

Using Your Business Knowledge

1. Not everyone believes in using credit. The following are statements that people who are for and against using credit might make. Read each one and then explain why you agree or disagree with each statement.

   a. "A bank card is nice to have. If I'm out of cash, I can still buy what I want."

   b. "I don't believe in using credit for most purchases. I pay cash for everyday items and use credit only for expensive items such as a new refrigerator, new carpeting, or a new car."

   c. "If I can't pay cash, I know that I can't afford it. I won't buy anything unless I can pay cash."

   d. "I often don't pay the full amount of my charge account when it is due; the finance charges are quite reasonable."

2. Many businesses would rather take credit cards than accept personal checks. Why do you think businesspeople feel this way?

3. Sue Ellen Ripley owns a sporting goods store and is considering joining a bank charge-card plan. Answer the following questions for her.

   a. What advantages would there be for her business if she did join?

   b. What will it cost her for the services the bank will provide?

   c. In what ways are the services the bank provides important?

4. Mark and Donna were discussing charge accounts. Mark said, "I don't like the gas company's budget plan—I have to pay more than I should during the warm months so they have my money to use and they don't pay me any interest." Donna gave several arguments in favor of the budget payment plan. If you were Donna, describe the features of a budget payment plan that might convince Mark the plan is a good one for most customers.

5. Jamie has a good part-time job and is a responsible person who takes good care of all of her possessions. Jamie wants to buy a VCR, but has not saved enough money to cover the cost. When she asked the salesperson if the store would extend credit, Jamie was told "No, you are too young." Jamie is 16 years old. What are some ways in which Jamie could get credit to purchase this VCR?

6. Why is it important not to leave any blank spaces in a loan agreement you sign?

13. What questions should be answered before signing a loan agreement?

Computing Business Problems

1. Alexis Ramirez bought three gallons of paint on credit. The paint cost $8.40 a gallon. A finance charge of $.25 was added to the purchase price of the paint. What was the total cost of Alexis' purchase?

2. Charlene Presley owns a pet store and hobby shop. She thinks she should join a bank charge-card plan so that she can better compete with some large department stores. Her credit sales each month on a bank-card plan will be about $10,000.

   a. If the bank plan she joins charges Ms. Presley 3 percent of her billings, how much would she pay for the bank's services in one month?

b. How much would the bank owe her for that month?

c. If her annual credit sales amount to $120,000, what would she pay for the bank's services for the year?

3. Eduardo Gomez bought 150 liters of gasoline for his motor home. He also needed 1.89 liters of oil. The gasoline cost $1.19 per gallon and the oil $2.29 per quart. What was the total amount of Eduardo's purchase? If he charged this purchase and paid $1\frac{1}{2}$ percent in finance charges on the amount purchased, how much would he have to pay?

4. Sue Perkowski has a charge account with a department store. Her account is billed to her on the first of each month, and she is expected to pay in full by the last day of the month. If she does not, the store charges her a $1\frac{1}{2}$ percent finance charge on the balance of the account. This past month Sue made the following purchases: two skirts at $15.55 each; one pair of children's shoes at $16.95; costume jewelry at $11.15; and a lamp at $22.10.

a. What is the total amount for which Sue will be billed on the first of each month?

b. If she pays only $20 on her account this month, what will be the amount of the finance charge when her bill comes next month?

Expanding Your Understanding of Business

1. Ask an older adult whom you know well about his or her use of credit. Find out how many credit cards are owned. Discover whether or not the person believes that people use too much credit today. Also discuss what advantages and disadvantages that person sees in the use of credit. Compare these answers with what is in your textbook, and prepare a report to give to your class.

2. Interview a banker about bank credit cards—select a bank that issues bank credit cards. Find out about the bank's involvement in bank credit card transactions. Then interview a local businessperson who allows customers to charge purchases using a bank credit card. Find out what she or he thinks about the use of bank credit cards from a business point of view. Compare the information received from these two sources. Prepare a short report to give to your class.

3. Stores may give a cash discount to customers who pay cash rather than charge a purchase so long as the store's policy is known and available to all customers. Why might a business offer a cash discount? What are some advantages and disadvantages to the store owner? to the customer? How might a regular customer who has been charging purchases for years feel when he or she finds out about the policy for the first time?

4. Get an application form that is used by a bank when a person wants to apply for a bank charge card. Note the information that is requested and compare it with information that is requested when someone applies for a loan. Do you think that bank charge cards are easier to obtain than are loans? Why or why not?

5. In most states, the age of majority has been lowered from 21 to 18 years. This change means that those who reach age 18 have the legal rights and duties of adults. How does this change affect an 18-year-old's ability to get credit? Is a person of this age able to make wise credit decisions? Give reasons for your opinion from the point of both the seller and the 18-year-old.

The Cost of Credit

Chapter 29

Chapter Objectives

After reading this chapter and completing the end-of-chapter activities, you will be able to:

1. *Explain why it is important to know the costs of credit.*

2. *State the formula for calculating simple interest.*

3. *Determine the amount of interest due when given the principal and a stated percentage rate for a period of days or months.*

4. *Determine the maturity date for a loan given the date on which it was made and the terms of the loan.*

5. *Explain what charges are included in the finance charge.*

6. *State what should be considered before taking out a loan or signing an installment sales contract.*

7. *Explain why it is important to shop for credit.*

The privilege of using someone else's money carries with it some costs. Interest is one of those costs. In a recent year, one of our largest corporations paid more than $1 billion dollars in interest; a small corporation paid more than $1 million dollars in interest. Debt owed by consumers also runs into the billions of dollars each year.

For the consumer, the cost of credit can create some problems or concerns. Here are two examples:

Rosalina likes to charge whatever she buys, regardless of the cost of the items. One day she wanted to buy a compact disc player, so she went to a company that lends money and borrowed the money that she needed. But now she has a problem. The total amount that she has to pay each month for her charge account and personal loan take too much of what she earns each month. The credit costs are more than she figured, and her money runs out before she can pay for things she needs now. What a dilemma! Through careless use of credit, she now cannot buy some of the things she really needs. She tied up too much of her future income with payments for her credit purchases.

Justin purchased a microcomputer on sale. He believed that he had made a good buy. Later, when his payments started, he reread the installment sales contract and discovered that the finance charges caused the total cost of his purchase to be quite high. He did not get the bargain he thought he was getting. Yet, it was the computer he needed, and he is satisfied with his purchase. However, the cost of credit added more to the price than he expected. He did not realize the cost of credit.

PAYING THE COST OF CREDIT

You have learned what credit is, how it is used, different types of credit, and some benefits and disadvantages of using credit. Now you need to learn about the cost of credit.

When credit is extended to you, expenses are incurred that must be covered. Expenses are covered by having finance charges added to the amount of credit extended; a major part of the finance charge is interest.

UNDERSTANDING HOW INTEREST IS COMPUTED

The amount of interest you must pay on a loan or charge account should be clearly understood. To determine the amount you have to pay, it is necessary to know three things:

1. **Interest rate**, the percentage that is applied to your debt expressed as a fraction or decimal.
2. **Principal**, amount of debt to which the interest rate is applied.

3. **Time factor**, the length of time for which interest will be charged.

Let's look at the way interest is computed on loans.

Computing Simple Interest

Interest is often expressed in terms of simple interest. **Simple interest** is an expression of interest based on a one-year period of time. The formula for computing simple interest is:

$$\text{I (interest)} = \text{P (principal)} \times \text{R (rate)} \times \text{T (time)}$$

If $1,000 (P) is borrowed at 9 percent (R) for one year (T), the amount of interest would be calculated as follows:

$$\text{I} = \$1,000 \times 9/100 \times 1 = \$90$$

In calculating the interest, there are three basic things to remember: (1) the interest rate must be expressed in the form of a fraction or decimal; (2) interest is charged for each dollar or part of a dollar borrowed; and (3) the interest rate is based upon one year of time. Here is how it works:

1. Interest is expressed as part of a dollar. This part of a dollar, or percent, is called the interest rate. Before using a percent rate in a problem, you

must change it to either a common fraction or a decimal. For example, an interest rate of 12 percent would be changed to a common fraction of 12/100 or a decimal of .12.

2. When an interest rate is expressed as 12 percent per year, you must pay 12 cents for each dollar you borrow for a year. At this rate, if you borrow $1, you pay 12 cents in interest. If you borrow $2, you pay 24 cents. If you borrow $10, you pay $1.20, and so on. The amount of interest charged is calculated by multiplying the principal by the interest rate and then multiplying that result by the time period. Suppose that you borrow $100 for one year at 12 percent per year. Here is how the amount of interest is calculated:

$$I = P \times R \times T$$
$$I = \$100 \times 12/100 \times 1 = \$12$$

3. If you borrow $100 at 12 percent for one year, you must repay the $100 plus $12 interest, as you have just seen. If you borrow the same amount of money at the same rate of interest for two years, you pay twice as much interest, or $24. If the money is borrowed for three years, you pay $36, and so on. The amount of interest on $100 borrowed at 12 percent for two years is computed as follows:

$$I = P \times R \times T$$
$$I = \$100 \times 12/100 \times 2 = \$24$$

How is interest calculated if you borrow money for less than a year? The amount of interest is based on the fractional part of the year. The fraction may be expressed either in months or in days. A month is considered to be one-twelfth of a year, regardless of the number of days in the particular month. If you were to borrow $100 at 12 percent for one month, the interest would be:

$$I = P \times R \times T$$
$$I = \$100 \times 12/100 \times 1/12 = \$1$$

When a loan is made for a certain number of days, such as 30, 60, or 90 days, the interest is determined by days. To make the computation easy, a year is usually considered 360 days. The interest on a loan for $100 at 12 percent for 60 days would be $2, as shown below.

$$I = P \times R \times T$$
$$I = \$100 \times 12/100 \times 60/360 = \$2$$

Finding Maturity Dates

The date on which a loan must be repaid is known as the **maturity date**. How is the maturity date determined? When the time of the loan is stated in months, the date of maturity is the same day of the month as the date on which the loan was made. If a loan is made on January 15 and is to run one month, it will be due February 15. If it is to run two months, it will be due March 15, and so on.

When the time of a loan is given in days, the exact number of days must be counted to find the date of maturity. First you would determine the number of days remaining in the month when the loan was made. For instance, if the loan were made on January 10, there would be 21 days to be counted in January. Then you would add the days in the following months until the total equals the required number of days. Suppose you wanted to find the date of maturity of a 90-day loan made on March 3. Here is how it would be done:

$$\begin{array}{l} \text{March — 28 days (31-3)} \\ \text{April — 30 days} \\ \text{May — 31 days} \\ \underline{\text{June — \ \ 1 day}} \\ \text{90 days} \\ \text{Due Date — June 1} \end{array}$$

Computing Installment Interest

Simple interest, as you have just learned, is calculated on the basis of one year of time. Installment credit, however, involves a monthly charge for interest on unpaid balances. An interest charge of 1 percent a month is the same as 12 percent for a year. If you borrowed $100 at 2 percent for one year at simple interest, you would repay $102 ($100 principal + $2 interest) at the end of one year. If you borrowed $100 at a monthly rate of 2 percent, you would repay $102 at the end of one month. Your interest charge, then, would be at a rate of 24 percent a year (2 percent x 12 months) since you had the use of the money for only one month.

The annual rate of interest, or annual percentage rate, must be stated on installment contracts. The **annual percentage rate (APR)** is a disclosure required by law, and it states the percentage cost of credit on a yearly basis.

On installment loans, interest is calculated on the amount that is unpaid at the end of each month. Suppose that Armando Rivera borrowed $120 and agreed to repay the loan at $20 a month plus $1\frac{1}{2}$ percent interest each month on the unpaid balance. His schedule of payments is shown in the first part of Figure 29-1. His father, Jason Rivera, obtained a loan of $1,000. He agreed to repay $100 per month including interest. Mr. Rivera's repayment schedule is shown in the second part of Figure 29-1. Both kinds of payment schedules are used in loan transactions.

Figure 29-1
Interest is
charged only on
the unpaid
balance of an
installment loan.
Payments may be
decreasing or
level, the same
each month until
the final payment.

A Decreasing Loan Payment Schedule. ($120 loan; 18 percent interest;
monthly payments are $20 plus interest.)

Months	Unpaid Balance	Interest Paid	Loan Repayment	Total Payment
1	$120	$1.80	$ 20	$ 21.80
2	100	1.50	20	21.50
3	80	1.20	20	21.20
4	60	1.90	20	20.90
5	40	.60	20	20.60
6	20	.30	20	20.30
Totals	—	$6.30	$120	$126.30

A Level Loan Payment Schedule. ($1,000 loan; 12 percent annual interest;
$100 monthly payments.)

Payment	Interest	Applied to Principal	Balance of Loan
			$1,000.00
$100.00	$10.00	$90.00	910.00
100.00	9.10	90.90	819.10
100.00	8.19	91.81	727.29
100.00	7.28	92.72	634.57
100.00	6.35	93.65	540.92
100.00	5.41	94.59	446.33
100.00	4.46	95.54	350.79
100.00	3.51	96.49	254.30
100.00	2.54	97.46	156.84
100.00	1.57	98.43	58.41
58.99	.58	58.41	—

With some loans, the amount of the interest is added to the amount you
borrow, and you sign a promissory note for the total amount. The note may
then be repaid in equal monthly installments. For instance, Sylvia Messinger
borrowed $100, signed a note for $108, and agreed to repay the loan in 12
monthly installments of $9.

If Sylvia had borrowed $100 for one year and paid $8 interest, the interest
rate would have been 8 percent ($8 ÷ $100 = .08 or 8%). But Sylvia repaid
the loan in monthly installments. She had the use of the entire $100 for only
one month and a smaller amount each succeeding month as she repaid the
loan.

DETERMINING OTHER COSTS OF CREDIT

When you use credit, you are not only using someone else's money, you are also spending your own future income. Interest paid on the amount charged or borrowed adds to the cost of what is purchased and to what must be repaid. While credit allows us to buy an item now rather than wait until later, the interest we pay may prevent us from buying something else we need. The money we use to repay debts, including interest and other charges, cannot be used for other purchases. This is what happened to Justin and Rosalina and is an example of opportunity cost. As you recall from Chapter 15, an opportunity cost is what you must give up when you buy one thing rather than another. If Justin was deciding whether to buy a new stereo system or a computer, the stereo system would be the opportunity cost of the computer.

Other costs of credit include charges such as service fees. These fees are added to the principal and interest and increase the amount that you owe. Lenders also commonly add an amount to cover the cost of credit insurance. **Credit insurance** is special insurance that repays the balance of the amount owed if the borrower dies or becomes disabled prior to the full settlement of the loan. Without credit insurance coverage, some lenders will not be willing to make a loan. These fees and insurance premiums add to the cost of credit and must be considered when determining credit costs.

KNOWING THE TOTAL FINANCE CHARGE

Before you borrow money or charge a purchase, you should have some idea of the cost for using the credit. In addition to interest, consider the other charges that may be made. The interest you pay may not cover all of the creditor's costs. Creditor's costs include the time and money it takes to investigate your credit history, process your loan or charge account, and keep records of your payments and balances. Costs of collecting from those who do not pay their accounts also may be an expense that is passed on to borrowers. As the debtor, the one who owes money to a creditor, you pay for the costs of credit.

To make you aware of the total cost of credit, a federal law requires that you be told of the total finance charge. The finance charge is the total cost of your loan including interest and all other charges. This finance charge must be stated in writing in your contract or on your charge account statement. Figure 29-2 shows how the annual percentage rate and finance charges are shown on a credit card bill and on an installment loan contract.

SHOPPING FOR CREDIT

If you have to borrow money or make a purchase on credit, you should consider not only the total cost but also the available alternatives. Check with several lenders and compare the APRs.

Figure 29-2 You must be informed about the cost associated with credit purchases.

DESCRIPTION		AMOUNT
PREVIOUS BALANCE		182.57
NEW PURCHASES	+	275.70
NEW CASH ADVANCES	+	.00
NEW MICHIGAN BANKARD PLUS™ PURCHASES	+	.00
CREDITS	−	.00
PAYMENTS	−	30.00
FINANCE CHARGE	+	4.70
NEW BALANCE	=	432.97
PAYMENT DUE DATE*		9/23/--

20989 7 28792

ACCOUNT INFORMATION	
DESCRIPTION	AMOUNT
MICHIGAN BANKARD PLUS BALANCE	.00
AVERAGE DAILY BALANCE	312.81

ANNUAL PERCENTAGE RATE 18%

*DATE NEW BALANCE MUST BE PAID IN FULL TO AVOID FINANCE CHARGE ON TRANSACTIONS BEING BILLED FOR THE FIRST TIME ON THIS STATEMENT (EXCEPT CASH ADVANCES AND MICHIGAN BANKARD PLUS PURCHASES).

NOTICE—SEE REVERSE SIDE FOR IMPORTANT INFORMATION

INSTALLMENT CONTRACT AND SECURITY AGREEMENT

Sergio Sound Systems, Inc.
The South Mall • Amarillo, TX 79199

I (we) the undersigned buyer(s) buy from, and grant a security interest, to SERGIO SOUND SYSTEMS, INC. in this property:

Quantity	Description	Amount	
1	Model XV-466 Turntable	400	00
Description of Trade-in:			
	Sales Tax	16	00
	Total	416	00

Insurance Agreement

Credit life insurance is available at a cost of $ _3.00_ for the term of the credit. The purchase of insurance is voluntary and not required for credit.

I want insurance.

Signed: _____ Date: _____

I do not want insurance.

Signed: _Maria Benitez_ Date: _1/15/19--_

Signed: _____ Date: _____

Buyer's Name _Maria Benitez_
Buyer's Address _805 Elberon Ave_
City _Amarillo_ State _TX_ Zip _79199_

1	Cash Price	$	400.00
2	Less: Down Payment	$ 40.00	
3	Trade-in	$	
4	Total Down	$	40.00
5	Unpaid Balance of Cash Price	$	360.00
6	Other Charges Sales Tax	$	16.00
7	AMOUNT FINANCED	$	376.00
8	FINANCE CHARGE	$	37.68
9	Total of Payments	$	413.68
10	Deferred Payment Price (1 + 6 + 8)	$	453.68
11	ANNUAL PERCENTAGE RATE		18.5 %

The Buyer(s) agrees to pay to SERGIO SOUND SYSTEM, INC. at their store the "Total of Payments" shown above in _12_ monthly installments of _34.47_ and a final installment of _34.51_. The first installment is due _February 15,19--_ and all other payments are due on the same day of the month, until paid in full. The finance charge applies from _1/15/19--_.

Signed: _Maria Benitez_ Date: _1/15/19--_

Notice to Buyer: You should get a copy of this contract when you sign. You can pay in advance the unpaid balance of this contract and get a partial refund of the finance charge based on the "Actuarial Method."

If you must purchase on credit, for instance, consider which charge card account will involve the lowest APR. If an installment sales contract is required, consider whether a personal loan from a financial institution may be cheaper for you.

When borrowing money, shop around just as carefully as you would for a new stereo, car, microcomputer, or any other major purchase. Borrowing money is costly, so make sure that you get the best loan. Some of the things you should check include the annual percentage rate, the amount of the monthly payments, and the total cost of the credit. Figure 29-3 shows information that was gathered by a person who wanted to borrow $4,000 to buy a car. Note the differences in the monthly payments, the total payments, and the cost of the credit.

Figure 29-3
Which loan is the best?

			Comparison Chart		
Lender	**APR**	**Loan Length**	**Monthly Payment**	**Total Payment**	**Cost of Credit**
A	11%	3 yrs.	$131	$4,716	$ 716
B	11%	4 yrs.	$103	$4,944	$ 944
C	12%	4 yrs.	$105	$5,040	$1,040

If you can afford the higher payments, you would borrow from lender A and make payments for only 36 months. Your total cost would be the smallest. If you cannot afford lender A's monthly payments, you would select lender B. The monthly payments would be less, but you would pay for an additional 12 months. Your total cost would be $228 more than with lender A. You would reject lender C because the interest rate is higher than the rate for either A or B.

Increasing Your Business Vocabulary

The following terms should become part of your business vocabulary. For each numbered item, find the term that has the same meaning.

annual percentage rate (APR)
credit insurance
interest rate
maturity date

principal
simple interest
time factor

1. An expression of interest based on a one-year period of time.
2. The amount of debt to which the interest is applied.

3. The date on which a loan must be repaid.
4. The length of time for which interest will be charged.
5. Special insurance that repays the balance

of the amount owed if the borrower dies or becomes disabled prior to the full settlement of the loan.
6. The percentage cost of credit on a yearly basis.

7. The percentage that is applied to a debt, expressed as a fraction or decimal.

Reviewing Your Reading

1. What three things must you know to be able to calculate interest?
2. In calculating interest, how many days are normally considered to be in one year?
3. How is the maturity date of a loan determined?
4. What is the formula for simple interest?
5. What are some costs that can be included in a finance charge?

6. By law, what information must be disclosed by creditors to make it easier for a consumer to compare finance charges?
7. List some things you need to consider when making a decision about obtaining a loan or using an installment sales contract.

Using Your Business Knowledge

1. Steve Beyer has charge accounts at three different stores. He also has a bank charge card and an oil company credit card that he uses quite frequently. Last month he took out a personal loan that requires him to pay $60 a month for the next 18 months. The total of the payments he makes on his three charge accounts is $142 per month. His credit card accounts require him to pay $80 per month. His monthly income, after taxes and other deductions, is $750. His normal expenses for an apartment, utilities, car, food, clothing and other necessities amount to more than $500 per month. Should Steve continue to make more credit purchases? What problems does Steve face at this time? What cost of credit is he experiencing?

2. Find the date of maturity for each of the following notes:

Date of Note	Time to Run
March 15	4 months
May 26	3 months

Date of Note	Time to Run
July 31	5 months
April 30	30 days
October 5	45 days

3. Les Heddle checked into several loan possibilities. He needed $15,000 to do some remodeling in his upholstery shop. The Thrifty Loan Company offered him an APR of 16 percent for a three-year loan. Monthly payments, including finance charges, would be $555. The Greenback Bank offered him a five-year loan at 15 percent APR with a total monthly payment of $375. The Silk Purse Finance Lending Shop did not quote an APR figure but said "We have a 'no frills' loan policy, and you can have a four-year loan with monthly payments at the amazingly low figure of $496 per month." Construct a loan comparison chart similar to the one on page 425 and decide which loan would be the best for Les Heddle. Give reasons for your decision.

Computing Business Problems

1. Using the formula for simple interest, find the interest charge for each of the following amounts for one year.
   a. $100 at 10 percent interest rate
   b. $500 at 12 percent interest rate
   c. $1,000 at 18 percent interest rate
   d. $25,000 at 10 percent interest rate
2. Jennifer Ward owns a large ranch and has a chance to buy additional land next to her ranch. She would need to put in a road so that she could move equipment onto the new land. The gravel road would be 3.3 kilometers long and would cost $800 per kilometer.
   a. How much would the road cost?
   b. If Jennifer had to pay 14 percent interest on a two-year loan to pay for the road, how much interest would she pay over that period?

3. Before borrowing $200, Laura Demetry visited a small loan company and the loan department of a bank. At the loan company, she found that she could borrow the $200 if she signed a note agreeing to repay the balance in six equal monthly installments of $36.50. At the bank, she could borrow the money by signing a promissory note for $215 and repaying the balance in six equal monthly payments.
   a. What would be the cost of the loan at the small loan company?
   b. What annual interest rate would Laura be paying if she borrowed at the small loan company?
   c. What would be the cost of the loan at the bank?
   d. What annual interest rate would she pay if she borrowed at the bank?

Expanding Your Understanding of Business

1. Look for magazine articles that tell about experiences of people who are deep in debt or talk with someone involved with credit counseling and find out why people have credit problems. Record the reasons given and report them to your class.
2. People borrow money for many different reasons. Some people borrow money to consolidate their debts.
   a. What is meant by consolidating debts.
   b. Is there any advantage in consolidating debts and making a single monthly payment on a single loan?
   c. How might consolidating debts reduce the amount of each payment? Would the borrower be saving money?
3. Interview a banker and a loan company representative to find out what is included in their finance charges and how they report the charges to consumers. Also find out whether they use computer programs or printed installment payment schedules to determine installment payments. Discuss trends in interest rates and what they predict will be rates charged for loans over the next five years.
4. Credit laws, designed to protect consumers, have imposed requirements on lenders to provide certain kinds of information. These are called *disclosure laws*. Find out from lenders in your community what forms are used in reporting information to consumers who apply for loans. Obtain copies of the forms, if possible, or make notes on what information is provided in the forms. Compare the forms used by various lenders to see how they are similar or different in providing information for consumers. Discuss with other students the helpfulness of the information that is provided and ways in which the forms might be improved to make them easier to understand.

Credit Records and Regulations

Chapter 30

Chapter Objectives

After studying this chapter and completing the end-of-chapter activities you will be able to:

1. Explain what a credit application is and how it is used.

2. Identify three specific factors that make a person creditworthy.

3. Describe what a credit bureau does.

4. Identify information shown on a statement of account.

5. Explain why receipts, credit memorandums, and canceled checks are important.

6. Explain what should be done when errors are found in credit statements.

7. Explain how provisions of several credit laws help consumers.

8. Explain how a good credit record can be established.

Rick Moreno applied for a charge account. His twentieth birthday was only ten days away. The credit manager told Rick he was too young to acquire a credit card and denied Rick's application. Were Rick's rights violated?

Annie Deardorff left her credit card lying on a counter. When she returned 15 minutes later, it was gone and the sales clerk said that he had not seen it. She waited a few weeks to see whether it would be returned—it was not. She wrote to the credit card company and told them she had lost her card. Charges for more than $200 worth of merchandise were made to her card before she reported it lost. What mistakes did Annie make? What can she do now?

David Zobott received his charge account statement. It had several errors on it. There was one charge for a purchase he did not make, and the charge has shown up for the third month in a row on his statement. One of his purchases had been returned several weeks ago, and the credit did not show up on his statement. His last month's payment, which he made on time, also was not listed. What can David do about these errors?

Renee and Kendall Lauver had their loan application turned down. The loan officer had checked with the local credit bureau and explained that their credit record was not good enough. Renee and Kendall were shocked; they always had paid their bills on time, with only a few minor exceptions. They needed this loan for home improvements. What can they do to correct this problem?

The four situations described above could happen to anyone. There are laws and regulations to help consumers in these situations, and there are actions that consumers can take to avoid some of these problems. Let's find out what can be done. First, however, we need to learn what information creditors need to have about those who want credit.

UNDERSTANDING CREDIT INFORMATION

You should understand what lenders need to know in order to make a decision about whether to grant credit. Generally, they want to be assured of two things: (1) your ability to repay a debt and (2) your willingness to do so. You may say that you can handle the debt, and you may assure them you will repay the debt according to the terms of the agreement. However, they need to have some evidence. They want to lend money, but lenders must minimize their bad debts. Lenders need some proof that you are creditworthy.

Being **creditworthy** means that you have established a credit record that shows you are a good credit risk. Potential lenders will want to examine your credit record. Your **credit record** is a report that shows the debts you owe, how often you use credit, and whether you pay your debts on time.

There is other information that lenders will want to know. Lenders want to find out about your finances, such as how much you earn, what kinds of savings and investments you have, and whether you have any other sources of income. They may also want to know about your reliability, that is, your occupation, how long you have been employed with your present employer, how long you have lived at the same address, and whether you own or rent your home.

Credit Application Forms

When you apply for credit or a loan, you will be asked to fill out a credit application. A **credit application** is a form on which you provide information needed by a lender to make a decision about granting credit or approving a loan. Figure 30-1 is an example of a credit application. Read this application carefully and note the information that is requested. What information could you provide on an application of this kind?

One of the most important parts of the credit application is the listing of credit references. A credit reference is a business or an individual who is able to provide information about your creditworthiness. Your signature on the credit application gives a lender permission to contact your credit references and inquire about your credit record. Your signature also indicates that you understand the terms of the type of credit for which you are applying and that the information you have provided is true. The credit application needs to be filled out completely, accurately, and honestly. You should sign it when you understand it and have provided the requested information.

Credit Bureaus

In addition to checking with your employers, your landlord (if you rent a house or an apartment), and your credit references, usually a lender will check with a credit bureau. A **credit bureau**, or a credit reporting agency, is a company that gathers information on credit users and sells that information in the form of credit reports to credit grantors. Banks, finance companies, and retail stores are among the users of credit bureaus.

Credit bureaus keep records of consumers' debts but can record only information that is officially reported to them. Creditors often send computer tapes or other payment data to credit bureaus, usually on a monthly basis. The information shows if payments are up-to-date or overdue and if any action has been taken to collect overdue bills. Other information may be added to create a month-by-month credit history for the consumer accounts. Credit bureaus cooperate with each other and provide information to other credit bureaus. If you are new to a community and request credit, the local credit bureau can obtain information from the bureau in the community where you formerly lived. There are several credit bureau associations; one of the largest has about 1,500 credit bureaus among its membership.

Figure 30-1
It is important to fill in all of the blanks on a credit application.

CREDIT CARD APPLICATION

Important: Fill in all information requested below.

Second National BankCorp

1. Information About Yourself *(Name of person in whose name card will be issued)*

☐ Mr. ☐ Mrs. ☐ Miss ☐ Ms.   First Name   Middle   Last Name
(Courtesy titles are optional)

Home Address   Apt.   City   State   ZIP Code   How Long?
     Years _____ Mos. _____

Previous Address (if less than 2 years at present address)   Apt.   City   State   ZIP Code

Home Telephone   Business Telephone   Social Security Number   Date of Birth   No. of Dependents (Exclude Yourself)
( )   ( )

Are You a U.S. Citizen? ☐ Yes ☐ No   If No, Explain Immigration Status   Are You a Permanent Resident? ☐ Yes ☐ No   Do You: ☐ Own ☐ Rent ☐ Other   Monthly Rent or Mortgage $

2. Employment Information *(Your total yearly income from all sources)*

Employer   Address   City   State   ZIP Code

How Long? Years _____ Mos. _____   Occupation   Yearly Gross Salary $ Other Income*   Source

Former Employer (if less than 1 year with present employer)   How Long? Years _____ Mos. _____   *Note: Alimony, child support or separate maintenance income need not be disclosed if you do not wish to have it considered as a basis for paying this obligation.

Nearest Relative Not Living with You   Address   City   State   Relation   Telephone

3. Other Credit

Major Credit Cards (Visa, MasterCard, etc. . . .)   Account Number

Other Credit Cards (Dept. Stores, etc. . . .)   Account Number

Other Credit   Account Number

4. Banking Information

☐ Checking ☐ NOW Account   Name of Bank   City   Account Number

☐ Savings   Name of Bank (if different from above)   City   Account Number

☐ Other (Check here if you have any of the following:)   IRA   CD   Money Market Account Stocks/Bonds   Investments Cash Management Account

5. Joint Account Information *(Complete for joint account or if you are relying on the income of another person to qualify for an account)*

First Name   Middle   Last Name   Relation

Home Address   Apt.   City   State   ZIP Code

Home Telephone ( )   Business Telephone ( )   Social Security Number   Date of Birth

Employer   Address   City   State   ZIP Code

How Long? Years _____ Mos. _____   Occupation   Yearly Gross Salary $ Other Income*   Source

Former Employer   How Long? Years _____ Mos. _____   *Note: Alimony, child support or separate maintenance income need not be disclosed if you do not wish to have it considered as a basis for paying this obligation.

6. Additional Cards *(Complete this section if you want cards issued to additional buyers on your account.)*

1. Spouse   First Name   Middle   Last Name

1. Other   First Name   Middle   Last Name

7. Signatures

I authorize the Second National BankCorp to check my credit record and to verify my credit, employment and income references. I have read the important information on the reverse side.

X _____ X _____
Applicant's Signature   Date   Joint Applicant's Signature   Date

I understand that Second National BankCorp may amend the account terms and charges specified in the Cardmember Agreement in the future.

Illus. 30-1
Credit bureaus keep confidential records of consumers' debts and provide these records only to those who have a legitimate reason for examining them.

Your credit record with a bureau is used to grade you as a credit risk. Credit bureaus do not make value judgments about any individual; they simply gather facts as reported to them. Your credit record is confidential. That is, it can be obtained only by you or those who have a legitimate reason for examining it.

Figure 30-2 is an example of a credit report that may be issued by a credit bureau. You will note that the top half contains background information about the individual, while the bottom half lists information about the individual's accounts and payment history. Note that at the bottom there is a reference to a public record showing a dispute between the consumer and a creditor that was settled in a small claims court. All of this information is of interest to credit grantors.

Documenting Your Credit History

Information provided on credit applications must be verified to assure its accuracy. Present and former employers can verify the dates of employment and salary figures. Banks and other financial institutions can report whether the applicants have the accounts listed on the applications. Landlords can indicate the length of time tenants have been renting and whether they pay their rent on time. Other creditors can report on how credit applicants make payments to their accounts and how they repay their loans.

Figure 30-2 An example of a credit report.

	Date Received 4/11/90	**CONFIDENTIAL**
FOR FIRST NATIONAL BANK Arborville, MT 83206	Date Mailed 4/11/90	**-FIRST AVENUE- CREDIT BUREAU**
	In File Since APRIL 1980	Member Associated Credit Bureaus, Inc.
	Inquired As: JOINT ACCOUNT	

REPORT ON:	LAST NAME SOCOL	FIRST NAME ROBERTA	INITIAL G.	SOCIAL SECURITY NUMBER 123-45-6789	SPOUSE'S NAME HENRY R.
ADDRESS: 5421 MAPLE AVENUE	CITY ARBORVILLE	STATE: MT	ZIP CODE 83206	SINCE: 1983	SPOUSE'S SOCIAL SECURITY NO. 987-65-4321

COMPLETE TO HERE FOR TRADE REPORT AND SKIP TO CREDIT HISTORY

PRESENT EMPLOYER: THE ARTIST'S LOFT, INC.	POSITION HELD: DEPT. MGR.	SINCE: 10/85	DATE EMPLOY VERIFIED 12/85	EST. MONTHLY INCOME $4,000

COMPLETE TO HERE FOR EMPLOYMENT AND TRADE REPORT AND SKIP TO CREDIT HISTORY

DATE OF BIRTH 5/25/60	NUMBER OF DEPENDENTS INCLUDING SELF: 3	☒ OWNS OR BUYING HOME	☐ RENTS HOME	☐ OTHER: (EXPLAIN)
FORMER ADDRESS: 321 FIRST AVE.	CITY: ARBORVILLE	STATE: MT	FROM: 1975	TO: 1983
FORMER EMPLOYER: O'NEILL & ASSOCIATES	POSITION HELD: SALESPERSON	FROM: 2/81	TO: 9/83	EST. MONTHLY INCOME $1,560
SPOUSE'S EMPLOYER: TRI-CITY DEPT. STORE	POSITION HELD: ASSIST. MGR.	SINCE: 4/84	DATE EMPLOY VERIFIED 12/84	EST. MONTHLY INCOME $2,500

CREDIT HISTORY (*Complete this section for all reports*)

WHOSE	KIND OF BUSINESS AND ID CODE	DATE REPORTED AND METHOD OF REPORTING	DATE OPENED	DATE OF LAST PAYMENT	HIGHEST CREDIT OR LAST PAYMENT	BALANCE OWING	PAST DUE AMOUNT	PAST DUE NO. OF PAYMENTS	NO. MONTHS HISTORY REVIEWED	30-59 DAYS ONLY	60-89 DAYS ONLY	90 DAYS AND OVER	TYPE & TERMS (MANNER OF PAYMENT)	REMARKS
2	FIRST MONTANA BANK B 12-345	2/6/90 AUTOMTD.	12/89	1/90	2000	1100	-0-	-0-	2	-0-	-0-	-0-	INSTALLMENT	$100/MO.
3	SMITHSON'S DEPT. STORE D 54-321	2/10/90 MANUAL	4/85	1/90	650	100	-0-	-0-	12	-0-	-0-	-0-	REVOLVING	$ 25/MO.
2	MULTIBANK CREDIT CARD N 01-234	12/12/89 AUTOMTD.	7/86	11/89	790	100	100	1	12	1	-0-	-0-	OPEN	30-DAY

PUBLIC RECORD: SMALL CLAIMS CT. CASE #SC1001 PLAINTIFF: APPLIANCES UNLIMITED, INC.
AMOUNT $225 PAID 4/4/85
ADDITIONAL INFORMATION: REF. SMALL CLAIMS CT. CASE #SC1001—5/30/85 SUBJECT SAYS CLAIM PAID
UNDER PROTEST. APPLIANCE DID NOT OPERATE PROPERLY.

If you list a personal reference because you do not have sufficient business credit references, the person you list can indicate how he or she feels you conduct your personal business affairs. School personnel can indicate how reliable and trustworthy you were in school. In each case, the reference checked merely helps the credit manager to get a better picture of you as a credit risk so that an accurate appraisal of your creditworthiness can be made.

AVOIDING CREDIT RECORD PROBLEMS

You can help maintain a good credit record by keeping track of your purchases and payments. When you buy on credit, you should keep your copy of the sales slip or credit card receipt for your own records in the event a problem with billing arises. The businessperson will retain the other copies for billing purposes.

Checking Your Statement of Account

You will receive a statement of account on a regular basis, usually monthly. The **statement of account** or, simply, a **statement** is a record of the transactions that you have completed with a business during a billing period. For credit card accounts, the statement lists all of your purchases from various businesses. Most statements show:

- The balance that was due when the last statement was mailed.
- The amounts charged during the month for the merchandise or services you bought.
- The amounts credited to your account for payments made during the month or for merchandise returned.
- The current balance, which is the balance from the last statement, plus interest charges and the amounts of any new purchases, minus the amounts credited to you (old balance + interest + purchases - payments = current balance).
- The minimum amount of your next payment and when it is due.

Most statements are prepared by computers. A statement serves two basic purposes: (1) it shows you how much you owe, and (2) it gives you a record of your business transactions. A statement is shown in Figure 30-3.

You should check the accuracy of the statement by comparing it with your copies of sales slips and with your record of payments and credit memorandums. A **credit memorandum** is a written record of the amount subtracted from your account when you return merchandise. If you discover an error on a statement, you should notify the seller at once.

Credit card fraud is a major problem reported by the Federal Trade Commission. To avoid being defrauded, your credit card account statements need to be checked very carefully for errors. One system used by consumers is to keep a file of sales slips when a credit card is used—each form normally has "sales draft, cardholder copy" printed on it. It is yours; keep it. When the statement arrives, check the items on the statement against the sales slips on file. If a charge is shown on the statement for which you do not have a sales draft, check that charge and report any error to the bank or credit card company immediately. Staple to the statement the sales slips for the items

Figure 30-3 Monthly statements give you important information that should be checked carefully.

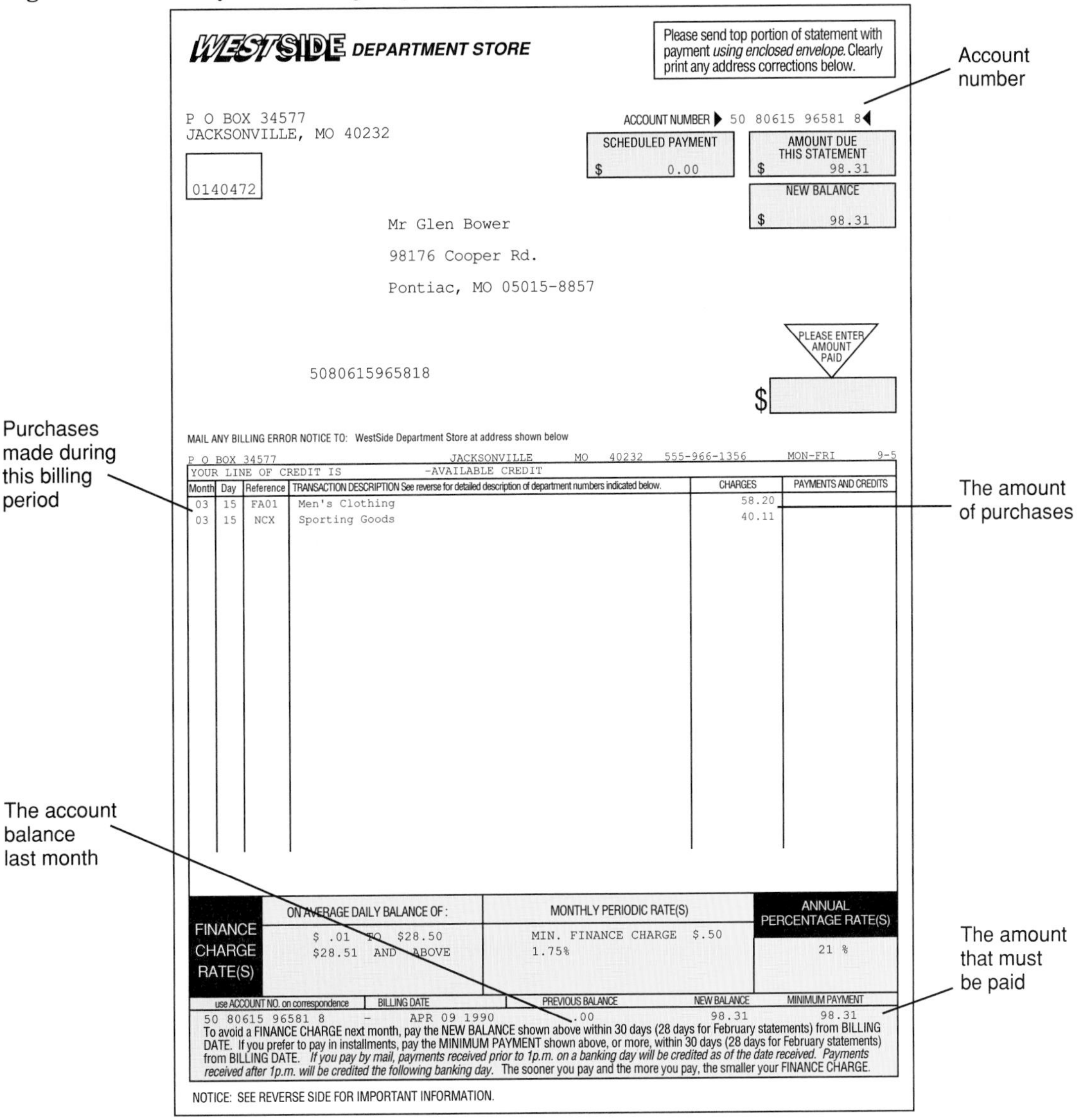
Account number
Purchases made during this billing period
The amount of purchases
The account balance last month
The amount that must be paid

WESTSIDE DEPARTMENT STORE

Please send top portion of statement with payment *using enclosed envelope.* Clearly print any address corrections below.

P O BOX 34577
JACKSONVILLE, MO 40232

0140472

ACCOUNT NUMBER ▶ 50 80615 96581 8◀

SCHEDULED PAYMENT	AMOUNT DUE THIS STATEMENT	NEW BALANCE
$ 0.00	$ 98.31	$ 98.31

Mr Glen Bower
98176 Cooper Rd.
Pontiac, MO 05015-8857

PLEASE ENTER AMOUNT PAID $

5080615965818

MAIL ANY BILLING ERROR NOTICE TO: WestSide Department Store at address shown below
P O BOX 34577 JACKSONVILLE MO 40232 555-966-1356 MON-FRI 9-5

YOUR LINE OF CREDIT IS -AVAILABLE CREDIT

Month	Day	Reference	TRANSACTION DESCRIPTION See reverse for detailed description of department numbers indicated below.	CHARGES	PAYMENTS AND CREDITS
03	15	FA01	Men's Clothing	58.20	
03	15	NCX	Sporting Goods	40.11	

FINANCE CHARGE RATE(S)	ON AVERAGE DAILY BALANCE OF:	MONTHLY PERIODIC RATE(S)	ANNUAL PERCENTAGE RATE(S)
	$ .01 TO $28.50	MIN. FINANCE CHARGE $.50	
	$28.51 AND ABOVE	1.75%	21 %

use ACCOUNT NO. on correspondence	BILLING DATE	PREVIOUS BALANCE	NEW BALANCE	MINIMUM PAYMENT
50 80615 96581 8 -	APR 09 1990	.00	98.31	98.31

To avoid a FINANCE CHARGE next month, pay the NEW BALANCE shown above within 30 days (28 days for February statements) from BILLING DATE. If you prefer to pay in installments, pay the MINIMUM PAYMENT shown above, or more, within 30 days (28 days for February statements) from BILLING DATE. *If you pay by mail, payments received prior to 1p.m. on a banking day will be credited as of the date received. Payments received after 1p.m. will be credited the following banking day.* The sooner you pay and the more you pay, the smaller your FINANCE CHARGE.

NOTICE: SEE REVERSE SIDE FOR IMPORTANT INFORMATION.

listed on the statement and file them for future reference. Also compare payments and previous balances with your records.

Keeping Accurate Records

Another thing that you can do to help avoid credit record problems is to keep your own records. This is a good personal business practice that too often is not followed.

Many errors are simply honest mistakes, and businesses are as eager to correct them as you are. Your creditworthiness may be at stake, and the business's reputation may be hurt by bad publicity if errors are not corrected. When you receive a sales slip, a credit memorandum, or a monthly statement, you should examine it to make sure that it is correct.

When making a payment by check, write the date and the check number on the statement. Keep your statements and sales slips. They will be valuable in the future if any questions arise as to whether they have been paid. You should be able to prove that payment was made. In Chapter 25, you learned that a canceled check is valuable as evidence that payment has been made because it has the endorsement of the payee on the back.

When you do not pay by check, you need some other method of showing that you have made payment. A written form that acknowledges that payment was made is called a **receipt**. The receipt form has spaces for entering the number of the receipt, the date, the name of the person making payment, the amount of the payment in words, the reason for the payment, the amount in figures, and the signature of the person receiving the payment. A stub is filled out to show the same information. Figure 30-4 shows a receipt properly filled out. Each stub and receipt is numbered so that the customer's receipt can be compared with the creditor's stub if a dispute arises.

Sometimes a receipt is not given. Instead, the word "paid" is written or stamped on the bill or statement. The date and the initials or signature of the one who received your money should be included.

Figure 30-4
Tracy has given Tami receipt for her $50 deposit on a school ring.

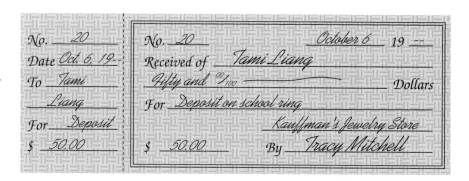

PROTECTING YOUR RIGHTS

Most businesses are honest and forthright in their business dealings. Nevertheless, it has been necessary for our federal and state governments to pass laws to protect consumers who engage in credit transactions. The Truth in Lending law of 1968 launched a series of laws that deal with various aspects of credit and lending practices. It was followed in 1980 by the Truth in Lending Simplification Act.

The **Truth in Lending law** requires that you be told the cost of a credit purchase in writing before you sign a credit agreement. It requires, for instance, that the APR and total finance charge be clearly stated. The Truth in Lending law also covers credit card problems. The law limits your liability to $50 for unauthorized credit card purchases made prior to notification of the issuer. You are not liable for any fraudulent charges made after you have notified the credit card company—even if someone charges several hundred dollars before you report your card missing. You can notify the company by telephone, but you should also put your notification in writing, citing the date of the phone call. Annie Deardorff does have a problem since she waited too long to report the loss of her credit card. She could be liable for the more than $200 charged before she reported her lost card.

The **Equal Credit Opportunity Act** prohibits creditors from denying credit because of age, race, sex, or marital status. Young people who may have just entered the labor market cannot be denied credit based only on their ages. Older, possibly retired, people also have special protection under this act. Married women who previously found it difficult to establish credit in their own names now have a legal right to do so. Under this law, a woman has a right to her own credit if she proves to be creditworthy.

Rick Moreno was not treated correctly. Unless his state still requires age 21 for the legal age to enter into a contract, he could not be denied credit based on his age alone. His creditworthiness would have to be investigated. He could insist on this and take the matter to court if necessary.

Another important piece of legislation is the Fair Credit Billing Act. The **Fair Credit Billing Act** is a law that requires prompt correction of billing mistakes when they are brought to the attention of a business in a prescribed manner. To get a correction of an error, you must notify the creditor *in writing* within 60 days after your statement was mailed. A good rule is to report errors as soon as you discover them. Then the following four points are important:

- While waiting for an answer, you are not required to pay any amount in question.
- Your complaint must be acknowledged by the creditor within 30 days unless your statement is corrected before that time.
- You do not pay finance charges on any amount in error.
- If no error is found, the creditor must bill you again and may include finance charges that have accumulated plus any minimum payments that were missed while the statement was being questioned.

David Zobott, if he followed the procedure described above, would not have to pay the amounts in question on his statement. If he did not report the errors in writing on a timely basis, he may have difficulty proving his dispute. This law is designed to cover situations such as his.

The Fair Credit Billing Act also provides that you may withhold payment of any balance due on defective merchandise or services purchased with a credit card. Your first step should be to contact the business and try to resolve the problem; many situations can be corrected if the complaint is made in a courteous but firm manner. The law does protect you if you have made this ''good faith'' effort.

The **Fair Credit Reporting Act** is the law that gives consumers the right to know what specific information credit bureaus are providing to potential creditors, employers, and insurers. It provides that if credit is denied on the basis of information in a credit report, the applicant must be given the name, address, and phone number of the credit bureau that provided the information. In addition, credit records for both a husband and wife are kept if both are responsible for the debt. This allows a credit history to be developed for each spouse.

Prior to this law being passed, many consumers were unaware that reports on their bill-paying habits were available to potential lenders. This act made those reports available to the consumer and provided ways in which information could be accessed and corrected. It also requires that any information dealing with bankruptcy that is more than ten years old must be automatically deleted. Any other adverse information must be deleted if it is more than seven years old.

Renee and Kendall Lauver have a right to see their credit bureau report. They requested it and did not have to pay to see it since they had been denied credit. They discovered two errors. In their former community, there was a couple with a name similar to theirs, the Lavers. That couple's credit record was bad, and some of their unpaid debts showed up on the Lauver's report. Also, one bill that was disputed with a local retailer was recorded as not being paid.

The Lauver's had a right to demand that the error of recording someone else's bad credit habits be removed from their record. They also were permitted to write a brief statement giving their side of the disputed bill with the local retailer. After taking these two actions, their good credit record was reestablished and they received the loan they needed.

BUILDING YOUR OWN CREDIT RECORD

Laws are important to have, and it is important for consumers to know their rights under those laws. However, building your own good record of creditworthiness is even more important.

What You Can Do Now

To some extent you can begin building a credit record while you are still in school. Since trust and reliability are important when it comes to matters of credit, you can help to establish yourself by having a good record of grades and school attendance. Both employers and creditors know that behavior patterns developed in school tend to carry on after graduation.

In addition, it is good to have both a checking and a savings account. If you have a balance in each account and do not overdraw your checking account, a lender can see that you can handle money. Making regular deposits to your savings account also suggests that you will be a good credit risk.

Some people establish credit records by charging small purchases. For instance, if you buy a sweater on credit and make the payments according to the agreement, you have taken an important step toward proving you are a good credit risk. Or you may want to pay off your account within 30 days and avoid an interest charge. Either way you will be building a good credit record.

Having a good part-time or full-time employment record also helps to establish a good credit record. Changing jobs often does not look good to a creditor. Being on a job for two or more years is a positive part of a good credit record.

How to Get Help

If you find that you just cannot pay your bills when they are due, you should follow these four steps: First, contact your creditors and explain your situation. Second, make a realistic proposal for when and what you can pay;

Illus. 30-2
Buying a sweater on credit and making the payments according to the agreement is one way to establish a credit record.

don't just say "I can't pay." Third, keep any promises you make. Fourth, make a written copy of your agreement to avoid disagreements later.

You may be able to work out a debt-repayment plan. A **debt-repayment plan** is an agreement developed cooperatively by a creditor and a debtor to reduce payments to a more manageable level and still pay off the debt. This plan is good for both the creditor and the debtor.

One thing to avoid is being misled by advertisements such as this: "Erase bad credit! 100% guaranteed." Claims such as these are fraudulent. No one can unconditionally correct a bad credit record—it does not work that way. If you need help with a consumer credit problem, there is a National Foundation for Consumer Credit in Silver Springs, Maryland, that provides counseling help at little or not cost to consumers. This nonprofit organization has more than 280 offices located in 44 states. Consumer Credit Counseling Services should be used when the need arises.

Increasing Your Business Vocabulary

The following terms should become part of your business vocabulary. For each numbered item, find the term that has the same meaning.

credit application   *Equal Credit Opportunity Act*
credit bureau   *Fair Credit Billing Act*
credit memorandum   *Fair Credit Reporting Act*
credit record   *receipt*
creditworthy   *statement or statement of account*
debt-repayment plan   *Truth in Lending law*

1. A form on which you provide information needed by a lender to make a decision about granting credit or approving a loan.
2. A company that gathers information on credit users and sells that information in the form of credit reports to credit grantors.
3. An act that prohibits. creditors from denying credit because of age, race, sex, or marital status.
4. A written form that acknowledges payment was made.
5. A written record of the amount subtracted from an account when merchandise has been returned.
6. A record of the transactions that you have

completed with a business during a billing period.
7. A law which requires that you be told the cost of a credit purchase in writing before you sign a credit agreement.
8. An agreement developed cooperatively by a creditor and debtor to reduce payments to a more manageable level and still pay off the debt.
9. A law that gives consumers the right to know what specific information credit bureaus are providing to potential creditors, employers, and insurers.
10. A law that requires prompt correction of billing mistakes when they are brought to

the attention of a business in a prescribed manner.

11. Having established a credit record that shows you are a good credit risk.

12. A report that shows the debts you owe, how often you use credit, and whether you pay your debts on time.

Reviewing Your Reading

1. What two things do lenders want to know before making a decision about granting credit?

2. Name three things lenders want to know about your finances and five things about reliability.

3. What is the purpose of a credit application? Why do credit references have to be listed?

4. What does your signature on a credit application signify?

5. What is the purpose of a credit bureau? Who uses its services?

6. What are some examples of the information contained in a credit bureau report?

7. In what ways is a receipt important? What information does it contain?

8. In what ways is a credit memorandum important?

9. What use might a debtor have for canceled checks?

10. What information is shown on a statement of account?

11. What is the procedure for checking a credit card account statement?

12. What are examples of laws that help protect consumers in credit transactions? What kinds of protection do they provide?

13. What should be done when errors are found in credit statements?

14. What are some things that can be done to build a credit record?

15. What kinds of help are available to debtors who have credit problems?

Using Your Business Knowledge

1. Sergio Torres operates a book store. One day Bill Cross, a total stranger, asked if he could buy a set of encyclopedias on credit. Mr. Cross explained that he had just moved into town two weeks ago. The moving expenses took most of his cash, but he has a good job and will be able to pay $30 a month beginning next month.
   a. What other information should Sergio get from Mr. Cross?
   b. What sources of information could Sergio use before making a final decision?
   c. Would you extend credit to Mr. Cross? Why or why not?

2. Cheryl Oakwood wants to open an account in the Hewitt Road Department Store. She objects, however, to giving the credit man-ager information about such things as where she has other charge accounts, whether she owns real estate, where she works, and in which bank she maintains an account.
   a. Why did the credit manager want this information?
   b. In what ways could a credit bureau report help this manager?
   c. Does Cheryl have a right to refuse to give this information? If so, can credit be denied her?

3. Donna Stratford has been working on her first job for seven months. Her checking account has a balance of $159. She has also put aside $50 in cash for an emergency. She wants to buy a clock radio which sells

for $69.95 at a store that offers credit. Donna has never used credit and would like to establish a credit rating. What can she do to get a credit record started? What advice would you give her if she decided to buy this clock radio on credit?

4. Below is a list of some consumer transactions. For each, explain whether there would be a cash receipt, a credit memorandum, a canceled check, or a credit card sales slip. Also explain how and why each record should be saved, if you believe it should be saved.
   a. Paid cash for flowers that have been ordered in advance
   b. Bought a pair of shoes using a credit card
   c. Returned a pair of slacks, purchased a week ago on a charge account, because they did not fit

Computing Business Problems

1. The Country Boutique grants open credit to people who have been steady customers. Today the boutique received checks in the mail from several customers as shown below:

Name	Amount Owed	Amount Paid
Enrique Navarro	$ 44.22	$44.22
Lynne Goldberg	10.00	5.00
Eloise Little	102.67	50.00
Sam Nader	54.89	25.00
Ruth Smith	19.35	19.35

   a. What was the balance in each account?
   b. What was the total amount received from charge customers?

2. Linda Spencer made the following credit purchases: gloves, $18; 2 purses at $23 each; necklace, $55; 3 pairs of shoes at $42 each. Later she returned the gloves and one purse and received a credit memorandum.

d. Paid $35 in cash toward a $170 balance owed on a charge account with a local store
e. Wrote a check for $125 to pay off a credit card account balance

5. Suzanne Winters does not believe in buying anything on credit. She says that too many people get into trouble using credit cards and that there are too many errors made in credit transactions. She also believes that there is no protection for consumers using credit and no help if they get into credit difficulties. Explain to Suzanne ways in which laws protect consumers who engage in credit transactions and tell her about some of the kinds of help that are available for consumers who have credit problems.

a. What was the total of Linda's purchases before she returned the gloves and the purse?
b. What was the amount of the credit memorandum?
c. How much did she owe after she received the credit memorandum?

3. Paul Zabawa bought some materials needed for the boat he was building. He purchased the following: 250 meters of board, $3.80 per foot; 90 meters of fabric, $8.15 per yard; and 50 liters of marine varnish, $26.95 per gallon.
   a. What was the total amount of his purchase?
   b. If he were offered a 4 percent discount for paying cash, how much would he save on this purchase?

4. Dixie Kauffman used her bank charge card for the following purchases: Earl's Clothing Store, 2 shirts at $14 each; Wingo's

Hardware Company, 2 gallons of paint at $10.75 each; PaDelford Family Restaurant, $24.75. A credit slip from Wingo's Hardware Company for $10.75 was received. Dixie's statement showed a balance of $152 from the previous month plus a finance charge of $2.28.

a. If Dixie pays her account in full, how much will she pay?

b. If she decides to make a minimum payment of $30, how much will she still owe?

c. If the finance charge is $1\frac{1}{2}$ percent per month on the unpaid balance, what will be the finance charge shown next month if she only pays the $30 this month?

Expanding Your Understanding of Business

1. When businesses have difficulty in collecting amounts that customers owe them, they sometimes hire collection agencies. Prepare a report on collection agencies. Tell what they do, what methods they use, and what their services cost. You should be able to find most of the information you need in the library. However, you might call or visit a local collection agency to get additional information. Collection agencies are listed in the Yellow Pages of your telephone book.

2. States set a limit on the interest rate that can be charged for different kinds of credit. Find out what the maximum allowable interest rates are in your state. Write a report on what you discover.

3. Assume that you checked your credit bureau record and discovered an error: an account with a local department store reportedly was overdue twice during the past year. Actually you had paid the correct amount on time in each instance, but your payment had been credited to someone else's account. After checking with the store's credit manager, you were able to have the situation corrected with the store, but apparently the correction was not reported to the credit bureau. Write a statement of no more than 100 words to correct the information in your credit bureau record.

4. The Equal Credit Opportunity Act permits lenders and creditors to use a credit scoring system. The credit scoring system assigns points to various factors that relate to whether a person is a good credit risk. Find out more about credit scoring systems by visiting your library and reading articles discussing these systems. Visit a retail store, a bank, or some other lending institution and learn what you can about the experience that businesses have had with credit scoring. If you can, bring an example of a credit scoring system to class for discussion.

5. What credit counseling services are available in your community? Check the Yellow Pages of a telephone directory and look through advertisements in local newspapers for the names, addresses, and telephone numbers of credit counseling services. Also find out if your county has a Cooperative Extension Office; if so, check to see if they offer credit counseling as part of their services. Interview a credit counselor or a manager in the office to see what kinds of credit problems seem to occur and the solutions that are used. Also include a reference to personal bankruptcy as a solution of last resort and its affect on the individual and his or her credit rating. Report your findings to your class and discuss them with the members of your class to see how they view credit counseling and bankruptcy.

Career Category: Credit

In Unit 8, you learned about the important role credit plays in our economy. Most individuals and businesses find it necessary to use credit for some purchases. As a result, many workers are involved in the processing of credit transactions.

Job Titles: Job titles commonly found in this career area include:

Credit Clerk
Credit Authorizer
Credit Reporter
Loan Clerk
Loan Officer
Credit Department Manager
Credit Union Manager
Credit Bureau Clerk
Credit Bureau Manager
Credit Counselor

Employment Outlook: The demand for workers in credit-related occupations is expected to be above average through the next decade. An increasing use of credit by both consumers and businesses will cause the demand for credit services to continue, although automation will tend to lessen that demand. Professional employment in credit counseling very likely will increase steadily as individuals and families seek help with credit management problems.

Future Changes: New developments in computer applications and systems for handling credit transactions will affect the need for credit workers who normally handle paperwork and routine activities.

What Is Done on the Job: Clerical workers in this area perform functions similar to clerical workers in other areas of work. They must keep accurate records of amounts borrowed, paid, and owed by customers. They must be efficient in working with numbers and must be able to handle confidential information in a responsible way.

Managers and other professional workers must decide whether to grant credit or extend a loan. They must analyze information and provide explanations for their actions.

Credit counselors meet with people who have credit problems and who seek help. The counselor must analyze credit problems and help clients move toward solutions.

Education and Training: High school graduates with good clerical skills will find employment in this career area. Job applicants who have continued their education beyond high school with courses in credit, finance, and counseling will be able to obtain higher level posi-

tions. In addition to a knowledge of credit laws, financial operations, and management procedures, professional credit workers must have good public relations and communications skills.

Salary Levels: Salaries vary widely but are competitive with salaries paid to similar workers in other career areas. The average annual salaries for credit clerks and credit authorizers range from $10,000 to $15,000; managerial and loan officer positions pay in the $20,000 to $60,000 range, depending upon the experience of the worker and the size of the business.

For Additional Information: Interviewing a credit worker from a local credit bureau, visiting the loan department of a bank or credit union, or observing the credit department of a retail store are good ways to get additional information on this career area. A speaker from a credit counseling service can provide up-to-date information on credit counseling work. Special sources of information include the following:

Consumer Credit Career Information Kit
International Consumer Credit Association
243 N. Lindbergh Blvd.
St. Louis, MO 63141

Careers in Collections
American Collectors Association
P.O. Box 35106
Minneapolis, MN 55435

Opportunities in Credit Management
National Association of Credit Management
475 Park Avenue
New York, NY 10016

Planning Your Savings and Investments

Unit Goals

After studying the chapters in this unit, you will be able to:

1. *Explain why savings plans are of interest to investors.*
2. *Describe a variety of savings plans that can be used by investors.*
3. *Give examples of how stocks and bonds fit into an investment plan.*
4. *Describe other investments, including real estate, that are considered by investors.*

Chapter 31
Creating a Savings Plan

Chapter 32
Using Your Savings Plan

Chapter 33
Investing in Bonds and Stocks

Chapter 34
Considering Other Investments

Two Well-Known Dates in Our Stock Market History

Business Brief

There are two well-known dates in the history of our stock market. One is Thursday, October 24, 1929, a day when the market crashed and ushered in the Great Depression of the 1930s. The other is Monday, October 19, 1987, a day when the Dow

Jones Industrial Average (a measure of how stocks are doing price-wise) plunged 568 points—an all-time record.

Had you been living in the early 1930s, you would have witnessed the disaster that followed the market's crash. Many people and businesses suffered huge financial losses. Bank failures were common, and business bankruptcies occurred throughout the country. Many individuals committed suicide because they were financially ruined; they had invested money they could not afford to risk, and they lost all of it.

You were alive during the crash of 1987, but you did not witness what was seen in the early 1930s. In many respects, after the crash of 1987 business went on as usual. Our economy stayed strong. Banks stayed open. People continued to make investments.

Many people did lose money in the 1987 crash, but they were not ruined financially. Some businesses were hurt and had to lay off some of their employees, but most did not have to close. As a result of the crash, many small businesses found it more difficult to raise needed capital. The crash of 1987 was not a disaster—just a bad day.

What accounted for the difference? For one thing, today people cannot buy as much stock on credit—known as margin buying—as they could in 1929. Banks are better regulated and managed than they were in the 1930s. The average investor has learned from past experience, is wiser in the market, and has a variety of investments for protection against any one investment going bad.

There has been a great deal of discussion about the crash of 1987 and what can be done to avoid another crash in the future. Some actions have been taken to help correct problems that were revealed during that crash. Forty-five million individual investors, compared to fifty-five million before the crash, continue to view the stock market as a good personal money management tool. Investors tend to be more cautious now, and many investment plans avoid having only high-risk stocks in them. More investors also use mutual funds to allow them to invest with others in a variety of stocks and bonds.

Our stock market is a unique tool of capitalism and an essential part of our market economy. Without a properly functioning stock market, many businesses would be unable to raise money needed to expand operations, buy new equipment, and employ additional workers. Consumers would be unable to invest in stocks for a greater return on their money. With both businesses and consumers benefiting from the stock market, it is safe to say that the market is here to stay.

Source: "Meltdown Monday," *Reader's Digest* (February 1988): 59.

Creating a Savings Plan

Chapter 31

Chapter Objectives

After studying this chapter and completing the end-of-chapter activities, you will be able to:

1. *Explain why it is important to have a savings plan.*

2. *Describe different ways to put money aside as savings.*

3. *Explain how interest makes your savings grow.*

4. *Explain why safety and yield are important to savers.*

5. *Describe what is meant by liquidity.*

6. *Give an example of how savings help our economy.*

You have learned about the use of credit and how it is important to consumers and businesses. U.S. consumers are especially good at using credit, and they use a lot of it. Some believe they use too much. U.S. consumers, on the other hand, do not save much of what they earn. In fact, compared to people of other nations, such as Japan, U.S. consumers save the lowest percentage of their incomes.

Developing a savings plan should be part of each person's financial program. Savings are used to buy the goods and services we need and want as well as to prepare for future expenses and emergencies. Savings also help to keep our economy healthy when those savings are invested and used by businesses to expand their operations. Saving a part of your income should become a regular, important habit.

HAVING A SAVINGS PLAN

Putting money aside in a systematic way to help reach an established financial goal is what is meant by a **savings plan.** How much you save, where you put your savings, and what you save for are important personal decisions. People save different amounts of money for different reasons and in different ways. For instance, Josie Coramoto's parents have had a savings plan for years. Today they use their savings to buy real estate. They bought their home and make monthly payments on their mortgage. In addition, they make payments on ten acres of land they bought in a newly developed lake area. Mr. and Mrs. Coramoto also believe it is important to have money in the bank that can be used for emergencies. Every week they deposit 10 percent of their income into their savings account.

Josie's older brother buys stocks and bonds with part of his wages. He is planning for his retirement years. Josie takes a certain amount of the money she earns baby-sitting and puts it in an envelope, which she keeps in a drawer in her room. As soon as she saves enough, she plans to buy her own stereo.

There is one common trait in Josie's family: all family members save. Each member, however, has a different savings plan. All except Josie invest their savings. **Investing** means using your savings to earn more money for you. Josie is saving but not investing. She has a savings plan, but it offers no opportunity to earn money. How will you save and invest your money?

WATCHING YOUR SAVINGS GROW

Saving a regular amount of money, even a few dollars at a time, is an important habit. It is the first step in a savings plan that can be important to you in the future. In addition to putting money aside as savings, you should have those savings work for you—that is, earn interest. Interest, as you learned in Chapter 22, is money you receive for letting others, such as financial institutions, use your money for loans and other investments. In addition to keeping your money safe, financial institutions reward you for making your money available to them. Savings put to work to earn interest are one form of investment.

Earning Interest

When savings are invested and the income from them is also invested, the increase over a number of years is larger than many people realize. For example, David Skinner is able to save $50 a month. In a year, his savings will amount to $600. In 10 years, he will have saved $6,000. If he deposits his money in a savings account that earns 6 percent interest paid every three months, his savings will increase rapidly as interest is added to his account. At the end of 10 years, he will have more than $8,200 in his account rather than $6,000. His savings will have grown by more than $2,200.

David realizes the importance of this increase in his savings. He looks at a chart (see Figure 31-1) to see how much his savings will grow if he saves for a longer period. At 6 percent, his $50-a-month savings will grow to $14,500 in 15 years. Since interest rates change, David's account may grow even more. At the 6 percent rate, the interest he receives by the fifteenth year is more than the $50 he was putting in each month. He could actually start taking out $50 each month without decreasing the amount he has on deposit.

Figure 31-1
Interest helps
savings grow.

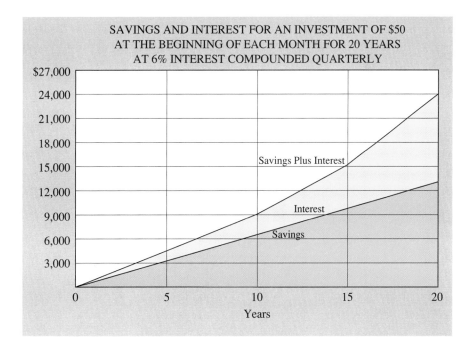

He would have a permanent income of $50 a month. Often people fail to do this kind of planning for the future. Figure 31-1 shows how interest can cause savings to grow over a period of years.

Earning Compound Interest

Have you heard about the magic of compounding? There really is no magic in it, but the compounding of interest often is referred to in that way. Compounding makes your savings grow faster than simple interest, and after a number of years, the difference is quite significant. **Simple interest** is interest that is computed only on the amount saved; **compound interest** is computed on the amount saved plus the interest previously earned.

In David's case, he is earning compound interest; that is, he is earning interest on the interest that is accumulating in his account. For example, simple interest of 10 percent on $1,000 is $100. However, if the interest is compounded, then the interest computed at the end of the next year will be based on $1,100 ($1,000 + $100 interest). The 10 percent interest earned would amount to $110. Interest the following year would be figured on $1,210 ($1,100 + $110) and would amount to $121. When interest is compounded, the amount of interest paid increases each time it is figured. If the interest were not compounded, the interest paid would be $100 each year.

Interest can be compounded daily, monthly, quarterly (every three months), semiannually (twice a year), or annually. The use of computer programs to calculate interest makes compounding relatively easy. The more frequent the compounding, the greater the growth in your savings. Figure 31-2 shows how rapidly monthly savings of different amounts increase when interest is compounded quarterly at 6 percent.

Figure 31-2 Even small amounts grow when interest is compounded.

Monthly Savings	End of First Year	End of Second Year	End of Third Year	End of Fourth Year	End of Fifth Year	End of Tenth Year
$ 5.00	$ 61.98	$ 127.76	$ 197.76	$ 271.68	$ 350.32	$ 822.16
10.00	123.95	255.52	395.15	543.35	700.47	1,644.32
25.00	309.89	638.79	987.87	1,358.38	1,751.62	4,110.79
30.00	371.86	766.55	1,185.45	1,630.05	2,101.94	4,932.95
35.00	433.84	894.30	1,383.02	1,901.73	2,452.26	5,755.11
50.00	619.77	1,277.58	1,975.74	2,716.75	3,503.24	8,221.59

Making Time Work for You

You may not have a large amount of money to save at any one time. In fact, you may be like many people who have to build up their savings with just a dollar or two at a time. Do not wait until you have a large sum to put into a savings account; rather, open one as soon as you can. With compounding, as you have learned, the length of time makes a difference. Take advantage of the time factor.

SELECTING YOUR SAVINGS PLAN

You will find financial institutions willing to accept small amounts of savings. Some savings plans are set up to encourage small sums to be set aside, and interest on those plans is paid at regular intervals. Banks, credit unions, and savings and loan associations usually welcome small as well as large savings deposits.

Being Careful Where You Put Your Money

Your savings will grow if invested wisely. The American humorist Will Rogers is quoted as saying, ''It's not the return *on* my money I am concerned about, it is the return *of* my money.'' Today, most financial institutions—as you learned in Chapter 22—have their savings accounts insured up to very large sums. It assures you that your money will be returned to you when you need it.

Suppose you lend $100 to someone who promises to pay it back with 15 percent interest at the end of one year, a rate higher than banks pay. If the loan is paid back, you will receive $115 ($100 + $15 interest). However, if the borrower has no money at the end of the year, you may get nothing back. You may lose both the $100 you loaned and the $15 interest you should have earned. Investments are satisfactory when the safety of the amount invested and the interest to be paid can be depended upon. **Safety** is assurance that the money you have invested will be returned to you.

Not all investors need the same degree of safety. Someone may have enough money to make 20 different investments. If one of them is lost, the investor still has the other 19. On the other hand, suppose that a person has only a small amount of money and makes only one investment. One loss would be serious. If you have limited funds, you should be careful to make investments that are as safe as possible.

When deciding how to invest your savings, there are several things to consider. In addition to considering the safety of your savings, you should consider the plan's earnings. You should also determine how quickly you can get your money out of your investment if you need it.

Paying Attention to Yield

A good savings plan should earn a reasonable amount of interest. That is, it should have a satisfactory yield. The **yield** is the percentage of interest that will be added to your savings over a period of time. Sometimes yield is referred to as the *rate of return*. Figure 31-3 shows the value of an original investment of $100 in 20 years at several different yields.

Figure 31-3
While a higher yield means greater growth, it may also mean greater risk.

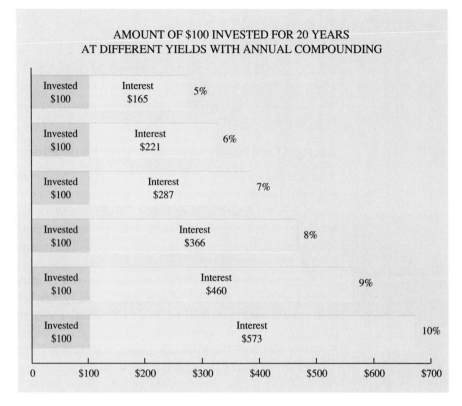

AMOUNT OF $100 INVESTED FOR 20 YEARS
AT DIFFERENT YIELDS WITH ANNUAL COMPOUNDING

Invested $100	Interest $165	5%
Invested $100	Interest $221	6%
Invested $100	Interest $287	7%
Invested $100	Interest $366	8%
Invested $100	Interest $460	9%
Invested $100	Interest $573	10%

0      $100 $200 $300 $400 $500 $600 $700

Usually the higher the yield, the greater the risk of loss. Loans to the federal government are the safest. When money is loaned to individuals or businesses, it usually earns higher interest rates than those paid by the government because there is less safety. For example, while the government is paying 6 percent interest, one business may pay 8 percent and a business that presents a greater risk may have to pay 12 percent.

The offer of a low rate of interest, however, does not guarantee safety. Similarly, high rates of interest do not mean that a loss will surely occur. The higher yields mean that investors generally believe that the situation involves a higher risk.

Getting Your Money When Needed

When an investment can be turned into money quickly, it is said to be a **liquid investment**. This feature of an investment is important if you should need money to take care of emergencies. Suppose, for example, that you have $5,000 on deposit in a bank. If you need money right away, you usually can go to your bank and withdraw it immediately. On the other hand, suppose you own a piece of land that you bought for $5,000. The land may be a safe investment and yield a satisfactory return; however, if you need money at once, you may find it difficult to sell the piece of land right away. You might even have to sell it for less than you paid for it if you cannot wait for a buyer who is willing to pay your price.

When you make a number of investments, you do not need to have all of them in a liquid form. How much you need in liquid investments will depend upon your own situation.

UNDERSTANDING HOW SAVINGS AFFECTS THE ECONOMY

Your savings serve a very useful economic purpose. Invested money can be used to operate a business, a government, or some other organization. A business often must borrow money to operate and/or expand the business. We, as individuals, borrow money from banks and other institutions to buy what businesses produce. The money we borrow from a financial institution is someone's invested savings. Our economic system would be significantly weakened without individuals' savings and investments. Your invested savings contribute to keeping our economic system healthy.

Illus. 31-1
Funds invested are used by businesses to expand their operations.

Increasing Your Business Vocabulary

The following terms should become part of your business vocabulary. For each numbered item, find the term that has the same meaning.

compound interest
investing
liquid investment
safety

savings plan
simple interest
yield

1. Interest computed on the amount saved plus the interest previously earned.
2. The percentage of interest that will be added to your savings over a period of time.
3. Putting money aside in a systematic way to help reach an established financial goal.
4. Interest that is computed only on the amount saved.
5. An investment that can be turned into money quickly.
6. Using your savings to earn more money for you.
7. Assurance that the money you have invested will be returned to you.

Reviewing Your Reading

1. What are several reasons why individuals should have a savings plan?
2. What are four different ways of saving?
3. When does money saved become an investment?
4. Why is it important to save even a small amount of money periodically?
5. Why is interest that is compounded better than interest that is not compounded?
6. What will be the total savings if $10 is deposited monthly at 6 percent interest compounded quarterly for a period of ten years? (Use Figure 31-2 on page 452.)
7. Suppose you save $20 a month. If your savings plan compounds interest monthly, should you wait six months and invest $120 at that time, or should you make deposits each month? Why?
8. Cindy Redmond has $500 in a savings account that is paying her 6 percent interest. A friend, Rosalind Tate, knows of a local business project where the $500 could be invested at a 10 percent rate of return. What might be the advantages and disadvantages for Cindy of taking her money out of her savings and putting it into this other investment?
9. Which of the following investments are liquid?
   a. Land
   b. A bank savings account
   c. A loan made to a friend
10. What are some advantages of a savings plan for you as an individual? for the economy?

Using Your Business Knowledge

1. Yolanda Miller has a pizza business, which she operates out of her home, and she makes a nice profit. She keeps all of her business cash in a small fireproof safe in her basement. She has accumulated more than $2,000—more than she needs to buy

supplies and meet unexpected business expenses. She wants to be sure that her money is safe and that she can get it when she needs it. What advice can you give Yolanda so that she can make better use of her money?

2. Donald Gorski has been saving money for the past year since he started working part time. He keeps the money in a metal box in his bedroom. Donald's mother gives him $10 for every $100 saved to help him pay for a new car when he graduates from high school in two years. Donald has saved almost $1,000. Someone told him about a new business that pays 20 percent on money it borrows. Should Donald consider lending his money to this business? Why or why not?

3. Ella Chapman, a wealthy businessperson, invests $5,000 in a newly organized manufacturing company. Frank Brokaw owns a small house and has $5,000 in a savings account. He knows of Ella's investment. Because she has a reputation for being a good investor, Frank decides to invest in that company, too. Does the fact that the investment may be a good one for Ella Chapman mean that it is also a good investment for Frank? Explain your answer.

4. Jennie Wolfe has inherited $25,000. She graduated from high school three years ago, has a good job in an accounting firm, is renting a small apartment with a friend, and has established a savings plan that she has followed regularly for the past two years. She does not want to take a chance on losing any of this inheritance, and yet she wants to get a good yield from investing it. She also feels that she will not need any large amount of cash for the next several years. What advice would you give Jennie regarding how she should invest her inheritance?

5. Paul Chan wanted to borrow $1,000 from his cousin, Gloria Hung. Paul offered to pay 20 percent annual interest although the usual loan rate was about 11 percent. What are some possible reasons for Paul's willingness to pay a higher interest rate? Gloria has several thousand dollars in a savings account that earns only 5.5 percent interest. What advice would you give Gloria regarding this new investment possibility? Should she consider a loan to Paul to be a safe investment? Why or why not?

Computing Business Problems

1. There are several different savings plans. Regardless of which plan is selected the important point is saving on a regular basis. Even small amounts add up to large sums in a short time. How much will each person below save in one year (365 days) if he or she saves the following amounts without interest being added?
   a. Charles Jason—10 cents a day
   b. Carla Spivak—75 cents a week
   c. Alice Farney—$5 every two weeks
   d. Nolan Robinson—$10 a month

2. Ramon Valdez wants a savings plan that will permit him to buy a stereo that costs $270.
   a. How much will he have to save each month to be able to make his purchase at the end of 6 months? at the end of 12 months? If he saves at the 12-month rate, how much longer would he have to save to buy a stereo that costs $450?
   b. Ramon learned that interest can double the amount of money you deposit if you leave it on deposit long enough. To find the number of years required to double the amount deposited, divide 72 by the

interest rate. If Ramon deposited $180, how long would it take for his deposit to double if this account paid 6 percent interest? 8 percent interest? 12 percent interest?

3. Cindy Hamon deposited $50 in her bank account each month for 15 years.

a. What is the total amount that she has invested?

b. How much money is in her account if her deposits earn 6 percent interest compounded quarterly? (See Figure 31-1 on page 451.)

Expanding Your Understanding of Business

1. If you deposit money in a savings account at a bank, savings and loan association, or credit union, the financial institution usually will have insurance that will protect your deposit and return it to you when you ask for it. In the meantime, you will be paid interest on the amount deposited. Why do financial institutions insure savings accounts and also pay interest on your deposits?

2. What would happen in your community if the banks and other lending institutions ran out of money to lend and businesses and consumers were not able to borrow the needed money? What businesses or industries might be hurt the most by this kind of situation?

3. Look through some advertisements of financial institutions to see if any encourage saving small amounts of money. You might want to visit a local financial institution and talk with someone about its policy regarding individuals who want to save only small amounts of money. You may find that some institutions have service charges for deposits and withdrawals if the amount on deposit is a small amount. Report your findings to your class.

4. Steve Bella has decided to save $30 monthly and to invest the money in a bank that pays 6 percent interest compounded quarterly. While he does not know how many years he will be saving and investing

this money, he would like some idea as to the total amount he will have each year for up to five years. Using the table in Figure 31-2, prepare a rough chart for Steve much like the one shown in Figure 31-1.

5. If everyone began saving money and did not buy things such as cars, furniture, household appliances, and new houses, problems would result. If no one buys, businesses will not make sales, factories will not need to produce goods, and, as a result, many people will lose their jobs. Ideally, what part of a person's income should be saved? Are there general rules for spending and saving for individuals? for families?

6. Lending institutions now compute interest for many differing time periods. Visit some lending institutions in your area and find out how much interest you could receive if you were to deposit $500 for one year. Find out what rates of interest would be paid and at what time period they would be compounded. Report your findings to your class; compare answers with other members of your class.

7. Find out from your local banks or savings and loan associations what kinds of investments they have made in your community with the money that has been placed in savings accounts in their institutions. Analyze how they have helped your community.

Using Your Savings Plan

Chapter 32

Chapter Objectives

After studying this chapter and completing the end-of-chapter activities, you will be able to:

1. *Explain how to open and use a savings account.*

2. *Compare a money market account with a Super NOW account.*

3. *Describe a certificate of deposit (CD) and explain its advantages and disadvantages.*

4. *Explain why an individual retirement account (IRA) should be considered.*

5. *State at least four questions to be answered when selecting a financial institution for your savings.*

When you decide to put your savings into an investment that will earn interest, you have a number of decisions to make. These decisions involve a wide variety of savings opportunities offered today by our economy's financial institutions.

Josie Coramoto's grandfather often tells her about how banks operated in his day. He explains that there was basically just a passbook savings account that paid interest of about one or two percent. People in his day never heard about all of those newfangled ideas, such as NOW accounts, money market accounts, and certificates of deposit. And now they even have something called an IRA. In his day, he said, Ira just referred to one of his best friends. He admits that we have a real advantage today but also says that life was indeed simpler in his day.

Savings accounts continue to be a popular part of most consumers' savings and investment plans. It is easy and convenient to make systematic deposits to a savings account, and those accounts pay an established rate of interest while keeping money safe. Let's take a look at the variety of savings accounts that can be considered for your savings plan.

REGULAR SAVINGS ACCOUNTS

Savings accounts may be opened in a commercial bank, a savings bank, a savings and loan association, or a credit union, if you are a member of the credit union. Young children and retired people, as well as those of ages in between, have savings accounts in one or more financial institutions. In a recent year, 72 percent of U.S. consumers had a savings account in one or more financial institutions and 63 percent had regular passbook savings accounts.

Illus. 32-1
Savings accounts are offered at a variety of financial institutions.

Opening Your Savings Account and Making Deposits

Opening a regular savings account is similar to the procedure for opening a checking account, which you learned about in Chapter 23. You will have to fill out a signature card, make a deposit to your account of at least $1, and receive either a savings account passbook or a savings account register. A **savings account passbook**, as shown in Figure 32-1, shows your deposits, withdrawals, interest earned, and the balance of your account. The bank teller will record each transaction in your passbook. If a **savings account register** is used, you must record each deposit or withdrawal as it is made. You must also add the interest when the bank reports it to you. The passbook or register is your record of what is in your savings account.

Figure 32-1
A savings account passbook provides a handy and complete record of your account transactions.

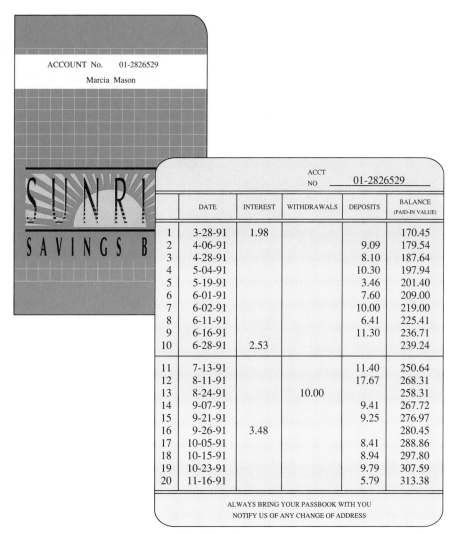

ACCOUNT No.   01-2826529
Marcia Mason

	DATE	INTEREST	WITHDRAWALS	DEPOSITS	BALANCE (PAID-IN VALUE)
1	3-28-91	1.98			170.45
2	4-06-91			9.09	179.54
3	4-28-91			8.10	187.64
4	5-04-91			10.30	197.94
5	5-19-91			3.46	201.40
6	6-01-91			7.60	209.00
7	6-02-91			10.00	219.00
8	6-11-91			6.41	225.41
9	6-16-91			11.30	236.71
10	6-28-91	2.53			239.24
11	7-13-91			11.40	250.64
12	8-11-91			17.67	268.31
13	8-24-91		10.00		258.31
14	9-07-91			9.41	267.72
15	9-21-91			9.25	276.97
16	9-26-91	3.48			280.45
17	10-05-91			8.41	288.86
18	10-15-91			8.94	297.80
19	10-23-91			9.79	307.59
20	11-16-91			5.79	313.38

ACCT NO   01-2826529

ALWAYS BRING YOUR PASSBOOK WITH YOU
NOTIFY US OF ANY CHANGE OF ADDRESS

The bank will periodically send a statement to you showing deposits, withdrawals, and any added interest. The statement will show the balance of your account as of the date of the statement. It is important for you to update your record and reconcile it with the bank statement. Errors you discover should be reported to the bank immediately.

When making a deposit, you fill out a deposit slip much like the ones used in making a checking account deposit. You present this slip, your passbook, and the money or checks you are depositing to the bank teller. The teller then enters the deposit in your passbook. If your bank uses savings account registers or electronic funds transfer, you will be given a receipt for your deposit. You must then enter the deposit on your register. You may also mail in your deposits.

Withdrawing Your Money

Normally, checks cannot be written against a savings account. If you need money that is in your savings account, you must fill out a withdrawal slip. A **withdrawal slip** is a written request to take money out of your account. You give the withdrawal slip and your passbook to the bank teller. Your withdrawal is then recorded in your passbook and your new balance is shown. Usually money cannot be withdrawn from a passbook savings account unless the passbook is presented.

Before any withdrawal can be made, a teller must check the bank's record to be sure that you have enough money in your account to cover the withdrawal. If you are withdrawing money using electronic funds transfer, the bank computer will automatically check the balance in your account. The bank's record is official; if there is a difference between the balance in your register or passbook and the bank's record, the error must be corrected. After the withdrawal is recorded on the bank's record, you will receive your money.

If you use a savings account register or are withdrawing money using electronic funds transfer, the withdrawal should be recorded in your register. Keeping your record of the account balance is important. Figure 32-2 shows how one person recorded entries in a savings account register.

To discourage customers from using a regular savings account as a checking account, banks sometimes restrict the number of withdrawals that can be made. They may also charge a service fee for withdrawals. NOW (negotiable orders of withdrawal) accounts, as discussed in Chapter 22, should be used if you can maintain the minimum balance required. Although the number of checks you can write may be limited, you have the advantage of earning interest on your deposits.

Figure 32-2
If a savings account register is used, it is your responsibility to record each account transaction in the register.

Date	Memo	(-) Amount of Withdrawal	(+) Amount of Deposit	(+) Interest Credited	Balance
					0 00
July 2	opened account		35 00		+35 00
					35 00
July 25	part of summer earnings		50 00		+50 00
					85 00
Aug. 5	birthday gift from parents		25 00		+25 00
					110 00
Aug. 28	supplies for school	19 00			-19 00
					91 00
Sept. 1	interest received			67	+ 67
					91 67
Sept. 19	automatic teller	25 00			-25 00
					66 67

SPECIAL SAVINGS ACCOUNTS

Savings institutions earn money by using your deposits to make other kinds of investments. The amount they can earn depends in part on how much money they have available to invest, how long they can invest it, and current interest rates. For example, special accounts may require a minimum deposit of $100 to $5,000, and you must agree to leave that amount on deposit for several months or years. Therefore, if you make large deposits and leave that money in your account for the specified time period, the savings institution can earn higher yields on its investments. They can then pay higher interest rates on your special account.

Special savings accounts are given different names by different institutions. The amount of interest earned also varies. To earn a higher rate of interest, there usually are three special conditions that you need to keep in mind:

1. A minimum deposit ($100, $250, $500, $1000, or more) may be required.
2. Your money must be left on deposit for a certain period of time. This periods varies from a few days to several years.
3. If your money is withdrawn before the stated time, much of your interest may be lost and other penalties may be assessed.

Figure 32-3 lists a variety of savings accounts. Note the minimum deposits required, the length of time the deposits must stay in the financial institution, and the yield that is possible from each of the accounts. Figure 32-4 on page 465 shows how one bank describes its savings plan. Note the variation in frequency of interest payments, accessibility of funds, and special fees to be paid.

Figure 32-3
Not all savings accounts are the same. You need to know the conditions of the account you select.

	Minimum Deposit	Maturity	Annual Yield
Passbook Savings	Varies	None	5.50%
NOW Accounts	Varies	None	5.00%
Super NOW Accounts	$1,000	None	Yields vary, average 5.25%
7-to-31-Day Time Deposits	$1,000	7-31 days	Yields vary
Money Market Deposit Accounts	$1,000	None	Yields vary, average 5.75%
	Varies	3 months	Yields vary, average 7.50%
Short-Term Certificates	Varies	6 months	Yields vary, average 7.75%
	Varies	12 months	Yields vary, average 8.00%
	Varies	2$\frac{1}{2}$ years	Yields vary, average 8.25%
Long-Term Certificates	Varies	48 months	Yields vary, average 8.50%
	Varies	60 months	Yields vary, average 8.75%
IRA Certificates	Varies	Varies	Yields vary

Money Market Accounts

One of the special savings accounts that is available to consumers and allows them to earn higher yields is the money market account. A **money market account** is one that pays a variable interest rate based on rates paid to holders of short-term government debt, namely U.S. Treasury bills. Interest paid on money market accounts reflects interest being paid in the money markets.

Money market accounts generally do not require long-term deposits but usually have minimum deposit and balance requirements. With these accounts, the interest paid will vary daily or weekly. It is important to know the current rate being paid in the money markets when opening one of these accounts. Normally the yield from money market accounts will be higher than regular savings but somewhat less than long-term CDs.

Figure 32-4 Financial institutions must inform their customers about the savings plans and services they offer.

Savings Plans	Minimum Deposit	Term of Interest Rate	Frequency of Interest	Accessibility	Fees Accessed
Statement Savings	$50	Fixed at 5$^1/2$%	Quarterly	Anytime	When the balance falls below $100 at anytime during a calendar quarter, no interest will be paid for that quarter and a fee of $3 will be assessed.
The Money Market Account	$2,500	Varies weekly	Monthly	Anytime	When the balance falls below $100 at anytime during a monthly statement cycle, no interest will be paid for that month and a fee of $3 will be assessed.
7-31 Day Certificate	$2,500	Fixed for 7-31 days	Varies	At maturity	None
91 Day Certificate	$2,500	Fixed for 91 days	Varies	At maturity	None
26 Week Money Market Certificate	$2,500	Fixed for 26 weeks	Varies	At maturity	None
18 Month Small Saver Certificate	$500	Fixed for 18 months	Varies	At maturity	None
30 Month Certificate	$500	Fixed for 30 months	Varies	At maturity	None
Individual Retirement Account (Fixed Rate)	$50	Fixed for 18 months	Varies	At maturity	None
Individual Retirement Account (Variable Rate)	$50	Varies monthly	Varies	At maturity	None

Certificates of Deposit

Long-term time deposits that have certain restrictions and pay higher interest rates than regular savings accounts are commonly referred to as **certificates of deposits (CDs)**. When you purchase a CD, you usually receive a numbered certificate (see Figure 32-5) instead of a passbook or a register. The certificate indicates how much you deposited, what the interest rate will be, and when you may withdraw your deposit plus interest. It lists the rules and regulations that must be followed for the certificate to be honored and the higher interest rate to be paid. It also states the penalties for withdrawing your deposit before the maturity date. To cash your CD, you must present and endorse the certificate at the financial institution.

Super NOW Accounts

As you learned in Chapter 22, NOW accounts are a special type of savings account on which checks can be drawn. A NOW account is a combination checking/savings account that earns higher interest than do regular savings accounts.

Some NOW accounts are commonly referred to as **Super NOW accounts** because they require higher minimum deposits and pay higher rates

Figure 32-5 CDs are attractive to many investors.

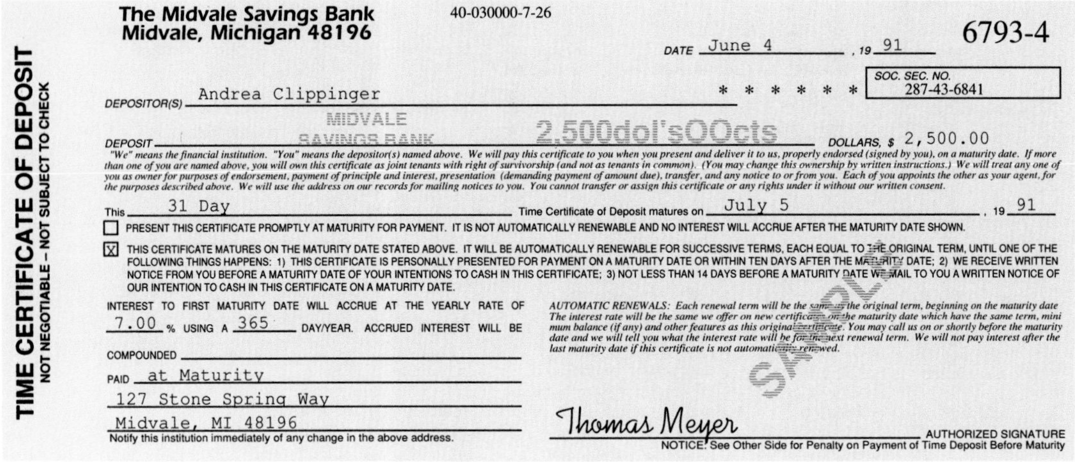

TIME CERTIFICATE OF DEPOSIT
NOT NEGOTIABLE – NOT SUBJECT TO CHECK

The Midvale Savings Bank
Midvale, Michigan 48196

40-030000-7-26

6793-4

DATE June 4 , 19 91

DEPOSITOR(S) Andrea Clippinger

* * * * * *

SOC. SEC. NO.
287-43-6841

MIDVALE
SAVINGS BANK

2,500dol'sOOcts

DEPOSIT

DOLLARS, $ 2,500.00

"We" means the financial institution. "You" means the depositor(s) named above. We will pay this certificate to you when you present and deliver it to us, properly endorsed (signed by you), on a maturity date. If more than one of you are named above, you will own this certificate as joint tenants with right of survivorship (and not as tenants in common). (You may change this ownership by written instructions.) We will treat any one of you as owner for purposes of endorsement, payment of principle and interest, presentation (demanding payment of amount due), transfer, and any notice to or from you. Each of you appoints the other as your agent, for the purposes described above. We will use the address on our records for mailing notices to you. You cannot transfer or assign this certificate or any rights under it without our written consent.

This 31 Day Time Certificate of Deposit matures on July 5 , 19 91

☐ PRESENT THIS CERTIFICATE PROMPTLY AT MATURITY FOR PAYMENT. IT IS NOT AUTOMATICALLY RENEWABLE AND NO INTEREST WILL ACCRUE AFTER THE MATURITY DATE SHOWN.

☒ THIS CERTIFICATE MATURES ON THE MATURITY DATE STATED ABOVE. IT WILL BE AUTOMATICALLY RENEWABLE FOR SUCCESSIVE TERMS, EACH EQUAL TO THE ORIGINAL TERM, UNTIL ONE OF THE FOLLOWING THINGS HAPPENS: 1) THIS CERTIFICATE IS PERSONALLY PRESENTED FOR PAYMENT ON A MATURITY DATE OR WITHIN TEN DAYS AFTER THE MATURITY DATE; 2) WE RECEIVE WRITTEN NOTICE FROM YOU BEFORE A MATURITY DATE OF YOUR INTENTIONS TO CASH IN THIS CERTIFICATE; 3) NOT LESS THAN 14 DAYS BEFORE A MATURITY DATE WE MAIL TO YOU A WRITTEN NOTICE OF OUR INTENTION TO CASH IN THIS CERTIFICATE ON A MATURITY DATE.

INTEREST TO FIRST MATURITY DATE WILL ACCRUE AT THE YEARLY RATE OF
7.00 % USING A 365 DAY/YEAR. ACCRUED INTEREST WILL BE

COMPOUNDED

PAID at Maturity

127 Stone Spring Way
Midvale, MI 48196
Notify this institution immediately of any change in the above address.

AUTOMATIC RENEWALS: Each renewal term will be the same as the original term, beginning on the maturity date The interest rate will be the same we offer on new certificates on the maturity date which have the same term, mini mum balance (if any) and other features as this original certificate. You may call us on or shortly before the maturity date and we will tell you what the interest rate will be for the next renewal term. We will not pay interest after the last maturity date if this certificate is not automatically renewed.

Thomas Meyer

AUTHORIZED SIGNATURE
NOTICE! See Other Side for Penalty on Payment of Time Deposit Before Maturity

of interest. The required minimum balances for Super NOW accounts must be maintained in order to qualify for the higher interest rate.

Suppose Michele Moberg has $2,000 to invest and goes to a local financial institution to invest it. She is told about a Super NOW account that earns 6 percent interest compared to a regular NOW account that yields 5.5 percent, or a basic savings account that yields 4.8 percent. With the Super NOW account, Michele would have to keep a minimum balance of $1,000 to earn the higher interest rate. Since she is quite sure that she can maintain the $1,000 minimum balance for several years, she chooses the Super NOW account for her investment. However, if the balance of her accounts drops below the minimum balance set by her bank, the amount of interest she earns would be adjusted to a lower rate for the period of time that her account balance was below $1,000.

DECIDING WHERE TO PUT YOUR SAVINGS

Many types of financial institutions offer savings plans to consumers. Commercial banks, savings banks, savings and loan associations, and credit unions all provide regular and special savings accounts. There are some firms that also offer financial services, such as Sears, Roebuck and Co.; these are often referred to as *nonbanks*. The institution you choose depends upon your individual financial needs.

Personal Desires

In choosing a financial institution for your savings, your personal needs and desires are important. Your answers to questions such as the following can help you choose the institution that is best for you:

- How much interest do you want to earn?
- Will you earn simple interest or compound interest? If it is compounded, how frequently is interest added?
- What services are offered that are important to you?
- Does the institution offer help in selecting the best savings plan from among their options?
- What are the institution's business hours? Does it offer electronic banking services for after-hours transactions?
- Is the institution conveniently located?
- How safe is your money with that institution?

The institution you select should offer a variety of savings and investment opportunities as well as friendly, efficient services.

Protection for Your Savings

Having an assurance that you will get back the money you deposit into a savings account is an important consideration. The safety of your investment is something you need to examine before depositing your savings into one of the savings plans. As you learned in Chapter 22, special insurance funds have been set up to protect the amounts on deposit in savings accounts. These include the Federal Deposit Insurance Corporation (FDIC), the Savings Association Insurance Fund (SAIF) which is a subdivision of the FDIC, and the National Credit Union Administration (NCUA).

If one of your investment goals is *safety*, it is wise to check on deposit insurance before you invest. Asking the question, "Is my deposit *federally insured?*" is appropriate when selecting a savings plan.

CONTRIBUTING TO AN IRA

Our federal tax laws permit you to plan ahead for your retirement in a unique way. You can do this by placing wage or salary earnings in an account that you designate as an individual retirement account. An **individual retirement account (IRA)** is a tax-sheltered retirement plan that allows certain workers to invest up to $2,000 annually and pay no tax either on that sum or on its earnings until the money is withdrawn.

In a recent year, for instance, a single worker who earned less than $25,000 per year in salary or wages could deposit up to $2,000 in an IRA and then deduct that amount from the adjusted gross income when filing a federal income tax form. Also, any interest earned on that IRA would be tax deferred. In that same year, individuals earning between $25,000 and $35,000 could deduct a reduced portion of earned annual income. Single workers earning $35,000 or more could not deduct any wages or salary from the adjusted gross income. The interest earned on a nondeductible IRA, however, would still not be taxable until withdrawn. When you consider the impact of earnings accumulating tax deferred, the IRA can be an attractive investment.

Because an IRA is considered to be a retirement plan, penalties are assessed if withdrawals are made prior to age $59^1/_2$. The penalty is a percentage of the amount withdrawn, and income tax also must be paid. An exception is made, however, if you incur a permanent disability and need to withdraw funds from an IRA.

In a calendar year, the law allows individuals to change from one IRA investment to another without penalty as long as funds are not withdrawn for more than 60 days. When you are ready to set up an IRA, you should consult a financial institution representative on current laws and procedures for establishing an IRA.

Most financial institutions offer a variety of IRA plans. Money market accounts and CDs are commonly used for IRAs. Annuities (which you will learn about in Chapter 42) as well as mutual funds and common or preferred stocks (which you will learn about in Chapter 33) are among the kinds of investments that can be considered when setting up an IRA.

Increasing Your Business Vocabulary

The following terms should become part of your business vocabulary. For each numbered item, find the term that has the same meaning.

certificates of deposits (CDs)
individual retirement account (IRA)
money market account
savings account passbook

savings account register
Super NOW accounts
withdrawal slip

1. A written request to take money out of your account.
2. Long-term deposits that have certain restrictions and pay higher interest rates than regular savings accounts.
3. A record in which you must record each deposit or withdrawal as it is made from your savings account; you must also add the interest when the bank reports it to you.
4. A special account that pays a variable interest rate based on rates paid to holders of short-term government debt.
5. A tax-sheltered retirement plan that allows certain workers to invest up to $2,000 annually and pay no tax either on that sum or on its earnings until the money is withdrawn.
6. Special savings accounts that require higher minimum deposits and pay higher rates of interest.
7. A record that shows your deposits, withdrawals, interest earned, and the balance of your savings account; the bank teller records each transaction.

Reviewing Your Reading

1. Why do savings accounts continue to be a popular part of the savings and investment plans of most consumers?
2. What types of businesses offer savings accounts?
3. What steps would you follow in opening a savings account?
4. What is the purpose of a savings account passbook or register?
5. How does a depositor withdraw money from a savings account?
6. Why do financial institutions pay higher interest rates on special savings accounts?
7. Name three conditions that a depositor must accept to earn a higher rate of interest on a special savings account.
8. What are some conditions that must be met with Super NOW accounts?
9. What are two restrictions placed on IRAs?
10. Why is it important to have a long-range goal when putting money into an IRA?
11. What are some questions you should ask when choosing a financial institution where you will put your savings?

Using Your Business Knowledge

1. What characteristics of savings accounts make them especially good for students?
2. Financial institutions commonly pay a higher interest rate on special savings accounts than they do on regular accounts. Explain how they can afford to pay a higher interest rate on special accounts.
3. Why is a Super NOW account attractive to some investors? What are some reasons why a consumer might or might not want to put savings into a Super NOW account? Why is a higher deposit limit set for Super NOW accounts?
4. What are some procedures that you should follow if you receive a savings account register rather than a passbook for your savings account? When should withdrawals and deposits be recorded in your register? How should the monthly or quarterly statements be used?
5. What is wrong with each of the following statements made by students who are discussing investing their savings?
   a. Most savings accounts are alike, so why bother to shop around?
   b. Credit unions are run by labor unions.
   c. All young people should have IRAs.
   d. It isn't important to keep your passbook record up-to-date because the bank has the official record.
   e. Always put your money in the savings plan that pays the highest interest regardless of your investment goal.

Computing Business Problems

1. Joanne Olson plans to deposit $8 a month in a savings account.
   a. How much will she deposit in the first 6 months?
   b. If she then increases her monthly deposit to $11, how much will have been deposited in 12 months?
   c. How much will she have deposited in the first 18 months of her savings plan?
2. Three people have the following amounts deposited in regular savings accounts at different places: Dan Schweizer, $10,000 in a commercial bank; Margaret Zimmerman, $20,000 in a savings bank; and Stephanie Nudo, $45,000 in a savings and loan association. Each financial

institution has insurance on account balances up to $100,000.
a. What is the total amount of money invested by all three depositors?
b. How much money would be lost, if any, by each depositor if all of these savings institutions went bankrupt?

3. Bernard Stahl can earn 5 percent on a regular savings account, 8 percent on a CD, and 11 percent on a money market account.
   a. If he invests $5,000, how much interest (compute simple interest) will he earn in one year in each of these plans?
   b. How much more will he earn on the money market account than he would with the regular savings account?
   c. If he decided to invest $2,000 in each plan, how much total interest (compute simple interest) would he earn in one year? In five years?

4. In a recent year, U.S. financial institutions had the following record of accounts and deposits:

	Savings Deposits
Savings accounts	$396 billion
NOW accounts	232 billion
Money Market accounts	571 billion

a. What percentage of the total of those deposits were each of the different savings plans?
b. If the total saved in each plan increases 10 percent each year, what would be the total of those deposits the following year?

5. The table below shows the amount of money in savings deposits in four types of financial institutions for two recent years.

	Savings Deposits (In Billions of Dollars)	
	Year 1	Year 2
Commercial banks	$576.4	$1,023.8
Savings banks	158.2	163.1
Savings and loan associations	431.0	566.2
Credit unions	53.1	90.0

a. What were the total deposits in all four types of financial institutions in each year?
b. Which two institutions had the largest deposits in Year 2?
c. In which type of institution did deposits increase the most in dollars from Year 1 to Year 2?
d. What was the percent of increase between Year 1 and Year 2 in deposits received by credit unions?

Expanding Your Understanding of Business

1. Most savings institutions have a rule that permits them to delay the withdrawal of money from savings accounts if necessary. One bank has the following provision:

"While it is extremely unlikely, the bank reserves the right to require depositors to give 30 days written notice of intent to withdraw funds." Why would institutions have such rules if they are seldom used?

2. The government does not guarantee that all investments will be successful. For example, it does not provide insurance for investments in land, stocks and bonds, or small businesses. Since it does not provide insurance against losses in other investments, why did it set up the Federal Deposit Insurance Corporation to insure deposits in banks?

3. A savings bank advertises its services under these headings: Business Services, Special Services, Savings Plans, Checking Accounts, and Loan Services. Under savings plans, it lists Golden Passbook, Certificates of Deposit, Regular Passbook, Individual Retirement Account, and Statement Savings Account. Each of these savings plans has special features and earns a different rate of interest. Visit one of your community's banks, or get some descriptive literature from them, and make a report to your class on the different kinds of savings plans they offer. Find out what rules affect each of the plans and what the interest rates are for each plan.

4. In recent years, a large number of financial institutions—including banks and savings and loan associations—have gone bankrupt. In some instances, depositors lost their money; in other cases, they eventually received the amount they had on deposit. Check the files of newspaper reports and determine reasons why financial institutions fail and under what circumstances depositors received or did not receive their money. Discuss why our government does so much to help financial institutions get out of financial difficulty.

Investing in Bonds and Stocks

Chapter 33

Chapter Objectives

After studying this chapter and completing the end-of-chapter activities, you will be able to:

1. *Give three reasons why organizations sell bonds.*

2. *Explain how investing in bonds is different from investing in stocks.*

3. *Discuss U.S. government securities as an investment.*

4. *Describe investment services offered by brokers.*

5. *Read and explain information included in bond and stock market listings.*

6. *Discuss investment clubs and mutual funds.*

7. *List questions that should be answered when deciding whether or not to invest in stocks.*

Depositing money in a savings account is an easy way to invest money. As you have learned, the variety of savings accounts available has made them popular with many consumers. However, there are other good ways to invest, too, such as buying bonds and stocks. Some people do not consider investing in bonds and stocks because they are unsure about the safety of such investments. Let's consider Alex Mendoza, for example.

Alex earns $45,000 a year as a data processing manager while his wife, Terress, earns $80,000 a year as an orthodontist. They have $22,000 in a savings account and have only a small mortgage on their home. They also have a good insurance plan. One of Alex's friends suggested that he would get a better return on his money by investing in **securities**—a general term for bonds and stocks that are sold by corporations and governments to raise large sums of money. Alex has heard about people who lost money by investing in bonds and stocks and wonders if securities would be a good investment for his family.

Alex is right to be concerned about the safety of investments. If you have only a small amount of savings, your money should be invested where it is safe. But Alex can increase the earnings on his savings and still have safe investments. After they learn more about bonds and stocks, Alex and Terress will be in a position to decide whether or not to invest in securities.

INVESTING IN BONDS

Bonds are sold by the federal government, by local and state governments, and by many corporations. Because there are so many types of bonds, it is helpful to know the answers to two questions: What is a bond? Why are bonds sold?

A **bond** is a printed certificate with a promise to pay a definite amount of money at a stated interest rate on a specified maturity date. Bonds are similar to promissory notes, which were discussed in Chapter 28. When you buy a bond, you are lending money to the organization selling the bond. You become the organization's creditor. Each bond has its face value printed on the front of the certificate. The **face value** is the amount being borrowed by the seller of the bond. Interest is paid periodically to the investor based on that amount and the stated interest rate. The face value is paid to the bond owner on the bond's maturity date.

Corporate and Municipal Bonds

Bonds are sold to raise large sums of money for a specific purpose. A corporation may want to build a new office building. A city may want to build a new park or a new school. Bonds issued by corporations are called

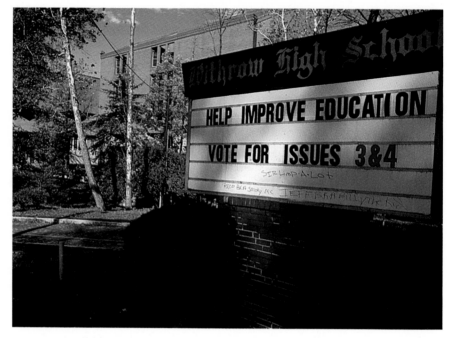

corporate bonds. Bonds issued by local and state governments are called **municipal bonds,** or **munis**.

Municipal bonds have an advantage over corporate bonds since federal and/or state income tax may not have to be paid on the interest earned on the municipal bonds. People buy municipal bonds even though the interest rate usually is not as high as that offered on corporate bonds in order to avoid paying taxes. Corporate and municipal bonds normally are sold in amounts of $1,000 or larger. Municipal bonds also are generally considered by most investors to be safer investments than corporate bonds.

Bonds are bought and sold in bond markets. Figure 33-1 gives an explanation of listings for the corporate bond market. Note that the prices are stated in 100s, but the bonds are sold in $1,000 denominations (ten times the listed amount). Therefore, a bond quoted at $101^1/_2$ (the AbbtL bond) costs $1,015.00 (101.50 x 10 = $1,015.00). These bonds closed up (+) 1 from the previous day; that is, they sold for $10 (1 x 10) more today than yesterday.

The price that investors are willing to pay for a bond depends upon the bond's stated interest rate. If interest rates in general are higher than the bond's rate, investors will want to buy the bond for less than its face value. On the other hand, if the bond's interest rate is higher than interest rates in general, the sellers of bonds will want to receive more than its face value. Bond prices are determined by buyers and sellers in the bond market.

Figure 33-1 Bonds that are traded on the exchanges are listed daily in newspapers.

Bonds			Cur Yld	Vol	Close	Net Chg.
AbbtL	9.2	99	9.1	5	101½	+1
(1)	(2)	(3)	(4)	(5)	(6)	(7)

CORPORATION BONDS
Volume, $37,268,000

Bonds	Cur Yld	Vol	Close	Net Chg.
AbbtL 9.2 99	9.1	5	101½ +	1
AetnLf 8⅛ 07	8.9	19	91½	...
AirbF 7½ 11	cv	10	109 +	½
AlaP 9 2000	9.2	11	97¾	...
AlaP 8⅞ 03	9.2	10	96¾	...
AlaP 8¼ 03	8.9	10	92½ −	1½
AlaP 10½ 05	10.2	5	103	...
AlaP 8⅞ 06	9.1	6	97¾ +	¾
AlaP 8¾ 07	9.1	10	96¼ −	⅛
AlaP 9½ 08	9.5	5	100 +	1
AlaP 9⅝ 08	9.5	5	101¾ +	1½
AlskAr 6⅞ 14	cv	5	102½	...
AlskH 17¾ 91	15.7	5	113¼	...
viAlgl 10.4 02f	...	13	49½ −	1
AlldC zr92	...	44	75 +	¼

Explanatory Notes: zr – zero coupon
                    f – dealt in flat

1. AbbtL (Abbott Laboratories) is the corporation that issued the bond. If a *vi* appears before the name, it indicates that the corporation is involved in some form of bankruptcy.

2. The original rate of interest paid on the face value of the bond.

3. Year in which the bond matures is 1999.

4. Current yield based on the selling price of the bond. If a *cv* appears in this column, it refers to a convertible bond, which can be traded for stock in the corporation.

5. Number of bonds traded that day which had a face value of $1,000 each.

6. The final price for a bond that day; e.g., $1,015.

7. Change in the closing price compared with the previous day; e.g., $10.

U.S. Savings Bonds and Other Federal Securities

One of the safest investments in securities, and one that is especially desirable for the investor who has only a small amount to invest, are U.S. government savings bonds. Figure 33-2 shows an example of a Series EE savings bond. Series EE savings bonds, which come in denominations from $50 to $10,000, pay interest through a process called *discounting*.

Figure 33-2
A Series EE
savings bond
with a face value
of $100.

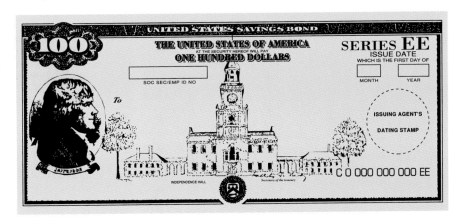

A Series EE bond is bought at half its face value. A $50 bond costs $25, and at the end of its full term pays at least $50. The difference between the purchase price and the redemption value is the interest earned. The interest earned is determined by the length of time the bond is held. All savings bonds mature in ten years.

The convenience of buying U.S. government EE bonds is an attractive feature to some investors. Amounts can be deducted, for instance, from a person's paycheck and accumulated until a bond can be purchased in the employee's name. A weekly deduction of $10 would result in a $100 EE bond being acquired after five weeks. This approach is an easy way for someone to get started on an investment program.

The U.S. government also sells Series HH savings bonds. These bonds are available to investors in face values from $500 to $10,000, are not discounted, and pay a fixed rate of interest through a check mailed to the investor. Series HH bonds are different from EE bonds in three important ways:

1. EE bonds pay interest only when the bond is cashed, while HH bonds pay interest directly to the bondholder semiannually.
2. EE bonds can be purchased at financial institutions throughout the United States and through payroll deduction plans, while HH bonds are available only in exchange for eligible EE bonds or savings notes called Freedom Shares.
3. There is an annual purchase limit of $30,000 (face value) on EE bonds, but there is no such limit on HH bonds.

The federal government also issues Treasury bonds and Treasury notes. The difference between the two is the length of time it takes them to mature. The notes mature in two to ten years, the bonds in ten years or more, and both are issued in denominations from $1,000 to $1,000,000. The U.S. government also borrows money for immediate cash needs through short-term securities called Treasury bills, which mature in 3, 6, or 12 months. The smallest denomination in which a Treasury bill can be purchased is $10,000.

INVESTING IN STOCKS

Investing in stocks is quite different from investing in bonds. When you invest in bonds, you lend money. When you invest in stock, you become a part owner of a business. As you learned in Chapter 6, you become a stockholder when you buy one or more shares in a corporation. Ownership is shown by a printed form known as a stock certificate. If a business is profitable, part of the profits may be paid to the stockholders in the form of dividends.

The opportunity to earn a high rate of return attracts many people to invest in stocks. However, the risk of losing your money is usually greater with stocks than with bonds. A corporation must pay bondholders the rate of interest promised before it can pay any dividends to stockholders. If there is not enough money left to pay dividends or if the corporation decides to use the money earned for business expansion, stockholders receive no dividends. If a corporation goes out of business, a stockholder may get little or nothing back from the investment. Bondholders, on the other hand, may get back the amount invested plus interest.

Stocks have a market value. The **market value** of a stock is the price at which a share of stock can be bought and sold in the stock market. The market value is the truest indicator of the value of a share of stock. The market value can change rapidly and frequently. If the business is doing well, the market value usually goes up; if the business has a poor record, the market value usually goes down. The market value also may be affected by other factors, such as the overall health of the economy and whether we are in a positive or negative phase of a business cycle, as discussed in Chapter 4.

Preferred Stock

Preferred stock is one of two main classes of stock issued by corporations. **Preferred stock** has priority over common stock in the payment of

Illus. 33-2
As a common stockholder, you own part of a corporation.

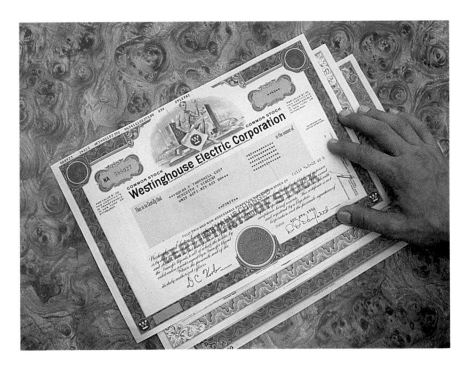

dividends. A preferred stockholder, for example, is paid first if profits are used to pay any stock dividends.

The dividends paid to preferred stockholders are usually limited to a rate stated on the stock certificate. Preferred stock may also have priority on the return of the amount invested if the corporation goes out of business. Preferred stock is less risky than common stock. However, preferred stockholders generally have no voting rights at annual meetings of the corporation.

Common Stock

Common stock is a certificate that represents ownership in a corporation and a right to share in its profits. Common stock has no stated dividend rate. As part owners of the corporation, common stockholders are invited to the annual meetings of the corporation and are entitled to one vote per share of common stock owned.

Common stockholders receive dividends only after preferred stockholders are paid their share of any dividends. Yet, if the profits of a company are large, the common stockholders may receive more in dividends than preferred stockholders. For example, suppose that a company has issued $100,000 worth of common stock and $100,000 worth of preferred stock with a stated dividend rate of 6 percent. If the company earns a profit of $20,000 and pays dividends, preferred stockholders would be paid $6,000 in dividends ($100,000 x .06 = $6,000). The remainder, or $14,000 ($20,000 -$6,000 = $14,000), would be available to pay dividends to the common stockholders. If all of the profits are paid out in dividends, the common stockholders would be paid $14,000, a return of 14 percent.

MAKING YOUR STOCK SELECTION

Buying a stock that is right for you is an important decision. The prices at which stocks are being bought and sold are readily available through stock market listings in newspapers. Examine Figure 33-3 which gives an explanation of the stock market listing from *The Wall Street Journal. The Wall Street Journal* specializes in providing financial information of interest to investors. Many other newspapers have special business sections devoted to providing this kind of information.

Help in Buying and Selling Stock

Stocks normally are bought and sold through stockbrokers. A **broker** is a licensed specialist in the buying and selling of stocks and bonds. Through brokers, stockholders state prices at which they are willing to sell their shares. Interested buyers tell brokers what they would be willing to pay for

Figure 33-3 *The Wall Street Journal* provides important information on stocks being traded.

52 Weeks		Stocks	Sym	Div	Yld %	PE	Vol 100s	Hi	Lo	Close	Net Chg.
Hi	Lo										
$27^7/_8$	$14^1/_2$	AAR	AIR	.44	1.9	17	160	$23^3/_8$	$22^3/_4$	$23^1/_8$	$+^3/_8$
(1)	(2)	(3)	(4)	(5)	(6)	(7)	(8)	(9)	(10)	(11)	(12)

**Quotations as of 4:30 p.m. Eastern Time
Friday, December 9, 19--**

52 Weeks		Stocks	Sym	Div	Yld %	PE	Vol 100s	Hi	Lo	Close	Net Chg.
Hi	Lo										
$27^7/_8$	$14^1/_2$	AAR	AIR	.44	1.9	17	160	$23^3/_8$	$22^3/_4$	$23^1/_8$	$+^3/_8$
$10^1/_8$	$8^3/_4$	ACM OppFd	AOF	1.01	11.4	...	x94	9	$8^7/_8$	$8^7/_8$	$+^1/_8$
$12^1/_8$	$10^3/_4$	ACM Gvt Fd	ACG	1.26a	11.7	...	x392	$10^7/_8$	$10^5/_8$	$10^3/_4$	$+^1/_8$
$10^1/_8$	10	ACM MgdIncFd	AMF	.08e	.8	...	x558	10	$9^7/_8$	$9^7/_8$	...
$12^1/_8$	$10^3/_8$	ACM SecFd	GSF	1.26	12.0	...	1234	$10^5/_8$	$10^1/_2$	$10^1/_2$	$-^1/_8$
$10^1/_2$	$8^3/_8$	ACM SpctmFd	SI	1.01a	11.4	...	624	$8^7/_8$	$8^3/_4$	$8^3/_4$	...
$5^3/_8$	$2^5/_8$	AMCA	AIL	.12e	3.7	...	133	$3^3/_8$	$3^1/_4$	$3^1/_4$	...
$6^1/_8$	$3^5/_8$	AM Int	AM	...	...	...	620	$4^3/_4$	$4^5/_8$	$4^5/_8$	$-^1/_8$
$23^1/_4$	$18^1/_8$	AM Int pf		2.00	9.4	...	49	$21^1/_4$	21	$21^1/_4$	...
55	$28^3/_8$	AMR	AMR	...	...	9	4206	54	$52^3/_4$	$53^7/_8$	$+^7/_8$
$9^1/_2$	$5^3/_8$	ARX	ARX	...	...	10	70	$5^7/_8$	$5^5/_8$	$5^7/_8$	$+^1/_4$
$54^1/_4$	$35^1/_4$	ASA	ASA	3.00a	7.7	...	235	39	$38^3/_4$	39	$+^1/_8$
$20^1/_4$	$11^3/_8$	AVX	AVX	.12e	.7	11	86	$16^5/_8$	$16^1/_4$	$16^5/_8$	$+^1/_8$
$52^3/_8$	$42^3/_8$	AbbotLab	ABT	1.20	2.5	15	5907	$47^5/_8$	$47^1/_8$	$47^1/_2$	$+^1/_4$
$21^3/_4$	$15^3/_8$	Abitibi	ABY	1.00	...	...	59	$16^3/_8$	16	$16^3/_8$	...
$13^7/_8$	$7^1/_2$	AcmeCleve	AMT	.40	5.2	...	75	$7^7/_8$	$7^5/_8$	$7^5/_8$	...
$8^5/_8$	$5^7/_8$	AcmeElec	ACE	.32b	5.4	26	7	$5^7/_8$	$5^5/_8$	$5^7/_8$	...
$29^1/_2$	$13^1/_2$	Acuson	ACN	...	...	23	99	$25^3/_8$	$24^3/_4$	$24^3/_4$	$-^1/_4$
17	$14^1/_2$	AdamsExp	ADX	1.82e	12.2	...	164	$14^7/_8$	$14^3/_4$	$14^7/_8$	...
$16^7/_8$	$7^7/_8$	AdvMicro	AMD	...	...	13	7649	$7^1/_2$	$7^3/_8$	$7^3/_8$	$-^3/_8$

1. Highest price paid for AAR common stock during the past 52 weeks.

2. Lowest price paid for AAR common stock during the past 52 weeks.

3. The company name abbreviated. If the stock quoted is preferred, the letters *pf* are shown.

4. AAR's ticker tape symbol.

5. The current dividend in dollars per share based on the last dividend paid.

6. The dividend yield based on the current selling price per share.

7. The P/E ratio, comparing the price of the stock with the earnings per share.

8. The number of shares traded; expressed in hundreds. An underline below the stock listing indicates that the stock on that day had a large change in the volume of shares traded.

9. Highest price at which shares changed hands during the day.

10. Lowest price at which shares changed hands during the day.

11. Closing price per share for the day.

12. The change in the closing price today compared with the closing price on the previous day. If the price changed more than 5 percent, the entire stock listing appears in bold type.

those shares. The brokers then work out a price that is acceptable to both buyers and sellers. The highest, lowest, and closing prices for stocks sold each day are included in the stock market listing, as noted in Figure 33-3.

For their services, brokers charge a fee called a **commission.** Brokers work through **exchanges**, which are business organizations that accommodate the buying and selling of securities. The best known exchange is the New York Stock Exchange in New York City. The American Stock Exchange, also in New York City, and the Midwest Stock Exchange, in Chicago, also are major exchanges. Brokers throughout the nation deal directly with these exchanges by telephone and computer.

There are two kinds of brokers with whom you can do business: full-service and discount brokers. A *full-service broker* is one who provides you with information about securities you may want to buy. Full-service brokers work for brokerage houses that have large research staffs. A *discount broker* basically places orders for you and offers limited research and other services; they charge lower commissions than do full-service brokers. Investors who have a great deal of information available to them and who can

Illus. 33-3
Exchanges
specialize in
buying and
selling stocks and
bonds.

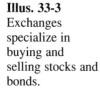

Illus. 33-3
Exchanges
specialize in
buying and
selling stocks and
bonds.

do their own research can save money on commissions by dealing with discount brokers.

Questions to Be Answered

In selecting a stock to buy, you should learn something about the business record of the corporation. There are a number of sources of information that can be used, including *Moody's Handbook of Common Stocks*, *Value Line*, and *Standard and Poor's Encyclopedia of Stocks*. Publications such as these provide information such as the company's net worth, its indebtedness, its income, its profit and dividend history, and the current outlook for the company's product or service. These publications often are available in public libraries.

Among the questions that should be answered concerning a company in which you may invest are the following:

- Has the company been profitable over a period of years?
- Have the company's managers made good business decisions?
- Does the company have growth potential in coming years?
- Does the company have an unusual number of large debts?
- How does the company compare with others in its industry?

There are some other considerations, too. The yield of a stock is important if your goal is to earn a good return from your investment. Suppose, for example, that the XYZ Corporation is paying a quarterly dividend of $.60 a share. The total dividend for the year would be $2.40, and if the stock is selling for $40 a share, the current yield (return) would be calculated as:

$$\text{Dividend Yield} = \frac{\text{Dividend per Share}}{\text{Market Price per Share}} = \frac{\$2.40}{\$40} = .06 \text{ or } 6 \text{ percent}$$

The price of a stock also will be important, and many investors look at the stock's **price-earnings ratio (P/E)**, the ratio of a stock's selling price to its earnings per share. The P/E is shown in stock market listings such as the one shown in Figure 33-3 on page 479. The P/E gives you an indication whether the stock is priced high or low in relation to its earnings per share. For instance, if a company has 100,000 shares of stock and it earns a net profit of $150,000, it has earned $1.50 ($150,000 ÷ 100,000 = $1.50) per share. If the stock is selling for $30 per share, its P/E is 20 ($30 ÷ 1.50 = 20). In a recent year, the average P/E for stocks traded on the New York Stock Exchange was 15. The P/E ratio, the yield, and other information about the company is information used by investors in deciding whether to buy a stock.

INVESTING WITH OTHERS

Some investors like to join with others in making investments. There are several advantages in doing so. Investment clubs and mutual funds are two common ways you can pool your investments.

Investment Clubs

An **investment club** is a small group of people who organize to study stocks and to invest their money. An agreement is usually drawn up which states how often the club will meet and how much the members will invest each month. At the meetings, members report on stocks they have studied. The group makes decisions on what stocks to buy. The club's earnings are shared in proportion to the members' investments. Brokers often help groups form investment clubs.

One advantage of an investment club is that membership encourages regular saving. Another advantage is that you learn a great deal about how to judge a stock. Members of the club spread their risk because the combined funds of all members are used to buy stocks in a number of corporations. If the club loses money on one investment, the loss may be offset by other investments that do quite well.

Mutual Funds

Investment clubs are not available to everyone. You may not want to take the time needed to study the stock market and make investment decisions. A good understanding of securities, however, is needed to make wise decisions. A mutual fund is another way to join with others in investing.

Mutual funds are funds set up and managed by investment companies that receive money from many investors and then usually buy and sell a wide variety of stocks or bonds. Mutual fund investors own shares of the mutual fund. Part of the dividends received from the fund's investments is used to pay operating expenses of the fund. The amount that is left may be distributed to the mutual fund shareholders as dividends or reinvested in the fund.

There are many mutual funds available to investors today, and the funds have many different objectives. For instance, some emphasize investing in growth stocks, some emphasize stocks that pay high dividends, and some emphasize international stocks. Selecting a mutual fund in which to invest also requires you to consider your investment objectives before selecting a particular fund.

DECIDING WHETHER OR NOT TO BUY SECURITIES

The decision whether or not to invest in stocks must be made carefully. One important guideline in the decision is whether you can afford to lose part or all of your investment. If you have to sell your stock or your mutual fund when an emergency arises, it might sell for much less than the amount that you paid for it. Before investing in securities, you should have adequate savings in a safe place, such as a bank savings account. You also should have sufficient insurance coverage. The money invested in securities should not be needed to meet your basic living expenses.

Ask yourself which of these factors are most important to your personal investment plan: safety, liquidity, or rate of return? From your answer, an investment plan can be selected. As shown in Figure 33-4, no single investment can give you the highest possible return and still be very liquid and safe.

Figure 33-4
Your investment goals will determine which investments are best for you.

Which Investment?	How Safe?	How Liquid?	How Is Rate of Return?
Savings accounts	Excellent	Excellent	Fair to good
Savings bonds	Excellent	Very good	Good
Other bonds	Very good	Good	Good
Preferred stocks	Fair to good	Good	Very Good
Common stocks	Fair	Good	Poor to excellent

Increasing Your Business Vocabulary

The following terms should become part of your business vocabulary. For each numbered item, find the term that has the same meaning.

bond
broker
commission
common stock
corporate bonds
exchanges
face value

investment club
market value
municipal bonds or munis
mutual funds
preferred stock
price earnings ratio or P/E
securities

1. A licensed specialist who helps investors buy and sell stocks and bonds.
2. Bonds issued by local and state governments.
3. A general term for bonds and stocks that are sold by corporations and governments to raise large sums of money.
4. A printed certificate with a promise to pay a definite amount of money at a stated interest rate on a specified maturity date.
5. Stock that has priority over common stock in the payment of dividends.
6. A fee charged by brokers for their services.
7. Funds set up and managed by investment companies that receive money from many investors and then usually buy and sell a wide variety of stocks or bonds.

8. The price at which a share of stock can be bought and sold in the stock market.
9. Stock that represents ownership in a corporation and a right to share in its profits, but has no stated dividend rate.
10. A small group of people who organize to study stocks and invest their money.
11. Business organizations that accommodate the buying and selling of securities.
12. The amount borrowed by the seller of a bond.
13. Bonds issued by corporations.
14. The ratio of a stock's selling price to its earnings per share.

Reviewing Your Reading

1. Why do businesses and other organizations sell bonds?
2. How much does a $50 series EE bond cost? What is the term for the difference between the purchase price and the face value?
3. What are some differences between series EE and HH bonds?
4. In what ways is investing in bonds different from investing in stocks?
5. What are some differences between preferred and common stock?

6. What kinds of information are provided for investors through bond and stock market listings?
7. What are some services that a broker offers individuals who are interested in buying stocks? Compare full-service with discount brokers.
8. What sources of information are available to investors about bonds and stocks?
9. Who selects stocks to be purchased by an investment club?

10. What are some advantages of investing through a mutual fund?
11. What are some important questions to ask when deciding whether or not to purchase stocks?

Using Your Business Knowledge

1. Why should investors have a savings account and an insurance plan before investing in stocks?
2. Why does the government pay a higher rate of interest on Series EE bonds held for their full time than if cashed in earlier?
3. Why do municipal bonds usually pay a lower rate of interest than corporate bonds?
4. Company A wants to borrow $1,000. Company B wants to borrow $10,000. Company C wants to borrow $1,000,000. Which business is most likely to issue bonds? Why?
5. Give several reasons why people buy stocks even though they are not as safe as some investments.
6. Why would a broker be interested in helping a group of people form an investment club?
7. Susan Haugen bought $5,000 worth of gold mining stocks a few years ago. Last week she received a letter saying that the company went out of business. It could not operate profitably so it closed down. How much of her investment might Miss Haugen lose?
8. Brian Anderson wants to invest in stocks that will be very safe, highly liquid, and earn an excellent return. What is wrong with his investment goals?
9. Patty Ritz decided that she wants to invest some money in securities. She has not studied bonds or stocks and knows very little about how to get started. What advice would you give to Patty?
10. Examine Figure 33-1 on page 475 and answer the following questions:
    a. What was the closing price for AlskH bonds?
    b. What is the interest rate on the AlskH bond?
    c. What is the yield on the AetnLf bond?
    d. What is the maturity date for the AlaP $10^{1}/_{2}$ 05 bond?
    e. Which bond had the highest daily volume of bonds sold?
11. Examine Figure 33-3 on page 479 and answer the following questions:
    a. What was the closing price for AAR stock?
    b. How many shares of AAR were traded that day?
    c. What was the P/E for AbbotLab?
    d. Did the closing price for AbbotLab stock go up or down from the previous day? How much was the change?
    e. What is the yield (percentage) on ASA stock?

Computing Business Problems

1. Shana Lindsay bought the following Series EE bonds: three $50 bonds and one $5,000 bond.
   a. How much did she pay for the bonds?
   b. How much will the bonds be worth when the stated time period is reached?
   c. How much interest will she have earned when the stated time period is reached.

2. Jerome Aili owns five Morgan Enterprises bonds, each with a face value of $5,000. Morgan Enterprises pays 8 percent interest on the bonds it has issued.
   a. How much interest does Jerome receive each year on each bond?
   b. What is the total amount of interest Jerome receives each year?
   c. If the interest payments are made semiannually to each bondholder, how much total interest does Jerome receive every six months?
3. At the stock exchange, the last sale on Tuesday for the Dandy Auto Corporation was $9.50. The next day it closed at $11.
   a. How much was the net change from Tuesday to Wednesday?
   b. By what percent did the stock increase in value between the close of the first day and the close of the second day?
   c. How much would 100 shares have cost on Tuesday at the closing price?
4. Investors sometimes refer to a "discomfort index." This index is the sum of the inflation rate and the unemployment rate. Using the data below, compute the discomfort index for each of the five years.

Year	Inflation Rate	Unemployment Rate
A	4.6%	5.9%
B	11.1	7.3
C	6.3	8.9
D	3.2	6.8

Which year had the highest discomfort index? How much higher was the highest year compared with the lowest year?

5. The P/E is the ratio of a stock's earnings per share compared with the price per share. For each of the following stocks, compute the P/E:

Stock	Earnings per Share	Price per Share
X	$1.16	$ 47.50
Y	.59	7.63
Z	3.69	136.50

If each of the above stocks had a P/E of 18, what would be the per-share selling price of each stock?

6. Using the table shown below, compute the yield for each of the stocks listed.

	Price Paid	Annual Dividend
Consolidated Engineering	$48	$2.40
Electro-Jet Company	50	3.00
Federated Industries	30	1.60
Instrumentation, Inc.	30	1.30
Magus Corporation	38	1.90
Seaboard Steel	65	2.60

Expanding Your Understanding of Business

1. U.S. savings bonds pay competitive rates of interest today. For many years, they paid relatively low rates of interest. Give several reasons why the rate has been increased.
2. Within a few weeks, the market price of a stock decreased from 32\frac{3}{4}$ per share to 26\frac{1}{2}$. Find out several possible causes for such a decrease.
3. Check the library to find what each of the following pairs of terms about stocks and bonds means:
   a. Registered bond and coupon bond
   b. Callable bond and convertible bond
   c. Par value stock and no-par value stock
   d. Cumulative preferred stock and noncumulative preferred stock
   e. Load fund and no-load fund
4. The National Association of Investment Clubs (NAIC) can be of great assistance to people who want to form an investment club. Through research in your library, by writing to the NAIC, or by contacting a stockbroker, make a report on the specific aids available for people interested in organizing an investment club. Why might it be a good idea for someone unfamiliar with stocks to join an investment club?
5. The financial or business section of many daily newspapers includes a list of mutual funds. Study such a list and answer the following questions:
   a. Which fund has the highest price per share? The lowest?
   b. What is the difference in meanings between the headings ''bid'' and ''asked''? (Check the library for your answer.)
6. Some stocks are sold in over-the-counter markets or OTC markets. The National Association of Securities Dealers (NASD) has instituted a reporting system known as NASDAQ, the National Association of Securities Dealers Automated Quotations. Learn what you can about OTC stocks and NASDAQ. Also learn why some stocks are listed OTC rather than being on one of the regular stock exchanges. (Your library may have information available or a local brokerage office can help you.)

Considering Other Investments

Chapter 34

Chapter Objectives

After studying this chapter and completing the end-of-chapter activities, you will be able to:

1. *Discuss the advantages and disadvantages of owning a place in which to live.*

2. *Describe four major costs associated with owning a house.*

3. *Differentiate between conventional mortgages and ARMs.*

4. *Indicate why real estate is a common investment.*

5. *List several agricultural and nonagricultural commodities that can be considered for investments.*

6. *Discuss collectibles as a form of investment.*

In addition to the variety of investments you have learned about, other investment opportunities are available. For instance, you might consider investing in real estate, commodities, precious metals, coins, stamps, or antiques. As with other investments, you must know what you are buying and what the potential is for gaining or losing money. **Real estate**—land and anything that is attached to it—is one investment that most people eventually acquire.

GETTING STARTED IN REAL ESTATE

Getting started with real estate for most people means finding a place in which to live. Jeff and Carrie Redfield were newlyweds who were starting a new life away from their families. They could not afford to buy a house, although buying a house was a goal they set for themselves.

Renting a Place in Which to Live

Jeff and Carrie met their housing needs by renting a low-rent apartment. As renters, they were freed from much of the work and expense of repairing the property, fixing the plumbing, and so forth. It was also easier for them to move to a new location when they changed jobs. As tenants, they took care of their rented property, but they were not able to call the apartment their own. Jeff and Carrie knew that someday they wanted to own a house and yard that they could maintain and fix up just the way they wanted. To realize their goal, they saved as much money as possible for a down payment on a house.

Owning a Mobile Home

Jeff and Carrie did well in their jobs and felt ready to settle down. They had their first child and decided it was time to examine the housing market. Houses were too expensive for them, but they did find a mobile home in a good location that they could afford. They purchased the mobile home and took their first step in the direction of becoming real estate owners.

The biggest advantage to owning a mobile home was having a place they could call their own. Borrowing money to help buy the mobile home was not a problem. Their monthly payments were not any more than the rent they had been paying, and they were able to continue to put aside some savings for their future house purchase.

INVESTING IN REAL ESTATE

After several years, Jeff and Carrie realized that they needed more space. They now had two children and still hoped to realize their dream of owning a house in a nice neighborhood. Jeff and Carrie sold their mobile home for almost what they had paid for it. Keeping it in good condition paid off; it had been a good investment for them. The experience they had in renting an apartment and owning a mobile home helped them know what kind of house they desired. They were ready for the next step in real estate ownership.

Home Ownership

Their dream came true—they bought a house. Jeff and Carrie felt proud about owning a house. They also experienced a feeling of security. But now they had a mortgage, and their monthly payments were much higher than the rent or mobile home loan payments they were used to making. They now had to watch their spending more carefully.

Mortgages

Unless you are a very rich person, you will need to obtain a mortgage when you buy a house. A **mortgage** is a legal document giving the lender a claim against the property if the principal, interest, or both are not paid as agreed. Mortgages generally are long-term loans, usually for 10, 20, or 25 years, that require monthly mortgage payments. Mortgage payments often include taxes and insurance in addition to a percentage of the principal and interest charges. Figure 34-1 shows what monthly payments would be required to cover the principal and interest for mortgages of 10, 20, and 25 years at a 12 percent interest rate.

Figure 34-1
The monthly house payment is usually the family's largest monthly expenditure.

Amount Borrowed	10 Years	20 Years	25 Years
$ 5,000	$ 71.74	$ 55.06	$ 52.57
10,000	143.48	110.11	105.23
20,000	286.95	220.22	210.65
30,000	443.42	330.33	315.97
40,000	573.89	440.44	421.29
50,000	717.36	550.55	526.62

Interest rates on mortgages are traditionally set for long periods of time and do not change during the life of the mortgage. This type of mortgage is called a **fixed rate mortgage**. Market interest rates, however, generally increase or decrease quite a bit during the life of a mortgage depending upon economic conditions. Therefore, lenders also offer an **adjustable rate mortgage (ARM)**. The interest rate of an ARM is raised or lowered periodically depending upon the current interest rate being charged by lenders. Monthly payments for ARMs often are lower, especially in the early years of the mortgage, compared with fixed rate mortgages.

Realtors and Lawyers

Buying a house is not a simple matter. Most home buyers need the help of a real estate agent, sometimes referred to as a Realtor. A **Realtor** is someone who is trained and licensed to help with the buying and selling of real estate. Both those who buy and sell real estate may require the assistance of a Realtor. Someone who wants to sell a house contacts a Realtor who then helps to set the selling price and lists the house for sale. Someone who wants to buy a house contacts a Realtor who helps the person decide what is wanted in a house. The Realtor will have many listings of houses for sale and will arrange for the prospective buyer to view the house.

There are important legal concerns when purchasing real estate, and both a realtor and a lawyer should help you with the transaction. A lawyer will help assure that your property has no claims against it, such as back taxes and liens. You need to have your own lawyer represent you in the transaction to help avoid future legal problems.

When buying a house, it is also important to have an appraiser report on the value of the house. An **appraiser** is one who is trained to estimate the value of property and who can give an official report on its value. Such things as the quality of construction, the location, and the price of similar houses are taken into account in the appraisal.

Illus. 34-1
Most home buyers need the help of a real estate agent.

The Cost of Home Ownership

While there are some important advantages to owning your own property, there are some disadvantages, too. For most people the advantages outweigh the disadvantages. Let's consider some costs, such as property taxes, insurance, upkeep, and interest, that go along with owning your own real estate.

Property taxes vary greatly from state to state and community to community, but generally they are about 3 percent of the market value of the property. Taxes are based on the **assessed value**—the amount that your local government determines your property to be worth for tax purposes. Assessed values are normally lower than the market value, often only about half. The Redfield's house has a market value of $90,000, but it was assessed at $45,000. A tax rate of $60 per $1,000 of assessed value would result in annual taxes of $2,700. This rate is 6 percent of the assessed value but only 3 percent of the market value.

Property insurance is another cost, but it is essential. The value of the house, its construction material, its location with respect to other buildings, and the availability of fire protection are among factors affecting the cost of homeowner's insurance. (See Chapter 37 for more information about homeowners insurance.) Typical insurance costs are about one-half of 1 percent of the market value of the house. The Redfield's pay $450 per year for their insurance, and they cannot afford to be without it.

The cost of **upkeep**—maintaining your property in good condition—is important in home ownership. Annual upkeep costs average about 2 percent of the property's value. Jeff and Carrie's costs for upkeep are about $1,800 per year. Postponing repairs or not taking good care of the house and yard through regular maintenance can be very costly in the end.

Interest payments add to the cost of the house. For instance, 12 percent interest for 25 years results in payments that more than triple the amount borrowed—a total of $126,387 is paid on $40,000 borrowed. The interest paid is part of an advantage of home ownership, too.

Advantages of Home Ownership

The advantages include a tax benefit that results when the interest paid can be included as a deductible expense on a tax return. Real estate taxes are generally a deductible expense.

From an investment standpoint, the increase in equity is an important consideration. **Equity** is the difference between what your house and property are worth and the amount owed on the mortgage. Equity builds up over the years and increases rapidly in the last few years of a mortgage. Because of **appreciation**, a general increase in the value of property that occurs over a period of time, homeowners gain value. After Jeff and Carrie

Illus. 34-2
Many hidden
expenses and
responsibilities
accompany home
ownership.

lived in their home for ten years, its market value had increased to $124,000 and their debt decreased to $55,000; their equity was $69,000.

In the final analysis, pride in ownership—one of our basic rights in a democracy—is the overriding advantage of owning a piece of real estate.

Condominiums

In recent years, condominiums, or condos, have become popular. A **condominium** is an individually owned unit in an apartment-like building or complex where maintenance and yard work are normally taken care of for a service fee. Life-style changes affect the type of housing needed. Later in their lives, the Redfield's found it difficult to handle the upkeep of their home. Their house was bigger than needed since their children had grown up and moved out. They looked at a variety of condos, found one they liked, sold their house for a profit, and moved into the condo.

Other Real Estate Investments

There are other types of real estate investments, too. Some people buy two-family houses, called *duplexes*, and live in one half while renting the other half. Real estate investors may buy an apartment building and hire someone to manage it. Still other investors buy vacant land in hopes of selling it when the market value increases substantially.

Another type of real estate investment is the purchase of resort or recreational property on a time-sharing basis. Time-shared property purchase plans are popular in many areas of our country. In these plans, there are a number of time-share owners. A schedule is followed to determine who will occupy and enjoy the property at certain times of the year. The property is normally used by owners for short periods of time, such as a week or two each year. Time-share plans allow people to acquire part ownership in high-cost property they could not otherwise afford to purchase by themselves.

INVESTING IN COMMODITIES

Another type of investment considered by experienced investors is commodities. Commodities include grain, livestock, precious metals, currency, and financial instruments. Generally commodity investing is considered to be speculative. A **speculative investment** is one that has an unusually high risk. Commodity investors deal in **futures**; that is, a contract for a commodity purchased in anticipation of higher market prices for their commodity in the near future.

Commodity Exchanges

Commodities are bought and sold on exchanges similar to stock exchanges. Buyers and sellers are represented by traders on the exchanges. The best known exchange, the Chicago Board of Trade (CBOT), was established in 1848 to provide a central market for agricultural products and to help avoid the huge price fluctuations that had been taking place in the market. The CBOT is governed by the Commodity Futures Trading Commission (CFTC) and the National Futures Association (NFA).

Agricultural Commodities

Agricultural products, such as corn, soybeans, and wheat, are examples of commodities traded on the CBOT. Agriculture producers sell their crops in advance of a harvest at a price that they believe is a good deal for them. A farmer, then, will know in advance how much he or she will receive for a crop. The buyers assume that the price of the crop will go up when harvested so that they can earn a profit on what it sells for at that time. Many conditions affect the agricultural commodities that are traded, such as weather conditions, international trade agreements, and worldwide demand and supply.

Gold, Silver, and Other Precious Metals

Precious metals are of major worldwide importance. Gold and silver have been traded on commodity markets for centuries. Gold has the longest history as a monetary commodity, going back to gold coins that were circulated as early as 500 B.C. Gold is also highly prized for both ornamental and industrial reasons. More recently other metals, such as copper and platinum, have been added. Prices of these metals are affected by a variety of factors.

Price fluctuations can be illustrated with gold. In 1879, gold sold for $18.79 per ounce. Its price (value) rose gradually but steadily through the years because of its scarcity. In 1979, one century later, the price of gold jumped to $850 per ounce and fluctuated wildly for several years. In 1980, the price fell to $490 and then gradually increased again to $711. A year later it had a high of $599 and a low of $390, eventually its value stabilized at about $500 per ounce.

Precious metals are quoted as spot prices per one troy ounce. The **spot price** is the price quoted for precious metals in the world markets. For instance, in August of 1989, the spot price for gold in London and New York was $374 per troy ounce.

Illus. 34-3
Commodities, such as livestock, grain, and gold, are considered to be speculative investments.

Money invested in precious metals does not earn interest. If you hold gold, silver, or platinum, you might profit by selling them later at a price higher than what you paid. Gold and other precious metals have one more advantage: Many investors see them as protection against currency becoming worthless. Gold is recognized for its value throughout the world and can be used in trading for goods and services when money is not accepted.

Currency and Financial Instruments

Currency, such as the U.S. dollar and the Japanese yen, and financial instruments, such as Treasury bonds and Treasury bills, also are traded on the Chicago Board of Trade. The price of currency and financial instruments is affected by a country's economic outlook and by the market rate of interest. Here again, investors buy currency or financial instruments expecting the prices to increase in the future so that they can sell them to others at a profit.

INVESTING IN COLLECTIBLES

Another form of investment that is popular with many people is collectibles. **Collectibles** are items of personal interest to the collectors that can increase in value in the future. Examples are stamps, coins, baseball cards, and antiques.

One of the advantages of collectibles is the personal pleasure that comes through the process of buying, collecting, storing, arranging, and displaying

Illus. 34-4
Collecting stamps and baseball cards combines a pleasurable hobby with an investment.

what is collected. Often organizations of collectors are formed. For example, stamp clubs around the country bring together stamp collectors who buy, sell, trade, display, and discuss their stamps. Baseball card trading takes place in scheduled events in huge arenas as well as over kitchen tables. Antique dealers and collectors gather for major events in which they buy and sell their items. For many people, this type of investing combines a pleasurable hobby with an investment. For others, collectibles are purchased purely as an investment.

The possibility of the average purchaser of collectibles making a large profit on what is collected is not great. Rare stamps, coins, and antiques, which may cost several hundred dollars or thousands of dollars, tend to be those items on which a considerable profit can be made for those who speculate in them. The wise investor in collectibles studies the market, knows the product well, and analyzes the risk to be taken.

Increasing Your Business Vocabulary

The following terms should become part of your business vocabulary. For each numbered item, find the term that has the same meaning.

adjustable rate mortgage (ARM)
appraiser
appreciation
assessed value
collectibles
condominium
equity
fixed rate mortgage

futures
mortgage
real estate
Realtor
speculative investment
spot price
upkeep

1. Land and anything that is attached to it.
2. Someone who is trained and licensed to help with the buying and selling of real estate.
3. An individually owned unit in an apartment-like building or complex where maintenance and yard work are normally taken care of for a service fee.
4. A general increase in the value of property that occurs over a period of time.
5. The cost of maintaining your property in good condition.
6. One who is trained to estimate the value of property and who can give an official report on its value.
7. The difference between what your house and property are worth and the amount owed on the mortgage.
8. A traditional mortgage with an interest rate that does not change during the life of the mortgage.
9. The amount that your local government determines your property to be worth for tax purposes.
10. A mortgage for which the interest rate is raised or lowered periodically depending upon the current interest rate being charged by lenders.

11. A legal document giving the lender a claim against the property if the principal, interest, or both are not paid as agreed.
12. The price quoted for precious metals in the world markets.
13. Items of personal interest to collectors purchased in anticipation of an increase in value in the future.
14. An investment that has an unusually high risk.
15. A contract for a commodity purchased in anticipation of higher market prices in the near future.

Reviewing Your Reading

1. Name two advantages of owning a house and two advantages of renting an apartment.
2. Why is owning a mobile home a good way for some people to get started in home ownership?
3. What costs, in addition to the original investment, are included in the cost of owning a house?
4. On the average, the annual cost of taxes is what percent of the market value of the property?
5. What is often included in mortgage payments in addition to principal and interest charges?
6. What factors help determine the amount charged for insurance on a house?
7. The annual costs for upkeep average what percent of the property's value?
8. Name some ways of investing in real estate other than buying property in which you will live.
9. In what ways can Realtors, appraisers, and lawyers help in real estate transactions?
10. What are some agricultural products that are traded on commodity exchanges?
11. What is the CBOT, and why was it formed?
12. Give examples of precious metals that are traded.
13. What can affect the price of currency and financial instruments that are traded as commodities?
14. What makes collectibles attractive to many investors?
15. What is good advice for "wise investors" who purchase collectibles and other forms of investments?

Using Your Business Knowledge

1. Blair West owns a house that has a value of $80,000. For the past three years, the upkeep has averaged less than $500 a year. Can Blair assume that his expenses will be only $500 in future years?
2. Why is a condominium often desirable to retired people? to others?
3. What can you do to help assure the increase in value of a home you purchase?
4. Under what circumstances is an adjustable rate mortgage better for a buyer than a fixed rate mortgage?
5. Robin Greer has decided to purchase a house. She has also decided to take care of all the details herself and avoid paying a Realtor, an appraiser, or a lawyer. Why might Robin find that her decision is not a good one?
6. Mei-ling Shen has been collecting coins for several years. She estimates that they are worth about $2,000. Someone told her that she could make more money investing in commodities. She is considering selling her collection and going into commodities. What advice would you give Mei-ling?

Computing Business Problems

1. The Brocks own a house valued at $65,000 and they have a balance on their mortgage of $40,000. Last year they had the following expenses:

Interest on mortgage $4,000
Upkeep   900
Insurance   250
Taxes   1,500

   a. What was the total of their expenses for last year?
   b. What is the amount of equity the Brocks have in their house?

2. Don Smith invests $10,000 with a group that buys apartment buildings as investments. At the end of the first year, he received earnings of 10 percent of his investment.
   a. What amount did he receive the first year?
   b. If he receives the same amount for the next six years, what is the total he will receive?

3. Bill Fields has been renting an apartment for three years and pays $250 per month for rent. He has an opportunity to buy a house that will require him to pay $320 per month as a mortgage payment.
   a. In one year, how much more will he have to pay for house payments than he now pays for rent?
   b. During the first year, 90 percent of each payment will be for interest and 10 percent will be for principal repayment. What will be the amount he pays for interest for the year? for principal repayment for the year?

4. Gold is considered to be a good investment in addition to real estate, stocks, and bonds. Yet the price of gold has changed drastically over the past few years. Gold is priced on the basis of troy ounces. The chart on this page shows the price per troy ounce of gold over a three-year period. Use the chart to answer the following questions:
   a. What was the highest price paid for gold in the first year? the second year? the third year?
   b. How much did the price of gold increase from the beginning of the first year to the end of the second year? What was the percent of increase?

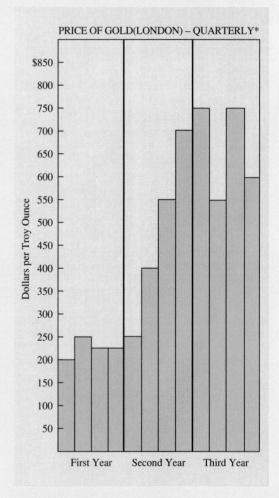

*At the end of each quarter, rounded to the nearest $25.

Source: First National Monetary Corporation.

c. How much did gold decrease in price from the beginning of the third year to the end of the third year? What was the percent of decrease?

5. Steve Lincoln bought 30,000 bushels of corn in the future's market at $2.98 a bushel. The price of corn rose to $3.02 a bushel.

a. What was Steve's total dollar profit on this investment?

b. What was his percentage gain?

c. If the price of corn had dropped to $2.90 a bushel, what would have been Steve's loss in total dollars?

d. What would have been his percentage loss?

Expanding Your Understanding of Business

1. Investigate the changes in rents charged for apartments in your community over the past five years. What factors have caused rents to increase or decrease? Report your findings to your class.

2. Visit a local Realtor's office or invite a Realtor to speak to your class. Find out what you can about the changing values of real estate in your community. Also find out about some of the problems that people are having today with the purchase of houses and other real estate.

3. Call or visit a bank or savings and loan association. Ask for information about getting a mortgage on a home costing $50,000. Get answers to the following questions and make a report to your class:

a. What is the minimum down payment needed?

b. What is the average interest rate for a fixed rate mortgage?

c. What is the current rate on an adjustable rate mortgage?

d. What is the monthly payment on a 25-year loan at the current interest rate if the minimum down payment is made?

e. If you decide to repay the loan early, will there be a financial penalty?

4. Investing in precious metals is an investment alternative that is attractive to many people. Precious metals commonly purchased by investors today include gold, silver, platinum, and copper. Check several newspapers and magazines or talk with precious metal dealers to determine the current price of each of these metals. Find out what trends there have been in the price of each precious metal. Do you consider investing in one or more of these precious metals to be a good idea? Why or why not?

5. Cooperatives are places to live that are somewhat like condominiums. Through research in your library, find out what cooperatives are and how they are like and unlike condominiums. Make a report of your findings.

6. Do some research on the operations of the Chicago Board of Trade (CBOT). Try to find out what terms such as hedging, day trader, forward contract, and time limit order mean as they are used on the CBOT. Report your findings to your class.

Career Focus

There are many ways in which people can save and invest their money. Some people turn to savings and investment workers for guidance and assistance in choosing just the right plan. This results in employment opportunities for those interested in helping others plan their financial futures.

Job Titles: Job titles commonly found in this career area include:

Securities Clerk
Real Estate Clerk
Order Clerk
Comparison Clerk
Figuration Clerk
Transfer Clerk
Margin Clerk
Receive and Deliver Clerk
Securities Analyst
Stockbroker
Stock Specialist
Investment Adviser
Investment Counselor
Financial Planner
Real Estate Agent
Real Estate Broker
Real Estate Appraiser

Employment Outlook: The job demand in this career area is expected to be better than average with securities salespeople and real estate agents being in highest demand. Clerical workers are used in a variety of areas with securities and real estate firms; the need for clerical workers in this career area will parallel the general trend.

Future Changes: It is anticipated that more and more individuals will find it possible and desirable to become involved in securities investments; this will tend to increase the demand for securities sales workers. The stock market crash of 1987 reduced the number of securities industry employees for a period of time, but a growth in the number of workers employed began again in 1989. Also, as the use of automation increases and as banks and discount brokers expand their securities sales operations, the need will be somewhat lessened. Real estate workers will be needed to respond to what is anticipated to be a growing demand for housing and other properties.

What Is Done on the Job: Clerical workers in this area perform a variety of functions

related to the purchase and sale of stocks and real estate. Familiarity with legal terminology as well as savings and investments technical terms is desirable.

Securities analysts work with market, economic, and company data to determine the desirability of investing in certain stocks. Sales workers generally serve as brokers; they meet with those who wish to sell or buy securities or real estate and work out a price acceptable to both parties. The sales worker handles legal forms and documents and may specialize in certain kinds of securities or real estate. Financial planners help individuals with all areas of planning for savings and investments and may attain a certified financial planner designation.

Education and Training: Clerical workers must possess good clerical skills and be especially reliable since large amounts of money are involved in daily transactions.

Sales workers must obtain a state license to sell securities and/or real estate. A college education with courses in finance, real estate, market-ing, and economics is desirable. College degrees are commonly required.

Salary Levels: Salaries vary widely with levels of work, experience, and geographic area. Brokers and sales agents generally work on a commission basis. Financial planners may charge a fee, earn a commission on sales, or both. Beginning securities salespeople average about $1,300 per month; with experience, they eventually will earn in the $40,000 to $90,000 annual salary range.

Additional Information: A visit with workers who are involved with real estate, stock market, and financial planning dealings will give you some additional insight into this career area. Reading periodicals about careers will also add to your information about this career area.

Protection from Economic Loss

Unit Goals

After studying the chapters in this unit, you will be able to:

1. *Explain how insurance can help protect you against economic loss.*
2. *Describe how each of the six categories of vehicle insurance protects you from economic loss.*
3. *Give examples that show why property insurance is needed.*
4. *Explain what life insurance is designed to do.*
5. *Explain why health insurance is important.*

The Liability Insurance Crisis

Business Brief

One of the forms of economic loss you can suffer is through lawsuits that are decided against you as a result of injury or damage that you may have caused to someone else. Insurance that protects you from this form of loss is called *liability*

insurance. Liability insurance has been the source of a great amount of discussion in the press, among consumer groups, and within the insurance industry. The attention given to liability insurance results from the large monetary awards that are given as compensation by juries to people who have been found to have been harmed by another person or business.

For example:

- In a Texas case, the color of a tricycle has forced a toy manufacturer to agree to a multimillion dollar settlement in a case involving the severe injury of a young boy. The victim, who was riding a black tricycle, was crossing the street from a shady area when he was struck by a car. The parents claimed that the tricycle's manufacturer was at fault because the dark color of the tricycle made it too difficult for the driver to see the child.

- In Nebraska, the owner of a golf cart is suing the manufacturer for several million dollars for bodily injury resulting from burns received when the golf cart, without a gas cap, overturned, caught fire, and severely burned the driver. The owner is claiming that the cart should have been manufactured with a loss-proof fuel cap.

And in response:

- A western state governor has signed a bill that places a one million dollar limit on awards in medical liability cases.
- A southern governor has signed a product liability act that protects manufacturers from liability unless damages are caused by an unreasonably dangerous characteristic of the product and the product was being used in a manner that could reasonably have been anticipated by the manufacturer.

In the past few years, there has been a dramatic growth in liability claims. This dramatic growth has been labeled as the "liability crisis" by the insurance industry. The multimillion dollar awards that have been paid out by insurance companies have resulted in severe financial problems for insurance companies and in increased costs for purchasers of insurance.

The good news is that there has been a slowdown in liability claims in the last few years. The reason for this slowdown seems to have occurred because some state legislatures passed laws that limit liability and liability-related awards. There has also apparently been a change in the public's attitude regarding liability suits. This change in attitude has probably resulted from the large amount of publicity associated with the liability crisis. The legal community has been given signals by insurance companies that the awards being paid were excessive, resulting in serious problems for sellers and buyers of liability insurance.

Source: Sean Mooney, "The Liability Crisis: Where Are We Now?" *Insurance Review* XLIX, no. 12 (December 1988): 46.

Chapter 35

Chapter Objectives

After studying this chapter and completing the end-of-chapter activities, you will be able to:

1. *Name several economic losses that people commonly risk.*

2. *Describe how insurance protects against financial losses.*

3. *List four kinds of insurance protection that are important to most people.*

4. *Explain what it means to be self-insured.*

5. *Name the most important factor that determines the level of insurance premiums.*

6. *Explain how everyone benefits from fewer insurance claims.*

7. *Describe how insurance provides economic security.*

Most of us have an adequate amount of economic resources to take care of our daily needs. We can pay for an occasional car repair, pay the rent or house payment on time, and afford a trip to a physician when we become ill. Many people even have a modest amount of savings that would help cover an economic emergency.

Few people, however, have the $15,000 it might take to replace a stolen car, the $80,000 it might take to rebuild a burned home, or the $100,000 or more to pay the hospital and medical costs associated with a long, serious illness.

Stolen or wrecked automobiles, storm or fire damage to houses, and serious health problems affecting people are only a few of the events reported daily in the newspaper. You can probably think of a problem such as an accident, an illness requiring hospitalization, property damage, or some other loss that has affected you or someone you know within the past year. Unfortunately, events like these are common. Perhaps these events will not happen to you very often, but you will probably experience at least one of them in your lifetime.

THE RISK OF ECONOMIC LOSS

Even if you are very careful, you will not be able to avoid all losses. You can, however, protect yourself against economic loss. **Economic loss** occurs when something that has some financial value is lost or destroyed. That is, economic loss usually costs money. For example, the loss of an heirloom

Illus. 35-1
The cost of replacing or repairing this stolen car might be very expensive.

ring would certainly be a family tragedy. Family members would be unhappy about the loss of an irreplaceable piece of family property. A portion of the loss (the unhappiness) is noneconomic. The ring, however, has economic value, perhaps thousands of dollars. Therefore, losing it could be seen as an economic loss.

Understanding the Kinds of Risk

Risk can be thought of as the possibility of incurring a loss. **Economic risk** can be related to property liability and one's own personal well-being. The economic risks that we may experience can be placed into three categories: personal risks, property risks, and liability risks.

Personal risks are risks associated with illness, disability, loss of income, unemployment, old age, and premature death. The risks of damage to or loss of property due to theft, wind, fire, flood, or some other hazard are called **property risks**. While personal and property risks involve economic losses to you, **liability risks** are potential losses to others that occur as a result of injury or damage that you may have caused.

Sharing Economic Risk

You can avoid a large economic loss by sharing the loss with other people. Suppose you and nine of your friends have new bicycles each worth about $300, and you decide to form an organization called the Bicycle Owners Insurance Association (BOIA). The purpose of the BOIA is to protect members from financial loss should one of the member's bicycles get stolen. To provide protection, each member agrees to share the cost of a stolen bike. Therefore, if your bike is stolen, each member (including yourself) would contribute $30 to buy a new one (see Figure 35-1).

If you were not a member of the BOIA and your bike was stolen, you would have to pay the total cost ($300) of a new bike if you wanted another one. As a member, it would only cost you $30. When a member loses a bike, each member suffers only a relatively small economic loss. In that way, the members help one another by sharing the risk of economic loss.

Defining Insurance

It would not be practical to share all losses as the BOIA does. There are too many kinds of risks and too many people to be protected. Loss protection must be carefully planned. **Insurance** is the planned protection provided by sharing economic losses. You will learn about several kinds of insurance in this unit, but they all have one thing in common. They provide you with the peace of mind that comes from knowing you are protected from economic loss. With insurance, a house fire, car accident, appendectomy, or early death will not cause you or your survivors economic difficulties.

Figure 35-1
Providing
insurance for
most risks is not
as simple as it
was for the
Bicycle Owners
Insurance
Association.

Join the **Bicycle Owners Insurance Association** Today!

Member
$30.00

COST TO REPLACE A STOLEN BICYCLE:

Nonmember
$300.00

Insurance companies are the businesses that provide planned protection against economic loss. Insurance companies, similar to the BOIA, agree to assume certain economic risks for you and to pay you if a loss occurs. The person for whom the risk is assumed is known as the **insured** or the **policyholder.** To show that risk has been assumed, the company issues a contract. That contract is called a **policy** and states the conditions to which the insurance company and the policyholder have agreed. For example, a policyholder may agree not to keep gasoline in the house, not to allow an unlicensed person to drive an insured car, or not to go skydiving. If a loss is experienced that is covered by insurance, the policyholder must file a claim with the insurance company. A **claim** is a policyholder's request for payment for a loss that is covered by the insurance policy.

As compensation for assuming a risk, the insurance company requires that the policyholder pay a certain amount of money. The amount the policyholder must pay for insurance coverage is called a **premium**. The insured usually makes payments once a month, once every six months, or once a year. The premiums from all the policyholders make up the funds from which the company pays for losses. Premium rates charged by insurance companies are reviewed by a state **insurance commission**. This is a state agency that makes sure that insurance premium rates and practices are fair.

THE TYPES OF INSURANCE

Both consumers and businesses are able to buy insurance to cover almost any kind of economic loss. Violinists can insure their fingers, professional athletes can insure against injuries, and writers may insure their manuscripts. Businesses are able to insure against the loss of rent from property damaged by fire, injury to consumers caused by a faulty product, or theft by employees. The kinds of insurance protection that will be important to most people, however, are insurance for automobiles and homes, life insurance, health insurance, and insurance for income security. You will learn about vehicle, property, life, and health insurance in the next four chapters. Insurance for income security will be presented as a part of Chapter 42.

Policyholders should know exactly what protection is provided by the kinds of insurance they have. Some people have failed to tell their insurance companies about losses they have suffered because they did not know that their policies covered those losses. Other people have assumed that losses they suffered were covered by their insurance, only to find out by reading their policies that the losses were not covered.

Some individuals, families, and businesses have decided that the best way to protect against economic losses is through self-insurance. **Self-insurance** means that the individual, family, or business assumes the total risk of economic loss. For instance, a family might regularly place money in a savings account to cover possible financial losses. Most families, however, would find it almost impossible to self-insure against economic catastrophes such as the cost of an extended illness or the cost of replacing a house that was destroyed by a fire.

Large businesses or institutions are sometimes able to insure themselves against certain kinds of losses. A company might, for example, determine that the average cost for damages to its fleet of company cars is $25,000 per year. It then establishes a special self-insurance fund for this purpose each year. In this way, the business can insure itself against the economic losses associated with automobile damage.

THE COST OF INSURANCE

The premium charged for each type of policy is determined partly by the past experiences of insurance companies in paying for the kinds of losses covered by each policy. For example, insurance companies have found that a

20-year-old driver is a greater risk because he or she is more likely to have an auto accident than a 40-year-old driver. Therefore, car insurance premiums for 20-year-old drivers are higher than they are for older drivers. Premiums are also affected by the cost of replacing the insured item. Premiums on a more expensive car would be higher. In general, the more claims the company has to pay, the higher the premiums.

Insured people also play an important part in determining the cost of insurance. They can reduce property losses by being careful. Locking doors and driving defensively, for example, will help to reduce losses associated with thefts and automobile accidents. Practicing good health habits will reduce life and health insurance claims. On the other hand, if losses paid by insurance companies increase because of policyholders' carelessness or poor health habits, premiums will usually increase.

Everyone benefits if the losses covered by insurance decrease. Assume, for example, that there is a decline in losses caused by fire and that fire insurance premiums are reduced as a result. If your family owns a house and has fire insurance on it, you gain directly because you pay lower premiums. If a business owner pays lower premiums, expenses will be less and prices on goods and services may be less. Anything that you can do to reduce losses covered by insurance helps you and the entire community.

Illus. 35-2
You can help reduce losses by practicing safety and security.

THE PURCHASE OF INSURANCE

Insurance protection can be acquired in several ways. Sometimes an employer will provide insurance for you. For example, sometimes all or part of life and/or health insurance premiums will be paid by an employer. In other cases, you will buy insurance directly from an **insurance agent**. An important part of an insurance agent's job is to help you select the proper kind of protection from economic loss. There are two basic types of insurance agents. One works for a large insurance company and sells only policies written by that company. The other is an independent agent who may sell many kinds of policies from a number of different companies.

INSURANCE FOR ECONOMIC SECURITY

Insurance is important to everyone because it provides economic security. If you had no insurance, you could probably take care of small losses such as those resulting from minor accidents. However, a large loss from a fire or serious illness could be a real financial hardship. Protection against such major events gives everyone a feeling of security.

Illus. 35-3
A good agent is very important to you when purchasing insurance.

Insurance also helps our economy. Insurance makes it possible for many people and businesses to do things they otherwise could not do. Suppose that someday you want to buy an $80,000 home but can make only a $10,000 down payment. You will need to borrow $70,000. It is very doubtful that anyone would lend you that amount at a reasonable rate if the house were not insured. Money to buy a new car cannot be borrowed at a reasonable rate unless the car is insured against risks such as theft and collision.

The money collected from premiums is invested. Many insurance companies, mainly life insurance companies, also use premiums to make loans. The loans are used to build government and private business projects, which help our economy grow.

Insurance companies also perform educational services by conducting campaigns on safety, health, and accident prevention. They conduct these activities to help reduce both losses and premiums.

Increasing Your Business Vocabulary

The following terms should become part of your business vocabulary. For each numbered item, find the term that has the same meaning.

claim
economic loss
economic risk
insurance
insurance agent
insurance commission
insurance companies

insured or policyholder
liability risks
personal risks
policy
premium
property risks
self-insurance

1. When something that has some financial value is lost or destroyed.
2. Risks associated with illness, disability, loss of income, unemployment, old age, and premature death.
3. The possibility of incurring a loss related to property liability and one's own personal well-being.
4. The planned protection provided by sharing economic losses.
5. Businesses that provide planned protection against economic loss.
6. The person for whom risk is assumed by an insurance company.

7. A contract that states the conditions to which the insurance company and the policyholder have agreed.
8. The risk of damage or loss of property due to theft, wind, fire, flood, or some other hazard.
9. A state agency that makes sure that insurance premium rates and practices are fair.
10. A person who sells insurance.
11. A policyholder's request for payment for a loss that is covered by the insurance policy.
12. The amount that a policyholder must pay for insurance coverage.

13. Potential losses to others that occur as a result of injury or damage that you may have caused.

14. When an individual, family, or business assumes the total risk of economic loss.

Reviewing Your Reading

1. Name several possible economic losses that people face.
2. Describe a loss that is *not* economic.
3. How does insurance protect against financial losses?
4. What are some unusual kinds of economic losses against which people may be insured?
5. List the three types of economic risks.
6. Name four kinds of insurance protection that are important to most people.
7. How do insurance companies use the premiums they collect?
8. What does a state insurance commission do for consumers?
9. Give three examples of how people benefit from fewer insurance claims.
10. How can policyholders influence the cost of insurance?
11. Why aren't most people able to use a self-insurance plan?
12. What is the main factor that determines the cost of insurance premiums?
13. How does insurance provide economic security?

Using Your Business Knowledge

1. How would the need for insurance against property risks differ between a family and a business?
2. Some people feel most comfortable when they are insured for almost every loss—large or small. Others believe that most people can handle small losses and favor insuring against only major or catastrophic losses. In which group would you place yourself? Why?
3. Develop a list of ways you could reduce the property risks associated with a home or an apartment.
4. The residents of a subdivision with 100 homes decided that they can save money by providing their own fire insurance. Since the houses in the area are of equal value, each owner agrees to contribute $800. The money is to be placed in a savings account in a bank. When a homeowner suffers a fire loss, the loss would be paid out of this account. Do you think this is a wise plan? Why or why not?
5. Why do you think insurance companies are willing to spend large amounts of money on health and safety education?

Computing Business Problems

1. Linda Caldwell is a 25-year-old computer technician living in an apartment. She pays the following insurance premiums every year: life insurance, $225; renter's insurance, $165; automobile insurance, $595; and health insurance, $650.

   a. What is the total annual cost of Linda's insurance premiums?
   b. If she paid her insurance premiums in equal monthly payments, how much would her total monthly insurance cost be?

2. A fire and casualty insurance company collected $978,000 in premiums in one year. That same year, the company paid out $821,520 in claims. What percentage of the premiums did the company pay out in claims?

3. Erin Michael's auto insurance company believes it can reduce its premiums by an average of 10 percent. This reduction is possible because of lowered speed limits with fewer and less costly accident settlements. Erin's last annual premium was $380.

   a. How much will she save if the proposed premium reduction is put into effect?
   b. What will be the amount of her new premium?

4. A fish wholesaling business decided to self-insure itself for damage to the property it owned. The property includes several forklifts, a large warehouse, office equip-ment, and a great deal of fish-handling equipment. The owners decided to put $47,000 in the self-insurance account the first year. Claims against the account that year were as follows:

One burned forklift	$6,500
One computer ruined by an electrical surge	3,200
Hail damage to the warehouse roof	7,400
One fish conveyer damaged by a supplier's truck	3,700

   a. What was the total of the property claims for the year?
   b. Was any money remaining in the account at the end of the year? If so, how much?
   c. What percent of the account was paid out in claims?

Expanding Your Understanding of Business

1. As you know, one may purchase certain kinds of insurance from an insurance company agent or from an independent agent. Talk with one of each and develop a list of advantages associated with buying insurance from each.

2. It has been said that some people are "insurance poor." That means that they are insured against so many possible economic losses that paying all of the premiums is a financial hardship for them. How do you think the condition of being "insurance poor" might develop? What is the danger of not having enough insurance?

3. Some states carry no insurance on state-owned buildings. Why do you think they do this? What would they do in case of a loss?

4. Examine two or three issues of your local newspaper. Look for news items reporting injuries to people or property damage. Think about the types of mishaps reported and the cost involved. Which of the situations may have been covered by insurance? Prepare a short report on your findings.

5. Contact a representative of the insurance commission of your state. Report on its purpose and the types of activities in which it is involved. Find out whether it investigates complaints from policyholders.

Vehicle Insurance

Chapter 36

Chapter Objectives

After studying this chapter and completing the end-of-chapter activities, you will be able to:

1. *List the six basic types of automobile insurance coverage.*

2. *Identify who is covered by bodily injury liability coverage.*

3. *Explain what type of property is covered by property damage liability coverage.*

4. *List the factors that determine the cost of automobile insurance coverage.*

5. *Describe financial responsibility laws.*

6. *Explain the purpose of an assigned-risk plan.*

7. *Explain what no-fault insurance laws are.*

Americans love their cars; they are a source of pleasure for many. Cars are interwoven in our lives. For most, they are the means by which we get to and from our workplace. We go to church, to school, to the movies, and on extended vacations in them. We wash them, wax them, brag about them, and complain about them. We build houses (garages) for them and sometimes give them names. Some people even cry when they are sold.

Cars are also the source of major economic risks. One in four drivers has an accident every year. In a recent year, there were almost 34 million auto accidents resulting in 48,700 deaths and 5.4 million injuries. The economic losses due to these accidents amounted to $85 billion. The costs of treating injured people and repairing damaged property could easily bring financial ruin to the people who must pay. Court action is costly, and awards to injured people and to owners of damaged property have increased tremendously. *Vehicle insurance* is designed to provide protection from the financial risks involved in owning and driving a car or another vehicle.

THE ECONOMIC RISKS OF CAR OWNERSHIP

If you own or lease a car, you must have adequate insurance. You will discover as you study this chapter that there really is no choice if you are a responsible person. The only choices are associated with how much and what kind of vehicle insurance you need.

Illus. 36-1
Sometimes as a result of jury awards, the cost of an auto accident can be very high.

Protection from the economic risks of car ownership is available with an automobile insurance policy. <u>You can buy insurance to protect yourself from the financial loss caused by almost anything that could happen to your car. You can also buy</u> **automobile liability insurance** <u>to protect yourself against financial loss if you injure someone else or damage someone else's property in an automobile accident.</u>

Sometimes an accident is unavoidable; that is, no one can be directly blamed for it. In most cases, however, someone is at fault. The person who is found to be at fault normally is responsible for damages and financial losses that result from the accident. <u>Although you may think you are completely faultless, you can be sued. If you are insured, your insurance company will provide legal defense for the suit. If the court decides that you are legally liable for injuries and damage to property, your insurance company will pay the costs up to the limits stated in your insurance policy.</u>

Several kinds of protection are available through companies that provide automobile insurance. This coverage is available in different combinations and for different amounts. Although some of the coverage can be bought separately, most car owners buy package policies that include most or all of the necessary coverage. There are two main categories of automobile insurance: <u>bodily injury coverage and property damage coverage.</u> Figure 36-1 summarizes the types of automobile insurance coverages.

Figure 36-1
The six types of automobile insurance coverage.

A Summary Chart of Automobile Insurance Coverages		
Types of Coverage	**Coverage on**	
Bodily Injury Coverages	**Policyholder**	**Others**
Bodily Injury Liability	NO	YES
Medical Payments	YES	YES
Uninsured Motorist Protection	YES	YES
Property Damage Coverages	**Policyholder's Automobile**	**Property of Others**
Property Damage Liability	NO	YES
Collision Insurance	YES	NO
Comprehensive Physical Damage	YES	NO

Source: Insurance Information Institute.

BODILY INJURY COVERAGE

The first major type of automobile insurance that you will read about are in the personal risk and liability risk categories you learned about in

Chapter 35. Bodily injury coverage includes bodily injury liability, medical payments, and uninsured motorist protection. These three types of bodily injury coverage are the source of most of the money paid in claims by auto insurance companies. In a recent year, the average bodily injury claim paid was $7,847.

Bodily Injury Liability Protection

Bodily injury liability coverage protects you from claims resulting from injuries or deaths for which you are found to be at fault. This type of insurance covers people in other cars, passengers riding with you, and pedestrians. It does not cover you or, in most cases, your immediate family.

Dollar amounts of bodily injury coverage are generally expressed as two numbers divided by a slash, such as 25/50, 50/100, or 100/300. The first number refers to the limit, in thousands of dollars, that the insurance company will pay for injuries to any one person in an accident. For example, if you had bodily injury coverage of 25/50 and had an accident for which you were found to be at fault, the insurance company would pay up to $25,000 if just one person were injured. The second number, in this case 50, refers to the limit, in thousands of dollars, that the insurance company would pay if more than one person were injured.

Some states have financial responsibility laws that require as little coverage as 10/20, but car owners should consider carrying much larger amounts. It is not unusual for juries to award an injured person $100,000 or more. If this happened to you and you only had 10/20 coverage, your insurance company would pay the $10,000 limit and you would have to pay the rest. Additional coverage is not very expensive, often only a few more dollars.

Medical Payments Protection

Through **medical payments coverage**, policyholders and their family members are covered if they are injured while riding in their car or in someone else's car. It covers them if they are walking and are hit by a car. Guests riding in the insured car are also protected.

Medical payments insurance also covers the costs of medical, dental, ambulance, hospital, nursing, and funeral services. Payment, up to the limit stated in the policy, is made regardless of who is at fault in the accident. Normally car owners purchase medical payments insurance along with their bodily injury liability coverage.

Uninsured Motorist Protection

In some cases, injuries are caused by hit-and-run drivers or by drivers who have no insurance and inadequate money to pay claims. Therefore, insurance companies make available **uninsured motorist coverage** to protect against these drivers. It is available only to those people who carry bodily injury liability coverage. In addition to covering the policyholder and family members, it also covers guests riding in the policyholder's car. Unlike medical payments coverage, which pays regardless of who is at fault in the accident, uninsured motorist protection covers the insured person only if the uninsured motorist is at fault.

PROPERTY DAMAGE COVERAGE

There are three types of automobile insurance designed to protect you from economic loss due to damage to the property of others and to your car. They are property damage liability, collision, and comprehensive physical damage. While the claims paid in these categories average only about $1,500 per claim, it is still important to have these coverages.

Property Damage Liability

People who drive a car are responsible for damage caused to another's property. **Property damage liability coverage** protects you against claims if your car damages someone else's property and you are at fault. The damaged property is often another car, but it may also be property such as telephone poles, fire hydrants, and buildings. Property damage liability insurance does not cover damage to the insured person's car.

Illus. 36-2
You can buy insurance against loss associated with property damage caused by a car.

Collision Insurance

A recent study by the Alliance of American Insurers showed that the money it would cost to repair a new Buick Skylark that was wrecked would be more than the cost of two new ones. The total included the cost of parts and paint but not labor to do the job. Rising insurance rates reflect the fact that coverages which pay for collision damage usually account for approximately two-thirds of the total cost of an insurance policy.

Collision coverage protects a car owner against financial loss associated with damage resulting from a collision with another car or object or from the car turning over. It does not cover injuries to people or damage to the property of others. Most collision coverage is written with a deductible clause. **A deductible clause** indicates the amount car owners are willing to pay themselves for damage to their autos in the event of an accident. This means that the insured may agree to pay the first $100 or $200 of damage to the car in any one collision and the insurance company agrees to pay the rest. Larger deductible amounts are available and reduce the premium paid by the policyholder.

Collision coverage does not provide for payment of damages greater than the car's value. Suppose your car receives $2,500 in damages in a collision with another vehicle. If your car has a value of only $2,100, the collision coverage would pay $2,100, not $2,500. Collision coverage should not be carried on a car that is of little value because the cost of repairing the car may be more than the car is worth. The car's worth is normally set by a book that reports the value of similar cars that have been sold recently.

Comprehensive Physical Damage

Even if you do not have an accident with another vehicle, your car can still be damaged or destroyed. The car could be stolen, or it could be damaged by fire, tornado, windstorm, vandalism, or falling objects. **Comprehensive physical damage coverage** protects you against almost all losses except those caused from a collision or from the car turning over.

If your car is totally destroyed or stolen, the amount paid to you is not necessarily equal to the amount you paid for the car. Rather, it is equal to the car's estimated value at the time of the loss. Suppose your car costing $9,000 is stolen soon after you buy it. The insurance company will probably pay you almost as much as the car cost, perhaps $8,500. However, if the car is stolen two years after you buy it, the insurance company may pay you only $5,500. The car has grown older and its value has decreased.

THE PURCHASE OF AUTO INSURANCE

People in the United States spent more than $81 billion in a recent year on auto insurance policies. This expenditure is more than 50 percent of all of the money spent on insurance. This indicates that a great deal of money is spent insuring cars and other vehicles. That money should be spent wisely and carefully. Therefore, car owners need to understand how to get the most protection for their insurance dollar.

Determining Insurance Rates

There are several factors that an insurance company may use to determine the cost of automobile insurance. Some of those factors include:

- Your age and other characteristics, such as accident record, marital status, or academic standing.
- The purpose for which you use your car.
- The value and type of car.
- The community in which you live.
- Types of coverage and deductibles.

Since some drivers are more likely to have accidents than others, they must pay higher premiums. To determine premium rates, drivers are classified according to age, marital status, driving record, and scholastic achievement. The lowest rates are reserved for the best risks, those least likely to have an accident. The cost of insurance is usually higher when one of the drivers in the insured's family is under age 30 than it is if all family drivers are over age 30.

The purpose for which a car is driven and the number of miles it is driven in a year are also important in determining insurance rates. Cars used for business purposes are generally driven more miles in a year than are cars driven for pleasure and are therefore more likely to be involved in an accident.

The value of your car naturally has an important effect on the cost of insurance. Premiums for collision coverage and comprehensive physical damage coverage must be higher for a car worth $12,500 than for a car worth only $6,000. The insurance company runs the risk of paying out much more to the insured if the $12,500 car is destroyed or stolen. The type of car also affects the rate. If you have a high-performance car or an expensive sports car, you may have to pay higher rates.

Rates for automobile insurance are not the same everywhere. Rates vary from state to state and even from city to city within a state. Auto insurance rates are also affected by the population in a particular area and the number of accidents that occur over a certain period of time in the area. Insurance companies gather statistics on the dollar amount of claims paid for an area and base their insurance rates on this information.

The cost of your auto insurance will also vary according to the types of coverage you have and the amounts of the deductibles you choose. Naturally, the more coverage you carry, the higher the cost.

Reducing the Cost

By planning your auto insurance purchase carefully, you may save a great deal of money. For example, the extra amount charged for young drivers may be decreased if they have completed an approved driver education course. Companies in most states offer young people a good-student discount. The discount may amount to as much as 25 percent of the premium.

Choosing the Company

Just as auto insurance premiums vary with the conditions associated with your car and your driving, they also vary from company to company. It pays to shop around and compare rates.

While it is very difficult to find out all of the possible rates from all companies, you should compare a few companies. The cost of the insurance will depend greatly on your choice of coverage.

INSURANCE FOR OTHER VEHICLES

Insurance on motorcycles, recreational vehicles, and snowmobiles is similar in some respects to automobile insurance. For example, bodily injury liability, property damage liability, collision, and comprehensive physical damage insurance are the most important coverages on these vehicles. The engine size and value of the vehicle are the important factors in determining

Illus. 36-3
Poor grades can keep you from earning an auto insurance discount.

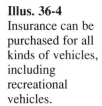

Illus. 36-4
Insurance can be purchased for all kinds of vehicles, including recreational vehicles.

the cost of insurance. Generally, the larger the vehicle, the higher the insurance cost.

LEGAL ASPECTS OF VEHICLE INSURANCE

Each year, our society becomes more complex with the passage of additional laws. Some of these laws relate to our vehicles and more specifically to our vehicle insurance. All owners of vehicles should know about compulsory insurance laws, financial responsibility laws, assigned-risks plans, and no-fault insurance laws.

Compulsory Insurance Laws

Thirty-nine states have adopted **compulsory insurance laws** that require you to carry certain types of automobile insurance before your car can be licensed. In those states, you may not register a car or obtain a license to drive without presenting proof of having the minimum amounts of insurance coverage required.

Financial Responsibility Laws

All states have some kind of financial responsibility law. **Financial responsibility laws** provide that if you cause an accident and cannot pay for the damages either through insurance, your savings, or the sale of property, your driver's license will be suspended or taken away. Most of these laws make you legally liable (responsible) for any damages you cause to people or their property.

Assigned-Risk Plans

Usually because of bad accident records, some drivers are unable to buy auto insurance in the normal fashion. Because of this, every state also has an **assigned-risk plan**. Under this plan, every auto insurance company in the state that sells liability insurance is assigned a certain number of high-risk drivers. That number is based on the amount of insurance each company sells. Using this plan, each company has to insure a fair proportion of high-risk drivers. The insurance industry calls this their shared insurance market. Drivers in high-risk categories must, of course, pay much higher premiums than those who are not high risks.

No-Fault Insurance Laws

In an effort to speed up the payment of claims and reduce the hardship of long delays, **no-fault insurance laws** have been adopted by some states. Under these laws, people injured in an automobile accident are required to collect for their financial losses—such as their medical bills, loss of wages, and other related expenses—from their own insurance companies no matter who is at fault.

Let's look at an example. Steve Gibson, who is insured with Vehicle Insurance Company, and Pamela Ross, who is insured with State Insurance Company, are injured in a serious two-car accident. Under no-fault insurance, Gibson would collect from Vehicle Insurance and Ross's claims would be paid by State Insurance. It would not be necessary to decide whether Gibson or Ross caused the accident.

No-fault insurance laws vary in some ways from state to state. Ordinarily the right to sue is retained for the more serious injury cases and for death. In such cases, it is necessary to decide how much each driver was at fault in the accident.

Increasing Your Business Vocabulary

The following terms should become part of your business vocabulary. For each numbered item, find the term that has the same meaning.

assigned-risk plan
automobile liability insurance
bodily injury liability coverage
collision coverage
comprehensive physical damage
   coverage
compulsory insurance laws

deductible clause
financial responsibility laws
medical payments coverage
no-fault insurance laws
property damage liability coverage
uninsured motorist coverage

1. Insurance coverage that provides medical-expense protection for the policyholder, immediate family members, and guests while in the insured person's car.
2. Auto insurance that provides coverage to high-risk drivers who are unable to purchase insurance in the normal fashion.
3. Insurance coverage that protects you against almost all losses except those caused from a collision or from the car turning over.
4. A plan in which people injured in auto accidents are required to collect for their financial losses from their own insurance companies no matter who is at fault.
5. Insurance coverage that protects you from claims resulting from injuries or deaths for which you are found to be at fault.
6. A clause in an insurance contract that indicates the amount car owners are willing to pay themselves for damage to their autos in the event of an accident.
7. Laws whereby your driver's license will be suspended or taken away if you cause an accident and cannot pay for the damages either through insurance, your savings, or the sale of property.
8. The general term used to describe insurance that you buy to protect yourself against financial loss if you injure someone else or damage someone else's property in an automobile accident.
9. Laws that require you to carry certain types of automobile insurance before your car can be licensed.
10. Insurance coverage that protects a car owner against financial loss associated with damage resulting from a collision with another car or object or from the car turning over.
11. Insurance coverage that protects the policyholder and immediate family members against losses resulting from injuries caused by a hit-and-run driver or by a driver who has no insurance and inadequate money to pay claims.
12. Insurance coverage that provides protection against claims if your car damages someone else's property and you are at fault.

Reviewing Your Reading

1. What is the purpose of vehicle insurance?
2. What are the six basic types of automobile insurance coverage? Into what two categories can they be grouped?
3. What type of auto insurance protects you against damage caused by a hit-and-run driver?
4. What can happen to an uninsured motorist who is found to be at fault in an accident, but does not have enough money to pay for the damages?
5. If you are protected by an automobile insurance policy and are sued as the result of an accident, how will the insurance company help you?
6. If a driver carries medical payments coverage, in which of the following situations will benefits be paid?
   a. A passenger in the driver's car is injured.
   b. The driver is injured in an accident.
   c. The insured person is crossing the street and is struck and injured by a passing car.
7. Is the average amount of claims higher for the area of bodily injury coverage or property damage coverages?
8. What does 100/300 mean in terms of bodily injury liability coverage?
9. Why would someone be required to purchase insurance from an assigned-risk plan?

10. What are no-fault insurance laws?
11. What factors determine the cost of insurance coverage?
12. Some automobile insurance companies give premium discounts to certain drivers. Name two types of drivers likely to receive discounts.

Using Your Business Knowledge

1. If you lost control of your car on an interstate highway and drove across the median and hit an oncoming car, what types of insurance would pay the other driver's accident expenses?
2. If there was a four-car pileup in foggy conditions on the interstate highway, how would claims be settled in a state with a no-fault insurance law? What would happen in a state without such a law?
3. Chris Engleman had four small auto accidents and three traffic tickets in one year. His auto insurance company canceled his policy because of his driving record. Chris wants to continue to be an insured driver. What is his next option?
4. Which type of automobile insurance coverage would Jane Edmunds need in order to be covered in the following situations?
   a. Jane, in an attempt to avoid hitting a dog in the street, ran into a parked car.
   b. Jane's daughter, who was riding in the back seat, was injured when Jane ran into the parked car.
   c. During a storm, a heavy tree branch damaged Jane's car, breaking the windshield and denting the hood.
   d. Jane was found to be at fault in an accident in which a pedestrian was injured.
5. How do financial responsibility laws benefit you?
6. Jim Pikkert was the driver at fault in an accident in which his three passengers were badly hurt. The court awarded two of the injured people $30,000 each, and it awarded the third person $45,000. Pikkert had bodily injury liability coverage in the amount of 50/100. Was this enough insurance to protect him from financial loss? Why or why not?
7. If your car hits a parking meter, breaks the meter, and you are found to be at fault, what coverage should you have?
8. Tell why you think it is less important to carry collision coverage on a ten-year-old car than on a three-year-old car. Are there circumstances when you may still want to have collision coverage on a ten-year-old car?

Computing Business Problems

1. Karen Samson carried a $200 deductible collision insurance policy on her automobile. She had an accident that was determined to be her fault. The cost of repairing her car was $750. How much of the repair bill would her insurance company pay?
2. The number of cars in the assigned-risk plans in a recent year was 6,786,630. New Jersey had 1,638,404 of these and North Carolina had 820,327. What percentage of the total did each of these states have? (Round to the nearest whole percentages.)
3. When Erik England drove 53 kilometers round-trip to work each day, his auto insurance premium was $350 a year. Erik changed jobs and now drives 24 kilometers round-trip. His insurance company gives a 10 percent premium discount to policyholders who drive less than 25 kilometers to and from work each day.

a. How much will he save per year?

b. How much is Erik's present premium?

4. Joan Nordland is a college student. She took a driver education course while in high school. She also earned an overall scholastic average of B+ in her college work. These qualify her for a driver educa- tion discount of 20 percent of the premium and a good student discount of 15 percent of the premium for her auto insurance.

a. If the standard premium for her policy is $450 per year, how much will Joan pay for her auto insurance this year?

b. How much will she save?

Expanding Your Understanding of Business

1. Ralph and Marvin had an accident in which one person was slightly injured. Although there appeared to be great damage to the two cars, Ralph suggested that they give each other their license numbers and driver's license information, and then leave. Marvin believed that they should call the police and wait for an officer to come. With whose position do you agree? Check with your local police department and report to the class on what to do at the scene of an accident. Check with an insurance agent to learn the procedure for reporting an accident to your insurance company.

2. Check with an insurance agent to find out what should be done about insurance coverage if:

a. You sell your car and buy a new one.

b. You sell your car four months before your policy expires and you do not plan to buy another car.

c. Conditions of driving change, such as use of the car, number of drivers of the car, or a move to another location.

Property Insurance

Chapter 37

Chapter Objectives

After studying this chapter and completing the end-of-chapter activities, you will be able to:

1. *Identify three types of economic losses against which property insurance protects.*

2. *Explain what kind of protection is provided by personal liability coverage.*

3. *Explain why personal liability coverage is so important today.*

4. *Explain the difference between real property and personal property.*

5. *Distinguish between homeowners policies and separate policies.*

6. *Name six examples of perils against which a basic homeowners policy provides protection.*

7. *Explain why a person who rents an apartment needs property insurance.*

A large portion of people's earnings is spent acquiring various kinds of property. People buy clothes, dishes, toys, and other inexpensive items. These items are sometimes stolen, broken, or misplaced, usually with relatively minor economic consequences. However, people also spend money to buy expensive jewelry, furniture, sound equipment, cameras, and houses. If something happens to one of these things the economic loss could be very large.

Property insurance is designed to protect you from the personal and financial hardships you would experience if some of your property were lost due to fire, theft, vandalism, floods, windstorms, or other hazards. Property owners also are at risk of being sued by people who are injured on their property. Because the risks of loss in such situations are high, property owners should carry property insurance.

IDENTIFYING HOME AND PROPERTY PROTECTION

Home and property insurance protects you against three kinds of economic loss: (1) damage to your home or property, (2) the additional expenses you must pay to live someplace else if your home is badly damaged, and (3) liability losses related to your property.

Illus. 37-1
You may have more property than you think you have.

Damage to Home or Property

Fires cause almost $9 billion worth of damage every year. Much of this damage is to homes. The dollar amount of damage goes up almost every year. Homes and other expensive property should be insured for fire damage as well as damage caused by vandalism, unavoidable accidents, and natural disasters such as lightning, earthquake, wind, and flood. If your home or property experiences damage and you are insured, the insurance company will pay all or a portion of the cost of repair or replacement.

Additional Living Expenses

If a fire or other disaster strikes your home, one of the first shocks you will experience is that you do not have a place to live. You may have to move into a hotel, motel, or furnished apartment while your home is being repaired. Insurance for additional living expenses will help to pay for the expenses you would incur if something happened to your home.

Liability Protection

The third kind of loss, liability loss, is protected by personal liability coverage. **Personal liability coverage** protects you from claims arising from injuries to other people or damage to other people's property caused by you, your family, or your pets. If a neighbor trips on your sidewalk and you are shown to be at fault, personal liability coverage will pay for any medical and

Illus. 37-2
If your home was destroyed by fire, insurance would pay for the repairs and for temporary living expenses.

legal costs up to a stated limit. If a child damages a car in an adjacent driveway with her tricycle, claims will be paid through the provisions in the policy of the child's family that covers liability for physical damage to the property of others.

These kinds of events may seem remote and rather trivial but often court awards to those who suffer the damage or injury are neither remote nor trivial. In fact, these awards (and consequently premiums) are increasing so quickly that the insurance industry often refers to it as the insurance liability crisis. Awards to injured people for millions of dollars are not uncommon. It is vitally important that everyone have some form of liability protection from economic loss.

UNDERSTANDING PROPERTY INSURANCE POLICIES

When considering the purchase of property insurance, you must first decide what should be insured and against what perils it should be insured. **Perils** are the causes of loss, such as fire, wind, or theft. Property permanently attached to land, such as a house or garage, is known as **real property**. Property not attached to the land, such as furniture or clothing, is known as **personal property**. Real and personal property may be protected by individual policies or by a combination homeowners policy. If you are a renter, there are also special policies that will cover your property.

Individual Policies

A property owner can buy separate policies that insure against certain perils. For example, a **standard fire policy** insures against losses caused by fire or lightning. **Extended coverage** can be included in a standard fire policy. This expands the coverage to include damage caused by perils such as wind, hail, smoke, and falling aircraft, among other things.

Policies also may be purchased separately for damage caused by flood in a flood-prone area. It is also possible to purchase insurance against economic losses caused by earthquakes. Neither of these two perils is typically covered in other policies. The advantage of purchasing separate policies is that the combination of policies purchased can be fitted to individual needs.

Homeowners Policies

The most common form of home and property insurance policy sold today is a homeowners policy. The **homeowners policy** is a very convenient package-type insurance policy designed to fit the needs of most homeowners wishing to insure their homes and property. A homeowners policy almost always comes in three forms. The number of perils covered by a homeowners policy depends on whether the insured chooses the basic form, the broad form, or the comprehensive form.

Illus. 37-3
Flood damage is not a normally included peril in a homeowners policy.

The basic form of a homeowners policy insures property against the first 11 perils listed in Figure 37-1. The broad form, which is very widely purchased, covers 18 different risks. The comprehensive form covers all perils shown in Figure 37-1 and many more. It is sometimes referred to as an all-risk policy. Actually, such a policy insures against all perils except those excluded by the policy. Personal liability coverage is included with all forms of the homeowners policy.

With a homeowners policy, you are as protected as you would be if you bought several different policies. Yet the cost of a homeowners policy is usually 20 to 30 percent less than if the same amount of coverage were obtained by buying separate policies.

Renters Insurance

Many people in our society rent homes or apartments. They fill these dwellings with their personal property. They have many of the same property and liability insurance needs as homeowners. In response to this, the insurance industry has developed a **tenants policy** that is a package property and liability policy appropriate for renters. It covers household goods and personal belongings and provides protection against the same kinds of perils covered by homeowners policies, including personal liability coverage. Even though renters insurance is not very expensive, many renters do not purchase it as they should. They may fail to see the need and often suffer later because of a loss.

Figure 37-1 Perils covered by homeowners policies.

PERILS AGAINST WHICH PROPERTIES ARE INSURED THROUGH A HOMEOWNERS POLICY

COMPREHENSIVE | **BROAD** | **BASIC**

1. Fire or lightning
2. Loss of property removed from premises endangered by fire or other perils
3. Windstorm or hail

4. Explosion
5. Riot or civil commotion
6. Aircraft
7. Vehicles
8. Smoke

9. Vandalism and malicious mischief
10. Theft
11. Breakage of glass constituting a part of the building

12. Falling objects
13. Weight of ice, snow, sleet
14. Collapse of building(s) or any part thereof
15. Sudden and accidental tearing asunder, cracking, burning, or bulging of a steam or hot water heating system or of appliances for heating water

16. Accidental discharge, leakage or overflow of water or steam from within a plumbing, heating or air-conditioning system or domestic appliance
17. Freezing of plumbing, heating and air-conditioning systems and domestic appliances

18. Sudden and accidental injury from artificially generated currents to electrical appliances, devices, fixtures and wiring (TV and radio tubes not included)

All perils EXCEPT earthquake, flood, war, nuclear accidents, and certain others. (Check policy for details.)

PURCHASING PROPERTY INSURANCE

As when making other large insurance purchases, a wise consumer will work to find the most appropriate property protection at the lowest cost. That involves making certain that the property is insured for the correct amount and that the factors affecting property insurance costs have all been carefully considered.

The value of a home and furnishings represents the largest investment that many people make. It makes good sense to protect that investment with a carefully selected insurance plan.

Buying the Correct Coverage

Suppose that Melinda Powell built her house in 1988 for $90,000 and she insured it for that amount. It might cost $105.000 to build a similar house today, so the house has a current replacement value of $105,000. Yet, if Miss Powell's house is completely destroyed by fire, the insurance company may pay her only $90,000. Some insurance companies provide for automatic increases in property coverage as the price level increases. Others will pay the current replacement value if the property is insured for at least 80 percent of that replacement value.

Building costs and property values have increased greatly in recent years. Property owners should review the value of their property and insurance coverage every few years. They should determine the cost of replacing their property and make sure that their insurance policies give enough protection.

Special care should be taken to estimate accurately the value of personal property. Since personal property includes many different items, some may be overlooked if a careless estimate of value is made. Most homeowners policies provide personal property coverage at 50 percent of policy value. For example, if your home is insured for $80,000, your personal property is insured for 50 percent of $80,000 or $40,000. The value of personal property that you collect over the years is often surprisingly high. In many cases, a homeowner's personal property is worth considerably more than 50 percent of the coverage on the home. Additional coverage is available for a slightly higher premium.

Understanding Homeowners Insurance Premiums

The price that homeowners pay for insurance on homes and furnishings is based on a number of factors. One of the most important is the estimated danger of loss based on the insurance company's past experiences. In addition to the loss experiences, an insurance company considers the following factors in determining homeowners insurance premiums:

- The value of the property insured.
- The construction of the building; that is, whether it is made of brick, wood, or concrete, and the construction of the roof.
- The type of policy (basic, broad, or comprehensive).
- The number of perils covered.
- The distance to the nearest fire department and water supply.
- The amount of deductible (the higher the deductible, the lower the premium).

You should consider these factors carefully first when purchasing or building a home and then when buying insurance on that home and your property.

MAKING A CLAIM

In the unhappy event that you should have to make a claim to your insurance company for a property loss, you will want to be well prepared. You should keep a list of personal property that you have insured. The list, called an **inventory**, should include: (1) the original cost of each article, (2) when the article was purchased, and (3) how long the article is expected to last. The age of an insured article of personal property is quite important. As most property becomes older, it gradually wears out and decreases in value. This decrease in value, called **depreciation**, usually affects the amount the insurance company will pay if the property is destroyed. For example, a sofa costing $700 that is expected to last ten years would depreciate $70 each year. Its value after five years would be $350.

As soon as possible after you discover a loss, you should file a claim with your insurance company. However, before the company will pay, you must provide proof of your loss. This is not a problem with real property. A representative of the insurance company, called an **adjuster**, can look at the damaged property, determine the extent of loss, and pay you according to the terms of the policy. The destroyed contents of a house, however, would pose a problem. In order to prove the amount of personal property loss, you must know the approximate value of each article damaged or destroyed.

In addition to maintaining an up-to-date personal property inventory, some insurance companies suggest taking photographs or videos of your furniture and other property. These pictures can be used to support claims. Insurance companies can provide you with inventory forms and information about how to make claims for losses.

Illus. 37-4
Videotaping your property will enhance your property inventory.

Increasing Your Business Vocabulary

The following terms should become part of your business vocabulary. For each numbered item, find the term that has the same meaning.

adjuster
depreciation
extended coverage
homeowners policy
inventory
perils

personal liability coverage
personal property
real property
standard fire policy
tenants policy

1. Property that is permanently attached to land.
2. Additional protection of property that covers damage caused by perils such as wind, hail, smoke, and falling aircraft, among other things.
3. Insurance that protects you from claims arising from injuries to other people or damage to other people's property caused by you, your family, or your pets.
4. A basic type of property insurance that protects against losses caused by fire or lightning.
5. Property that is not attached to the land.
6. A package-type insurance policy designed to fit the needs of most homeowners wishing to insure their homes and property.

7. The decrease in the value of property as it becomes older and wears out.
8. Insurance for those who rent which covers household goods and personal belongings and provides protection against the same kinds of perils covered by homeowners policies, including personal liability coverage.
9. A list of goods showing the original cost of each item, when it was purchased, and how long it is expected to last.
10. The causes of loss, such as fire, wind, or theft.
11. An insurance company representative who determines the extent of loss and pays insureds according to the terms of the policy.

Reviewing Your Reading

1. List the three kinds of economic losses for which home and property insurance provides protection.
2. Tell why personal liability coverage is so important today.
3. What kind of loss would you have to suffer in order to take advantage of additional living-expense coverage in your insurance policy?
4. What kind of protection is provided by personal liability coverage?
5. Describe the difference between real property and personal property.

6. Name two prominent perils that are not covered in most homeowners policies.
7. Describe the difference between buying separate home and property insurance policies and buying a homeowners policy.
8. Name six examples of perils against which a basic homeowners policy will insure you.
9. How does extended coverage affect the standard fire policy?
10. Which homeowners policy covers more perils, the comprehensive or the broad policy?

11. Why would a person who rents an apartment purchase property insurance? What kind of policy should a renter purchase?

12. How is the cost of property insurance determined?

Using Your Business Knowledge

1. In a recent year, several homes in a Colorado canyon were destroyed when a heavy rain in the Rocky Mountains caused the river flowing through the canyon to rise several feet above its normal level. Do you think those canyon residents who had homeowners policies suffered any financial losses? Why or why not?

2. It snowed in Ames one night in February, and Art Shold did not take the time to shovel the snow from his front steps. Two days later a salesperson slipped on Art's snow-covered steps and broke an arm. The salesperson has asked Art to pay the medical expenses associated with the broken arm. Will Art's homeowners policy cover the expenses?

3. The Conforths had a serious home fire. They had an adequate fire insurance policy in force, but they had a very difficult time listing for the insurance adjuster all of the possessions they lost in the fire. What advice would you give to others in the Conforth's neighborhood who might be in this position some day?

4. Barbara Derrick's property is covered by the basic form of homeowners insurance. Against which of the following losses is she insured? Which of the losses would be covered if she had the broad coverage?
   a. A smoldering fire breaks out in a bedroom closet and her clothing is damaged by smoke.
   b. Her home is broken into and vandalized, but nothing is stolen.
   c. A storm knocks out the electricity for two days in mid-winter and the pipes burst, causing flooding.

Computing Business Problems

1. If Marilyn Wilhelm owned a home worth $98,000 and wanted to be certain it was insured for at least 80 percent of its value, for how much should it be insured?

2. A thief broke the lock on Don Gleason's garage and stole the following items:

   15 liters of oak stain,
      valued at $4.25 a liter
   6 liters of motor oil,
      valued at $1.45 a liter
   3 kilograms of 2.5 cm finishing nails,
      valued at 85 cents a kilogram
   68 meters of 2.5 cm x 30.5 cm pine
      shelving, valued at $4.50 a meter

   Since Don had recently bought these items and had not yet used any of the material, for what amount should he make his claim under his homeowners policy?

3. The Popovs were shopping for property insurance policies when they found a basic homeowners policy that would cost them $140 per year. The total of three separate policies that would cover all of the same perils would be $175. What percent of the total of the three separate policies would the Popovs save by buying the homeowners policy?

4. Kathleen Christensen lives in an apartment. Her furniture and other personal property are covered under a tenants policy. Miss Christensen's apartment was broken into and the following items were stolen:

A stereo, bought 3 years ago for $350
  and estimated to last 10 years
A camera, bought 4 years ago for $160
  and estimated to last 10 years
A suede jacket, bought 2 years ago for $80
  and estimated to last 5 years

If the insurance company pays Miss Christensen the estimated present worth of the lost articles, what amount will she receive?

Expanding Your Understanding of Business

1. What do you think the insurance industry means by the insurance liability crisis?
2. Determine why insurance companies sell combination property insurance policies called homeowners policies. Why can they sell package-type policies at discount rates compared to separate policies?
3. Property insurance policies usually set certain limits on the amount of protection allowed for such personal property as stamp and coin collections, jewelry, furs, and rare paintings. Why are such limitations established? If a person wants to be covered for the full value of such property, what can he or she do?
4. Why do you think only three in ten renters has a renters insurance policy.

Life Insurance

Chapter 38

Chapter Objectives

After studying this chapter and completing the end-of-chapter activities, you will be able to:

1. Explain why people need life insurance.

2. List four basic types of life insurance.

3. Distinguish between term life insurance and whole life insurance.

4. Describe the procedure for buying life insurance.

5. Name the three factors that determine the cost of life insurance.

The life insurance industry in the United States is big business, and it's growing bigger every year. Look at these facts that were compiled in a recent year.

- Purchases of life insurance totaled nearly $1.4 trillion.
- Life insurance benefit payments totaled $71.4 billion.
- Assets of life insurance companies exceeded $1 trillion.
- Purchases and benefits of life insurance have gone up for the twentieth year in a row.
- Life insurance was owned by 81 percent of American households.
- The average amount of life insurance per household is $102,200.

These are interesting facts and astounding numbers. They suggest that life insurance is a powerful force in our economy. It follows that the study of life insurance is something you, along with millions of others, should consider. You need to have answers to several questions such as: What kind of life insurance should be bought? How much life insurance does a person need? Where should life insurance be purchased?

WHAT DOES LIFE INSURANCE DO?

Life insurance protects survivors against the financial loss associated with dying. There are several other reasons for purchasing life insurance, but it is most often designed to provide financial protection and security for families in the case of the death of a provider. Specifically, it is designed to replace

Illus. 38-1
The life insurance industry is a very large one employing many people.

a loss of income for those who are financially dependent upon another person. Life insurance can also be considered a means of saving or investing, but its primary purpose is always protection against financial loss.

WHO NEEDS LIFE INSURANCE?

People with dependents usually need life insurance. A *dependent* is a person who must rely on another for financial support. You will one day need to ask the question, ''What would happen to the people who are financially dependent on me if I died tomorrow?'' If they could not live financially in the manner in which they lived before your death, you probably need life insurance.

Another common, though far less important, reason for buying life insurance is to assure that there is enough money to cover ''final expenses.'' Many people believe that everyone should have enough life insurance to cover funeral and burial or cremation expenses.

WHAT ARE THE TYPES OF LIFE INSURANCE?

Originally life insurance was very simple. You paid a fee (premium) each year and, if you died, your family or heirs were paid a sum of money. Like much of life, it is not as simple now. Insurance companies now offer a variety of plans that meet the different insurance needs of individuals.

Illus. 38-2
People with dependents need adequate life insurance to insure against financial loss.

A recent high school graduate would not have the same life insurance needs as someone who is ready to retire. A young single person has insurance needs that are different from those of a married person with small children. To provide for the different types of protection that are needed, insurance companies offer a variety of policies. The four basic types of life insurance are term life, whole life, variable life, and universal life.

Term Life Insurance

Term life insurance provides financial protection from losses resulting from loss of life during a definite period of time, or term. It is the least expensive form of life insurance. It is also the *only* form of life insurance that is purely life insurance; all the rest have savings or investment features added to them.

Policies may run for a period of from 1 to 20 years or more. If the insured dies during the period for which the insurance was purchased, the amount of the policy is paid to the beneficiary. A **beneficiary** is the person named in the policy to receive the insurance benefits. If the insured does not die during the period for which the policy was purchased, the insurance company is not required to pay anything. Protection ends when the term of years expires.

By paying a slightly higher premium, a person can buy term insurance that is renewable, convertible, or both. A **renewable policy** allows the policyholder to continue term insurance for one or more terms without taking a physical examination to determine whether she or he is still a good risk. A **convertible policy** allows the insured to have term insurance changed into another type of permanent insurance without taking a physical examination.

Term insurance policies may be level term or decreasing term. With **level term insurance**, the amount of protection and the premiums remain the same while the insurance is in effect. With **decreasing term insurance**, the amount of protection gradually becomes smaller, but premiums remain the same during the term.

An example of decreasing term insurance is **mortgage insurance**. It protects homeowners from losing their homes in case an insured dies before the mortgage is paid. Suppose the Hanson family bought an $80,000 house on which they made a down payment of $10,000 and took a 30-year mortgage for the remaining $70,000. The Hansons want to be sure that the mortgage will be paid if one of them should die, so they buy a $70,000 mortgage insurance policy. The amount of coverage decreases as the Hansons repay what they have borrowed, so the amount of coverage is about the same as the decreasing balance of the debt.

Whole Life Insurance

Whole life insurance is permanent insurance that extends over the lifetime, or whole life, of the insured. It offers more than financial protection at death.

Illus. 38-3
Mortgage insurance can help assure that a house is paid for if a homeowner should die.

Whole life builds cash value that can be borrowed to help families meet financial emergencies, pay for special goals, or provide income for retirement years. **Cash value** refers to the amount of money or sum received should a policyholder decide to give up the protection provided by a policy. All life insurance *except* term insurance has cash value. The cash value that accumulates is not taxable until you cash in a policy.

One type of whole life insurance is called a **straight life policy**. Premiums for straight life insurance remain the same each year as long as the policyholder lives. Some whole life insurance policies are intended to be paid up in a certain number of years and are called **limited-payment policies**. They may also be designated by the number of years the insured agrees to pay on them, such as 20-payment life policies. They are like straight life policies, except that premiums are paid for a limited number of years—20 or 30, for example—or until a person reaches a certain age, such as 60 or 65. Limited-payment policies free the insured from paying premiums during retirement when income may be lower.

Variable Life Insurance

Variable life insurance is a type of life insurance plan that resembles an investment. This plan lets the policyholder choose among a broad range of investments including stocks, bonds, and mutual funds. The death benefits and cash values of variable life policies vary according to the yield on the investments the policyholder selects.

The insurance company first designates an amount of the variable life premiums to cover the insured's expenses. The remaining amount is placed in an investment account. Both the death benefit and the cash value rise and fall with the success of the investment account of your choosing.

A minimum death benefit is guaranteed, but there is no guaranteed cash value. The minimum death benefit, in relation to premiums paid, is well below other types of life insurance. On the positive side, however, a strong rate of return on the investment account can increase the cash value and the death benefit well above the guaranteed level.

Universal Life Insurance

Universal life insurance provides both insurance protection and a substantial savings plan. The premium that you pay for universal life insurance is divided three ways. One portion of it pays for insurance protection. A second portion is taken by the insurance company for its expenses. The third portion is placed in interest-earning investments for the policyholder. The most important feature of universal life insurance is that the savings portion of the policy earns a variable (and usually higher) interest rate than is paid on other cash value insurance. The yield on the savings portion tends to rise or fall with the Consumer Price Index. Figure 38-1 compares the features of the different types of life insurance.

Combination Life Insurance Policies

The life insurance policies you have just read about can be combined or modified by an insurance agent and his or her company to meet your special needs. A combination plan that is popular with many people is a variable universal life policy. *Variable universal life insurance* combines features of variable and universal life policies. This policy combines the investment options of variable life insurance with the flexible premium and death benefit of universal life insurance. It is a good way to have insurance and to accumulate assets while deferring taxes on those assets.

WHAT ARE THE ECONOMICS OF LIFE INSURANCE?

Virtually everyone needs life insurance of some sort. Few of us have the financial resources necessary to pay the costs that can overtake us as the result of someone's death.

The Purchase of Life Insurance

In order for a life insurance program to be most effective for you, it must be suited to your needs and your family's. The answers to the following questions will help to determine that suitability:

Comparison of Alternative Life Insurance Programs

	Term Insurance	Straight Life	Limited Life	Variable Life	Universal Life
Premium	Starts out low but increases every few years on a preset schedule	High but usually stays constant	Higher than straight life insurance but constant	Fixed and regular	Varies (within limits) at the discretion of the policy-holder
Payment Period	Specified number of years—normally 5, 10, or 15 years	Life of the insured	Specified number of years—normally 20 or 30 years	Specified period	Specified period
Cash Value	None	Some cash value	More cash value than straight life but less than variable insurance	Varies with the rise or fall in the value of the investment account	Varies with the interest rate paid on the cash value, which the company can change from time to time
Death Benefit	Fixed	Fixed	Fixed	Death benefit always exceeds cash value	Can vary (within limits) at discretion of policyholder
Purposes	Protection for a specified period of time; to cover specific and temporary risks	Protection for life; some cash value for insured	Protection for life; some cash value for insured	Life insurance plus an opportunity to select different cash value invest-ment options	Life insurance with a fairly high rate of return on cash value

Figure 38-1 Alternative life insurance programs.

- How much money do you want to leave your dependents?
- How much income will you need when you retire?
- What can you afford to pay for your life insurance needs?

Answers to these questions will help you purchase the best life insurance program for you.

To buy life insurance, you frequently apply for a policy through an insurance agent. Normally you will be required to take a physical examination so that your state of health can be determined. Assuming that you have no serious health problems, you then pay a premium and receive your life insurance policy. If you are in poor health or work in a dangerous occupation, you may be considered a poor risk. For example, if you drive racing cars to earn a living, you are in a dangerous occupation. Even if you are in poor health or work in a dangerous job, you may be able to obtain insurance. However, you will probably pay higher premiums than people who are in good health and are employed in less hazardous occupations.

When you buy life insurance, you will be asked to name a beneficiary. This is most often a spouse or one or more children. You may insure not only your own life, but also the life of any other person in whom you have an insurable interest. To have an **insurable interest** in the life of another person, you must receive some kind of financial benefits from that person's continued life. You have, for example, an insurable interest in the lives of your parents. You do not have an insurable interest in a stranger's life. A partner in a business has an insurable interest in the life of his or her partner.

Illus. 38-4
Life insurance may be more expensive for someone in a hazardous occupation.

The insurable interest must exist at the time the policy is started, but generally it need not exist at the time of the loss.

The Cost of Life Insurance

In addition to the health and occupation of the insured, the cost of a life insurance policy depends on the type of life insurance being purchased and the age of the person being insured. In purchasing a whole life policy, the premiums for straight life insurance are higher than those for term insurance, but the annual premium stays the same throughout the insured's life. The premiums on limited-payment life insurance are higher than those for straight life insurance, but they are payable for only a limited number of years. Although the premiums on a 20-payment life policy are payable for only 20 years, the policy remains in force for the lifetime of the insured.

An insurance policy that covers a group of people is called **group life insurance**. The group acts as a single unit in buying the insurance. Our U.S. market economy tends to recognize efficiencies and savings that result in selling multiple quantities. You can often buy three pounds of hamburger for a lower per-pound price than buying just one pound. You can sometimes travel 1,000 miles by air for only a few dollars more than 500 miles. So it is, too, with insurance. The cost of group life insurance is less than the cost of a similar amount of protection bought individually because insurance covering many people can be handled economically in one policy.

Most group life insurance contracts are issued on a term basis through employers. Some policies, though, are available through unions, professional associations, and other similar organizations. Group life insurance is most often issued on a term basis, but whole life policies may also be purchased. The amount of protection available to an individual under a group insurance plan is generally limited. Many people, therefore, supplement their group insurance with policies of their own.

The Cash Value of Life Insurance

As long as they are kept in force, whole life policies, variable life policies, and universal life policies accumulate cash value. The longer you keep your policy, the higher its cash value will be. If you give up or surrender your policy, you are paid the amount of the cash value. If you need money but do not wish to cancel your policy, you can borrow from the insurance company an amount up to the cash value. If you should die before the loan can be repaid, the unpaid amount will be deducted from the face value of the policy when your survivors are paid. *Face value* is the amount of insurance coverage that will be paid upon the death of the insured.

Cash value life insurance can be seen as a savings plan as well as financial protection for beneficiaries. The return on your money in the cash value portion of life insurance is often not large. However, cash value insurance plans have a built-in savings feature for people who lack the discipline to save for the future.

Increasing Your Business Vocabulary

The following terms should become part of your business vocabulary. For each numbered item, find the term that has the same meaning.

beneficiary
cash value
convertible policy
decreasing term insurance
group life insurance
insurable interest
level term insurance
life insurance

limited-payment policies
mortgage insurance
renewable policy
straight life policy
term life insurance
universal life insurance
variable life insurance
whole life insurance

1. Life insurance that covers a group of people who are usually employed by the same company or are members of the same organization.
2. A whole life policy intended to be paid up in a certain number of years.
3. The person named in an insurance policy to receive the insurance benefits.
4. A life insurance policy that protects homeowners from losing their home in case an insured dies before the mortgage is paid.
5. The amount of money or sum received should a policyholder decide to give up the protection provided by a policy.
6. A life insurance policy that provides financial protection from losses resulting from loss of life during a definite period of time.
7. A term life insurance policy that may be changed into another type of permanent insurance without taking a physical examination.
8. Life insurance which provides both insurance protection and a substantial savings plan.

9. One type of whole life insurance for which premiums remain the same each year as long as the policyholder lives.
10. A term life insurance policy that allows the policyholder to continue the term insurance for one or more terms without taking a physical examination to determine whether she or he is still a good risk.
11. Insurance designed to protect survivors against the financial loss associated with dying.
12. A financial interest in or benefit from the continued life of a person.
13. Term life insurance on which the amount of protection and the premiums remain the same while the insurance is in effect.
14. Permanent insurance that extends over the lifetime of the insured.
15. Term life insurance on which the amount of protection gradually becomes smaller, but the premiums remain the same during the term.
16. Life insurance that lets the policyholder select from a range of investments.

Reviewing Your Reading

1. Why do people need life insurance?
2. What is a secondary reason for buying some type of life insurance?
3. What question should you ask yourself to determine whether or not you need life insurance?
4. What must you do to buy life insurance?
5. What is a dependent?
6. What determines whether you have an insurable interest in someone else's life?
7. List the four basic types of life insurance.
8. What is the only form of life insurance that has no investment or savings feature?
9. What does it mean if a term life insurance policy is convertible? What does it mean if it is renewable?
10. In what way is a limited-payment policy different from a straight life policy?
11. For what purposes might someone borrow from the cash value of life insurance?
12. Explain why a variable universal life policy is referred to as a combination plan.
13. Why is the cost of group life insurance less than the cost of insurance that is bought individually?
14. What three factors determine the cost of life insurance.
15. What advantage does cash value life insurance have to a person who lacks the discipline to save for the future?

Using Your Business Knowledge

1. Tell why the loss of income to a family is of greater concern than the loss of property.
2. Do you think the Board of Directors of the Ellingson Plastics Company has an insurable interest in the company's chief chemist? Why or why not?
3. What happens to the insurance protection of a whole life policy if the insured borrows the cash value of the policy?
4. What purpose does a physical examination serve during the process of purchasing a life insurance policy?
5. What kind of life insurance policy would you recommend for each of the following people?
   a. Jim Edgar, age 27, wants to buy a policy on which the premiums will be as low as possible for the next ten years.
   b. Sonja Kilmer, who works as a mechanic, wishes to have maximum protections for her invalid and widowed mother in case anything should happen to Sonja.
   c. Julie Van Hovel, age 45, wants to buy a policy that will not require payment of any premiums after she retires.
6. Why should a term policy that is renewable or convertible cost more than one which is not?
7. When a person buys life insurance as a member of a large group, no physical examination is ordinarily required. Why do you think this is so?
8. A wide variety of life insurance policies is available for purchase. Why do you think this is so?

Computing Business Problems

1. People who have cash value life insurance can borrow up to the cash value of the policy from the insurance company. Gary Hardesty had a $50,000 life insurance policy with a current cash value of $7,000. He decided to borrow $5,000 from that

amount to make a down payment on a small house he wanted to buy.

   a. If he died before repaying the loan, how much insurance would his beneficiary receive?

   b. If Gary repays the loan in one year at 8 percent annual interest, what is the total amount he will pay back?

2. John Larson needed $2,400 for one year's tuition at a technical school. He decided to borrow the money from a bank for four years and pay $600 of the principal each year, plus interest of 12 percent a year on the unpaid balance. To be sure that his debt would be paid if he should die, he took out a $2,400, four-year decreasing term insurance policy with an annual premium of $22.

   a. How much did John pay in premiums and interest each year?

   b. What was the total cost of premiums and interest for the four years?

3. Bruce Wright is having the physical examination required for his life insurance policy. His height is 185 centimeters, and his weight is 115 kilograms. The doctor's chart shows that the best weight for someone Bruce's height is 92 kilograms. The insurance company charges 10 percent more than standard rates for overweight people.

   a. If the standard annual premium for the insurance that Bruce wants is $1,350, what will his annual premium be?

   b. Approximately how many pounds must he lose to qualify for the standard premiums?

Expanding Your Understanding of Business

1. Term life insurance premiums are higher per thousand dollars of coverage for people who are older because an older person is more likely to die sooner. Make a list of reasons why life insurance premiums might be higher for some categories of people.

2. If the rate of return on the investment portion of a life insurance policy is six percent, why would the insurance company charge eight percent for a policy loan?

3. There is a great deal of debate in the insurance industry and among consumers regarding the merits of term and cash value life insurance. Research the subject and prepare a list of the positive and negative aspects of each type of life insurance. That research should include reading articles in consumer and insurance magazines and talking with consumers and insurance representatives.

4. Variable life insurance is a relatively new type of insurance. Describe one unique advantage and one unique disadvantage associated with the purchase of this type of life insurance policy.

Health Insurance

Chapter 39

Chapter Objectives

After studying this chapter and completing the end-of-chapter activities, you will be able to:

1. *Explain why it is so important to have health insurance.*

2. *Describe the most common types of coverage available in health insurance policies.*

3. *Explain how deductible and coinsurance clauses in a health insurance policy work.*

4. *Name the most common sources of health insurance.*

5. *Identify three health insurance programs operated by government agencies.*

One day while at work, Kim Chong, who is an independent computer consultant, noticed that she was having some vision problems. She was having a difficult time reading the print on the pages produced by her computer printer. She ignored the problem for a week. Soon, however, she decided that she must solve the problem and went to see her eye doctor. After some tests, she was referred to a specialist who, after more tests, diagnosed a tumor on Ms. Chong's brain, which was affecting her vision. She was immediately scheduled for surgery.

The good news: The surgery was successful; the tumor was not cancerous. Now, six years later, Ms. Chong has apparently made a complete recovery. And, yes, the bad news: The total amount of the medical bills was very large—more than $130,000. Ms. Chong had no health insurance.

Everyone should be covered by health insurance. Almost no one has enough money to pay the extremely large medical bills associated with a catastrophic illness. *Health insurance* provides protection against the economic hardships associated with paying for medical care and the loss of income that results when an injury or illness prevents you from working. Health insurance is similar to the other forms of insurance. You pay premiums for a policy that guarantees protection. When you are ill and need money to pay medical bills, the insurance company will pay up to specified amounts.

Illus. 39-1
Ms. Chong has experienced a complete recovery from very expensive surgery.

MEDICAL INSURANCE

A variety of health-related insurance is available. Each kind provides for a different type of coverage. Four categories of health insurance can be classified as medical insurance: (1) hospital expense, (2) surgical expense, (3) regular medical expense, and (4) major medical expense.

Hospital Expense Insurance

When an illness or injury requires you to be hospitalized, **hospital expense insurance** usually pays most or all of the charges for your room, food, and such items as use of an operating room, anesthesia, X rays, laboratory tests, and medicines. Because of the high cost of hospitalization, more people purchase hospital expense insurance than any other kind of health insurance. In fact, more than 181 million Americans are covered by hospital expense insurance.

Hospital expense insurance can be purchased from insurance companies or from nonprofit corporations. The most well-known nonprofit organization that offers hospital insurance is Blue Cross. Blue Cross plans usually pay hospitals directly for care provided to their policyholders. If expenses go beyond the amount covered by the Blue Cross contract, the patient must pay the difference.

Surgical Expense Insurance

Surgery is one of the major reasons for hospitalization and is normally very expensive. **Surgical expense insurance** covers all or part of the surgeon's fees for an operation. The typical surgical policy lists the types of operations that it covers and the amount allowed for each. Some policies allow larger amounts for operations than others. This, of course, requires that a higher premium be paid. Surgical expense insurance is frequently bought in combination with hospital expense insurance.

Surgical expense insurance can be purchased from insurance companies or from nonprofit organizations such as Blue Shield. Unlike Blue Cross, Blue Shield plans cover mainly medical and surgical treatment rather than hospital care. Most Blue Shield plans list the maximum amounts that will be paid for different types of surgery. They also cover the doctor's charges for care in the hospital and some plans pay the doctor's charges for office or home care.

Regular Medical Expense Insurance

Sometimes normal care provided by a physician can be quite expensive. **Regular medical expense insurance** pays part or all of the fees for nonsurgical care given in the doctor's office, the patient's home, or a hospital. The policy states the amount payable for each visit or call and the maximum number of visits covered. Some plans also provide payments for

X-ray and laboratory expenses. This type of insurance is usually combined with hospital and surgical insurance. The protection provided by these three coverages is referred to as **basic health coverage**.

Major Medical Insurance

Ms. Chong's problem was a good example of why people need major medical insurance. Long illnesses and serious injuries can be very expensive. Bills of $50,000 to $100,000 and even more are not unusual. **Major medical expense insurance** provides protection against the high costs of serious illnesses or injuries. It complements the other forms of medical insurance. Major medical expense insurance helps pay for most kinds of health care prescribed by a doctor. It covers the cost of treatment in and out of the hospital, special nursing care, X rays, psychiatric care, medicine, and many other health care needs. Maximum benefits range up to $250,000 and higher.

All major medical policies have a deductible clause similar to the one found in automobile collision insurance, as described in Chapter 36. With this clause, the insured agrees to pay the first part—perhaps $500 or more—of the expense resulting from sickness or injury. Major medical policies also usually contain a coinsurance clause. A **coinsurance clause** means that the insured will be expected to pay a certain percentage—generally 20 or 25 percent—of the costs over and above the deductible amount.

Illus. 39-2
Major medical expense insurance protects families from the high cost of serious injuries or long illnesses.

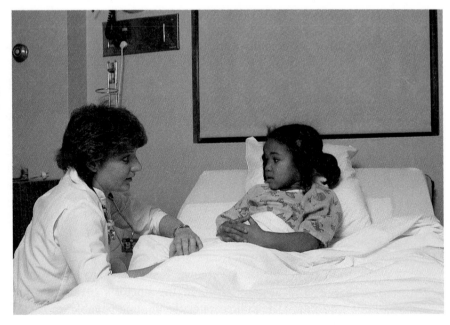

The deductible clause discourages the filing of minor claims. The coinsurance clause encourages the insured to keep medical expenses as reasonable as possible. Thus, both clauses help to make lower premiums possible because they help to lower payments of insurance claims.

Comprehensive Medical Policy

A combination of hospital, surgical, regular, and major medical insurance in one policy is called a **comprehensive medical policy**. This insurance retains the features of each of the separate coverages such as deductibles, amounts payable, limits, and the like. A combination of coverages is usually less expensive than the total of the separate coverages.

DENTAL EXPENSE INSURANCE

Insurance to help cover dental expenses was first offered in the 1960s and now covers about 40 percent of the population. **Dental expense insurance** helps pay for normal dental care, often including examinations, X rays, cleaning, fillings, and more complicated types of dental work. It also covers dental injuries resulting from accidents. Some dental plans contain deductible and coinsurance provisions, while others pay for all claims. Dental expense insurance is offered mainly through group plans and is still growing in popularity.

VISION CARE INSURANCE

A new type of health insurance coverage is **vision care insurance**, which covers eye examinations, prescription lenses, frames, and contact lenses. Vision insurance usually does not cover such things as tinted lenses, coated or plastic lenses, nonprescription lenses, and vision training. Coverage is usually available through group plans offered by a number of insurance companies. The popularity of vision care insurance results from the recognition by many individuals and employers who help pay for group plans that eye care health is very important.

DISABILITY INCOME INSURANCE

There is one form of health insurance that provides periodic payments if the insured becomes disabled as a result of illness or accident. **Disability income insurance** protects you against the loss of income because of a long illness or an accident. The insured receives weekly or monthly payments until he or she is able to return to work. Disability income policies frequently include a waiting period provision which requires that the insured wait a specified length of time after the disability occurs before payment begins. The purpose of the waiting period is to deter people from making frequent claims for small losses. Infrequent claims reduce premium costs.

SOURCES OF HEALTH INSURANCE

Where can you acquire health insurance? Health insurance is available from several sources and in many different forms. You can buy health insurance as an individual or as a member of a group. Private companies and government agencies provide many kinds of health insurance.

Group Health Insurance

The most popular way to buy health insurance is through a group. As with group life insurance, group health insurance policies are made available by employers to their employees and by unions and other organizations to their members. The company, union, or organization receives a master policy. The members who are insured under the plan are given membership cards to indicate their participation in the plan. Companies that sponsor group policies often pay part or all of the premium costs for their employees. The cost of group health insurance is lower per insured than the cost of a comparable individual policy. This is possible because insurance companies can administer group plans more economically, thus lowering costs for each person in the group.

Individual Health Insurance

Some people are not members of a group and are not eligible for group health insurance. They may be self-employed, for example, and have no employer to help buy health insurance for the group. One alternative is to buy individual health insurance. Individual health insurance is health insurance that is available to individuals and is adaptable to individuals' health insurance needs. Individual health insurance policies are usually rather expensive, require a physical examination, and have a waiting period before the policy is in force.

Health Maintenance Organizations

There is a form of health care coverage that has been developed as an alternative to health insurance. **Health maintenance organizations (HMOs)** normally consist of a staffed medical clinic organized to serve its members. You may join an HMO for a fixed monthly fee. As a member, you are entitled to a wide range of health care services. HMOs emphasize preventive care. Early detection and treatment of illnesses help to keep people out of hospitals and keep costs down.

HMOs are increasingly popular. From mid-1971 to the present, the number of HMOs increased from 33 to 626 and the number of members or subscribers increased from 3.6 million to 27.8 million.

Preferred Provider Organization

A new alternative to the HMO is the **preferred provider organization (PPO)**. This health insurance delivery system involves a group of physicians, a clinic, or a hospital contracting with an employer to provide medical services to employees. Employees are encouraged, but not required, to use the PPO's services through financial incentives. The employee is usually able to get medical treatment through the PPO at a significant discount. Employees are free, however, to seek medical treatment elsewhere and may be partially reimbursed for out-of-pocket medical expenses.

State Government Assistance

An important health insurance program established by state governments is workers' compensation. **Workers' compensation** is an insurance plan that provides medical and survivor benefits for people injured, disabled, or killed on the job. Accidents may occur on almost any job. Employees may suffer injuries or develop some illness as a result of their working conditions. To deal with this problem, all states have passed legislation known as workers'

Illus. 39-3
Worker's compensation provides medical and survivor benefits to workers who have been injured, disabled, or killed as a result of their working conditions.

compensation laws. These laws provide medical benefits to employees who are injured on the job or become ill as a direct result of their working conditions. Under these laws, most employers are required to provide and pay for insurance for their employees.

The benefits provided through workers' compensation vary from state to state. In some states, all necessary expenses for medical treatment are paid. In others, there is a stated payment limit. Usually there is a waiting period of a few days before a worker is eligible for loss-of-income benefits. If unable to return to the job after this waiting period, the worker is paid a certain proportion of wages as benefits. This usually amounts to about two-thirds of the worker's normal wages. Payments are also made to dependents if the worker is killed in an accident while on the job.

State governments also administer a form of medical aid to low-income families known as **Medicaid**. The federal government shares with states the cost of providing health benefits to financially needy families. A financially needy family is one whose income provides for basic necessities but who could not afford adequate medical care or pay large medical bills.

The services covered by Medicaid include hospital care, doctors' services, X rays, lab tests, nursing home care, diagnosis and treatment of children's illnesses, home health care services, and family planning. States may provide additional services.

Federal Government Assistance

The nation's social security laws provide a national program of health insurance known as **Medicare**. It is designed to help people age 65 and older and some disabled people to pay the high cost of health care. Medicare has two basic parts: hospital insurance and medical insurance.

The hospital insurance plan includes coverage for hospital care, care in an approved nursing home, and home health care up to a certain number of visits. No premium payments are required for the hospital insurance, and almost everyone 65 years old and older may qualify.

The medical insurance portion of Medicare is often called supplementary or voluntary medical insurance. The services covered under this plan include doctors' services, medical services and supplies, and home health services. The medical insurance requires a small monthly premium. The federal government pays an equal amount to help cover the cost of the medical insurance. Some features of the Medicare plan are similar to the deductible and coinsurance provisions in other health policies.

THE COST OF HEALTH INSURANCE

No matter who pays the premium, the cost of health insurance, like the cost of health care, is very high. In fact, the cost of health care has been increasing two to three times faster than the rate of inflation. The cost of insurance to cover health care is usually determined by at least four factors: the extent of the coverage, the number of claims filed by policyholders, the age of the policyholder, and the number of dependents. You will have little control over your age and the number of people dependent on you. You can, however, make sure you buy only the kind and amount of insurance you need. You can also take good care of yourself and be careful not to abuse your benefits by using medical services when they are unnecessary. By doing so, you will be doing your part to keep health insurance costs down.

Increasing Your Business Vocabulary

The following terms should become part of your business vocabulary. For each numbered item, find the term that has the same meaning.

basic health coverage
coinsurance clause
comprehensive medical policy
dental expense insurance
disability income insurance
health maintenance organizations
   (HMOs)
hospital expense insurance
major medical expense insurance

Medicaid
Medicare
preferred provider organization
   (PPO)
regular medical expense insurance
surgical expense insurance
vision care insurance
workers' compensation

1. Insurance that combines hospital, surgical, regular, and medical insurance into one policy.
2. Insurance that protects a worker against the loss of income because of a long illness or accident.
3. Insurance that pays part or all of the fees for nonsurgical care given in the doctor's office, the patient's home, or a hospital.
4. Organizations that provide complete health care to their members for a fixed monthly payment.
5. A combination of hospital, surgical, and regular medical expense insurance.
6. Insurance that helps pay for normal dental care and covers dental injuries resulting from accidents.
7. Insurance that provides medical and survivor benefits to people injured, disabled, or killed on the job.
8. Insurance that provides benefits to cover part or all of the surgeon's fee for an operation.
9. Medical expense assistance administered by state governments to financially needy families.
10. Insurance that pays most or all of the charges for room, food, and other hospital expenses that the insured person incurs.
11. Insurance that provides protection against the high costs of serious illnesses or injuries.

12. Health insurance provided by the federal government for people age 65 and older and some disabled people.
13. A provision in which the insured will be expected to pay a certain percentage of the costs over and above the deductible amount.
14. Insurance that covers eye examinations, prescription lenses, frames, and contact lenses.
15. A group of physicians, a clinic, or a hospital that contracts with an employer to provide medical services to employees.

Reviewing Your Reading

1. What kind of health insurance is purchased most often?
2. What are the two types of losses for which health insurance provides protection?
3. What well-known nonprofit organization offers health insurance?
4. What are the four basic types of coverage provided by medical insurance? Explain the kinds of expenses each covers.
5. How does a deductible clause in a health insurance policy work?
6. What types of dental care are covered by a dental expense policy?
7. Why is being insured under an individual health insurance policy more expensive than under a group policy?
8. What three health insurance programs are operated by government agencies?
9. What are the two basic parts of the Medicare plan?
10. What kind of health insurance covers you if you are injured on the job?
11. What has been happening to the cost of health care?

Using Your Business Knowledge

1. Debra Pope is studying to be a commercial artist and has a part-time job to help pay her college expenses. She does not have health insurance because she believes she cannot afford it. She also believes that she does not really need health insurance.
   a. Give several reasons why Debra should protect herself with some type of health insurance.
   b. Where might she find a policy at a reasonable premium?
   c. What can she do to keep the policy premium at a reasonable level?
2. Many major medical policies contain a coinsurance clause. These policies are usually less expensive than a policy without such a clause. What advice would you have for a person or group considering purchas-

ing a major medical expense insurance policy containing a coinsurance clause?
3. The federal government in recent years has put a great deal of emphasis on programs that are designed to provide medical benefits for the elderly. Why do you think this has happened?
4. The Carney family is trying to determine which kinds of health insurance coverage would best fit their needs. On one hand, they believe that a Blue Cross hospital expense plan and a Blue Shield surgical expense plan would be sufficient. On the other hand, a major medical plan might better serve their needs. Mr. and Mrs. Carney are both 48 years old and are employed by the same company. They have two children. There is a history of

heart disease in Mr. Carney's family, and Mrs. Carney smokes cigarettes. They have about $20,000 in a savings account. What advice would you offer this family based on their health insurance needs?

5. Why do you think a health insurance agent would suggest the addition of major medical expense coverage to a health insurance policy?

6. Why do you think an employee of a company would be willing to use a prepaid health plan, such as HMOs or PPOs, to satisfy health care needs?

Computing Business Problems

1. Ernest Chamberlain is considering job offers from two different companies. The jobs seem equally desirable to him. The Star Fire Company provides health insurance benefits to their employees that total $140 per month. The Axelrod Company provides no health insurance for its workers. How much money would the Star Fire health insurance benefit be worth to Ernest each year?

2. In a community with a population of 5,000, the following numbers of people are covered by the types of health insurance indicated:

Hospital expense	4,600
Surgical expense	3,200
Regular medical expense	3,000
Major medical expense	3,900
Dental expense	2,000
Vision care expense	700
Disability income	3,000

a. What percent of the people in the community are covered by each type of insurance?

b. In one year, 235 people covered by surgical expense insurance presented claims totaling $176,250. What was the amount of the average claim?

3. Many communities have blood banks that collect blood from donors. They make it available to local hospitals for transfusions for people who are ill or who are accident victims. During a recent blood drive, the Columbus Blood Bank collected 675 pints of blood from donors.

a. How many liters did they collect?

b. How many milliliters did they collect?

4. Karl Powell was hospitalized as a result of a skiing accident. His medical expenses were as follows:

6 days in hospital	$ 350 per day
Lab tests and X ray	$ 585
Surgeon's fee	$1,375

Karl is covered by hospital expense insurance, which pays the cost of his hospital room for up to 120 days for any one illness. Coverage for lab tests, X rays, and other hospital extras is limited to $500. His surgical expense insurance plan limits benefits to $1,200 for the type of surgery involved.

a. What was the total cost of Karl's medical services?

b. How much of this total cost was paid by his insurance?

c. How much of the medical cost did Karl have to pay?

Expanding Your Understanding of Business

1. It has been stated in many ways that the cost of health care is very high. Interview a health insurance agent or read magazine articles on the subject and develop a list of

ways you would suggest to help lower these costs.

2. One of the stated goals of health maintenance organizations is to keep people healthy through preventive care. Are there any health maintenance organizations in your community? If there are, see what their brochures have to say about preventive care. Report your findings to your class.

3. Schools often arrange with an insurance company to provide students with coverage that protects the students in case of accidents on the way to and from school and on school grounds. They also provide coverage for members of school athletic teams. Does your school provide such coverage? If so, how much does it cost? What coverage is provided?

4. As good health care has become more difficult for individuals to afford, the federal government has become active in providing health services, especially for the elderly. Some characterize this government activity as a move toward socialized medicine. Read about socialized medicine and tell why you do or do not favor government involvement in health care.

Career Focus

The insurance industry is a people-oriented business that has a large number of workers in a wide variety of jobs. The basic task of most employees is to participate in determining and satisfying customers' insurance needs.

Job Titles: Job titles commonly found in this career area include:

Agent
Insurance Clerk
Claims Adjuster
Underwriter
Claims Examiner
Data Processing Manager
Insurance Broker
Insurance Investigator
Actuary
Policywriter
Accountant

Employment Outlook: With the installation of sophisticated data processing equipment, the growth of employment opportunities within the insurance industry is expected to slow somewhat through the year 2000. Most of these job openings will result from the need to replace workers who will retire or transfer to other jobs. The employment of insurance workers such as agents and brokers who work outside the office contacting clients is expected to grow more rapidly. The opportunities will be best for ambitious people who enjoy sales work and who develop skills in a wide range of insurance and financial services. The volume of insurance sales is expected to grow through the year 2000, indicating an increasing demand for workers in the insurance industry. That growth plus a rather

high turnover of insurance agents and brokers will cause this field to continue to be a popular employment area.

Future Changes: The demand for insurance workers will probably always be dependent on the volume of future sales. This volume will probably increase rapidly over the next decade as many more workers enter the 25-54 age group—an age period when insurance is especially important. People in this group have the greatest need

for life and health insurance and protection for homes, cars, and other possessions.

What Is Done on the Job: Many of the positions within the insurance field require fre-

563

quent contact with clients—both clients who may buy or who have bought insurance. Claims adjusters and claims examiners, for instance, must meet with policyholders when they investigate a claim and decide how much, if anything, should be paid. They must treat policyholders fairly and courteously. Agents, those workers who find new customers and sell them the kinds of insurance needed, also may deliver claim checks to those who have had a loss. Agents must be able to get along well with people. All workers who have contacts with the public should have pleasant manners and should be able to talk easily with a great variety of people. An honest desire to help people is also important for workers in this career area.

Some insurance specialists must be very good in math and statistics. Actuaries, for example, are responsible for determining the risks assumed by insurance companies when they sell policies. Accountants and data processing managers also are important in making sure that appropriate records are maintained and analyzed. Actuaries, accountants, and data processing managers work together as an important management team.

Education and Training: Insurance companies usually prefer employees with college training. Many companies, however, are willing to hire high school graduates, especially people who are ambitious. Many community colleges and other colleges and universities offer training in insurance to help prepare workers for this industry.

In addition, all states require people who market insurance to be licensed by the state. The license is issued only after the applicant has passed a test.

Salary Levels: The salaries paid in the insurance field vary a great deal. They are competitive with salaries paid to people with comparable skills in other businesses. The largest single group of employees is sales agents and insurance brokers. As beginners, they are guaranteed a moderate salary and later begin earning good commissions as a percentage of their insurance sales.

A typical salary for a new agent is about $1,800 per month. Life insurance sales agents with five or more years experience will earn about $50,000 per year, with many eventually earning more than $100,000 per year.

For Additional Information: Most insurance companies are eager to provide information free of charge to people interested in their business. Information on state licensing requirements can be obtained from the department of insurance at any state capital. Information about careers in insurance is also available from the following organizations:

American Council of Life Insurance
10001 Pennsylvania Avenue, N.W.
Washington, DC 20004

The National Association of Life
   Underwriters
1922 F Street, N.W.
Washington, DC 20006

Insurance Information Institute
110 William Street
New York, NY 10038

Alliance of American Insurers
1501 Woodfield Rd., Suite 400
Schaumburg, IL 60173

Independent Insurance Agents of America
100 Church Street
New York, NY 10007

National Association of Professional
   Insurance Agents
400 N. Washington Street
Alexandria, VA 22314

Financial Management

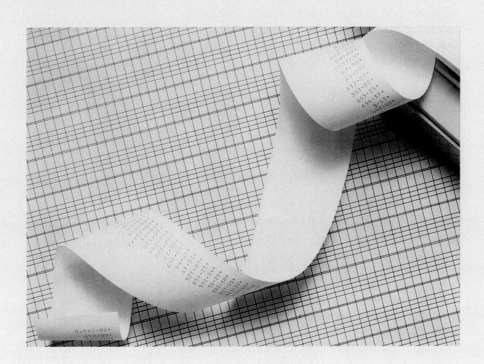

Unit Goals

After studying the chapters in this unit, you will be able to:

1. *Explain the importance of wise money management for individuals and families.*
2. *Describe how to create and use a budget for an individual family.*
3. *Discuss the steps involved in developing and using a financial plan.*

Financial Management—A Skill for Everyone

Business Brief

What do a $1 million lottery winner, Coleco Industries, and New York City have in common? Despite having lots of money, each has experienced financial difficulty.

A recent winner of the Maryland lottery ended up in debt, despite receiving $50,000 a year for 20 years. She squandered her income on nonessentials, leaving an inadequate amount of money for medical expenses and taxes. Coleco, while having great financial success with the Cabbage Patch doll products, spent large amounts of money to develop other products that were not well received by consumers. In the mid-1970s, New York City had financial problems as a result of spending much more than it collected in taxes.

Having large sums of money does not mean that a person or organization can ignore financial management activities. Every individual, family, business, and government unit must go through a series of steps when managing their finances.

First, there is the process of setting goals. Financial goals for a household may be to buy a house, to take a vacation, or to save for retirement. The goals of a business, commonly called organizational objectives, may be quite different from those of an individual or family. A main goal of a business involves increasing income from sales and reducing operating costs. In a similar manner, government has a goal to efficiently use its tax revenue in a cost-effective manner to serve the needs of the public.

The second step in financial management deals with creating a budget. Most of us are familiar with individual or family budgets. A business must also establish a budget. It must decide whether to use its money to buy additional computer equipment or to modernize its stores, offices, warehouses, and factories. Governments, too, cannot spend unlimited amounts of money. A government's budget reflects decisions about what is important and how available revenue will be spent.

The third step in the process involves an identification of the sources of funds. Whether for an individual, business, or government, available funds can only come from two sources—income and borrowing. You may already be receiving money, or an income, from a job. A business receives its income from the sales of goods and services. And a government, such as New York City, has tax revenue as its source of income.

Debt financing is an important part of financial management. As we all know, individuals, businesses, and governments borrow to help finance their activities. Remember, however, that borrowing is only a temporary source of funds. Unlike a regular income, the debt (along with interest) must be repaid. An ability to use credit wisely is vital to successful financial management, whether you are managing personal finances, running a business, or making decisions in government.

The final step in the financial management process involves evaluation of progress; in other words, is progress being made toward certain goals? Estimating revenue or income and comparing actual expenses each month with planned expenses is the heart of the evaluation process.

Foundations for Sensible Money Management

Chapter 40

Chapter Objectives

After studying this chapter and completing the end-of-chapter activities, you will be able to:

1. *Develop money management goals.*

2. *Discuss the importance of making decisions.*

3. *Identify the elements of personal financial statements.*

4. *Create a personal balance sheet.*

5. *Develop a personal income statement.*

6. *List techniques of wise money management.*

Money plays an important role in many of our daily activities. You will need to make many decisions about how to spend your money on the things you want. If you are like most people, you will never have enough money to buy everything you want. The satisfaction you get from spending your money will depend to a large extent upon the quality of your financial decisions.

The one thing most of us have in common is a desire to use wisely the money we have so that our needs, wants, and goals will be satisfied. While no individual, family, or organization is likely to have every desire met, various money management techniques can help you use wisely the financial resources that are available to you.

MONEY MANAGEMENT

As a high school graduate, you are likely to earn close to $1 million in your lifetime. If you become a college graduate, you can expect to earn even more. While this may seem like a great deal of money, remember that you will be responsible for many living expenses. You will have to pay for food, housing, clothing, transportation as well as other goods and services you need and desire. Upon beginning a career and living on your own, you will face the same problem you face now—having a limited amount of money to pay for all the goods and services you want and need.

This basic economic problem, which was discussed in Chapter 1, can be resolved by learning to carefully manage your money and to live within your income. **Income** is the money you receive from work that you do and from money that you invest. As you know, a person's income will vary based on the type of work he or she does. Your income will also be influenced by the level of education and amount of experience you have.

Money management refers to the day-to-day financial activities associated with using limited income to satisfy your unlimited needs and wants. Money management involves getting the most for your money through careful planning, saving, and spending; it involves creating and using a plan for spending.

Many people have the wrong idea about money management. They think it means pinching pennies, doing without things, and not having any fun. They are wrong. If you learn to manage your money well, you will be able to buy the things you really want that you may not have been able to buy before. Planning ahead and deciding what is really important will help you to have money to spend on the things you enjoy.

Developing Goals

Money management starts with setting attainable financial goals. **Goals** are those things you want to achieve; they may be short-term or long-term goals. A short-term financial goal, for example, might be to pay off debts or to purchase a compact disc player. Long-range goals often involve large amounts of money. A family's long-range goal might be to take a trip to a foreign country or to provide college educations for the children. A personal long-range goal might be to open your own business.

Goals are personal. They are not the same for all people, or even for everyone within a given age group. Goals are affected by such things as a person's age, family situation, interests, and values. Financial goals, as they relate to developing and implementing a financial plan, will be discussed in greater detail in Chapter 42.

Making Decisions

Money management can be seen as part of the process for making the economic decisions that were discussed in Chapter 1. Money, of course, is limited and individuals and families must decide how to use the money that is available to them. The main decisions we each make involve three areas:

1. *Paying for basic needs.* Needs are those things that are necessary for survival such as food, clothing, and shelter. Everyone's basic needs, however, are not exactly the same. Needs depend on where you live and what life-style you follow. If you live in a southern city, for example, you have different transportation and clothing needs from those who live on a large ranch in a northwestern state. For some people, an apartment is ideal; others may need a house. In any case, after you have met these basic needs, you must decide how to use the money that remains.

Illus. 40-1
Saving for a vacation is a long-range goal for many families.

2. *Saving for future expenses.* After providing for your basic needs, you should decide how to prepare for large expenses in the future. As you learned in Chapter 31, you do this by developing a savings program. Everyone has special reasons for saving. Maybe you want to buy a car or save for college, or perhaps you want to start a business that requires expensive equipment. Unless you manage your money wisely and plan your savings, you may not be able to do or buy the things you want.

3. *Spending discretionary income.* The third decision you must make when managing your money is how to spend any money you have available after you have taken care of your basic needs and future expenses. These funds are referred to as **discretionary income**. This is income you spend to buy the things you want for pleasure, satisfaction, and comfort. Discretionary income, for example, is spent on such things as entertainment, travel, compact discs, or hobby supplies. Spending discretionary income is usually more fun than buying basic items or saving and can be seen as your reward for good money management.

Buying Wisely

Most of us have more needs and wants than we could ever hope to satisfy. We must stretch our limited incomes as far as possible. Wise buying is an important way to stretch your income.

As discussed in Unit 5, to buy wisely you must gather information carefully before making your purchases. You must plan your purchases so that you buy the right good or service at the right time and at the right price. Unplanned buying often leads to disappointment and wasted money. Planned buying leads to better use of money and greater satisfaction from the things you buy.

Using Possessions Properly

After careful planning and buying, you should use your possessions properly. Using your possessions carelessly wastes money. Clothing must be cleaned and repaired or it may become unwearable. Automobiles and motorcycles need regular tune-ups and oil changes. Things you own will give you greater satisfaction and last longer with proper care. Taking care of your possessions is an important part of money management.

Living Within an Income

Do you ever run out of money before the end of the month? Many people have that problem. They have not learned to live within their incomes. Living on the amount that you have available is a central idea in money management. Creating and using a budget to help you live within your income is discussed in the next chapter.

Illus. 40-2
Proper use and
care of your
possessions is an
important part of
wise money
management.

YOUR CURRENT FINANCIAL POSITION

The process of good money management starts with knowing your current financial position. When viewing a baseball or football game, most people want to know the score as the game progresses. In the money management game, score is kept with the use of financial statements. The two most common financial statements are the balance sheet and income statement.

Creating a Personal Balance Sheet

"How much money do you have?" may be the first question many people would ask when measuring your financial situation. The answer to that question, however, would not give the entire picture since most people have other items of value besides money. A **balance sheet** reports what a person or family owns as well as owes. It is also called the *statement of net worth*.

The main components of a balance sheet are displayed in Figure 40-1 and consist of the following categories:

1. **Assets** are items of value and include such things as money in bank accounts, investments, furniture, clothing, automobiles, jewelry, and rare coins. The current value of all assets of an individual or family is the first thing reported on a balance sheet.

Figure 40-1 A personal balance sheet is used to report your current financial position.

ASSETS   LIABILITIES

NET
WORTH

2. **Liabilities** are amounts owed to others. These debts may include credit
   card balances, automobile loans, a home mortgage, or personal loans.
   Total liabilities are the second item on a balance sheet.
3. **Net worth** is the difference between a person's or family's assets and
   liabilities. This difference represents the amount of money that could be
   claimed if all assets were sold for cash and all debts were paid off. For
   example, if a family has $163,000 in assets (including the value of a
   home and other valuables) and has $98,000 in debts (mainly the home
   mortgage), the family has a net worth of $65,000.

A balance sheet is a helpful way to measure a financial situation. Every
business will prepare a balance sheet either once a month or every three
months to determine if the value of the company has increased or decreased.
In the same way, a balance sheet can help an individual or family in
measuring its financial situation.

Creating a Personal Income Statement

A balance sheet reports assets, liabilities, and net worth on a given date.
Almost everyday, however, business transactions occur that change these
balance sheet items. For example, when you make a loan payment, the
amount of your liabilities decreases. If you save part of your earnings, your
assets and net worth increase. To examine changes in a person's net worth,
another financial statement can be helpful. An **income statement** reports the
inflow and outflow of money for a given period of time, such as for a month.
As shown in Figure 40-2, there are two major components of an income
statement: income and expenses.

The first part of an income statement reports your financial inflow, or
income. This is the money you have available to spend as a result of working

Figure 40-2 A personal income statement reports your income and expenses.

FINANCIAL INFLOW

- Wages
- Salary
- Tips
- Interest
- Dividends
- Bonus
- Gifts
- Other Income

FINANCIAL OUTFLOW

- Housing Costs
- Food
- Clothing
- Transportation
- Health Care
- Insurance
- Gifts and Donations
- Recreation and Entertainment

NET INCREASE
OR DECREASE
IN NET WORTH

or from other income such as interest earned on your savings. When preparing an income statement, you should first report your **net income**, or **take-home pay**, which is the amount received after taxes and other deductions have been subtracted from your total earnings. Your take-home pay is used on your income statement since this is the amount you actually have available to spend.

The next step necessary for creating an income statement is to maintain records of all spending. The amounts spent for food, clothing, transportation, and other living costs are called **expenditures**. Keeping track of how much is spent for various living expenses will help you to plan and control your spending. In the next chapter, you will see how your personal income statement can be used to develop a budget.

The final step in preparing the income statement is to subtract your total expenditures from your total income. If you have spent less than you had in income, the difference represents an increase in your net worth. Most likely this amount will be kept in savings for future needs or wants. If you spent more than you had in income, you either had to use some of your savings or had to use credit to pay these additional expenses. As you can easily see, if you spend more than you have available for too many months, you will eventually use up all of your savings or get into credit difficulty.

MANAGING YOUR MONEY WISELY

While effective money management may seem like a lot of trouble, poor money management practices can result in a poor credit rating, arguments with family members about money, and money shortages, to name just a few problems. For wise money management, practice the following behaviors on a regular basis:

- *Plan carefully.* Setting goals and knowing what you really need and want will help you to avoid financial difficulties while also obtaining enjoyment from the resources you have available.
- *Make wise decisions.* By using the decision-making process discussed in Chapter 1, you will be able to make effective use of your limited resources.
- *Use information.* Much is written about budgeting and financial planning. Articles in magazines, such as *Money* and *Changing Times*, can help you better understand and take action on your money matters.
- *Compare products and prices.* As discussed in Unit 5, comparison buying—achieved by reading ads, using label information, and analyzing different brands—can help you get the most for your money. Being a wise consumer is one of the basic principles of effective money management.

Increasing Your Business Vocabulary

The following terms should become part of your business vocabulary. For each numbered item, find the term that has the same meaning.

assets
balance sheet
discretionary income
expenditures
goals
income

income statement
liabilities
money management
net income or take-home pay
net worth

1. The financial statement that reports what a person or family owns as well as owes.
2. Income available to spend after money has been set aside for basic needs and future expenses.
3. The difference between a person's or family's assets and liabilities.
4. Day-to-day financial activities associated with using limited income to satisfy unlimited needs and wants.
5. The amounts spent for food, clothing, transportation, and other living costs.
6. Amounts owed to others.
7. The financial statement that reports the inflow and outflow of money for a given period of time.
8. The things you want to achieve.
9. The amount received after taxes and other deductions have been subtracted from total earnings.
10. Items of value.
11. The money you receive from work that you do and from money you invest.

Reviewing Your Reading

1. What activities are associated with money management?
2. List four factors that affect a person's goals.

3. What are the three main decisions associated with money management?
4. List four goods or services for which you might spend discretionary income.
5. How is proper use of your possessions part of good money management?
6. What are the three main components of a balance sheet?

7. What is the purpose of an income statement?
8. What must a person or family do if more money is spent than is received in a certain month?
9. Name four wise money management techniques.

Using Your Business Knowledge

1. Describe the difference between short-term and long-term goals. Give two examples of each type.
2. List some items that might be a want for one person but a need for someone else.
3. What are some actions people can take to use properly their possessions and avoid wasting money?
4. Identify each of the following items as an asset or a liability:

a. Money owed to the dentist
b. An automobile
c. Clothing
d. Savings account
e. Credit card balance
f. Amount due for a personal loan
g. 100 shares of stock

Computing Business Problems

1. The Gage family's assets total $134,500. Their total liabilities are $57,800. What is the amount of their net worth?
2. Mike Collins has a monthly income of $1,510. Each month Mike has to make a loan payment of $135 for his car. What percentage of his income is used for the automobile loan payments?
3. Dorothy Christensen decided to change the oil and filter in her car. She bought five quarts of 10W40 multiweight oil for $1.35 per quart and an oil filter for $4.29.
   a. How much was the total bill for the oil and filter, including 5 percent sales tax?

   b. How much did Dorothy save if a service station would have charged her $18 for the oil and filter change?
4. Beth Hamlin is a computer software marketing representative. She earns a basic salary of $250 per month plus a commission that is 5 percent of her sales. In addition, Beth earns $70 in interest and dividends.
   a. In a month with $48,000 in sales, what would Beth's total income be?
   b. What percent of her total income is from each item (basic salary, commission, and interest and dividends)?

Expanding Your Understanding of Business

1. Prepare a list of problems that could be the result of poor money management. Talk to several people about the techniques they use to achieve good money management.

2. "The more you earn, the more you spend." Do you agree or disagree with this statement? Why? How does a person's life-style relate to this statement?

3. Besides the money they spend themselves, teenagers have another important effect on the American economy. This effect results from what they have to say about how their family's money is spent. In what ways does having a teenager in the family influence a family's spending?

4. Contact a major company to obtain a copy of its annual report, or check with your local library to see if annual reports are available. Find the balance sheet and income statement for the corporation. How is the information on these financial statements similar to the information that appears on the balance sheet and income statement for an individual or family?

Budgeting Your Finances

Chapter 41

Chapter Objectives

After studying this chapter and completing the end-of-chapter activities, you will be able to:

1. *Describe the steps involved in the budgeting process.*

2. *List the ways in which a budget can be of value to an individual or family.*

3. *Discuss the importance of goals in the budgeting process.*

4. *Give three examples of fixed expenses.*

5. *Name eight categories that could be used for a budget.*

6. *Explain why budgets must be revised from time to time.*

Dana Collins has saved $750 for a school trip from her earnings. She will compete in the regional finals of theater competition in the drama category. Funds are needed to cover travel, lodging, and food expenses. Two days before she is scheduled to leave, Dana receives a letter requesting a $200 deposit to reserve her place at the college she plans to attend next fall.

Dana, however, remembers that she put aside part of her earnings in a special savings account. She will be able to pay the $200 deposit. Dana's ability to develop and use a plan for saving and spending resulted in her achieving two goals—competing in the regional competition and starting college next fall.

WHAT IS A BUDGET?

By developing a specific plan for saving and spending income, you will be able to make wise personal economic decisions. A **budget** allows you to meet your personal goals with a system of saving and wise spending. Your plan may be a simple record of how much money you make, how much you plan to spend, and how much you want to save. Or, your budget may be a more detailed record that includes specific amounts to be spent in categories such as food, clothing, and transportation. A good budget should take very little of your time, but it should be specific enough to provide needed information on your spending and savings plans. Having a written budget is an important phase of successful money management.

THE BUDGETING PROCESS

The main purposes of a budget are to help you (1) live within your income, (2) achieve your financial goals, (3) buy wisely, (4) avoid credit problems, (5) plan for financial emergencies, and (6) develop good money management skills. The process of creating and using a budget is shown in Figure 41-1. These steps can be used by any individual, family, or organization to assist them in using available financial resources.

Figure 41-1 A budget is an important component of successful money management.

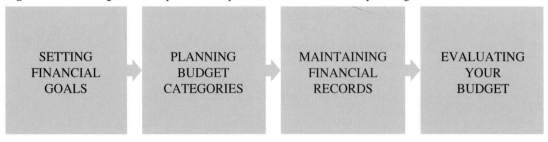

Setting Financial Goals

As mentioned in the previous chapter, your goals are the starting point of any financial decision. These future plans assist you in deciding how you want to spend and save your money. If you want to set aside money for college, you are likely to budget more for savings. If you are currently working at a job that requires you to spend a large portion of your income for transportation, you are likely to budget more for transportation.

Using the financial statements explained in Chapter 40 can also help you develop financial goals. Your balance sheet presents your current financial position. An income statement reports how you have spent your money over a certain time period, such as a month. By reviewing these documents you can decide where you would like to be financially and develop your budget accordingly.

Planning Budget Categories

Many financial advisers recommend that an amount be set aside for savings as the first component of a budget. If savings are not considered first, other expenses may use up all of the available income and leave nothing for future goals. After savings, two other types of living expenses must be considered: fixed and variable expenses. **Fixed expenses** are costs that occur regularly and are for the same amount each time. Examples of fixed expenses are rent, mortgage payments, and insurance premiums.

Variable expenses are living costs involving differing amounts each time and are usually more difficult to estimate. These types of expenses include food, clothing, and utilities, such as telephone and electricity. Certain types of variable expenses, such as medical and dental costs, may occur less frequently and may be large when they do occur. Such expenses must be provided for in the budget. If budget categories are not created for these variable expenses, bills for these items could result in using up a large part of your savings.

The amount budgeted for savings and other expenditures is referred to as an **allowance**. This is the amount of money you plan to use for a certain budget category. While the budget categories can vary for different personal and family situations, savings and expenses are often classified under eight main divisions:

1. *Savings.* Savings accounts, government bonds, stocks, and other investments.
2. *Food.* Food eaten at home and meals eaten away from home.
3. *Clothing.* Clothing, shoes, dry cleaning, sewing supplies, and repairs.
4. *Household.* Rent, mortgage payments, taxes, insurance, gas, electricity, coal, fuel oil, telephone, water, household furnishings, household supplies, painting, and repairs.

Illus. 41-1
Certain types of
living expenses,
such as telephone
bills, will vary
from month to
month.

5. *Transportation.* Automobile payments, insurance, automobile upkeep and operating costs, public transportation fares, and auto and drivers' licenses.
6. *Health and personal care.* Medical and dental expenses, medications, eyeglasses, hospital and nursing expenses, accident and health insurance, hair care costs, and children's allowances.
7. *Recreation and education.* Books, magazines, newspapers, theater tickets, concerts, vacations, school expenses, hobbies, radio, television, musical instruments, and club dues.
8. *Gifts and contributions.* Donations to church, charitable contributions, and personal gifts.

The logical question at this point is, "How much should I set aside for each category?" The answer to this question will be determined by several factors. Planned spending for various budget categories will depend on income, family size, ages of children, the current cost of living in your area, work-related expenses as well as personal values, needs, and goals.

The income statement discussed in Chapter 40 can help you develop budget categories. This financial statement reports the categories in which your money has been spent and provides a basis for your budget. Other assistance for developing a budget can come from government reports on family spending or from articles in personal finance magazines, such as

Changing Times and *Money*. Figure 41-2 provides some suggested percentages for typical budget categories. In addition to this information, your budget should also consider estimates for future income and living expenses. The Martinez budget, as shown in Figure 41-3, is an example of a family budget for one month.

Figure 41-2
The amount set aside for various living expenses will vary depending upon the family situation and life-style.

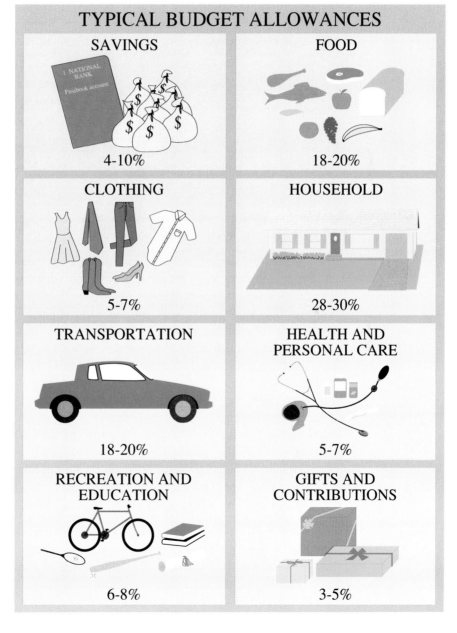

TYPICAL BUDGET ALLOWANCES

SAVINGS
4-10%

FOOD
18-20%

CLOTHING
5-7%

HOUSEHOLD
28-30%

TRANSPORTATION
18-20%

HEALTH AND PERSONAL CARE
5-7%

RECREATION AND EDUCATION
6-8%

GIFTS AND CONTRIBUTIONS
3-5%

Figure 41-3
The Martinez family's monthly budget.

The Martinez Household Monthly Budget January, 19--				
Estimated Income			*Estimated Expenditures*	
Manuel's net income	1,325	00	Savings	225	00
Lydia's net income	1,250	00	Food	500	00
			Clothing	175	00
			Household	725	00
			Transportation	475	00
			Health & Personal Care	150	00
			Recreation & Education	200	00
			Gifts & Contributions	125	00
Total Income	2,575	00	Total Savings & Expenditures	2,575	00

Maintaining Financial Records

After planning a budget, individuals and families should set up an income and expenditure record to find out if their plan is working. An example of this type of document is shown in Figure 41-4. The first line of this report shows the monthly income available to the family ($2,575) and the budget allowances for each budget category.

The first payment entry of the month was for money put into a savings account. By setting aside that amount first, the family could be sure of saving part of their income. Entries for expenditures were recorded each Saturday and at the end of the month, except for especially large payments which were recorded immediately. Since the family pays most bills by check, a checkbook is an easy reference for the information needed to prepare the income and expenditure record. Incomes were entered on the days they were received, and all columns were totaled at the end of the month.

Evaluating Your Budget

At the end of the month, it is necessary to compare actual spending with the budgeted amounts. Any difference between these two amounts is called a **budget variance**. If actual spending is greater than planned spending, such as for the Martinez's ''Clothing'' and ''Household'' categories, it is referred to as a *deficit*. When actual spending is less than the budgeted amount, as

Figure 41-4 An account record of income and expenses is an important part of the budgeting process.

The Martinez Household
Income and Expenditures Record

Date		Explanation	Totals		Distribution of Savings and Expenditures							
			Receipts	Payments	Savings	Food	Clothing	House-hold	Trans-portation	Health & personal care	Rec. & Educ.	Gift & Contrib.
		Budget $2,575			225 00	500 00	175 00	725 00	475 00	150 00	200 00	125 00
Jan 1990	1	Balance	300 00									
	2			225 00	225 00							
	7			345 00		95 00	50 00	30 00	30 00	75 00	20 00	45 00
	14	Manuel's Salary	662 50	199 00		80 00	29 00	5 00	20 00	10 00	45 00	10 00
	15	Lydia's Salary	625 00									
	16	Mortgage Payment		650 00				650 00				
	17	Car Payment		325 00					325 00			
	21			250 00		95 00	40 00	60 00	20 00		25 00	10 00
	28	Manuel's Salary	662 50	281 00		90 00	87 00	3 00	30 00	6 00	60 00	5 00
	29	Lydia's Salary	625 00									
	31	Totals	2,875 00	2,275 00	225 00	360 00	206 00	748 00	425 00	91 00	150 00	70 00
	31	Balance		600 00								
			2,875 00	2,875 00								
Feb.	1	Balance	600 00									

with their "Food" and "Transportation" categories, a *surplus* occurs. A category by category comparison allows you to find areas where changes in the budget may be appropriate.

CHARACTERISTICS OF A SUCCESSFUL BUDGET

A difference between the actual amount spent and the budgeted amount does not automatically mean a change in your spending plan is necessary. Your budgeted amount may still be appropriate with a slight deficit or surplus occurring every couple of months in certain categories. However, if you expect continued higher or lower spending in a certain category, a change in your budget is probably needed. A budget must be realistic. It should reflect your current income and planned spending.

A budget should also be flexible. When unexpected expenses arise, your spending plan should be able to handle these living costs. Every few months, an individual or family should evaluate the budget to determine if it still is appropriate.

A successful budget must be well planned and clearly communicated to those involved. All members of a family should discuss financial goals, wants and needs, and plans for spending. In addition, the best spending plan should be written so that all affected by it can review its components. Your written budget can be kept in a notebook or in a specialized budgeting book purchased from an office supply store. Most important, the budget format should be simple. If it is too detailed and difficult to understand, family members may not be willing to use the spending plan.

As personal computers have become more common, people are using computerized budgets. A spreadsheet program, as discussed in Unit 6, can be used to record and process financial information. In addition, a wide range of software designed for home and family budgets is available, ranging in cost from under $10 to several hundred dollars.

OTHER METHODS OF BUDGETING

While a written budget is most common, and usually the most appropriate, other types of savings and spending plans are also used. Some people believe a checkbook is an effective budgeting system. However, a checking account does not serve the purpose of planning for spending. Your checks are a record of purchases and paid bills, but you still need a plan for using income.

Many people will say they keep their budgets ''in their heads'' rather than on paper. This simple system may work for an individual with limited income and few financial obligations, but a family with a larger income and more living expenses would find it ineffective. A person with a mental budget is also in danger of forgetting how much is to be spent on certain items.

Another system used by families is envelopes or folders marked with labels such as ''Food,'' ''Housing,'' and ''Automobile Expenses.'' Each envelope or folder contains the budgeted amount of money, and expenses are paid from the available money in the envelopes. With a budget of this type, there is the danger of keeping large amounts of cash in the home to cover expenses.

Illus. 41-2
Successful
budgeting
requires
involvement by
all household
members.

Increasing Your Business Vocabulary

The following terms should become part of your business vocabulary. For each numbered item, find the term that has the same meaning.

allowance
budget
budget variance

fixed expenses
variable expenses

1. Costs that occur regularly and are for the same amount each time.
2. The amount budgeted for savings and other expenditures.
3. A plan that allows you to meet your personal goals with a system of saving and wise spending.

4. Living costs involving differing amounts each time and are usually more difficult to estimate.
5. A difference between actual spending and planned spending.

Reviewing Your Reading

1. What are six ways in which a budget can help you?

2. What is the first step in the budgeting process?

3. Why should savings be the first amount considered in planning budget categories?
4. Name some examples of fixed expenses.
5. Why are variable expenses more difficult to budget for than fixed expenses?
6. What factors influence the amount set aside for various budget categories?
7. Does a budget variance mean that you should change your spending plan?

8. What are the characteristics of a successful budget?
9. Is a checkbook a type of written budget? Explain.
10. What types of budgets are available for use by an individual or a family?

Using Your Business Knowledge

1. "If you only spend money on things you really need, you will always have money for the things you really want." Do you agree with this statement? Explain your answer.
2. Some people believe they make enough money and do not have to have a budget. Explain why you believe this statement is true or not?
3. Some people claim that living by a budget is too structured and restrictive. That is, they do not like to live such a planned and strict economic life. What would you say to those individuals who have that point of view in order to convince them that budgets can be helpful to everyone?
4. Every week Chris Thorson puts any amount he has not spent during the week into a savings account. If he needs more money than he has during a week, he withdraws it from his savings. Is Chris following a good money management plan? Explain.
5. Consider a family of four people: the mother, a supermarket manager; the father, a department store salesperson; and two children, ages 14 and 11.
   a. List four fixed expenses that this family would likely have each month.
   b. What are some variable expenses that they are likely to have?
   c. How are the family's expenses different from those of other families with younger children or no children?

Computing Business Problems

1. Mary and Fred James budgeted $260 a month for groceries. During the month, they spent $87, $62, $28, $49, and $38 at the supermarket.
   a. What was the total amount spent for food?
   b. Did Mary and Fred have a budget deficit or surplus for food? What was the amount?
2. You are currently budgeting $650 for insurance costs, and you expect the premiums to increase by 7 percent for next year. How much should you budget for insurance next year?
3. A family has $2,050 to spend each month. They plan to spend $425 on food, $150 on clothing, $710 on rent, $175 on transportation, and want to save $160.
   a. What percentage does the family plan to spend on each item?
   b. How much does the family have available to budget for other living expenses?

Expanding Your Understanding of Business

1. Talk to family members, neighbors, and friends about the types of budgets they use. How helpful are these budgets for achieving financial goals?

2. What are some methods that could be used to help you save money for future expenses or financial goals?

3. Locate an article in a magazine or newspaper, or obtain information from the federal government, on the amount families spend on various budget categories. Discuss the personal and economic factors that influence budgeting with your class.

4. From newspapers, the library, or other information sources, try to find out how much money was budgeted for the following items by your city, town, or county.
   a. Education (schools)
   b. Streets and highways
   c. Police department
   d. Fire department
   e. Public library
   f. Parks

Planning Your Financial Future

Chapter 42

Chapter Objectives

After studying this chapter and completing the end-of-chapter activities, you will be able to:

1. Explain four advantages of financial planning.

2. List the five financial planning steps.

3. Give examples of financial goals.

4. Explain how a financial plan is implemented.

5. Describe two forms of income insurance.

6. Ask at least three questions useful in choosing a financial planner.

As you begin your study of this final chapter, you might reflect for a moment on the valuable things you have learned in your introduction to business course. You have had an opportunity to examine the roles of business, government, labor, and consumers in our economy. You have learned about how technology affects business. Many aspects of finance and credit have also been covered, and you have acquired information about saving, investing, protecting, and managing money.

In order to put into practice all that you have learned about our economy and about earning and saving money, you must have a plan. Successful coaches talk about game plans. Travel agents refer to vacation plans. Builders must have house plans. And successful consumers and businesspeople must have a financial plan. A **financial plan** is a report that summarizes your current financial condition, acknowledges your financial needs, and sets a direction for your future financial activities. **Financial planning** includes evaluating one's financial position, setting financial goals, and guiding activities and resources toward reaching those goals.

THE NEED FOR FINANCIAL PLANNING

Everyone should have a carefully developed financial plan. Your financial plan should encompass all that you have learned about good money management, should be developed thoughtfully, and should be evaluated and updated frequently. A well-developed financial plan can make your financial life a great deal more satisfying and stress free. Ultimately, it will become a blueprint for an improved standard of living. Financial planning will offer you several specific advantages:

- Your financial uncertainties will be reduced.
- You will gain more control of your financial affairs.
- Your family or associates will have a way of knowing more specifically of your financial affairs in case there is a need for them to assume control of your finances.
- Earning, spending, protecting, and saving your resources will be more systematic.

Financial planning should follow a set of steps. These steps will be a reflection of the decision-making process, as discussed in Chapter 1. The first step in the process is to analyze your current financial condition. You should list your assets and liabilities, as discussed in Chapter 40. The second step is to develop your financial goals. What short-term and long-term objectives do you have? Next, you must create your financial plan. This will take the most time and require the most thought; it may also require additional help from a financial planner. The fourth step is to actually implement the plan. This may involve buying or selling things, moving bank accounts, acquiring insurance, or any number of financial activities. Finally, you will frequently evaluate and revise your financial plan.

DETERMINING YOUR FINANCIAL CONDITION

The first step in financial planning is usually a careful and honest analysis of where you are financially. You must determine your current financial position in terms of income, savings, investments, property, living expenses, insurance, and money owed. This step is thought by many to be a prerequisite to the development of financial goals.

A Financial Inventory

Taking an inventory of your financial affairs is a lot like a physician giving you a physical examination. As the doctor's exam requires an assessment of your health, your financial inventory includes a careful appraisal of your finances. This inventory is most frequently completed through the use of the personal balance sheet, which you read about in Chapter 40. Completing a financial inventory will provide you with the beginning of a more orderly financial life as well as serve as an important first step in financial planning.

Illus. 42-1
The first step in financial planning is determining your current financial condition.

A Personal Financial Filing System

In order to keep your financial statement current and to keep all of your records orderly and within easy reach, you will need a personal financial filing system. Handling your financial affairs is a little like operating a small business. You will have taxes to pay, income to track, insurance to buy, charge accounts to monitor, and savings to manage—to name just a few items.

Well-organized files are valuable to financial planning. Rather than try to break down all of your different financial activities into numerous individual files, it is probably simpler to maintain a few basic categories. These files should contain all of the documents and records associated with such things as contracts, bills, receipts, bank balances, and legal papers. The contents of these files will become an invaluable resource to you as you progress with your financial planning.

SETTING FINANCIAL GOALS

Once you have a clear understanding of your financial condition, you will be able to develop a realistic set of financial goals. Financial goals are usually stated in dollar amounts. Examples of some financial goals are:

- Saving $2,000 in one year.
- Purchasing a $200 bicycle in June.
- Increasing your income by $2,000 by your twentieth birthday.
- Paying off your $750 credit card balance by March.

You will notice each goal requires that you save or acquire a specific amount of money in a specific period of time. These goals are very simple, straightforward, and relatively short term. However, financial goals associated with a financial plan are often more complex and achievable only over a long period of time. They might include such objectives as:

- Owning your own home by age 40.
- Paying for a college education for your daughter.
- Taking a trip to Europe in five years.
- Receiving a retirement income equal to 50 percent of your salary at age 64.

In the process of developing and carrying out your financial plan, you will quickly discover that it is often necessary to compromise short-term goals in order to accomplish long-term ones. You may have to forgo a movie to pay for a bicycle. In any event, without establishing goals, it will be difficult for you to measure your financial progress through your life cycle.

A Financial Life Cycle

Most people's lives follow a predictable pattern called a *life cycle*. Each stage of your life is distinguished by unique characteristics, requirements, and expectations. For example, during the teen years, people are exploring career options, developing plans for eventual independence, evaluating future financial needs and resources, and developing an understanding of the financial system. In their twenties, people are training for careers, establishing households, marrying, and having children.

The thirties and forties sometimes involve more education, more children, developing retirement plans, paying for children's education,

Illus. 42-2
Each stage of your financial life cycle will be different.

investing, and estate planning. In the fifties and sixties, people tend to guard their assets more carefully, work toward financial security, and reevaluate living arrangements.

Each of these life stages has financial matters that need attention. That attention can be provided through the development of a good financial plan. Remember, a good plan is one that is flexible and useful throughout several life cycles.

Retirement and Estate Planning

Although it seems a long time off, retirement is considered by many people to be the heart of financial goal setting. The chances are very good that you will spend many happy and healthy years in retirement. They will be happier and healthier if you have done some financial planning that results in an adequate supply of money during those years.

Estate planning involves the accumulation and management of property during one's lifetime and the distribution of one's property at death. It is a part of retirement planning and is an integral part of financial planning. It has two parts. The first consists of building your estate through savings, investments, and insurance. The second consists of planning for the transfer of your estate, at your death, in the manner that you wish.

CREATING YOUR FINANCIAL PLAN

After you have established your financial goals, you can begin to plan for the income you will need to achieve these goals. Some may think that income is not possible to plan for or control because it is money received from someone else. To an extent that is correct, but there are aspects of income that can be planned. Or more precisely, you can develop strategies that will help you acquire the amount of income you want when you want it.

For example, if you want more income, you might ask for a raise, become qualified for a better paying job, get an additional part-time job, or invest in securities. You can also time your income so that you have money coming in when you want it. This can be done by investing at certain times, seeking increased salary at certain times, or by asking that you be paid on certain days of the month. Develop and write a plan for generating income that is consistent with your financial goals.

IMPLEMENTING YOUR FINANCIAL PLAN

Implementing your plan may involve a wide variety of actions. You may need to move your savings to an account in which you will earn a higher interest rate. You may buy a bond. Maybe you will begin to work more hours on your part-time job to earn more money. As you can see, the list of implementation possibilities is endless. The point is: For your plan to lead to the satisfaction of your goals, you must carry it out.

Insuring Your Current Income

There are some safeguards you should take to assure the success of your plan. They involve protecting your income so that it contributes to your goals. Insurance is available that will provide an income to those who fear the two most common causes of loss of income: disability and unemployment.

Disability income insurance helps replace income that is lost when you cannot work because of an illness or injury. Many different disability income policies are available. The amount of each payment, the length of the waiting period before benefits are paid, and the length of time that payments are made should be chosen on the basis of your needs. Most companies from which you can buy disability income insurance will pay from 40 to 60 percent of your salary while you are disabled. However, before the benefits begin, there is usually a waiting period from 1 week to 90 days after you are disabled. As with other kinds of insurance, the more benefits provided, the higher the price for coverage.

One of the most important forms of income protection comes through the federal government's Social Security system. The Medicare program, which you learned about in Chapter 39, is one part of the Social Security system. The other part is **retirement, survivors, and disability insurance**. This part of the insurance system provides pensions to retired workers and their families, death benefits to dependents of workers who die, and benefits to disabled workers and their families. More will be said about retirement benefits later in this chapter.

Unemployment is another hazard to a financial plan. To reduce the financial hardship of unemployment, most states have an unemployment insurance program that they operate in cooperation with the federal government. **Unemployment insurance** provides cash payments for a limited time to people who are out of work for a reason other than illness. The local unemployment office will provide guidance to help you find a new job, but if no suitable job is found, you may receive payments to replace part of your lost wages.

Guarding Your Future Income

The success of any financial plan is largely dependent on a continuing stream of future income. Once people retire, their salaries stop, but they continue to need money to cover living expenses. There are several ways for workers, sometimes with the help of their employers and the government, to insure that they will have an adequate income during their retirement years.

PENSIONS

A **pension** is a series of regular payments made to a retired worker under an organized plan. Many employers offer plans that provide monthly payments to retired workers. Similar plans are often established by professional and trade associations or unions. To qualify for a pension under most pension plans, you must work for the same organization for a minimum number of years. Some workers retire on pensions together with their Social Security benefits.

SOCIAL SECURITY

The basic idea of **Social Security** is simple. During working years, employed people pay Social Security taxes. The taxes are deducted from the employees' paychecks. Employers match the amounts paid by their employees. Self-employed people, such as farmers and small-business owners, pay the entire tax themselves.

The taxes collected are put into a special trust fund. When a worker retires, becomes disabled, or dies, monthly payments from the trust fund are made. The amount of benefits received depends to a great extent on how long a worker was employed and how much a worker earned while employed.

Those who are covered by Social Security can receive the full amount of the monthly payments to which they are entitled when they reach age 65.

Illus. 42-3
Social Security provides monthly payments when a worker retires, becomes disabled, or dies.

Starting in the year 2000, the age at which full benefits are payable will be increased in gradual steps until it reaches age 67. This will affect people born in 1938 or later.

If they choose, people can retire as early as age 62 by accepting lower payments. Workers may be entitled to full benefits if they become disabled at any age before 65. If an insured worker dies, monthly benefits are also payable to a surviving spouse and/or dependent children.

INDIVIDUAL RETIREMENT ACCOUNTS

People can also develop their own retirement income plans. The most popular of these plans is the individual retirement account (IRA). As described in Chapter 32, this is a tax-sheltered retirement plan in which people can annually invest earnings up to a certain amount. The earnings contributed and the interest earned are tax free until the time of withdrawal at age $59\frac{1}{2}$ or later.

ANNUITIES

An amount of money that an insurance company will pay at definite intervals to a person who has previously deposited money with the company is called an **annuity**. An annuity is an investment plan for retirement income that is usually purchased from an insurance company. You pay the insurance company a certain amount of money either in a lump sum or in a series of payments. In return, the company agrees to pay you a regular income beginning at a certain age and continuing for life or for a specified number of years.

EVALUATING AND REVISING YOUR FINANCIAL PLAN

A financial plan must be flexible. It is important to view your financial plan as a fluid, changeable report that will accommodate opportunity. If your plan is not producing the expected results, you must make changes. You may need to sell certain securities that are not "producing," or save more of your income each week in order to meet the goals set forth in your plan.

New financial options that you should consider and make part of your plan become available from time to time. The IRA you learned about is a good example of such an option. Several years ago this form of retirement option was not available.

SELECTING A FINANCIAL PLANNER

Developing a financial plan is not a simple task. Doing your own financial planning requires a great deal of time, information, and patience. There are

Illus. 42-4
A financial plan
can be revised at
any time.

professionals called *financial planners* who can help you. A financial planner should have at least two years of training in securities, insurance, taxes, real estate, and estate planning and have passed a rigorous examination.

There are some questions you can ask to help you choose a financial planner. They are:

- What experience and training does the financial planner have?
- Is the financial planner willing to supply you with references?
- Does the financial planner have a good reputation among other financial professionals?
- What are the financial planner's charges?

A financial planner will want to ask you some questions as well. You will need to have some idea of what your financial goals are. You must be prepared to describe your financial inventory. You should be willing to share information about your income, expenditures, and savings. With this information and your cooperation, together you can create a useful financial plan.

Increasing Your Business Vocabulary

The following terms should become part of your business vocabulary. For each numbered item, find the term that has the same meaning.

annuity
estate planning
financial plan
financial planning
pension

retirement, survivors, and disability
    insurance
Social Security
unemployment insurance

1. An activity that involves the accumulation and management of property during one's lifetime and the distribution of one's property at death.
2. A report that summarizes your current financial condition, acknowledges your financial needs, and sets a direction for your future financial activities.
3. An activity that includes evaluating one's financial position, setting financial goals, and guiding activities and resources toward reaching those goals.
4. Insurance that provides cash payments for a limited time to people who are out of work for a reason other than illness.

5. A series of regular payments made to a retired worker under an organized plan.
6. An amount of money that an insurance company will pay at definite intervals to a person who has previously deposited money with the company.
7. A tax that is put into a trust fund and provides certain benefits to retirees or beneficiaries.
8. The part of the Social Security system that provides pensions to retired workers and their families, death benefits to dependents of workers who die, and benefits to disabled workers and their families.

Reviewing Your Reading

1. What four advantages does financial planning offer you?
2. List the five steps in financial planning.
3. How do you determine your current financial position.
4. What is the purpose of a personal financial filing system?
5. How are financial goals usually stated?
6. Why is retirement planning important?

7. What are the two most common causes of loss of income?
8. From what type of business is an annuity normally purchased?
9. List three questions that you should ask when choosing a financial planner.
10. What two things influence the amount of benefits a worker receives from Social Security?

Using Your Business Knowledge

1. Why do you think it is important for your family or associates to have a way of

knowing more specifically about your financial situation?

2. Explain why financial planning is important, regardless of the size of one's financial situation.
3. List two of your short-term and one of your long-term financial goals.
4. Tell in your own words how people's financial goals change throughout their life cycle.

5. Why would you want to insure your income?
6. Give examples of activities that might be involved in implementing your financial plan.

Computing Business Problems

1. If you are a woman who is 65 years old and the average life expectancy for women indicates that you will have an estimated 19 more years of life, to what age are you likely to live?
2. If the Coopers invest $31,700 on January 1 in an account that pays 7.34 percent simple annual interest, how much interest will they earn by December 31 of that same year?
3. Your grandparents are both age 64 and are earning $52,000 per year. Their goal is to retire on an income equal to 50 percent of their salary earned at age 64. How much income will they need to have in retirement to achieve that goal?
4. You earn $25,000 per year and receive an automatic annual increase of 5 percent per year. You become disabled after you receive one 5 percent raise. You are protected by disability income insurance that pays 60 percent of your salary. How much would your annual salary be if you were disabled for one year?
5. Shelly Meinke is about to retire. She will collect a pension from a New York gas and electric company where she has been employed, as well as Social Security from the government. She has always planned to spend her retirement years in Florida, but she is worried about missing her children and grandchildren who live in New York. She plans to return to New York twice a year by car for a visit. The distance from New York City where she lives to her new home in Florida is 2,050 kilometers. How many kilometers will she travel the first year, counting the initial trip to Florida from New York?

Expanding Your Understanding of Business

1. The normal retirement age for people is 65. Some decide to retire earlier than that and others later. What are the financial implications of choosing an earlier or later retirement?
2. Investigate the pension plans of several of your local businesses, industries, or institutions. Answer the following questions for each organization:
   a. What is the minimum number of years you must work for this organization in order to qualify for the pension plan?
   b. Are there other qualifications that must be met? If so, what are they?
   c. How and when is the pension paid out?
3. State some ways that you might increase your income.
4. In selecting a financial planner, it has often been suggested that one should never take advice from someone who has something to sell. While this is a generalization, what wisdom do you see in its meaning?

Career Focus

You have just finished reading about the importance of keeping accurate and up-to-date financial records for yourself. If you find this activity to be enjoyable and satisfying, you might consider a career in accounting.

Job Titles: Job titles commonly found in this career area include:

Accountant
Accounting Clerk
Auditor
Bank Teller
Bookkeeper
Cost Accountant
Data Entry Clerk
Inventory Clerk
Payroll Clerk
Public Accountant
Tax Accountant

Employment Outlook: Because the volume of business transactions is expected to grow rapidly, there will be a corresponding increase in the need for workers who can keep financial and accounting records. Because the occupational area is exceptionally large, replacement needs produce many job openings each year. While little change is expected in the number of people employed as accounting clerks and bookkeepers through the year 2000, the need to replace workers who transfer to other occupations or leave the labor force will still remain.

Future Changes: The most significant change that is occurring in accounting is the increasing use of computers to record, store, and manipulate data. The sophisticated software packages that now are available make accounting work much easier and faster and permit employers to do much more work with the same number of employees. Success in accounting is likely to require skills in using computers and software.

What Is Done on the Job: Accounting clerks and bookkeepers maintain systematic and up-to-date records of accounts and business transactions. They also prepare periodic financial statements showing all money received and paid out. The specific duties of accountants vary with the size of the business. However, virtually all of these workers use calculators and work with computers. In small businesses, a general bookkeeper handles all the financial record keeping of business transactions, such as orders and cash sales. Accounting clerks also check money received against money paid out to be sure accounts balance, calculate the business's payroll, and

make up employees' paychecks. They prepare and mail customers' bills and answer telephone requests for information about orders and bills. In larger businesses, several accounting clerks may work under the direction of an accounting supervisor. In these organizations, workers often specialize in certain types of work. Some, for example, prepare statements of a company's income from sales or its daily operating expenses. Others record business transactions, including payroll deductions and bills paid and due, and compute interest, rental, and fee charges. They may also key vouchers, invoices, and other financial records.

Accounting workers must be good at working with numbers and details. They need to be very accurate and orderly in their work.

Education and Training: The minimum requirement for an accounting position is a high school education. Courses in business math and accounting are necessary in order to meet minimum requirements for most accounting jobs. Accounting courses from a community or junior college would be appealing to some employers. Accounting clerks who enroll in college accounting programs may advance to higher level accounting positions.

Salary Levels: Average annual earnings for accounting clerks are about $18,000 per year, ranging from $15,000 to $22,000 per year. Ten percent of them earn more than $30,000. Accountants may be in business for themselves and can earn more.

For Additional Information: Many associations, government agencies, and other organizations provide useful information on accounting careers. State employment service offices and *The Occupational Outlook Handbook* can also provide sources of information on this career area. Specific information about careers in accounting is available from:

American Institute of Certified Public
  Accountants
1211 Avenue of the Americas
New York, NY 10036

National Association of Accountants
10 Paragon Drive, Box 433
Montvale, NJ 07645

Finding and Using Information Sources

In this age of technological advancement and increased knowledge, it is impossible for you to know everything about our complex economic system. You should, however, know where to seek the information you need when you need it. By knowing what type of information is available and where to find it, you will be able to locate the desired facts and figures quickly.

LIBRARIES

Public libraries and school libraries are among the most common and frequently consulted sources for business information. You are free to visit public libraries to read books, newspapers, and magazines. Some libraries keep files of clippings on important topics. In some of the larger libraries, films and recordings can be borrowed. Public, school, and college libraries contain those reference books most likely to help you when you need to find specific information on almost any subject, including business. Helpful librarians will assist you.

In some parts of the country, traveling libraries called bookmobiles circulate through rural and suburban areas. Special libraries are maintained by many large businesses, trade associations, and clubs. Microfilms of documents or technical and scientific reports may sometimes be obtained from government and university libraries. Also, many libraries now have back issues of major newspapers on microfilm.

Databases

Modern libraries also have databases available for looking into a variety of subjects. Databases are often on-line and information is retrieved from data banks located throughout our country by using computer terminals. Some databases have information stored on disks that are available in the libraries and that are updated periodically.

General Reference Sources

Many books are designed as sources of information. When you want information of any kind, consider first the possibility of finding it in a general reference book. If one of the popular reference sources does not contain the information needed, consult a librarian or the card index in the library.

Dictionaries

The dictionary is probably the most widely used reference book. Its chief purpose is to give the spelling, pronunciation, and meaning of words; however, most dictionaries provide other useful information. Some of the more commonly used types of dictionaries are listed below.

- *Unabridged dictionary.* This is a complete dictionary giving more information about words and their meanings than smaller editions do. Unabridged dictionaries provide additional information such as the following: guide to pronunciation; abbreviations; punctuation and grammar; rules for spelling, forming plurals, and capitalizing; drawings and illustrations; tables of measures and weights, kinds of money used throughout the world, and common language phrases.
- *Abridged dictionary.* This is a condensed or shorter version of a larger dictionary. It is a handy reference on the spellings and meanings of words. An abridged dictionary may contain some of the special features of the unabridged dictionary.
- *Thesaurus.* This is a book of synonyms (words similar in meaning) and antonyms (words opposite in meaning).
- *Special dictionaries.* Special kinds of dictionaries are published for use in such fields as medicine, law, and business. Dictionaries of special interest to businesspeople and students would include *Finance and Investment* by Moore, the *Dictionary of Advertising* by Irvin, the *Dictionary of Business and Economics* by Ammer, and the *Dictionary of Business Information* by Georgi.

Encyclopedias

The most complete source of general information is the encyclopedia, which contains information taken from all fields of knowledge. Encyclopedias, like dictionaries, are published in brief as well as in comprehensive editions. Both one-volume editions and complete sets are available. Junior editions are also published for school-age children.

Encyclopedias are also published for special fields of interest such as business, education, engineering, sports, and religion. Munn's *Encyclopedia of Banking and Finance* and *Standard and Poor's Stock Market Encyclopedia* are examples in the business area.

Almanacs

An almanac is a publication with facts and figures about government, population, industries, religions, museums, education, cost of living, national defense, trade, transportation, and many other subjects. The *World Almanac* and the *Information Please Almanac* are two books of facts that are published annually. They are among our most popular up-to-date references. Paperbound editions of these almanacs can be purchased at many bookstores.

Atlases

An atlas is a book containing maps of regions and countries of the world. It includes information on populations, products, climate, history, and commerce. An atlas is very helpful in learning the location or the size of a city or a country or the agricultural and commercial products of an area.

Directories

A directory is a book listing names of people living in a certain place or engaged in a particular business, trade, or profession.

- *Telephone*. The telephone directory gives the names, addresses, and telephone numbers of people and businesses who have telephones. Some telephone directories contain a civic section that provides a highway map of the city, information about the business and industry of the city, a list of parks and playgrounds, and a summary of traffic rules. Most telephone directories have a classified section—the Yellow Pages. This is a listing of the names, addresses, and telephone numbers of suppliers of goods and services. The names are arranged in alphabetical order under headings that describe the types of businesses and services.
- *City*. A city directory lists the names, occupations, and addresses of people 18 years old and older who reside in the city for which the directory is compiled. Other information usually given includes the names of businesses, streets, clubs, churches, museums, and other institutions in the city. It is among the most useful directories to people interested in business.
- *Government*. The *Congressional Directory* and the *Congressional Record Abstracts* contain information about the federal government including the names of members of Congress. The *Book of the States* and the *Municipal Yearbook* provide similar information about state and local

governments. Another important source, published annually by the federal government, is the *United States Government Manual*. This is a valuable reference book for students, teachers, businesspeople, lawyers, and others who need information about the functions, publications, and services of U.S. government agencies.

- *Computers*. Special publications dealing with computers are being developed to help users of the technology. Examples are *Baker's Complete Sourcebook of Personal Computing* and the *Data Base Directory*, published by Knowledge Industry Publications in cooperation with the American Society for Information Science.
- *Special types*. Special types of directories include those of national businesses, public schools, school teachers and administrators, clubs, associations, and newspapers and periodicals. These can usually be found in libraries.

Books of Statistical Information

Statistics are facts that can be stated in the form of numbers. There are several excellent sources of statistical information. In addition to the almanacs previously mentioned, there are the *Statistical Abstract of the United States*, the *Statesman's Yearbook*, the *Census Reports*, *Standard & Poor's Statistical Service*, and the *American Statistics Index*.

Guides to Reading

Magazines or periodicals contain many current articles on various business concerns and other subjects not found in books. Because there are so many magazines, it is impossible for anyone to find all of the desired information without some aid. This aid is supplied by guides—sometimes referred to as indexes. Perhaps the most commonly used guide is the *Readers' Guide to Periodical Literature*. This guide provides an index to articles appearing in almost 200 current magazines. It is published twice a month, except for one issue in February, July, and August. Once a year, one large volume is published that combines all of the listings from the indexes issued during the preceding 12 months.

The *Education Index* and the *Business Education Index* cite articles that appear in journals of particular interest to educators. The *Public Affairs Information Service Bulletin* and the *Business Periodicals Index* will also assist you in locating articles and other literature on public affairs and business topics.

Some of the larger newspapers publish their own guides that assist readers in locating articles of interest in their newspapers. Examples of these are the *New York Times Index* and the *Wall Street Journal Index*. The *Newspaper Index* indexes news items and other articles in the *Chicago*

Tribune, the *Washington Post*, the *New Orleans Times Picayune*, and the *Los Angeles Times*.

Newspapers

Almost everyone refers to daily newspapers for information on radio and television programs and for announcements of movies showing at the theaters. If you are planning a trip, you may check on weather forecasts and road condition reports. Newspapers also inform us of scheduled lectures, exhibits, concerts, school affairs, sports events, and other activities. Major newspapers print information about economic conditions, prices of commodities, cost of living, prices of stocks and bonds, and other information of interest to businesspeople and consumers.

SPECIALIZED REFERENCE SOURCES

There is a wealth of information in almost any special field. You may be familiar with such special references as the *Official Baseball Guide* for baseball fans and the *Radio Amateur's Handbook* for ham radio operators. Directories, yearbooks, handbooks, and other references are available to hobbyists, artists, musicians, entertainers, workers in technical professions, ethnic groups, and many others. A few of the more widely used special reference sources are described in the following paragraphs.

Information for Travelers

Two commonly used sources of information for travelers are:

- *Road maps*. In addition to highway routes, many road maps show places of interest, camping sites, parks, lakes, street layouts of larger cities, and other details.
- *Guides and directories*. The *Hotel and Motel Red Book* gives information about the location and size of hotels and motels, room rates, and hotel services for thousands of hotels and motels in the U.S. and in many foreign countries. The *Official Airline Guide* contains airline schedules, fares, and information such as airmail rates, car rental services, and conversion of dollars to foreign currencies. The *Rand McNally Campground and Trailer Park Guide*, revised annually, contains a list of thousands of campgrounds and trailer parks in the United States and Canada.

Information for Consumers

Three popular monthly magazines, *Money*, *Consumer Reports*, and *Consumers' Research Magazine*, contain facts and advice about products and services used most by consumers. Organized consumer groups and the federal government publish newsletters and other literature of particular interest to consumers.

Many useful government bulletins, some free and others available at little cost, can be ordered from the Superintendent of Documents, U.S. Government Printing Office, Washington, DC 20402. Many libraries have the *Monthly Catalog of U.S. Government Publications*, which lists by subject all federal government publications issued during the preceding month. Bulletins of value to consumers are often available from Better Business Bureaus, labor unions, colleges, government agencies, and other public and private organizations.

Information for Business

The U.S. Department of Commerce issues many reports and studies of value to large and small businesses. It publishes *Survey of Current Business*, a monthly periodical with articles and statistics on business activity and economic conditions. The U.S. Department of Labor issues the *Monthly Labor Review* which gives information on prices, wages, and employment. National, state, and local chambers of commerce also provide many kinds of useful reports.

The *Economic Almanac* is prepared by the Conference Board. It is a standard source of facts on current business and economic developments.

Much information about business activity can be found in the financial pages of daily newspapers. Other publications such as *Fortune* and *Business Week* are devoted primarily to business and its activities. A business can subscribe to special newsletter services, such as *The Kiplinger Washington Letter*, for information not usually published in newspapers and magazines.

Many handbooks describing principles, practices, and methods for certain specialized fields of business are available. Among the handbooks of special interest to businesspeople are:

- *Accountants' Handbook*—a general reference book in accounting, containing answers to accounting problems and presenting the principles of accounting.
- *Financial Handbook*—a guide to solving financial problems such as financing the growth and operation of a business and raising new capital for expansion.
- *Office Administration Handbook*—a comprehensive volume focusing attention on the human relationships involved in the management of offices. It includes chapters on testing, hiring, supervising, training, and promoting office workers and on office systems, policies, work procedures, correspondence, layouts, equipment, and data processing developments.

- *Marketing Handbook*—a reference book that discusses all phases of the marketing process such as advertising, sales promotion, and marketing research.

Almost every field of business has its special trade directory. For example, special directories are published for people in such businesses as advertising, retailing, insurance, real estate, banking, plastics manufacturing, air transportation, and frozen food processing.

Information about People

Encyclopedias tell about great people of history. Other reference books give information about men and women now living. The best-known books of this type are *Who's Who* and *Who's Who in America. Who's Who* gives a summary of the lives and achievements of outstanding people living throughout the world. *Who's Who in America* lists mainly those leaders living in the United States. Books similar to these are also published for special groups, such as *Who's Who in Finance and Industry, Who's Who of American Women*, and *Who's Who in Black Corporate America*, and *American Men* and *Women of Science*. Another popular reference about people is *Current Biography*, which includes sketches about individuals, many of various nationalities, who have become prominent because of their recent accomplishments.

Information about Occupations

Two important government publications giving information on occupations are the *Dictionary of Occupational Titles* and the *Occupational Outlook Handbook*. Another very worthwhile reference for junior and senior high school students is the *Encyclopedia of Careers and Vocational Guidance*. This extensive compilation is published in two volumes. Volume I contains practical guidance material and broad articles on opportunities in some 70 major industries or areas of work. Volume II contains more than 200 articles on specific occupations, such as bank teller, stenographer, travel agent, hotel manager, buyer, economist, accountant, automobile mechanic, glazier, and watch repairer. These articles give detailed information about the nature of work, requirements, methods of entry, earnings, and sources of additional information.

Because of the recent emphasis on career education, school libraries in particular have acquired more information on different occupations. This information is presented not only in book form, but also through films, microfilm, games, and computers. Several databases contain up-to-date information about careers.

Appendix B

This arithmetic review will be especially helpful to you in solving many of the end-of-chapter problems in this text and the common arithmetic problems you will encounter in business. These suggestions deal with a few of the kinds of calculations that are the most troublesome.

MULTIPLYING NUMBERS ENDING WITH ZERO

When multiplying two numbers, if one or both of the numbers have zeros at the extreme right, place the zeros to the right of an imaginary line, multiply the numbers to the left of the line, and bring down the total number of zeros to the right of the line.

Examples:

$$
\begin{array}{r|l}
36 & \\
\times 25 & 00 \\
\hline
180 & \\
72 & \\
\hline
900 & 00 \\
\end{array}
\qquad
\begin{array}{r|l}
36 & 00 \\
\times 25 & \\
\hline
180 & \\
72 & \\
\hline
900 & 00 \\
\end{array}
\qquad
\begin{array}{r|l}
36 & 0 \\
\times 25 & 00 \\
\hline
180 & \\
72 & \\
\hline
900 & 000 \\
\end{array}
$$

DIVIDING BY NUMBERS ENDING WITH ZERO

When the divisor is 10, 100, 1,000, etc., move the decimal point in the dividend one place to the left for each zero. Moving the decimal point one place to the left divides a number by 10; two places to the left, by 100; three places to the left, by 1,000; etc.

Examples:

$$16.8 \div 10 = 1.68 \qquad\qquad 5,732 \div 1,000 = 5.732$$
$$246.9 \div 100 = 2.469$$

$930.9 \div 30 =$

$3\overline{)93.09}$

$\quad31.03$

When the divisor is 20, 400, 3,000, etc., drop the zeros in the divisor, move the decimal point in the dividend one place to the left for each zero, and divide by the remaining number 2, 4, 3, etc.

Other Examples:

$65.8 \div 200 =$

$2\overline{).658}$

$\quad.329$

$8,428 \div 4,000 =$

$4\overline{)8.428}$

$\quad2.107$

USING DECIMALS

When people find the use of decimals difficult. Knowing and following a few simple rules will help improve your calculations using decimals.

1.   Adding numbers with decimals—keep all decimal points in line.

Examples:

33.65	26.5
72.85	.4
2.10	385
+ 30.00	400.329
138.60	+ .07
	812.299

2.   Subtracting numbers with decimals—keep decimal points in line.

Example:

392.6   ← fill out spaces to the right with zeros →   392.600

– 8.794   – 8.794

                                                  383.806

Subtract 12.678 from 36   36.000

                        −12.678

                         23.322

3. Multiply numbers with decimals.

Example: Multiply 7.46 by 3.2

```
      7.46
×     3.2
      1492
     2238
   23.872
```

a. Keep right margin even.
b. Keep figures in line.
c. To position the decimal point in the product, count all digits to the right of the decimal points in the two original figures—in this case three—count off that number of places from the right in the product, and set the decimal point.

4. Always multiply by the simpler number.

Example: Multiply 3.7 by 327.4. This is the same as multiplying 327.4 by 3.7, which is simpler.

```
      327.4
×       3.7
      22918
       9822
    1,211.38
```

5. Dividing numbers with decimals.

First example: 129.54 (Dividend) ÷ .34 (Divisor) =

```
.34)129.54
```

```
      381.(Quotient)
.34)129.54
    102
    275
    272
     34
     34
```

To the right of the decimal point in the dividend count as many places as are to the right of the decimal point in the divisor. Set the decimal point in the quotient at this point. Keep figures in line.

Second example: 420 ÷ 75 =

```
       5.6
75) 420.0
    375
    450
    450
```

The decimal point is always at the extreme right of whole numbers although it is not shown. When dividing, a decimal point may be placed at the right of the dividend and zeros added as needed.

MULTIPLYING BY PRICE FIGURES

Dealers frequently price items for sale at such figures as 49¢, $5.98, $99.95, etc. This is done because a price of $99.95, for example, seems less to the prospective buyer than an even $100.

Let us assume that 27 items are purchased at $.99 each.

The usual method of multiplication:

$.99
× 27
693
198
26.73

A simpler method:

27
× $ 1.00
27.00
− .27
$26.73

(1) Multiply by the next higher number containing zeros—in this case $1.00.
(2) If the price figure ends in 99¢, subtract 1¢ for each item purchased—in this case 27¢.

Other examples:

If the price figure ends in 98¢, subtract 2¢ for each item purchased—in this case 64¢.

($.02 × 32 = $.64).

32 items at $4.98

32
× $ 5.00
$160.00
− .64
$159.36

If the price figure ends in 97¢, subtract 3¢ for each item purchased—in this case $2.13.

($.03 × 71 = $2.13).

71 items at $9.97

71
× $ 10.00
$710.00
− 2.13
$707.87

In some cases, the use of a calculator may make the simpler method of multiplying by price figures unnecessary.

USING FRACTIONAL PARTS OF $1.00 IN MULTIPLYING

While goods and services may be priced at any figure, prices are frequently expressed in fractional parts of $1.00, $10.00, $100.00, etc., that can be calculated easily and quickly. For example, 50 cents is $1/2$ of $1.00; 25 cents is $1/4$ of $1.00; $33 1/3$ cents is $1/3$ of $1.00. Thus:

24 items selling for $1.00 each would cost	$24.00
24 items at 50¢ each would cost $1/2$ of $24 or	$12.00
24 items at 25¢ each would cost $1/4$ of $24 or	$ 6.00
24 items at $33 1/3$¢ each would cost $1/3$ of $24 or	$ 8.00

With a little practice, many similar calculations can be made mentally. While there are many fractional parts of $1.00, the ones shown below will be very helpful to you from time to time in making your arithmetic calculations. This skill will be especially useful to you when comparing the prices of goods and services.

Fractional Part of $1.00	Halves	Thirds	Fourths	Sixths	Eighths
$1/8$					$.12\frac{1}{2}$
$1/6$				$.16\frac{2}{3}$	
$1/4$			$.25		
$1/3$		$.33\frac{1}{3}$			
$3/8$					$.37\frac{1}{2}$
$1/2$	$.50				
$5/8$					$.62\frac{1}{2}$
$2/3$		$.66\frac{2}{3}$			
$3/4$			$.75		
$5/6$				$.83\frac{1}{3}$	
$7/8$					$.87\frac{1}{2}$

You already know several of the above fractional parts of $1.00, and with practice you will be able to use those and others quickly and accurately. Four different types of calculations are involved. Master as many of them as you are able.

First type:

1. Numerator of fractional part is, "1," that is $1/8$, $1/6$, $1/4$, etc.
2. There is no remainder; that is, the calculations come to even dollars.

Example:

How to calculate:
12 items at $1.00 each would cost $12.00
50¢ is $1/2$ of $1.00; hence, at 50¢, 12 items will cost $1/2$ of
   $12 or . . . . $ 6.00

Other examples:

$$32 \times \$.12\frac{1}{2} \ (32 \times 1/8) = \$ \ 4.00$$
$$36 \times \$.16\frac{2}{3} \ (36 \times 1/6) = \$ \ 6.00$$
$$48 \times \$.25 \quad (48 \times 1/4) = \$12.00$$
$$39 \times \$.33\frac{1}{3} \ (39 \times 1/3) = \$13.00$$
$$48 \times \$.50 \quad (48 \times 1/2) = \$24.00$$

Second type:

1. Numerator of fractional part is "1."
2. There is a remainder; that is, the calculations will result in dollars and cents.

Example:

$$33 \times \$.25 = \$8.25$$

How to calculate:

33 items at $1.00 each would cost $33.00

25¢ is $^1/_4$ of $1.00; hence, at 25¢ 33 items will cost $^1/_4$ of
$33 or 8^1/_4$; $^1/_4$ of $1.00 is 25¢, thus . . . . $ 8.25

(*Note:*   The fraction of a dollar obtained will always be one of the fractions illustrated on page 614 so that once these fractional parts are mastered there is nothing new to be learned.)

Other examples:

$$39 \times \$.16^2/_3 = \$ \ 6^3/_6 = \$ \ 6.50 \ \ (^3/_6 = \ ^1/_2 = .50)$$
$$37 \times \$.25 \ \ \ = \$ \ 9^1/_4 = \$ \ 9.25$$
$$28 \times \$.33^1/_3 = \$ \ 9^1/_3 = \$ \ 9.33*$$
$$25 \times \$.50 \ \ \ = \$12^1/_2 = \$12.50$$

(*Since 1¢ is our smallest coin, if the final fraction is $^1/_2$ or more, the last figure is raised 1 penny; if less than $^1/_2$, the fraction is dropped. *Note*:   Some retailers convert every fraction to 1¢, even if the fraction is less than $^1/_2$.)

Third type:

1. Numerator is other than "1."
2. There is no remainder.

Example:

$$48 \times \$.75 = \$36.00$$

How to calculate:

Think of $.75 as $^3/_4$ of $1.00 and solve by cancellation.

$$48 \times \$.75 \left(\overset{12}{\cancel{48}} \times \frac{3}{\cancel{4}} \right) = \$36.00$$

Other examples:

$$24 \times \$.37^1/_2 \left(\overset{3}{\cancel{24}} \times \frac{3}{8} \right) = \$ \ 9.00$$

$$32 \times \$.62^1/_2 \left(\overset{4}{\cancel{32}} \times \frac{5}{8} \right) = \$20.00$$

$$36 \times \$.66^2/_3 \left(\overset{12}{\cancel{36}} \times \frac{2}{\cancel{3}} \right) = \$24.00$$

Fourth type:

1. Numerator is other than "1."
2. There is a remainder.

Example:

$$34 \times \$.62^{1}/_{2} = \$21.25$$

How to calculate:
Think of $\$.62^{1}/_{2}$ as $^{5}/_{8}$ of 1.00; but since 8 does not divide evenly into 34, first multiply by 5 and then divide by 8.

$$\$34 \times 5 = \$170$$
$$\$170 \div 8 = \$21^{2}/_{8}$$
$$\$21^{2}/_{8} = \$21.25$$

$$34 \times \$.62^{1}/_{2} \left(34 \times \frac{5}{8} = \frac{170}{8} \right) = \$21.25$$

Other Examples:

$$61 \times \$.37^{1}/_{2} \left(61 \times \frac{3}{8} = \frac{183}{8} \right) = \$22.88$$

$$43 \times \$.66^{2}/_{3} \left(43 \times \frac{2}{3} = \frac{86}{3} \right) = \$28.67$$

$$21 \times \$.75 \quad \left(21 \times \frac{3}{4} = \frac{63}{4} \right) = \$15.75$$

$$23 \times \$.87^{1}/_{2} \left(23 \times \frac{7}{8} = \frac{161}{8} \right) = \$20.13$$

Note: You will discover that after the number is multiplied by the numerator, the remaining calculation is exactly like that in the second type above.

Fractional parts of other amounts:

To the student who is interested in developing greater skill in calculating fractional parts of other amounts, a few additional examples will demonstrate the large number of applications possible.

First example:

.05 is $^{1}/_{2}$ of	.10
.50 is $^{1}/_{2}$ of	1.00
5.00 is $^{1}/_{2}$ of	10.00
50.00 is $^{1}/_{2}$ of	100.00
500.00 is $^{1}/_{2}$ of	1,000.00

Thus:
$$\begin{cases} 24 \times & .05 = & 1.20 \\ 24 \times & .50 = & 12.00 \\ 24 \times & 5.00 = & 120.00 \\ 24 \times & 50.00 = & 1,200.00 \\ 24 \times & 500.00 = & 12,000.00 \end{cases}$$

Second example:

$.02^{1}/_{2}$ is $^{1}/_{4}$ of	.10
.25 is $^{1}/_{4}$ of	1.00
2.50 is $^{1}/_{4}$ of	10.00
25.00 is $^{1}/_{4}$ of	100.00
250.00 is $^{1}/_{4}$ of	1,000.00

Thus:
$$\begin{cases} 430 \times & .02^{1}/_{2} = & 10.75 \\ 430 \times & .25 = & 107.50 \\ 430 \times & 2.50 = & 1,075.00 \\ 430 \times & 25.00 = & 10,750.00 \\ 430 \times & 250.00 = & 107,500.00 \end{cases}$$

Determining Percentages and Interest in Business

Appendix C

Finding percentages and calculating interest are frequent functions in business. Every career in business demands some knowledge of percentages and interest. The well-prepared businessperson is comfortable with percentages and interest.

FINDING PERCENTAGES

Most business students find that the percent concept is very simple. Percent is derived from two Latin words, "per centum," meaning "by the hundred." You use a fraction whose denominator is always 100. The percent sign is %. Every percent figure can be expressed as either a common fraction or a decimal fraction.

Examples:

Percent		Common Fraction		Decimal Fraction
3%	=	3/100	=	.03
25%	=	25/100	=	.25
57%	=	57/100	=	.57

In fact, you never use the percent figure in calculating percent. You always change the percent figure to either a common fraction or a decimal fraction.

To find:

7% of $300:　multiply $300 \times \dfrac{7}{100}$ = $21.00; or $300 \times .07$ = $21.00

12% of $250:　multiply $250 \times \dfrac{12}{100}$ = $30.00; or $250 \times .12$ = $30.00

CALCULATING INTEREST

Interest is always expressed as a percent; but in calculating interest, both the percent and the length of time are considered.

Examples:

8% interest on $400 for 1 year = $400 \times .08 \times 1$ = $ 32.00
15% interest on $550 for 3 years = $550 \times .15 \times 3$ = $247.50

One method of calculating interest for less than one year is explained in Chapter 29 of this textbook and is reinforced in the examples that follow.

When you loan or borrow money for less than a year, the amount of interest is calculated on the fractional part of the year. The fraction may be expressed either in months or in days. A month is considered to be one twelfth of a year regardless of the number of days in the particular month.

Examples:

9% interest on $500 for 3 months = $500 \times .09 \times \dfrac{3}{12}$ = $11.25

11% interest on $900 for 4 months = $900 \times .11 \times \dfrac{4}{12}$ = $33.00

When a loan is made for a certain number of days, such as 30, 45, or 85 days, the interest is determined by days. To make the calculating easy, a year is usually considered to be 360 for most business applications.

Examples:

$7^1/2$% interest on $100 for 15 days = $100 $\times .075 \times \dfrac{15}{360}$ = $.31

$9^1/4$% interest on $2,000 for 85 days = $2,000 \times .0925 \times \dfrac{85}{360}$ = $43.68

CALCULATING INTEREST ON INSTALLMENT LOANS

The method of calculating the rate of interest on installment loans presented in Chapter 29 is sufficiently accurate for most purposes. For a more exact calculation of interest, the following method is presented.

Problem:

Evelyn Louis borrowed $120 from the small loan department of her bank and signed a note for $126. She agreed to pay back the balance in 8 equal monthly installments of $15.75. What annual rate of interest did she pay for the use of the $120 that she actually received? Assume that an interest rate of 12% a year, or 1% a month, was charged for the loan.

Solution:

The cost of the loan was $126 − $120 = $6. On this basis, the interest would have been:

$120.00 borrowed for 1 month @ 1% would cost $1.20
− 15.75 1st payment

104.25 borrowed for 1 month @ 1% would cost 1.04
− 15.75 2d payment

88.50 borrowed for 1 month @ 1% would cost 89
− 15.75 3d payment

72.75 borrowed for 1 month @ 1% would cost 73
− 15.75 4th payment

57.00 borrowed for 1 month @ 1% would cost 57
− 15.75 5th payment

41.25 borrowed for 1 month @ 1% would cost 41
− 15.75 6th payment

25.50 borrowed for 1 month @ 1% would cost 26
− 15.75 7th payment

9.75 borrowed for 1 month @ 1% would cost 10
− 15.75 8th payment

Interest cost if the money had been borrowed at 1%
a month, or 12% a year $5.20

Notice that the interest was figured on the total $120 for the first month only, because the borrower had the use of the entire amount only during that month. During the second month, the interest was figured on $104.25, as $15.75 was repaid at the end of the first month. The amount on which the interest was figured was decreased in a like manner for each month during the time of the loan.

At 1% a month, or 12% a year, the interest would have been $5.20. The actual cost of the loan was $6. How many times greater was this actual cost than $5.20? This may be found by dividing $6 by $5.20:

$$\$6 \div \$5.20 = 1.1538$$

The amount actually paid was, then, 1.1538 times greater than the amount would be if the rate had been 1% a month, or 12% a year. Since interest rates are stated on a yearly basis, the actual rate was:

$$12\% \times 1.1538 = 13.85\%$$

CALCULATING INTEREST ON INSTALLMENT PURCHASES

The method of calculating the rate of interest on installment purchases is similar to the method of calculating the rate of interest on installment loans.

Problem:

William Regier bought a radio on the installment plan from Super Sounds for $102. A down payment of $12 was made at the time of the purchase, and $9 was paid at the end of each of the following 10 months. The radio could have been purchased for $92 in cash. What rate of interest was paid for the privilege of buying on installments?

Solution:

The amount that William paid for the privilege of buying on installments is found by subtracting the cash price of the radio from the installment price of the radio.

$102 the installment price of the radio
− 92 the cash price of the radio
$ 10 the amount paid for the privilege of buying on installments

The radio could have been purchased for $92 in cash. A down payment of $12 was made. The cash price was therefore $80 more than the down payment. William could have bought the radio for cash if he had borrowed $80 from some other source. He was, then, in reality borrowing $80 from the Super Sounds. This may be shown as:

$92 the price that would have been paid if the purchase had been for cash
−12 the down payment at the time of the purchase
$80 the amount borrowed from the dealer

If William had borrowed $80 from some other source at a rate of 1% a month, or 12% a year, the interest would have been found as follows:

$80 borrowed for 1 month @ 1% would cost . . . . $ .80
− 9 1st payment

71 borrowed for 1 month @ 1% would cost 71
− 9 2d payment

62 borrowed for 1 month @ 1% would cost 62
− 9 3d payment

53 borrowed for 1 month @ 1% would cost 53
− 9 4th payment

44 borrowed for 1 month @ 1% would cost 44
− 9 5th payment

35 borrowed for 1 month @ 1% would cost 35
− 9 6th payment

26 borrowed for 1 month @ 1% would cost 26
<u>− 9</u> 7th payment

17 borrowed for 1 month @ 1% would cost 17
<u>− 9</u> 8th payment

8 borrowed for 1 month @ 1% would cost 08
<u>− 9</u> 9th payment

Interest cost if the money had been borrowed at 1% a
month, or 12% a year $3.96

Notice that the interest was figured on $80 for the first month only since William had the use of this amount during that month only. During the second month, the interest was figured on $71 because $9 was repaid at the end of the first month. The amount on which the interest was figured was decreased in a like manner for each installment paid.

At 1% a month, or 12% a year, the interest was $3.96. The actual cost for the loan was $10 ($102 - $92 = $10). How many times greater was this actual cost than $3.96? This may be found by dividing $10 by $3.96:

$$\$10 \div \$3.96 = 2.5252$$

The amount actually paid, then, was 2.5252 times greater than the amount would have been if the rate had been 1% a month, or 12% a year. The actual rate, then, was:

$$12\% \times 2.5252 = 30.30\%$$

Using the Metric Measurement System in Business

The metric system of measure is used in business by most nations in the world. Because of our great amount of trade with other countries, the United States has taken some steps toward conversion to the metric system. The change to metric is being made gradually. Some U.S. businesses and industries have already made the change, and you should become familiar with the metric system.

There are some things about the metric system that may already be familiar to you. For example, if you have been to a track or swimming meet or have seen one on television, you know that the distances are sometimes measured in meters, not in feet, yards, or miles. Food is often labeled to show amounts in grams as well as pounds or ounces. Meters, kilometers, and grams are examples of metric units of measurement.

BASIC METRIC UNITS

To use the metric system, you will measure weight (or mass), distance, volume, and temperature differently from the way you are accustomed to measuring them. Once you become familiar with it, the metric system is actually simpler to use than the U.S. system. Metric has very few base units, while the U.S. system uses many base units.

The kilogram is the metric base unit of weight. A kilogram is equal to a little over two pounds. The kilogram and units based on the kilogram are used instead of ounces and pounds.

The meter is the metric base unit of distance. A meter is a little longer than a yard. The meter and a few other units based on the meter are used to measure the things we now measure in inches, feet, and miles.

The cubic meter is really the metric base unit of volume. However, for most measurements of volume, you will use the liter. A liter is equal to a little more than a quart. You will use the liter in place of the fluid ounce, the pint, the quart, and the gallon.

The degree Celsius (named after the Swedish astronomer Anders Celsius), once called the centigrade degree, is used instead of the Fahrenheit degree to measure temperature.

Figure D-1 gives you some idea of how these metric units of measure compare with U.S. units.

Figure D-1 Some common units of measure in the U.S. and metric systems.

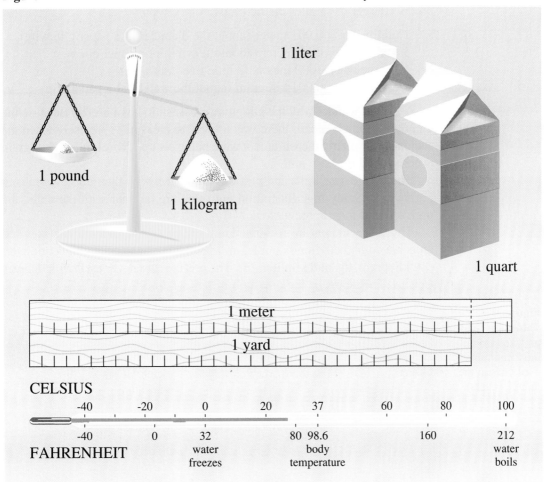

METRIC PREFIXES

Any measure can be expressed in the base units of the metric system. However, this can be awkward if very large or very small numbers are involved. By using prefixes with the units of the metric system, you can express measurements in a more convenient way. Since the metric system is a decimal system (that is, it is based on the number 10), the prefixes all mean to multiply or divide the unit by 10, 100, or 1000. There are quite a few metric prefixes, but the ones that are used in this book and in most business applications are:

> milli = one one-thousandth or 1/1000 or 0.001
> centi = one one-hundredth or 1/100 or 0.01
> kilo = one thousand or 1000

Prefixes are added to or taken away from the names of the base units to produce larger or smaller metric units. For example:

> 1 millimeter = 0.001 meter (about the diameter of a paper clip wire)
> 1 centimeter = 0.01 meter (about the width of a paper clip)
> 1 kilometer = 1000 meters (a little over half a mile)
> 1 gram   = 0.001 kilogram (about the weight of a paper clip)

You may wonder why the kilogram, a base unit, has a prefix. Because the gram is extremely small, there was no way to measure it precisely when the standards for metric measurement were being set up. Therefore, the kilogram is considered the base unit.

The metric base units and prefixes are shown with their abbreviations in Figure D-2. Study this illustration until you are familiar with the units, the prefixes, and their abbreviations.

The abbreviations are combined in the same way that metric prefixes and units are combined. For example, millimeter is abbreviated mm; centimeter, cm; kilogram, kg; and kiloliter, kL. The prefixes are never used with degrees Celsius. The degree is the only unit of temperature.

Figure D-2
These units and prefixes are the most commonly used ones in the metric system.

Unit	Abbreviation	Use
kilogram	kg	weight
meter	m	distance
liter	L	volume
degree Celsius	°C	temperature

Prefix	Abbreviation	Meaning
milli	m	1/1000
centi	c	1/100
kilo	k	1000

USING UNITS AND PREFIXES CORRECTLY

It would not mean much to say that a pill weighs 0.0001 kilogram or that the distance between two towns is 77 058 meters. That would be like telling someone that the distance to the next service station is 10,560 feet instead of 2 miles. (As you see here, in the metric system a space is used instead of a comma to show thousands when grouping five or more digits.)

You would not say that your bicycle weighs 12 000 grams, but that is weights 12 kilograms. The kilogram is ordinarily used wherever we are used to using pounds. The milligram, a very small measure, is used a great deal in the medical and scientific fields. Pills prescribed by doctors are often measured in milligrams.

Meters are used where we are accustomed to using feet or yards, and millimeters usually replace inches for short measurements. Centimeters are used for some measurements such as the dimensions of household objects, for example towels and sheets, and personal measurements, for example your height.

The liter replaces the fluid ounce, the pint, the quart, and the gallon for small quantities. Gasoline in a car's tank would be measured in liters, but the amount of gasoline in a large storage tank would be measured in kiloliters. The milliliter is used to measure very small quantities such as medicine dosages or amounts of liquid ingredients in recipes.

CHANGING FROM ONE SYSTEM TO THE OTHER

To use the metric system well, you must learn to think in terms of metric units. However, until you get used to doing this, it is sometimes easier to convert the metric units into units you know. Figure D-3 tells you how to convert some commonly used metric units to their U.S. equivalents and some U.S. units to their metric equivalents. The numbers that you are to multiply by have been rounded off to make them easier for you to use and remember.

Take a look at Figure D-3 on the next page; then study these examples.

If you buy a 6-ounce bag of candy, what is its weight in grams?

6 ounces $\times$ 28 = 168 grams

If you have 9 meters of masking tape, how many yards of tape do you have?

9 meters $\times$ 1.1 = 9.9 yards

What is the volume in liters of 5 quarts of oil?

5 quarts $\times$ 0.95 = 4.75 liters

If the temperature is 77°F, what is the temperature in degrees Celsius?

77 − 32 = 45

5/9 $\times$ 45 = 25°C

Figure D-3 Table of approximate metric-to-U.S. and U.S.-to-metric conversions.

Approximate Conversions from U.S. to Metric and Metric to U.S.

	When You Know:	You Can Find:	If You Multiply By:
Distance	inches	millimeters (mm)	25.4
	inches	centimeters (cm)	2.5
	feet	meters (m)	0.3
	yards	meters (m)	0.91
	miles	kilometers (km)	1.61
	millimeters (mm)	inches	0.04
	centimeters (cm)	inches	0.4
	meters (m)	inches	39.4
	meters (m)	feet	3.3
	meters (m)	yards	1.1
	kilometers (km)	miles	0.6
Weight (Mass)	ounces	grams (g)	28
	pounds	kilograms (kg)	0.45
	grams (g)	ounces	0.035
	kilograms (kg)	pounds	2.2
Volume	pints	liters (L)	0.47
	quarts	liters (L)	0.95
	gallons	liters (L)	3.8
	liters (L)	pints	2.1
	liters (L)	quarts	1.06
	liters (L)	gallons	0.26
Temperature	degrees Fahrenheit	degrees Celsius (°C)	5/9 (after subtracting 32)
	degrees Celsius (°C)	degrees Fahrenheit	9/5 (then add 32)

Glossary

A

ability test. A test that measures how well a job applicant can perform certain job tasks.

adjustable rate mortgage (ARM). A mortgage for which the interest rate is raised or lowered periodically depending upon the current interest rate being charged by lenders.

adjuster. An insurance company representative who determines the extent of loss and pays insureds according to the terms of the policy.

allowance. The amount budgeted for savings and other expenditures.

annual percentage rate (APR). The percentage cost of credit on a yearly basis.

annuity. An amount of money that an insurance company will pay at definite intervals to a person who has previously deposited money with the company.

antitrust laws. Laws designed to promote competition and fairness and to prevent monopolies.

application form. A document used by an employer that asks for important information related to employment.

appraiser. One who is trained to estimate the value of property and who can give an official report on its value.

appreciation. A general increase in the value of property that occurs over a period of time.

arbitrator. A person who makes a legally binding decision to resolve labor-management differences.

articles of partnership. A written agreement made by partners in forming their business.

artificial intelligence (AI). Programs that enable computers to reason, learn, and make decisions using logical methods similar to the way humans do.

assessed value. The amount that your local government determines your property to be worth for tax purposes.

assets. Items of value.

assigned-risk plan. Auto insurance that provides coverage to high-risk drivers who are unable to purchase insurance in the normal fashion.

automatic teller machine (ATM). A computer terminal provided by a bank to receive, dispense, and transfer funds electronically for its customers.

automobile liability insurance. The general term used to describe insurance that you buy to protect yourself against financial loss if you injure someone else or damage someone else's property in an automobile accident.

B

balance of payments. The difference between the total amount of money that flows into a country and the money that flows out of a country for investments, tourism, and non-trade items.

balance of trade. The difference between a country's total exports and total imports of merchandise.

balance sheet. The financial statement that reports what a person or family owns as well as owes.

bank draft. A check that a bank official draws on the bank's deposits in another bank.

bank reconciliation. A statement showing how the checkbook balance and the bank statement were brought into agreement.

bankruptcy. A situation in which a business does not have enough money to pay its creditors even after selling its equipment and other capital resources.

bank statement. A report sent by the bank to a depositor showing the status of his or her account.

base year. The year chosen to compare an item, such as price, to the same item in another year.

basic economic problem. The problem—which faces individuals, businesses, and governments—of satisfying unlimited wants with limited resources.

basic health coverage. A combination of hospital, surgical, and regular medical expense insurance.

beneficiary. The person named in an insurance policy to receive the insurance benefits.

blank endorsement. An endorsement consisting of the endorser's name only.

blue-collar workers. People whose work involves the operation of machinery and equipment.

board of directors. A group of people elected by stockholders to guide a corporation.

bodily injury liability coverage. Insurance coverage that protects you from claims resulting from injuries or deaths for which you are found to be at fault.

bond. A printed certificate with a promise to pay a definite amount of money at a stated interest rate on a specified maturity date.

boycott. A refusal by workers to handle or buy the products of a company involved in a labor disagreement.

brand name. A name given to a product or service by a manufacturer that is intended to distinguish it from other similar and/or competitive products or services.

broker. A licensed specialist who helps investors buy and sell stocks and bonds.

budget. A plan that allows you to meet your personal goals with a system of saving and wise spending.

budget charge account. A credit plan which requires that payments of a certain fixed amount be made over several months.

budget variance. A difference between actual spending and planned spending.

business. An establishment or enterprise that supplies goods and services in exchange for some form of payment.

business cycle. The movement of our economy from one condition to another and back again.

C

canceled check. A check that has been paid by the bank.

capacity. The factor in credit that refers to a customer's ability to pay a debt when it is due.

capital. The factor in credit that refers to the value of the borrower's possessions.

capitalism. An economic system in which most economic resources are privately owned and decisions about production are largely made by free exchange in the marketplace.

capital resources. Tools, equipment, and buildings used in producing goods and services.

career. A goal in life that is fulfilled through a job or a series of jobs.

career information interview. A planned discussion with a worker to find out about the work that person does, the preparation necessary for that career, and the person's feelings about that career.

career planning. The process of studying careers, assessing yourself in terms of careers, and making decisions about a future career.

cashier's check. A check that a bank draws on its own in-house funds.

cash value. The amount of money or sum received should a policyholder decide to give up the protection provided by a policy.

central processing unit (CPU). The control center of the computer.

certificate of incorporation. A document, generally issued by a state government, giving permission to start a corporation.

certificates of deposits (CDs). Long-term deposits that have certain restrictions and pay higher interest rates than regular savings accounts.

certified check. A personal check on which the

bank has written its guarantee that the check will be paid.

channel of distribution. *See* marketing channel.

character. The factor in credit that refers to a customer's honesty and willingness to pay a debt when it is due.

check. A depositor's written demand to a bank to pay out money from his or her account.

checkbook. A bound book containing blank checks and forms on which a depositor writes a record of deposits made and checks written.

check register. A separate form on which the depositor keeps a record of deposits and checks.

check stub. A form attached to a check on which a depositor keeps a record of the checks written and any current deposit.

chips. Tiny pieces of silicon that contain imprinted circuits.

claim. A policyholder's request for payment for a loss that is covered by the insurance policy.

clearance sale. A sale in which a price reduction is used to sell items that a store no longer wishes to carry in stock.

clearing a check. Returning a check to the drawer's bank to be paid and charged to his or her checking account.

clearing house. A place where member banks exchange checks to clear them.

closed shop. A business in which an employer agrees to hire only union members.

coinsurance clause. A provision in which the insured will be expected to pay a certain percentage of the costs over and above the deductible amount.

collateral. Property that is offered as security for some loan agreements.

collectibles. Items of personal interest to collectors purchased in anticipation of an increase in value in the future.

collective bargaining. Negotiations that take place between an organized body of workers and an employer which deal with wages and working conditions.

collision coverage. Insurance coverage that protects a car owner against financial loss associated with damage resulting from a collision with another car or object or from the car turning over.

commercial bank. A bank that offers a full range of financial services; sometimes called a "financial department store."

commission. A fee charged by brokers for their services.

common stock. Stock that represents ownership in a corporation and a right to share in its profits, but has no stated dividend rate.

communism. An economic system in which government owns most of the economic resources and has tight control over the production and distribution of goods and services.

comparison shopping. Comparing the price, quality, and services of one product to those of another product.

competition. The rivalry among businesses to sell their goods and services to buyers.

compound interest. Interest computed on the amount saved plus the interest previously earned.

comprehensive medical policy. Insurance that combines hospital, surgical, regular, and medical insurance into one policy.

comprehensive physical damage coverage. Insurance coverage that protects you against almost all losses except those caused from a collision or from the car turning over.

compulsory insurance laws. Laws that require you to carry certain types of automobile insurance before your car can be licensed.

computer-assisted design (CAD). Technological assistance used to create products styles and designs.

computer-assisted instruction (CAI). The use of computers to help people learn or improve skills at their own pace.

computer language. A system of letters, words, numbers, and symbols used to communicate with a computer.

computer literacy. The ability to use computers to process information or solve problems.

computers. Electronic devices designed to store, process, and report information.

computer virus. A program code hidden in a system that can later do damage to software or stored data.

condominium. An individually owned unit in an apartment-like building or complex where maintenance and yard work are normally taken care of for a service fee.

consumer. A person who buys and uses goods or services.

consumer finance companies. Financial institutions that specialize in making loans for durable goods and financial emergencies.

Consumer Price Index (CPI). An index that shows the changes in the average prices of goods and services bought by consumers over a period of time.

consumers' cooperative. An organization of consumers who buy goods and services together.

contract. An agreement to exchange goods and services for something of value.

convenience store. A small store that emphasizes the sale of food items, an accessible location, and long operating hours.

convertible policy. A term life insurance policy that may be changed into another type of permanent insurance without taking a physical examination.

cooperative. A business that is owned by the members it serves and is managed in their interest.

copyright. Protection of the work of authors, composers, and artists.

corporate bonds. Bonds issued by corporations.

corporation. A business made up of a number of owners but authorized by law to act as a single person.

cosigner. Someone who becomes responsible for payment of the note if you do not pay as promised.

cost-push inflation. A rise in the general level of prices that is caused by increased costs of making and selling goods.

credit. The privilege of using someone else's money for a period of time.

credit application. A form on which you provide information needed by a lender to make a decision about granting credit or approving a loan.

credit bureau. A company that gathers information on credit users and sells that information in the form of credit reports to credit grantors.

credit insurance. Special insurance that repays the balance of the amount owed if the borrower dies or becomes disabled prior to the full settlement of the loan.

credit memorandum. A written record of the amount subtracted from an account when merchandise has been returned.

creditor. A person or business that is owed money; one who sells on credit or makes a loan.

credit rating. A person's reputation for paying debts on time.

credit record. A report that shows the debts you owe, how often you use credit, and whether you pay your debts on time.

credit references. Businesses or individuals from whom you have received credit in the past and/or who can help verify your credit record.

credit union. A financial institution formed by workers in the same organization that serves only its members.

creditworthy. Having established a credit record that shows you are a good credit risk.

custom-based economy. An economic system in which goods are produced the way they have always been produced.

D

data. Facts in the form of numbers, alphabetic characters, words, or special symbols.

database. A collection of organized data whose elements are in some way related to one another.

database software. A computer program that processes an organized collection of information.

data processing. The rearrangement or processing of data to make it more useful.

debtor. One who buys on credit or receives a loan.

debt-repayment plan. An agreement developed cooperatively by a creditor and debtor to reduce payments to a more manageable level and still pay off the debt.

decreasing term insurance. Term life insurance on which the amount of protection gradually becomes smaller, but the premiums remain the same during the term.

deductible clause. A clause in an insurance contract that indicates the amount car owners are willing to pay themselves for damage to their autos in the event of an accident.

deficit. A situation that exists when government spends more than it collects.

deflation. A decrease in the general price level.

demand. The quantity of a product or service that consumers are willing and able to buy at a particular price.

demand deposit. Money put into a checking account.

demand-pull inflation. A general rise in prices in response to increased demand for products or services.

dental expense insurance. Insurance that helps pay for normal dental care and covers dental injuries resulting from accidents.

deposit. Money that is placed in a bank account by a customer.

deposit slip or deposit ticket. A form that accompanies a deposit and lists the items deposited—currency, coins, or checks.

depreciation. The decrease in the value of property as it becomes older and wears out.

depression. A phase of the business cycle in which unemployment and business failures are high and GNP is at its lowest point.

derived demand. A demand for factors of production affected by the demand for a product or service.

desktop publishing. A process of writing and designing high-quality publications with the use of microcomputers.

directed economy. An economic system in which government owns and controls the economic resources and makes all of the decisions regarding the production of goods and services.

direct marketing. The process through which goods are bought by the consumer directly from the producer.

direct tax. A tax that cannot be passed on to someone else.

disability income insurance. Insurance that protects a worker against the loss of income because of a long illness or accident.

discount stores. Large stores that sell large quantities of goods at low prices.

discretionary income. Income available to spend after money has been set aside for basic needs and future expenses.

disk drive. A device that is used to store information onto a magnetic disk so that the information can be recalled and used again.

displaced workers. Workers who are unemployed due to changing job conditions.

dividend. The part of the profits of a corporation that each stockholder receives.

domestic trade. The buying and selling of goods and services among people and businesses within the same country.

down payment. A payment of part of the purchase price that is made as part of a credit agreement.

drawee. The bank or other financial institution in which the account is held.

drawer. The owner of the account and the person who signs the check.

E

economic decision making. The process of choosing which want, among several wants being considered at a certain time, will be satisfied.

economic loss. When something that has some financial value is lost or destroyed.

economic resources. The means through which we produce goods and services.

economic risk. The possibility of incurring a loss related to property liability and one's own personal well-being.

economic system. A nation's plan for making decisions on what to produce, how to produce, and how to distribute goods and services.

electronic funds transfer (EFT). A system through which funds are moved electronically from one account to another and from one bank to another.

electronic mail. The delivery of correspondence through a computer system.

embargo. Stopping the importing or exporting of a certain product or service.

endorsement. Written evidence that you received payment or that you transferred your right of receiving payment to someone else.

entrepreneur. Someone who takes a risk in starting a business to earn a profit.

entrepreneurship. The process of starting, organizing, managing, and assuming the responsibility for a business.

Equal Credit Opportunity Act. An act that prohibits creditors from denying credit because of age, race, sex, or marital status.

equity. The difference between what your house and property are worth and the amount owed on the mortgage.

estate planning. An activity that involves the accumulation and management of property during one's lifetime and the distribution of one's property at death.

estate tax. A tax based on the value of a person's property when he or she dies.

exchanges. Business organizations that accommodate the buying and selling of securities.

excise tax. A tax on certain goods and services, generally included in the price of the item.

expenditures. The amounts spent for food, clothing, transportation, and other living costs.

expert systems. Programs that assist people in problem solving on technical topics.

exports. Goods and services sold to another country.

express warranty. A guarantee made orally or in writing that promises a specific quality of performance.

extended coverage. Additional protection of property that covers damage caused by perils such as wind, hail, smoke, and falling aircraft, among other things.

extractor. A business that grows products or takes raw materials from nature.

F

face value. The amount borrowed by the seller of a bond.

facsimile (FAX). A system in which a copy of a document is transmitted from one location to another through an electronic device that is connected to the telephone lines.

factors of production. *See* economic resources.

factory outlet stores. Stores selling products at low prices that sometimes have minor flaws.

failure. The closing of a business with a loss occurring to at least one creditor.

Fair Credit Billing Act. A law that requires prompt correction of billing mistakes when they are brought to the attention of a business in a prescribed manner.

Fair Credit Reporting Act. A law that gives consumers the right to know what specific information credit bureaus are providing to potential creditors, employers, and insurers.

Federal Deposit Insurance Corporation (FDIC). A federal agency that protects depositors' money in case a bank or financial institution that it regulates fails.

Federal Reserve System (Fed). A nationwide banking plan set up by our federal government to assist banks in serving the public more efficiently by supervising and regulating member banks.

finance charge. The additional amount you must pay for using credit, including interest and other charges.

financial plan. A report that summarizes your current financial condition, acknowledges your financial needs, and sets a direction for your future financial activities.

financial planning. An activity that includes evaluating one's financial position, setting financial goals, and guiding activities and resources toward reaching those goals.

financial responsibility laws. Laws whereby your driver's license will be suspended or taken away if you cause an accident and cannot pay for the damages either through insurance, your savings, or the sale of property.

fixed expenses. Costs that occur regularly and are for the same amount each time.

fixed rate mortgage. A traditional mortgage with an interest rate that does not change during the life of the mortgage.

flat tax. *See* proportional tax.

float. The time between the receipt of a deposit by the bank and its availability to the depositor.

floppy disks. Small, pliable oxide-coated plastic disks in protective covers that may be used to store programs or data.

forgery. The crime of writing another person's signature on the check without his or her authority.

franchise. A written contract granting permission to sell someone else's product or service in a prescribed manner, over a certain period of time, and in a specified area.

franchisee. The person or group of people who have received permission from a parent company to sell its products or services.

franchisor. The parent company that grants permission to a person or group to sell its products or services.

fraud. When inaccurate information is given to a customer in an effort to make a sale.

free enterprise system. *See* capitalism.

full endorsement. *See* special endorsement.

full-service bank. *See* commercial bank.

full-service stores. Stores that offer a wide variety of goods and emphasize customer service.

futures. A contract for a commodity purchased in anticipation of higher market prices in the near future.

G

gift tax. A tax imposed when an individual receives an amount of money or property greater than $10,000.

goals. The things you want to achieve.

goods. The things you can see and touch.

goods-producing industry. Businesses concerned with manufacturing various products.

government employment office. A tax-supported office that helps people find jobs and provides information about careers.

grade. An indication of the quality or size of a product.

graphics software. A computer program that prepares charts, graphs, and other visual elements.

grievance procedure. A process in a labor contract for solving differences between workers and management.

gross national product (GNP). The total value of all final goods and services produced in a country in one year.

gross profit. The difference between the selling price and the cost of merchandise sold.

group life insurance. Life insurance that covers a group of people who are usually employed by the same company or are members of the same organization.

guarantee. A promise by the manufacturer or dealer, usually in writing, that a product is of a certain quality.

H

hard disk. A disk that is built into the computer and is made from rigid material, which does not bend; allows storage of tens of millions of characters.

hardware. The components or equipment of a computer system.

health maintenance organizations (HMOs). Organizations that provide complete health care to their members for a fixed monthly payment.

homeowners policy. A package-type insurance policy designed to fit the needs of most homeowners wishing to insure their homes and property.

hospital expense insurance. Insurance that pays most or all of the charges for room, food, and other hospital expenses that the insured person incurs.

human resources. The people who work to produce goods and services.

I

implied warranty. A guarantee imposed by law that is not stated orally or in writing which requires certain standards to be met.

imports. Goods and services bought from another country.

impulse buying. Buying too rapidly without much thought.

income. The money you receive from work that you do and from money you invest.

income statement. The financial statement that reports the inflow and outflow of money for a given period of time.

income tax. A tax levied on the earnings of individuals and corporations.

indirect marketing. The process through which goods move through one or more middle firms between the producer and the consumer.

indirect tax. A tax that is passed on to someone else for payment.

individual retirement account (IRA). A tax-sheltered retirement plan that allows certain workers to invest up to $2,000 annually and pay no tax either on that sum or on its earnings until the money is withdrawn.

inflation. An increase in the general price level.

inheritance tax. A tax based on the value of property or the amount of money received from a person who has died.

injunction. A court order directing striking employees to go back to work.

input. Data entered into a computer.

installment loan. A type of loan in which you agree to make monthly payments in specific amounts over a period of time.

installment sales credit. A credit contract issued by the seller that requires periodic payments to be made at times specified in the agreement with finance charges added to the cost of the purchase.

insurable interest. A financial interest in or benefit from the continued life of a person.

insurance. The planned protection provided by sharing economic losses.

insurance agent. A person who sells insurance.

insurance commission. A state agency that makes sure that insurance premium rates and practices are fair.

insurance companies. Businesses that provide planned protection against economic loss.

insured. The person for whom risk is assumed by an insurance company.

integrated software. A computer program capable of performing more than one basic function.

interest. An amount paid for the use of money.

interest rate. The percentage that is applied to a debt, expressed as a fraction or decimal.

interstate commerce. Business transactions involving companies in more than one state.

intrastate commerce. Business transactions involving companies that do business only in one state.

inventory. A list of goods showing the original cost of each item, when it was purchased, and how long it is expected to last.

investing. Using your savings to earn more money for you.

investment club. A small group of people who organize to study stocks and invest their money.

investments. Savings that are put to work to earn more money.

J

job. A task or series of tasks that are performed to provide or help to provide a good or service.

job interview. A two-way conversation in which the interviewer learns about you and you learn about the job and the company.

joint account. A bank account that is used by two or more people.

L

label. A written statement attached to a product giving information about its nature or contents.

labor. *See* human resources.

labor union. An organization of workers formed to give workers greater bargaining power in their dealings with management.

letter of application. A sales letter about yourself written for the purpose of getting a personal interview.

level term insurance. Term life insurance on which the amount of protection and the premiums remain the same while the insurance is in effect.

liabilities. Amounts owed to others.

liability risks. Potential losses to others that occur as a result of injury or damage that you may have caused.

life insurance. Insurance designed to protect survivors against the financial loss associated with dying.

limited-payment policies. A whole life policy intended to be paid up in a certain number of years.

liquid investment. An investment that can be turned into money quickly.

loan credit. Borrowing money to be used later for some special purpose.

locational unemployment. Jobs are available in one place but go unfilled because workers who are qualified to fill those jobs live elsewhere and are not willing to relocate.

lockout. A situation in which management closes all of its facilities in an attempt to put pressure on striking employees.

M

mainframe. A large computer system, which can handle more instructions and process data faster than smaller computers.

major medical expense insurance. Insurance that provides protection against the high costs of serious illnesses or injuries.

manufacturer. A business that takes an extractor's products or raw materials and changes them into a form that consumers can use.

margin. *See* gross profit.

market economy. *See* capitalism.

marketing. The activities that are involved in moving goods from producers to consumers.

marketing channel. The path that a product travels from producer to consumer.

marketplace. Any place where buyers and sellers exchange goods and services for some form of money.

market value. The price at which a share of stock can be bought and sold in the stock market.

maturity date. The date on which a loan must be repaid.

mediator. A neutral person who recommends solutions to disputes between labor and management.

Medicaid. Medical expense assistance administered by state governments to financially needy families.

medical payments coverage. Insurance coverage that provides medical-expense protection for the policyholder, immediate family members, and guests while in the insured person's car.

Medicare. Health insurance provided by the federal government for people age 65 and older and some disabled people.

memory. Storage locations for the instructions and data that the computer will use.

menu. A list of computer functions that appear on the screen.

microcomputer. The smallest type of computer.

minicomputer. A computer that is smaller and less powerful than a mainframe.

mobility. The willingness and ability of a person to move to where jobs are located.

modem. A device that allows you to communicate with other computers through the use of telephone lines.

money management. Day-to-day financial activities associated with using limited income to satisfy unlimited needs and wants.

money market account. A special account that pays a variable interest rate based on rates paid to holders of short-term government debt.

money market rate. The current cost of money in the marketplace.

money order. A form of payment that orders the issuing agency to pay the amount printed on the form to another party.

monopoly. A business that has complete control of the market for a product or service.

mortgage. A legal document giving the lender a claim against the property if the principal, interest, or both are not paid as agreed.

mortgage insurance. A life insurance policy that protects homeowners from losing their home in case an insured dies before the mortgage is paid.

mouse. A hand-held device used to point to a certain command on the computer screen.

municipal bonds (munis). Bonds issued by local and state governments.

municipal corporation. An incorporated town or city.

mutual funds. Funds set up and managed by investment companies that receive money from many investors and then usually buy and sell a wide variety of stocks or bonds.

N

National Credit Union Administration (NCUA). A federal agency that insures depositors' funds in credit unions up to $100,000.

national debt. The amount of money owed by the federal government.

natural resources. Raw materials supplied by nature.

needs. Things that are necessary for survival, such as food, clothing, and shelter.

net profit. The amount left over after expenses are deducted from the gross profit.

net worth. The difference between a person's or family's assets and liabilities.

no-fault insurance laws. A plan in which people injured in auto accidents are required to collect for their financial losses from their own insurance companies no matter who is at fault.

NOW (negotiable order of withdrawal) account. A savings account on which checks can be drawn or a checking account that earns interest; each may require a minimum balance and may limit withdrawals.

O

open charge account. A credit plan in which the seller expects payment in full at the end of a specified period, usually a month.

opportunity cost. The value of any alternative that you give up when you buy something else or make another choice.

output. Data that has been processed into a useful form.

outstanding checks. Checks that have not been deducted from the bank-statement balance.

overdrawing. Writing a check for more money than is in one's account.

P

partnership. An association of two or more people operating a business as co-owners and sharing profits or losses according to a written agreement.

patent. The exclusive right given to a person to make, use, or sell an invention for a period of 17 years.

payee. The person to whom the check is written.

pension. A series of regular payments made to a retired worker under an organized plan.

per capita output. The figure that results from dividing the GNP of a country by the population of that country.

perils. The causes of loss, such as fire, wind, or theft.

personal data sheet. A summary of job-related information about yourself.

personal liability coverage. Insurance that protects you from claims arising from injuries to other people or damage to other people's property caused by you, your family, or your pets.

personal property. Property that is not attached to the land.

personal references. People who can give a report about your character, education, and work habits.

personal risks. Risks associated with illness, disability, loss of income, unemployment, old age, and premature death.

personnel interviewer. Someone who has special training in talking with job applicants and hiring new employees.

picketing. A situation in which union members carry signs to publicize their complaints.

piracy. Stealing or illegally copying software packages or information.

planned economy. *See* directed economy.

policy. A contract that states the conditions to which the insurance company and the policyholder have agreed.

policyholder. *See* insured.

postdated check. A check dated later than the date on which it is written.

preferred provider organization (PPO). A group of physicians, a clinic, or a hospital that contracts with an employer to provide medical services to employees.

preferred stock. Stock that has priority over common stock in the payment of dividends.

premium. The amount that a policyholder must pay for insurance coverage.

price earnings ratio (P/E). The ratio of a stock's selling price to its earnings per share.

price index. A series of figures showing how prices have changed over a period of years.

principal. The amount of debt to which the interest is applied.

printer. An output device that produces written results on paper.

private enterprise. The right of the individual to choose what business to enter and what to produce with only limited direction from the government.

private enterprise system. *See* capitalism.

private property. The right to own, use, or dispose of things of value.

producers' cooperative. An organization that farmers form to market their products.

productivity. The quantity of a good that an average worker can produce in one hour.

profit. Money left from sales after subtracting the cost of operating the business.

profit motive. The right to work for profit.

program. A series of detailed step-by-step instructions that tell the computer what functions to complete and when to complete them.

programmers. People who write the instructions to tell the computer what functions to perform.

progressive tax. A tax whose rate increases as the amount taxed increases.

promissory note. A written promise to repay based on the debtor's excellent credit rating.

promotional sale. A sale in which items are sold below their regular price to publicize the opening of a new store or location and to build acceptance for new products.

property damage liability coverage. Insurance coverage that provides protection against claims if your car damages someone else's property and you are at fault.

property risks. The risk of damage or loss of property due to theft, wind, fire, flood, or some other hazard.

property tax. A tax based on the value of the land and the buildings attached to the land.

proportional tax. A tax method in which everyone pays the same rate.

prosperity. A phase of the business cycle in which employment is high, wages are good, and GNP is high.

public services. Efforts of government, such as fire and police protection, which benefit citizens.

public utility. A business that supplies a service or product vital to all people and whose prices are determined by government regulation rather than competition.

Q

quota. A limit on the quantity of a product that may be imported or exported within a given period of time.

R

raised check. A check on which the amount has been dishonestly increased.

rate of exchange. The value of the money of one country expressed in terms of the money of another country.

real estate. Land and anything that is attached to it.

real property. Property that is permanently attached to land.

Realtor. Someone who is trained and licensed to help with the buying and selling of real estate.

receipt. A written form that acknowledges payment was made.

recession. A phase of the business cycle in which demand decreases, businesses reduce production, and unemployment rises.

recovery. A phase of the business cycle in which unemployment begins to decrease and GNP rises.

regular medical expense insurance. Insurance that pays part or all of the fees for nonsurgical care given in the doctor's office, the patient's home, or a hospital.

renewable policy. A term life insurance policy that allows the policyholder to continue the term insurance for one or more terms with-

out taking a physical examination to determine whether she or he is still a good risk.

restrictive endorsement. An endorsement that limits the use of a check to the purpose given in the endorsement.

retailer. A middle firm that sells directly to the consumer.

retirement, survivors, and disability insurance. The part of the Social Security system that provides pensions to retired workers and their families, death benefits to dependents of workers who die, and benefits to disabled workers and their families.

revenue. Income that government receives from taxes and other sources.

revolving charge account. A credit plan that allows purchases to be charged at any time but requires that at least part of the debt be paid each month.

right-to-work laws. Laws which state that no one can be required to join a union to get or to keep a job.

robots. Mechanical devices programmed to do routine tasks.

S

safe-deposit boxes. Boxes in a bank vault for storing valuables.

safety. Assurance that the money you have invested will be returned to you.

sales credit. Credit that is offered at the time of sale.

sales tax. A tax on goods and services that is collected by the seller.

savings account passbook. A record that shows your deposits, withdrawals, interest earned, and the balance of your savings account; the bank teller records each transaction.

savings account register. A record in which you must record each deposit or withdrawal as it is made from your savings account; you must also add the interest when the bank reports it to you.

savings and loan associations (S&Ls). Financial institutions that specialize in savings accounts and loans for mortgages.

savings banks. Banks that mainly handle savings accounts and make loans to home buyers.

savings plan. Putting money aside in a systematic way to help reach an established financial goal.

scarcity. *See* basic economic problem.

secured loan. A type of loan in which the lender has the right to sell property used as collateral to get back the amount of the loan in the event the loan is not repaid.

securities. A general term for bonds and stocks that are sold by corporations and governments to raise large sums of money.

self-insurance. When an individual, family, or business assumes the total risk of economic loss.

service business. A business that does things for you instead of making or marketing products.

service charge. A fee a bank charges for handling a checking account.

Service Corps of Retired Executives (SCORE). A group of retired executives who can provide assistance to small-business owners.

service-producing industry. Businesses that satisfy the needs of other businesses and consumers.

services. Things that satisfy our wants through the efforts of other people or equipment.

sharedrafts. Withdrawals made on a member's shares of ownership (deposits) in a credit union.

shareholder. *See* stockholder.

signature card. A card, kept by a bank, that shows the signatures of all individuals authorized to draw checks against the account.

simple interest. An expression of interest based on a one-year period of time; interest that is computed only on the amount saved.

single-payment loan. A type of loan in which you do not pay anything until the end of the loan period, possibly 60 or 90 days.

small business. A business that usually has the owner as manager, is not dominant in its field of operation, employs fewer than 500 people, and usually serves its nearby community.

Small Business Administration (SBA). A government-funded organization that helps small-business owners borrow money as well as manage their businesses more efficiently.

Small Business Institutes (SBIs). Programs offered in cooperation with colleges and universities to provide management counseling.

SMART card. A plastic card with a silicon chip for storing information.

socialism. An economic system in which government owns and operates a number of industries while providing for some degree of private property and private enterprise.

Social Security. A tax that is put into a trust fund and provides certain benefits to retirees or beneficiaries.

software. Instructions that run a computer system.

sole proprietorship. A business owned by one person.

special endorsement. An endorsement including the name of the person to whom the check has been transferred.

specialty stores. Stores that carry a wide variety of products in a narrow line.

speculative investment. An investment that has an unusually high risk.

spot price. The price quoted for precious metals in the world markets.

spreadsheet software. A computer program that uses a row and column arrangement of data to perform calculations.

standard fire policy. A basic type of property insurance that protects against losses caused by fire or lightning.

standard of living. As a measure of how well people in a country live, this term indicates the quantity and quality of wants and needs that are satisfied.

statement of account. A record of the transactions that you have completed with a business during a billing period.

stockholder. A person who owns stock in a corporation.

stopping payment. Instructing a bank not to pay a certain check.

straight life policy. One type of whole life insurance for which premiums remain the same each year as long as the policyholder lives.

strike. A situation in which employees refuse to work until their demands are met.

Super NOW accounts. Special savings accounts that require higher minimum deposits and pay higher rates of interest.

supermarket. A large, full-service food store that carries a wide variety of national, store, and generic brands at moderate prices.

supply. The quantity of a product or service that businesses are willing and able to provide at a particular price.

surgical expense insurance. Insurance that provides benefits to cover part or all of the surgeon's fee for an operation.

T

take-home pay. The amount received after taxes and other deductions have been subtracted from total earnings.

tariff. A tax that a government places on certain imported products.

technology. The use of automated machinery and electronic equipment to help increase the efficiency of labor.

telecommunications. The use of television, telephones, communication satellites, computers, and other electronic devices to transmit both visual and audio communication.

telecommuting. A term used to describe the activities of a worker using a computer at home to perform a job.

tenants policy. Insurance for those who rent which covers household goods and personal belongings and provides protection against the same kinds of perils covered by homeowners policies, including personal liability coverage.

tentative career decisions. A career decision that is subject to change or modification as new information is received.

terminal. The keyboard and visual display screen used to enter and view data.

term life insurance. A life insurance policy that provides financial protection from losses resulting from loss of life during a definite period of time.

time deposit. A deposit that usually will be left in the bank for a period of time.

time factor. The length of time for which interest will be charged.

trade association. An organization of businesses engaged in the same type of business.

trade credit. A business receives goods from a wholesaler and pays for them at a later specified date.

trademark. A word, letter, or symbol associated with a specific product or company.

traveler's check. A form designed for the traveler to use in making payments.

trust. The creditor's belief that the debtor will honor the promise to pay later for goods and services that have already been received and used.

trust companies. Banks that specialize in managing the money and property of others.

Truth in Lending law. A law which requires that you be told the cost of a credit purchase in writing before you sign a credit agreement.

U

unemployment insurance. Insurance that provides cash payments for a limited time to people who are out of work for a reason other than illness.

uninsured motorist coverage. Insurance coverage that protects the policyholder and immediate family members against losses resulting from injuries caused by a hit-and-run driver or by a driver who has no insurance and inadequate money to pay claims.

union shop. Exists when workers are required to join a union within a specified time after employment.

unit price. The price per unit of measure of a product.

universal life insurance. Life insurance which provides both insurance protection and a substantial savings plan.

upkeep. The cost of maintaining your property in good condition.

user-friendly software. A program that will tell you what to do next and will also help you when you make a mistake.

V

values. The things that are important to you in life.

variable expenses. Living costs involving differing amounts each time and are usually more difficult to estimate.

variable life insurance. Life insurance that lets the policyholder select from a range of investments.

venture business. A business that has been in operation for less than three years and has no employees other than the owner.

venture capital. Money used to start up a new small business or help a business expand during a growth period.

vision care insurance. Insurance that covers eye examinations, prescription lenses, frames, and contact lenses.

W

wants. Things which are not necessary for survival but which add pleasure and comfort to our lives.

warehouse market. A no-frills food outlet emphasizing the sale of large quantities of items at reasonable prices.

white-collar crime. An illegal act performed by office or professional workers while at work.

white-collar workers. People whose work involves a great deal of contact with other people and who work with or process information.

whole life insurance. Permanent insurance that extends over the lifetime of the insured.

wholesaler. A middle firm that sells goods to other firms like itself or to other retailers.

withdrawal slip. A written request to take money out of your account.

word processing. An office function that involves using electronic equipment to produce written material rapidly.

word processing software. A computer program used to create and revise written documents.

workers' compensation. Insurance that provides medical and survivor benefits to people injured, disabled, or killed on the job.

work force. All of the people age 16 and over who hold jobs or who are seeking jobs.

world, foreign, or international trade. Trade among different countries.

Y

yield. The percentage of interest that will be added to your savings over a period of time.

Index

Acknowledgments

For permission to reproduce the photographs on the pages indicated, acknowledgment is made to the following:

COVER PHOTOS
Earth, NASA; Oil refinery, © Eric Meola/The Image Bank; Sears Tower, © Wilfried Bauer/ The Image Bank

CHAPTER 1
p. 7, (top) Kerr-McGee Corporation, (bottom left) Photo courtesy of American Petroleum Institute, (bottom right) Courtesy of Chevron Corp.; p. 9, Photo courtesy of Disabled Children's Computer Group

CHAPTER 2
p. 19, U.S. Navy Photo; p. 21, World Bank Photo; p. 23, Photograph courtesy of Hewlett-Packard Company

CHAPTER 3
p. 33, Superstock; p. 38, TRW, Inc.

CHAPTER 4
p. 45, (top) Photo by Steve Costello/Marine World/Africa USA on San Francisco Bay; p. 52, Photo courtesy of NASA

CHAPTER 5
p. 66, Aetna Life & Casualty Co.; p. 73, INPUI Publications

CHAPTER 7
p. 98, (left) USDA by Wilson, (right) Photo courtesy of Lockheed Aeronautical Systems Co.; p. 106, Silvia Koner/COM-STOCK, INC.

CHAPTER 8
p. 119, (right) Bethlehem Steel Corporation; p. 121, General Motors Corporation

CHAPTER 9
p. 129, Bill Anderson/Super-stock, Inc.

CHAPTER 10
p. 143, (left) United States Department of Agriculture, (right) Alaska Division of Tourism; p. 146, Tennessee Valley Authority; p. 148, Superstock

CHAPTER 11
p. 154, Photo by W.R. Grace & Co.; p. 157, Courtesy of Jostens; p. 160, S. Barrow, Inc./Super-stock

CAREER FOCUS FOR UNIT 3
p. 164, Aetna Life & Casualty Co.

CHAPTER 12
p. 173, Peter Menzel/STOCK BOSTON, INC.

CHAPTER 13
p. 192, Courtesy of International Business Machines Corporation

CHAPTER 14
p. 198, Photo Courtesy of Carter Hewley Hale Stores, Inc.; p. 203, Laima Druskis/Taurus Photos

CAREER FOCUS FOR UNIT 4
p. 212, Reproduced with permission of AT&T Corporate Archives

CHAPTER 18
p. 257, Photo Courtesy of United States Department of Agriculture; p. 258, Century 21 Real Estate Corporation; p. 261, Michael Grecco/Stock Boston, Inc.

CAREER FOCUS FOR UNIT 5
p. 265, Courtesy of International Business Machines Corporation

BUSINESS BRIEF FOR UNIT 6
p. 268, Courtesy of International Business Machines Corporation

CHAPTER 19
p. 271, Courtesy of International Business Machines Corporation; p. 273, Courtesy of International Business Machines Corporation; p. 276, Photo courtesy of Cal-Comp

CHAPTER 20
p. 281, Courtesy of Honeywell, Inc.; p. 288, Photo courtesy of Hewlett-Packard Company; p. 289, Courtesy of International Business Machines Corporation

CHAPTER 21
p. 294, Courtesy of International Business Machines Corporation; p. 296, Courtesy of Compaq Computer Corporation; p. 297, Courtesy of International Business Machines Corporation; p. 299, Courtesy of General Motors Corporation

CAREER FOCUS FOR UNIT 6
p. 304, Photo courtesy of Apple Computers, Inc.

CHAPTER 22
p. 313, Federal Reserve Bank/Cleveland Branch; p. 319, R. Heinzen/Superstock, Inc.

CHAPTER 25
p. 360, Photo courtesy of Unisys Corporation

CHAPTER 28
p. 410, Photo courtesy of Aruba Tourist Authority

BUSINESS BRIEF FOR UNIT 9
p. 448, New York Convention and Visitor's Bureau

CHAPTER 33
p. 480, New York Convention and Visitor's Bureau

CHAPTER 34
p. 494, (top) USDA photo, (bottom left) USDA photo, (bottom right) Photo courtesy of AMAX, Inc., Greenwich, CT

CAREER FOCUS FOR UNIT 9
p. 500, Photo courtesy of International Business Machines Corporation

CHAPTER 35
p. 506, Superstock, Inc.; p. 511, Courtesy of American Brands, Inc.

CHAPTER 36
p. 516, Superstock, Inc.; p. 519, Superstock, Inc.; p. 523, Pace Arrow Motorhouse produced by Fleetwood Enterprises, Inc.

CHAPTER 37
p. 530, J. Jeffers/Superstock, Inc.; p. 532, Photo courtesy of Aetna Life Insurance

CHAPTER 38
p. 541, Warren Utzel/USDA; p. 546, Courtesy Indiana Department of Commerce

CHAPTER 39
p. 554, Brent Jones/Stock Boston; p. 557, Aluminum Company of America

CAREER FOCUS FOR UNIT 10
p. 563, David R. Frazier/TSW-CLICK/Chicago

CHAPTER 40
p. 569, Florida Department of Commerce

CHAPTER 41
p. 580, Charles Gupton/Stock Boston; p. 585, Jose Carrillo, Ventura, CA

CHAPTER 42
p. 592, (bottom right) Ernst Grasser/TSW-CLICK/Chicago